District Gazetteers of India Series 60

BENGAL DISTRICT GAZETTEERS

THE GAZETTEER OF SIKHIM

District Gazetteers of India Series 60

BENGAL DISTRICT GAZETTEERS

THE GAZETTEER OF SIKHIM

H. H. RISLEY

52 VOLUMES

(VOL. 49th)

GYAN

Published by

Gyan Publishing House
5, Ansari Road
Daryaganj, New Delhi-110002
Phone: 011-47034999, 9811692060
E-mail: books@gyanbooks.com

Distribution Network
gyanbooks.com
India, USA, Canada, UK, Australia, France

ISBN: 978-93-6208-448-4 (Set) 52 Volumes
978-81-212-5669-8 (HB)

First Published, 1894

2nd Impression 2024

Printed at: Gyan Press, Delhi.

BENGAL DISTRICT GAZETTEERS (VOL. 49th)
Author: H. H. Risley

LIST OF VOLUMES

S. NO.	ISBN NO.	VOL.	TITLE	AUTHOR	PRICE	PAGES
			ASSAM DISTRICT GAZETTEERS			
1	9788121286046	1st	Cachar	B. C. Allen	1200	300
2	9788121286039	2nd	Sylhet	B. C. Allen	1500	378
3	9788121286022	3rd	Goalpara	B. C. Allen	800	203
4	9788121286015	4th	Kamrup	B. C. Allen	1370	344
5	9788121286008	5th	Darrang	B. C. Allen	1450	364
6	9788121285995	6th	Nowgong	B. C. Allen	1120	280
7	9788121285988	7th	Sibsagar	B. C. Allen	1370	343
8	9788121285971	8th	Lakhimpur	B. C. Allen	1380	347
9	9788121285964	9th	Naga Hills and Manipur	B. C. Allen	1170	294
10	9788121285957	10th	The Khasi And Jaintia Hills, The Garo Hills And The Lushai Hills	B. C. Allen	1350	363
11	9788121285940	11th	The Sadiya and Balipara Frontier Tract	B. C. Allen	760	190
			BENGAL DISTRICT GAZETTEERS			
12	9788121218665	1st	Angul	L. S. S. O'Malley	500	168
13	9788121259644	2nd	Bakarganj	J. C. JACK	1350	194
14	9788121218689	3rd	Balasore	L. S. S. O'Malley	675	228
15	9788121259606	4th	Bankura	L. S. S. O'Malley	1390	199
16	9788121218368	5th	Bhagalpur	J. Byrne	580	194
17	9788121218283	6th	Birbhum	L. S. S. O'Malley	450	150
18	9788121259668	7th	Eastern Bengal and Assam - Bogra	J. N. Gupta	1320	188
19	9788121218344	8th	Burdwan	J. C. K. Peterson	680	227
20	9788121259545	9th	Calcutta District Gazetteer - Statistics, 1901 - 02		480	68
21	9788121218306	10th	Champaran	L. S. S. O'Malley	610	205
22	9788121259620	11th	Eastern Bengal District Gazetters - Chittagong	L. S. S. O'Malley	1500	216
23	9788121259569	12th	Chota Nagpur Tributary		180	26
24	9788121259422	13th	The Cooch Behar Gazette: Statistics		2040	292
25	9788121218405	14th	Cuttack	L. S. S. O'Malley	740	248
26	9788121261364	15th	Eastern Bengal District Gazetteers Dacca	B. C. Allen	800	207
27	9788121218429	16th	Darbhanga	L. S. S. O'Malley	540	180
28	9788121204965	17th	Darjeeling	L. S. S. O'Malley	500	248
29	9788121259460	18th	Eastern Bengal District Gazetteers - Dinajpur	F. W. Strong	1250	178
30	9788121259408	19th	Faridpur	L. S. S. O'Malley	980	140
31	9788121218467	20th	Gaya	L. S. S. O'Malley	810	270
32	9788121214025	21st	Bihar and Orissa District Gazetteer: Hazaribagh	E. Lister	950	234
33	9788121218320	22nd	Hooghly	L. S. S. O'Malley	1020	340
34	9788121218184	23rd	Bengal District Gazetteer Howrah	L. S. S. O'Malley	590	199
35	9788121259309	24th	Eastern Bengal and Assam - Jalpaiguri	John F. Gruning	1250	178
36	9788121259286	25th	Jessore	L. S. S. O'Malley	1340	192
37	9788121259248	26th	Khulna	L. S. S. O'Malley	1540	220
38	9788121259224	27th	Malda	G. E. Lambourn	940	134
39	9788121297912	28th	Manbhum	H. Coupland	1250	313
40	9788121218481	29th	Midnapore	L. S. S. O'Malley	750	252
41	9788121218580	30th	Monghyr	L. S. S. O'Malley	840	280
42	9788121259163	31st	Murshidabad	L. S. S. O'Malley	1750	250
43	9788121259583	32nd	Bengal District Gazetteers - Muzaffarpur	L. S. S. O'Malley	1300	188
44	9788121259149	33rd	Mymensingh	F. A. Sachse	1340	192
45	9788121259125	34th	Nadia	J. H. E. Garrett	1500	214
46	9788121259101	35th	Eastern Bengal and Assam - Noakhali	J. E. Webster	800	115
47	9788121218443	36th	Feudatory States of Orissa	L. E. B. Cobdenramsay	1180	395
48	9788121259088	37th	Pabna	L. S. S. O'Malley	990	142
49	9788121218504	38th	Palamau	L. S. S. O'Malley	570	190
50	9788121218627	39th	Patna	L. S. S. O'Malley	750	250
51	9788121218528	40th	Puri	L. S. S. O'Malley	980	328
52	9788121218740	41st	Purnea	L. S. S. O'Malley	660	220
53	9788121258944	42nd	Rajshahi	L. S. S. O'Malley	1500	216
54	9788121256674	43rd	Bihar and Orissa District Gazetteers: Ranchi	M. G. Hallett	1950	278
55	9788121258920	44th	Eastern Bengal and assam - Rangpur	J. A. Vas	1250	178
56	9788121218542	45th	Sambalpur	L. S. S. O'Malley	730	242
57	9788121214049	46th	Santal Parganas	L. S. S. O'Malley	1250	308
58	9788121218603	47th	Saran	L. S. S. O'Malley	570	190
59	9788121218641	48th	Shahabad	L. S. S. O'Malley	570	190
60	9788121256698	49th	The Gazetteer of Sikhim	H. H. Risley	2280	481
61	9788121218566	50th	Singhbhum, Saraikela And Kharsawan	L. S. S. O'Malley	840	280
62	9788121259446	51st	Eastern Bengal District Gazetteers - Tippera	J. E. Webster	1020	146
63	9788121259040	52nd	24 Parganas	L. S. S. O'Malley	1990	284

S. NO.	ISBN NO.	VOL.	TITLE	AUTHOR	PRICE	PAGES
			CENTRAL PROVINCES DISTRICT GAZETTEERS			
64	9789362085474	1st, Vol. A	Akola (Descriptive)	A. E. Nelson, C. Brown	1740	436
65	9789362087232	2nd, Vol. A	Amraoti (Descriptive)	S. V. Fitzgerald, A. E. Nelson	2100	524
66	9789362085191	3rd,Vol. A	Balaghat (Descriptive)	R. V. RUSSELL	860	216
67	9789362085986	4th, Vol. A	Betul (Descriptive)	R. V. RUSSELL	1220	306
68	9789362082039	5th, Vol. A	Bhandara (Descriptive)	R. V. RUSSELL	1170	292
69	9789362087713	6th, Vol. A	Bilaspur (Descriptive)	R. V. RUSSELL	1740	434
70	9789362084255	7th, Vol. A	Buldana (Descriptive)	A. E. Nelson	2170	543
71	9789362082107	8th, Vol. B	Chanda (Descriptive)	R. V. RUSSELL	940	234
72	9789362084576	9th	Chhattisgarch Feudatory State	E. A. De Brett	1760	440
73	9789362084873	10th	Chhindwara (Descriptive)	R. V. RUSSELL	1100	274
74	9789362086426	11th, Vol. A & B	Damoh (Descriptive and Statistical Tables 1891-1901)	R. V. RUSSELL	1660	414
75	9789362080240	12th, Vol. A	Durg (Descriptive)	A. E. Nelson	930	232
76	9789362080448	13th, Vol. A	Hoshangabad (Descriptive)	R. V. RUSSELL	1720	430
77	9789362080028	14th, Vol. A	Jubbulpore (Descriptive)	A. E. Nelson	1900	474
78	9789362088079	15th, Vol. A & B	Mandla (Descriptive and Statistical Tables 1891-1901)	R. V. RUSSELL	740	186
79	9789362086693	16th, Vol. A	Nagpur (Descriptive)	R. V. RUSSELL	1580	394
80	9789362085221	17th, Vol. A	Narsinghpur (Descriptive)	R. V. RUSSELL	1030	257
81	9789362086501	18th, Vol. A	Nimar (Descriptive)	R. V. RUSSELL	1200	299
82	9789362082145	19th, Vol. A	Raipur (Descriptive)	A. E. Nelson	1580	396
83	9789362085948	20th, Vol. A	Saugor (Descriptive)	R. V. RUSSELL	1140	285
84	9789362080318	21st, Vol. A	Seoni (Descriptive)	R. V. RUSSELL	930	232
85	9789362089625	22nd, Vol. A	Wardha (Descriptive)	R. V. RUSSELL	1210	302
86	9789362088468	23rd, Vol. A	Yeotmal (Descriptive)	R. V. RUSSELL	1110	277
87	9789362083500	24th, Vol. I, Pt. I	Gwalior (Text and Tables)	R. V. RUSSELL	1960	489
88	9789362081667	24th, Vol. I, Pt. II	Gwalior (Maps)	R. V. RUSSELL	790	198
89	9789362087478	24th, Vol. I, Pt. III	Gwalior (Village List)	R. V. RUSSELL	1620	406
90	9789362089731	24th, Vol. I, Pt. IV	Gwalior (Photos)	R. V. RUSSELL	2790	698
91	9789362088956	25th, Vol. II	Indore (Text and Tables)	C. E. Luard	2100	524
92	9789362088543	26th, Vol. III	Bhopal (Text and Tables)	C. E. Luard	1090	272
93	9789362082732	27th, Vol. IV	Rewah (Text and Tables)	C. E. Luard	1000	250
94	9789362087065	28th, Vol. V, Pt. A	Western States - Malwa (Text)	C. E. Luard	3050	762
95	9789362080707	29th, Vol. VI, Pt. A	Eastern States - Bundelkhand (Text)	C. E. Luard	1850	463
96	9789362086273	30th, Vol. VI, Pt. B	Eastern States - Bundelkhand (Tables)	C. E. Luard	1670	417
			GAZETTEER OF THE BOMBAY PRESIDENCY			
97	9788121283458	1st, Part I	History of Gujarat	Ed.: James M. Campbell	4500	644
98	9788121285599	1st, Part II	History of the Konkan Dakhan and Southern Maratha Country	Ed.: James M. Campbell	5870	840
99	9788121285575	2nd	Gujarat, Surat and Broach	Ed.: James M. Campbell	4150	598
100	9788121285551	3rd	Kaira and Panch Mahals	Ed.: James M. Campbell	2370	339
101	9788121285537	4th	Ahmedabad	Ed.: James M. Campbell	2600	372
102	9788121285513	5th	Cutch, Palanpur, and Mahi Kantha	Ed.: James M. Campbell	3330	478
103	9788121285490	6th	Rewa Kantha, Narukot, Cambay, and Surat States	Ed.: James M. Campbell	2030	290
104	9788121285476	7th	Baroda	Ed.: James M. Campbell	4550	652
105	9788121285452	8th	Kathiawar	Ed.: James M. Campbell	5300	758
106	9788121285438	9th, Part I	Gujarat Population - Hindus	Ed.: James M. Campbell	4450	636
107	9788121285414	9th, Part II	Gujarat Population - Musalmans and Parsis	Ed.: James M. Campbell	2120	304
108	9788121285391	10th	Ratnagiri and Savantvadi	Ed.: James M. Campbell	3500	501
109	9788121285377	11th	Kolaba and Janjira	Ed.: James M. Campbell	3550	513
110	9788121285353	12th	Khandesh	Ed.: James M. Campbell	4450	638
111	9788121285339	13th Part I	Thana	Ed.: James M. Campbell	2880	413
112	9788121285315	13th Part II	Thana	Ed.: James M. Campbell	2490	357
113	9788121285292	14th	Thana - Places of Interest	Ed.: James M. Campbell	4600	659
114	9788121285278	15th Part I	Kanara	Ed.: James M. Campbell	3250	468
115	9788121285254	15th Part II	Kanara	Ed.: James M. Campbell	2440	468
116	9788121285230	16th	Nasik	Ed.: James M. Campbell	4880	698
117	9788121285216	17th	Ahmadnagar	Ed.: James M. Campbell	5400	772
118	9788121285193	18th Part I	Poona	Ed.: James M. Campbell	4100	586
119	9788121285179	18th Part II	Poona	Ed.: James M. Campbell	3750	537
120	9788121285155	18th Part III	Poona	Ed.: James M. Campbell	3500	503
121	9788121285131	19th	Satara	Ed.: James M. Campbell	4840	692
122	9788121285117	20th	Sholapur	Ed.: James M. Campbell	3820	547
123	9788121285094	21st	Gazetteer of the Bomaby Presidency: Belgaum	Ed.: James M. Campbell	3590	514
124	9788121285070	22nd	Dharwar	Ed.: James M. Campbell	5880	841
125	9788121285056	23rd	Gazetteer of the Bombay Presidency:Bijapur	Ed.: James M. Campbell	4980	712
126	9788121285032	24th	Kolhapur	Ed.: James M. Campbell	3150	450
127	9788121285018	25th	Botany	Ed.: James M. Campbell	2850	408

S. NO.	ISBN NO.	VOL.	TITLE	AUTHOR	PRICE	PAGES
128	9788121284998	26th, Part I	Materials Towards a Statistical Account of the Town and Island of Bombay - History	Ed.: James M. Campbell	3525	504
129	9788121284974	26th, Part II	Materials Towards a Statistical Account of the Town and Island of Bombay - Trade and Fortifications	Ed.: James M. Campbell	3750	538
130	9788121284950	26th, Part III	Materials Towards a Statistical Account of the Town And Island of Bombay - Administration	Ed.: James M. Campbell	4840	702
131	9788121284936	27th	General Index	Ed.: R. E. Enthoven	2990	428
			MADRAS DISTRICT GAZETTEERS			
132	9788121258821	1st	Anantapur	W. Francis	1590	227
133	9788121258562	2nd	Malabar	C. A Innes & F. B Evans	4210	602
134	9788121258807	3rd	Bellary	W. Francis	2640	377
135	9788121258784	4th	Statistical Appendix For Chingleput		390	56
136	9788121258760	5th	Coimbatore	K. N. Krishnaswami Ayyar	4790	628
137	9788121232821	6th	Madras District Gazetteers District Gazetteer Cuddapah	C. F. Brackenbury	1950	285
138	9788121258722	7th	Statistical Appendix For Ganjam		510	73
139	9788121256759	8th, Vol. 1st	Godavari District Gazetteer	F. R. Hemingway	1280	320
140	9788121256797	8th, Vol. 2nd	Godavari District Gazetteer	F. R. Hemingway	340	83
141	9788121258685	9th	Statistical Appendix For Kistna		890	127
142	9788121258661	10th	Statistical Appendix For Kurnool		380	54
143	9788121258623	11th	Madura	W. Francis	2650	379
144	9788121258586	12th	Statistical Appendix For Madura		1040	148
145	9788121258647	13th	The Nilgiris	W. Francis	3060	437
146	9788121234283	14th	Madras District Gazetteers Gazetteer Of The Nellore District Brought Upto 1938			2110
386						
147	9788121258524	15th	North Arcot		830	118
148	9788121258500	16th, Vol. 1, Part I	Salem	F. J. Richards	2400	343
149	9788121258609	16th, Vol. 1, Part II	Salem	F. J. Richards	2520	360
150	9788121258463	17th	South Arcot	W. Francis	3360	480
151	9788121258487	18th	Statistical Appendix For South Canara		560	80
152	9788121258449	19th, Vol. 1st & 2nd	Tanjore: Main Volume and Statistical Appendix		2900	401
153	9788121258401	20th	Tinnevelly	H. R. Pate	3830	547
154	9788121258425	21st	Statistical Appendix For Tinnevelly		450	64
155	9788121258388	22nd, 1st & 2nd	Trichinopoly: Main Volume and Statistical Appendix	F. R. Hemingway	3410	487
156	9788121241960	23rd	Vizagapatam District Gazetteer	W. Francis	1520	385
			PUNJAB DISTRICT GAZETTEERS			
157	9788121255936	1st	Ambala District 1883-84		870	124
158	9788121255950	2nd	Amritsar		1650	236
159	9788121255974	3rd	Delhi		1820	260
160	9788121255998	4th	Ferozepore		1320	188
161	9788121256018	5th	Faridkot		490	70
162	9788121256032	6th	Gujranwala 1893-94		1780	254
163	9788121256056	7th	Gujrat	C. E. Luard	1590	228
164	9788121256070	8th	Gurdaspur 1891-92		1764	252
165	9788121256094	9th	Gurgaon 1883-4		1420	203
166	9788121256117	10th	Hazara	H. D. Watson	3200	458
167	9788121256131	11th	Hissar district and Lohar State		2570	367
168	9788121256155	12th	Hoshiarpur		1980	283
169	9788121256179	13th	Jhang		1490	213
170	9788121256193	14th	Jhelam		1410	202
171	9788121256216	15th	Jalandhar District 1883-84		750	108
172	9788121256230	16th, Vol. XIV-A	Jullundur District, with maps and Kapurthala		2786	398
173	9788121256254	17th, Pt. I	Kangra (Proper)		2030	290
174	9788121256278	17th, Pt. II	Kangra (Kulu, Lahual, Spiti)		2500	357
175	9788121256292	18th	Karnal		2700	386
176	9788121256315	19th	Kohat		2150	307
177	9788121256339	20th	The Lahore District 1883-84		1710	244
178	9788121256377	21st	Ludhiana and Maler Kotla		2350	335
179	9788121256391	22nd	Lyallpur		1029	147
180	9788121256414	23rd	Mianwali		1640	234
181	9788121256438	24th	Montgomery	P. J. Fagan	2230	318
182	9788121258357	25th	Multan (1901-02)	E. D. Maclagan	3360	480
183	9788121258692	26th	The Rohtak District 1883-84		1370	196
184	9788121258739	27th, Vol. III A	Dujana State 1904		600	16
185	9788121256476	28th	Shahpur District		2490	356
186	9788121256490	29th	Simla District		1110	159
187	9788121256513	30th	The Chamba State		2860	408

S. NO.	ISBN NO.	VOL.	TITLE	AUTHOR	PRICE	PAGES
188	9788121256537	31st	The Chenab Colony 1904		2170	310
189	9788121256551	32nd	Kalsia State		370	53
190	9788121256575	33rd	Suket and Mandi		1080	154
191	9788121256599	34th	Phulkian States, Patiala Jind And Nabha 1904		2898	414
192	9788121256636	35th	Simla Hill States		3100	443
193	9788121256650	36th	Sirmur		1280	183
			RAJPUTANA DISTRICT GAZETTEERS			
194	9789362089847	1st, Vol. I-A & B	Ajmer-merwara (Text and Statistics Tables)	C. C. Watson	1720	246
195	9789362088895	2nd. Vol. II-A & B	Mewar Residency (Text and Statistics Tables)	K.D. Erskine	2370	339
196	9789362087935	3rd, Vol. III-A & B	The Western Rajputana States Residency And The Bikaner Agency	K.D. Erskine	5000	718
			UNITED PROVINCES OF AGRA AND OUDH DISTRICT GAZETTEERS			
197	9789362080523	Vol. I	Agra	H. R. Nevill	3160	452
198	9789362084149	Vol. II	Aligarh	H. R. Nevill	1820	260
199	9789362081452	Vol. III	Allahabad	H. R. Nevill	2860	409
200	9789362085917	Vol. IV	Almora	H. G. Walton	2330	333
201	9789362089717	Vol. V	Azamgarh	D. L. Drake Brockman	2440	349
202	9789362089069	Vol. VI	Bahraich	H. R. Nevill	1970	281
203	9789362089670	Vol. VII	Ballia	H. R. Nevill	2450	350
204	9789362080974	Vol. VIII	Banda	D. L. Drake Brockman	2440	349
205	9789362082657	Vol. IX	Bara Banki	H. R. Nevill	2410	344
206	9789362089588	Vol. X	Bareilly	H. R. Nevill	2290	327
207	9789362088772	Vol. XI	Basti	H. R. Nevill	2250	321
208	9789362086556	Vol. XII	Benares	H. R. Nevill	3210	458
209	9789362089762	Vol. XIII	Bijnor	H. R. Nevill	2540	363
210	9789362087522	Vol. XIV	Budaun	H. R. Nevill	2650	378
211	9789362085665	Vol. XV	Bulandshahr	H. R. Nevill	2930	419
212	9789362080899	Vol. XVI	Cawnpore	H. R. Nevill	3090	442
213	9789362082237	Vol. XVII	Dehra Dun	H. G. Walton	2390	342
214	9789362089489	Vol. XVIII	Etah	E. R. Neave	2240	320
215	9789362086983	Vol. XIX	Etawah	D. L. Drake Brockman	1940	277
216	9789362081650	Vol. XX	Farrukhabad	E. R. Neave	2270	324
217	9789362083326	Vol. XXI	Fatehpur	H. R. Nevill	2640	377
218	9789362081018	Vol. XXII	Fyzabad	H. R. Nevill	2370	339
219	9789362086907	Vol. XXIII	Garhwal	H. G. Walton	1780	254
220	9789362085092	Vol. XXIV	Ghazipur	H. R. Nevill	2240	320
221	9789362083272	Vol. XXV	Gonda	H. R. Nevill	2310	330
222	9789362088185	Vol. XXVI	Gorakhpur	H. R. Nevill	2650	378
223	9789362082756	Vol. XXVII	Hamirpur	D. L. Drake Brockman	1940	277
224	9789362081780	Vol. XXVIII	Hardoi	H. R. Nevill	2350	336
225	9789362085641	Vol. XXIX	Jalaun	D. L. Drake Brockman	1650	236
226	9789362080998	Vol. XXX	Jaunpur	H. R. Nevill	2450	350
227	9789362088123	Vol. XXXI	Jhansi	D. L. Drake Brockman	2740	391
228	9789362081568	Vol. XXXII	Kheri	H. R. Nevill	2310	330
229	9789362088161	Vol. XXXIII	Lucknow	H. R. Nevill	2460	352
230	9789362081155	Vol. XXXIV	Mainpuri	H. R. Nevill	2440	348
231	9789362086839	Vol. XXXV	Meerut	H. R. Nevill	3040	434
232	9789362080400	Vol. XXXVI	Mirzapur	D. L. Drake Brockman	3400	486
233	9789362088666	Vol. XXXVII	Moradabad	H. R. Nevill	2660	380
234	9789362082213	Vol. XXXVIII	Muttra	D. L. Drake Brockman	3000	428
235	9789362083555	Vol. XXXIX	Muzaffarnagar	H. R. Nevill	3160	451
236	9789362080820	Vol. XL	Naini Tal	H. R. Nevill	2640	377
237	9789362087799	Vol. XLI	Partabgarh	H. R. Nevill	2180	312
238	9789362082022	Vol. XLII	Pilibhit	H. R. Nevill	2200	314
239	9789362085337	Vol. XLIII	Rai Bareli	H. R. Nevill	2250	322
240	9789362088901	Vol. XLIV	Rampur	H. R. Nevill	1640	234
241	9789362082664	Vol. XLV	Saharanpur	H. R. Nevill	3070	438
242	9789362088406	Vol. XLVI	Shahjahanpur	H. R. Nevill	2110	302
243	9789362089823	Vol. XLVII	Sitapur	H. R. Nevill	2220	317
244	9789362083913	Vol. XLVIII	Sultanpur	H. R. Nevill	1860	266
245	9789362081544	Vol. XLIX	Unnao	H. R. Nevill	2140	305

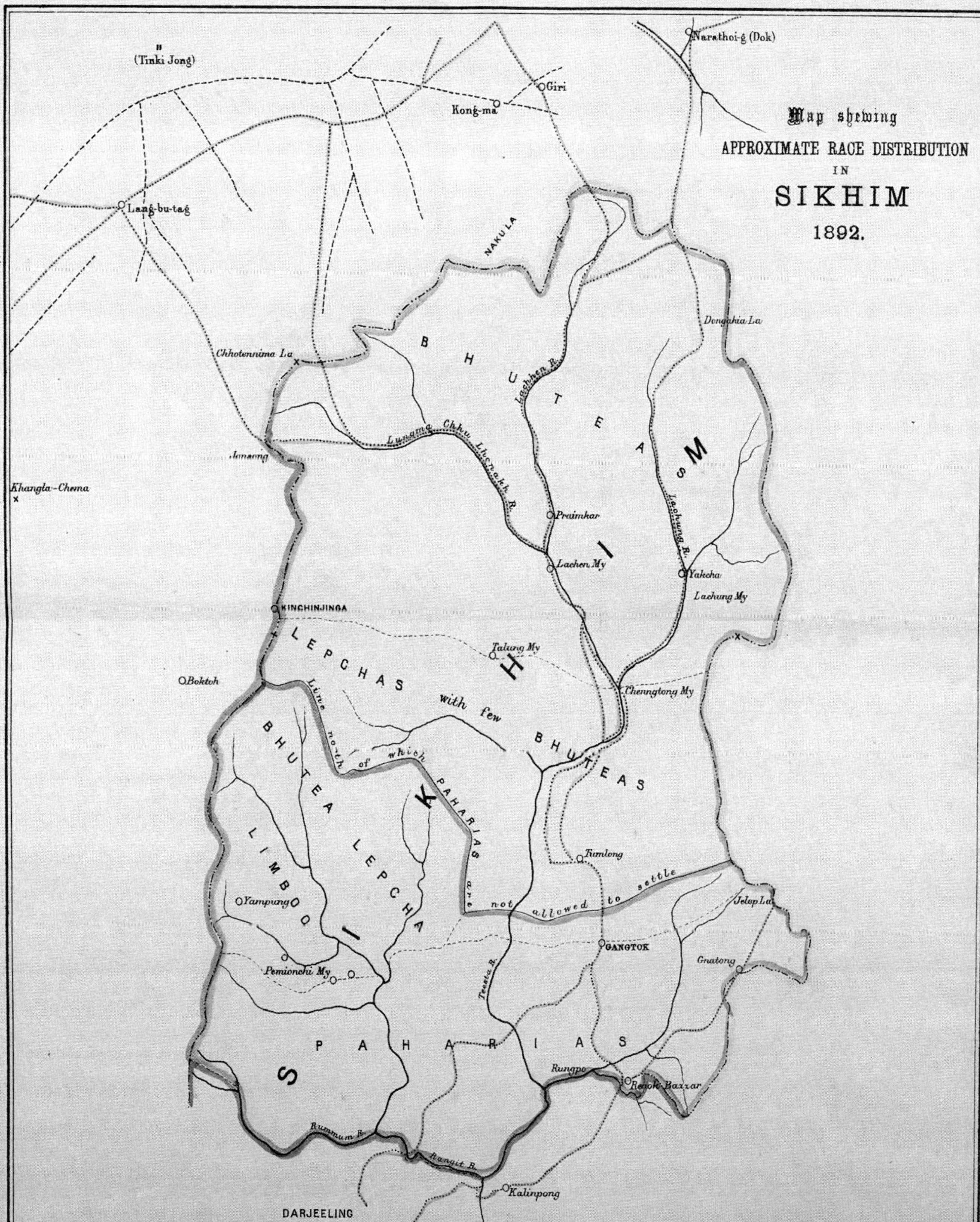

Reg. No. 585, Bengal, Rev.—Nov. 94.—500.

Litho., S. I. O., Calcutta.

THE

GAZETTEER OF SIKHIM.

WITH AN INTRODUCTION BY

H. H. RISLEY,

INDIAN CIVIL SERVICE, COMPANION OF THE INDIAN EMPIRE,
OFFICIER D'ACADÉMIE FRANÇAISE.

EDITED IN THE BENGAL GOVERNMENT SECRETARIAT.

Calcutta:
Printed at the Bengal Secretariat Press.
1894.

THE

GAZETTEER OF SIKHIM.

LIST

OF

SOME WORKS ON SIKHIM.

AITCHISON'S TREATIES (Volume I, 3rd Edition), Calcutta, 1892.

W. T. BLANFORD—"Journey through Sikhim," *Journal of the Asiatic Society of Bengal*, Volume XL, Part II, page 367, 1871.

CAMPBELL, DR.—"Papers on the Valley of Chumbi" in the *Journal of the Royal Asiatic Society* for September 1873.

———————— "Papers on the Relations with Sikhim and Nepal" in the *Oriental* of January 1874.

DESGODINS, C. H., ABBÉ—"La Mission du Thibet," Verdun, 1872.

EDGAR, SIR J. WARE, K.C.I.E., C.S.I.—"Report on a Visit to Sikhim and the Tibetan Frontier in 1873," Calcutta, 1874.

GAWLER, COLONEL J. C.—"Sikhim: with hints on Mountain and Jungle Warfare; exhibiting also the facilities for opening Commercial Relations through the State of Sikhim with Central Asia, Tibet, and Western China" (Stanford, 1873).

HODGSON, BRIAN HOUGHTON—"Essays on the Language, Literature, and Religion of Nepal and Tibet, with further papers on the Geography, Ethnology, and Commerce of those Countries," Trübner, 1874.

HOOKER, SIR J. D., K.C.S.I.—"Himalayan Journals; or Notes of a Naturalist in Bengal, the Sikhim and Nepal Mountains, &c.," Murray, 1854.

MACAULAY, COLMAN, C.I.E.—"Report of a Mission to Sikhim and the Tibetan Frontier," Calcutta, 1885.

SHERWILL, CAPTAIN—"Map of British Sikhim from surveys by—" published Calcutta, 1852.

TURNER, CAPTAIN SAMUEL—"Account of an Embassy to the Court of Tesho Lama in Tibet," 2nd Edition, London, 1806.

CONTENTS.

Chapter III.—The Temple and its Contents.

PAGE.

Chapter IV—Monkhood.

LIST OF FULL-PAGE ILLUSTRATIONS.

INTRODUCTION.

On the northern border of the British district of Darjeeling, the main chain of the Himalayas throws out to the southward two enormous spurs—the Singilela and Chola ranges. These almost impassable barriers enclose three sides of a gigantic amphitheatre, hewn, as it were, out of the Himalaya, and sloping down on its southern or open side towards the plains of India. The tracts of mountainous country thus shut in consist of a tangled series of interlacing ridges, rising range above range to the foot of the wall of high peaks and passes which marks the "abode of snow" and its offshoots. The steps of this amphitheatre make up the territory known as Independent Sikhim (Sukhim or 'new house'); the encircling wall of peaks and passes forms on the north and east the frontier of Tibet, while on the west and south-east it divides Sikhim and Darjeeling from Nepal, and the Dichu forms the boundary between Sikhim and Bhutan. Pursuing our simile a little further, we may add that the lower levels of the Sikhim amphitheatre, the valleys of the Tista and Balasan and Mahanadi rivers, are similar in character to, and virtually form part of, our frontier district of Darjeeling. The northern hills, on the other hand, whence the snow-fed torrents of the Lachen and Lachung struggle down through precipitous valleys to unite in the broader but hardly less turbulent Tista, are moulded on a grander and more markedly Himalayan scale. Geographically speaking, these heights are of closer kin to the snow-clad giants which dominate them than to the lower elevations and tamer scenery of Sikhim Proper. With the latter, indeed, all intercourse is cut off during five months of the year, and during this time the people of the highlands dwell apart except for occasional visits from traders, who find their way over the Kangralama pass in Tibet.

Physical features.

Of the early history of Sikhim a few doubtful glimpses reach us through the thick mist of Lepcha tradition. The Lepchas, or as they call themselves, the Rong-pa (ravine-folk), claim to be the autoch-thones of Sikhim Proper. Their physical characteristics stamp them as members of the Mongolian race, and certain peculiarities of language and religion render it probable that the tribe is a very ancient colony from Southern Tibet. They are above all things woodmen of the woods, knowing the ways of birds and beasts, and possessing an extensive zoological and botanical nomenclature of their own. Of late years, as the hills have been stripped of their timber by the European tea-planter and the pushing Nepalese agriculturist, while the Forest Department has set its face

Early history.

against primitive methods of cultivation, the tribe is on the way to being pushed out. The cause of their decline is obscure. There is no lack of employment for them: labour is badly wanted and well paid; and the other races of the Darjeeling hills have flourished exceedingly since European enterprise and capital have made the cultivation of tea the leading industry of the district. The Lepchas alone seem to doubt whether life is worth living under the shadow of advancing civilisation, and there can, we fear, be little question that this interesting and attractive race will soon go the way of the forest which they believe to be their original home.

The Sikhim Raj.

The legendary account of the founding of the Sikhim Raj connects the establishment of settled government in that country with the great ritualistic schism in the Tibetan Church. Tradition tells how three monks of the *dukpa* or red-hat sect, flying from the persecution set on foot by the reforming party in Tibet, met after many wanderings at the village of Yaksun, under Kinchinjunga. Here they sent for the ancestor of the Rajas of Sikhim, Pencho Namgay, an influential Tibetan then residing at Guntuk, and an alliance was formed, having for its object the conversion of the Lepchas to Buddhism, and the installation of Pencho Namgay as the Raja of the whole country. Both objects were attained. The easy-going Lepchas readily accepted the externals of Buddhism, monasteries and churches rose to preserve the memory of the missionary monks, and the descendants of the Tibetan settler are recognised to this day as the rightful rulers of Sikhim. The external policy of the petty princedom thus formed was determined by the manner of its creation. In the East religion is still a power, and all things take their colouring from the faith of the ruler. The chief of a barbarous tribe, raised to power by the ingenuity of Tibetan monks, must needs, in default of stronger influences, acknowledge the religious and political predominance of the rulers of Tibet. As the craving for ritual revived, and the hostility between the rival sects showed signs of abating, the religious and political bonds linking Sikhim with Tibet began to be drawn tighter. Doubtful questions of discipline and procedure were referred to Lhassa for the decision of the Dalai Lama, and his mandate was virtually, if not statedly, admitted to be the final appellate authority for Sikhim Buddhists. While this religious *rapprochement* was going on, the Rajas of Sikhim were brought within the attraction of a civilisation far higher than their own. Wool, silk, tea, all the comforts and ornaments of life, came to them from Tibet; while intercourse with other countries was difficult. Small wonder, then, that their continual effort was to show themselves to be thorough Tibetans; that the Tibetan language came into use at their court, and that their chief advisers were drawn from Tibetan monasteries. In course of time this connection grew to be closer, and the last three Rajas have married Tibetan wives, and have held landed property and owned herds of cattle in Tibet. Such marriages introduced a new and important factor into Sikhim politics. Women brought up in the dry keen air of Tibet could not stand the moist warmth of the Sikhim hills, drenched by the immoderate rainfall which prevails on the southern slopes of the Eastern Himalayas. Their influence, coupled with the Tibetan proclivities of their husbands, promoted by the Nepalese invasion of the country, induced the Rajas to transfer the head-quarters of their Government to the valley of Chumbi, one march to the Tibetan side of the Jelap pass. The prolonged residence of the chief in Tibetan territory had the worst effect on the internal administration of the State. Abuses of all kinds sprung up, while redress was hard to obtain. Lepcha interests were neglected, and Chumbi became the Hanover of Sikhim.

British intervention, 1817.

Meanwhile a still greater Power was being compelled, in spite of itself, to enter the field of East Himalayan politics. Already for thirty years the bigoted and warlike Hindus of Nepal had been harrying their peaceful Buddhist neighbours with cattle-lifting and slave-taking incursions. Before the year 1814 they had conquered and annexed the Terai or lower hills, lying between the Mechi and Tista rivers, and now covered by the valuable tea-gardens of the Darjeeling Terai. But for our intervention they would probably have permanently turned the whole of Sikhim and the hills south and west of the Tista into a province of Nepal. Peace had to be kept on the frontier, and the Government of India was the only Power willing or able to keep it. At the close, therefore, of the Goorkha war in 1817 we restored the Terai to Sikhim, and took such guarantees as were possible against a renewal of hostilities on our border. By the treaty of Titalya we assumed the position of lords paramount of Sikhim, and our title to exercise a predominant influence in that State has remained undisputed for seventy years, until recently challenged by the monastic party in Tibet.

Cession of Darjeeling, 1835.

Following our traditional policy, we meddled as little as possible in the affairs of Sikhim, and no further negotiations took place until 1834, when certain Lepcha malcontents, who had sought refuge in Nepal, made a raid on the tract ceded in 1817. Under pressure from us the refugees returned to Nepal, and the opportunity was taken by the Government of India to procure from the Raja of Sikhim the cession of the hill-station of Darjeeling and a small tract immediately surrounding it. Fifteen years afterwards Dr. Campbell, the Superintendent of

Darjeeling, and Dr. (now Sir Joseph) Hooker, while travelling in Sikhim with the permission of the British Government and the Raja, were seized and imprisoned by the influential monopolist, Namguay, popularly known as the *Pagla Diwán*, or "mad Prime Minister" of Sikhim. This treachery was punished by the annexation of the entire Terai, and a large area of the middle hills bounded on the north by the Great Rungeet river. But Namguay, though ostensibly dismissed from office, continued to exercise great influence through his wife, an illegitimate daughter of the Raja. Criminals were harboured in Sikhim, and British subjects were kidnapped from our own territory for the purposes of the slave-trade between Sikhim and Bhutan. Having exhausted all ordinary forms of protest, the Government of India found it necessary in 1860-61 to order the occupation of Sikhim by force under Colonel Gawler, accompanied by the Honourable Ashley Eden as Envoy and Special Commissioner. Our troops advanced to the Tista, the Raja accepted the terms offered, and in March 1861 a treaty was concluded at Tumlong, the capital of Sikhim, which regulates our relations with the State up to the present day. Its chief provisions are the following: "Criminals, defaulters, or other delinquents" are to be seized and given up on demand, and may be followed by our police. The ex-Diwan Namguay and all his blood relations are for ever banished from Sikhim, and excluded from the Raja's council at Chumbi. Trade monopolies, restrictions on the movements of travellers, and duties on goods passing between Sikhim and British territory, are abolished. Power is given to the British Government to make a road through Sikhim, and the Sikhim Government covenants to protect the working parties, to maintain the road in repair, and to erect and maintain suitable rest-houses for travellers. The slave-trade is prohibited. Our suzerainty in questions of foreign policy is recognised, and Sikhim undertakes not to cede or lease any portion of its territory, or to permit the passage of troops, without our consent. Finally, the Raja "agrees to remove the seat of his Government from Tibet to Sikhim, and reside there for nine months in the year." No more complete recognition of our supremacy in matters of external policy, and of our right to prescribe certain essential conditions of internal administration, could well be demanded.

Annexation of Morang, 1850.

Sikhim mediatised, 1861.

Up to this time, and indeed for some years afterwards, Tibet appears to have taken no active interest in the internal politics of Sikhim. The leading Tibetans, whether lamas or laymen, were unwilling to be mixed up in any way with Sikhim affairs, and looked with suspicion and dislike on the residence of the Raja at Chumbi, as likely to lead to dangerous political complications. Sikhim, again, though acknowledging the religious supremacy of the Dalai Lama, was as far as possible from posing as a vassal of her Eastern neighbour.

Relations of Sikhim and Tibet.

Notwithstanding the close matrimonial and proprietary connections between the reigning family and Tibet, the Raja had at no time put forward his relations with that country as a reason for failing to comply with the demands of our Government, nor had we in our dealings with him made allowance for any possible claims to suzerainty on the part of Tibet. No difficulty, therefore, was experienced in carrying out the terms of the treaty of 1861. Europeans travelling in Sikhim were cordially received by the lamas and people; surveys were commenced without hindrance; criminals were surrendered by the Sikhimese, or captured with their consent by the police of Darjeeling; freer intercourse with Darjeeling brought about the extinction of slavery; and many British subjects acquired landed property in Sikhim and held office under the Government of that country. The actions of the Raja himself showed a tendency to look to us rather than to Tibet for guidance and support. In 1873 he was permitted to visit Darjeeling, where he had an interview with Sir George Campbell. The results of this were that the allowance he received from us was increased from Rs. 9,000 to Rs. 12,000; and in the cold season of 1873-74 the Deputy Commissioner of Darjeeling was deputed to visit Sikhim and the Tibet frontier to enquire into the condition and prospects of trade with Tibet, and the advisability of making a road through Sikhim to the Tibetan frontier. In the course of this tour the Deputy Commissioner (Mr., afterwards Sir, John Ware Edgar, K.C.I.E., C.S.I.) visited all the passes of the Chola range, the eastern wing of the Sikhim amphitheatre, meeting the Raja and his chief officials and some officers of the Tibetan district of Phari. He discovered that the Tibetans were very jealous of our attempts to use the Sikhim Government and country in our efforts to open up trade with Tibet, and that the Chinese *ampa*, or Resident of Lhassa, had written to the Raja in the name of the Emperor of China, reminding him that he was bound to prevent the "Peling Sahibs" (Europeans) from crossing the frontier of Tibet, and warning him that if he continued to make roads for the Sahibs through Sikhim, "it would not be well with him." In deference to this feeling, no attempt was made by the Deputy Commissioner to cross the Tibetan frontier; but the discussions on the subject left no doubt as to the fact that the frontier line was the water-parting of the Chola range, and it was assumed throughout as a matter of course that Tibet had no right of interference, direct or indirect, in the country to the west of the frontier. She desired, in fact, nothing more than that her ancient solitary reign should remain unmolested by the approach of the European trader.

The following year witnessed a still more striking assertion of our supremacy. The sudden death of the Sikhim Raja gave the signal for the revival of an old intrigue to substitute a half-brother for the Raja's brother and heir, who was disfigured by a hare-lip. At this juncture the Deputy Commissioner of Darjeeling, acting in anticipation of the orders of the Government of India, caused the brother, the present Raja, to be proclaimed, and thus finally made an end of the intrigue. Not a whisper was heard on the frontier of remonstrance against this vigourous piece of king-making, and Tibet acquiesced silently in an act which struck at the root of any claim on her part to exercise a paramount influence in the affairs of the Sikhim State.

Proclamation of 1876.

The march of subsequent events was altogether in tune with our proclamation. In all our dealings with the Raja there never was a question raised as to the claim of Tibet to control him, while his absolute dependence on our Government was throughout acknowledged by him and his people. Sir Richard Temple, while Lieutenant-Governor of Bengal, made several excursions in Sikhim, and during his tenure of office a road was constructed through a portion of that country to the Tibetan frontier at the Jelap pass. In this work we received the active assistance of the Sikhim State, and met with no objections on the part of Tibet, though it was well known that the Government and people of that country looked on our proceedings with a certain amount of suspicion and uneasiness. We may even go so far as to credit with some political foresight an old Tibetan, who said to the Deputy Commissioner while some blasting operations were in progress on the road—"Sahib, the sound of that powder is heard at Lhassa!"

Seven years later, the question of promoting commercial intercourse with Tibet, which had dropped out of notice during the troubles in Afghanistan, was again pressed on the Government of Bengal in the general interests of British trade in the East. Mr. Colman Macaulay, Financial Secretary to that Government, was deputed to visit Sikhim and the Tibetan frontier in order to inquire into certain rumours of the stoppage of trade through Darjeeling by Tibetan officials; to ascertain whether a direct road could be opened through the Lachen valley between Darjeeling and the province of

Mr. Macaulay's proposed Mission.

Tsang, celebrated for the quality of its wool; and if possible to communicate, through the Tibetan officials at the head of the Lachen valley, a friendly message from the Government of India to the Minister at Tashe-lhunpo, the capital of Tsang. At Giagong in the north of Sikhim, Mr. Macaulay met the *Jongpen* or civil officer of the Tibetan district of Kamba, and collected much interesting information regarding the possibilities of trade between Tibet and India. In the following year, under instructions from the English Foreign Office, he visited Pekin, and obtained from the Chinese Government passports for a mixed political and scientific Mission to proceed to Lhassa for three or four months to confer with the Chinese Resident and the Lhassa Government on the free admission of native Indian traders to Tibet, and the removal of obstructions on the trade through Sikhim and Darjeeling, it being understood that no proposal for the general admission of Europeans would be brought forward.

Early in 1886 the Mission was organised, and assembled at Darjeeling with a small escort of native troops for the protection of the treasure and presents which it carried. While it was waiting to start, negotiations commenced with China concerning the north-eastern frontier of Upper Burma, then recently annexed, and in deference to Chinese susceptibilities the Government of India consented to forego their intention of despatching a Mission to Lhassa. This forbearance, though highly appreciated by China, seems to have been misunderstood by the monastic party in Tibet, whose desire to promote a policy of exclusion, and to maintain their own monopoly of trade with India, was connived at by the Chinese Resident. Arguing in true Asiatic fashion, the monks concluded that we broke up our Mission because we were afraid of them. They assumed a highly aggressive attitude, and sent a small body of Tibetan militia to occupy Lingtu, a point about twelve miles to the Sikhim side of the frontier, on the top of a high peak crossed by our road to the Jelap, one of the passes of the Chola range. Here the invaders constructed, at an elevation of 12,617 feet above the sea, a stone fort blocking and commanding the road; they warned off one of our native engineers, and announced their intention of stopping all trade by that route between Tibet and India. This open violation of territory under our protection was at first looked upon by us as a temporary outburst of Tibetan Chauvinism, which we could well afford to disregard. It was confidently expected that the mob of archers, slingers, and matchlockmen collected on a barren, windswept ridge at a height which even Tibetans find trying, would speedily fall away under stress of cold and starvation; and that the Chinese Government, moved partly by our diplomatic remonstrances, and partly by fear lest we should treat the Lingtu demonstration as a pretext for entering Tibet in force, would compel the Lhassa authorities to adjust their relations with Sikhim on a basis involving the recognition of our predominance in that State.

Tibetans occupy Lingtu, 1886.

Our expectations were signally disappointed. Not only did the Tibetans hold their ground at Lingtu with characteristic Mongolian obstinacy, but their refusal to receive letters or to enter into negotiations with us soon began to produce an alarming effect in Sikhim. When called upon to visit Darjeeling for the purpose of conferring with the Lieutenant-Governor concerning the affairs of his State, the Raja of Sikhim, after exhausting the standard Oriental excuses, replied in so many words that he and his people had in 1886 signed a treaty declaring that *Sikhim was subject only to China and Tibet.* He was therefore unable to come to Darjeeling without the express permission of the Tibetan Government. The history of this treaty is curious. It is alleged that in 1880 one of the Tibetan Secretaries of State, accompanied by a Chinese military officer, went to Paro, in Bhutan, for the purpose of settling some local disturbance. On their return to Phari, in Tibet, an attempt, at that time unsuccessful, was made to extract a similar agreement from Sikhim. Six years later, when our influence in Sikhim had begun to wane, the subject was reopened, and a formal treaty was signed at Galing, in Tibet, by the Raja, on behalf of the "people of Sikhim, priests and laymen." The treaty, which is couched in the form of a petition to the two Chinese Residents at Lhassa, set forth that some Europeans, after petitioning the great officers of China, have, to the detriment of religion, got an order to enter Tibet for trade. "From the time of Chogel Penchoo Namguay (the first Raja of Sikhim), all our Rajas and other subjects have obeyed the orders of China. . . . You have ordered us by strategy or force to stop the passage of the Rishi river between Sikhim and British territory; but we are small and the *sarkar* (British Government) is great, and we may not succeed, and may then fall into the mouth of the tiger-lion. In such a crisis, if you, as our old friends, can make some arrangements, even then in good and evil we will not leave the shelter of the feet of China and Tibet. . . . We all, king and subjects, priests and laymen, honestly promise to prevent persons from crossing the boundary."

Attitude of Sikhim Raja.

The Galing Treaty.

The ultimate aim of this singular document, in which we are referred to under the form of one of those composite animals familiar to students of Tibetan chronology, is illustrated and made clear by a very remarkable map found by a man of the Derbyshire Regiment in a house at Rinchingong, where a Tibetan General and Secretary of State were so nearly surprised by our troops that the tea they had been drinking was still hot in the cups when the house was entered. This map purports to show the tract of country extending from Phari to Darjeeling. At the latter place, temples, houses, trees, and a locomotive puffing smoke at the railway station, are depicted with much display of accuracy.

In one respect it is even more realistic than the medieval maps to which it bears a general resemblance; for the houses on either side of the Darjeeling spur are reversed in relation to each other, so that to bring them into their proper positions, the map, which is drawn on cloth, must be tilted up from below like the ridge of a tent. As a political manifesto, the map is of peculiar interest at the present time; and one is disposed to wonder that our barbarous neighbours should have been so ready to adopt one of the characteristic weapons of modern diplomacy. The Lingtu fort, with its block-house and wall, stands out in conspicuous disregard of proportion and perspective; while Tibetan territory (coloured yellow) is shown as extending to the Rishi river, about thirty miles in advance of the frontier hitherto recognised by all parties concerned. Although the borders of Tibet are to this extent enlarged, the assertion of her paramount authority over Sikhim is not indicated on the face of the map. So far at least as colouring goes, that State is not made out to be a part of Tibet. It is painted red, while the British district of Darjeeling is shown in a lighter shade of the same colour.

Map of Sikhim.

Had this been all—had an aggressive Tibet and a Tibetanising Raja of Sikhim been the only elements of danger that we were called upon to face—we might perhaps safely have indulged our national proclivities, and with some loss of prestige in Eastern Asia, have permitted the tangle to unwind itself. The Raja's announcement of his change of allegiance might have been looked upon as a meaningless flourish, to be punished by severe reproof and the stoppage of his subsidy; while the withdrawal of the Tibetans from Lingtu might ultimately have been brought about by the tardy action of China, which must sooner or later have called so unruly a vassal to order. But this door of escape from unwelcome action was absolutely closed by the state of feeling in Sikhim.

We may repeat here what has already been indicated above, that from the commencement of our relations with Sikhim there have been two parties in that State—one which may be called the Lepcha or national party, consistently friendly to our Government, and a foreign or Tibetan party, steadily hostile. The family of the chiefs has generally been by way of siding with the latter, partly in consequence of their habit of marrying Tibetan women, and partly through their fondness for Chumbi. Of late years a further complication has been introduced by the settlement of colonies of Nepalese in parts of Sikhim—a measure favoured by the Lepchas generally. These settlers look to us for protection in case of danger, and are naturally friendly to our Government; but their presence is regarded with disfavour by many

State of parties in Sikhim.

influential lamas, who allege that they waste the forests, allow their cattle to trespass, and make themselves unpleasant neighbours in other ways. In truth, however, the unwarlike Sikhimese have a wholesome dread of the fighting races of Nepal, and fear lest the industrious Newars who have settled along their southern border should be merely the forerunners of an invading army of Goorkhas. So long as these three parties maintained what may be called their natural relations, there was no fear of our influence declining, and the internal affairs of the country could be trusted to adjust themselves with the minimum of interference on our part. But when we came to inquire how things actually stood, and to look below the surface of the Lingtu demonstration, we were forced in spite of ourselves to admit that within the last three or four years some remarkable changes had taken place in the political situation. Tibet, as has already been pointed out, had assumed an attitude of unmistakable, though probably cautious, aggression; while the leaders of the Sikhim people, and Nepalese settlers with influence and property in that country, had begun to ask themselves seriously whether it might not be necessary for their ultimate safety to cast in their lot with the Tibetan party. These men, although as anxious as ever to keep up their former relations, and fully as hostile to Tibetan encroachment, had begun to doubt our desire or our ability to assist them, and openly expressed their fear of being "drowned," as they worded it, if they persisted in trying to swim against the current now running in favour of Tibet. The head of the Nepalese party, himself a resident of Darjeeling, explained in the clearest language that he would do anything we told him to do if assured of our support and ultimate protection; but that failing this guarantee, he must make his peace with the Tibetan party as the only hope of saving his property in Sikhim from confiscation, and his relatives there from imprisonment or death. The fact that this line was taken by a representative of the Nepalese settlers in Sikhim was of itself the clearest indication of the extent to which our influence had been undermined. Things must have gone very far before these settlers—people almost bigoted in their Hinduism, with just enough Mongolian blood in their veins to make them hate the Mongols—could bring themselves to contemplate the possibility of coming to terms with their ancient enemies. Things clearly had gone so far that unless we bestirred ourselves in a speedy and effective fashion, Sikhim would either become once for all a province of Tibet, or, if we were not prepared to acquiesce in that solution of the difficulty, would have to be regularly conquered by us with the people of the country either actively hostile, or, which is perhaps worse, sulkily and treacherously neutral. Some months before, representatiens had been made to China in the belief that her influence would suffice to bring about a peaceful settlement. But it is a far cry from Pekin to Lhassa; the wheels of State move slowly in China, and no effective action appears to have been taken. In default, therefore, of any means of introducing the Tibetans themselves to civilised methods of settling international disagreements, it was decided to send an ultimatum to the troops at Lingtu, warning them that if they did not abandon the post by the 14th of March they would be driven out by force of arms. Meanwhile, lest it should be supposed that even then we were not in earnest, the 32nd Pioneers, a very fine regiment of low-caste Sikhs, were sent forward to bridge the Rongli river, and His Excellency the Viceroy addressed a letter to the Dalai Lama, explaining the reasons which had induced him to take so decided a line of action.

Now this letter to the Dalai Lama raises, and in some degree answers, the very questions which the average English politician, with one eye on the fortunes of our Indian empire and the other on the prejudices of jealous or wavering constituencies, will naturally be forward to ask, What was there really to fight for? What is this Sikhim that it should become the Belgium of Asia? Why spend money and squander lives to maintain our influence in a petty sub-Himalayan princedom, merely because the chapter of accidents involved us in diplomatic relations with it seventy years ago? Are treaties so sacred in Europe that they must be deemed inviolable under the shadow of the Himalayas? If Tibet wants to have Sikhim, why should we not jump at the chance of cutting ourselves loose from uncomfortable obligations, and leave our barbarian neighbours to settle their differences within their own borders in their own way?

Our policy towards the East Himalayan States.

The answer to these questions, pertinent enough from certain points of view, involves the consideration of our general policy towards the East Himalayan States with which we come more or less into contact. Counting from the east, those States are—Tibet, Bhutan, Sikhim, and Nepal. In discussing our relations with them, the ground may be cleared by stating that under no circumstances now easily conceivable can we desire to annex any of the group. Concerning Tibet in particular, we may add, without much fear of contradiction, that the

Tibet.

Government of India, as such, wishes to have as little to do with it as possible. It lies on the other side of a great wall, which we, as the rulers of India, have not the smallest ambition to climb over. But here supposed commercial interests come in, and it is urged, on the strength of somewhat conjectural data, that Tibet offers a great market for certain articles of English manufacture. The Tibetans will take from us, we are told, any quantity of broadcloth, piece-goods, cutlery, hardware, and other odds and ends which are not worth mentioning. They may also, if their peculiar fancies are consulted, buy up a good deal of the Indian tea which fails to command a remunerative price in other markets. In return they will send us wool of admirable staple but dubious cleanliness, musk, ponies, yaks' tails, borax; and they may, if they can but get over their superstitious prejudices against mining, contribute to the solution of the currency problem by flooding the world with fresh supplies of gold. These possibilities, no less attractive than indefinite, have repeatedly been pressed upon the Government of. India; and the purely commercial arguments proper to the question have been coloured by the halo of mystery which surrounds the great inaccessible tableland of Eastern Asia. There lies the modern Brynhilde, asleep on her mountain-top; men call on the Viceroy of India to play the part of Siegfried, and awaken her from the slumber of ages. The spirit of adventure and science makes common cause with the commercial spirit in urging the most prosaic of Governments, troubled rather for its finances than its soul, to open up one of the dark places of the earth, and to enable many Englishmen to go where few Englishmen have been before. Doubtless this view of the matter is at first sight highly enticing. A gap in the botanical record needs to be filled; our maps of Tibet are still imperfect; and numerous ethnological problems crave solution. Tibet, once free to European travellers, promises all these things, and many more, to the scientific world hungering for fresh facts to assimilate. But who can doubt that the Government of India is right in putting on the drag and ignoring the few enthusiasts who grumble at its inaction? Who will deny that it would be a piece of surpassing folly for us to alienate a possible ally in China by forcing our way into Tibet in the interests of scientific curiosity, doubtfully backed by mercantile speculation? To meddle with Tibet against her will is like touching the springs of some strange machine, or handling a freshly caught animal. There is no telling what effect such experiments may produce. To this moment we cannot say for certain what set on foot the feeling of aggressive hostility which led the Tibetans to invade territory under our protection. Its outward and visible signs were obvious enough, and appeared, so far as any one could tell, to be of comparatively recent origin. Since Sir Joseph Hooker led the way in his famous journey through Sikhim, a number of Europeans, officials and others, have visited the passes of the Chola range which the Tibetans claimed as their own territory. All were more or less inclined to enter the *terra incognita* spread out before them; and all were stopped at the crest of the passes by a Tibetan guard, who displayed a placard inscribed with Tibetan and Chinese characters, and intimated by simple but significant gestures that if the English persisted in crossing the frontier, the throats of its guardians would assuredly be cut. So clearly, indeed, was the definition of the frontier understood by the Tibetans in 1849, that when Dr. Campbell was seized by the Sikhim people just below the Chola, the Tibetan guard, though remonstrating, could not interfere, because their jurisdiction ended at the crest of the pass. It may be added that the Tibetan Namguay, the "mad Minister" who was banished from Sikhim by the treaty of 1861, never ventured, at any rate in his public journeys, to cross the water-parting of the range, but invariably stopped on the Tibetan side. Within a few years all this was changed. In theory, at least, the placards were advanced to the Rishi, and nice scruples as to the exact location of the frontier gave place to a daring attempt to remove a peaceful neighbour's landmark.

One asks, almost in vain, what spell thus transformed the scene? Did some strange wave of religious fanaticism sweep over Tibet, overwhelming on one side the Roman Catholic Missions of Bathang, and on the other stirring the monks of Gyantsi and Tashelhunpo to organise an attack on Sikhim? The pointed reference to religion in the Galing treaty reads as if something of the sort had been in the air; and indications are not wanting of a tendency to resist Chinese interference, and to struggle against the policy which seeks to make Lhassa a Chinese Avignon, and to utilise the spiritual authority of the Dalai Lama as a check on possible Tartar outbreaks in Central Asia. On the other hand, the missionaries themselves, who might be expected to be the first to recognise a religious revival, do not appear to have observed any such movement. They affirm, with admirable frankness, that it was the Tibet Mission of 1886, or possibly the abandonment of the Mission, that troubled the political waters, and encouraged the monastic party in Tibet to persecute the rival Church in Bathang, and to interfere in the affairs of Sikhim. No doubt Monseigneur Biel at Ta-tsien-lu and Father Desgodins at Pedong are entitled to speak with much authority as to the political springs of action in Tibet; but one is inclined to question whether things Tibetan move so quickly as their theory would require. A cycle of Cathay, whether better or worse than twenty years of Europe, is certainly less fruitful of results; and it may be doubted whether any cause that only began to operate in 1886 could possibly, in the region of Tibetan politics, have produced a tangible effect by 1887. It seems, indeed, more probable that we must look further back for the real cause of the present difficulties: that the making of the Jelap road roused a feeling of suspicion which went on quietly spreading, and needed only some slight stimulus from our side to translate itself into action. Such a stimulus may have been given by the Tibet Mission, or by exaggerated rumours of the strength of the escort provided for it. Conjectures of this sort are, however, mostly vanity, and they are only mentioned here in order to show how little we know of what goes on in these regions of mystery, and to indicate the possible dangers of adopting a forward policy with the object of promoting freer commercial intercourse with British India. Such intercourse may, we believe, be trusted to grow up of itself in no very distant future. The Tibetan, whether monk or layman, has all the instincts of a born trader, and sooner or later he is bound to realise in what direction his advantage may be found. We, on the other hand, can well afford to wait an opportunity, and need not risk the substantial gain of our *entente cordiale* with China by clutching too eagerly at the problematic chances of Tibetan markets.

With regard to Bhutan we are in some respects more fortunately situated. No one wishes to explore that tangle of jungle-clad and fever-stricken hills, infested with leeches and the *pipsa* fly, and offering no compensating advantages to the most enterprising pioneer. Adventure looks beyond Bhutan; science passes it by as a region not sufficiently characteristic to merit special exploration. Our policy towards the Bhutanese, therefore, is determined solely by considerations of geographical position and diplomatic expediency, and has not to take account of pressure applied in the supposed interests of commerce or science. In point of fact, only one source of possible complications has to be borne in mind. Bhutan, as is generally known, is afflicted with a curious dual system of government, under which the Dharm Raja, or spiritual chief, is supplied by a series of incarnations which occur in the families of the chief officers of the State; while the temporal ruler, or Deb Raja, is supposed to be elected by the council of permanent ministers called the Lenchen. In practice, however, the Deb is nominated by whichever of the two governors of East and West Bhutan happens at the time to be the more powerful. The equilibrium thus arrived at is eminently unstable; rival parties are constantly struggling for power, and the work of government is lost in a whirl of intrigues and counterintrigues. This concerns us little, so long as the turmoil does not boil over into our territory. But the ruling classes of the State are still sore at the loss of the Duars, or "gates" of Bhutan, a level strip of country running along the foot of the hills, which we annexed at the close of the Bhutan war in 1865. Excellent tea land is found in the Duars, which now form part of the Jalpaiguri district, and a fringe of tea-gardens, giving occupation to a large number of European planters, extends along a portion of the Bhutan frontier. Many of these are within easy reach of a raid from the hills, and any circumstance which for a time over-clouded our influence in this part of the country might create a risk of a massacre of our planters or

Bhutan.

their coolies in the Duars, or force us to make an expedition into Bhutan to avert such a calamity.

Turning now to the western member of the East Himalayan group of States, we are struck by a remarkable contrast. Whatever else it may be, the Hindu kingdom of Nepal is certainly not a weak Government. Its methods are not exactly our methods, and its ways with political dissenters are exceedingly short. Nevertheless its officers hold regular trials, record evidence, and administer a rough sort of justice, which seems to be on the road to discarding barbarous punishments in the case of offences which are not of a political character. Nepal at any rate is civilised enough for us to have concluded with it an extradition treaty, which on the whole works fairly well; while in matters of revenue administration it is centuries ahead of Sikhim and Bhutan. Many of the leading men of the country have been educated in our schools; they take a just and intelligent view of Indian politics, and at the present day they are in no way inclined to underrate the length of the British arm. From the beginning of the Sikhim difficulty the Katmandu *darbar* has shown every disposition to make itself serviceable to us by communicating information and by warning us of certain manœuvres, such as poisoning springs, making attacks by night, and constructing booby traps, which are supposed to characterise the art of war as practised in Tibet. It has behaved, in short, in a manner befitting the governing body of a strong State, occupying country which we have no wish to annex, and recognising that its interests are in the main identical with ours. As a buffer between ourselves and the barbarous country beyond, Nepal leaves little to be desired.

Nepal.

The peculiar position of Sikhim renders it impossible for us to ignore it as we ignore Bhutan, or to treat it on terms of comparative equality as we treat Nepal. Sikhim cannot stand by itself, and if we withdrew our support, it must ultimately fall either to Tibet or to Nepal. But for our treaty obligations the latter consummation would hardly be one to be deeply regretted, but it is difficult to see how it could be brought about peaceably. The Tibetan party would certainly try to hold the country for themselves; and although the stronger races of Nepal would probably win in the long run, the period of transition would be one of intolerable anarchy. Once let our hold be relaxed, and Sikhim would become the Alsatia of the Eastern Himalayas, and such a state of things would react most formidably on the security of life and property in the great European settlement of Darjeeling. Every rood of land in that district that is not expressly reserved by Government for the cultivation of food-crops has already been taken up for tea, and a very large capital has been sunk in its cultivation, which gives

Sikhim.

employment to an enormous number of natives, mostly immigrants from Nepal. On all sides the hills are dotted with Europeans' bungalows; tea-gardens cover the slopes which face towards Sikhim; and the summer residence of the head of the Bengal Government is to all appearance within a stone's-throw of the stream which forms the boundary of British territory. The station of Darjeeling itself is no doubt adequately protected by the European troops stationed at the cantonment of Jellapahar; but a large number of outlying tea-gardens are absolutely at the mercy of possible raiders from Sikhim. Nor is it only the planters and their native labourers that have to be considered. Many of our subjects, Tibetans settled in Darjeeling, Lepchas, and Nepalese, have large transactions and interests in Sikhim, about which disputes constantly arise. For the last twenty-five years our relations with the Sikhim Government have been so close, and our hold over it so strong, that the Deputy Commissioner of Darjeeling has, as a rule, found little difficulty in settling such disputes when referred to him. Processes, both civil and criminal, issued by the Darjeeling courts, are virtually current in Sikhim, and the Darjeeling police have free access to the country. Sikhim, in fact, has been treated substantially as part of British India, subjected for political reasons to the nominal rule of a princelet of the Merovingian type. An instance of recent date will serve to illustrate what is meant. In July 1888 a murderous outbreak occurred in the Darjeeling jail; a warder was killed, and eight convicts escaped. Some fled to Nepal, others were believed to have taken refuge in Sikhim. In the case of Nepal no hot pursuit was possible; the frontier was close, and we could not follow our criminals over it. The utmost that could be done was to demand extradition through the Resident at Katmandu, sending a formal record of the evidence against the offenders, with proof of the nationality of each. In the case of Sikhim no such formalities were necessary. The Deputy Commissioner sent off a party of armed police with orders to arrest the runaways, wherever found, and bring them back at once. Now, if Sikhim were allowed to become a part of Tibet, cases of this kind would give rise to inconvenient negotiations, and might even become a cause of friction between our representative at Pekin and the Chinese Government. It must further be remembered that a Tibetan Sikhim would lack the stability, the common sense, and the capacity for gradual advance towards civilisation, which characterise the Nepal Government. An extradition treaty would hardly be workable, and every absconding criminal would become the subject of an irritating diplomatic wrangle.

Enough has perhaps been said to show that the obligation of driving the Tibetans out of Sikhim was imposed on us by the essential conditions of our policy towards the East Himalayan States; that this policy is a just and reasonable one; and that it involves the assumption on our part of no more authority than is necessary if we are to keep the peace in this particular corner of the Indian empire. To maintain this policy by the cheapest and most effective means was the sole object of the military operations commenced in March 1888, and terminated by the engagement of the 24th September of that year. For the better understanding of the principles on which this little war was conducted, a further glance at the conformation of the country will be needed. Lingtu, we have already explained, is a peak about twelve miles to the Sikhim side of the frontier, over the top of which our road runs to the Jelap pass. The sides of this peak are very precipitous, and the road could not have been taken along them except at great expense. A force holding Lingtu can therefore block the road, and can also command the steep downs below the Jelap, where Tibetan herdsmen pasture their sheep and cattle during the summer months. Both points probably counted for something with the Tibetans, who have a considerable, if not an excessive, sense of the value of position in warfare, and who seem also not to have overlooked the possible support which the habits of the herdsmen might give to the theory of a pastoral frontier extending to the Garnei. As a matter of fact, no such theory is at all tenable. The practice arises partly out of the necessities of the case—the pastures lie on both sides of the frontier, and cattle are bound to stray—and partly from the accident that a large part of the property owned in Tibet by the Rajas of Sikkim and their wives has consisted of cattle tended by Tibetan herdsmen, their servants. On the Singilela range, where it forms the border between Darjeeling and Nepal, Nepalese shepherds feed their flocks on either side of the frontier, paying grazing fees to our Forest officers—just as the Tibetans pay rent to the Raja of Sikhim for the period spent by them on the Sikhim side. But no Nepalese official would be so inconsequent as to make this a reason for asserting that the whole of the grazing tract belonged to Nepal.

At the beginning of hostilities, while our troops were being moved up from the plains, public opinion in India had hardly made up its mind to take tho Lingtu garrison seriously. A turn for cheap swagger is a prominent trait in the Tibetan character, and it seemed not impossible that in invading Sikhim, the lamas were merely "trying it on," and would withdraw their rabble directly the advance of our troops showed that we were in earnest. In order to leave open the door to an early reconciliation, and to make it clear that our only object was to restore the *status quo* in Sikhim, and to secure that country and Bhutan from future aggressive interference on the part of Tibet, General Graham was directed not to pursue the enemy across the frontier, unless it was absolutely necessary to do so for military reasons. These instructions were carefully observed. In the storming of the stockade at Jeyluk, a short distance below Lingtu, only thirty-two Tibetans were killed; and no attempt was made to pursue the Lingtu garrison, who fled from their fort when Sir Benjamin Bromhead and some men of the Pioneers reached the gate. The methods of defence adopted at Jeyluk recall some of the incidents of medieval warfare. Walls and stockades had been built across the most precipitous part of the road; the road itself was cut away so as to leave an impassable chasm; rocks and tree-trunks were piled at favourable points, with levers to hurl them down on an ascending enemy; and slings and arrows were freely, but vainly, used as our men advanced. The issue, one would think, might have shown that the weapons of Morgarten avail little against modern infantry. But the lesson was lost on the fanatical monks of the great monasteries around Lhassa. Their only answer to our pacific messages was to hasten up to the frontier all the troops they could collect, and to occupy the Jelap and Pembiringo passes with a continually increasing force. Meanwhile we had fortified the more sheltered and defensible position of Gnatong, about eight miles to the south of the Jelap, and lay waiting there for events to develop themselves. The whole of April and the early part of May were spent by the Tibetans in massing their troops on their own side of the passes. On the 22nd May, encouraged by a promise of victory from the "shaking oracle"[1] at Naichang, they attacked Gnatong in force, were repulsed with heavy loss, and retired over the Jelap.

Tibetans attack Gnatong, 22nd May 1888.

In order to avoid needless slaughter, our men were not encouraged to follow the flying enemy farther than was necessary to completely break up the attack and convince the Tibetans that they had been really defeated. This conviction, however, came slowly to those who had taken no part in the fight. Strange rumours of the prowess of "the Lama army" that was gathering at Lhassa found their way across the frontier; fresh troops were beaten up in all directions; terrible threats were conveyed to the leaders of the force on the frontier; and everything went to show that the counsels of the monastic party were still for open war. It is hardly surprising that this should have been so. The new *ampa*, despatched by China with instructions to bring about a peaceful settlement, had not yet arrived, and the lamas lacked the sagacity to perceive that we were only holding back in order to give him time to make his influence felt. To their eyes we appeared to forego without purpose our own advantage, and they

[1] This may refer to the use of an arrow as a sort of divining rod, described by Schlagintweit, "Buddhism in Tibet," or possibly to divination by the shivering of an animal, for which there are classical parallels.

drew from this the conclusions which most Asiatics would draw under similar circumstances.

Nevertheless, though the lamas knew it not, their obstinacy, wasting itself on our defensive tactics, was daily bringing us nearer to the real object of the campaign. At relatively small cost to ourselves, we were wearing out the resources of Tibet, and leading her on to strike the blow which should be our opportunity. The prisoners taken at Gnatong confirmed the reports received from our officers in Almora and Ladakh, that forced levies had been beaten up from the most distant provinces, and were fed and kept together with the utmost difficulty. The Tibetan commissariat is indeed somewhat less elaborate than our own. Forty pounds of barley-flour, half a brick of tea, half a pound of salt, half a small sheep's bladder of butter, and 3½*d.* to buy meat, are said to represent a month's rations for a fighting man; and it may be surmised that he gets little or no pay beyond this. But the simplest supplies are hard to obtain in a barren region intersected by mountain-ranges, and wanting in all effective means of carriage; while a militia snatched on the spur of the moment from pastoral and agricultural pursuits is proverbially unsuited for prolonged hostilities.

As soon, then, as it was clear that Tibetan patience was coming to an end, and that our forbearance was still mistaken for timidity, fresh troops were ordered up and preparations made for bringing the campaign to a close directly the rains were over. By the middle of August, General Graham had under his command at Gnatong a wing of the Derbyshire, the 32nd Pioneers (Sikhs), one of the newly raised Goorkha regiments, and six mountain guns—in all, nearly 2,000 men. After a month of waiting for fine weather, the conclusive engagement was brought on by the action of the Tibetans themselves. Two ridges, the Tukola and the Nimla, intervene between our position at Gnatong and the Kaphu valley, into which, as has been mentioned above, the Jelap and Pembiringo passes open. On the night of the 23rd September our advanced pickets came in as usual, and reported no unusual activity on the part of the Tibetans. At daylight on the morning of the 24th, the Gnatong garrison became aware that the enemy had advanced during the night four miles from their camp; had occupied the Tukola ridge, 13,550 feet above the sea, and 1,500 feet higher than Gnatong; and had built a stone wall two miles in length all along the crest of the ridge. Notwithstanding this marvellous piece of impromptu engineering, the weakness of their new position was apparent at a glance. The whole of their large force, numbering more than 11,000 men, was distributed in line along the wall; no attempt had been made to take advantage of the ground or to

Final defeat of Tibetans, 24th September 1888.

concentrate troops at points of importance; while the entire position was enfiladed by the Tukola peak, on which their right flank rested. Once in possession of this peak, less than a mile and-a-half from Gnatong, we could roll up the enemy's line at leisure, and the conformation of the ground was such that a force retiring towards the Jelap must need suffer terribly during its retreat. This fact determined the scheme of our attack. Approaching the Tukola peak by a route which covered them from the fire of its defenders, the Goorkhas carried the position by a rush, and their attack, combined with the parallel advance of the Pioneers, swept the Tibetans from the ridge. In their flight down that fatal hill, and the ascent of the Nimla ridge which lay between them and the Jelap, the ill-armed, undrilled militia whom the monks had sent forth as the army of Tibet lost nearly a tenth of their number in killed and wounded. On our side, Colonel Sir Benjamin Bromhead, commanding the 32nd Pioneers, was severely wounded in the attempt to take prisoners two Tibetans, whom he believed to have surrendered; one of the Goorkhas was severely and two Pioneers slightly wounded. No effort was made by the Tibetans to rally their broken troops or to keep up a running fight; the rout was complete. We bivouacked that night in the enemy's camp on the Jelap, and no resistance was offered to our advance upon Rinchagong next day. Straggling parties of the enemy were seen emerging from the Tibetan side of the Pembiringo pass, but they broke off into Bhutan as soon as they realised that we were about to enter Rinchagong, and the village was empty when our troops reached it. The march to Chumbi through the beautiful valley of the Mochu was a mere promenade, and our troops returned to Gnatong without seeing any more of the enemy.

There seems to be reason to believe that this unavoidably severe lesson has been taken to heart by the Tibetans. The force which was dispersed at Gnatong had been drawn from all parts of the country, and the knowledge of our overwhelming military superiority must by this time be so widely diffused that even the arrogance of the lamas can no longer affect to ignore it. Indications, indeed, are not wanting that the Tibetan claim to suzerainty over Sikhim had already been practically abandoned, though the Tibetans tried hard to retrieve their defeat in the field by a diplomatic triumph of the Fabian type, and seem for a time to have had the support of China in their ingenious efforts to tire out our representatives.

The Anglo-Chinese convention of 1890 secures the formal acknowledgment of our rights which the Gnatong victory entitles us to demand. At the close of a costly and vexatious campaign, carried on at an elevation never before reached by regular troops, and involving transport difficulties of the most serious kind, it was clearly essential to have something in the nature of a final settlement to show for our trouble.

But we can afford to be content with a distinct surrender of the indefinite claim to control the course of events in Sikhim which for the last three years has troubled the peace of our frontier and stopped all trade between Darjeeling and Tibet. Above all things, we have no call to irritate the Tibetans and possibly excite the jealous territorial susceptibilities of China by introducing stipulations granting to European traders or travellers the coveted right of exploiting the commercial and scientific treasures of the interior of Tibet. Traders would assuredly fall foul of the monopolies reserved to the monks of the great monasteries; while scientific research, however modest in its aims, could scarcely fail to come into collision with some form of religious or social prejudice. Here surely is one of the cases where "the half is more than the whole." Be the treaty never so meagre, we anyhow remain in possession of the disputed tract, while the roads and bridges made during the campaign ensure us the command of the passes against Tibetan inroads. Our influence is predominant in Sikhim; it has been vigorously asserted by the introduction of essential reforms in the government of the State, and we need not fear that it will hereafter be permitted to decline.

Most of all will our position be strengthened by the change which is insensibly but steadily taking place in the composition of the population of Sikhim. The Lepchas, as has been stated, are rapidly dying out; while from the west, the industrious Newars and Goorkhas of Nepal are pressing forward to clear and cultivate the large areas of unoccupied land on which the European tea-planters of Darjeeling have already cast longing eyes. The influx of these hereditary enemies of Tibet is our surest guarantee against a revival of Tibetan influence. Here also religion will play a leading part. In Sikhim, as in India, Hinduism will assuredly cast out Buddhism, and the praying-wheel of the Lama will give place to the sacrificial implements of the Brahman. The land will follow the creed; the Tibetan proprietors will gradually be dispossessed, and will betake themselves to the petty trade for which they have an undeniable aptitude.

The future of Sikhim.

Thus race and religion, the prime movers of the Asiatic world, will settle the Sikhim difficulty for us, in their own way. We have only to look on and see that the operation of these causes is not artificially hindered by the interference of Tibet or Nepal. The trade with Tibet which the Macaulay Mission was intended to develop may well be left for the present to take its chance. Such scanty data as are available do not appear to warrant a very high estimate of its value. Whatever it may be worth, it is bound sooner or later to seek out the shortest and cheapest route. The troubles of the last three years have of course diverted it to Nepal, and some time may elapse before it finds its way back to its former channel. But the roads made while hostilities were imminent must ultimately attract traffic to the railway at Darjeeling, and in this indirect fashion we shall realise the only tangible and substantial benefit likely to be derived from closer intercourse between India and Tibet.

H. H. RISLEY.

SIKHIM.

ITS GEOGRAPHICAL POSITION AND DESCRIPTION.

The Native State, commonly called Sikhim, is situated in the Eastern Himalayan Mountains, and is bounded on the north and north-east by Tibet, on the south-east by Bhutan, on the south by the British district of Darjeeling, and on the west by Nepal: it lies between 27° 5′ and 28° 10′ N. Lat., and between 88° 4′ and 88° 58′ E. Long., and comprises an area of 2,818 square miles.

The country may be briefly described as the catchment area of the head waters of the river Tista, and the boundary with Tibet is thus laid down in the Anglo-Chinese Convention of the 17th March 1890:—

"The boundary of Sikhim and Tibet shall be the crest of the mountain range separating the waters flowing into the Sikhim Tista and its affluents from the waters flowing into the Tibetan Mochu, and northwards into other rivers of Tibet. The line commences at Mount Gipmochi on the Bhutan frontier, and follows the above-mentioned water parting to the point where it meets Nipal territory."

The continuation of the above range southward as far as the source of the Rummam stream forms the western boundary.

The Rummam stream, until its junction with the Great Rungeet, and thence the latter river, separate Sikhim from British territory.

The boundary with Bhutan is ill-defined, but appears to be the Richi-Pangola range up to the plateau south-east of Lingtu, thence a line north-east to the trigonometrical station near Gnatong, and thence a straight line to Gipmochi. The natural boundary should be the river Dichu.

In the reigns of the earlier Sikhim Rajas their realms extended from the Arun river on the west to the Tegon La range on the east, and thus included the Tambur and Mochu valleys. In a Sikhim paper, which recites various old works, it is thus described:—"This sacred country (hBres-mo-kShong, which lies to the south-west of Lhassa) is bounded on the north by the 'Mon-Thangla' mountain,

Note.—A uniform system of transliteration has not been followed throughout the Gazetter: the style adopted by each contributor has been reproduced.

which is guarded by the spirit 'Kiting.' On the east lies the 'lTas-hGons' mountain. Its southern gate is 'Nagsharbhati,' which is guarded by 'Ma-mGon-lCham-Bral-Yab-lDud.' Its western gate, 'lTimar mChhod-rTen,' is guarded by the terrible female spirit 'Mamos.' The 'mDsod-lNga' mountains and the spirit 'Phra-Man-dGe-Man' of Zar guard it on the north."

Sketches from Nipal, vol. 1, pp. 53-54.

Dr. Oldfield, writing in 1858, makes the country subject to the Sikhim Rajas even more extensive:—"The hill country constituting the basin of the Kosi river is divided into two provinces or districts by the Arun river. The district lying on the right bank of the Arun, and extending between it and the Dud Kosi, is the country of the Kirantis—a hill tribe of low-caste Hindus, who once possessed considerable power and territory in these eastern hills, but were speedily reduced to submission by Prithi Narayan after his conquest of Nipal. The district lying on the eastern or left bank of the Arun, and extending from it to Sikhim,* is Limbuana or the country of the Limbus, another tribe of low-caste Hindus. It formerly belonged to Sikhim, but was conquered and permanently annexed to Nipal by Prithi Narayan. Previous to the Gorkha conquest of the valley of Nipal, the territories of the Niwar Kings of Bhatgaon extended eastward to the Dud Kosi river, which formed the boundary between the country of the Niwars and the country of the Kirantis."

* *i.e.*, the Sikhim of 1858.

Political Mission to Bhutan, p. 112.

The Hon'ble Mr. Ashley Eden in 1864 noticed that "Sikhim, though a very petty State then, was formerly a fair-sized country, reaching from the Arun river on the west to the Taigon Pass on the east, from Tibet on the north to Kissengunge in Purneah on the south."

In dealing with the reigns of the successive Sikhim Rajas it will be seen how, by degrees, Sikhim lost the bulk of its original territory.

The range of mountains that practically bound Sikhim on three sides form a kind of horse-shoe, which constitutes the watershed of the Rungeet and the Tista: while dependent spurs project from this horse-shoe and serve as lateral barriers to the basins of the Rungeet and the Tista's greater affluents, the Lachung, Lachen, Zemu, Talung, Rongni, and Rungpo-Chu. These basins have a southward slope, being broad at the top, where they leave the watershed, and gradually contracting like a fan from its rim to the handle, which is the Tista valley near Pashok.

On or near the outer range, commencing from the south-east, are the following peaks and passes:—

Richila, 10,370.—The trijunction point of Darjeeling, Sikhim, and Bhutan.

Pangola, 9,000.—The road from Sikhim *viâ* Memo-chen to Assom-Dok in Bhutan crosses the ridge here.

Lingtu, 12,617.—The erection of a fort by the Tibetans at this place in July 1886 led to the Sikhim expedition of 1888; the fort was captured on the 21st March of that year and destroyed.

Shalambi, 12,500.—A road to Bhutan starts from this place.

Gnatong, 12,606.—The British fort here is about 12,300 feet above sea level: was attacked by the Tibetans in force on the 22nd May 1888.

Gipmochi, 14,523.—The trijunction point of Sikhim, Bhutan, and Tibet.

Merugla, 15,271.

Pembiringo-la, 14,400.—More properly Pemaringong-la.—The pass that leads to the villages of Pema and Rinchingong in the Mochu valley.

Jendorhi, 15,516.

Jelep-la, 14,390.—Meaning "the smooth beautiful pass," the most frequented of all the passes opening out into the Mochu valley near Chumbi.

Chukurchi, 15,283.

Nathula, 14,400.—Pass leading to Pema.

Yak-la, 14,400.—Close to preceding.

Cho-la, 14,550.—Leads more directly to Chumbi than any of the above, and was formerly the main route from Sikhim to Phari.

Dopendikang, 17,325.

Gna-ri, 17,570.

Thanka-la, 16,000.—Leading out from the Lachung valley eastwards.

Ghora-la, 17,000.—Ditto ditto ditto.

Shu-Du-Tshenpa, 22,960.

Kangchinphu, 23,190, improperly styled Powhunri in the map.—This latter name really belongs to a mountain near Dubdi monastery.

Donkia-ri, 20,250.—Close to this peak is

Donkia-la, 18,100.—A pass once supposed to lead direct into Tibet, but in fact only joining the upper tracts of the Lachung and Lachen valleys of Sikhim.

Bhom-tsho, 18,000.—Leading from the Cholamoo-lake district into Tibet.

Kongra-lamu, 16,000.—The direct pass from Sikhim towards Kambagong: the actual boundary pass, called Sebu-la, is a little further north.

Chomiomo, 22,290.

Nakula, 17,000.

Choten Nyema, 19,000.—Formerly the direct route to the district of Ser-Tinki when that place belonged to Sikhim: now seldom used.

Jonsong-la, 22,350.—Almost unused.

Kanchinjingna, 28,156.

Kabru, 24,015.

Kangla-Nangma-la, 16,740.—Leading to Walloon-gola on the Nepalese-Tibetan frontier.

Kangrangla, 14,770.

Chiabhangan or Singali-la, 10,320.—The main pass on the chief route between Sikhim and Nepal.

Go-cha, 12,130.—Usually, but improperly, called Singa-le-la.

On the main ridge running south-east from Kanchinjingna and separating the Rungeet from the Talung Chu we meet with the

Guicha-la, 16,500.

Pandim, 22,020.

Narsing, 19,150.

On the ridge running due east and separating the Talung Chu from the Zemu are—

Simolchu (D. 2), 22,300.

Yeumtsola, 15,800.

Lama-anden or Tak-cham (D. 3), 19,210.

Other notable mountains and passes are—

Kangchinjhau, 22,550;

Sibula, 17,590;

Phalung, 16,150;

Chango-Khang, 20,990;

all on the range separating the Lachen-Lachung:

Phieungong, 12,130, on the road to the Chola, and

Jongri, 15,140, at the junction of the routes from the Guicha-la and Kangla-nangma-la.

Moinam, 10,637, and Tendong, 8,675, are conspicuous in the landscape, as viewed from Darjeeling.

There are no towns or even villages in Sikhim; the nearest approach to the latter is to be found in the collection of houses near the Raja's palaces at Tumlong and Gantok, round some of the larger monasteries, such as Pemiongchi, Tashiding, Phensung, and a few others at the copper mines of Pache near Dikkeling and the bazars at Rhenock, Pakhyong, the Rungeet and Rummam.

Round each monastery will be found separate houses in which the monks reside, but these are so few that the term "village," if applied to them, would be a misnomer.

In Sikhim there are some 36 monasteries, whose origin is detailed in subsequent chapters.

HISTORY OF SIKHIM AND ITS RULERS.

Before detailing the legendary history of the descent of the Sikhim Rajas, it may be as well to premise that the alleged Indian origin of the early Tibetan kings is without any real foundation, and is in itself a proof of the modern manufacture of their history, as it is merely an invention in common with the other Buddhist kings to affiliate themselves on to Sakya's stock. It will also be a mistake to take earlier accounts as history, as there is no real history of Tibet obtainable from indigenous sources previous to Srong-tsan Gampo's time, *i.e.*, the 7th century A.D. Insight into pre-historic Tibet is only obtainable from scattered accounts contained in Chinese records: while even at Srong-tsan's time, when the introduction of writing made records possible, history is so vague that the birth of that king himself may be any time between 600 and 627 A.D. The historical books credited to this epoch were probably written some centuries later.

It is believed in Sikhim that the Rajas of Sikhim came of Indian origin by descent through the first king of Tibet, Ñah-Thi-Tsanpo.

The appearance of this monarch in Tibet is usually supposed to have been as follows*:—The fifth son of King Prasenajit of Kośala was born with obliquely drawn† eyes, with blue eyebrows, webbed fingers, and two rows of full developed, pearly white teeth. His parents, in alarm at such a prodigy, placed the infant in a copper vessel and set it afloat on the Ganges. A poor cultivator found the infant and brought him up as his own. On attaining man's estate the prince felt he had been born to a higher state than that of a cultivator, and in a spirit of restless ambition set out northwards over the Himalayas in quest of some great exploit. With difficulty he reached the lofty snowy mountains of Lha-ri near the modern town of Tse-thang in Tibet. Descending into the plains of Tsan-than he was met by many natives of the country, who, struck with the graceful looks of the stranger, asked him respectfully who he was and whence he came. Not knowing their language, the prince could only reply by signs that he was a prince, and pointing up to top of Lha-ri wished them to understand that he had come from that direction. The Tibetans misunderstood his meaning, and assumed he was a god descended from heaven, and accordingly entreated him to become their king. On his assenting, they placed him in a chair and carried him on their shoulders in triumph to Yumbu Lagân, near the site of the present town of Lhassa. From having been carried on a "chair" on men's "backs," the prince

* For fuller details see S. C. Das's "Contributions on Tibet," J. A. S. B., No. 3, 1881.

† Another version states that the infant winked with the lower eyelids.

obtained his name Ñah-Thi-Tsanpo, the chair-borne king; *i.e.*, *g*Nah = back, Khri = chair, and pTsan-po = powerful one or king.

There may be another interpretation of the word, as applied to himself by the prince, viz., "the dead one," alluding to his having been rejected by his family, to whom he was now dead: the northern tribes frequently using the phrase "one borne on men's shoulder" to express euphemistically "one dead."

There is also another tradition in Tibet that Sakya Singh's son, Dachen Zing, had two sons, the younger of whom married, but had no children; the elder became a priest. On his death-bed he pointed out that his spirit would go out into two eggs: these his minister, Chulen Danwa Zangpo, hid in a sugarcane field. From these eggs sprang two boys: the elder became a priest, while the younger married and had three sons, of whom Sali-nim-mo went to Nepal, Palgyegel Zanpo to Kham, and the third Na-lag-chen (*i.e.*, he of the webbed fingers) entered Tibet and became the progenitor of Ñah-Thi-Tsanpo above.

The date of the birth of Ñah-Thi-Tsanpo is given as 416 B.C.

The twenty-seventh king in direct descent was Lha-Tho-Tho-ri Ñan-Tsan,* born about 441 A.D.,† in whose eightieth year there fell from heaven on the top of the great palace of Yumbu Lagân a precious chest, which was found to contain—

(1) Two books written with jewel water on gold leaves.
(2) A golden miniature shrine set with jewels and enclosing.
(3) A crystal gem and cup.

At that time there were no letters or alphabet in Tibet, but the Tibetans, though not knowing these books were scriptures, treated them with the greatest faith and reverence; while the king sitting in council was debating on the value and merit of the divine gift, a voice from heaven was heard saying that the books were scriptures, and that in the fifth generation the mystery of their contents would be revealed. The relics were thenceforth placed on a throne set with rubies and other jewels, lights were kept burning before them, and the people worshipped them under the appellation Tembosangwa‡ to the best of their ability.

The third in descent from Lha-Tho-Tho-ri was the blind king, who recovered his sight while worshipping the sacred relics at his coronation. As the first object he saw was an *Ovis ammon* sheep on the hill Tag-ri, he received the *sobriquet* of Tag-ri-nyan-ssig, the beholder (ssig) of a sheep (Nyan) on Tag-ri.

* Other accounts say that Lha-Tho-Tho-ri gNyan-bTsan is the same as Ñah-Thi-Tsanpo, and that the name, which means "the god from the high mountains," has reference to the prince's pointing up to the mountain whence he had come.

† Cs. 252 A.D. Cs. = Csoma de Koros.

‡ San-wa Nyanpo.

His son was Nam-ri-Sron-tsan, who introduced the knowledge of arithmetic and medicine from China, and also discoveréd the great salt mines of Chyan-gi-tshva.

His son Sron-tsan-Gampo was born A.D. 600-627.* Up to his time there was no written language in Tibet, but this monarch, seeing how essential a written language was both for religious and moral good government, sent his minister, Sambhota, with sixteen companions to Kasi (Benares) to study carefully the Sanskrit language and the sacred literature of the Indian Buddhists. In particular they were instructed to devise a written language for Tibet by adopting the Sanskrit alphabet to the phonetic peculiarities of the Tibetan dialect. On their return they framed the present two-fold system of Tibetan characters, viz., the "U-chan" or headed or capital letters, and the "U-med" or headless or running hand; the former adopted from Devanágarí, and the latter from the Wartu. Thus was introduced a copious system of written language intoTibet. This same monarch married two princesses from China and Nepal, then two great centres of Buddhism, and thus great influence was brought to bear for the propagation of Buddhism: practically his two wives converted him to Buddhism: he also founded the city of Lhassa and made it his capital.

His great-great-grandson was Thi-Sron-De-Tsan, the most illustrious king of Tibet, born about 730 A.D.† In his reign the Indian sage S'ánta Rakshita and Pandit Padma Sambhava from Udyayana came to Tibet and founded the great monastery of Samye. He left three sons, one of whom migrated eastwards and became Gyalpo‡ (or princelet) of Kham§-Miñag-Andong, one of the eighteen quasi-Tibetan principalities that were seized by China about 1732. This place is situated to the west of Ta-tsien-loo, between Litang and Dirghé.

Twenty-five generations later there was born a prince, who went with his five sons westwards on a pilgrimage to the Guru Chooi-wang at Lho-brag: owing to this visit he received his first appellation Zhal-nga-Guru-Tashe. He next went to Lhassa, where Jo-vo-Rimpoche Sakya Moonі‖ foretold to him that he should proceed south-west, where he would find a country Demo-shong. He accordingly went to Sakya. In this place the hierarch was then engaged in building the great

* Cs. 627 A.D.

† Cs. 728 A.D.

‡ It is said that one of his descendants summoned the Sakya Penchen Rimboche hGromgon hPhags-pa to Kham Minag, and by his worship and intercession with Guru Thamar-Yese-Ran-bar obtained a miraculous seal, set on one side with a ruby, engraved with a nine-horned scorpion. This mark of divine favour made him so famous that he became King of China and of Shö-ser as well as Kham.

§ Män Nya. *See* Rockbill's "The Land of the Lamas," pp. 218 and 345, where it is said this State was from 1864 to 1889 part of the Kingdom of Lhassa.

‖ Image brought by the Chinese princess, wife of Sron-tsan-Gampo.

hall of the hPhrul-pahi-Lha-khang monastery, which is supported by four immense wooden pillars,* besides 160 small ones: the building is seven stories high. These four pillars, that had defied the efforts of several thousand men to raise, Guru Tashe's eldest son succeeded in erecting in their proper positions. For this exploit his name was changed to Jo-khyé-Bumsa.† In Sakya Khyé-Bumsa married Guru-mo, the daughter of the hierarch. Shortly after the whole family removed to a place, north-west of Khambagong, called Pa-shi, where they built a monastery for 400 monks and left one of the brothers in charge: the others went on to Phari, where they built the Samdub Lhakang monastery: the father died here. Three of the brothers, Se-shing, Tsendong, and Kar-tshogs, migrated towards Hah in Bhutan, while Khyé-Bumsa proceeded first to Khang-bu Takloong, on the western branch of the Mochu, and then finally settled at Chumbi, where he built a house, the site alone of which now remains, to the north of the present palace.

From the first three brothers are descended the Bep-Tshan-Gye families alluded to subsequently.

It may here be mentioned that the worship of ancestors is in some families incumbent: the descendants of the three brothers continue the worship of their common ancestor, Guru-Tashe, and are known as the Tashe-pho-la (the worshippers of the ancestor Tashe), while Khyé-Bumsa's family, being separated from the main branch, fell back on the worship of Pa-shi, where their first temple was, and are now called Pa-shi-pho-la.

Several stories are told of the miraculous strength of Khyé-Bumsa, and his victory over Ngag-wang-ge-pü-pul-bar, a rival Bhutanese hero, which resulted in the present worship of Mt. Massong by the inhabitants of Chumbi and Hah. The Phari people worship Chumulhari.

Being childless, Khyé-Bumsa consulted his Lamas and was told to propitiate the heads of the Lepcha people. Accordingly, with a following of seventeen persons only, he crossed the Yak-la and Penlong and reached Sata-la near Rankpo: here he enquired who were the heads of the Lepchas, and was informed that they were Thekong Tek and his wife, Nyekong-Nal, but where they dwelt he failed to ascertain. Proceeding towards Gantok, they came across a very old man quite black from tilling his recently burnt field, but could get nothing out of him. Suspecting he knew more than he chose to

* These four pillars are called collectively "Ká-wa-ming-Ches-zhï;" individually the first pillar, called Karpod Zum-lags (white), came from Khongbu; the second, Serpod-Zum-lags (yellow), from the Mochu valley; the third, Marpo-Tag-d Zag (red), from Nyanam (near Nepal); and the fourth, Nakpo-Khun-shes (black), from Ladak.

† Jho-vo-Khyed-hBum-bSags, "the superior of 10,000 heroes."

tell, the Tibetan party hid themselves, and when the old man left off work, followed him secretly to a house which he entered. Obtaining at last an entrance, they found their old man clad in a robe adorned with animals' heads and seated in state on a daïs, worshipped by the other inmates, and thus discovered that he was the veritable Thekong Tek they were in search of. Khyé-Bumsa offered him many presents, and finally obtained a promise that he should become the father of three sons.* With this assurance he returned to Chumbi, where three sons were born to him. On making a second visit to Sikhim *viâ* the Chola, Thekong Tek met them at the cave of Pyak Tsé below Phieungong and did worship to them. When his boys were growing up, the father asked them what they wished to be. The eldest replied he should like to trade on the foibles of his fellowmen, the third said he should be content to get his living from the fruit of the soil, while the second declared that nothing less than the leadership of men would satisfy his ambition. According to these answers Khyé-Bumsa called the first *s*Kya-bo-rab,† or the swindler; the third son *g*Lang-mo-rab, or the ploughman; and the second Mi-tpon-rab, or the leader of men. Though their father remained and died at Chumbi, the three sons crossed the mountains and settled respectively at Living, Gantok, and Phodang Takse. At the same period some of their relatives from Hah arrived *viâ* Chumbi.

Kya-bo-rab or his descendants did not long remain at Living, but kept changing their residence, moving always eastwards: whence they obtained the family name of "Yul-tenpa," the exiles.

The descendants of "Lang-mo-rab" are known as the "Linzerpa," while both of these, as well as the descendants of Mi-tpon-rab, are sometimes styled Pyak-'Tsen-tarpa, from the place mentioned above.

Mi-tpon-rab, who had married a lady of Sakya, had four sons: the eldest was named Zhan-po-tar because‡ he was born at his maternal uncle's house; the second Tshes-bchu-tar, because born on the 10th day of the month; the third Nyi-ma Gyaspa, the chief born on a Sunday; and the fourth Guru-tashe, the saintly one.§ From these four brothers the four chief families of Sikhim, known as the sTong-hDu Rus-bzi, trace their descent; these are Zhang-tar-pa, Tshes-rGyud-tarpa, Nyi-ma Gyaspa, and Guru-tashe-pa. Tshes-bchu-tar had five sons and a daughter; the latter had a *liaison* with her father's orderly and bore a son. This disgrace so incensed the family of Kya-bo-rab that they murdered the guilty pair and cut off the ears of the child and

* He also prophesied that Bumsa's descendants should become lords of Sikhim, while his own people should become their raiyats.

† Rab means "to excel," "to surpass."

‡ *i.e.*, she returned to her family for her first confinement.

§ Because born while the Tashe-rubne worship was being celebrated.

called him Nyor-spog-pa-Tsho-pa. This outrage led to a long series of internecine strife, more particularly between the sons of Kya-bo-rab and Mi-tpen-rab, and their descendants. Gyelpa Achoo, the son of the former, succeeded by treachery in slaying Guru-Tashe near Sonamse, but some nine years later was defeated by Gyelpa Apha, Tashe's son, and had to flee from Rongni, where Apha had settled, to Thunporung, near Dikkeling; but this place was too close to his enemies, and he was forced successively to retreat to Patheng Ding and then to Dumsong and Daling. Gyelpa Apha was still not content and wrote to Bhutan for assistance, whereupon the Bhutanese General "Ari Sethe" attacked Gyelpa Achoo and his son Tshadoon Raja and killed them both near Ambiokh. From the other brothers the Yul-tenpa trace their descent.

At this date all the present subdivision of Kalimpong as far as the Tegonla range was known as the Moñ-loong-kha-bzi and belonged to Sikhim.

Owing to this blood feud, even now the Zhang-tar-pa will not eat with, marry, or enter the house of any Yul-tenpa. It is also said that tribute in kind paid by Yul-tenpas is kept separate and not allowed to be stored in the Raja's treasure house.

Guru Tashe's eldest son is called in full Zhal-nga-A-phag*: his son was Guru Tenzing, who was the father of Phun-tsho-Namgyel (Punchoo Namgay), who became the first Raja of Sikhim or De-jong Gyalpo.

PHUN-tSHOGS rNAM-rGYAL

(Penchoo Namgyé) was born in 1604 A.D., and passed his earlier years near Gantok. The story of his being summoned to Yoksom by the three Tibetan Lamas, and his being proclaimed the first Buddhist Gyalpo or King of Sikhim, has been told elsewhere. The date of his accession is given as 1641 A.D.

Very little is known of his reign: but in all probability he was chiefly engaged in subduing or winning over the chiefs of the petty clans inhabiting the country east of the Arun. It is said that with the aid of Lha-tsan Lama he overcame one Shintu Satichen, or Mangal Gyelpa; though the latter is considered to have been a Lepcha, the name sounds more like a Mangar one: this tribe occupied the valleys to the south of the Kanchinjingna-Everest range. The chief disappeared leaving no trace, after vowing he would petition the sun and moon for the injuries done him.

* This name was attributed to him by Lama Den-zin-pa of Pemiongchi and Labrong in the time of Cho-phoe Namgyé.

Penchoo married a relation at Gantok, who probably belonged to one of the Bep-Tshan-gye families, as the Tong-du-ru-zi at that time were too near of kin to him.

In this reign the monastery at Dubde was built and that at Sangachelling commenced under the direction of Lha-tsun Chhempoo, who also pointed out Pemiongchi as a proper site for a monastery for pure monks (Tasongs).

bsTAÑ (or rTEÑ)-bSRUNG rNAM-rGYAL

(Tensung Namgye), who was born in 1644, succeeded his father Penchoo about 1670.

His reign was not an eventful one. Lama Jig-med Gyatsho came from Tibet and succeeded Lha-tsun Chhempo as his incarnation: with his assistance the monastery at Sangachelling was completed: that establishment was open to all alike, no matter what their descent, so in accordance with the directions of Lha-tsun a third monastery or building was erected near Pemiongchi for persons of pure descent (Tibetan) only. This building was erected on a site about half a mile west of the present Gompa, and the remains of it are still to be seen. The palace at Rubdentse was also completed.

Tensung married three times: first, a lady from Tibet known by her family name Nyum-bi-enmo: by her he had a daughter, Pende Amo, destined to play an important and disastrous part in Sikhim history.

The Raja next married a lady, Deba-sam-serpa, from a family residing near Tinki-jong to the north-west of Sikhim: she bore him a son, Cha-dor Namgye, afterwards Raja.

He also married a daughter of a Limbu Raja, by name Yo-yo-hang, whose jurisdiction was to the west near the Arun river. With this lady came seven Limbuni maidens, who were married into the leading Sikhim families. By the Limbuni princess the Raja had two children: a son Shalno-Guru, who resided at Dingrong, but whose family is now extinct, and a daughter Pendi Tchering Gyenu, who married a member of the Nam-Tsang-korpa family.

PHYAG-rDOR-rNAM-rGYAL

(Chak-dor Namgyé) was the son by Raja Tensung's second wife (Deba-sam-serpa), and was born in 1686. He succeeded his father about 1700, but his reign was the reverse of his father's.

In his youth he seems to have mortally offended his half-sister Pende Amo (who also considered that she, as the elder, was entitled to the throne), so shortly after his accession the quarrel again broke out, and the latter invited the Bhutanese to invade Sikhim and attack her brother. This intrigue was for a time completely successful. The Deb Raja of Bhutan, sDe-po-bZi-rDar, sent a force, under his celebrated General rTa-pa-Nag-dWang Tin-les and the Dewan Phenlai, which overran Sikhim and seized the palace of Rubdentse and compelled Raja Chador to flee to Tibet *viâ* Ilam in Nepal. The Bhutanese held the country for some five or six years, and built forts at Ongdo-phodang near Pakhyong, at Takse-gong and Namgyel Tempoo.* The date of this Bhutanese invasion is variously given from 1700 to 1706.

Mr. Eden writes:—"The Sikhim Raja, who was quite a boy, fled to Lhassa, and the Lhassa Raja, Miung, taught him and supported him, and gave him some taluks, which the Sikhim Raja still holds in Tibet. When the boy had obtained sufficient knowledge and discretion, the Lhassa Raja gave him some men and told him to go back to his country: he sent messengers to raise the Sikhimese, and on hearing of his arrival the Bhutanese evacuated Sikhim and returned ignominiously to their own country." But in this account Mr. Eden seems to have by mistake ascribed some events in the life of the succeeding Raja Gyurme to his father Chador.

If the Reh Umig (chronicles†) of Yesés DPal hByor is to be trusted, it was to the court of the Mongol Prince Gyalpo Lha-bZan that Chador fled. Gyalpo Lha-bZan became Raja of Tibet in 1702-3, and defeated and killed his predecessor the great Viceroy sDe-Srid Sangs rGyas rGya-mTsho in 1704, whereas Phola Thege-bSod-nams-sTobs-rGyas, otherwise called Gyalpo Mi-wang, did not become Viceroy of Tibet until 1726-27.

Chador Namgyé remained several years in Lhassa, studying hard, and gradually rose in scholastic eminence, until he became rChi-Tung-yig to the Dalai Lama (Tshang-dWyans rGya-mTso). This hierarch by some is said to have led a gay and dissolute life, and was accordingly summoned to China to answer for his misconduct. He died or was murdered *en route* near Lake Kokonor in 1704 or 1707.‡ It was perhaps this departure of his patron for China that influenced Chador to return to Sikhim. However, return he did, accompanied by, or closely followed by, Lama sJig-med-Paw of Hug-pya-gLing in Tibet.

On the Raja's return the Bhutanese retired and evacuated all Sikhim west of the Tista, but they still maintained their position at

* They also constructed a flight or road of stone steps from the Rungeet up to Rubdentse, portions of which still remain.

† Translated by Babu S. C. Dass, J. A. S. B., vol. LVII, Part I, No. 2, 1889.

‡ According to Horace Della Penna (M., p. 320).

Fort Dumsong and retained what is now the Kalimpong district and up to Tegonla. Thus Sikhim lost the bulk of the Moñ-loong-kha-bzi.

His long sojourn amongst the learned priests at Lhassa had exercised a great influence towards monasticism in the Raja, and he accordingly on his return devoted himself to the cause of religion and learning. Aided and encouraged by Lama Jig-med-Paw, he founded the present monastery of Pemiongchi for Tasongs, and richly endowed it: the establishment was to consist of 108 monks, and the Raja himself shaved his head and became one of the first number: he also appointed 108 tGar-na-pa or lay officials to serve with the lamas and assist them in secular business. Among other works the Raja wrote a book on monastic discipline, called lChags-Yig, composed a religious dance, Rong-Chham, in honour of Takpoo or warlike demons, and designed an alphabet for the use of his Lepcha subjects.

The Raja's half-sister, Pende Amo, had meanwhile formed a *liaison* with mNgah-bDag-Rin-Chhen-mGön, who was the third lama in succession to Lama mNgah-bDag-Sems-dPah-Chhen-po, referred to in pages 10 and 123, and married him. The lama by his vows of the Rabjungpa sect, which were very strict, ought to have maintained the strictest celibacy, and in marrying Pende Amo had committed a mortal sin. In hopes of mitigating his spiritual punishment, and as an expiatory offering for her share of the offence, Pende Amo built the Chos-rGyel Lha Khang monastery at Tashiding and another at Senan: this was about the year 1716.

The tension between brother and sister still continued after Chador's return, and culminated in the latter causing her brother to be murdered* about the year 1717. Immediately afterwards Pende herself was strangled by orders of the Durbar, and her corpse burnt at a place called Pende Laptse near Niamtchi. Owing to her wickedness and power for evil, she has been looked upon as the incarnation of gZah-dMar-rGyan, an evil spirit, the wife of gZah-bDud-Ra-hu-la, who is credited also with causing the solar eclipses. It is not known whether she left any children.

For his services in the Dalai Lama's household, Raja Chador was given the fiefs of Piahte-gong (Pedi-gong) near Lake Yam-dok-tsho and of hRe-Rin-Chhen-rTse-Jong near Shigatzi in Tibet. These were enjoyed by his successors up to the beginning of the present century, when they were resumed by the Tibetan Government in Cho-phoe Namgyé's minority, in the confusion resulting from the Nepalese-Tibetan war.

* The Raja being unwell had gone to take a course of the hot springs at Raklong, and while in the bath his physician, at the instigation of Pende Amo, treacherously opened his veins, and he bled to death.

Chador married a lady from the province of U in Tibet, who is known as the "Lho-gyelma." By her he had a son, afterwards Raja hGyur-Med-rNam-rGyal: he is also credited with having a *liaison* with the wife of his Lepcha minister, Tasa Aphong, during her husband's absence on a mission to Tibet. A comparison of subsequent dates leads one to believe that the Raja concerned was more probably Ten-sung Namgyé.* The result of this union was a boy called Yúk-thing Arub. Mr. Eden thus narrates his history:— "During the war (in Chador Namgyé's reign) the Bhuteahs had seized and confined at Poonakh a Sikhim Chief named Athoop, the ancestor of the Gantoke Kazee, who confined Drs. Hooker and Campbell, and again fought with us in 1861. The Sikhim Raja on his return procured his release, and the Bhuteahs on setting him free bribed him to remain a friend to their Government. He had been well treated during confinement, and his son Joom-tashi, born during his captivity, turned out a thorough Bhuteah; he eventually became the most powerful man in Sikhim, and kept up continual correspondence with the Bhutanese; and some years later, when there was a dispute between Bhutan and Sikhim regarding the boundaries of the two countries, he treacherously gave up to Bhutan all the tract between the present (1865) Sikhim border and the Taigon pass, including Darling-cote, Jonksa, and Sangbe, which in those days were richly cultivated tracts."

As, however, Joom-tashi is looked up to as the ancestor of the present leading families in Sikhim, and was the father and grandfather of two of their famous men, Changzed Karwang and Kazee Satrageet, it is much more probable that Joom-tashi found himself unable to expel the Bhutanese from their position at Dumsong, and so had to accept the situation and the Tista boundary.

hGYUR-MED rNAM-rGYAL

(Gyurmé Namgué) was born in 1707, and ascended the guddee about 1717. He was at all events eccentric, if not actually weak in intellect.

He married a lady from Ming-do ling, a place south-east of Lhassa. She was so exceedingly plain that the Raja would not live or have anything to do with her: accordingly he removed himself to the Di-chhen-ling monastery. This house no longer exists, but was

* But the subject is still further obscured, unless Joom-tashi and Changzed Karwang *alias* Athing Thi-shé are one and the same person, as a deed, bearing Karwang's seal, is in existence dated "the 10th of the 3rd month of the Fire-bird year," corresponding about to our 1777 A.D. This particular deed is interesting as showing that at this time Ilam (now in Nepal) was then part of Sikhim and that slavery was in full force. Unfortunately the genealogies of the Rhenock and Gantok Kazis do not agree.

situated near Gyezing. The Rani continued to reside at Rubdentse near the Tasongs. The Raja, on the other hand, became more and more inclined to the Lepchas and their form of worship. Five of their priests, who gave themselves out to be the incarnation of Tesi (the Lepcha Guru Rimpoche), obtained immense influence over the Raja, and treated him in a most contemptuous manner, and arrogated so much to themselves that the Tasongs rose and successfully expelled them, the Raja himself being convinced they were Mu-thepa or impostors. Throughout this commotion the Raja harried and distressed his Limbu subjects so much by calling them out unnecessarily to fight and again to build forts and walls, that in despair they threw off their allegiance and joined Nepal, so thus Sikhim began to lose the Limbuana country.

Worn out by these dissensions and in disgust at having to return to his ugly wife, the Raja disguised himself as a fakir or religious mendicant and went on a pilgrimage to Tibet. No one in that country suspected his royal origin, until he came before dWangs-Chuk Dorze, the 9th Karmapa Lama. That ecclesiastic penetrated the king's disguise and treated him royally: in consequence the Karmapa Lama is much looked up to by the Sikhimese.

Being thus deserted, Rani Ming-do-ling also betook herself to Tibet.

Shortly after Raja Gyurme returned to Sikhim, but his behaviour was still inconsistent with his position, as he refused to remarry—a decision that gave his people and court much concern, as there was then no direct heir to the throne.

In 1734 the Raja was taken dangerously ill, and being on his death-bed was asked to name his heir. He replied, "his ministers need have no anxiety on the point, as they would find a young nun* tending cattle near Sing-Jyang:† the girl is a daughter of Neer-Gahden, of the Tak-chhungtar family, and has had a son by me." This son had been born at Ang-nye-khí-sa, and was called Namgye Penchoo. The Raja shortly afterwards died.

rNAM-rGYAL PHUN-TSHOGS

Was born in 1733.

At this date the Kazis or, more correctly, the Jongpens (local governors) were chosen from the fourteen leading families: the head among them was one Changzed Tamdi (rTa-mGrui) of the Tshé-chutar family: he headed the opposition and refused to acknowledge the legitimacy of Namgué Penchoo, and assumed the reins of government. For three years or so Tamdi and his party were successful, but finally

* Probably of Sangachelling.

† A grazing place near Dubde.

the Lepcha or national party in favour of Namgué Penchoo gained strength, and Tamdi was forced to flee to Lhassa and lay his cause before the Tibetans. During the quarrel there were several fights, and blood was shed on either side.

To settle this dispute and the succession, the Tibetans sent a commission under one Rabden Sher-pa* Gyalpa to make a full enquiry and report. Having once obtained a footing in Sikhim, Rabden Gyalpa was in no hurry to depart, and actually reigned for some five years, though pretending all the while he was still engaged on his enquiry.

During his regency he built forts at Karmie (Raja Tendook's seat) and at Mangsir at the head of the Chongtong spur.

In these days the Tasong monks of Pemiongtchi had a branch establishment at Rishehot opposite to Darjeeling, to which they used to resort in the hot weather and rains. The most celebrated among them was Lama Kang-chen-Ralpe-Dorje, a Tibetan from Sher. While at Rishehot he made friends with Changzed Karwang, described as a Lepcha minister, who was living in exile at Darjeeling. Karwang besought the Lama's aid and went to Karmie, where through the Lama's intercession he was introduced to, and pardoned by, the Regent Rabden, who hitherto had not taken up warmly the cause of Namgué Penchoo. Now, however, by the influence of Lama Ralpe, the Regent declared for Namgué Penchoo, and a national agreement or amnesty was drawn up and promulgated at Mangsir. This is known as the Mang-Sher-hDu-ma.

A copy unfortunately in detail is not forthcoming, but apparently under it the Lepchas obtained a greater share in the administration as Tumiyang or superintendents of cultivation, and some fixed system of revenue was devised. The names still survive and are—

(1) h Bah-pa.
(2) b Zo-lung, a tax on forest produce.
(3) Tshong-skyed, a custom or income-tax.

After this Rabden formally placed Raja Namgué Penchoo on the throne and returned to Tibet.

The Regent Rabden's eldest son was one Angel, whose daughter became Raja Namgué Penchoo's first wife. The lady, however, died from dysentery without having had any children.

Subsequently Raja Namgué married or, perhaps, more properly engaged himself to two ladies—(1) a daughter of Pishi-Tergyen of U, and (2) a daughter of Deba-Shamsher-Khiti-Phukpa. Being in a dilemma which lady to choose, the Raja sent and consulted the Sakya Penchen Rimpoche as to which lady he should marry, and the choice

* Also Shak-pa.

fell upon Deba-Shamsher-Khiti-Phukpa's daughter. By her the Raja had a son, Tenzing Namgué.

According to a proclamation dated 1826, Raja Chophoe records that "Karwang was really a slave, though his mother gave out he was the illegitimate son of the Raja. Karwang became so great that he put Raja Namgye Penchoo entirely aside, and gradually turned out all the old Jongpens and put his own sons in his stead, who began to use red seals and take the law into their own hands. Karwang finally joined the Limbus, and in this way caused the invasion of the Goorkhas." This is undoubtedly an exaggeration, as there exist several deeds stamped by Changzed Karwang, and the colour of the seal has always been black and not the royal red. Further, his son, Chothup, obtained his *sobriquet* of Satrajeet from his victories over the Nepalese.

bsTAN hDSIN rNAM-rGYAL

(Tenzing Namgué) was born about 1769, and succeeded his father in 1780 about.

He married Anyo Gyelyum, the daughter of Changzed Karwang, by whom he had a son, Choēphoe Namgué, born in 1785. About 1767 Deb Judhur rose into power and became Raja of Bhutan, while from 1765 to 1769 Raja Prithi Narayan Singh was making himself master of Nepal. With two such restless powers on either side it was not likely that a buffer State like Sikhim could escape the ravages of war.

About 1770 the Bhutanese had overrun all Sikhim east of the Tista, while some of their spies or scouts actually got as far as Mangbru below Barphung. The whole country, however, rose, and the Bhutanese, who seemed to have concentrated their main forces above the Ralong Samdong (bridge over the Tista), were utterly defeated and fled across the Tama-la precipice below Mafila; here the Sikhimese had prepared an ambuscade above and spiked the bottom of the precipice below: thus caught, the straggling forces were cut up to a man and perished miserably.

In 1775-76 Raja Sinha Protapa Sah, son and successor of Raja Prithi Narayan Sah, threatened the invasion of Sikhim; but the Tibetan general, Deba Patza *alias* Depön tPal-rTsal, was sent to make a diversion, and the Goorkha Raja at that time failed in his attempt. The war, however, was waged with varying success for several years. During this war Changzed Karwang's son, Changzed Chothup, *alias* Athingpoi, *alias* Satrajeet, greatly distinguished himself: the various names are those given him by the Tibetans, the Lepchas, and the Goorkhas. Under the first appellation he is known to have negotiated with the Bhutanese (probably after their defeat at Tama-la), and obtained the restitution of the Rhenock ridge and the neighbouring land at Pop-chu.

The second name was given him by the Lepchas in consideration of his having visited Pöd or Tibet, while the third commemorates his seventeen victories over the Goorkhas in the Terai and the Morung.

His military colleague was Deba Takarpo, the grandfather of the present Yangthang Kazi: the name given is merely the family and not the personal name, which was Jor-den (hByor lDan), *alias* Sang Rinzin (Tshang Rin-hZin).

This officer carried on the war successfully for a time and drove back the Goorkhas from Ilam and the hills; and his forces actually penetrated as far as Chainpore. Here near Bilungjong the Sikhimese general was defeated and slain, and his army dispersed, and in consequence of this defeat Satrajeet had also to retire from the Morung. The date of Deba's death and defeat was about 1787.

Active hostilities seemed to have then died out for a time, and Sikhim was lulled into a state of false security, when suddenly in 1788-89 a Goorkha force under General Jor Singh secretly crossed the Chiabhanjan pass and penetrated unobserved across the Kalhait. Rubdentse was surprised: there were no means of resisting, and the Raja and Rani had to fly precipitately without saving any property, save a mask of Kanchinjingna, which the Rani snatched from the altar and carried off in the bosom of her dress. gSol-tPon Tshang-rNam-rGyal, grandfather of the Phodang lama, took up the Raja's son gTsug-Phud-rNam-rGyal and bore him on his shoulders *viâ* Katong Ghát to the Mo-chu valley, and so close was the pursuit, that the fugitives had to subsist on turok or wild yams, which they dug up in the jungles. More troops were sent by the Goorkha General Damoodar Pandé, which overran and held possession of all Sikhim south and west of the Tista.

In 1790 the Raja went to Lhassa to obtain help, and the Tibetan Government promised to render help and arranged to send an army towards Nyanam (sMya-nam). Meanwhile Chothup, Jomgye, and Densa Siring wrote to Lhassa to say they had recovered Sikhim: the Tibetans in consequence were incensed and ceased preparations. In 1790 the Raja died, and the Tibet Government apparently gave his young son, Chophoe Namgyé, some presents and sent him back.

gTSUG-PHUD-rNAMGYAL

(Cho-phoe Namgyé) was born in 1785, and nominally succeeded his father in 1790.

In 1791 the Goorkhas made war with Tibet and sacked Tashe-lhunpo, but in the following year were defeated near Katmandu and had to sign an ignominious treaty. In this war a party of Tibetans are said to have reached Martam on the left bank of the Tista, but it is quite clear from the sites of the fortifications near Katong Ghát that the popular party in Sikhim successfully and without help prevented the Goorkhas crossing the Tista. In fact, in the proclamation referred to above, the Raja records that the Tibetans had refused Sikhim help or to listen to their representations, when peace was being made, on the ground that though Bhutan had rendered the Tibetans assistance, the Sikhimese had not. In consequence during the negotiations carried on by the Chinese General Hosi-Thang-thang, Sikhim was not represented, the Raja and his family were reduced to great straits, the boundary with Nepal was drawn back to the left bank of the Tista, and Tibet resumed the Raja's fiefs at Piahte Jong and Samye, and pushed its own boundary up to the Chola-Jelep range.

For some years Pemiongchi and all the South Tista tract paid rent to Nepal, until in 1815 the Nepalese were expelled by the British Government, who by the Treaty of 1817 restored all this country together with the Terai to the Sikhim Raja. But even then the Raja had to be content to see his western boundary thrown back from the Kankayi to the Phalut range and the Mechi river. This boundary appears to have been originally laid down by Major Barre Latter, who was accompanied by Nazir Chaina Tinjin, Macha Timbah, and Lama Duchim Longadoo. About the year 1814 the Raja commenced building a palace at Tumlong, which was henceforward to be the capital in preference to Rubdentse, considered insecure and too far distant from Tibet.

In 1819 a serious quarrel arose between the Raja and his minister, his own uncle Bho-lod, but was patched up and an agreement made. Another agreement was made the following year, and a third in 1824, but about that time his wife and child (the former seems to have been friendly to the minister) died, and the Raja, freed from all restraint, seemed determined to make away with his relative: so finally in 1826 Bho-lod was treacherously murdered near Tumlong by Tung-yik Menchoo, father of Dunya Namgye, better known as the Pagla Dewan. Bho-lod's cousin, Yuk-LhatGrup *alias* tkra-thup, fearing a similar fate, fled from Sikhim and took refuge at Unthoo in Nepal with some 800 of his Lepcha tribesmen.

Shortly after this disputes arose on the Sikhim and Nepal boundary, which came under the cognizance of the Governor-General's Agent for the North-Eastern Frontier and the Resident in Nepal. In 1828 Captain Lloyd was deputed to the Sikhim frontier in connection with these disputes. He penetrated the hills in company with Mr. J. W. Grant, the Commercial Resident at Malda, as far as

Rinchingpung. These gentlemen, attracted by the position of Darjeeling, brought it to the notice of the Governor-General, and it was resolved by Government to open negotiations with the Maharaja of Sikhim on the first convenient occasion for the cession of Darjeeling to the British Government in return for an equivalent in lands or money. This opportunity occurred in 1834-35, when the Lepcha refugees in Nepal made an inroad into the Sikhim Terai, and Colonel Lloyd was deputed to enquire into the causes of the disturbance. The refugees were obliged to return to Nepal, and the negotiation ended in the unconditional cession by the Maharaja of the Darjeeling tract under a Deed of Grant, dated February 1835.

In 1841 the Government granted an allowance of Rs. 3,000 per annum to the Maharaja as compensation for the cession of Darjeeling, and in 1846 a further sum of Rs. 3,000: in all Rs. 6,000 per annum.

The settlement of Darjeeling advanced rapidly, its population having risen from not more than 100 souls in 1839 to about 10,000 in 1849, chiefly by immigration from the neighbouring States of Nepal, Sikhim, and Bhutan, in all of which slavery is prevalent. There was free trade in labour and all other commodities, with forest land enough for all comers to settle in, and every encouragement given to the new arrivals. The increased importance of Darjeeling, under free institutions, was a source of early and constant jealousy and annoyance to the Dewan of the Maharaja, who was himself the monopolist of all trade in Sikhim, and this jealousy was shared in by the Lamas and other principal people in the country, who lost their rights over slaves settling as British subjects in our territory. The plan pursued was through reports and secret emissaries to frighten our new subjects, by declaring that they should be delivered up as escaped slaves to their former masters, and by discouraging the resort in every way of the Sikhim people to Darjeeling; added to which some British subjects were occasionally kidnapped to be sold into slavery, and there were frequent denials of aid in capturing and surrendering criminals. There has always been an arrangement for a mutual exchange of slaves between Sikhim and Bhutan, and Dr. Campbell, the Superintendent of Darjeeling, was constantly importuned by the Maharaja of Sikhim and his Dewan to get the British Government to follow a similar course with Sikhim, which was of necessity steadily refused.

In 1849 Dr. Hooker and Dr. Campbell, while travelling in Sikhim with permission of Government and the Maharaja, were suddenly seized and made prisoners. The object was to force Dr. Campbell to relinquish claims for the surrender of criminals; to make him, while in durance, agree to the dictation of the Dewan regarding the giving up of escaped slaves; and to detain him until these enforced conditions should be sanctioned by Government. Foiled by the declaration that whatever concessions might be extorted then would not be confirmed by Government, and intimidated by the declaration of the Governor-General that the Maharaja's head should answer for it if a hair of the head of Dr. Campbell or Dr. Hooker were hurt, the Sikhimese eventually released the prisoners on 24th December 1849.

In February 1850 an avenging force crossed the Great Rungeet river into Sikhim. The expedition resulted in the stoppage of the annual grant of Rs. 6,000 enjoyed by the Maharaja, the annexation of the Sikhim Terai, and of the portion of the Sikhim hills bounded by the Rummam river on the north, the Great Rungeet and the Tista on the east, and by the Nepal frontier on the west. This new territory was put under the management of the Superintendent of Darjeeling; the Dewan was ostensibly dismissed from office, and for some years matters proceeded smoothly and well between Sikhim and our Government. But this man having worked his way into power again through his wife, an illegitimate daughter of the Maharaja, the kidnapping of our subjects was resumed without the possibility of obtaining redress. In April and May 1860 two aggravated cases of kidnapping were reported to Government. All ordinary efforts to procure reparation having failed, the Governor-General in Council resolved to occupy the territory of the Maharaja lying to the north of the Rummam river and to the west of the Great Rungeet, and to retain it until our subjects were restored, the offenders given up, and security obtained against a recurrence of similar offences. On the 1st November 1860 the Superintendent of Darjeeling crossed the Rummam with a small force, and advanced as far as Rinchingpung. But he was eventually forced to fall back on Darjeeling. A stronger force was then despatched under command of Lieutenant-Colonel Gawler, accompanied by the Hon'ble Ashley Eden as Envoy and Special Commissioner. The force advanced to the Tista, when the Sikhimese acceded to the terms dictated by the Governor-General, and on the 28th of March 1861 a new treaty, consisting of twenty-three articles, was concluded by the Envoy with Maharaja Sikyong Namgyal, as his father, Maharaja Cho-phoe Namgyé, though alive and in Chumbi, was afraid to come over. Cho-phoe Namgyé died in 1863.

SRID-SKYONG-rNAM-rGYAL

(Sikhyong Namgyé) was born in 1819, and practically became Raja in 1861, though his father did not die until two years later.

The annual allowance of Rs. 6,000 forfeited in 1850 was in 1862 restored, as an act of grace, to the ruling Maharaja Sikyong Namgyé:

it was increased in 1868 to Rs. 9,000, and in 1873 to Rs. 12,000 on the understanding that it was granted without any reference to the increased value of Darjeeling and purely as a mark of consideration for the Maharaja.

In 1868 the Maharaja solicited permission for the return of the ex-Dewan, but the request was refused as being contrary to the 7th article of the Treaty of 1861, and likely to lead to intrigues for the succession.

But to understand this and subsequent events an examination of the family relations of Raja Cho-phoe Namgyal is necessary, and to explain these the following genealogical tree has been drawn out.

RAJA CHO-PHOE NAMGYAL.

Married five wives in succession, besides keeping a concubine (2a).

- (1)
  - (1) Daughter, married to Tarding of Tashelhunpo.
  - (2) Daughter, died unmarried.
  - (3) Son, Kupgain of Labrong, died unmarried.
- (2)
  - (1) RAJA SIKYONG NAMGYAL, died childless. His widow, Pending, was the first wife of RAJA THOTHUB, to whom she bore three children.
  - (2) Kuzhoo Lhase, died childless.
  - (3) Avatar of Namchi, died unmarried.
- (2a) A maidservant to (2).
  - Illegitimate children.
    - (1) Daughter, married as his first wife DEWAN NAMGAY (Pagla Dewan).
    - (2) CHANGZED GELONG KAR-PO, married after the decease of RAJA CHO-PHOE his widow MEN-CHI, by whom he had TINLE NAMGYAL, who at present styles himself KUZHOO LHASE.
- (3) Died childless.
- (4) Tanna Dinga, died childless.
- (5) Men-chi.
  - Before her marriage had borne two children.
    - (1) Daughter, married to a Kazi in Tibet.
    - (2) SERINGPUTTI, married as his second wife to DEWAN NAMGAY.
  - Legitimate.
    - (1) THOTHUB NAMGYAL, Raja of Sikhim, who had by RANI PENDING
      - Namgyal Dumo.
      - TCHODA NAMGYAL.
      - CHOTAL.
    - (2) Daughter, a nun at Tumlong.
  - After Raja Cho-phoe's death, married Changzed Kar-po, and by him bore Tinle Namgyal.

Neither Cho-phoe nor Sikyong Rajas appear to have taken much interest in the administration, and so in consequence of their relationship by marriage and birth, first Dewan Namgay and after his banishment, in a lesser degree, Changzed Kar-po became the really influential personages in the State. Dewan Namgay* was anti-English in feeling and conduct, while Changzed, on the other hand, pretended much sympathy for the English.

In 1873 Raja Sikyong Namgyé, accompanied by his half-brother, the present Raja Thothub Namgyé, and his half-sister Seringputti, and Changzed Gelong Kar-po, visited Sir George Campbell, then Lieutenant-Governor of Bengal, at Darjeeling.

Raja Sikyong Namgyel died in April 1874, and unsuccessful intrigues were attempted to set aside the accession of Thothub Namgyé in favour of Tinle Namgyé (born in 1866), but were defeated by the prompt action of the then Deputy Commissioner of Darjeeling, Mr. J. Ware Edgar (now Sir John Edgar).

mTHU-sTOBS-rNAM-rGYAL

(Tho-tub Namgye) was born in 1860, and on the death of his half-brother both ascended his throne and married his widow, a lady of Tashelhunpo by name Pending. She died in childbirth in 1880, leaving three children by Thothub, viz., a daughter, Namgyel Dumo, born in 1876, and two sons; the elder Tchoda-Namgyé, heir to the Raj, born in 1877, and the younger Chotal, born in 1879, supposed to be the incarnation at Phodang of Sikyong Namgyel.

In October 1875 Sir Richard Temple had a friendly interview with the Raja and Changzed Kar-po at Chomnaga near the Cho-la pass. At this interview the Raja expressed his desire that the British Government should undertake arrangements for the conservation of the sál, pine, and other forests in his territory, but nothing was actually carried out.

The Maharaja was invited to be present at the Imperial Assemblage at Delhi on the 1st January 1877, but as he was unable to attend, his banner, medal, and ring were duly presented to him at Tumlong by Mr. Edgar mentioned above.

Some complications which had arisen as far back as 1872 between one Luchmee Das Prodhan, the head of the Nepalese Newars in Darjeeling, and the Lassoo Kazi, the Sikhim Vakil in Darjeeling, but had been smoothed over, again became prominent in 1878, so that in November of that year the present Raja and

* Died in 1888.

Changzed Kar-po came to Kalimpong to meet the Hon'ble Sir Ashley Eden, the then Lieutenant-Governor of Bengal. The question of Nepalese settling in Sikhim was there discussed, and Nepalese settlers were admitted in certain parts under certain restrictions. This agreement, owing to the intrigues of the exiled Dewan Namgay, the Dorjee Lopen of Pemiongchi and Norden Gelong, tahsildar at Kalimpong, did not work well, and events culminated in the disturbances and fight at Rhenok in 1880. Mr. A. W. Paul was then sent to settle matters at Tumlong, and a fresh agreement was drawn up and promulgated on the 14th April 1880. This, with some slight modifications arranged by the Phodang Lama and the Dorjee Lopen, worked well.

Changzed Kar-po, after a visit to Giantzi, where he met the Chinese Amban and some of the Tibetan officials, died in 1879. This visit apparently took place shortly after the interview with Sir Ashley Eden, and appears to have resulted in some secret agreement with Tibet and the investiture of Thothub Namgyé with a Chinese button of the 1st rank (plain coral).

As stated above, Rani Pending died in 1880, and these two deaths threw the whole power of the State into the hands of the old Rani Men-chi and Dewan Namgay, who naturally, from living wholly at Chumbi, favoured Tibetan interests and the cause of young Tinle, then growing up to manhood.

Raja Thothub meanwhile lived peacefully at Tumlong and evinced no disposition to contract a second marriage. However, pressure seems to have been brought to bear on him, and so having obtained two elephants from the Government of Bengal in 1881, he sent them to the Grand Lamas at Tashelhunpo and Lhassa, in charge of Nudup Gyaltsen (brother of the Phodang Lama) and the Rhenok Kazi. These officers, when at Lhassa, arranged a marriage between the Raja and the daughter of Shafe Utok, one of the leading men in Tibet.

Unfortunately the old Rani and her son Tinle, accompanied by Dewan Namgay, followed shortly afterwards in 1882-83, and, apparently in furtherance of their design to place Tinle in direct succession to the Raj, broke off this match, and secured as a wife to the Raja the daughter of an inferior officer in the Dalai Lama's court, known as Leden-se. It is said that the old Rani had to execute a bond, guaranteeing that the Raja of Sikhim would receive the girl as his Rani; but without the slightest attempt at a show of decency, the girl immediately went to live with Tinie, and by the time the party returned from Lhassa to Chumbi, she was very far gone in pregnancy, and in fact bore two children before Raja Thothub ever saw her. All this helped the intrigues in favour of Tinle, as his joint marriage with Leden-se's daughter is pointed out as proving Thothub and Tinle are legitimate brothers, and so both of the Royal family, polyandry being permissible under Tibetan law. The real facts as to Tinle's parentage have been given above.

Raja Thothub up to 1884 remained in Sikhim and refused to have anything to do with the girl, but in 1885 the influence of Tinle became too great, especially as the Deputy Commissioner himself approved of his going to Chumbi to learn what was being done regarding the dispute between Bhutan and Tibet and the interruptions to trade. Accordingly Raja Thothub went over to Chumbi nominally to pay his respects to the Shafe Rampa. Subsequently the Raja was requested to remain at Chumbi, while the Macaulay Mission was in progress in 1886. In that year, after the stoppage of the Macaulay Mission, the Tibetans advanced into Sikhim and built a fort at Lingtu which they persistently refused to evacuate. The Raja remained at Chumbi, notwithstanding the remonstrances of the Indian Government and the stoppage of his pension, until December 1887, when he returned to Gantok, in the meantime having made an agreement with the Tibetans at a place called Galing. In March 1888 the Sikhim Expeditionary Force was sent against Lingtu, which the Tibetans were compelled to evacuate, and in September the campaign ended with the complete expulsion of the Tibetans across the Jelep.

In December 1888 the Chinese Resident, His Excellency Shêng Tai, arrived at Gnatong, and negotiations were opened with a view to a settlement of the Sikhim-Tibetan dispute, but were unsuccessful, and so were formally broken off on the 11th January 1889.

On the arrival in Darjeeling of Mr. James H. Hart, of the Chinese Imperial Customs Service, fresh attempts at the solution of our difficulties were made, and after long interchange of views, negotiations were re-opened towards the close of 1889, and resulted in the convention signed in Calcutta on the 17th March 1890.

In June 1889 Mr. J. C. White, Executive Engineer, was appointed Assistant Political Officer at Gantok to advise and assist the Maharaja in his administration of the country. A representative Council selected from the chief men in Sikhim was also established with the same view.

Good roads have been opened from Pedong in British territory to the Jelep pass and to Tumlong, properly bridged throughout. Iron bridges have also been constructed across the Tista, the Rungeet and other streams, and communication throughout Sikhim has been very greatly improved.

POPULATION, TRIBES, AND CHIEF FAMILIES OF SIKHIM.

A census taken in Sikhim in February 1891 roughly divides the population as follows :—

Race or caste.	Males.	Females.	Children.	Total.
Lepcha ...	2,362	2.399	1,001	5,762
Bhutea ...	1,966	1,960	968	4,894
Limbu ...	1,255	1,159	942	3,356
Gurung ...	1,108	1,047	766	2,921
Murmi ...	801	778	1,288	2,867
Rai, Jimdar, &c. ...	742	691	587	2,020
Khambu ...	726	648	589	1,963
Kami ...	626	464	580	1,670
Brahman ...	521	372	521	1,414
Mangar ...	363	346	192	901
Chetri ...	303	253	273	829
Newar ...	240	183	304	727
Slaves ...	124	99	103	326
Dirzi	102	92	93	287
Miscellaneous, including troops ...	350	72	99	521
	11,589	10,563	8,306	30.458

Of the above, the Limbus, Gurungs, Murmis, Khambus, and Mangars are more or less allied, while the others, excepting the Lepcha and Bhutea, are later immigrants from beyond the Arun in Nepal: thus, roughly speaking, it may be said that there are three main stocks in Sikhim :—

the oldest and perhaps aboriginal inhabitants of Sikhim were the "Rong," or, as we know them from their Nepalese title, "the Lepchas;"*

the next in importance, if not in antiquity, come the Kham-pa or Kham-ba, the immigrants from the Tibetan province of Khams; commonly called Bhuteas;

while the Sikhim Limbus rank as last and least: these belong to what Mr. Risley styles the Lhása Gotra, as they are believed to have migrated to Sikhim from Shigatsi, Pénam, Norpu, Khyongtse, Samdubling, and Gyangtse, places in the Tibetan province of Tsang, south of the Tsanpo.

All the families in Sikhim belong to one or other of these strains, or to an admixture of them, as intermarriages are allowed.

* Dr. Waddell in a separate article has shown that the Lepchas are probably Indo-Chinese cognate with the tribes of the Naga Hills, and entered the Sub-Himalayas *viâ* the Assam valley.

The royal family belong to the second of the above.

The descendants of Khyé-bum-sar are divided into six families, viz.—

Pyak-Tsen-Tar Pu-pun-Sum.*

(1) Yul-tenpa or Yul-thon-pa.
(2) Lingzerpa.
(3) Zhan-tar-pa or Zhan-po-tar.
(4) Tshé-gyu-Tarpa or Tshés bChu-tar.
(5) Nyim-Gyé-pa.
(6) Guru-tashe-pa.

(3)–(6) forming the Tong-du-ru-zi, or "the four families of a 1,000 collections."

But with Khyé-bum-sar came other† Tibetans or Kham-pas, who founded the eight families now known as the hBeps-mTshan-bGyad, or the tribe of "the eight respectable names."

There is some confusion as to the exact names of these eight sub-families and the order in which they rank, but the following is fairly correct:—

1. Pon-pa.
2. rGañ-sTag-Pu-Tshogs or tGon-gSang-pa.
3. Nam-gTsang-sKho-pa or sKor-pa.
4. sTag-Chhung-Tar-pa.
5. tKar-Tshogs-pa.
6. Grong-sTod-pa.
7. bTshun-rGyal-pa or rGyas-pa.
8. mDo-Khang-pa or Kham-pa.

In all there are thus fourteen original main families of Tibetan origin in Sikhim, if we do not include a fifteenth, the Pu-Tshogs Nier-pok, descended from the illegitimate grandson of Tshé-bChu-tar referred to in page 9 above: the representatives of this branch have dwindled considerably and are in low circumstances near Chongpon close to Pemiongchi.

These fourteen main families have the right to be admitted to the Tasong monastery at Pemiongchi without payment of nuzzur or entrance fees.

The Pon-pa are again subdivided into five, viz.—

(*a*) Nag-lDig.
(*b*) Lha-bSungs.
(*c*) Yos-lChags.
(*d*) Na-pon.
(*e*) Pon-Chhung-pa.

* "Pu-pun-Sum" means "the three brothers."

† As mentioned above, Khyé Bamsa had three brothers, who migrated to Hah in Bhutan, whence their descendants migrated into Sikhim.

Besides the above there are other families of Tibetan origin which form Mr. Risley's Rui-chhung (*i.e.*, little families). These came into Sikhim at various times since the establishment of the Raj, and are divided into groups (named after their place or manner of origin). The chief and most important are the—

(i) Pu-Tsho-po-pa.
(ii) Lag-lDingpa.
(iii) rGod-Rong-pa.
(iv) Gyeng-pa.
(v) sTod-pa.
(vi) Shar-pa.
(vii) hBar-Phong-Pu-Tsha-po (Barphungpuso).
(viii) A lDan-Pu-Tsha-po (Adinpuso).

The above families are admitted into the Pemiongchi monastery, but only on payment of heavy entrance fees.

Of these the (v) sTod-pa or Tumu-sTod-pa, so called from their having first settled in Tumu or the upper Mo-chu valley, are again subdivided into—

(*a*) Toi-Lha-goi-pa or sTod-Lha-rGod.
(*b*) Toi-Jám Yang-pa or sTod-hJam-tByangs.
(*c*) Toi-Chhu-khápa or sTod-Chhu-kha-pa.

After all the above come others, such as the—

(2) Chombi-pa, immigrants from Kham in Tibet and Hah in Bhutan to the lower reaches of the Mochu near Chumbi. The following subdivisions are given:—

(*a*) Lham-tar or Lha-ma-tar.
(*b*) Gué-ne-pu-Tshogs or tGé-bsNyen-pu-Tsha-pa.
(*c*) Agon or Ang-tGon.
(*d*) Athub-pu-Tshogs.
(*e*) Do-Shoi-pa or rDog-Zhod-pa.
(*f*) Khimbarpa or Khyim-hPar-pa.

In the north the Lachen-Lachung valleys have been colonised by other immigrants from Hah and Paro in Bhutan, who are now called the—

(3) Lopon Lhundub.

There are other families also whose names are in many cases derived from local features: among them are found the—

(4) (*a*) A-som-pa.
(*b*) Mang-sPod-pa.
(*c*) Na-Mangs.
(*d*) Shag-Tshang-pa.

(*e*) rDo-hRob-pa.
(*f*) sGang-rGyab-pa.
(*g*) La-hog-pa.
(*h*) Mang-Tshang-pa.
(*i*) sPa-Thing-pa.
(*j*) Peng-ri-pa.
(*k*) Ka-gyé-pa.
(*l*) Dobta-po, to whom belong Dunya Namgué (the Pagla Dewan) and his father, Tungyik Menchoo, murderer of Bholod.

Among the above, the traditions regarding the ancestors of the Lag-lDingpa (ii) and rGod-Rong-pa (iii) are curious. To the south-east of Pema-kod-chen lies the country of Lho-tawa, inhabited by cannibals; at their weddings it is customary to kill and eat the bride's father or mother, should the hunters, sent to forage for the feast, return empty-handed. Many years ago the sons of Guru Chhod-wang and of another learned lama, in hopes of improving their minds, as they were not as clever as their fathers, went on a pilgrimage to Tsari and Pema-kod. One evening they arrived at an old woman's hut at Lho-khabta and took shelter there. The woman informed them that the owner of the hut had gone out hunting in order to procure some game to celebrate the marriage of his son, and added that if the hunters were unsuccessful, she would be killed and eaten at the first day's feast; while if they continued unsuccessful, the two lamas would be killed and eaten on the second and third days of the ceremony. On hearing this the travellers were naturally very much alarmed, and begged the old woman to show them some means of getting away and so saving their life. She instructed them that at the distribution of her remains the men of the house would probably offer the lamas one of her arms to be cooked in a curry: that if they did so, the lamas should beg for the hand instead, on pretence that in a previous existence the old woman had been a great hero and the hand was more precious. If the lamas obtained the hand, then there was hope for them, and they should that very day at midnight decamp from the house, taking with them the dead hand. Matters turned out as predicted: the old lady was killed for the feast to welcome the bride's arrival, and the lamas succeeded in obtaining the hand, and escaping with it that night. In the morning the men of the house, missing the lamas, followed on their tracks, tracing them like dogs by the scent. Seeing them coming, the lamas climbed up a high tree: soon the hunters with their noses to the ground came to the foot of the tree and there lost all further trace. The others with those hunting by scent got angry with the latter and threw them down on their backs to kill them: in this position the hunters were obliged to look up and so saw the lamas in the tree, and pointed up with their fingers; taking this as a sign of resistance, the others cut off the hands, before an explanation of the signs could be given. Learning, however, where the lamas were, the men began to cut down the tree. Rather than fall alive into the hands of such barbarians, the lamas determined to kill themselves by flinging themselves off the tree. They tried to do this, but the one who held the woman's hand was miraculously wafted through the air, still clinging to the hand, and safely transported to Lhobrak. The other was transformed into the semblance of a vulture and flew into some thick forest, whence he subsequently made his escape. In commemoration of this event the first lama obtained the name of Lag-lDing-pa, "the hand-flyer," and the latter of rGod-Rong-pa, "the wild bird (the lammergeyer) of the crags."

The first La-ding-pa connected with Sikhim was called Lama Thampa Phur-gyel, literally the Holy Flying King: he is said to have been able to fly all over the Tumo valley, Rinchingong and Nyam-nag-tsho. This miraculous power of flight is attributed to more than one lama at Sikhim. Thus just below Tashiding is pointed out a rock, called Urgyen-phur-sa, because Padmasambhava is said to have flown thence.

The Barphungpuso (vii) and Adinpuso (viii) have hitherto been thought to be pure Lepcha or Róng families, and General Mainwaring considers that the first is Bar-fóng-mo="the flowing from on high," and the second A'-den="the created, fashioned, formed," the two combined being equivalent to "the patricians and plebians." The following accounts given by members of the two families are entirely different:—

The original ancestor of Tekong-tek, the old Lepcha chief in the time of Jo-khyé-Bum-sar, came of divine orgin, Tekong-tek being the sixth in direct descent. From Tekong-tek or one of his brothers came one Tasa Aphong some five or six generations later, who was a leading Lepcha and a minister under Raja Ten-sung Namgué.* His wife was also a Lepchani. The husband in course of duty was sent on a mission to Tibet which lasted some time. In his absence the Raja formed an attachment for his Minister's wife, and by him she became the mother of a son, who was called Yukthing Adub or Arub. This boy grew up and rose to the office of Treasurer to Raja Chador Namgue. When the latter fled to Ilam and Tibet on the invasion of the Bhutanese, Adup was in charge of the palace of Rubdentse, and thus fell into the hands of the Bhutanese, who brought him prisoner to Hah in Tibet. Here from an incestuous marriage there was born to him a

* Tasa Aphong originally held a small post or tahsilship at his native place hBar-phag, and his full title was Túmiyáng Thekong Tasa Aphong of hBar-phag; this was contracted to Bar-phag A-phong, and thence to Bar-phong: hence his descendants (Pu-tsho) are now known as "the Bar-phong-pu-tsho."

son, called from his birthplace at Dzom-thang near Paro in Bhutan, Dzom-tashi.* This man is known by several names, such as Athing Thi-she, Yuk-thing De-si, but is best known by his Tibetan title Changzed Karwang or Karwie. Some details of his life are given under the reigns of Rajas Chador, Gyur-me, Namgué Penchoo, and Tenzing Namgué.

Karwang was twice married, viz., to the daughter of one Yuk-Dagom of the Ta-karpo family and to a Limbu or Mangar lady, and had eighteen children: of these some eight or nine only need be mentioned.

By the second lady we find the following:—

(1) Namgyel Tshiring.	(3) Dzomgyel (Jomgyé).
(2) Ka-bhi Changzed.	(4) Könga.

By the first lady:—

(5) Athing-poï.	(6) Tateng Athing.

And three daughters:—

(7) Añyong-poi.	(8) Añyo Gyalyum.	(9) Añyo Chu-wa.

(1) Namgyel Tshiring was the ancestor of the present Barmik Kazi Dorze Dadup: he was also called "Den-chap," from having acted as Regent of Sikhim during the Raja's absence, and the title is said to be still continued in the family.

(2) Ka-bhi Changzed was the celebrated General Satrajeet or Changzed Chothup: he had only a daughter, married to Yapa-Tsi-suh of the Ta-karpo family, who thus became his adopted son; from them is descended the present Rhenock Kazi, Rinzing Namgyel.

(3) Dzomgyel is the ancestor of the three Kazis of Entchi, Ramtik, and Tatong (Gantok).

(4) Könga was appointed Kazi of Kotah (*i.e.*, Ilam): he had two children, Da-thup† (tGra-thup) and Gerong Danen, a lama of Pemiongchi. The former again had two sons, one the father of the old Lassoo Kazi, who succeeded Tchebu Lama as Sikhim Vakil in Darjeeling, and the other Namgyé, father of Yuk Sirman Kazi of Kotah, whose son Man Bahadur married Raja Tendook's daughter. Gerong Danen forsook his vows, and marrying in his old age became the father of Sinkoop, the old Dharm din Kazi, who was the grandfather of the present youth Kazi Badur, and of Yuk Sateng *alias* Bidoor

* More probably Karwang was the son of Dzom-tashi.

† *See* p. 19.

Kazi of Ilam, who was also at one time Soobah of Darjeeling. The monument so conspicuous on the ridge in the Bhutea Busti (Do-chúk) was erected to the memory of his wife, Yang-chen, half-sister to Raja Tendook.

(5) Of Athing-poï nothing seems to be known.

(6) Tateng Athing, better known as Changzed Bho-lod or Ba-lu, became Minister to his sister's son, Raja Chophoe Namgyé, and was murdered owing to the intrigues of Tung-yik Menchoo, father of the Dewan Dunya Namgué, better known as the Pagla Dewan. Tateng Athing was the father of Gelong, the present Tateng Kazi, whose grandson, Dorje Tchiring, has married Raja Tendook's daughter.

Nothing is known of the daughters (7) and (9), but (8) Añyo Gyalyum was married to Raja Tenzing Namgyé, and became the mother of Raja Chophoe Namgyé.

It will be seen from the above that though the Barphongpuso were made Kazis or Jongpens of the chief Lepcha districts, their descent is not a purely Lepcha one.

The Adinpuso have still less claim to the title of Lepcha. Their legendary history is to the effect that some generations before the accession of Raja Penchoo to the throne of Sikhim, three brothers from Khams-A-lDan-Chhos-hKhor-gLing in Tibet came *viâ* Lhassa and Tsang down the Lachen-Lachung route into Sikhim. At Ringon the eldest brother was so terrified at the awful hills and rocks and the difficulties of the road that he turned back. The two other brothers persevered until they were stopped near sBas (Bé) by a red demon, called bTsan-rNams-rGyal-mThon-po, who only let them pass on condition that their descendants should regularly do him worship. The younger brother subsequently settled at Mangbru and the elder at Barmyak.

The more probable account is as follows:—In the middle of the thirteenth century the hierarch at Sakya was the great hGro-mGon-hPhags-pa, who was the spiritual guide to Prince Khublai, afterwards the Emperor Sa-chhen of China and the founder of Peking. In 1251 this monarch presented the learned lama with the thirteen provinces of Tibet, called Khri-sKor-bChu-gSum, in recognition of his sanctity and ability. A few years later the lama made a journey to Mongolia (and perhaps China). On his return journey about 1264 he brought with him from Kham one Na-tWang-Ton-Grub, a native of Kham-Aden. After some residence at Sakya the latter was advised by the lama to travel south and seek his fortunes in Sikhim, and so came as far as Talung, which he made his home. His son, Tsé-tWang-rNam-rGyal, removed to Tung-sBong (Ting-bong), where he married a Lepchani wife. Their son, bKra-gShi-Ton-Grub, and grandson, bSam-hPhel, settled lower down the Talung valley at

Lingthem. The latter's son, Tshe-hPhel, resided at Yul-sBar-Phag. Tse-phel had two sons, Ye-shes and rDo-rJe, who crossing the Tista settled at Rin-tGon (Ringim). Dorje's son, Nor-Pu-tWang-hDus, had again two sons, who are the ancestors of Raja Tendook's and Tchehu Lama's families. The following is their genealogical tree :—

NOR-PU-TWANG-HDUS.

Lha-Tren-Norpu.	Tshe-ring-tWang-hDus, who lived at first at Kubbi near Tumlong and thence removed to Gantok.
Kham sTong lDan-brTan-hDsing.	Norpu-Tshe-ring of Namphak.
Kham-Las-hGrubs.	Norpu Ta-brGyas of Geyzing.
Na-Skyes (Jongpen of Barmie).	rDorje of Chongpong.
sDsong A-hDams.	bDe-Chhen-Skyabs of Yoksom.
Dsong Khyung hDus.	A-lu.
sDsong Ras-lChog.	Norpu-rGyal-mTshan.
sDsong tPal-hByor.	Lha-rGyal.
sDsong-Lhun-hGrubs-Phun-Tshogs *alias* sDsong-hBrug-bGyas.	A-Sras.
Raja Tendook and others as detailed below.	Lha-Chhos.
	rTsis-pu Lama.

It will thus be seen how little Lepcha blood there is in the two chief families of the Adinpuso stock. It is stated that De-Chhen-kyab was one of those who hailed Penchoo Namgué Raja at Yoksom in 1641.

It may be interesting to note that Doobgye (Tendook's father), though Jongpen of Barmie, went to Nagri as captain in the Sikhimese army, fought there against the Nepalese, and assisted Major Latter to lay down the present boundary between Sikhim and Nepal. He had two wives: by the elder, a daughter of the Pad-gLing Lama, he had two sons, Dawa Sring and Yit-tam Sring, now a Jongpen in Nepal; by the younger wife, who was the daughter of the hGu-ling Jongpen, a Barphongpuso by family, he had three sons who lived to grow up, viz., hBrug-brTan-hDsin, Bahadur, and Tendook Pulgor. Doobgye had also two illegitimate sons, Rabden Tsiring and Rinchen Long-dol, Jongpen of Pachim, both of whom have served as interpreters to Government.

There are, however, several Lepcha families still existing, particularly along the banks of the Talung river and its vicinity. Among them the following may be noted, many of whom derive their patronymic from the places they settled in :—

(1) Singyang-mo, spread over Eastern Nepal: Tekong Solon was one of their ancestors.
(2) Luksom-mo or Yoksom-mo, from the place of that name.
(3) Si-ming or Sungut-mo, whose head-quarters are near Rungli Rungliot, and to whom is allied the family of the Khangsar Dewan and Phodang Lama.
(4) Tuk-nyil-mo live near Cheumthang.
(5) Sambo-mo or Sumba-putsho occupy Namtheng near Chidam.
(6) Turgok-mo live near Rinchingpung.
(7) Rong-gong-mo are a numerous clan and came from Rong-gong near Ilam.
(8) Kheng-bo, from the place of that name near Ilam.
(9) Nam-chhyo-mo occupy Sidhi and Karmie, and had as their Jongpen Chado, father of the Phodang Lama, and after him Lachoo, Chobu Lama's father.
(10) Guling-mo, near Ilam in Nepal.
(11) Samdar-mo ditto.
(12) Kotha-mo, from Kotah near Ilam.
(13) Barmyak-mo.
(14) Sungphung-mo, ditto.
(15) Namtchi-mo were formerly subordinate to the Gnabdeh Lama's people, but subsequently were granted a special Jongpen.
(16) Sam-ling-mo in Nepal.
(17) Mong-mong-mo near Dentem, whose headman is the Sing-li Mapen.
(18) Talong-mo, near Dharm-den.
(19) Sang-pu-mo occupy Lingmo, which was given to the Song Jongpen, an uncle of Tchebu Lamas.
(20) Song-mo, closely allied to preceding.
(21) Namphak-mo, whose lands were given to the Phodang Lama.
(22) Re-doo-mo live near Rinchingpung and are under the Sikhim Raja direct.
(23) Kubbi-mo, from the place of that name near Tumlong.
(24) Fok-ram-mo and
(25) Rongeu-ram-mo live near Lingthem.
(26) Rangit-ram-mo, near the head of the Rungeet.
(27) Rathong-ram-mo and
(28) Rangbi-ram-mo near the Rathong.
(29) Lo-so-mo at Tassiding.
(30) Kalét-ram-mo from the Kulhait river.
(31) Lingdam-mo are at Ilam in Nepal.

(32) Rhenok-mo at Rhenok in Sikhim.
(33) Yong-bi-mo at Kotah in Nepal.
(34) Chong-khey-mo at Phoogurhi near Merig in Darjeeling.
(35) Lingdong-mo at Mangbru.
(36) Yok-cho-mo at Phensung.
(37) Re-ma-song near Ramtik.
(38) Na-be-mo in the Dik-chhu valley.
(39) Sangmi-po, though sometimes styled Lepchas, are really Limbus.

Many of the smaller families give a mythical origin to their ancestors, and trace their descent from spirits or demons, the offspring of an alliance between a rock or tree and a pond. To these they always assign a known location.

The most celebrated of their mythical heroes are reported to have disappeared from earth through various caves that are still pointed out.

The origin of the LIMBUS is veiled in great obscurity, though the most received account relates that they came from Kasi (*i.e.*, Benares).

But the following, taken from an old Limbu manuscript, may be interesting:—

According to Yak-thum (Limbu) tradition, in the beginning existed almighty god Tagyera Ningwa Puma. His spirit entered into Mubuk Wa-ma and caused him to create woman out of bamboo ashes and fowls' droppings: she was called Muzina Kye-ong-ma, and married the wind. They had a son by name Susu-weng Hara-weng. He went a-hunting one day and met two women whose origin is unknown. They bore to him respectively a son, Suwangbe-ba, and a daughter, Laha-dang-ma: these two marrying became the progenitors of the whole human race.

After creating woman, Mubuk Wa-ma seated himself on the right side of Khamba-karma (Mt. Kanchinjingna), and proceeded to invent four different kinds of alphabets.* These were—(1) Shyang-bed, (2) Athar-bed, (3) Jajur-bed, all written on paper, and (4) Riki-bed, written on a doe-skin, and for many eras after their construction were, however, lost.

The direct descendants of Suwangbe-ba are not known, but one branch appears at Kasi (Benares) in the persons of four brothers. One of these penetrated direct into the hills, where there was uninhabited country, and settling there, his descendants were known as the "Khambung-ba," or "lords of the soil." This may be the Phedhap or Bhuiphuta branch. Another brother settled in "Sukhi-gang-zi."

* Dr. Waddell points out that this is merely a clumsy way of citing the four Hindu veds or scriptures, viz., Sáma, Atharwa, Yajur and Ríg veds.

His descendants were called "Kasi-thang-ba," or "the arrivals from Kasi."

The other brothers travelled east into the hills, whence their descendants found their way westward at a subsequent period: hence they were known as the "Muna-pemba," or "the late comers." They are now better known as the Lhasa Gotra, from having come from the direction of East Tibet. In this branch there were again four brothers, the two kings U-ba-hang and Chang-ba-hang, and Kajung-ma and Gammi-ma: the two first names have evident reference to the two Tibetan Provinces of U (Lhassa) and Chang (Tashelhunpo); and in consequence of this latter, or because they came from the north (Chang, *lit.* Pyang), the Limbus derive their *sobriquet* of Chang. Dr. Waddell explains that the name Limbu has been given them by the Nepalis: they call themselves *Yákthumba* (or Yák-herds), and the Lepchas and Bhuteas call them *Tshong* (which in the vernacular means 'a merchant,' and the Limbus were the chief cattle-merchants and butchers in Sikhim).

It has been mentioned above that Mubuk Wa-ma had invented and hidden four different kinds of "Bed" (the Limbu for books). These were found the (1) by Bishu Karma, the protecting deity or ruler of the Kamis; the (2) by Mahisur, a Bhutea lama; the (3) by Bishun Raja, the head of the Brahmans, and forms the present Deva-nagari; while the (4) was found by the two Limbu Rajas mentioned above. Unfortunately the doe-skin on which the characters had been written had expanded and contracted so much with alternate damp and heat that the writing was undecipherable, and the Limbu alphabet remained lost. Many generations later the great Limbu Siri-jungna, called also the Dorze Lama of Yangrup, in a vision saw Mubuk Wa-ma, who pointed out where another copy of the Limbu writings, inscribed on stone, was to be found. The saint thus found them, and dictated to his eight chief disciples what now remains of Limbu literature. Siri-jungna was, however, in this betrayed to the Raja of Sikhim and the Tasong monks. They in jealousy or from fear of the Limbus, now becoming a united and separate people, tried to shoot him. In this they failed, as also in an attempt to drown him; so finally capturing him alive, they filled his mouth with fowls' dung, whereupon his spirit fled away in the form of a bird. Singha Raja was at that time King of Nepal. It may be, as Mr. Risley mentions, this Raja was Prithi Narayan Singh, but in that case it is singular all authentic history of Siri-jungna should have been lost in less than 100 years.*

* Babu S. C. Dass in his "Narrative of a Journey to Lhassa," page 6, states that the famous Srijanga, the deified hero of the Limbus, appeared probably in the 9th century, and is identified by the cis-Himalayan Bhuteas with an incarnation of Padma Sambhava. It is also said that he was born 95 years after Bikramjit's era, *i.e.*, about 38 A.D.

Another interpretation of Kashi and Lhassa Gotras is that the former are Limbu on both sides, whereas the latter are the offspring of a Limbu father, but a Tibetan mother.

The country between the Arun and Kankaye was originally peopled by Limbus, who were distributed over ten districts, each subject to their own headman, Soubah or petty Raja, who looked on his district as his own property. From this division into "ten" (Das), the Limbus are often known as "Das Limbus," and from their headman derived their title of "Soubah." These ten main divisions (or Thums) derive their names either from the name of the locality itself or from the number of the separate "Thars" or subdivisions, with whom the Goorkha Government made settlement, after the conquest of the Newar Raja and submission of the Limbu Soubahs. It seems that the Limbus were not conquered by the Goorkhas, but voluntarily submitted, and in consequence retain several privileges; among others, the right to guard the Walloon passes.

The Thums named from their locality are—

Yangrup.	Mewa or Mai-khola.
Tambarkhola.	Phédháp.

The second class comprise the remaining six Thums, viz.—

Charkhola (four).	Terathar (thirteen).
Panch-thar (five).	Atharai (eighteen).
Chothar or Soodap Chatharea (six).	Chaubisa (twenty-four).

The Thars or Septs embraced in these ten Thums are very numerous, but a full account will be found in Mr. Risley's "The Tribes and Castes of Bengal."

Of other tribes in Sikhim the Newars are the most enterprising and influential, though their number is small. Their history is, however, in no way connected with that of Sikhim. An interesting account of the Newars is to be found in Dr. Oldfield's "Sketches from Nepal."

The Gurungs live chiefly in Western Sikhim, and are well versed in sheep grazing.

The Mangars formerly occupied parts of the Kangpa-chen and Tambur valleys, but were expelled, and their power broken by their rivals, the Sherpa Bhuteas: the last of their chiefs is rumoured to have died near Pomong (in the Darjeeling Government Cinchona estate).

NOMENCLATURE OF PLACES.

The Tibetan names for Sikhim are pronounced Denjong, Demojong and Demoshong, though actually spelt hBras-lJongs, hBras-ma-lJongs and hBras-gShongs, and mean "the country or valley of rice." In Chinese this same word has been corrupted into Chê-Mêng-Hsiung. The great Dutch traveller Van de Putte, who travelled in Tibet about the year 1730, in his sketch map called Sikhim "Bra-ma-scjon," which is evidently the "hBras-ma-lJongs" above, while Horace della Penna in the same century speaks of the Kingdom of "Bregion" or "Bramashon:" the former must be a corruption of "hBras-lJongs."

In Tibetan the people of Sikhim are often called "Rong-pa," or "the dwellers in the steep country." The term "Mon-pa," or "dwellers in the lower country," is used occasionally to describe the Lepcha inhabitants. The first appellation must not, however, be confounded with the similar word by which the Lepchas speak of themselves; and which means "the squatter in," or "care-taker" of "the country of caves" (Ne láyang).

What the derivation of Lepcha is cannot be ascertained. It must, however, be remembered that the English form of spelling the word is incorrect and out of keeping with the local pronunciation, which is "Lap-cha" or "Lap-che," the former being the more common and probably the correct one. Dr. Waddell writes: "As the term '*Lapcha*' is of Nepalese origin, and the Parbatiya dialect of the Nepalese consists mainly of pure Sanskrit roots, the word 'Lapcha' may perhaps be derived from '*lap*,' speech, and '*cha*,' vile = the vile speakers—a contemptuous term with reference to their non-adoption of the Parbatiya language like the rest of the 'Nepalese' tribes." Another authority enquires whether it may refer to the Hindi 'Lap-thi,' the name of a kind of skate fish, *i.e.*, of a flat fish, a term which may have been applied by the Goorkhas to the Lepchas on account of the flatness of their faces. None of these derivations are convincing, but none are offered by the people themselves.

"The etymology of the modern name of Sikhim," as Dr. Waddell writes, "is not at all clear. It is generally alleged by the Lepchas and Bhuteas to be a Parbatiya name applied to the country by the conquering Goorkhas. As the great majority of the Parbatiya words are derived almost directly from the Sanskrit, I venture to suggest that its most probable derivation is from the Sanskrit शिखिन, *Sikhin* = crested. This would characterise the leading feature of the approach from the Nepal side—a long high ridge with Kanchinjingna 28,000 feet and Kabur 22,000 feet in its middle separates this country from Goorkha territory; and being shut off from Bhutan by another high ridge, the intervening narrow tract which constitutes Sikhim presents within itself an unusual number of ridges (crests) running more or less in N. to S. direction transverse to the vista from Nepal. This name is not at all likely to be related to Skt. सेक, *sek*, to wet or moisten, for the climate of Sikhim does not appear to be more moist than that of the adjoining portion of Eastern Nepal. Nor does the conjecture seem tenable that it is a Parbatiya translation of one of the vulgar forms of the Bhutea name for the country, viz., 'Demo-jong,' or 'the happy country,' from सुख, *sukhi*, happy, as this word is never spelt or pronounced with a *u*, and the country was a most inhospitable one."

Dr. Waddell, however, is not correct in saying that the word is never spelt or pronounced with an "u;" on the contrary, it is more often pronounced with an "u" than with an "i," and so may have been derived from two Limbu words "Su," new, and "Khim," a house or palace: and the name was first given to the country when the Tibetan Penchoo Namgué, the first Raja, built a "new palace" at Rubdentse and established a new kingdom. Curiously enough in an old map in Hamilton the place where Rubdentse stands is marked "Sikhim," and it may be noted that Kirkpatrick, writing in 1793, speaks of "the town and district of Sookhim," and of a place Sikhem in the itinerary from Bijapore to Daling, and this place would fall somewhere near the Rungeet. It is clear, therefore, that the name was originally given to a place and not a country.

Nearly every place in Sikhim that has a name has been so called from some special or striking natural feature, or in commemoration of some event that has occurred there: and connected with all the more conspicuous places there is often a legend attached. A few of the best known are here given, though the list of examples might be indefinitely enlarged.

As might be expected, names of Lepcha origin are chiefly found in the southern or lower portions of Sikhim, while Nepalese or Pahariya names are very rare and modern. The bulk of the derivations are Tibetan.

In Lepcha "Rang or Rung" means "a stream" and "Ung or Ong" "water." In Tibetan "Chhu" is "water or stream," "Tsho" (properly *m*Tsho) "a lake or pond," "Ri" "a mountain," "La" "a pass," "Kang" (pro. Kangs) "perpetual snow," "Chheñ" "great or full of," "Thang" (vulgarly "Tong" or "Tang") "a plain or meadow."

Omitting affixes denoting river, mountain, &c., we find the following Lepcha names for rivers:—

"Rang-nyét" (Rungeet) = "the two streams," as there are two main branches, the Little Rungeet in British territory and the

Great Rungeet rising from the south-east flank of Kanchinjingna. If, however, the name is pronounced Rung-nyēēt, it means "the good river."

"Rang-nyu" (our Tista) = "the straight river," so called, according to Dr. Waddell, because "this river, though receiving the full force of the Rungeet at right angles, still continues in its straight unaltered course, its direction being unaffected by this great accession of waters, or more probably because of its straight course across the plain after leaving the hills, in contrast to the other great effluent river of Sikhim, the *Māhaldi Ung*)Ang. 'Mahananda)', which means 'the bent moving water' with reference to this river, as seen from the hills, taking a very sudden bend to the right on reaching the plains." Another derivation is from "A-nyung," "deep," but this seems far-fetched, as there are a number of shallows even in its lower course. There is a third meaning given, viz., "the great river," from "A-nyoo." It may also mean "the mother river" from a tradition that tho Tista and Rungeet were born in the Himalayas and started for the plains, the former carrying a mountain-snake and the latter a pheasant. To find food for the bird, the Rungeet had to wander hither and thither, whereas the Tista went straight and arrived at Rangli first: the Rungeet, finding the Tista had the start, was very angry and threatened to return, whereon the Tista consented to be his wife and carry him on her back: and the curious way the Rungeet waters, which are always dark, overrun the white stream of the Tista at the junction is pointed to as a symbol of this union.

Ratong, "the surging swallowing one," the main source of the Rungeet, a glacier-fed rapid torrent subject to sudden and destructive flood.

Rilli=Ri-li, "the twisting one," but the name of this stream is often pronounced Rongli, so the derivation seems doubtful.

Rungneac="Rung-nyak," the black or dark stream which in Pahariya is called Kali jhora, an obvious corruption of "Kala jhora," an exact translation of the Lepcha.

Ryott=Ri-yot, "the rapid loosened stream," from its precipitous impetuous course, falling several thousand feet in a few miles.

In mountain names occur these—

Senchal=Shin-shel-hlo. Shin, cloud and mist-enveloped; shel, to be wet or dank; and hlo, a mountain, "the damp misty hill." This is Dr. Waddell's interpretation, and to the habitués of Darjeeling no name could be more appropriate for the highest hill near the station.

Phallut=Fok-lut, "the bare or denuded peak," as it is bare of trees and in striking contrast to its neighbour.

Singalela=Singli-la, "the hill or pass of the wild alder" (*Betula Bhojpattra*), because covered with the tree of that name. Near these places is Subarkum=Sabar-kam, "the musk deer hunter's shelter or cave." Quite recently musk deer were found here.

Sandakphu. Dr. Waddell translates this name to be "the height of the poison plant:" a translation only natural, when aconite and poisonous rhododendron used to be so common that sheep and cattle passing over had to be muzzled. The other classical interpretation, "the height where to obtain meditation," seems very far-fetched. The Pahariyas (Limbus) called a neighbouring and conspicuous hill "Sindok-kok-ma," literally "the high ridge," so it is much more probable that this name was erroneously transferred to our "Sundukphoo," which was formerly known to the Lepchas as "Tam," which means a plateau.

Tendong, "the up-raised horn," is the mountain which the Lepchas assert arose when all the country was under water, and supported a boat containing a few persons, all other people being drowned. The hill rose up like a horn (hence its name) and then subsided to its present form. To this day at the commencement of the rains a monk is sent from the neighbouring monastery of Niamtchi to the top of Tendong, where he has to remain during the wet season, praying hard that a second flood may not be sent. This tradition of a flood is traceable in another Lepcha name.

Rungli Rungliot (lit. Rungion Rung liot), "the waters of the Tista (Rungniou) have come this far and retired," and a cliff or cutting is pointed out as the channel by which the waters subsided. But the story has been metamorphosed and now runs, that the Balasun courted the Rungeet, daughter to the Tista, and at last persuaded her to elope. The pair got as far as the Ghoom range, which the Balasun safely crossed. The Rungeet's strength failed her, and she fell back again into her old valley. The angry father pursued the Balasun, but only succeeded in reaching Rungli Rungliot. Another version makes out that the Balasun came over to steal the fish (and not the daughter) of the Tista and succeeded; in fact until very recently no fish could be caught with a line in the latter river. There is also a tradition of a tower of Babel built at Dharmdin; it had nearly reached the moon, when word was sent down to send up a hook to throw over the horn of the moon: this command was misunderstood, and the people below cut away the foundations, so the building fell and killed numbers: a mound of stones and potsherds is shown to this day, and the tribe concerned (now extinct) were called "Na-ong" or "the blind fools."

Pankim. Dr. Waddell translates this "The King's Minister," supposed to be an attendant of Kanchinjingna. The Tibetan equivalent is very similar to Pal lDen. It may, however, be of Lepcha origin, and mean the Hill of the Goddess. It may also mean the conical hill with a point like a needle.

Phieungong, "the home of the dwarf bamboo" (*Thamnoculamus Falconeri*), is a hill covered with the "Phieun," whence one of the finest views in Sikhim is obtainable.

Rong-li, "the hut of the Lepcha" (Rong), is applied to several Lepcha settlements.

Pashok=Pa-zok, means a "jungle" or "forest," or the place where bamboos are split, thus corresponding to the common Paharia appellation Chatai-bans given to many places where mats are plaited from strips of bamboo.

Yoksom, the meeting place of the "three Lamas," where they selected Penchoo Namgué as Raja of Sikhim.

Ramtek was the first place where Penchoo Namgué stopped on his way from Gantok to Yoksom, before his accession; it was inhabited by Lepchas, who on being told by Penchoo of his divine mission, called the place after him, "the departure of the god," referring to Penchoo's journey.* It may, however, have reference to the deposition (departure) of their own kingdom which was to result from this journey.

Of Tibetan names there are many examples, such as—

La-chhen and La-chhung, the big pass and the little pass, whence rise two of the main streams of the Tista. The Donkhia (hBr Dong-khyags), the real pass at the head of the latter valley, is very steep, high and dangerous (whence the name, the pass where even the wild yak is frozen), much more so than the Kongra lama (Kangdu lama), "the pass of our exalted lady;" hence the names seem inappropriate. This is, however, explained by saying that La-chhen is a long wide sloping ascent and descent, whereas the La-chhung is short and steep. Notwithstanding the present spelling, it is probable the words were Lam-chhen and Lam-chhung, the highway and the byeway, which exactly hits off the physical natures of the two routes. The La-chhen village is more often called Lam-teng.

Nemitzo, pronounced Men-mo-tsho, "the lake of the demoness."

Tsho-la-mo (Cholamoo), "the lake of our lady or the goddess," being close to Kongra lama.

Bidang tsho (properly hBri-thang-tsho), "the lake of the cow-yak."

Tanitzo=Tanyek-tsho, "the lake of the horse-tail or the horse-hair noose."

---

* Penchoo being an educated, intelligent person, was looked upon by the ignorant Lepcha as a superior being, a deity.

The reason for these names is very obscure.

In mountains and passes we have such names as Kanchinjingna =Kang-chhen, "great snow," mDzöd, "treasury," and lña, "five." The legend has it there are five treasures to be found in the mountain, but it may have reference to the five peaks forming the mountain.

Kanchinjhau, the bearded Kanchin (rGyau, the beard), perhaps so called from the way the lower ice and snow slip down from its southern face. The flat near it is Giaogong (properly rGyau-gong), "the bearded hill."

Gipmochi, properly Gyé-mo-chhen, the trijunction of the boundaries of Tibet, Sikhim, and Bhutan.

Chumulhari (properly Jo-mo-lha-ri), "the hill of our lady-goddess."

Chomiomo (properly Jo-mo-Yúm-mo), "the mount of our lady-mother," and said to be the wife of the neighbouring Kanchinjhau: a small peak between the two is pointed out as their child.

Cho-la (properly kTso-la), "the principal pass," being the main pass between Lower Sikhim and Chumbi. Chomnaga should be kTso-nags-go, "the head of the great forest," a place at the foot of the Chola pass.

Yak-la, the pass used by yak-graziers.

Gnatui-la (properly rNa-thös-la), "the pass of the listening ear."

Jelep-la, "the easy, level pass," a very appropriate name, if this pass is compared with others.

Pembyringo is usually called gDong-lam, "the road of the face," also very appropriate if it means one's face is terribly cut up by the winds, that make this otherwise easy pass inconvenient for several months in the year.

Gnatong is spelt in Tibetan Ñags-thang and not Nag-thang: the former means the "forest-meadow," as it is situated close to large pine forests; the latter "black-meadow," which has no local significance, unless it refers to the black pine trees.

The British Fort Graham or Fort Gnatong is not really situated at Gnatong, but at Dulpong. The meaning of this word is "the place of victory or the subduing," very prophetic of the two crushing defeats of the Tibetans on the 22nd May and the 23rd September 1888. The word for victory is spelt "hDul." There is another word rDul, meaning "dust' or "dung," also appropriate, as the place was crowded with yak and cattle stations.

Lingtu=Lung-thur, "the descent into the valley."

Phadenchen, "the pigs' wallowing place," from its being damp and muddy.

Sedongchen, "full of Sé-trees (sDong)," a tree whose leaves cause great itching and even blisters.

Rhenock=Ri-Nag, "the black hill." This is the ordinary accepted spelling, but it may be a corruption from Ri-sÑa, the hill whose outline is like that of a nose (sNa); there are several places of this name in Tibet, and the same termination is seen in "Lho-na" (Hooker's Thlonok), "the south face."

Merig, "the burnt hill."

Gantok, "the high hill."

Rubdenchi=Rab-gDañ-tsé, "the height of the chief residence" (palace).

Barmie=hBar-Nyag, "the rough notch or ridge." hBar may also mean burnt.

Barphung, "the collection of burnings."

The following are the names of more than one place:—

Laghyap=La-rGyap, "the back of the pass," *i.e.*, the first halting place on the other side of the pass.

Byutan may perhaps mean "the meadow of the cow-yak," a place where calves are usually tethered.

Sebula=bSil-bu or gSer-bu-la, "the cold pass;" perhaps it is "Sil-bu-la," a "fragment," a side pass, which exactly describes one or two of the passes called "Sebula." It may again be Ser-bu-la, "the pass of hail," or Serpala, "the yellow pass."

Chak-chu=Tsha-chhu, "a hot spring."

Samdong=Zam-gDong, "the bridge-face" (or head), *i.e.*, the place facing a bridge.

Of Pahariya or Nepalese the most striking is Chiabhangan, "the hollow where one peeps over," referring to the main pass between Sikhim and Nepal. Bhangan or Bunjang means a hollow or depression in the ridge of a mountain chain, so is equivalent to the Tibetan "la;" thus we have at the head of the Little Rungeet the pass or dip of Mani-bhangan (mani=tomb or monument), so called from the monument there.

A Pahariya evidently in good faith explained that the Tista was so called because it was the boundary of Tibet, *i.e.*, "Tibetstan."

As mentioned above, Sundukphoo may be a word of Limbu origin.

SIKHIM LAWS.

The following is a short account of the Sikhim Laws as translated from a manuscript copy obtained from the Khangsar Dewan. The language used in this book is difficult, and thanks are due to the Phodong Lama and Lamas Shorab Gyatsho and Ugin Gyatsho for the help they have given.

History.

The Sikhim laws are founded on those spoken by Raja Me-long-dong,[1] who lived in India before the time of Budda (914 B.C.). This Raja is mentioned in the Ka-gyur[2] in the 31st chapter.

They were again written by Kun-ga-gyal-tsan*[3] of Sa-kya-pa, who was born in 1182. He was King of 13 provinces in Tibet, and has called the laws† Tim-yik-shal-che-chu-sum or Chu-dug,[4] there being two sets, one containing 13 laws and the other 16.‡ These are practically the same. The laws were again written by De-si-sangye Gya-tsho,[5] who was born in 1653 and was a Viceroy of Tibet. They were called by him Tang-shel-me-long-nyer-chik-pa.§[6]

The first set of laws deal with offences in general; the second set forth the duties of Kings and Government servants, and are simply an amplification of some of the laws contained in the former.

SUMMARY OF THE SIXTEEN LAWS.

No. 1.—General Rules to be followed in time of War.

(*a*) It is written in the Ka-gyur that before going to war the strength of the enemy should be carefully ascertained, and whether any profit will be derived from it or not. It should also be seen if the dispute cannot be settled by diplomacy before going to war. Care should also be taken that by going to war no loss be sustained by your Government. Whatever the cause of dispute, letters and

[1] Me-long-gdong.
[2] bkah-hgyur-mdo-sa-pa.
[3] Kun-dgah-rgyal-mtsan.
[4] khrims-yig-zhal-lcbe-bchu-gsum.
[5] sde-srid-sangs-rgyas-rgya-mtso.
[6] dang-shel-me-long-gnyer-gchig-pa.
* Full name Sa-skya-penṭi-ta-kun-dgah-rgyal-mtsan.
† The law of 13 cases.
‡ The book containing the 16 laws is supposed to have been amplified from the 13 laws by De-si-sangya Gya-tsho.
§ The 21 laws as clear as crystal.

messengers between the contending parties should on no account be stopped, and messengers should be properly treated. Any one coming with overtures of peace should be well received.

(*b*) Should two or more enemies combine against you, no means should be left untried to separate them, and if possible to bring one over to your side, but false oaths should not be resorted to, nor the using of God's name.

(*c*) The lie of the ground should be well examined to see how the roads run, and whether your position is strong.

(*d*) If it is necessary, other methods having failed, to go to war, you should all combine, and being of one mind should attack. See that there are no sick, lazy, or timid in the ranks, but only those who fear not death. See that your own soldiers obey the law, and all should obey the orders of the General. Experienced men should only be sent, and not those who look after their own interest only.

The army should be divided into three divisions under the command of different officers. The General and his staff should be trusted men who can guide the army: they should do their work thoroughly. Your horses, tents, and arms should be kept in good order. A doctor, diviner, astrologer, and lama should be appointed.

The tents should be properly arranged the first day, and this arrangement adhered to so as to prevent confusion. On moving, the fires should first be put out, the wounded should be cared for, and in crossing rivers order should be kept, and those behind should not push forward. Things found should be returned without asking a reward, and should not be concealed or kept. Thieves are not to be flogged, but only to have their hands tied behind them, but they may be fined. Should any one kill another by mistake, he must pay the funeral expenses. Should any combine and kill another, they must pay twice the fine laid down by law. Any disputed loot must be drawn for by lots between the contending parties.

The General should appoint sentries, who must look to the water-supply and see they become not easily frightened. They should allow no stranger to enter the camp armed, but should be careful not to kill any messenger. If a sentry kills a messenger coming to make peace, he shall be sent to his home in disgrace on some old, useless horse with broken harness.

No. 2.—For those who are being Defeated and cannot Fight.

When a fort is surrounded, those in the fort should remain quiet and should show no fear. They should not fire off their arms uselessly and with no hope of hitting the enemy. The well within the fort should be most carefully preserved. Those within the fort should not be allowed to communicate with the enemy for fear of treachery. They should not be lazy. Until peace is declared the messenger should receive no reward.

Should you be defeated, you must give up your arms, and those who give them up must not be killed. Should any one kill one who has given up his arms, he must be derided and scoffed at as a coward.

If during a conflict you capture a General or officer of rank, you should bind his hands in front with a silk scarf; he should be allowed to ride his own horse or another good horse, and should be treated well, so that in the event of your ever falling into his hands he may treat you well also. Any other prisoners should have their hands tied behind them and they should be made to walk. Officers should be placed on old, worn-out horses with broken harness and rope stirrups. Should an army be defeated and be obliged to fly, nothing should be said to them, but they should not be rewarded or receive any presents, even though the leader be a great man. The prisoners should receive what is necessary for subsistence and also expenses for religious ceremonies, and men of rank should be treated well and with consideration.

A man can only make a treaty for himself and his descendants.

No. 3.—For Officers and Government Servants.

These should leave off their own work and apply themselves entirely to Government work, should obey the orders of the Viceroy and head of the Church, should not change the shari (hat sects) and Tub-tha (religious sects).

In the fifth month they should kill no animals, and the Raja's store should be well kept, so that there be no deficiency. They should repair the images, temples and books, and all passes and roads. Also on the 10th of this month the "dadok" ceremony must be performed.*

If a man be sent on private business, the name of Government should not be used. Debts may be recovered through officers, who should patiently hear the case and not give arbitrary orders. They should give just judgment and not favour those who can reward them. They should enquire diligently into all cases, and leave no case undecided, so that all men can say your work has been well done.

No. 4.—Law of Evidence.

You should listen carefully to what is said by both parties. Equals by birth should be heard at the same time and place. Those that are

* This puja is performed in order to send our enemies away.

not equals should be heard separately. Should any one not agree to your decision, he can be fined.

If the evidence be false, both parties are fined according to which has given the most false evidence.

If after a decision has been given the parties wish to compound between themselves, one-half of the fine only is imposed.

No. 5.—Grave Offences.

There are five sins:

(1) Murder of mother, (2) murder of holy men, (3) murder of father, (4) making mischief amongst Lamas, and (5) causing hurt to good men. There are also the sins of taking things from Rajas and Lamas for our own use; causing a good man to fall through no fault of his own; administering poison; killing any one for gain; causing strife in a peaceful country; and making mischief.

For the above offences punishments are inflicted, such as putting the eyes out, cutting the throat, having the tongue cut out, having the hands cut off, being thrown from cliffs, and being thrown into deep water.

No. 6.—Fines inflicted for Offences in order to make people remember.

Certain crimes may be punished by money fines, varying in accordance with the gravity of the offence.

When a number of men have committed dacoity, they may be fined from 15 to 80 gold srang.* For small offences smaller fines are imposed, and can be paid either in money or in kind; the amount to be settled by the officer trying the case.

No. 7.—Law of Imprisonment.

Any one rioting, using arms, and disputing near the court can be imprisoned. Thieves and those who destroy property, and those who do not obey the village headman, those who give bad advice, those who abuse their betters, can be bound and put in the stocks and fined according to the law, and are only released if petitioned by some one in authority who makes himself responsible for his fine.

* Note.—One srang = one oz.

No. 8.—For Offenders who refuse to come in an Orderly has to be sent expressly to enquire about the case.

A messenger who is sent off at a moment's notice should receive 3 patties* of barley per diem for food and a small sum in money, according to the importance of the case in which he is employed, but the messenger's servants should not be fed. The messenger is allowed one-fourth of the fine for his expenses.

Should an agent not settle a case properly, he must return to the villagers what he took, otherwise the villagers will have much trouble given them.

The agent should report having received the fine on penalty of forfeiting one-fourth what he has taken. When a fine is imposed, it should be at once collected, no excuse being taken. If an agent is sent to collect rent, he should be fed twice by the headman.

Of stolen property recovered by an agent, the Government receive one-tenth value.

No. 9.—Murder.

For killing a man the fine is heavy—even up to many thousands of gold pieces. In the Tsalpa law book it is written that if a child, a madman, or animal kills any one no fine is taken, but that money must be given by the relations of the first two for funeral expenses, and one-fourth of that amount must be given by the owner of the animal towards these expenses.

Should one man kill another and plead for mercy, he must, besides the fine, give compensation and food to the relative of the deceased.

Should a man kill his equal and the relatives come to demand compensation, he must give them 18oz. of gold in order to pacify them. The price of blood should never be too much reduced, or a man may say, "If this is all I have to give, I will kill another."

The arbitrator must take the seal of each party, saying they will abide by his decision, and they must each deposit 3oz. of gold as security.

Fines can be paid in cash, animals, and articles of different kinds.

The price for killing a gentleman who has 300 servants, or a superintendent of a district, or a Lama professor, is 300 to 400oz. gold srang. For full Lamas, Government officers, and gentlemen with 100 servants the fine is 200oz. of gold.

For killing gentlemen who possess a horse and 5 or 6 servants, working Lamas, the fine is 145 to 150oz. of gold.

* 17 patties = 1 maund or 82lbs.

For killing men with no rank, old Lamas, personal servants, the fine is 80oz. of gold.

For killing a man who has done good work for Government the fine is 50 to 70oz. of gold.

For killing common people and for villagers the price is 30 to 40oz. of gold.

For killing unmarried men, servants, and butchers the price is 30 gold srang.

And for killing blacksmiths and beggars 10 to 20oz. of gold.

These prices can also be paid in grain. The prices for funeral expenses must be paid within 49 days.

On the fines being paid, a letter must be written and a copy given to each party, saying that everything has been settled. If a case is re-opened, a fine must be paid by him who opens the case. The murderer must write to the effect he will not commit such a crime again. Part of the fines can be given towards the funeral expenses of the deceased.

No. 10.—Bloodshed.

In the old law it is written that for any drop of blood shed the price varies from one to one-quarter zho.* A man may even be beheaded for wounding a superior. For wounding his own servant a man is not fined, but he must tend the wounded man. Should two men fight and one wound the other, he who first drew his knife is fined, and he who is wounded must be tended by the other till his wounds be well. The fines are payable in money or kind. Should one man wound another without any fight, he is fined according to the law of murder.

If in a fight a limb or an eye is injured, the compensation to be given is fixed by Government.

No. 11.—For those who are False and Avaricious the following Oaths are required.

If it is thought a man is not telling the truth, an oath should be administered. At the time of taking an oath powerful gods should be invoked, and those who are to administer the oath must be present. It is writen in ancient law that the bird of Paradise should not be

* The word 'zho' means a drachm, or as a coin two-thirds of a rupee.

killed, the poisonous snake should not be thrown down, the raven should not be stoned, and the small turquoise should not be defiled. Thus pure Lamas and monks should not be sworn.

Magicians, shameless persons, women, fools, the dumb, and children should not be sworn.

Men should be employed who know both parties and are intelligent and truthful. Those willing to take an oath should be of equal rank. When all are present, the case should first be settled, if possible, by arbitration. If this fails, the ordeal either by hot stones or boiling oil is resorted to. That by oil: The oil must be supplied by Government and must be pure. It is boiled in a pan at least 3 inches deep. In the oil a black stone and a white stone are placed of equal size and weight. He who has to take the oath must first wash his hands in water, in milk, and in widow's urine. His hand is then bound in a cloth and sealed. This is done a day or two before the ordeal in order to give him a chance of confessing. The vessel with the boiling oil is then placed so that the stones cannot be seen, and he has to take one out. If he takes out the white one without any burn, he wins his case. He who gets the black stone is sure to be burnt and loses his case. Should he who gets the white stone be slightly burnt, it means he has partially spoken the truth and wins half his case.

That by hot stone: The stone is made hot by the blacksmith, taken out of the fire with tongs, and placed on a brass dish. The man's hands are washed as before, examined to see what marks there are on it produced by labour, and the hot stone placed in the palm. With the stone he must walk 4 to 7 paces. His hand is then bound up and left for 3 to 7 days. On examination if there are no marks, or if there is a long mark called rdo-lam, he wins his case. He also wins his case if the stone bursts three times in being heated. It depends on the number of marks how much of his case he wins.

A cloth and a rug have to be paid as expenses, and the brass vessels go to the blacksmith. In order to test the oil for boiling, a grain of barley is thrown in: if it flies into the air, the oil is ready.

Whilst placing his hand in the oil or holding the hot stone, a statement in writing of the case is placed on the person's head.

The ordeal by oil may be gone through without using the stone.

Mud and water can be used in place of oil. Hot iron used to be employed in place of the stone, but is now discontinued.

No. 12.—THEFT.

For taking a Jongpen's or other great man's things, 10,000 times their value has to be given in return. For taking a Lama's things

80 times their value has to be given, a neighbour's things 9 times, and a villager's 7 times. For taking a stranger's things 4 times.

Beggars who steal from hunger have only to give back what they took.

Should one man accuse another falsely of stealing, he must give him as compensation what he accused him of stealing.

Should a man find anything on the road and without telling take it for himself, he must be fined double its value; but should he tell, he receives one-third the value. Should any one recover stolen property, but not be able to catch the thief, he receives half of the property recovered.

Should any one find a horse, any cattle, yaks or sheep and keep them for a year without finding the owner, he receives one-fourth the value, provided he has not in the meantime used the animals for his own benefit.

Should any one wound a thief he is not fined.

If a thief whilst running away be killed by an arrow or stone, a small fine only is taken.

Should any one having caught a thief kill him, he is fined according to the law of murder. The reward for catching a thief is from 1 to 5oz. of gold, according to the amount of the property stolen.

No. 13.—Disputes between near Relatives. Between Man and Wife and between Neighbours who have things in common.

If a husband wishes to be separated from his wife, he must pay her from 18 zho, the amount varying in accordance with the length of time they have been married.

If the wife wishes to leave her husband, she must pay him 12 zho and one suit of clothes. The wife on separation also receives the clothes given to her at her marriage, a list of which is always taken, or its equivalent in money.

Should there be children, the father takes the boys and the mother the girls; the father paying from 5 to 15 zho for each son, called the price of milk. If the woman has committed no fault, she receives her ornaments.

Should a family wish to separate, a list of the whole property should be taken and divided according to circumstances. The father and mother are asked with whom they would like to live, and if there is any dispute about it, lots are drawn. The married children's property is first separated from the rest, and if any children are going to school, their expenses must be taken from the whole before decision.

No. 14.—Taking another's Wife or Adultery.

The old law runs that if any one takes a Raja's or Lama's wife, he may be banished, have his hands cut off, or his penis cut off. He may also have to pay a weight in gold equal to his penis and testicles. For violating a woman of different position 3oz. of gold have to be paid to the woman's relations and 4 gold srang to Government, besides many things in kind.

For violation of a woman of the same position, 2 or 3 gold srang and several kinds of articles have to be paid.

If the woman goes of her own accord to the man, he has only to pay 1 gold srang and three kinds of articles.

Should one man's wife entice another married man to go with her, she has to pay seven things in kind.

Should a man and woman cohabit on a journey there is no fine.

No. 15.—Law of Contract.

Should any one take a loan of cattle, yaks, sheep, &c., and they die in his charge, he must pay for them. Should they die one night after being returned, it is the owner's loss. If they die before midnight of the night they are returned, the borrower has to pay.

Should a horse die whilst on loan from a wound, one-fourth to one-third its value will have to be paid.

Should any one having made an agreement to take anything refuse to take it, the articles being good, he must pay one-fourth its value. If there be any mistake in an account, it can be rectified up to one year.

No. 16.—For Uncivilized People.

Such as Bhuteas, Lepchas, Mongolians, who know no law, therefore what is written below is not required in Tibet. The Mongolians also have their own law, written by Raja Kesar, of which we know little.

Any Government messenger must be supplied with what he wants (such as horses, food, &c.), and if not provided he can take them. Also whilst halting he must be supplied with food and fire. But the messenger must not draw his sword or use his bow, or he will be liable to a fine, and he must only take what is necessary to the performance of the Government work.

MARRIAGE CUSTOMS OF THE SIKHIMESE.*

[These customs have been gathered from actual observation, and are the customs now observed amongst the Bhuteas.]

If the eldest brother takes a wife, she is common to all his brothers.

If the second brother takes a wife, she is common to all the brothers younger than himself.

The eldest brother is not allowed to cohabit with the wives of the younger brothers.

Should there be children in the first case, the children are named after the eldest brother, whom they call father.

In case 2, after the second brother, &c.

Three brothers can marry three sisters, and all the wives be in common, but this case is not very often seen. In such a case the children of the eldest girl belong to the eldest brother, &c., if they each bear children. Should one or more not bear children, then the children are apportioned by arrangement. Two men not related can have one wife in common, but this arrangement is unusual.

A man occasionally lends his wife to a friend, but the custom is not general and uncommon.

If a girl becomes pregnant before marriage and afterwards marries the father of the child, the child is considered legitimate, but the man is fined a bull or its equivalent, which go to her relatives. Should the man by whom the girl was made pregnant not marry her, and should she afterwards marry another, the child remains with the woman's brothers or relatives. A woman is not considered dishonoured by having a child before marriage.

The marriage ceremony consists almost entirely in feasting, which takes place after the usual presents have been given to the girl's relations. These presents constitute the woman's price, and vary in accordance with the circumstances of both parties.

The only religious ceremony is performed by the village headman, who offers up a bowl of marwa to the gods, and presenting a cup of the same marwa to the bride and bridegroom, blesses them, and hopes the union may be a fruitful one. Lamas take no part in the ceremony.

The marriage tie is very slight, and can be dissolved at any time by either the man or the woman.

A man may marry his mother's brother's daughter, but he can marry none of his other first cousins till the second generation. Their system of relationship is peculiar and interesting, and is given below.

* Sikhim, Tibetans and Bhutanese.

Regarding succession the following order seems to be generally, though not always, used:—

1. Son.
2. Grandson, &c., through the males.
3. Brother by same mother.
4. Father's brother's son, „ sister's son, Mother's brother's son, „ sister's son — by choice.
5. If only distant relatives, they only receive a portion, a portion going to the Lamas and the remainder to Government.
6. If no relatives, funeral expenses, &c., to the Lamas and the remainder to Government.

NOTES ON THE GEOLOGY AND MINERAL RESOURCES OF SIKHIM.

By P. N. Bose, B.Sc. (London), F.G.S., *Deputy Superintendent, Geological Survey of India.*

(i) Physical Geography.

Sikhim is essentially a mountainous country without a flat piece of land of any extent anywhere. The mountains rise in elevation northward. The high serrated, snowcapped spurs and peaks culminating in the Kanchanjinga, which form such a characteristic and attractive feature in the scenery of Sikhim, are found in this direction. The northern portion of the country is deeply cut into steep escarpments, and, except in the Lachen and the Lachung valleys, is not populated. Southern Sikhim is lower, more open, and fairly well cultivated.

This configuration of the country is partly due to the direction of the main drainage, which is southern. The Himalayas on the Indian side must have sloped to the south from the earliest geological times when the gneiss which constitutes their main body was elevated. For all the later rocks—the submetamorphic slate group, the coal-bearing Damudas and the tertiaries—which fringe the outer Himalaya are evidently formed of detritus carried from the north.

The physical configuration of Sikhim is also partly due to geological structure. The northern, eastern and western portions of the country are constituted of hard massive gneissose rocks capable of resisting denudation to a considerable extent. The central and southern portion, on the other hand, is chiefly formed of comparatively soft, thin, slaty and half-schistose rocks which are denuded with facility, and it is this area which is the least elevated and the best populated in Sikhim.

The trend of the mountain system, viewed as a whole and from a distance, is in a general east-west direction. The chief ridges in Sikkim, however, run in a more or less north-south direction, as, for instance, the Singalela and the Chola ridges. Another north-south ridge runs through the central portion of Sikhim separating the Rungeet from the Tista valley; Tendong (8,676 feet) and Moinam (10,637 feet) are two of its best known peaks. This north-south direction of the principal ridges is due, no doubt, to the original southern slope of the Himalaya. The Rungeet and the Tista which form the main channels of drainage, run nearly north-south. The valleys cut by these rivers and their chief feeders are very deep. The valleys of the

Rungeet, of the Tista, and of their chief tributaries are generally not less than 5,000 feet in depth. They are rather open towards the top, but usually attain a steep gorge-like character as we approach the beds of the rivers. As a consequence of this, and also of the comparative insalubrity of the lower portion of the valleys, all the monasteries and principal villages are situated at an elevation ranging from 4,000 to 6,000 feet.

The snowcapped jagged ridges in the northern portion of the country send down glaciers* which at present usually come down to about 13,500 feet; those from the Kanchanjinga appear to descend about a thousand feet lower. The perpetual snow line in Sikhim may be approximately put down at 16,000 feet, so that the glaciers descend 3,500 to 2,500 feet below that line. Formerly they used to descend much lower than at present. Lachung, for instance, of which the elevation is 8,790 feet, stands at the foot of an immense terminal moraine. The Bidangcho lake, on the road between Gnatong and Jalep pass, at an elevation of 12,700 feet, is dammed at the southern end by a bank of boulders which are distinctly of glacial origin. Moraines occur also about Thangme in the Pragchu valley, north of Jongri, at an elevation of about 13,000 feet. The retreat of the glaciers backwards towards their gathering ground or the *névé* in these cases has been recent, and the ancient moraines witnessing their advance are still *in situ.* But the excessive rainfall of Sikhim, amounting annually to probably no less than 200 inches, makes the removal and re-arrangement of the glacial boulders a question of very short time; and once brought within the action of the torrential streams, the boulders soon lose all traces of their glacial origin. The peculiar configuration of the hills passed over by glaciers is also soon lost owing to pluvial denudation. The glacial valleys, as for instance the Pragchu, the Lachen, and the Lachung valleys, are open and ⌣ shaped; and this shape is one of the most reliable evidences of their origin. But after the retreat of the glaciers, the streams taking their place cut the valleys down deeply into V-shaped gorges, and the striking distinction between glacier and river valleys is soon effaced. Thus owing to the excessive rainfall, traces of past glacial action are liable to extinction in Sikhim; and it is impossible to tell how far the glaciers extended in comparatively remote times. The lowest height of glacial extension, for which I found unmistakeable evidence, is that of Lachung (8,790 feet). Below Lachung also down to a height of about 7,000 feet, the valley is open and has a glacial look about it.

* The writer has described some of the Sikkim glaciers visited by him in a paper containing extracts from the Journal of a trip to the glaciers of the Kabru, Pandim, &c. published in the "Records of the Geological Survey of India," Vol. XXIV, pt. 1.

Valleys to which glaciers come down, or whence these have but recently retired, abound in small lakes or tarns which are dammed in at the outlet by moraines. The Bidangcho lake, 3 miles north-east of Gnatong, is the best instance I came across of a glacial lake in a valley whence the glacier has recently retired. It is 1⅓ mile in length, and its greatest breadth is ½ mile.

The following hot springs are known in Sikhim :—

1. *Phut Sachu*—On the east side of the Rungeet river, 2 miles north-east of Rinchingpong monastery, situated amongst dark coloured massive siliceous limestones. Hot fetid water bubbles up at several spots. Temperature at one spring 100·4°F. The springs are situated in the bed of the river which at the time I visited them (March) was dry. These springs are referred to in Dr. Oldham's "Thermal Springs of India" (Vol. XIX, pt. 21, p. 32) as "Phugsachu."

2. *Ralong Sachu*—On the west bank of the Rungeet river, about 2 miles N.N.W. of Ralong monastery. Elevation about 3,100 feet. Situated amongst finely laminated phyllites with abundance of vein quartz, at a height of about 100 feet above the bed of the river. Hot water flows out through fissures at several places. The temperature of the hottest spring close to where it comes out is 131°F.; in a reservoir constructed for bathing purposes, it is 118·4°F. The temperature of another spring close to where the water flows out is 114·8°; in the reservoir it is 107·6°. [The temperature of a stream close by was found to be 53·6°.] A whitish deposit, which effervesces strongly on the application of hydrochloric acid, is formed at the mouths of the springs. It is stained green in places with carbonate of copper, due, no doubt, to the springs passing through cupriferous ores. It is very likely these springs that are referred to in Dr. Oldham's list as "Puklaz Sachu, about one day's journey from the monastery of Pemlong" (*op. cit.*, p. 32). Probably "Pemlong" is meant for Ralong.

I heard of a hot spring about half a mile north of Ralong Sachu, which I had no time to visit.

3. *Yeumtang*—On the east bank of the Lachung river, half a mile below Yeumtang. Though I passed the springs I could not get at them owing to the bridge over the Lachung not having been constructed at the time of my visit (May). They are described in Dr. Oldham's list (*op. cit.*, p. 32) :—"The discharge amounts to a few gallons per minute ; the temperature at the source is 112½°, and in the bath 106°. The water has a slightly saline taste ; it is colourless, but emits bubbles of sulphuretted hydrogen gas, blackening silver."—(*Hooker, Him. Journ.*, 1855, *Vol. II, p.* 126.)

4. *Momay.*—"Hot springs burst from the ground near some granite rocks on its floor, about 16,000 feet above the sea, and only a

mile below the glacier [of Kinchinjhow], and the water collects in pools: its temperature is 110°, and in places 116°."—(*Hooker, Him. Journ.*, 1855, *Vol. II*, *p.* 140; *see also Dr. Oldham*, op. cit., *p.* 33.)

(ii) GEOLOGY.

1.—*The Gneissic Group.*

The rocks belonging to this group are the oldest, and constitute the main body of the Himalayas. From near Kurseong, south of Darjeeling, to the northern frontier of Sikhim it is uninterruptedly traced over a distance of some 75 miles in a straight line; whereas all the later rocks—the submetamorphic slate group, the Damudas, and the tertiaries—together cover an area in the outer Himalayas nowhere more than six miles in width.

Two forms of the gneiss are met with :—

(*a*) In Southern Sikhim, approximately south of the parallel of Jongri and Boktola (about lat. 27° 250′), the gneiss is highly micaceous and frequently passes into mica schists. Both muscovite and biotite occur, the former predominating. Hornblende, garnet, and schorl are the chief accessory minerals. Bands of quartzite are common. Veins of calcite occur at places, as near Lingtu by the road to Gnatong. The gneiss is well foliated, and exhibits strongly marked features of disturbance, in that it is much folded and crumpled, especially in the extreme south about Darjeeling. The prevailing strike is WNW—ESE.

(*b*) In Northern Sikhim, as north and south-west of Jongri, about Lachung, &c., the gneiss is not quite so micaceous. Muscovite is either rare or is entirely absent. Schorl and hornblende are the chief accessory minerals. Intrusive granitic rocks occur as dykes and sheets; in some of them muscovite is well developed.

The northern gneiss agrees in some of its petrological characters with the central gneiss of Stoliczka. As the southern gneiss, however, was uninterruptedly traced into it, and as no physical break was perceptible anywhere, they are very likely of the same age. Mr. Medlicott takes the same view in the "Manual of Indian Geology."*

The relation between the gneissic group and the next group (the Dalings), which includes submetamorphic slates, phyllites, &c., is far from clear. At the eastern boundary between the two groups which passes by Gantok, the present capital of Sikhim, the latter apparently

* *Op. cit.*, pp. 597—614.

underlie the gneiss, the dip of both being north-eastern. So do they also at the western boundary, which passes by Pemiongchi, the first monastery in Sikhim, the dip there being north-western. At the southern boundary, which is in the Darjeeling district, and which appears to be faulted, the dips of both the groups are southern. Wherever the junction between the two groups is observed, the Dalings appear to underlie the gneiss; and the fact that the former pass into mica schists at places near the junction makes it appear as if there was a passage from the one to the other group. Indeed, Mr. Mallett considered the gneiss as moro recent than the Dalings.* But the former being presumably the older rock, it would be preferable to find some other explanation for the apparent underlie of the Dalings.

The fact that near the junction everywhere the gneiss dips in the same direction as the Dalings, shows that the former was largely affected by the disturbing forces which tilted up the latter.

2.—*The Dalings.*

This name was given by Mr. Mallet to a group of submetamorphic rocks after a place called Daling in the Darjeeling district. Phyllites form the predominant rocks in this group. At the boundary between it and the gneissose rocks, they pass into silvery mica schists; in fact, in this position the passage is sometimes so gradual, that it is difficult to say where the one group begins and the other ends. Dark clay slates with thick quartzite bands prevail near Chakang, Pachikhani (south of Pakyang), &c.; the workable copper ores invariably occur amongst these rocks. Gritstone is sometimes met with as just south of Namchi; but conglomerate never. Impure siliceous limestone is found north-east and north-west of Namchi, and highly carbonaceous shales occur in the Mangpur jhora just south of Namchi, by the Rungeet east of Chakang, and by the Rummam near Gok (south of Chakang).

Igneous rocks are rare. A rather thick band of gneissose granite was met with between Murtam and Ramtpek which continues for some distance northward as well as southward, forming the serrated peaks D: 5 and Maphila. It is probably of intrusive origin. An unquestionably intrusive dioritic-looking rock was encountered penetrating through slates by the road between Song and Tikobu.

The Sikhim Dalings occur somewhat in the form of a dome-shaped anticlinal. On the south side the dip is southern; east of the Rungeet it is chiefly E.N.E.; west of that river the inclination is

* "Memoirs, Geological Survey of India," Vol. XI, pt. 1, p. 42.

north-western; and on the north side, as near Ralong, the dip is mainly northern. The southern boundary between the Dalings and the gneissose rocks which passes a little north of Darjeeling was shown by Mr. Mallet to be faulted. The eastern boundary passes by Gantok, and the western by Pemiongchi. As in the case of the Damuda-Tertiary and the Daling-Damuda boundaries in the Sub-Himalayas, both of these boundaries may represent "lines of original contact, possibly modified by subsequent faulting."* The Daling rocks would in this case have to be supposed as deposited in a lake of which steep gneiss escarpments formed the sides: the lower gorge of the Tista below its junction with the Rungeet which, except close to its debouchure, is composed of Daling rocks, forming the outlet of such a lake. The Dalings, it should be noted in this connection, unquestionably bear the impress of lacustrine, rather shallow water deposits, false bedding being noticeable at places. In fact, they recall to one's mind the micaceous clays and sandstones of Tertiary age in the outermost fringe of the Sub-Himalayas. By subsequent tangential pressure which caused their disturbance, the Dalings would be tilted up against the original gneiss escarpments in such a manner as to present an appearance of conformable underlie and of faulting. The greater metamorphism of the Dalings at the boundary between them and the gneissose rocks (a fact which has been noted before) may be accounted for by the greater pressure to which they would be subjected there owing to the resistance offered by the older gneissose rocks.

The Dalings have suffered considerable disturbance. The slates and phyllites frequently exhibit crumbling and contortion; and the dips are, as a rule, rather high, being seldom below 45°.

The following sequence of strata in ascending order is met with near Chakang:—

(*a*) Massive, coarse quartzites or quartzite sandstones with a lenticular band of carbonaceous shales.
(*b*) Dark slaty shales which are cupriferous at places.
(*c*) Phyllites passing into micaceous schists at places.

(iii) ECONOMIC GEOLOGY.

1.—*Copper.*

General remarks.—Copper ores are very widespread in Sikhim, and constitute the main source of its prospective mineral wealth.

* "Memoirs, Geological Survey of India," Vol. III, pt. 2, p. 102: Vol. XI, pt. 1, p. 48; "Records, Geological Survey of India," Vol. XXIII, pt. 4, p. 244.

The following generalisations arrived at by Mr. Mallet with regard to the copper ores of the Darjeeling district *generally* hold true for Sikhim also:—

(1) "All the known copper-bearing localities are in the Daling beds. Some are, it is true, situated in the transition rocks between the Dalings and the gneiss, but none in the genuine gneiss itself.

(2) "The ore in all is copper pyrites, often accompanied by mundic. Sulphate, carbonate, and oxide of copper are frequent as results of alteration of the pyrites, but they occur merely in traces.

(3) "The ore occurs disseminated through the slates and schists themselves, and not in true lodes."*

With regard to the first generalisation, it may be noted that copper ores have been found at several places noted below, in the gneiss itself, though usually within a short distance of its junction with the Dalings. The gneiss ores, however, do not appear to be so rich as those in the Dalings, and have never been worked. With regard to the third generalisation, the ore in one case at least, that of Pachikhani, appears to occur in true lodes.

Within the Dalings, the richest ores (those of Pachikhani and Rathokhani, for instance) occur amongst greenish, rather soft, slaty shales. The gangue in this case consists of the shale, much hardened by infiltrated quartz, or of quartz alone.

The method of copper-mining adopted in Sikhim is very similar to that generally pursued in India in most native operations, and has been fully described by Mr. Mallet in his geological account of Darjeeling. His description,† with some additions, is, however, repeated here for easy reference.

The Sikhim mines greatly resemble magnified rabbit-holes: meandering passages are excavated with little or no system beyond following, as far as possible, the direction of the richest lodes; and although some precaution is taken to support the roof in the more shaky places by timber props, the number of galleries fallen in or abandoned show how inefficiently this is done. The shafts are always driven vertically in from the face of a cliff or declivity, as no attempt at systematic pumping is ever made. Should the shaft become flooded or too damp to permit of the water being kept down by gravitation or simple bailing, it has to be abandoned. Poor shafts are immediately deserted if richer ore is found near, long before the former, under a better system, would be worked out.

The passages vary according to the height and thickness of the lode, and average about three to four feet in height and width; but

* Memoirs, Vol. XI, pt. 1, p. 72.

† *Op. cit.*, p. 69.

where the rock has not yielded a paying proportion of ore, they are contracted to a size barely sufficient to admit a man's body. Access to the interior of the mines, therefore, is gained by crawling on "all fours," and in the narrowest parts by lying flat on the face and progressing after the manner of serpents. As a natural consequence of such a primitive system, the excavations cannot be carried beyond a very trifling depth, as compared to European mines.

The ore is got out by manual labour, no machinery or even blasting being resorted to. The tools generally used are an iron hammer and an ordinary wedge or chisel (*cheni*), which is held by a strip of split bamboo twisted round it. Small picks are also sometimes employed. The lights used are torches made of thin strips of bamboo about a foot long, which burn for a minute and-a-half or even less. This necessitates the presence of two men, one to hold the light, while the other chisels out the ore.

Mallet says the smoke from the bamboo is less irritating to the eyes than that from other kinds of wood. No explosion from gas has ever been known; blasting by powder is very seldom resorted to.

The miners are all Mangars by race, and called Agris: the men excavate the ore in large lumps and the women carry it to the surface in very small bamboo baskets about 9 inches by 12 inches, which are called "jak;" they are of elongated form so as to be readily taken along the narrow passages. Further, the jaks are taken out by relays of men or boys, who push or carry them from one to the other. From the pit's mouth women carry the ore away in ordinary baskets to the nearest streams and wash it.

After a preliminary breaking up of the larger pieces and rejection of the refuse, the picked ore is broken up small on flat stones with hammers of iron, and not now-a-days by hammers formed of quartzite or other hard rock, tied into forked sticks as described by Mallet. This pounded ore is called "dhan." This is roughly sorted, small pieces of nearly pure copper are taken direct to the miner's home, while the more impure pieces are taken to a shed near a stream, where it is beaten into coarse powder by heavy round hammers or in stone hand-mills called "jhatoo."

Near a convenient watercourse a succession of troughs called "khali" are built up: the troughs are made of rough planks fixed on the ground, one forming the bottom, which has a slight incline, and the others fixed on edge. In form and size the troughs resemble small coffins, but the top and lower end are open: water from the stream is conducted into these troughs, which are placed one just above another in a continuous straight line. The quantity of water allowed to flow into the trough is regulated by a clay dam at the upper end, the surplus water flowing off in a parallel channel. In the case of very dirty "dhan" the powdered ore is put through a wooden sieve, the refuse called "maddam" being thrown away, while the other portion, chan chamru, is again ground in the "jhatoo" and afterwards washed.

The powdered ore is now washed in these troughs, and continually agitated by the hand: in this way the dust and lighter particles containing but little ore get washed down the troughs by the flowing stream, leaving only the heavier particles containing copper ore.

These copper particles are taken to the blacksmith's house, where the smelting operations are carried out. These blacksmiths belong to the "Muhur" branch of the "Kamis."

The ore, whether in pure lumps or in powder as above mentioned, is taken to the smelting house (afur), in which there is a furnace ("tora") built down into the floor and lined with some neatness with refractory clay, about 18 inches deep, a foot square at the top, and tapering a good deal towards the bottom. Small charcoal is first filled in to a depth of about a foot and beaten down by a wooden rammer till a saucer-shaped floor of coarsely powdered charcoal is formed, sufficiently compact to prevent the products of the smeltings sinking into it. These protect it from the blast, and it is besides too compact to burn easily. There is no orifice in this part of the furnace. Two clay tuyeres dip nearly vertically about three inches into it from the top, and are respectively connected with skin bellows by horizontal tubes about a yard long. The tubes are formed of clay mixed with chopped straw, and are moulded on a straight stick, which is subsequently withdrawn.

The furnace thus prepared is lighted up with charcoal, and the bellows at each side worked alternately. When at its full heat the powdered ore is sprinkled in at short intervals, until a sufficient amount of regulus or chakhoo, as it is called by the smelters, has collected at the bottom of the furnace, covered by the lighter slag. The charcoal is then raked away and the surface of the slag ("keet") cooled with a whisp of wet straw tied to a stick. The solidified cake is removed and the fresh surface cooled: in this way the slag is taken off in two or three successive cakes, leaving the heavier and more perfectly fluid regulus behind, which is afterwards cooled and extracted.

The regulus is then pounded and ground in the jhatoo, mixed with an equal amount of cowdung, and made into balls about the size of oranges, often called "paira." After drying, a quantity of these are spread on a layer of charcoal in a place surrounded by stones and covered with charcoal, then a second layer of balls, and then more charcoal. The whole is then ignited, and the regulus thus roasted with free access of air; this roasting lasts nearly twenty-four hours.

The roasted balls are subsequently broken up and ground, and the powder sprinkled into the furnace (tora) in the same way as the original ore.

The copper was formerly exported to Nepal, but for the last two years importation has been stopped by the Nepalese Government, for what reason is not known; in consequence the Newar lessees have a large stock of copper in hand, the cost of manufacture being estimated at Rs. 23 a maund, while the price in Calcutta is only Rs. 20. It will not pay to export, and consequently the stocks are held over for a rise in the market or the reopening of Nepal. It is suspected that the closure of Nepal was carried out with a view to prevent emigration of the Kami class. At present Russian copper is used here, chiefly in sheets: the price in Calcutta is Rs. 29 a maund. It does not require to be re-infused before being wrought into manufactured articles, whereas Sikhim native copper does, and loses 20 per cent. in weight in the operation.

The usual transit charge in Nepal is one anna per dharni (2½ seers) (here a dharni is 3 seers, but in Nepal it is 2 seers 10 chitaks).

In Nepal there are several copper mines, much drier than those in Sikhim.

Deep mining is not practised, owing chiefly to the want of suitable apparatus for draining the mines. At Pachikhani, the only place where copper ores are worked on a tolerable scale in Sikhim, the deepest mine goes down only to about 55 feet; and I found water had collected to such an extent even at this depth that the miners were talking of abandoning it, though the ore is very rich. Many mines, as, for instance, those of Tukkhani (south of Namchi), have been abandoned owing to the difficulty of draining the water with the primitive appliances used by the miners. As the ore almost invariably gets richer with depth,* deeper working at the abandoned mines with improved appliances may be reasonably expected to yield good results. Mining under the present conditions may be said to be abandoned just when it begins to be most profitable.

The miners are all Nepalese, and belong to the caste of Mangars. The men and boys work in the mines, and the women dress the ore. Smelting of the dressed ore is performed by the caste of Kamis or blacksmiths. This is considered a very low caste; and a Kami would not be allowed to enter the house of a Mangar or any other Hindu of a higher social status. The houses of the Mangars run north-south, whereas those of the Kamis have their length directed east-west; so that in a

* This was unquestionably found to be the case at Pachikhani, the only place where I could compare surface with comparatively deep-seated ores. A specimen of picked ore from the surface yielded on assay 14·06 per cent. of copper, whereas one taken at random from a depth of about 50 feet from surface gave 20·31 per cent.

mining village like that of Pachikhani it is easy to distinguish the house of a miner (belonging to the caste of Mangar) from that of a smelter (Kami). Scarcely any mining work is done during the rains, and even in the working season, which extends from October to June, an occasional heavy shower often puts a stop to it for days. On the occasion of my last visit to the mines (11th April 1891), I found only a few women dressing the ore, and there was no one working at the mines owing to the heavy rainfall of the previous day. The number of men, women, and children who find employment one way or another—mining, dressing the ore, smelting, &c.—probably does not exceed 300 any day.

The miners work in gangs on their own account and not for hire, each gang under a headman. For every five seers of copper turned out, one goes to the Kami or the man who conducts the smelting, and four remain as the share of the miners. The whole of the copper turned out must be sold to the party who has the lease of the mines, called *taksari*, at a price fixed by him. The average annual outturn at Pachikhani is estimated at about 6,000 dharnis, or 450 maunds of copper, valued at Rs. 12,000, at the rate of Rs. 2 per *dharni*, which is the price paid by the lessee to the miners. If we take the average number of the men, women, and children maintained by the mines at 200, Rs. 60 falls to the share of each individual; which, considering that but little mining work is done during the rains, is a very fair wage. Indeed, the mining people here are probably better off than in most other parts of India. They are well housed, well clad, and well fed, and the women make a fair show of trinkets.

2.—*Ore locations.*

Copper ores occur at the following localities :—

1. *Pachikhani.*—The only place besides Rathokhani where copper ores are worked at present. The old mines, which are now deserted, were situated close to the junction of the Rorochu and the Rahrichu just by the Gantok road. The mines worked at present occur a mile further north, about 3 miles south of Pakyang, also close to the Gantok road. The roofs of the galleries in the old Pachikhani have fallen in, as is the case with all deserted mines. At the entrance of one of the galleries I found stalactitic and stalagmitic deposits stained green by carbonate of copper, also traces of copper pyrites in slaty rocks. The dip is north-eastern; but, on the east side of the Rorochu, it is E.S.E. The stream probably marks the position of a fault.

The new Pachikhani stands on slaty shales which have a greenish hue when wet, but appear grey when dry. These are superposed by schistose quartzite, in which very thin slightly greenish foliæ of shaly matter occurs. The strike varies between NW—SE and WNW—ESE, and the dip is north-eastern, about 35°.

There are five principal galleries. The drift which was being worked at the time of my visit was found to be about 4 feet in height and 3 feet in width. The roof is supported by timbering on a large scale. Chips of bamboo are used as lights. The gangue consists of quartz and much hardened shale; soft slaty shale is the country rock. The ore is extracted from the veinstone by chisel and hammer. The richest ore occurs at the deeper and suddenly sloping end of this drift, below 40 feet; but the miners were there in water and were talking of ceasing to go any further down. If the water were let out—and this could be done without serious difficulty by proper contrivances—I have no doubt the ore would be found to go down much deeper. Here we have to all appearance a true lode. It is about 4 feet in thickness and nearly vertical.

The ore is, as usual, copper pyrites mixed with a little mundic. The analysis of a sample taken at random from this deeper part gave 20·31 per cent. of copper. I was informed at the mines that one maund of ore yielded 20 seers of *cheku* (*regulus*), and that 4 seers of *cheku* gave one seer of copper, so that from a maund of ore there is obtained about 5 seers, or 12 per cent. copper. The copper is sent from the mines in flat pieces. It is again refined by those who work it up into vessels. Five seers of mine copper yield four on being refined.

2. *Rhenock.*—About half-way between Pachikhani and Rhenock, on the south side of the Rungpo (or the Rarhichu as it is called on map) and close to the bridge over it, there is exposed a fine section of the Dalings in which indications of copper are found. The cupriferous rocks in descending order are—

Slaty shales with bands of segregated quartz in which traces of copper pyrites are found.

3″ quartz with copper pyrites.	Dip ENE about 45°.
1′ slaty shales.	
6″ quartz with copper pyrite shales.	

Here the ore apparently occurs in segregated veins parallel to the bedding.

3. *Lingui.*—About two miles to the east of the last-named locality, and a mile south of Lingui monastery at the junction of the Rungpo and the Ronglichu, copper pyrites occur in highly quartzose gneiss dipping NE about 45°. The cupriferous band was found to extend about 100 yards and is about 6 feet in thickness.

4. *Ronglichu.*—About three miles* east-north-east of the Ronglichu rest bungalow, at the junction of a stream coming down from Pangola with the Ronglichu, I picked up a few pieces of schistose quartzite in which copper pyrites and bornite (?) are disseminated along foliation planes. I did not find the ores *in situ*. I have no doubt they occur some distance up the stream towards Pangola. In this case the ores occur in the heart of the gneissose group.

5. *Lindok.*—About half-way on the new road between Gantok and Tumlong, close to the village of Lindok, there occurs interstratified with gneiss, talcose schists with pyrite, chalco-pyrite, bornite, copperas and blue vitriol with small traces of epsomite. The thickness of the cupriferous band in a stream just by the road was found to be about 2 feet, and it was traced for about 38 feet: dip 40° ENE. A little to the south-east of the stream, also by the road, there is similar schist with copper ores in the gneiss, but the thickness here is not more than 7 inches.

6. *Bhotang.*—Situated about 6 miles east-south-east of Pachikhani, close to the junction of the Tista and the Rungpo, along a precipitous scarp of slaty rocks overlooking the Tista. The mines here were worked for about 20 years and abandoned only last year. Lachmi Das, proprietor of Pachikhani, was the lessee. The average annual outturn was about 300 *dharnis*, or 225 *maunds* of copper. The ore as usual is chalco-pyrite, occurring in a hard jaspery-looking rock; but it is much mixed up with iron pyrites, more so than at Pachikhani. There are two ore-bands parted by 10 or 12 feet of slaty shales, which too are more or less impregnated by ore. Of these two bands, the upper averages about 3 feet in thickness, and the lower 2 feet 6 inches. They run parallel to bedding and appear to be what are called segregated veins. The dip is about 45° E. to ESE. Levels are driven along the courses of the ore-bands. One I entered has gone for about 54 feet and then stopped owing to water filling in. If the water were let off, there is no reason why the ore should not be found workable deeper down.

The ore-bands can be traced with the eye for some 200 feet along the strike on the north side. South of the levels they run for about 25 feet, and are then faulted against greyish and greenish soft slaty shales dipping north-eastward. On the south side of the fault the ore-bands are met with at a height of about 100 feet above those on the north side.

An average sample from the old working yielded on assay 12·21 per cent. of copper.

* It may be observed that distances throughout this paper are measured as the crow flies.

7. *Barmiak.*—Near Barmiak, just south of the new bridge over the Tista at a place called Lingyathang, I found on the east bank of the Tista, traces of copper ore in some detached blocks of quartzite.

There is also copper ore near the head of a stream south of Barmiak, called Kalok jhora.

8. *Namphak.*—There were found minute traces of copper pyrites in a detached block at this village, close to the Tumlong road between it and the Tista.

9. *Dajong.*—Close to the head of the Rangpochu, about 3 miles north-west of Yangong monastery, steep scarps of the Dalings are seen from a distance to be stained green by carbonate of copper at places. The place is almost inaccessible, and I could not explore it well within the time at my disposal. At one spot about a mile-and-a-half east of Dajong there were met with chalco-pyrite along with peach and iron pyrites in some profusion in quartzitic rocks. The percentage of copper, however, appears to be too low to pay for working.

10. *Temi.*—About three miles west-north-west of this village, close to the source of a stream called Rimpichu, there was found copper pyrites in some abundance in very hard quartzitic rocks.

Trial pits were opened both here and at Dajong last year by a Nepalese named Parsa Sing, but have been abandoned.

11. *Tukkhani.*—These mines are situated along a feeder of the Mangpur jhora, a tributary of the Rungeet, three miles due south of Namchi. They were deserted some time ago owing to the excavations filling in with water. The ore is said to have been of excellent quality, better even than that of Pachikhani, though now but little is seen of it, the galleries having fallen in. Deep mining here would, I have no doubt, give good results. The annual outturn of Tukkhani used to be about the same as that of Pachikhani—about 450 maunds. The lessee was Luchmidas. The country rock is slaty shales similar to those of Pachikhani.

12. *Mik.*—Two miles north-east of Tukkhani, close to the village of Mik, just by the Namchi road, copper pyrites were found disseminated in some very hard quartzites.

13. *Mongbru.*—A mile north-east of this village, and about three miles south-south-west of Ralong monastery, close to the junction of a stream flowing from Rabongla with the Rungeet, there occur copper pyrites in clay slates with segregated quartz.

14. *Rinchinpong.*—Copper ores occur near this place, close to the source of a feeder of the Kulhait. The rock as usual is clay slate. The ores were worked on a small scale last year, but have been given up, as they did not pay.

15. *Bam.*—Two miles and-a-half south-south-west of Rinchinpong monastery, close to the village of Bam, there occur, by the Risi, copper

ores in slaty shales with segregated quartz. The ore-bearing band was found only 6 inches in thickness at one place. The ore is found in traces on both sides of the river. The dip here is NW about 65°.

16. *Rathokhani.*—Close to the village of Chakang. The mines here are the oldest in Sikhim, and were in working at the time of Mr. Mallet's survey of the Darjeeling district.* The ore (copper pyrites) occurs in slaty shales as well as in lenticular bands of segregated quartz, especially in the latter. Mr. Mallet found 9·1 per cent. of copper in a carefully selected average sample; it is not, therefore, nearly so rich as that of Pachikhani. The ore is confined to the east side of a ravine which apparently marks the position of a fault: east of it the strata are inclined south-east to north-north-east, whereas west of it the strata exhibit the normal dip of these parts, viz., north-west. The workings extend for about 100 yards on the east side of the strike of the strata. The main drifts run parallel to the bedding; but meandering passages across it in all directions also exist. The ore here appears to occur in segregated veins parallel to bedding, and there did not appear to be any indication of a true lode. Still the oriferout beds may, I think, be advantageously followed deeper down. The difficulty of drainage has led to their abandonment; and at present the miners burrow here and there on a small scale.

Masses of quartz rock containing copper pyrites are found in the bed of the Ratho, a short distance below the mine. An average sample yielded on analysis 6·38 per cent. of copper.

3.—*Summary and concluding observations.*

The following is a summary of the copper localities mentioned above:—

(*A*).—*In the Dalings.*

(1) Mines now worked	Pachikhani, Rathokhani (on a very small scale).
(2) Mines recently abandoned ...	Old Pachikhani, Bhotang.
Mines abandoned and wholly choked up	Tukkhani.
Localities where trial openings have been made and abandoned.	Dajong, Rinchinpong, Temi.
Localities not yet tried	Rhenock, Bam, Mongbru, Barmiak, Namphak, Mik.

(*B*).—*In the Gneissic rocks.*

Localities not yet tried ...	Lindok, Lingui, Ronglichu.

The Nepalese miners have a very keen eye for copper ores; and the localities where they have been mining or rather burrowing—

* *Op. cit.*, p. 75.

Tuk, Bhotang, Ratho, and Pachi—are certainly the most promising in all Sikhim. They work, however, in a primitive fashion, and the depth of the drifts which they run for the ore is limited by the water level of the nearest stream. As soon as a drift fills in with water which cannot be easily let out, it is abandoned. The deepest mine scarcely ever goes down below 70 feet from the surface; that at Pachikhani has scarcely reached this depth, and the miners intend abandoning it already, owing to the difficulty of draining it, though the ore is found to get richer with depth. It was chiefly this difficulty of draining that led to the abandonment of Tukkhani, Bhotangkhani, and partly also of Rathokhani. I have no doubt Pachikhani also will be deserted as soon as the surface ores have been worked out. Deep mining on modern methods at these places, especially at Pachikhani, is likely to yield a very fair return.

Of the four places just mentioned, Pachikhani appeared to me the most promising. This may partly be due to the fact that, owing to the works here being in progress, I could see for myself the exact mode of occurrence of the ore. However, as the existence of at least one good lode here is known, this place ought to be tried first, in case Sikhim should attract mining enterprise, which it is likely to do in the near future. There are other reasons also in favour of Pachikhani. A sample taken from the lode just mentioned yielded 20·31 per cent. of copper; and from what the miners told me the average yield from the entire mine is about 12 per cent. (five seers of copper from one maund of ore). On the other hand, the picked ore from Rathokhani was found by Mr. Mallet to contain not more than 8 or 9 per cent. of copper. At Bhotang, the ore appeared to me to contain rather too much mundic. From what the miners who had worked at Tukkhani told me, the ore there at the point where it was given up was richer even than that of Pachikhani. I would not place much reliance upon such a statement uncorroborated by samples. Still from all accounts, Tukkhani would be a very favourable place for trial, after Pachikhani.

Of the other localities the surface indications at Rhenock appear to be rather favourable.

IRON

Occurs chiefly as pyrites in association with chalco-pyrite. It is most plentiful at Bhotang, where magnetite also occurs. The iron ores have nowhere been put to any economic use.

LIME.

There is a vein of calcite in the gneiss at Lingtam, about three miles north-east of the Ronglichu rest bungalow. Lime was experimentally made from it, but it did not turn out quite satisfactory, being rather dark coloured. There are beds of limestone in the Dalings north-east and north-west of Namchi, but it is as a rule too impure to yield good lime. Lime in Sikhim is invariably made from tufaceous deposits which abound in the vicinity of the limestone beds, especially at Vok near Namchi, whence large quantities of lime used at one time to go to Darjeeling.

Garnet

Is abundant in the gneiss and mica schists at places. But it does not appear to be fit for the market.

NOTE ON AGRICULTURE IN SIKHIM.

Rice, chum, unhusked rice, rad. There are 12 kinds of rice grown in Sikhim—

1, hbras-chung, grown in damp land, in which it will mature, but is better for being transplanted when about 12 inches high into irrigated ground. It is the earliest crop, being sown in December and harvested in March.

2 and 3, la-dmar and san-kha, are grown in the lower valleys, and seldom seen above 4,500 feet. The cultivation is similar to that in the plains: the plants are sown in nurseries, and transplanted when large enough into irrigated ground. These are sown in August and cut in December.

4 to 12, rang-ldan, tso-hbras, dbang-hbras, khab-hbras, hdam-hbras, phag-hbras, kho-smad, kha-hzis and rtsong-hbras, are grown on dry land, that is, not irrigated. The best ground is that which has lain fallow for some years, and on which there is a heavy undergrowth of jungle. This is cut, burnt and carefully dressed, and excellent crops are obtained. These are sown in March and cut in August.

From one measure of seed in good ground the yield varies from twenty to fiftyfold.

La-dmar, san-kha and hbras-chung are considered the best varieties. Paddy husking is only done by each house as required, and is carried out in a most primitive fashion. The paddy unboiled is placed in a hollow piece of timber called htsom, and pounded with a long wooden mallet called htsom-phu.

The preparations made from rice are—1, marwa; 2, dbyon, a kind of rice-cake fried in butter; 3, a-rag, a spirit; 4, hbras-sgnos, parched rice; 5, hbo-dker, boiled and parched rice; 6, hbras-su, chura.

Other crops—

Bhoota, kin-rtsong, of which there are four kinds, distinguished by their colour—viz., white, red, yellow, and black. Almost any soil will do and any elevation up to 6,200 feet. This is the staple food of the Paharias. In low-lying land it is sown in March, and according to elevation in the high grounds as late as May and June.

The quantity obtained varies from twenty to hundredfold.

Marwa, me-chag, a millet. There are 13 kinds—Bsam-shing, shags-chag, sga-ser, mang-dkar-ma, bze-hbogs, tsigs-nag-ma, phags-hgyugs, dung-dkar-ma, gong-tses-ma, dker-hjom-la, sla-gsum-ma, ser-rgyug-ma, ma-la-dkar-mo.

These are sown in March and cut in July and August. The yield varies from forty to one hundred and fiftyfold.

Me-chag is used almost entirely in the preparation of chang, marwa, but is occasionally ground and made into chupatties, and the flour is also used to eat with tea.

Hbog-ma, a millet, of which there are four kinds—dkar, dmar, khyimn-shig, spre-hjug.

These are used for making chang, a-rag, and are used, when boiled, for food.

Bra-hu, buckwheat, of which there are five kinds—dkar-hgor-ma, bra-nag, hgyas-ra, kha-hjug-ma, bra-chung—used for making chang, a-rag and chupatties.

Sla-sum-ma, a kind of me-chag, used in the same manner.

Na, wheat, five kinds—dkar, dmar, nag, spre-hjug-ma, mgo-rog-ma.

Gyo, barley, only one kind. Both wheat and barley are only grown in small quantities on account of the danger of the crops being destroyed by hailstorms, which are very prevalent in March and April just as the crops are ripening.

Rdo-gson, dhal, three kinds—dkar, nag, and one other, no name—only grown in small quantities; sown in September and cut in January.

Mustard, three kinds—yung-dkar, yung-nag and pad-sgang—grown for oil.

Ko-ko-la, cardamom, grown in irrigated ground with plenty of shade and good drainage; that is, the plants generally grow in running water. The crop is much prized and of considerable value, varying from Rs. 30 to Rs. 45 a maund. The cultivation of cardamom is increasing rapidly, many new plantations having been laid out this year.

Marwa, chang, is a kind of beer brewed by everyone in Sikhim, and might be called their staple food and drink. It is prepared from a great variety of seeds and plants. The following is a list of most of them, both cultivated and wild:—

Cultivated: me-chag, wheat, barley, bra-hu, rice, rkang-ring, shum-hbem, tsong, and Indian-corn.

Wild: elephant creeper, yams of all kinds, ra-ling, hbar-neg, spa-sko two kinds, spa-lo-hi, dun, and hbyam.

This drink is universal, very refreshing and sustaining, and very slightly intoxicating. It is drunk, warm generally, from a bamboo through a straw or thin hollow bamboo.

The preparation is as follows:—

The seed is soaked in water for two nights, then husked, washed and boiled; the water is then drained off and the seeds kept for half an hour in the vessel. The seed is then spread on a bamboo mat, and in winter the spice, &c., added before the seed is quite cold; in summer when cold. The "spice" is first well mixed, then spread on a bed of ferns covered with plantain leaves and in winter with a blanket.

After 48 hours the fermentation is ready; this is known by the smell, and the marwa is stored in baskets lined with half-dried plantain leaves. It is ready to drink in 3 days, but is better kept for 8 days.

Spice consisting of spen-hgram (leaves of a tree), chilly, ginger, chiretta, kag-hbim, are used according as the marwa is required to taste sweet, bitter, sour, or hot.

The spices are used in the following proportions:—Mix one seer rice flour with 2oz. of spice. This is mixed wet and dried, and it depends on the strength of this how much is used, but approximately one ounce is used to a maund of seed.

Tea.—This varies from our mode of making it, inasmuch as it is churned with butter and salt, till the butter is so mixed with the tea leaves, hot water, and salt that there is no grease floating on the surface. The tea plant is only grown in very small quantities, and no systematic cultivation is resorted to. The leaf usually made into tea comes from Tibet in the form of brick tea. Tea is made from the following plants:—

Tea, hdong-rna-mchogs, dbya-li, rang-spo-mchu-dog, phi-chung-skyag-ko, chestnuts, rtsi, sim-rtsi, aru, skyi-hdabs, shing-skyur, spem-po-rdo-hkyabs, cha-ru, mi-tog-dbyang-hzin, and rgen-mtsen-ldan.

The following is a complete list of the wild and cultivated fruits, vegetables, edible roots, &c., obtained in Sikhim and used by the inhabitants as food:—

Fruits cultivated—

Orange.	Bread-fruit.	Apple.
Mango.	Citron.	Pear.
Peach.	Lemon.	Pomegranate.
Walnut.	Guava.	Pineapple.

Plantain, 2 kinds.

Vegetables cultivated—

Sugarcane, 3 kinds.	Radish.
Pumpkin, 2 kinds.	Turnip.
Chilly, 5 kinds.	Garlic.
Brinjal, 3 kinds.	Onion.
Cucumber.	Hu-si (spice).
Tomatos, 2 kinds.	Ginger, 2 kinds.
Hsbrul-tsod, 2 kinds (a kind of cucumber).	Potatoes, 2 kinds.
Khag-tig, 2 kinds.	Yams, 6 kinds.
Mustard, 3 kinds.	Do-hu (a kind of yam).

Jungle products used for food—

La-spa-mchod-ma.
Ting-ku-mchod-ma.
Wild figs, 2 kinds.
Phang-ski.
Mu-si.
Spom-si, 4 kinds.
Ken-dang.
Spag-ko, 2 kinds.
Ga-dhor-spes (wild mango).
Lta-si.
Sung-lum.
Nyor-chung.
No-shel.
Cha-tses (raspberry), 5 kinds.
Chestnut, 3 kinds.
Hbrom-kes.
Chi-chung-sdong-nyel, 2 kinds.
Rtseg-rtseg-ru-bhi.
Hber-heg.
Ske-skyum.
Hbah.
Hum-pa-do-rog, 2 kinds.
Kling-shu.
Gues-chung-spes.
A-um-la.
A-ru-ra, 2 kinds.
Ltog-tos.
Khum-dgos.
Mu-ti-spes.
Cane shoots, 2 kinds
Bamboo shoots, 15 kinds.
Ra-mje-dong.
Stag-kya-dong.
Dos-mo-dong (elephant creeper).
Ding-hbram-dong.
Yams, 11 kinds.
Fungi, 18 kinds.
Nettles, 6 kinds.
Hbab-mchod.
Rdum-rug.
Sken-tung.
Chu-ten.
Kang-ki-rig.
Mgo-ned.
Mus-la.
Btang-sku.
Sug.
Si-khag.
Pha-ru.
Dbu-shul.
Bam-chag.
Chu (a water weed).
Ben-spu-dog.
Na-res.
Khung-rug.
Dugig-s.
La-sgog, 2 kinds (wild onion).
Spyan-res.
Ba-sho-kha.
Gua-lhag (wild plantain).
Hzas-bhag.
Tig-bhig, 5 kinds (a bean).

Fibres.—Cotton is grown in small quantities in the lower valleys. (*See* "Statistical Account of Bengal," vol. X, page 96.) Jute is not grown in Sikhim.

Wild fibres.—The natives employ the large nettle (so-ris) for making cloth, which is said to be very durable.

Land measurement.—The land is usually measured for cultivation by the number of pattis of seed that can be sown in it. Amongst the Paharias the rent recoverable is calculated by the number of pattis sown. *See* Statistical Account of Bengal, vol. X, page 99, from "In the hills" to "a small field of 1¼ bighas."

Cattle.—There are three kinds of cattle in Sikhim—

1. *Ba-glang.*—These are the larger cattle, and are by far the best. They are owned chiefly by the Lepchas and Bhuteas. Many of this cattle are driven up to 13 and 14,000 feet for grazing.

A good cow fetches from Rs. 30 to Rs. 45.

An ox or bull from Rs. 20 to Rs. 25.

2. *Nam-thong* (*Paharia cattle*).—These are much smaller, and fetch from Rs. 15 to Rs. 25 only.

3. *Thang* (*plains cattle*).—These are considered the worst of all, and only fetch from Rs. 12 to Rs. 15 each.

Yaks.—There are three kinds—

1. *Lho-gyag.*—These are the large yaks found only in Sikhim and Chumbi. They are considered the best, and fetch from Rs. 25 to Rs. 30 each. Yak milk is of excellent quality, containing a very large proportion of butter fat.

The males are used for pack animals, but not to such an extent as in Tibet.

2. *Bod-gyag.*—These are similar to the above, but are very much smaller. The price varies from Rs. 20 to Rs. 25.

3. *A-yu.*—These are polled yaks, and some very fine specimens have been seen in the higher valleys of Sikhim. There are also half-breed cattle from bull yaks and cows. These are considered the best of all the cattle for giving milk.

Sheep, 5 kinds—

1. *Ha-lug.*—A black sheep comes from Bhutan, the wool of which is coarse.

2. *Bod-lug.*—The ordinary Tibetan sheep, small, but much prized for its wool, which is of excellent quality.

3. *Byang-lug.*—Also from Tibet.

4. *Sog-lug.*—The large-tailed sheep, very seldom seen in Sikhim.

5. *Phe-dar.*—The Paharia sheep, a much larger animal, which lives low down. The wool is coarse.

The price of sheep varies considerably, being from Rs. 3 to Rs. 9, according to size and kind. The Paharia fetches the highest price.

Goats, 2 kinds—

1. *Ra.*—The small goat, smaller than that in the plains.

2. *Bod-ra.*—The small long-haired Tibetan goat. It does not do well down in the hot valleys.

Wages—

Coolie, 2 annas to 8 annas a day.
Mason, 8 ,, 1 rupee ,,
Carpenter, Rs. 30 to Rs. 50 a month, and are almost impossible to get.

Prices—

Rice, Rs. 4-8 to Rs. 5-8 per maund.
Marwa, 8 seers per rupee.
Bhoota, Re. 1 to Rs. 3-4 per maund.
Dhal, 8 seers per rupee.

VEGETATION.

NOTE.—The works consulted for this paper are Hooker's "Himalayan Journals;" Hooker and Thomson's "Flora Indica;" "Hooker's Flora of India;" Clarke's "Ferns of Northern India;" King's "Annals of the Royal Botanic Garden, Calcutta;" Gamble's "Trees, Shrubs and Large Climbers found in the Darjeeling District," and Watt's "Dictionary of Economic Products."

J. GAMMIE—19-9-91.

SIR J. D. HOOKER, who is the greatest authority on the vegetation of Sikhim, in his Introductory Essay to the Flora Indica, divides the country into three zones. The lower, stretching from the lowest level up to 5,000 feet above the sea, he called the tropical zone; thence to 13,000 feet, the upper limit of tree vegetation, the temperate; and above, to the perpetual snow line at 16,000 feet, the Alpine. In describing the aspect of the country he says that up "to an elevation of 12,000 feet, Sikhim is covered with a dense forest, only interrupted where village clearances have bared the slopes for the purpose of cultivation." At the present time, however, this description does not apply below 6,000 feet, the upper limit at which Indian-corn ripens; for here, owing to increase of population, almost every suitable part has been cleared for cultivation, and trees remain only in the rocky ravines and on the steepest slopes where no crop can be grown; but above 6,000 feet the face of the country still remains comparatively unaltered. He continues—"The forest consists everywhere of tall umbrageous trees; with little underwood on the drier slopes, but often dense grass jungle; more commonly, however, it is accompanied by a luxuriant undergrowth of shrubs, which render it almost impenetrable. In the tropical zone large figs abound, with *Terminalia*, *Vatica*, *Myrtaceæ*, Laurels, *Euphorbiaceæ*, *Meliaceæ*, *Bauhinia*, *Bombax*, *Morus*, *Artocarpus*, and other *Urticaceæ* and many *Leguminosæ;* and the undergrowth consists of *Acanthaceæ*, Bamboo, several *Calami*, two dwarf *Arecæ*, *Wallichia*, and *Caryota urens*. Plantains and tree-ferns, as well as *Pandanus*, are common; and, as in all moist tropical countries, ferns, orchids, *Scitamineæ*, and *Pothos* are extremely abundant. Few oaks are found at the base of the mountains, and the only conifers are a species of *Podocarpus* and *Pinus longifolia*, which frequent the drier slopes of hot valleys as low as 1,000 feet above the level of the sea, and entirely avoid the temperate zone. The other tropical Gymnosperms are *Cycas pectinata* and *Gnetum scandens*, genera which find their north-western limits in Sikhim.

"Oaks, of which (including chestnuts) there are upwards of eleven species in Sikhim, become abundant at about 4,000 feet, and at 5,000 feet the temperate zone begins, the vegetation varying with the degree of humidity. On the outermost ranges, and on northern exposures, there is a dripping forest of cherry, laurels, oaks and chestnuts, *Magnolia*, *Andromeda*, *Styrax*, *Pyrus*, maple and birch, with an underwood of *Araliaceæ*, *Hollböllia*, *Limonia*, *Daphne*, *Ardisia*, *Myrsine*, *Symplocos*, *Rubi*, and a prodigious variety of ferns.

"*Plectocomia* and *Musa* ascend to 7,000 feet. On drier exposures bamboo and tall grasses form the underwood. Rhododendrons appear below 6,000 feet, at which elevation snow falls occasionally. From 6—12,000 feet there is no apparent diminution of the humidity, the air being near saturation during a great part of the year; but the decrease of temperature effects a marked change in the vegetation. Between 6,000 and 8,000 feet epiphytical orchids are extremely abundant, and they do not entirely disappear till a height of 10,000 feet has been attained. Rhododendrons become abundant at 8,000 feet, and from 10,000 to 14,000 feet they form in many places the mass of the shrubby vegetation. *Vaccinia*, of which there are ten species, almost all epiphytical, do not ascend so high, and are most abundant at elevations from 5,000 to 8,000 feet.

"The flora of the temperate zone presents a remarkable resemblance to that of Japan, in the mountains of which island we have a very similar climate, both being damp and cold. *Helwingia*, *Aucuba*, *Stachyurus*, and *Enkianthus* may be cited as instances of this similarity, which is the more interesting because Japan is the nearest cold damp climate to Sikhim with whose vegetation we are acquainted. At 10,000 feet (on the summit of Tongloo) yew makes its appearance, but no other conifer except those of the tropical belt is found nearer the plains than the mountain of Phalūt, on which *Picea Webbiana* is found, at levels above 10,000 feet. *Abies Brunoniana* and the larch are found everywhere in the valleys of the Lachen and Lachung rivers, above 8,000 feet.

"A subtropical vegetation penetrates far into the interior of the country along the banks of the great rivers; rattans, tree-ferns, plantains, screw-pines, and other tropical plants occurring in the Ratong valley, almost at the foot of Kanchinjinga, and 5,000 feet above the level of the sea. With the pines, however, in the temperate zone, a very different kind of vegetation presents itself. Here those great European families which are almost entirely wanting in the outer temperate zone become common, and the flora approximates in character to that of Europe. Shrubby *Leguminosæ*, such as *Indigofera* and *Desmodium*, *Ranunculaceæ* (*Thalictrum*, *Anemone*, *Delphinium*, *Aconitum*, etc.), *Umbelliferæ*, *Caryophylleæ*, *Labiatæ* and *Gramineæ* increase in numbers as we advance into the interior. The air becomes drier, and from the increased action of the sun the temperature does not diminish in proportion to the elevation, the summers being warmer, though the winters are colder. The forests at the same time become more open, and are spread less uniformly over the surface, the drier slopes being bare of trees, and covered with a luxuriant herbaceous vegetation. It is only in the upper part of the valley of the Tista, however, above the junction of the Lachen and Lachung, that this change becomes marked; and from the rapidly increasing elevation, not only of the surrounding mountains, but of the floors of the valleys, it proceeds with great rapidity, and the temperate soon gives place to an Alpine flora.

"The sub-Alpine zone in Sikhim scarcely begins below 13,000 feet, at which elevation a dense rhododendron scrub occupies the slopes of the mountains, filling up the valleys so as to render them impenetrable. Here the summer is short, the ground not being free of snow till the middle of June. It is, however, comparatively dry, and the Alpine flora very much resembles that of the Western Himalaya and (in generic types at least) the Alps of Europe and Western Asia; while as we advance towards the Tibetan region we have a great increase of dryness, so that a Siberian flora is rapidly developed, which at last entirely supersedes that of the sub-Alpine zone, and ascends above 18,000 feet."

Sir J. D. Hooker's own collection of Sikhim plants amounted to 2,920 species, of which 150 were ferns. Assuming that he failed to get 25 per cent. of the plants during his short residence, the total of about 4,000 species of flowering plants and ferns together for Sikhim will be arrived at, and be very near the real number. Owing to the humid climate of Sikhim, and the absence of excessive cold at any season of the year over the greater part of it, the prevailing vegetation is of an evergreen character. A few trees, and two tree-ferns growing at elevations under 6,000 feet, have the abnormal habit of shedding their leaves and remaining bare during part of the warmest and wettest seasons when their neighbours are making their most vigorous growth; whilst other trees, chiefly of higher elevations, have the ordinary habit of shedding their leaves towards the end of autumn and remaining bare till spring. The vast majority, however, of the Sikhim trees and shrubs are evergreen. As might be expected from the dripping nature of the climate, ferns are a predominating feature of the vegetation generally, but more especially of that of the extra dripping and misty region lying between 5,000 and 9,000 feet, where they are to be seen on every rock, on the stems of trees, and growing on the ground. Mr. C. B. Clarke, in his valuable paper on the Ferns of Northern India, published in the Linnean Society's Journal for 1879, enumerates eight species of tree-ferns and 248 of stemless and sub-arborescent sorts found between Nepal and Assam. Probably over 200 of them are indigenous to Independent Sikhim. There are, besides, several species of *Lycopodium* and *Selaginella*, which are usually associated with the true ferns. Above 5,000 feet the European club-moss (*Lycopodium clavatum*) is in great abundance and luxuriance on the ground and rocks in open spaces, and several handsome tasselled species of the same genus are pendent on the limbs of trees. Of the eight species of Sikhim tree-ferns noted by Clarke, five are found between the lowest levels and 4,000 feet, and three between 3,500 and 7,000 feet. They are all most graceful objects and form a striking feature in the landscape wherever they occur, but more especially so in the moister, uncultivated valleys, where, undisturbed, they attain their full luxuriance, and are found either as isolated individuals, in small groups, or in extensive groves. Their average height is about twenty feet, but plants of forty and fifty feet are not very uncommon. The eight species are included in two genera, viz., two in the genus *Hemitelia* and six in *Alsophila*. The sori are placed on cup-shaped receptacles in the former, whilst in the latter they are exinvolucrate as in *Polypodium*, from which the genus *Alsophila* is separated more on account of the gigantic size of its component species than by any very definite character. *Hemitelia decipiens* ranges from low elevations to 4,000 feet, where it is replaced by its congener *H. Brunoniana*, which ascends to 7,000 feet, the limit of tree-fern vegetation in Sikhim. Both the *Hemitelias*, but especially *decipiens*, have stipes densely armed with short, stout wrickles. For ready identification the *Alsophilas* may be divided into two groups; one comprising the species with single or rarely once-forked stems, and the other those with many-branched stems bearing numerous heads of fronds at different heights on the same plant. To the first group belong *A. glauca*, which grows at elevations under 4,000 feet, and is distinguished by the bluish-hue of its stipes and grayish under-surface of the fronds, and *A. latebrosa*, closely resembling *Hemitelia Brunoniana*, and with the same distribution, but distinguished by its exinvolucrate sori. The species falling into the second group are *A. glabra*, the most tropical of the tree-ferns, recognized by the V-shaped arrangement of the sori; *A. Andersoni*, growing generally in dense shade by banks of streams below 3,500 feet, resembles *A. glabra* in growth, but is of a dull dark green colour, and its sori are in almost parallel lines; and *A. Oldhami* and *A. ornata*, both of the upper forests lying between 4,500 and 6,000 feet.

A. Oldhami, which grows gregariously, is, perhaps, the most elegant of all the Sikhim tree-ferns, and is common, but *A. ornata* is rather rare. Both have the strange habit of shedding their fronds in the wettest and warmest season of the year and remaining bare for several weeks. The pith of the stems of three species, *H. decipiens*, *A. Oldhami*, and *A. Andersoni*, is eaten by the Lepchas when there is dearth of other and more wholesome food. They also use the same substance for making their "marwa" beer when the supply of the *Elusine* or marwa grain is exhausted. It is dried in the sun, fermented, and afterwards put in a bamboo cylinder with water in the usual way of making marwa beer, and the liquor sucked through a thin reed placed in the middle. Of the other kinds of ferns, the genera more abundant in species are *Davallia*, *Pteris*, *Asplenium*, *Nephrodium*, *Polypodium*, and *Acrostichum*. *Osmunda regalis*, the Royal fern of Europe, is to be found, as are also the European Moonwort and Adder's-tongue ferns. *Angiopteris evecta*, which is found from the hottest parts up to 6,000 feet, attains to gigantic proportions, especially in the cool forests, where its massive fronds grow to more than five yards in length and three in breadth, with a spread over all, measuring from tip to tip of opposite fronds, of eight yards. At the bases of the fronds are succulent appendages which the Lepchas cook and eat in times of scarcity. They also habitually use the young fronds of several species as a vegetable, and very excellent they are when properly cooked. There are four *Adiantums* or Maidenhairs, two of which, *lunulatum* and *candatum*, cover the banks of the roads in many places at the lower elevations in the rainy season, and *pedatum* and *venustum* grow at the cool heights of 6—10,000 feet. In the valley of the Rungeet a handsome climbing fern, *Acrostichum palustre*, clothes the trunks of tall trees, and a *Lygodium* which climbs on grasses and the smaller shrubs is common up to 4,000 feet. The two *Gleichenias* found in Sikhim are also of a scandent nature. The largest one, *glauca*, which has a superficial likeness to the ubiquitous Bracken, forms almost impenetrable thickets, 15 or 20 feet in height, in places at 6,000 feet and above. Of the kinds found growing on rocks and trees the most delicately beautiful are the *Hymenophyllums* and *Trichomanes*, popularly known as Filmy ferns. There are 8 sorts of them, mostly confined to the cool, moist forests over 5,000 feet. The Irish Filmy (*Trichomanes radicans*) is the largest, covering the faces of large rocks under dense shade, and its fronds growing to over a foot in length; whilst those of *Hymenophyllum Levingii* barely exceed an inch or an inch and-a-half in length. Many of the *Davallias*, *Polypodiums*, and *Aspleniums* are very beautiful and graceful on the rocks and trees during the rainy season, and the bird's-nest fern (*Asplenium nidus*) and *Drynaria coronans*, with their large, massive fronds, are always conspicuous objects; the former mostly growing on rocks and stems of trees under shade, and the latter encircling the trunks of trees under full exposure to the scorching sun of the lowest elevations up to 4,000 feet. Of the large and more remarkable of the species growing on the ground, none excel *Polypodium ornatum* in beauty or elegance. Its fronds are sometimes small, but usually about six or seven feet long, and sometimes as long as 20 feet and of proportionate width, but whether large or small it is always an object of admiration. It hardly ascends over 4,000 feet elevation.

The orchid family is also extensively represented in Sikhim, there being from 350 to 400 species out of an estimated total of 5,000 for the whole world. Although none of the Sikhim orchids have flowers equal in size or colour to many of the South American species, yet several are hardly second in beauty or in popular estimation. They may be divided into two classes, viz., the epiphytal, which attach themselves to rocks and trees but do not derive any nourishment from them, and the terrestrial, which grow on the ground. A few are parasitical on roots of trees. In Sikhim the first-named class is the more numerous and better known; and the more important of its genera are *Dendrobium*, *Cœlogyne*, *Cymbidium*, *Vanda*, *Arachnanthe*, *Saccolabium*, *Ærides*, and *Phalænopsis*. Among the terrestrial sort are *Calanthe*, *Goodyera*, *Pogonia*, *Anæctochilus*, *Arundina*, *Habenaria*, *Satyrium*, *Diplomeris*, and *Cypripedium;* and of the parasitical the most notable are the *Galeolas*, which grow on the decaying roots of trees and have flowering stems over six feet high. Their flowers are yellow and the seed-pods not unlike those of the Vanilla.

Perhaps the most popular genus of the orchid family in Sikhim is *Dendrobium*, of which there are about 40 species; one-third of them having large, showy flowers, and the remainder are mostly pretty, but small and rather inconspicuously flowered. The best known, and at the same time the finest, is *nobile*, which is common from 1,000 up to 5,000 feet, growing on trees and rocks. Its flowers are borne on erect stems, and are variable in colour, but usually white, broadly tipped with purple. *Densiflorum*, which grows at the same altitudes, is equally common and has dense bunches of yellow flowers. *Calceolaria*, the largest both in growth and in flower, of the Sikhim *Dendrobiums*, smells strongly of Gregory's powder. Its flowers vary in colour from white and pinkish to golden yellow, and the lip is pouch-shaped. *Amœnum* is common on trees from 3,000 to 4,000 feet and is slender stemmed, with very numerous smallish flowers, white tipped with violet and purple, and smelling strongly of violets. Other showy *Dendrobiums* are *Hookeriana*, whose flowers are golden yellow with a deeply fringed lip spotted with purple; *chrysanthum*, *Gibsonii*, *Ruckeri*, and *fimbriatum*, all also yellow, and *amplum*, *Farmeri*,

Pierardi, *longicornu*, and *sulcatum*. The next genus in importance, *Cœlogyne* (including the section *Pleione*, popularly known in Europe as Himalayan crocuses), comprises about 20 species, of which *cristata* is the most in favour with orchid fanciers in Europe. It has egg-shaped bulbs on long trailing stems, and very large snow-white flowers with a yellow stained lip, on long racemes. It may be seen clothing rocks and the stems of large trees between 4,000 and 6,000 feet. *Corymbosa* and *ochracea* are similarly coloured, but much smaller, the former being found up to 9,000 and the latter to 7,000 feet. Both are very common. There are four species of the section *Pleione*, all of them pretty. They are stemless, their flowers springing from a pseudo bulb, usually when bare of leaves. The most abundant is *præcox*, which has large rosy-purple flowers, and is found between 5,000 and 8,000 feet. It flowers in the autumn. *Maculata*, which flowers at the same season, is white spotted with purple, and is not uncommon on the stems of *sál* trees between 2,500 and 3,500 feet. *Humilis* flowers in the spring at elevations from 6,000 feet upwards, and is white, streaked brown on the lip. The fourth species, *Hookeriana*, ascends as high as 10,000 feet, and produces rosy-purple flowers about the beginning of the rainy season. There are about 10 sorts of *Cymbidium*, the most of them with long grassy leaves and many-flowered drooping racemes. The majority of them belong to the cool forests above 5,000 feet, but a few are natives of the hottest valleys. *Eburneum*, which is one of the hot valley sorts, has large ivory coloured flowers, faintly stained with peach on the lip, and sweet scented. *Giganteum* and *grandiflorum* are very fine sorts of the cooler forests. *Arachnanthe Cathcartii*, which was considered by the great botanist, Lindley, to have the most remarkably shaped flowers of all orchids, grows on trees, in densely shaded places, between 2,000 and 4,500 feet. It has thick, fleshy flowers, of 2½ inches diameter, whitish, closely barred with chocolate, and the lip curiously hinged. *Rhynchostylis retusa* and *Ærides affine*, of the hot valleys, have both bottle-brush spikes of flowers of a purplish colour; and *Ærides odoratum* and *Saccolabium ampullaceum*, of the same parts, are favourite species.

The terrestrial species, on the whole, do not at present hold a high place in popular estimation, but many of them are well worth cultivating. *Phajus Wallichii*, which grows in marshy places, below 4,000 feet elevation, has large, richly coloured flowers on spikes over 2 feet high, and *Arundina bambusæfolia* exceeds 6 feet in height, and flowers more or less during the greater part of the year. Its flowers, which are large, are of a pinkish colour with a bright purple lip. *Anœctochilus Roxburghii* is a small plant with velvety leaves netted with golden nerves, and grows under shade between 2,000 and 4,000 feet; and several other species have also exceedingly pretty foliage although their flowers are inconspicuous. One lady's-slipper orchid (*Cypripedium venustum*) is found from 1,000 up to 4,000 feet, and two others at over 10,000 feet. Nowadays few of the Sikhim orchids have much commercial value in Europe, as the greater number of the species considered worth growing by orchid fanciers are already common in collections, and can be bought from the English nurserymen at a cheap rate. But few of the species can survive the Calcutta climate for more than two or three years, and still fewer will flower satisfactorily there a second year. There are, however, several sorts that do thrive well in Calcutta, and *Phajus Wallichii*, the finest of all the Sikhim ground orchids, is one of them. At the Botanical Gardens it has continued to multiply and flower to perfection for many years, and *Arundina bambusæfolia* has also flowered there fairly well for several years when treated as a semi-aquatic. Of the epiphytal sorts *Vanda teres* is most at home at Calcutta, and even there requires full exposure to the sun to flower freely. *Dendrobium Pierardii* also thrives well, as might be expected from the fact of its being found in parts of the plains of Bengal as well as in Sikhim. *Dendrobium calceolaria* does well too, either as a basket plant or planted in ordinary soil if well drained and raised above the surrounding ground. A few of the other *Dendrobiums*, such as *Farmeri*, *nobile*, and *fimbriatum*, *var. oculata*, struggle on for several years, but, generally speaking, the Sikhim orchids are disappointing in Calcutta unless arrangements are made for their frequent renewal.

The natural order *Scitamineæ* is largely represented by both wild and cultivated species. It includes the gingers, turmerics, plantains, cardamoms, *Hedychium*, *Costus*, *Alpinia*, etc. Ginger and turmeric are cultivated for consumption in the country but not for export. One cardamom, the *Bara Elainchi* (*Amomum subulatum*), is cultivated extensively under the chequered shade of trees and shrubs, at low elevations, in places capable of being irrigated at the proper seasons. It is a most profitable crop, and there appears to be a market in Bengal for all that can be produced. The seeds of one or two of the wild sorts are also used, but for home consumption only, and they make rather indifferent substitutes for the cultivated one. The fibre of an *Alpinia* is occasionally used for making floor mats of a durable quality, and *Phrynium* leaves form the water-proof layer of the *Ghums*, or rain mats, so useful as rain protectors in field work and in load carrying. The *Hedychiums* are all showy, and a yellow and a white-flowered variety of the species *coronarium* are almost the only indigenous plants cultivated by the natives for the sake of their sweet-scented flowers. *Gardnerianum*, which is common between 4,000 and 7,000 feet, is the most conspicuous of the genus, having large bold spikes of yellow flowers formally arranged in seven or eight vertical rows. All the family, but especially the two above-named species, are a great attraction to the Sphinx moths which visit them freely after dusk. A *Curcuma,* which sends up flower spikes with bright pink-coloured bracts in spring, is a striking and abundant plant on dry ridges below 4,000 feet. There are five species of wild plantains, all very common; but their fruits are of but little economic value, being a mass of black seeds embedded in a little sweet pulp and enclosed in a skin. One of the species, in the young stage, has, occasionally, prettily variegated leaves.

The Arum family is also an important one in Sikhim, and one of its members, the gigantic *Pothos,* perhaps the noblest of all climbers, is among the most prominent objects of the cool forests where it clothes the huge trunks of trees with its handsome foliage. Fortunately for the lover of the beautiful, its leaves are uneatable by cattle, and it is thus enabled to develop its full beauty; but a smaller-leaved sort, associated with it, is periodically denuded of its leaves for cattle fodder, and its use is said to cause a considerable increase in the yield of milk, and to rapidly bring calves into good condition. The leaf stalks of a wild Caladium are largely used, in a cooked state, for feeding pigs; and ten or a dozen sorts are cultivated for their tubers as ordinary articles of food. The roots of several *Arisœmas* of the high levels are eaten by the poorer inhabitants of those infertile parts after they have been fermented for some days, and then boiled to ensure the dissipation of their poisonous matter. But at the best they are unwholesome food, and Hooker remarks that they cause bowel-complaints and loss of hair and skin. A few of them have elegant foliage and strange looking flowers with tendrils, of half a yard in length, from the tops of the spadices; and in autumn and winter they brighten up the roadsides with their large bunches of shining red fruit, which are greedily eaten by the Crimson Tragopan pheasant. The flower of an *Amorphophallus* which grows below 4,000 feet, and flowers at the beginning of the rainy season, has a disgusting and far-reaching odour of carrion.

The palms are but sparingly represented, and that mostly by the rattans. One of them, *Calamus montanus,* was formerly much used as suspending ropes of the foot-bridges across the large rivers, for which it was admirably adapted on account of its lightness, great length, and enormous strength, but owing to the spread of cultivation it is now scarce. From *Calamus inermis* are got the best alpenstocks of the district, and *C. leptospadix* is a favourite plant with palm cultivators on account of its light feathery foliage, which is very elegant. *Plectocomia himalayana,* another rattan, ascends to 6,500 feet, often forming impenetrable thickets in the forests. By means of its strongly incurved spines it climbs to the tops of the tallest trees, from which, in autumn, depend its enormously-long clusters of fruit. It is used for making baskets and tying fences. A stemless date (*Phœnix acaulis*) of the hottest valleys bears a poor sort of edible fruit; and the leaves of *Wallichia densiflora* are a good cattle fodder, and from their midribs are made the coarse hair brooms used by the natives. *Caryota urens* is a large tree of over 40 feet in height, bearing huge fronds of wedge-shaped leaflets, resembling some of the maiden-hair ferns on a gigantic scale. In Ceylon it is tapped for its juice, which yields jaggery, and sago is made from its pith. In Sikhim its juice is not extracted, but the Lepchas cut down the large trees to procure the pith, from which a kind of sago is made, and make walking-sticks and knife-handles out of the wood. They do not appear to make any use of the fibre which it yields in abundance, but Gamble says:—"The leaves give the *kittul fibre*, which is very strong, and is made into ropes, brushes, brooms, baskets, and other articles; the fibre from the sheathing petiole is made into ropes and fishing lines." And, according to Watt, it is expected that the fibres sewn closely together in bands will be an excellent substitute for whalebone in corset-making. Watt also says of it, quoting Roxburgh:—"This tree is highly valuable to the natives of the countries where it grows in plenty. It yields them, during the hot season, an immense quantity of toddy or palm wine. I have been informed that the best trees will yield at the rate of 100 pints in the 24 hours. The sap in some cases continues to flow for about a month. When fresh the toddy is a pleasant drink, but it soon ferments, and when distilled becomes arrack, the gin of India. The sugar, called jaggery, is obtained by boiling the toddy. The pith or farinaceous part of old trunks is said to be equal to the best sago; the natives make it into bread, and boil it into thick gruel; these form a great part of the diet of those people, and during famine suffer little while those trees last. I have reason to believe this substance to be highly nutritious. I have eaten the gruel, and think it fully as palatable as that made of the sago we get from the Malay countries." As the tree is of most luxuriant growth, at suitable elevations in Sikhim it may yet be found of considerable economic value to the inhabitants.

Of bamboos there are about twenty species. Those growing at elevations exceeding 5,000 feet have thin stems, but several of the lower level species have stems of great girth and length. Of them *Dendrocalamus Hamiltonii* (Po, Lep.) is the commonest and as useful as any. It is used for building huts, &c., and carrying water, and its leaves are a good horse fodder. Its young shoots when about a foot long are cooked and eaten. *Dendrocalamus Sikkimensis* (Pag-riang, Lep.) has large brown stems which are equally useful, and by many is considered the handsomest of the Sikhim bamboos. *Bambusa nutans* (Mahlu, Lep.) also grows to a great size, and has a nearly solid stem which is much prized in hut building for its lasting qualities, and for prayer flagstaffs. *Arundinaria Hookeriana* (Prong, Lep.) of the upper forests has often stems of a beautiful bluish colour, and *A. racemosa*, the Maling of the Nepalese, yields the best pony fodder of all the bamboo tribe, and from its stems the best roofing mats are made. Of the smaller sorts several grow so thickly together, over considerable areas, that even a small dog cannot make its way through them; and the most of the species flower simultaneously at intervals of about a quarter of a century, and then die. The more noteworthy of the large grasses which are very conspicuous objects in the autumn are a few species of *Arundo* with large, loose, cottony panicles, and several of *Saccharum* and *Imperata* with smaller compact panicles of similar composition. They are rare in forests, but are apt to become troublesome pests in land that has been cleared for cultivation. Their leaves are extensively used for thatching houses. *Thysanolana acarifera* is a tall tufted grass with broad, bamboo-like leaves and spikes of minute flowers arranged in large spreading panicles, which are much used as brooms. *Anthistiria gigantea* and a reed (*Phragmitis*) abound in swampy places on sunny slopes up to 5,000 feet. Small herbaceous forms are few in species and in individuals in the tropical and lower part of the temperate zones, but are common in the interior at higher elevations. *Poa annua*, an English grass, following the tracks of men and quadrupeds in all temperate regions, grows from the perpetual snow line down to 4,000 feet, and is abundant on cleared camping-grounds and by roadsides. The Dutch clover, another European introduction, is often associated with it.

The rhododendrons may be called the glory of Sikhim, so grandly beautiful are they, and also so abundant; so much so, in fact, that they abound in places to the exclusion of almost everything else. There are about thirty species, varying in size from the gigantic *R. grande*, a tree of 30 to 40 feet in height, and trunk girthing up to 5 feet, down to the prostrate *R. nivale*, barely rising two inches above the ground. A few species are sparingly found as low as 6,000 feet, but the majority of them grow between 9,000 feet and 14,000 feet, and four species (*lepidotum*, *nivale*, *setosum*, and *anthopogon*) ascend so high as 15-16,000 feet. At about 6,000 feet the large flowered *Dalhousiæ* begins to appear. It is a small straggling shrub, and as it is usually epiphytic on the tops of tall trees, it is hardly noticed till the fallen flowers direct attention to it. *Falconeri* is a large gregarious shrub, growing between 9,000 and 13,000 feet, with big leathery leaves felted on the underside with rusty-coloured hairs. The widely distributed species, *arboreum*, is common up to 10,000 feet. Only one species, *R. cinnabarinum*, is said to be poisonous.

Hooker mentions that "many of his young goats and kids died after eating it, foaming at the mouth and grinding their teeth. When the wood is used as fuel it causes the face to swell and the eyes to inflame;" and he notes that the honey of the wild bee is much sought after, except in spring, when it is said to be poisoned by rhododen dron flowers. A small tree, *Pieris ovalifolia*, is interesting on account if its wide altitudinal distribution, ranging from a little above sea level to 10,000 feet elevation.

Sikhim is almost as famous for its Primulas as for its rhododendrons, and they also affect high elevations. There are from 30 to 40 species; the majority of them growing at altitudes from 12—15,000 feet, two or three only being found below 10,000 feet, and about an equal number so high as 16-17,000 feet. *P. Sikhimensis* which is found from 11—15,000 feet, and resembles a gigantic cowslip, is one of the very few Sikhim primroses which really thrive in England, where the majority of them merely survive long enough to flower once in a miserable sort of way and then die. This is to be regretted, as all are beautiful, and they are very varied in colour, some being white, and others yellow, blue, pink, or purple, which is the prevailing colour.

Among numerous notable herbaceous plants are several species of *Meconopsis*, fritillaries, deadly aconites, gentians, violets, geraniums, potentillas, saxifrages, balsams, many species of *Pedicularis*, *Crawfurdia*, *Didymocarpus*, *Chirita*, *Smialacina*, jatamansi, and rhubarbs, one of which, *Rheum nobile*, was considered by Hooker the handsomest herbaceous plant in Sikhim, and he thus describes it:—"On the black rocks the gigantic rhubarb forms pale pyramidal towers a yard high, of inflated reflexed bracts, that conceal the flowers, and overlapping one another like tiles, protect them from the wind and rain; a whorl of broad green leaves edged with red spreads on the ground at the base of the plant, contrasting in colour with the transparent bracts, which are yellow, margined with pink. It is called 'Tchuka,' and the acid stems are eaten both raw and boiled; they are hollow and full of pure water: the root resembles that of the medicinal rhubarb, but is spongy and inert; it attains a length of four feet and grows as thick as the arm. The dried leaves afford a substitute for tobacco; a small kind of rhubarb is, however, more commonly used in Tibet for this purpose." It may be mentioned that in the late military expedition to the Tibetan frontier a batch of plants of this rhubarb growing in a sequestered valley were mistaken in the distance, one misty morning, for a surprise party of the Tibetan army.

Among the more remarkable of the climbing plants of the "tropical zone" are one or more species of each of the following genera, viz., *Thunbergia*, *Beaumontia*, *Bauhinia*, *Chonemorpha*, *Aristolochia*,

Vitis, *Porana*, *Uvaria*, *Hibiscus*, *Aspidocarya*, *Mucuna*, *Entada*, *Rubia*, *Argyreia*, *Clematis*, *Hodgsonia*, etc.; and of the "temperate zone" *Edgaria*, *Stauntonia*, *Thunbergia*, *Clematis*, *Rubus*, *Cissus*, *Porana*, *Rosa*, *Mucuna*, *Hedera*, *Lonicera*, *Rubia*, *Jasminum*, etc. Among the "tropical zone" shrubs are *Osbeckia*, *Oxyspora*, *Plectranthes*, *Clerodendron*, *Buddleia*, *Desmodium*, *Rubus*, *Polygala*, *Saurauja*, *Leea*, *Indigofera*, *Trevesia*, *Mussœnda*, *Ixora*, *Coffea*, *Morinda*, *Tabernœmontana*, *Dœdalacanthus*, *Barleria*, *Phlogocanthus*, *Justicia*, *Pavetta*, etc.; and of the "temperate zone" *Daphne*, *Edgeworthia*, *Luculia*, *Leycesteria*, *Ardisia*, *Buddleia*, *Hydrangea*, *Vaccinium*, *Rubus*, *Hypericum*, *Saurauja*, *Reinwardtia*, *Skimmia*, *Melastoma*, *Helwingia*, *Brassaiopsis*, *Aucuba*, *Mussœnda*, *Polygonum*, *Strobilanthes*, etc.

The trees of the "tropical zone" more worthy of mention for their useful or ornamental properties belong to the genera *Shorea*, *Cedrela*, *Morus*, *Quercus*, *Castanopsis*, *Artocarpus*, *Bombax*, *Canarium*, *Talauma*, *Schima*, *Ficus*, *Gynocardia*, *Æsculus*, *Mangifera*, *Albizzia*, *Bauhinia*, *Terminalia*, *Eugenia*, *Duabanga*, *Bassia*, *Alstonia*, *Wightia*, *Callicarpa*, *Gmelina*, *Cinnamomum*, *Bischoffia*, *Mallotus*, *Betula*, *Alnus*, *Iuglans*, *Engelhardtia*, *Salix*, *Populus*, *Phyllanthus*, *Symplocos*, *Phœbe*, *Cordia*, *Podocarpus*, *Pinus*, etc.; and of the "temperate zone," *Magnolia*, *Michelia*, *Quercus*, *Bucklandia*, *Ficus*, *Ilex*, *Acer*, *Cornus*, *Andromeda*, *Prunus*, *Taxus*, *Abies*, *Larix*, *Juniperus*, *Betula*, *Machilus*, etc.

Dr. King in his Annals of the Royal Botanic Garden, Calcutta, describes about 17 species of figs from Sikhim, ten oaks, and four chestnuts. Several of the figs are mere shrubs; a few are climbers, and the others lofty trees. The leaves of many of them are prized as fodder for milch cows, and are said to cause an increased yield of milk. *Ficus elastica* yields rubber of excellent quality when care is taken to collect it free from impurities, but the tree is not abundant enough naturally to render it of much commercial importance. The fruits of several species are eaten, but are insipid and greatly inferior to the ordinary cultivated figs. Several of the oaks and chestnuts yield excellent building timber, and the seeds of the chestnuts, although small, are good to eat. The sâl (*Shorea robusta*) is one of the best known and durable of timbers in India. Formerly there were magnificent forests of it along the Rungeet, but they have had to give way to the cultivator, and but little of their former magnificence now remains. *Magnolia Campbelli* is unsurpassed as a flowering tree. It is a large deciduous tree, producing magnificent rosy-purple flowers in spring, before the leaves expand, calling to mind the flowers of some of the water-lilies, which they strongly resemble. *Michelia excelsa* produces white flowers in great profusion, at the same season of the year, and its timber is one of the most useful for general purposes. From the seeds of *Gynocardia odorata*, a common tree of the lower forests, is got the chálmugra oil, which is of good repute in the treatment of leprosy and other skin diseases. A large mulberry (*Morus lævigata*) yields a timber second to none in Sikhim for its lasting and other good qualities, and its leaves, and those of the small species (*Morus indica*), are good for feeding silkworms. A large proportion of the Sikhim trees yield very inferior quality timbers, and care has to be exercised in their selection for building purposes. For instance, the timbers of *Bombax*, *Duabanga* and a *Canarium* are so unenduring that tea boxes made of them occasionally crumble to pieces within two years, and sometimes in less than one.

Many of the woody nettles (*Böhmeria*, *Villebrunea*, *Debregeasia*, &c.), yield excellent fibre, but as yet their extraction has been found too slow and expensive for them to be commercially remunerative, but the Lepchas make fishing-lines, &c., out of them for their own use. *Urtica crenulata* is the most dreadful of all the nettle tribe. It is found in the warm valleys up to 4,000 feet, and grows to 12 or 15 feet in height with large, glossy, innocent-looking leaves which are seemingly devoid of stinging hairs, but are extremely virulent, their stings causing great pain which lasts for several days and may bring on serious illness. Rubbing the affected parts with opium liniment has been found to give almost instantaneous relief. One or two of the cinnamons produce bark and leaves with aromatic properties, and are used for home consumption and sometimes sold in the local bazars. The leaves of *Callicarpa* are said to be useful in asthmatical complaints. A coarse, strong paper is made from the bark of *Daphne cannabina* and *Edgeworthia Gardneri*, two handsome flowered shrubs growing in the forests over 5,000 feet, and the root bark of a *Morinda* is used at home, and also exported to a small extent for dyeing. Several of the raspberries yield large crops of fairly good fruit. The fruit of the wild mango is eatable, and that is the best that can be said for it. *Wightia gigantea* is an extraordinary epiphytic tree, of great size, which embraces its foster parent with its numerous horizontal roots and ultimately strangles it. Gamble mentions that the Lamas make their idols out of its wood. The wood of *Gmelina arborea* is used by the Nepalese turners for making bowls and other domestic utensils, and the leaves are largely given to cattle. Among the flowering shrubs epiphytic on trees are *Vacciniums* of sorts, several species of *Hoya*, *Æschynanthus*, *Hymenopogon* and misletoe, and there are several species of the parasitical *Loranthus*.

The Lepchas find innumerable things to eat in the jungles in the shape of fruits, leaves, piths of stems, roots and flower buds. They also eat an enormous variety of fungi, and seldom make a mistake in collecting them, but occasionally a whole family does get poisoned. Some of the sorts resemble those commonly eaten in Europe and grow on the ground, but others, and they the best flavoured sorts, grow on dead trees, and are slimy, unwholesome-looking things.

The principal cultivated crops of the Lepchas are their own peculiar varieties of rice, which require no irrigation, and several wet sorts, millets of various kinds, maize, buckwheat, mustard, radishes, turnips, potatoes, climbing beans, yams, caladiums of sorts, pumpkins, cucumbers, plantains, capsicums, ginger, turmeric, cardamoms, cassava, cotton, &c., &c.

THE VEGETATION OF TEMPERATE AND ALPINE SIKHIM.

BY GEORGE A. GAMMIE.

THE following account of the vegetation of a restricted area of Sikhim is based on observations made during journeys through the interior of the country and its frontier tracts in the summer of 1892. Some portions of this paper are verbatim extracts from a report submitted to the Government of Bengal after my return. I have not hesitated to avail myself of information from Sir J. D. Hooker's invaluable "Himalayan Journals" whenever I consider that the opinion of a botanist of world-wide experience, even in such an early period of his career, would throw a clearer light on many questions which one with infinitely less knowledge and grasp of details would, perhaps, attempt to answer by the use of vague conjectures.

All tracts above an elevation of 10,000 feet are treated of as Alpine. Under the term "Temperate Region" is included only the country contained in the Lachen and Lachung valleys with their ramifications up to 10,000 feet.

It is true that many parts of Sikhim, such as the higher levels of the spurs proceeding from the Singalelah and other ranges, are temperate in their thermometric conditions, but the region to which the designation is strictly confined is called so on botanical considerations. Its climate, drier and more sunny in summer, favours the existence of a vegetation in many ways radically different from that of the moist outer ranges. As the botany of these has already been dealt with in a former chapter, it will be only alluded to for the sake of comparison when such a course becomes necessary for the more perfect apprehension of any subject under discussion.

The Temperate Region.—The hamlet of Cheongtong (Choongtam), at the junction of the Lachen and Lachung rivers, marks the entrance to this exceedingly interesting botanical area. The two valleys through which these head waters of the Tista flow, run northwards to the stupendous masses of the Himalayan axis which divides Sikhim from Tibetan territory. They are separated by a lofty range extending southwards from Kinchinjhow, and even at its termination it is 10,000 feet in elevation. The floors of both valleys are nowhere broad, and their flanks rapidly attain high altitudes, so that the area in which temperate forms of plants flourish is circumscribed in extent.

The Lachung Valley.—The trade route up the Tista valley passes through tropical forests and cultivation as far as Cheongton, where the air becomes appreciably cooler and where plants unknown to an inhabitant of the lower valleys attract our notice. The first indication of the transition of the flora is the presence of a tall *Anemone* (*A. vitifolia*), a taller thistle (*Cincus involucratus*), a leguminous plant (*Astragalus pycnorhizus*) creeping over the sand, a composite (*Eupatorium cannabinum*) and a common fragile climber with pretty blue flowers (*Leptocodon gracilis*). All these, with many more which could be enumerated, prevail as far as the village of Keadom. This is situated on a large open expanse which enjoys such a balmy climate in summer that, although it lies at an elevation of 6,600 feet, cereals such as Indian-corn, *Eleusine*, &c., are successfully grown. On the outer ranges, owing to the humidity and want of sunshine during the rains, these crops cannot be profitably cultivated above 5,000 feet.

The dense forests of tall trees terminate some distance above Keadom, and are replaced by grassy slopes on which grow more scattered trees. The character of the vegetation completely alters, and an abundance of species of plants unknown in other parts of the country flourish in profusion, their many-hued flowers endowing the landscape with a bright and cheerful appearance, conrtasting strongly with the dark green wealth of foliage whose monotonous aspect at lower levels tires the traveller's eye with its unbroken uniformity.

The arboreal and shrubby vegetation consists of *Xanthoxylum*, *Hydrangea*, *Rosa macrophylla* and *R. sericea*, *Prinsepia utilis*, *Pyrus*, *Rhus*, *Pieris ovalifolia* and *P. formosa*, *Rhododendron arboreum*, *R. setosum*, Maples, Oaks, Poplar, Holly, Hazel, &c. Others are *Leycesteria formosa*, *Buddleia macrostachya* and *B. Colvillei*, *Berberis* of several species, *Rubus niveus* with palatable fruits and the box-like *Sarcococca pruniformis*. The most conspicuous climbers are *Aristolochia Griffithii* with strongly-ribbed cylindrical fruits, *Hollbœllia latifolia*, a *Polygonum* and a few species of leguminous and cucurbitaceous plants. Of herbaceous plants, *Euphorbia Sikkimensis* is most abundant, but the variety of composite and umbelliferous plants is the most prominent feature. *Aster Sikkimensis*, *Erigaon multiradiatus*, *Eupatorium*, *Saussurea*, *Inula Hookeri*, *Lactuca*, and *Senecio* are most common.

Lilium giganteum grows on the verges of streams, fully deserving its specific name by attaining a height of ten feet; a smaller congener, *Lilium roseum*, with pink flowers is rarer. *Roscoea alpina* is seen everywhere, and the flat tops of many rocks are brightened by the yellow flowers of *Spathoglottis ixioides*. *Satyrium nepalense*, a pink-flowered orchid, most sweetly scented, accompanies it, and there are many species of *Habenaria*. Other plants worthy of mention are tall Balsams, *Thalictrum*, *Halenia*, *Swertia*, *Geranium*, Thistle, Wormwood, and *Polygonum molle. Aconitum uncinatum*, remarkable in its genus by its scandent habit, is extremely localized, and does not exist beyond a radius of two miles from Lachung village.

The handsome fern *Osmunda Claytoniana* overruns large areas in the manner of the bracken at lower elevations. Two species of *Leucostegia* with hay-scented fronds, *L. Hookeri* and *L. membranulosa*, and a large form of *Pleopeltis simplex* grow in a wood about 8,000 feet in elevation. *Goniophlebium ebenipes* occurs in dense clusters on the tops of many of the numerous rocks.

Woodwardia radicans, *Cheilanthes albomarginata*, *Pteris dactylina*, *Adiantum pedatum*, *Botrychium ternatum*, all rarer in other parts, are common along the course of the Lachung, as is also the ivy, which has a very restricted distribution in this country. Here it rambles up the stems of trees in a simple unbranched manner, which gives it a widely different appearance from the same plant in Europe which clothes trees, old walls, and buildings so densely.

The peach and apricot, said to have been introduced from Tibet, are cultivated by the villagers. *Pyrus Sikkimensis*, the Sikhim crab-apple, is common. Agriculture is not pursued in earnest by the people, their only crops being scanty fields of barley, radishes, and turnips. The temperate region is eminently distinguished by its variety of coniferous trees. *Picea Morinda* and *Tsuga Brunoniana* are found between 8 and 11,000 feet. The former is a tall, conical tree, with thick trunk and dark green pendulous branches; the latter has spreading branches drooping at the extremities, and bears very small cones. *Larix Griffithii*, the only Himalayan larch, grows only in Eastern Nepal, Sikhim, and Bhutan, and previous to its re-discovery by Dr. Hooker, its existence was known only from a note in Griffith's Journals. Young trees of this are commonly gregarious, and remind one of the gigantic *Lycopodia* which once grew on the earth. Full-grown specimens are pyramidal in outline, and attain a height of sixty feet. The branches are long and pendulous, supporting erect, cylindrical cones resembling those of *Picea Morinda.* It first appears at 8,000 feet, becomes plentiful at 9,500 feet, and ascends to 12,000 feet. It is the only deciduous conifer in Sikhim, the leaves falling in autumn to be renewed in the succeeding summer. All these conifers are often infested with a lichen, *Usnea barbata*, which hangs in long grey streamers, giving the scenery a quaintly antique appearance. I was told that, when reduced to straits for food, the Tibetans boil and eat this uninviting plant, finding it to be as nourishing and satisfying as flesh diet.

As I did not visit the Lachen valley, I can give no detailed account of its vegetation; but, judging from Sir J. D. Hooker's descriptions, its flora is in most ways identical with that of the Lachung valley. I may, however, safely conclude this part of my paper by quoting the remarks which this illustrious traveller makes concerning the variety of the vegetation in the temperate region from a geographical standpoint. These remarks relate primarily to the flora of the Lachen valley at Lamteng, but they are equally applicable to that of Lachung.

"At first sight it appears incredible that such a limited area, buried in the depths of the Himalaya, should present nearly all the types of the flora of the north temperate zone; not only, however, is this the case, but space is also found at Lamteng (and Lachung also) for the intercalation of types of a Malayan flora, otherwise wholly foreign to the north temperate region. A few examples will show this. Amongst trees the conifers are conspicuous, and all are of genera typical both of Europe and North America: namely, silver fir, spruce, larch, and juniper, besides the yew; there are also species of birch, alder, ash, apple, oak, willow, cherry, bird-cherry, mountain ash, thorn, walnut, hazel, maple, ivy, holly, *Andromeda*, *Rhamnus*. Of bushes, rose, berberry, bramble, rhododendron, elder, cornel, willow, honeysuckle, currant, *Spiræa*, *Vilurnum*, *Cotoneaster*, *Hippophæ*. Herbaceous plants are far too numerous to be enumerated, as a list would include most of the common genera of European and North American plants. As an example, the ground about my tent was covered with grasses and sedges, amongst which grew primroses, thistle, speedwell, wild leeks, *Arum*, *Convallaria*, *Callitriche*, *Oxalis*, *Ranunculus*, *Potentilla*, *Orchis*, *Chærophyllum*, *Galium*, *Paris*, and *Anagallis*, besides cultivated weeds of shepherd's purse, dock, mustard, mithridate cress, radish, turnip, *Thlaspi arvense* and *Poa annua*. Of North American genera not found in Europe, were *Buddleia*, *Podophyllum Magnolia*, *Sassafras?* *Tetranthera*, *Hydrangea*, *Diclytra*, *Aralia*, *Panax*, *Symplocos*, *Trillium*, and *Clintonia*. The absence of heaths is also equally a feature in the flora of North America. Of European genera not found in North America, the Lachen (and Lachung) valleys have *Coriaria*, *Hypecoum*, and various *Cruciferæ*. The Japanese and Chinese floras are represented by *Camellia*, *Deutzia*, *Stachyurus*, *Aucuba*, *Helwingia*, *Hölbellia*, *Hydrangea*, *Skimmia*, *Eurya*, *Anthogonium*, and *Enkianthus*. The Malayan by *Magnolia*, *Talauma*, many vacciniums and rhododendrons, *Kadsura*, *Daphniphyllum*, *Marlea*, both coriaceous and deciduous leaved, *Cælogyne*, *Oberonia*, *Eulophia*, *Calanthe*, and other orchids; *Ceropegia*, *Parochetus*, *Balanophora*, and many *Scitamineæ;* and amongst trees by *Engelhardtia*, and various laurels." To those interested in problems connected with geographical botany this statement supplies ample food for reflection. When the surrounding unknown countries shall have been explored and their botanical characteristics detailed, it may be possible to trace back the march of these far-reaching genera of plants to their starting-points.

The Alpine Region.—This region extends from 10,000 feet to 19,000 feet, above which elevation plants of even the most humble and degraded forms are altogether absent. The included tracts are the Singalelah ranges and slopes of Kanchinjingna, the upper levels of the Lachen and Lachung valleys, with their flanks, and the Chola Range.

The Singalelah Range and the slopes of Kanchinjingna.—The Singalelah Range, forming the political boundary between Sikhim and Nepal, springs from Kanchinjingna and extends southwards to the plains of Bengal. The Nepal frontier road terminates at the staging bungalow of Cheabhanjan, and from thence the only path available for marching is the sheep path running onwards to the grazing grounds which lie towards Jongri. The only large trees existing in the country travelled over are *Abies Webbiana*, *Juniperus pseudo-Sabina*, and *Juniperus recurva.* The silver fir extends to 13,000 feet, the junipers to 15,000 feet. Where the former is only a small, stunted, weather-worn tree, the other, a prostrate, intricately branched shrub. For many miles the path runs through woods of *Rhododendron arboreum*, *R. cinnabarinum*, *R. Falconeri*, *R. barbatum*, *R. campanulatum*, and *R. Hodgsoni*, *Acer caudatum*, *Betula utilis*, *Pieris ovalifolia*, *Prunus rufa* *Pyrus foliolosa*, *P. macrophylla*, &c. Here also are seen the last examples of the Bamboo tribe, *Arundinaria spathiflora* (so named from the spathe-like sheaths on the divisions of its inflorescence), and *A. racemosa*, not the large form so common at Tongloo and near Darjeeling, but a small variety rarely exceeding a height of three feet. The young culms of these bamboos are used as food by the Bhutias and the Gurung shepherds of Nepal who frequent the whole range with their flocks during summer. The upper limit of these bamboos is 13,000 feet, from thence upwards only small tufted species of grasses abound. The shrubby vegetation already enumerated grows so densely that few herbaceous plants can exist beneath it. Beautifully green moss carpets the boulders, and *Saxifraga ligulata*, *Potentilla*, *Clintonia*, *Polygonum*, and two species of ferns are the commonest plants. On open knolls, which occur but rarely, *Gaultheria nummularia*, small willows, and the heather-like *Cassiope fastigiata* cover the ground with their dense growths. Towards the termination of the range rhododendrons and other shrubs grow more sparsely, thus favouring the existence of a greater variety of herbaceous plants. Two remarkable gentians attract our notice: *Gentiana stylophora*, with large, terminal, greenish-yellow, lily-like flowers, and *Swertia Hookeri*, conspicuous by its brown leaves and inflorescence growing together in whorls on a stem often six feet high. Primroses become more abundant, the prevalent species being the water-loving *P. Sikkimensis* and *P. reticulata*, and also those growing on dry ground, such as

P. Stuartii, *P. denticulata*, *&c.* In shallow streams various species of *Sedum* of the section *Rhodiola*, and the golden *Chrysosplenium alternifolium* are common in the clefts of stones, partly submerged in the water. Near the camping-ground of Megu can be found a quantity of *Polypodium clathratum*, a fern separated by Clarke from *P. lineare* which it superficially resembles. It is thin and flacid in texture and dries black; the peculiarly-shaped scales covering the sori, which suggested the trivial name, alone serve to readily distinguish it from its congeners. *Woodsia lanosa* affects the same habitat. The latter is by no means a common fern, and its minute size assists to make it more difficult to find. *Cryptogramme crispa* is another equally interesting fern which is abundant in most parts of Sikhim between 13 and 15,000 feet.

On leaving the Singalelah Range properly so called and emerging under the stupendous masses of rock which extend in all directions from Kanchanjingna, a remarkable change of scenery is experienced. For a short distance the terraces are covered with a thick turf of grasses and sedges, amongst which are innumerable plants of *Primula Stuartii* and *Anemone.* The faces of many rocks are covered with cushions of saxifrages growing in hard, moss-like clusters, spangled with white and yellow flowers. Further on, the ground is covered with enormous accumulations of boulders which support no vegetation except humble mosses, which are perennially moist from the water which trickles over the whole surface of the slopes. Sir J. D. Hooker, in his admirable account of the Physical Geography of Sikhim, thus explains the cause of this barren desolation:—"Glaciers again descend to 15,000 feet in the tortuous gorges which immediately debouch from the snows of Kanchinjingna, but no plants grow on the *debris* they carry down, nor is there any sward of grass or herbage at their base, the atmosphere immediately around being chilled by enormous accumulations of snow, and the summer sun rarely warming the soil."

The presence of one plant alone in this and other similar places prevent the imputation of almost absolute sterility which they would otherwise deserve. This is the truly remarkable and unique plant *Rheum nobile*, the gigantic rhubarb of Sikhim. It thrives best on inaccessible ledges of precipices. As Sir J. D. Hooker says, "it forms pale pyramidal towers a yard high, of inflated reflexed bracts that conceal the flowers, and, overlapping each other like tiles, protect them from the wind and rain; a whorl of broad green leaves edged with red spreads on the ground at the base of the plant, contrasting in colour with the transparent bracts which are yellow, margined with pink." He considered it to be the handsomest herbaceous plant in Sikhim, and mentions that the acid stems are eaten both raw and boiled, that they are hollow and full of pure water, and that, although the root resembles medicinal rhubarb, it is spongy and inert. The dried leaves are used as a substitute for tobacco, according to the same authority. The plant is, in all truth, beautiful to close inspection, but the thought of it will recall to the traveller's mind the barren crags where it delights to grow, and where it heightens the depressingly weird effect of such scenery by its cadaverous stove-like stem.

A short reprieve from views of desolation is granted by a steep descent into the valley of the Runghi river at Gambothan. The sheltered position of this place favours the growth of large pine trees, and copses of *Salix Wallichiana* fringe the river banks. A steep ascent to the summit of the ridge beyond terminates on a broad open plateau called Bokto, which, being covered with grass, is a favourite sheep-grazing station. Another descent and ascent follow over the valley of the Yangsap through dense growths of rhododendrons, *Abies Webbiana*, *Pyrus foliolosa* and *P. microphylla*, &c. Beyond are two small plains and low ridges bearing only closely-cropped grass, with thickets of small rhododendrons here and there in sheltered hollows. Another valley, the Ratong, again intervenes, and we emerge in the elevated tracts close to the eternal snows. The ground is covered thickly with grassy turf. On the high knolls other vegetation is scanty, comprising, however, amongst a few others, a plant of doubtful affinity—*Oresolen Wattii*—spinose-stemmed *Astragali* and *Anemone*. The celebrated collecting ground of Jongri is a good type of the more sheltered situations. Here many plants constitute a luxuriant herbage, such as *Potentilla peduncularis*, *P. microphylla*, *P. coriandrifolia*, *P. albifolia*, *Geum elatum*, *Primula reticulata*, *P. Stuartii*, *P. pusilla*, *P. glabra*, *Pedicularis siphonantha*, *Geranium polyanthes*, *Ranunculus affinis*, *Meconopsis simplicifolia* and *Phlomis sp*. Here also can be found that intensely bitter-rooted plant *Picrorhiza kurrua*, of repute as a febrifuge and tonic amongst the Tibetans; and *Chrysanthemum Atkinsoni*, bearing golden flower heads, and worthy of note as being the only representative of its genus in Sikhim. Various species of *Primula* not known to exist elsewhere have been discovered by several collectors at Jongri and in its vicinity. Another fact worthy of record is that a majestic species of poppy is cultivated near the huts. It is a *Meconopsis* near *M. simplicifolia*, but grows in dense clusters two to three feet high. The flowers vary in diameter from five to seven inches, are an intensely vivid blue on opening, and change before fading away into purple.

The superabundance of rhododendrons is the glory of the Singalelah Range. The equally moist Chola Range also possesses them in the same abundance, and the whole Alpine region of Sikhim can boast of them in a lesser degree. One, *R. nivale*, a humble soil-embracing plant inhabiting the desolate slopes of Donkia and Kinchinjhow, between 17 and 18,000 feet, bears the honour of being the most Alpine woody plant in the Himalayas.

For miles and miles the traveller trudges by sheep paths through impenetrable scrubs of rhododendrons. Their flowers are of varied colours, but none are blue. They are devoid of strong perfume, with the exception of *R. Anthopogon*, *R. setosum* and *R. nivale*. These three when bruised or trodden upon, exhale an overpowering scent from the superficial glands with which they are crusted, aggravating the headaches suffered by every one at high elevations. The discomfort is intensified in bright weather, as the warmth engendered by the sun causes the vapours to rise in greater volume. Many loads of their twigs are annually collected and taken to the Buddhist temples of Sikhim, where they are burned as incense. They are also of much service in camp, as they burn readily when lighted, a consideration of extreme importance in a country where the wetness of ordinary wood causes such delay in obtaining brisk fires.

By comparison with the drier regions of Upper Sikhim, the chief characteristics of the vegetation along the Singalelah Range are its poverty in variety of forms, and its wealth in individual species of rhododendrons. Sir J. D. Hooker, in his appendix on the Physical Geography of Sikhim, thus explains the cause of this peculiarity:—"The banks (of rivers between 8,000 and 14,000 feet are generally covered with rhododendrons sometimes to the total exclusion of other wooded vegetation, especially near the snowy mountain, a cool temperature and great humidity being the most favourable conditions for the luxurious growth of this genus." Such conditions prevailing throughout the Singalelah Range, due to its proximity to Kanchinjingna, account for the overwhelming abundance of rhododendrons, and may also be accepted as probable reasons for the comparative absence of variety in herbaceous plants, most of which would be unable to maintain a struggle for existence in such an adverse climate and against such formidable competitors.

The Alpine part of the Lachung Valley and its surrounding heights.—The first quickly obtainable introduction to the flora of this district can be had by visiting the Tankra mountain which overlooks the eastern bank of the river. A magnificent forest of enormous pine trees extends without a break from 9,500 to 12,500 feet.

Polypodium subamœnum, *P. Hendersoni*, *P. hastatum*, and *P. erythrocarpum* depend gracefully in large clusters from their stems. A great variety of plants grows along the banks of the rapidly flowing Tunkra river, a tributary of the Lachung. Here, as elsewhere, edible fruits are few in number, the only plants yielding them being *Fragaria Daltoniana*, a strawberry with long oval fruits, and *Fragaria vesca*, the wild strawberry of Europe, both possessing the well-known and appreciated flavour; various species of *Ribes* bear racemes of red and yellow fruits reminding of red currants. No species of *Rubus*, strange to say, grows above 13,000 feet.

Other noteworthy plants were two species of *Cremanthodium*, *Polygonum vaccinifolium*, *Oxyria digyna*; *Pedicularis* of several species, all with purple flowers, *Potentilla fruticosa*, yellow and white saxifrages, *Epilobium*, *Lactuca macrantha*, *Parnassia*, and aconites. Above the region of trees is a dense low growth of *Rhododendron campanulatum*, the unfolding leaves of which colour the landscape with a dark glaucous tint. The bladder-headed *Saussurea obvallata* thrives on the damp verges of water-courses, and bumble bees affect its fœtid flower-heads which are enclosed in white inflated papyraceous bracts. Equally remarkable plants are the woolly *Saussurea* (*S. gossypiphora*), delighting to grow in sandy *debris*, appearing at first sight as balls of white fleecy wool. The young flower-heads are completely enveloped in their soft protective covering: but when the florets expand, a ring opens on the top disclosing the inflorescence inside. In similar situations is found *Crepis glomerata*, whose carrot-like stem buried in the ground is flattened on a level with the surface and bears a broad head of yellow flowers surrounded by small radiating leaves pressed closely to the soil. *Rheum nobile* is common, and ascends to 17,000 feet. Between the minor pass of Kanko and the glacier below Tankra La, there are multitudes of bright-hued flowering plants mostly confined to the sloping banks of the streams. On the Kanko La itself there are three small localized primroses—*P. uniflora*, *P. muscoides* and *P. soldanelloides*—*Ligularia*, brown and yellow *Chrysosplenium*, yellow saxifrages, blue and yellow forms of *Corydalis*, several species of *Pedicularis* and blue gentians. Dr. Hooker enumerated the plants to be found on the bleak pass of Tankra:—"A pink-flowered *Arenaria*, two kinds of *Corydalis*, the cottony *Saussurea*, diminutive primroses, *Leontopodium*, *Sedum*, *Saxifraga*, *Ranunculus hyperborea*, *Ligularia*, two species of *Polygonum*, a *Trichostomum*, *Stereocaulon* and *Lecidea geographica*, not one grass or sedge. In addition to these I found *Meconopsis horridula*, a lovely plant belonging to the *Papaveraceæ*, an order with notoriously delicate flowers. It affects the most inclement situations, sheltering itself under the shade of large rocks.

The fragrant spikenard (*Nardostachys Jatamansi*) is plentiful in the depression below the Tankra peaks, and *Picrorhiza Kurrooa*, intensely bitter when chewed, is abundant about 14,000 feet, as are species of *Lagotis* which bear a superficial resemblance to the latter. The only woody plant beyond the Kanko La is the humble *Diplarche pauciflora*.

Another interesting Alpine tract of comparatively easy access from Lachung is the Lebu valley, through which runs the scarcely used trade route to Tibet over the Ghoro La, the second highest pass in Sikhim, being at an elevation of 17,000 feet. The northern side of this valley is enclosed by an almost continuous precipitous spur, broken in one place only by a deep forest-clad depression; the range on the other flank is more gently sloped, and is covered with forest and succeeding smaller vegetation, and is more diversified by ravines. From 13 to 15,000 feet there is an impenetrable growth of rhododendrons and willows, with numerous small trees of *Pyrus foliolosa* and *P. microphylla;* and intermingled with grass under these bushes is an equal luxuriance of herbs, such as aconites, *Senecio*, *Saxifraga*, *Prunela*, *Potentilla*, *Polygonum*, and thistles. *Cnicus eriophoroides*, which is moderately common in most valleys, is so abundant as to be a perfect pest. From 14 to 15,000 feet the vegetation is more sparse and scattered, being chiefly *Rhododendron campanulatum* and *R. anthopogon*.

From 15,000 feet to the pass the floor of the valley is broad and swampy. *Sedum* of many species are common amongst the stones, and *Rheum nobile*, descending at last from what would be its more congenial perches in other valleys, is found in numbers over the level surface. Dense stiff growths of *Ephedra vulgaris*, a plant of the order *Coniferæ*, abound on steep banks. Its presence is always a certain witness of the proximity of the dry, arid regions of Tibet. Saxifrages, *Allardia*, *Meconopsis horridula*, *Cyananthus*, gentians, *Saussurea* of three spiecies, *Rhododendron nivale*, some grasses and sedges almost complete the scanty details of the vegetation. *Saussurea tridactyla*, growing at the foot of the ascent to the pass, is the last flowering plant seen, and the rocks above, suffering continual denudation by the weather, do not bear either mosses or lichens.

Numbers of yaks are grazed in this valley up to 17,000 feet, cattle range up to 13,000 feet. These animals possess sufficient instinct to avoid eating the poisonous aconites, which at their highest attained levels grow only to the height of the accompanying low herbage. Goats and Tibetan ponies, from the information I gathered, share in the same knowledge; while sheep, strange to say, must be muzzled or driven quickly through areas infested with these plants. One of the rhododendrons, also, is equally poisonous to animals. The species known to possess this property is *Rhododendron cinnabarinum.* Honey, which is collected in spring, but at no other time of the year, is said to be rendered deleterious by the admixture of nectar from rhododendron flowers.

By travelling up the main Lachung valley one arrives at the flat of Yeumtong, standing at the entrance to the Alpine zone extending northwards to Tibet. A thick turf of grass covers the surface of the flat, and on it grows a yellow Anemone (*Anemone obtusiloba*) with leaves appressed to the ground, a surculose saxifrage, the dandelion (*Taraxacum officinale*), the aromatic yellow *Elsholtzia eriostachya*, and groups of *Senecio diversifolius.* Other plants are *Pedicularis tubiflora*, a small floating *Ranunculus*, *Meconopsis simplicifolia* and *M. Nepalensis*, *Salvia glutinosa*, *Lychnis nutans*, *Cucabalus baccifer*, and *Asarum himalacium.* Aroids of the genus *Arisœma* are common. In early summer their tuberous roots are prepared and used for food according to the method described by Sir J. D. Hooker. As the people neglect agricultural pursuits, they depend almost entirely on the milk and its products from the yaks and cattle for their sustenance. When this source of nourishment is withheld in the early part of the year, they are driven to utilize the nauseous food obtained from Aroids, which causes disastrous results if continued for a time.

In this and all other valleys, every range facing a southerly direction, in even the least degree, is, in summer, exposed to the full force of the southerly winds, laden with mist and drizzling rain, which blow with increasing violence as the day advances, to die away only at night. These continuous currents rapidly denude the surface, wash down the superincumbent earth, and wear away rocks which become precipices or crags of fantastic shapes. Vegetation, therefore, cannot find permanent foothold under such adverse circumstances, and its abundance, of trees especially, is confined to the sheltered flanks on the opposite side where a copious rainfall is absorbed by the deep and fertile soil.

At the highest elevations where vegetation is naturally more scanty, the valleys are broader and their bounding spurs are comparatively lower in altitude. The currents, therefore, act equally in all directions, causing the whole area to assume an uniformly bleak and desolate appearance.

From Yeumtong to Momay Samdong an ascent of four thousand feet has to be effected. The distance is not great, but the steepness of the intervening tract rapidly discloses a radical change in the aspect of the country and of its vegetation. A forest of silver fir, maples, birch, *Pyrus*, rhododendrons, willows, and other trees and shrubs extends to 13,000 feet; for a few hundred feet farther some scattered black juniper trees occur; an equal distance upwards is occupied by smaller rhododendrons and willows; above, the valley is broad with enormous rocks on its surface and supports low-growing plants only.

Of this place Sir J. D. Hooker gives the following description:— "It was a wild and most exposed spot; long stony mountains grassy on the base near the river; distant snowy peaks, stupendous precipices, moraines, glaciers, transported boulders and rocks rounded by glacial action, formed the dismal landscape which everywhere met the view. There was not a bush six inches high, and the only approach to a woody plant were minute creeping willows and dwarf rhododendrons with a very few prostrate junipers and *Ephedra*. The bottom of the Lachung Valley at Momay is broad, tolerably level and grassy. The ground was marshy and covered with cowslips, *Ranunculus*, grasses and sedges, *Cyananthus*, blue asters, gentians, etc. Wild clover, shepherd's purse, dock, plantain, and chickweed are imported here by yaks; but the common *Prunella* of Europe is wild, and so is a groundsel-like *Senecio Jacobæa*, *Ranunculus*, *Sibbaldia* and 200 other plants." In addition may be noted some small species of *Pedicularis* and *Draba;* also *Mandragora caulescens* (belonging to the same genus as the well-known mandrake of scripture, to which in former times many magical virtues were ascribed). It is difficult to obtain perfect specimens of this plant as yaks are so partial to it.

The Donkia Pass, at an elevation of 18,000 feet, is situated seven miles above Momay, and the path to it runs over a broad, boulder-strewn valley, with shallow streams meandering through it. Some lakes are passed, all surrounded by marshy bogs where many plants grow. During the ascent the vegetation becomes more and more scanty, and the rocky heights rising steeply on either side from the pass are sterile. One *Arenaria* ascends to the summit, and a woolly *Saussurea* and *Delphinium glaciale* are last seen at the base of the steep path winding a few hundred feet up to the pass. The last-named smells most disagreeably and strongly of musk, and the natives assert that the musk-deer derives its scent from feeding on this plant—an absurd belief, as the plant grows only at high altitudes far above the habitat of the animal. The shallow waters of the stream flowing from Kinchinjhow and Donkia to Momay support quantities of reddish-brown *Sedum* and *Rheum nobile*. Gentians predominate, and all have bright blue flowers which unfold in every brief glimpse of sunshine. *Allardia glabra*, an aromatic plant with large flowers like purple Chrysanthemums, grows in low dense tufts. *Aconitum napellus*, which gradually decreases in size as it ascends, is here reduced to a minute plant with two or three leaves and one flower. Other plants are—*Ranunculus lætus*, *Cyananthus* of two species, the Edelweiss (*Leontopodium alpinum*), *Erigeron*, *Cremanthodium reniforme*, *Lactuca*, *Dubyæa*, *Crepis glomerata*, *Saussurea*, and the curious lichen-like *Antennaria muscoides*.

The prevailing feature of the vegetation growing from 17,000 feet upwards is the variety of plants growing in dense, hard, hemispheric tufts, such as *Arenaria*, *Saxifraga*, *Saussurea*, *Astragalus*, and *Myosotis Hookeri*. The flora on the moraines of the Kinchinjhow glacier at 16,000 feet furnishes an instance of what may be expected in such situations. *Eriophyton himalaicum* is common. It is a white, woolly Labiate, rooting in loose sandy *debris*, with bright blue flowers peeping from under the leaves. The other plants are a minute *Saxifraga* with extensive runners, a small gentian with quadrifarious leaves, *Pedicularis* of three species, *Festuca* and *Carex*. *Potentilla fruticosa* also exists here, but I have never seen it elsewhere in such an inclement situation. It is in its largest and most developed form, covered with leaves and flowers.

The Chola Range.—This range commences from the Donkia Mountain and runs southward, forming the political boundary between Sikhim and the Tibetan province of Chumbi. The hills intervening between it and the plains are of low elevation, few exceeding 7 to 8,000 feet, so that there is no barrier in front to prevent its receiving the full brunt of the rainy monsoon.

It is, therefore, exposed to the same influences as the Singalelah Range, and its climate being identical, the features of the vegetation are also similar. We have already seen that the drier air of the Lachen and Lachung valleys is an important factor towards the existence of an unique flora; here, we find, at temperate elevations, a vegetation in every way the same as that of like tracts on the outer hills; and, as the plants of the Singalelah Range have been mentioned in some detail, it is scarcely necessary to reiterate for the sake of this district.

To reach the Chola Pass, the best route to take is the road followed by the Sikhim rajas on their annual journeys to Chumbi, where they used to go to escape the heavy rains of Sikhim so disliked by Tibetans, who are denizens of an almost rainless climate.

After crossing the river Ryott below Tumlong, the path leads up a continuously steep ridge as far as Pheunggong—12,130 feet. Up to 10,000 feet, there is a dense forest of temperate trees and shrubs. *Gamblea ciliata*, a well-marked Araliad, is common, as is also *Quercus semicarpifolia*, an oak occurring but rarely in other parts of the country. At 7,000 feet are plants of *Decaisnea insignis*, a remarkable plant of which Sir J. D. Hooker gives an excellent description. From 6,000 feet upwards, on this ridge, can be found every species of rhododendron existing in Sikhim with the exception of *Rhododendron nivale*. Such a specific concentration of the genus has absolutely no parallel in any other part of Sikhim. The rainfall of the whole range must be excessive, judging from the manner in which these plants grow.

At Pheunggong the long continuous ascent terminates, and for a short distance the path runs along the level summit. *Abies Webbiana* is first seen here. The two junipers also grow on the range, but no other conifer accompanies them. A descent to the river Rutto follows, and the track runs along its course to the pass. It is a broad grassy valley with scattered pine trees, and is bounded by rocky hills, towards the head being bleak and stony with scanty vegetation. At

Barfonchen is a quantity of *Scopolia lurida*, *Aconitum Napellus*, *Elsholtzia strobilifera* and many other plants. On rocks near the river are plants of *Cathcartia villosa*, a papaveraceous plant of localised distribution. The Chola Pass itself is a barren depression, overlooking a precipitous defile. Between Chamanako and Nathu La to the eastward, are two spurs covered with an almost uninterrupted scrub of rhododendrons. Immediately below the pass is a large extent of pasture land, marshy in many places. The most striking plants are *Chrysanthemum Atkinsoni*, with finely divided foliage and bright yellow flowers; *Saussurea* of many species, some with fern-like leaves resembling small Alpine *Asplenium;* a large *Senecio; Parnassia*, *Calathodes*, primroses and others. Beyond Nathu La is a long transverse trough-like valley terminating under Zeylap La. It contains several lakes with marshy banks; before reaching the small plain of Kapup, a deep ravine, which has to be crossed, discloses a view of a magnificent lake whose surface appears black from the reflection of extensive pine forests which grow down to it from every side. A great part of the area on this march is covered with *Polygonum campanulatum;* and the spikenard (*Nardostachys Jatamansi*) is extremely common. Kapup, immediately at the foot of the valley leading up to Zeylap La, is like an oasis in the desert, as the hills above are rocky and bare. The plants seen during the ascent are those characteristic of the elevation 13 to 14,500 feet.

The following is a table of the Dicotyledonous orders of Alpine Sikhim, with the numbers of their component species:—

Ranunculaceæ	38	Caprifoliaceæ	19	Scrophularineæ	43
Magnoliaceæ	1	Rubiaceæ	7	Lentibulariaceæ	2
Berberidæ	4	Valerianaceæ	3	Gesneraceæ	2
Papaveraceæ	5	Dipsaceæ	7	Acanthaceæ	4
Fumariaceæ	9	Compositæ	110	Selagineæ	2
Cruciferæ	29	Campanulaceæ	14	Labiatæ	22
Caryophyllaceæ	29	Vacciniaceæ	2	Chenopodiaceæ	3
Tamariscineæ	1	Ericaceæ	35	Polygonaceæ	24
Hypericineæ	5	Diapensiaceæ	1	Aristolochiaceæ	1
Geraniaceæ	11	Primulaceæ	40	Laurineæ	6
Leguminosæ	16	Styraceæ	1	Santalaceæ	1
Rosaceæ	40	Oleaceæ	2	Euphorbiaceæ	2
Saxifragaceæ	36	Asclepiadaceæ	4	Urticaceæ	10
Crassulaceæ	13	Loganiaceæ	1	Cupuliferæ	5
Onagraceæ	7	Gentianaceæ	26	Salicineæ	12
Umbelliferæ	29	Boragineæ	13	Coniferæ	8
Araliaceæ	6	Solanaceæ	2		

An analysis of the list proves that this region does not possess any Dicotyledonous order pecular to itself. Twenty-four of the orders are represented more or less all over the world, generally in temperate regions; nine are confined to the North Temperate zone, one—*Selagineæ*—is South African, with the exception of the *Globularia* of Europe and *Lagotis*, a Himalayan, Arctic, and Alpine genus.

A further examination brings to light the fact that every order in this region (likewise in all others where they prevail) abounds in plants having brightly-coloured flowers, excepting the *Apetalæ*, and, even in those, the high level Euphorbias are differentiated sufficiently by their showy involucral leaves; therefore, to apply the case shortly without putting forward an absolute assertion, of the 50 orders named above, only seven can be characterized by having inconspcuous flowers.

There are a few details in the phenomena of vegetation in the Alpine region of Sikhim which are deserving of a brief notice.

The first is the preponderance of shrubby and herbaceous plants with bright-coloured flowers. For these the only fertilizing agents are apparently bees, of which there are a great variety of species, belonging to the kind known as bumble bees in England. Other orders of insects are rare; and butterflies, flying as they do in countless multitudes at lower levels, are here too uncommon for their agency to be taken into serious consideration.

As the higher orders of plants require the aid of insects for their propagation, it naturally follows that, as bees are here the commonest group of insects, the flowers from which they extract nectar and pollen for honey, will enjoy most opportunities for the due perpetuation of their race, those which require specialized forms of insects, such as flowers with elongated and narrow corollas, will be entirely absent, diœcious forms with inconspicuous flowers will share the same fate; and the only species adapted to survive this restricted method of existence will be plants with bright shallow flowers, with coloured bracts surrounding a less apparent inflorescence, or with broad corolla tubes into which bees can enter with ease.

The structure of the prevalent orders shows that the plants most fitted by nature for the visitation of bees and similar insects are the commonest at high elevations. As plants with brightly-coloured flowers will naturally first attract the attention of insects, it would appear that they have become so for no other definite reason, although the greater intensity of light consequent on a more attenuated and clearer atmosphere has also been advanced as an explanation of the fact.

With the exception of the musk *Delphiniums*, many labiates, composites, and some primroses, all the plants are remarkably devoid of odour. No rhododendron has scented flowers, and the species of that genus abounding in aromatic glands over their whole surface are low-growing bushes, extensively gregarious, which may have acquired their peculiar character to guard them against cattle and other herbivorous animals.

The second class of noteworthy plants are those manifestly endowed with protection from the moisture and inclemency of the climate As examples, the following may be cited: *Rheum nobile*, *Eriophyton Himalaicum*, *Saussurea obvallata*, and *Saussurea gossypiphora*. *Rheum nobile* has the divisions of its inflorescence hidden under overlapping bracts; the leaves of *Eriophyton* are of the same service to its flowers; *Saussurea obvallata* has flower heads enclosed in a hollow ball of inflated papery bracts; while *Saussurea gossypiphora* is completely enveloped in a woolly covering. Were all the plants found in company with these furnished with similar or equally efficacious protection, the fact would admit of easy solution; but the majority are absolutely naked as regards vestiture, and no reason can be advanced to prove why a few species, belonging to widely different orders, should be invested with safeguards against climate and other circumstances, while most of their congeners are destitute of such aids for successful existence. Although these protected plants are seemingly more adapted to their environment, they certainly cannot show, by numerical superiority, that they have gained any advantage in the struggle for life.

The last class of vegetation to be noted is composed of the procumbent species of rhododendron (*R. nivale*), with *Diplarche multiflora* and *D. pauciflora*, and many plants of diverse genera (some formerly enumerated) growing in dense, hard, hemispheric tufts. The situations in which these plants are found produce numbers of others, of normal form, distinctly Siberian in character. Two reasons may explain these curious methods of growth—one, that plants growing so closely to the ground benefit from the heat absorbed by the stony soil, their density of growth assisting them to conserve the warmth thus obtained; another, that their humble stature saves them from being broken by the winds which blow continuously over this region. Their habit, together with their small harsh leaves, may also save them from being browsed on by animals.

Grasses and sedges form a close herbage over many tracts, and the same winds, which probably force the bulk of high Alpine vegetation to creep on the soil, assist in the scattering of their pollen and seeds. The pollen and seeds of *Coniferæ* and the light feathery seeds of willows are carried hither and thither by the same means. The fructification of Alpine plants is another subject which would well repay a more than casual investigation.

The list of orders with soft, fleshy fruits is short; for instance, *Berberideæ*, *Rosaceæ* (*Pyrus*, *Fragaria*), *Saxifragaceæ* (*Ribes*), *Caprifoliaceæ*, *Vacciniaceæ*, *Ericaceæ* (*Gaultheria*). *Solanaceæ*, *Laurineæ*, are nearly all that could be comprised in this section. The remaining orders and a part of those already given yield dry, uneatable fruits with usually numerous and small seeds. How the distribution of the lighter seeds is effected is a question easily answered when we remember the power of the ever-blowing gales. Of birds, which are everywhere known as active agents for the dispersal of plants, the finches, so numerous at high elevations in summer, must bear a large share in the task of aiding the spread of plants with large seeds.

Enough has been said to point out the infinite variety of the vegetation of the Sikhim Himalaya, which contains in its whole extent types of every flora from the tropics to the poles, and probably no other country of equal or larger extent on the globe can present so many features of interest or so many problems for the solution to the thoughtful naturalist.

BUTTERFLIES.

NOTE.—The works consulted for this paper are "The Butterflies of India, Burmah and Ceylon," by L. de Nicéville, and "Catalogue of the Lepidoptera of Sikhim," by H. J. Elwes and Otto Möller.

J. GAMMIE—21-9-91.

BUTTERFLIES are extremely abundant in Sikhim. In the Catalogue of the Butterflies of Sikhim, published in 1888 by Elwes and Möller, 536 species are enumerated, besides 8 more they were doubtful about. But probably the species discovered since, and others still to be discovered, will bring the number up to about 600, and this in a small country of only 1,800 square miles. In the warmer valleys butterflies are to be found in every month of the year, but are comparatively scarce from the end of November till after the middle of March. Some of the species which are abundant at the lowest elevations are also found more or less sparingly over a wide range of altitude; as high as 8—9,000 feet, but the majority of the cool-forest loving species never by any chance go down to the hot valleys. In the lower valleys the collector should start soon after the middle of March and keep on till the end of November if he wishes to make a full collection. At these low elevations the warmth alone, without sunshine, is sufficient to keep the insects in movement; but in the cool forests of the higher altitudes few are to be seen unless the sun is shining; and the season begins a month or two later and ends as much earlier. The genus *Papilio* is strikingly represented in Sikhim by no fewer than 42 species. About one-half of the species remain always below 5,000 feet, at which height they are few in numbers, the majority keeping below 3,500 feet, and are most numerous thence to the bottoms of the valleys. They all frequent flowers, but several of them are oftener to be seen feeding on the roads and riversides, especially on damp spots. Of the well-known green species, with longish tails and blue or green spots on the hindwing, there are four species, of which *paris* and *ganesa* are the commonest, but they keep to the lower slopes, hardly ascending above 4,000 feet. *Krishna* and *arcturus* which resemble them, but have a distinguishing yellow bar across the forewing and lower part of the hindwing, have a much wider range, ascending to 9,000 feet, but rarely being found in the hot valleys. *Machaon*, a European species, is not found below 10,000 feet or so, and *gyas* keeps above 5,000. *Glycerion* and *paphus* have semi-transparent wings of a lace-like pattern, with long slender tails to the hindwings, and are of a very elegant shape. They are found from low elevations up to 4,000 and 9,000 feet respectively. *Teinopalpus imperialis* and two *Ornithopteras*, which belong to the same order as the *Papilios*, are among the most splendid of the known butterflies. The former is never found below 5,500 feet and seldom lower than 7,000, and is commonest over 8,000 feet, where it frequents cleared grassy spots within heavy forest. On the upperside it is green with yellow spots on the hindwing, and the long tails are tipped yellow; on the underside the middle part of both wings is green and the outer part of the forewing brown barred with black; the outer part of the hindwing is spotted yellow as on the upperside. The *Ornithopteras* measure from 6 to 8 inches across, and their coloration is both bold and pleasing, the forewing being wholly of a velvety black, and the hindwing golden-yellow scolloped with black. They keep mostly to the warmer slopes under 4,000 feet, where they frequent flowering trees.

Of the family *Morphinæ*, two species of *Thaumantis* (*diores* and *ramdeo*), believed to be seasonal forms of one and the same species, are most gorgeously coloured, being black with large spots which cover a great part of both fore and hind wings, of a brilliant metallic, changeable blue, and measure 4¾ inches across the outspread wings. They avoid the direct sunlight and dodge about among the scrub growing under the deep shade of tall trees in the hottest and moistest valleys. Frequently associated with them is *Stichophthalma camadeva*, of similar habits and among the largest of the Sikhim butterflies, being from 5 to 6¼ inches in expanse. It is more soberly coloured on the upperside than the *Thaumantis*, being chiefly white and brown, but the underside is showier, having a row of five red ocelli with black irides on each wing and other pretty markings. *Kallima inachus*, one of the oak-leaf butterflies, has a marvellous resemblance to a dead leaf when it is at rest with its wings folded over the back and showing the underside only, the leaf-stalk, veins, &c., being excellently mimicked. This mimicry is supposed to be protective to the insect, but this is doubtful as, when flying about, and protection most needed, it exhibits its upperside, which is a deep violet-blue with a conspicuous yellowish bar across the forewing, apparently quite as much designed to attract attention as the underside is for concealment. The Lepchas, with better discernment than the Europeans, call it the chestnut-leaf, to which it bears a closer resemblance than the oak-leaf. At times immense crowds of butterflies, composed of many species, may be seen feeding on certain spots by river-sides in the lower valleys, probably where large animals go nightly to drink; and many species may be caught on a single tree when covered with its scented flowers, but these are the common sorts; the rare ones have to be hunted for in more out-of-the-way places and prized when found. Among the smaller sorts there are about 100 of the *Hesperiidæ* or "skippers," chiefly dull coloured. The *Lycænidæ* or "blues" are represented by no less than 125 species, many of them of surpassing beauty. The males of three common species of *Ilerda* are beautifully marked with changeable metallic hues on the upperside of the forewing: *epicles* with violet, *androcles* with green, and *brahma* with golden-bronze. They are all abundant at elevations varying from 3—9,000 feet, and are an inch and-a-half or less across. Others are blue of many shades, and many have long slender tails. The male of *Zephyrus duma*, which is found from 7,000 feet upwards, is altogether of a brilliant gold-green on the upperside, but the female is a dowdy brown. The periodical occurrences of many of the "blues," and also of some of the other butterflies, is perplexing; one year a species may be in the greatest abundance everywhere, and then for several years be very scarce without any apparent cause. Other genera, comprising large or remarkable species, are *Danais*, *Euplœa*, *Zophoessa*, *Elymnias*, *Melanitis*, *Discophora*, *Enispe*, *Cethosia*, *Cynthia*, *Helcyra*, *Sephisa*, *Apatura*, *Junonia*, *Neptis*, *Stibochiona*, *Hypolimnas*, *Argynnis*, *Limenitis*, *Athyma*, *Euthalia*, *Vanessa*, *Cyrestis*, *Charaxes*, *Dodona*, *Abisara*, etc.

Moths.

The moths are not yet so well known as the butterflies, notwithstanding they are the more interesting race from an economic point of view. Sikhim is exceptionally rich in species. Already about 1,500 have been classified, but many are still undescribed, and probably their number will ultimately be found to exceed 2,000. The majority of the Sikhim moths are rather small in size, but several are among the largest of the insect race. The largest of them all is the Atlas-moth (*Attacus atlas*), which is sometimes nearly a foot across. Its caterpillars feed on many kinds of leaves, but those of the sâl tree are their favourite food. Next in size come several species of the genus *Actias*, of which *selene* is the most common. It is of a pale green colour with a pinkish spot partly edged with a black crescent on each wing, and has long slender tails. It measures about eight inches across the forewings, and nearly as much from the shoulder to the tip of the tail. Several species spin tussur-like silk cocoons, but as yet none have been procured in sufficient quantity to enable their commercial value to be tested. They are well worth enquiring into, however, and may yet prove a source of income to the inhabitants. The more promising species appear to be one or two species of *Antheræa* which yield, to the non-professional eye, a thread of excellent quality and colour, and in considerable abundance. Their caterpillars feed on oaks and *Engelhardtia spicata* (mahwa of the Nepalese), a common tree of a wide range, being found from the bottoms of the lower valleys up to 5,000 feet. *Theophila Huttoni*, whose caterpillars feed on the leaves of *Artocarpus chaplasha*, spins a cocoon not unlike the domesticated silk-worm, *Bombyx mori*, of Europe and Asia. *Bombyx mori* itself is not recorded from Sikhim, and probably does not occur there in a wild state. Attempts are now being made to introduce it on a commercial scale, and if successful must prove of great benefit to the Lepchas, who are sadly in need of some such cottage industry. Other insects numerously represented in Sikhim are beetles, bugs, grasshoppers, leaf-insects, praying-insects, walking-stick insects, dragon-flies, ants, lantern-flies, *Cicadæ*, etc.

It might be noted that the Lepcha collectors of Sikhim are most skilful, and would compare favourably with those of any country in the world: they are the only race in Hindostan who have names for the different species of butterflies.

N.B.—*Attacus cynthia* and *Cricula trifenestrata* are also hopeful species and are very common. *A. cynthia* is more than a hopeful species, it = *A. ricini* or the "ende" silkworm of commerce. *Cricula trifenestrata* has no silk worth the trouble of reeling. A hand-book on the Indian Moths is now in course of preparation by Mr. G. F. Hampson.

A LIST OF THE BUTTERFLIES OF SIKHIM.

By LIONEL DE NICÉVILLE, F.E.S., C.M.Z.S., &c.

The list of the butterflies of Sikhim here given is largely based on a somewhat similar list by my friends Messrs. H. J. Elwes and the late Otto Möller, which appeared in the Transactions of the Entomological Society of London for 1888, pages 269—464, and is illustrated with four plates, Nos. viii—xi. I have added many (94) species to the list, which then numbered 537 species, and have brought up the nomenclature to date. The notes on the times of appearance and the actual spots where the various species occur are largely taken from the above-cited paper, but I have not thought it necessary to give these notes in quite such detail, and occasionally I have found it advisable to add to them from my personal experience of Darjeeling and its neighbourhood, which extends over 15 years, during which time I have visited it annually and at nearly all seasons of the year. This list is probably now nearly complete, as Sikhim has been most thoroughly explored for butterflies, and not more than 50 species at a maximum await discovery. As regards the order adopted in this list, I have followed that of Mr. F. Moore in "Lepidoptera Indica" as far as the book has been published; afterwards I have taken the sequence of the species adopted in my own work, "The Butterflies of India, Burmah and Ceylon," which at present ends at the family *Lycænidæ;* finally, for the family *Hesperiidæ* I have followed Lieutenant E. Y. Watson's Classification and Revision of the Genera, as given in the Proceedings of the Zoological Society of London for 1893, pp. 3—132, and plates i—iii.

As the atmospheric effects in that part of Darjeeling which lies to the east of the Tista river, and which is included in the Daling Division of that district, are so different from those of the whole of the rest of the district, it might be expected that the fauna should also vary. The part of the Daling Division referred to is bounded on the north by a very high continuous ridge of hills, running in the following order from west to east:—Songchongloo (6,264 feet), Lolagaon (6,000 feet), Sichoor (5,836 feet), Nankfloo (7,108 feet), Labah (7,000 feet), Pankasarri (8,112 feet), and Richila (10,400 feet), and continued thence by a series of unnamed peaks along the south bank of the Né Chu to Namchala (7,852 feet) and the Jaldoka River, or Dé Chu, from the east bank of which the ridge rises again to be continued far into Bhutan. This ridge seems to form a natural breakwater for rain-clouds coming from the plains, and the average annual rainfall is more than double that of the station of Darjeeling. The measured rain taken for the last seven years on a ridge opposite Daling Ma and on the west bank of the Chel River or Ché Chu yields an annual average of 224·42 inches; while, had a record been kept of the rainfall on those spurs directly under Pankasarri and Richila, it would be found to far exceed this. On this account and by consequent causes the development of some species of butterflies is more favoured in this part, and many species, which have hitherto been found rarely, or have not been recorded from Sikhim and from Darjeeling to the west of the Tista, occur more plentifully in Daling. Although it might be argued that the fauna of this part of the country should be more appropriately included with that of Bhutan, of which country it was formerly a part, yet, as it is now placed in the Darjeeling district, it must be taken along with it.

To make the list as complete as possible I have added all the species which are known to me to occur in Bhutan, that country and Sikhim being conterminous. The species recorded from Bhutan only are few in number, and most of them may be expected to occur in Sikhim also. Indeed, in the case of many of them, as they have been procured by native collectors only, it is a little doubtful whether they really came from Sikhim or from Bhutan.

Family NYMPHALIDÆ.

Subfamily DANAINÆ.

1. DANAIS (Tirumala) LIMNIACE, Cramer.

Rare in Sikhim; occurs only in the Terai at the foot of the hills, and in the low hot valleys in May and June.

2. DANAIS (Tirumala) SEPTENTRIONIS, Butler.

A common species at low elevations, where it is found throughout the year. It occurs also in Western China.

3. DANAIS (Limnas) CHRYSIPPUS, Linnæus.

Not very common, and occurs only in the lower valleys. The aberration or "sport" named *D. alcippus* by Cramer and *D. alcippoïdes* by Moore, and which is found in Africa right across India to Burmah, in the Malay Peninsula, and in Sumatra, has never been recorded from Sikhim.

4. DANAIS (Salatura) GENUTIA, Cramer.

A very common species at low elevations, occurring throughout the year. It is not known if in Sikhim it has the habit of "swarming" or "assembling," as I have observed it to do in mid-winter in Calcutta. It is found in Western and Central China.

5. DANAIS (Parantica) MELANOÏDES, Moore.

Occurs commonly at low elevations throughout the year.

6. DANAIS (Caduga) MELANEUS, Moore.

Less common at low elevations only than any of the species previously named except *D. limniace*, Cramer. It is found in Western and Central China.

7. DANAIS (Caduga) TYTIA, Gray.

The rarest of all the species of the genus occurring in Sikhim except *D. limniace*, and is found at a higher elevation than any of them, flying as high as 9,000 feet above the sea in native Sikhim.

8. EUPLŒA (Crastia) CORE, Cramer.

A butterfly more of the plains than of the hills, found somewhat commonly at low elevations throughout the year. Mr. Moore gives *Crastia vermiculata*, Butler, from Sikhim instead of *E. core*, but Sikhim examples are typical *E. core*; and even were they typical *E. vermiculata*, I am not prepared to admit that species as distinct; at best it is but a "local race," and may be only a seasonal form. Further, the *Tronga nicevillei* described by Mr. Moore in Lep. Ind., p. 77, pl. xx, figs. 1, 1*a*, *male;* 1*b*, 1*c*, *female* (1890), from the Sunderbuns near Calcutta, is not only in my opinion of the same subgenus as *E. core*, but is at best a local race (possibly a seasonal winter form) only of that species.

9. EUPLŒA (Penoa) DOUBLEDAYI, Felder.

Heer P. C. T. Snellen has recently pointed out that the *Euplœa alcathoë* of Godart, by which name this species is usually known, is an Amboina butterfly and does not occur in India, so Felder's name must be adopted for the species. It is very rare in Sikhim, though quite common in Assam. In the Indian Museum, Calcutta, there is a single male example obtained by Schlagintweit, and in 1889 Major C. A. R. Sage obtained another specimen. These are all the examples I know of from Sikhim.

10. EUPLŒA (Penoa) DEIONE, Westwood.

Rather rare, and only occurs in the low valleys. In Daling it is found more commonly.

11. EUPLŒA (Trepsichrois) LINNÆI, Moore.

This species is more generally known as *E. midamus*, Linnæus. It is the commonest species of the genus occurring in Sikhim, and actually swarms at times in the low valleys. It is found in Western and Central China.

12. EUPLŒA (Danisepa) DIOCLETIANUS, Fabricius.

A somewhat rare species, occurring only at low elevations, I have seen it flying once only in Sikhim. Mr. Moore in "Lepidoptera Indica" has given a new name, *Danisepa ramsayi*, to the Nepal and Sikhim form of this species, which is the whitest of all. The Assam,

Burmah, Malay Peninsula and Sumatran form he calls *Danisepa rhadamanthus*, Fabricius, and places "*Papilio*" *diocletianus*, Fabricius, which was first used of the two names for this butterfly, as a synonym. I am unable to draw any line of division either between the specimens themselves (as they gradually grade the one into the other) or geographically between the whitest form of the species from Nepal and the darkest form from Sumatra, so the oldest name is here adopted for the species; which may, however, to be precise, be known as *E. diocletianus*, local race *ramsayi*.

13. Euplœa (Pademma) klugii, Moore.

A very rare species in Sikhim, occurring only in the Terai and in the low outer valleys. I have recently pointed out (Journ. Asiat. Soc., Bengal, vol. lxi, pt. 2, page 237, 1892), how excessively variable this species is. Two local races are found and meet in Sikhim, *E. kollari*, Felder, and the typical form, *E. klugii*, Moore. The former is but slightly blue-glossed on the upperside, the latter brilliantly so. There is every gradation between the two forms. Colonel Swinhoe has recently added to the very extensive synonymy of this species by describing a *Pademma hamiltoni*, var. nov., from the Khasi Hills. This "new variety" is not only an inconstant form of *E. klugii*, but it is more than that, being an absolute synonym of *Pademma regalis*, Moore.

14. Euplœa (Isamia) rogenhoferi, Felder.

Very rare, and occurs only in the low outer valleys and in the Terai from April to November. It is found more commonly in Daling and Bhutan.

15. Euplœa (Stictoplœa) harrisii, Felder.

This is another protean species, as I have pointed out recently in the Proceedings Asiat. Soc., Bengal, 1892, page 158. The Sikhim form is fairly constant, and may be known as a local race as *E. binotata*, Butler. It is by no means common in Sikhim, and is found only in the lowest valleys.

Subfamily Satyrinæ.

16. Anadebis himachala, Moore.

Wholly a forest butterfly, occurring only at low elevations rather locally. It is found also in Assam and Upper Burmah.

17. Mycalesis (Virapa) anaxias, Hewitson.

Not uncommon at low elevations. Seasonal dimorphism occurs in this species, but not to a very marked extent.

18. Mycalesis (Gareris) sanatana, Moore.

The dry-season form of this species (true *M. sanatana*) occurs commonly in forests at low elevations in the spring, while the wet-season form (*M. gopa*, Felder) is found in the same places during the rains. Intermediate forms are found when there is heavy rain at the commencement of the year. It occurs commonly in the Khasi Hills and in Upper Burmah.

19. MYCALESIS (Orsotriæna) MEDUS, Fabricius.

Occurs at low elevations only, and is fairly common. *M. medus* is the wet-season, ocellated form; while *M. runeka*, Moore, is the dry-season, non-ocellated form. This latter is found with or without the median white band on the underside.

20. MYCALESIS (Calysisme) PERSEUS, Fabricius.

Rare in the low valleys. *M. perseus* is the dry-season form, while *M. blasius*, Fabricius, is the wet-season form.

21. MYCALESIS (Calysisme) MINEUS, Linnæus.

Mr. Moore records this species from Sikhim. The wet-season form is *M. mineus*, while the dry-season form is *M. otrea*, Cramer.

22. MYCALESIS (Calysisme) VISALA, Moore.

This is the commonest species of the genus occurring in Sikhim, and is found up to about 5,000 feet elevation above the sea. *M. visala* was named from a dry-season form; the wet-season form has not been named. Mr. Moore thus describes the male secondary sexual characters of *M. mineus* and *M. visala*:—

M. mineus.

Upperside, hindwing, with a subbasal tuft of pale ochreous hairs overlapping a glandular patch of *blackish scales.*

Underside, forewing, with a glandular patch of *blackish scales* on the middle of the submedian nervure. The patch, as seen under the microscope, is composed of densely-packed but loosely raised, overlapping, large, broad, oval scales with even front edges. Compared with the patch of yellow scales on the forewing of *M. visala*, that of *M. mineus* is two-thirds less in size, the scales are less closely packed, are more laxly raised, and are narrower both anteriorly and posteriorly.

M. visala.

Upperside, hindwing, with an elongated glandular patch of *pale yellow scales*, overlapped by the subbasal yellow tuft; these scales being of exactly the same size, form, and disposition, as those present on the patch on the underside of the forewing, the overlapping hairy tuft consisting of long straight filaments, each arising from a distinctly visible minute round pore.

Underside, forewing has the glandular patch on the submedian nervure two-thirds larger than that in *M. mineus*, extending from the middle of the vein to the transverse discal pale band, and is composed of *pale yellow scales*; these scales (as seen under the microscope) are very densely packed, overlap each other, are slightly raised, are large and rather long, broad and somewhat broadest anteriorly, with evenly-rounded front edge, and very short peduncle; no slender intervening scales present;—this patch in *M. mineus* being short, situated on the middle of the vein, and composed of differently-shaped blackish scales.

23. MYCALESIS (Pachama) MESTRA, Hewitson.

Has frequently been brought into Darjeeling from the neighbourhood of Buxa in Bhutan by the Lepcha collectors employed by Messrs. Otto and F. A. Möller, A. V. Knyvett and G. C. Dudgeon. It may be found in Sikhim proper also, as it flies at Daling in May and August from 5,000 to 7,000 feet elevation. It does not appear to occur under two seasonal forms.

24. MYCALESIS (Pachama) SUAVEOLENS, Wood-Mason and de Nicéville.

Like *M. mestra*, Hewitson, this species appears to have only an ocellated form. It is very rare in Sikhim, being found by the late Otto Möller on a single spot on the Tukvar spur below Darjeeling at 3,000 feet in thick forests during April and May. Mr. G. C. Dudgeon has specimens from Sivoke and Bhutan taken in March, April, May, and July.

25. MYCALESIS (Samanta) MALSARA, Moore.

Occurs at low elevations only. It has very distinct seasonal forms, the rainy-season form being true *M. malsara*, the dry-season form is *M. rudis*, Moore.

26. MYCALESIS (Samanta) NICOTIA, Doubleday and Hewitson.

The rains-form, true *M. nicotia*, is very much rarer than the dry-season form, *M. langi*, de Nicéville. It is found from 3,000 to about 5,000 feet on paths through the forest, as are all the species of the genus.

27. MYCALESIS (Samanta) MISENUS, de Nicéville.

A very rare species, occurring in Sikhim in April and May at low elevations only. It appears to possess an ocellated form only. It is found in the Khasi Hills also. Mr. Leech has described a local race from Western China as *M. misenus*, var. *sericus*.

28. MYCALESIS (Samanta) HERI, Moore.

Occurs not uncommonly near Buxa, Bhutan; a few specimens have been brought in by the Lepcha collectors from Sikhim, and it is found in Nepal and Kumaon. I have seen an ocellated form only.

29. NEORINA HILDA, Westwood.

A rather high elevation butterfly, occurring in heavy forests in the rains at 7,000 to 9,000 feet. It swarms on Songchongloo in the Daling division of Darjeeling.

30. LETHE (Rangbia) SCANDA, Moore.

This lovely butterfly is confined to Sikhim, Bhutan, and the Khasi Hills. It occurs in dense forests at from 6,000 to 8,000 feet elevation.

31. LETHE (Rangbia) BHAIRAVA, Moore.

Rare in Sikhim and Bhutan, occurring from 6,000 to 8,000 feet elevation. It is found commonly in Daling on Labah and Rissoom; and the female, unlike *L. scanda*, Moore, is almost as plentiful as the male.

32. LETHE (Rangbia) GULNIHAL, de Nicéville.

Described from Bhutan, but may also be found in Sikhim. It is a very rare species, and the male only is known.

33. LETHE (Rangbia) LATIARIS, Hewitson.

Double-brooded, appearing in April and May and again in October at low elevations. Mr. Dudgeon records it only from Daling from 6,000 to 8,000 feet.

34. LETHE (Debis) KANSA, Moore.

A common species in the forests, and is found in the low hot valleys and up to 9,000 feet from April to October.

35. LETHE (Debis) SINORIX, Hewitson.

Rare in Sikhim, but occurs more commonly to the eastwards in Bhutan and Assam. It is found from Sivoke up to Rissoom (6,600 feet). I have lately rediscovered the allied *L. samio*, Doubleday and Hewitson, in Java. It was described from "East India."

36. LETHE (Debis) MEKARA, Moore.

A common species at low elevations wherever bamboo grows, on which its larva feeds. It occurs throughout the warmer months. The spring broods are lighter and brighter coloured than the broods emerging in the rains.

37. LETHE (Debis) CHANDICA, Moore.

Rarer than *L. mekara*, Moore, but occurs at the same times and places. Mr. Leech has described a local race from Western, Central and Eastern China as *L. chandica*, var. *cœlestis*.

38. LETHE (Debis) DISTANS, Butler.

An excessively rare species in Sikhim. The writer possesses a single female example from Sikhim, and a single male from the Khasi Hills. Mr. Moore suggests that *L. distans* may ultimately prove to be the dry-season form of *L. chandica*. The latter species is by no means rare, and it is highly improbable that the dry-season form of it should occur so extremely seldom as *L. distans* does.

39. LETHE (Debis) VINDHYA, Felder.

Very rare in Sikhim, more common to the east in Bhutan and Assam. It has been taken at Mongpoo at 3,800 feet in August. The species exhibits slight seasonal variation, the specimens flying in the spring being lighter coloured, more red, than those flying in the rains. The wet-season form is true *L. vindhya*, the dry-season form is *L. dolopes*, Hewitson.

40. LETHE (Debis) SERBONIS, Hewitson.

Occurs only at high elevations, 7,000 to 9,000 feet elevation, from June to September, in heavy forest.

41. LETHE EUROPA, Fabricius.

Occurs rarely in the low outer valleys and Terai. It is found also at Foochau in China.

42. LETHE DYRTA, Felder.

At low elevations only, and is rather a scarce insect in Sikhim. I have taken it in the Duars in dead winter at an elevation but a few hundred feet above the sea. It is far commoner in the Western Himalayas. It occurs right across China to Foochau.

43. LETHE ROHRIA, Fabricius.

Common almost throughout the year at low elevations. The spring brood is much more brightly red-coloured on the underside than the broods occurring later on in the year. It is a common species in Western, Central, and Eastern China.

44. LETHE DINARBAS, Hewitson.

Occurs in forests at 7,000 to 9,000 feet, and is not particularly rare, swarming all along the ridge from Songchongloo to Pankasarri in Daling. Mr. Moore in "Lepidoptera Indica," vol. i, page 266, refers the figure I gave of this species in Journal. Asiatic Soc., Bengal, vol. lv, pt. 2, page 250, pl. xi, figure 4, *female* (1886) to *L. hyrania*, Kollar. Mr. Moore quite correctly limits that species to the Western Himalayas, and *L. dinarbas* to the Eastern Himalayas and Assam, though Colonel Swinhoe (as I believe quite erroneously) records both from the Khasi Hills. My figure was taken "from a specimen from native Sikhim in Mr. Otto Möller's collection," and is a true *L. dinarbas*.

45. LETHE BRISANDA, de Nicéville.

Described from near Buxa in Bhutan. It is not improbably a Sikhim species also.

46. LETHE (Dionana) MARGARITÆ, Elwes.

A rare species obtained by the native collectors only near Buxa, Bhutan. It is, I believe, the largest known species of the genus *Lethe*.

47. LETHE (Tansima) VERMA, Kollar.

Distinctly rarer than *L. rohria*, Fabricius, which it most closely resembles. It is found from 4,000 to 8,000 feet almost throughout the year. It is recorded from Western China by Mr. Leech.

48. LETHE (Sinchula) SIDONIS, Hewitson.

A common species from April to November on the road round Birch Hill in Darjeeling, and on the cart road between Ghoom and

Kurseong through the forest, but is rare to the east of the Tista river. It flies in all weathers, and settles on ordure on the roads.

49. LETHE (Sinchula) VAIVARTA, Doherty.

Originally described from Kumaon. Mr. Otto Möller's collectors brought in a pair of specimens in August from Bhutan.

50. LETHE (Sinchula) NICETELLA, de Nicéville.

Found at high elevations only, 7,000 to 8,000 feet; where it occurs it is found in thousands. This is one of the few species which become rarer to the east of Darjeeling.

51. LETHE (Sinchula) SIDEREA, Marshall.

A very rare species, recorded by H. J. Elwes from Tendong, native Sikhim, 7,000 feet, in the rainy season and November, and by Mr. Dudgeon from Daling. It is found also at Moupin in Western China.

52. LETHE (Sinchula) MAITRYA, de Nicéville.

Occurs in enormous numbers from 9,000 to 12,000 feet on the Singalela range in July and August. Elwes records it also from Bhutan, and it was first discovered in the Western Himalayas.

53. LETHE (Sinchula) NICETAS, Hewitson.

Far rarer than *L. nicetella*, de Nicéville, and is found at 7,000 to 8,000 feet in the rains. Occurs less rarely on the Daling hills at the same elevation in May and June.

54. LETHE (Sinchula) VISRAVA, Moore.

Excessively rare in Sikhim, more common to the eastwards in Bhutan. It occurs at Pankasarri in the Daling division. I have only seen one female, which was in Otto Möller's collection; that sex was described by Hewitson as a distinct species under the name of "*Debis*" *deliades*.

55. LETHE (Kerrata) TRISTIGMATA, Elwes.

Very rare, and occurs on the Singalela range at 9,000 to 10,000 feet in June and July.

56. LETHE (Putlia) BALADEVA, Moore.

Rather rare. Elwes records it from Tonglo in July, Ghoompahar in June, and Tonglo and Tendong in August. It swarms in Daling at 8,000 feet. I do not think the genus *Zophoessa*, Doubleday and Hewitson, of which *Z. sura*, Doubleday and Hewitson, is the type, can be maintained as distinct from *Lethe*. Until recently, *baladeva* has always been placed under that genus.

57. LETHE (Putlia) RAMADEVA, de Nicéville.

Very rare; occurs at Tonglo in July and August, and in Bhutan in June.

58. LETHE (Zophoessa) SURA, Doubleday and Hewitson.

I have taken this species in the Birch Hill Park, Darjeeling, in October; it is found from 5,000 to 8,000 feet in forests from June to November, and is rather common. In May it swarms on the dark forest roads in Daling, and is always found at a higher elevation than *L. dura*, Marshall.

59. LETHE (Zophoessa) DURA, Marshall.

The type specimen was ticketed by Colonel G. F. L. Marshall, R.E., "Lower Thoungyeen forests, Upper Tenasserim, May." I cannot help thinking that there is some mistake with regard to this locality. No other species of *Zophoessa* is known to occur in Burmah at practically the level of the sea; the type specimen is unique, and its capturer, Major C. T. Bingham, has never obtained a second specimen, though during the last ten years he has collected over and over again through these forests. The type specimen agrees absolutely with examples from Bhutan, and my impression is that it came from thence and not from Burmah. Anyhow, Mr. Moore's *Zophoessa gammiei* (Lepidoptera Indica, vol. i, page 294, pl. xci, fig. 3, *male*, 1892), from Bhutan, is an absolute synonym of *Z. dura*. Mr. Moore had only the original description and figure of *Z. dura* to guide him when he described *Z. gammiei*. He may have been further misled by Mr. Elwes' figure of this species, which was taken from a female example, not from a male as stated. Other synonyms are "*Debis*" *moupinensis*, Poujade, and *Zophoessa libitina*, Leech, from Western and Central China.

Z. dura is a somewhat rare species, and has been obtained by native collectors in Bhutan in September, and by Mrs. Wylly at Kalimpong. It is local and swarms in May on the Nim ridge in bamboo jungle at an elevation of 4,500 to 5,000 feet. It has the same habits as *L. sura*.

60. LETHE (Zophoessa) GOALPARA, Moore.

Native collectors bring in this species in thousands. It occurs in the interior at from 6,000 to 8,000 feet. Mr. G. O. Dudgeon has never noted a specimen from east of the Tista river or from Bhutan. Nor have I seen a female, though I have constantly looked for it amongst the numerous males that have passed through my hands.

61. LETHE (Zophoessa) ATKINSONIA, Hewitson.

Occurs at high elevations, 8,000 to 9,000 feet, in July and August. It is not common, but occurs throughout Sikhim and Bhutan as far as the Sankosh river.

62. LETHE (Zophoessa) ELWESI, Moore.

Occurs commonly on the Singalela range from 9,000 to 12,000 feet elevation in July and August. Mr. Moore considers this species to be sufficiently distinct from the Western Himalayan form

(*Z. jalaurida*, de Nicéville) to constitute a local race. Mr. Leech records *Z. jalaurida* from Western China.

63. LETHE (Zophoessa) MOELLERI, Elwes.

Far rarer than *L. elwesi*, Moore. Occurs on the Singalela range from 9,000 to 11,000 feet in July.

64. BLANAIDA BHADRA, Moore.

This species is usually placed in the genus *Neope*, Moore, which is preoccupied through *Neopus*, a genus of birds. *B. bhadra* occurs in the hot low valleys from 1,000 to 4,000 feet from May to December. It flies through dense bamboo jungle, on which its larva feeds.

65. BLANAIDA PULAHA, Moore.

Occurs on the Singalela range, 9,000 to 11,000 feet, in July and August, rather commonly. Mr. Leech has described a local race from Central China as "*Neope pulaha*, var. *ramosa*.

66. PATALA YAMOÏDES, Moore.

Better known as *Zophoessa yama*, Moore, which Mr. Moore now restricts to the Western Himalayas. It is rare in Sikhim, and is found only in the interior at Tendong, 6,000 to 7,000 feet, in June and July. In Daling in suitable places it is perhaps the commonest butterfly in May, swarming at 6,000 feet; it also occurs in Bhutan. Mr. Leech has described a local race of "*Neope*" *yama* as var. *serica* from Western and Central China.

67. ORINOMA DAMARIS, Doubleday.

Rare. I have taken it twice only, once in the bed of a "jhora" or hill-stream, once in forest. It occurs from 2,000 to 6,000 feet.

68. RHAPHICERA SATRICUS, Doubleday.

Not very common. Found in forests at 6,000 to 8,000 feet. It occurs also in Western China.

69. RHAPHICERA MOOREI, Butler.

In Sikhim it occurs only in the interior, from 9,000 to 11,000 feet, in July.

70. CHONALA MASONI, Elwes.

Until recently, this butterfly has always been placed in the genus *Lethe*. It is found only far in the interior at great elevations, and in Bhutan, and is rare.

71. AULOCERA BHAHMINOÏDES, Moore.

This is the Sikhim form of *A. brahminus*, Blanchard. It occurs at high elevations in the interior only.

72. Aulocera chumbica, Moore.

This is a recently described species from the "Chumbi Valley, Sikhim-Tibet."

73. Aulocera loha, Doherty.

In Sikhim Mr. Elwes took this species on the Singalela range at from 10,000 to 12,000 feet in July. It occurs also in Kumaon and Western China.

74. Aulocera padma, Kollar.

Mr. Moore does not record this species in his "Lepidoptera Indica" from Sikhim, but only from the Western Himalayas. I believe it does occur in Sikhim, though I possess no specimen from thence. It is found actually in the station of Darjeeling (all the other species of the genus are only found in the interior), Mr. Elwes and I having both seen a specimen on the north side of Birch Hill. There is one specimen from Sikhim in Mr. Otto Möller's collection. It occurs also in Bhutan and in Western China.

75. Aulocera saraswati, Kollar.

Restricted to the Western Himalayas by Mr. Moore. It certainly occurs far in the interior of Sikhim also; many specimens from thence have passed through my hands.

76. Parœneis sikkimensis, Staudinger.

This butterfly has hitherto been recorded from India as *Œneis pumilus*, Felder. Mr. Elwes (Trans. Ent. Soc. Lond., 1893, page 459) says that it "is unquestionably an *Aulocera*." However, Mr. Moore has made a new genus for it, which may perhaps stand, as *P. pumilus*, and its numerous named forms differ greatly in *facies* from the butterflies hitherto placed in *Aulocera*. *P. sikkimensis* is excessively rare, and I believe has only been obtained twice by some plant collectors sent into the Chumbi valley by Messrs. J. Gammie and H. J. Elwes in 1881 and 1884.

77. Ypthima baldus, Fabricius.

Hitherto known from India as *Y. philomela*, Johanssen. It is common in Sikhim at low elevations. The ocellated, wet-season form is true *Y. baldus*; the dry-season form is *Y. marshallii*, Butler.

78. Ypthima methora, Hewitson.

The rainy-season form of this species has alone been named. It is very rare in Sikhim, occurring probably at rather low elevations at Pashok and in the interior. Mr. Dudgeon has captured it at 3,000 feet.

79. Ypthima sakra, Moore.

The commonest species of the genus occurring in Sikhim, found everywhere from 2,000 to 8,000 feet elevation. It has only one (ocellated) form. Mr. Leech records it from Western China.

80. Ypthima avanta, Moore.

This species has two seasonal forms: *Y. ordinata*, Butler, is the wet-season form; true *Y. avanta* the dry-season form. I possess a single large female specimen only of this species from Sikhim, captured by my friend the late Otto Möller in the Terai on 10th July, 1881. It is found in Central China.

81. Ypthima huebneri, Kirby.

The ocellated form occurring in the rains is true *Y. huebneri;* the dry-season, non-ocellated form is *Y. howra,* Moore. In Sikhim it is confined to the Terai, being a butterfly of the plains rather than of the hills.

82. Ypthima newara, Moore.

Occurs locally in Sikhim from the Terai up to about 5,000 feet from May to September, and is not common. Mr. Leech describes a local race from Central China as *Y. newara*, var. *chinensis.*

Hemadara narasingha, Moore, was originally described as an "*Ypthima*" from Sikhim, but it almost certainly does not occur there. It has recently been rediscovered at Bernardmyo in Upper Burmah at 5,400 feet elevation above the sea.

83. Callerebia annada, Moore.

Occurs only in the interior, and has been obtained occasionally only by the native collectors in native Sikhim and Bhutan. Mr. Moore has (erroneously I believe) recorded *Dallacha hyagriva,* Moore, and *Callerebia scanda,* Kollar, from Darjeeling.

84. Zipœtes scylax, Hewitson.

Neither rare nor common. It occurs at low elevations only throughout the year except in the three coldest months. I have recently received it from Upper Burmah. It frequents dark places near water.

85. Ragadia crito, de Nicéville.

Has only so far been obtained by native collectors near Buxa, Bhutan, but possibly occurs in Sikhim also. It is a local species, and is found commonly where it occurs in August. Mr. Elwes records it from Margherita in Upper Assam.

86. Melanitis ismene, Cramer.

A very common species; occurs from the level of the Terai up to 7,000 feet. It is highly seasonally dimorphic, the wet-season form being usually referred to as *M. leda,* Linnæus, but Messrs. Butler and Moore both declare that true *M. leda* is a distinct species from Amboina. That being so, the wet-season form will stand as *M. determinata,* Butler, and the dry-season form as true *M. ismene,* Cramer.

87. Melanitis bela, Moore.

Rather rare in Sikhim, and occurs only at low elevations. The wet-season form is *M. aswa*, Moore, and *M. tristis*, Felder; the dry-season form is true *M. bela*.

88. Melanitis zitenius, Herbst.

Commoner than *M. bela*, less common than *M. ismene*. In Sikhim it is found at low elevations. It is seasonally dimorphic as usual, though less markedly so than the other species in the genus; the wet-season form has not been named; the dry-season form is the true *M. zitenius*, as is also *M. duryodana*, Felder.

89. Cyllogenes suradeva, Moore.

Very local, occurring at Singla at about 2,000 feet, from April to June. I suspect it is single-brooded.

90. Cyllogenes janetæ, de Nicéville.

A very rare species, which has hitherto only been obtained by native collectors at or near Buxa in Bhutan, and by Mr. W. Doherty in the Naga Hills.

Subfamily Elymniinæ.

91. Elymnias undularis, Drury.

Occurs in the Terai and at low elevations only in the outer valleys, where it is common.

92. Elymnias malelas, Hewitson.

Usually known as *E. leucocyma*, Godart, described from Java, but Heer P. C. T. Snellen has recently pointed out that the description of *E. leucocyma* refers to a butterfly allied to, if not identical with, *E. undularis*, Drury, and does not at all apply to the present species. That being the case, the name given to it by the late Mr. Hewitson is adopted. It is not a rare species in Sikhim at low elevations, and is generally found where plantains are growing, on which the larva feeds.

93. Elymnias timandra, Wallace.

It is more than probable that the name given to this butterfly by Mr. A. R. Wallace should fall before *E. lais*, Cramer, the two species hardly at all differing, and Cramer's name being the older. It is excessively rare in Sikhim. I have seen only two specimens from thence, both females, which were taken in the low hot valleys. Mr. Dudgeon's collection also contains three females, one from the Tista valley, and two from the Geet valley (2,000 feet).

94. Elymnias (Dyctis) patna, Westwood.

Not very common in the low valleys up to 3,000 feet from April to October; in the latter month I have captured it in the Runjit valley.

95. Elymnias (Dyctis) vasudeva, Moore.

Rather rare at low elevations throughout the hot months, but it seems to extend to a greater altitude than any of the others of the same genus.

Subfamily Morphinæ.

96. Amathusia portheus, Felder.

Rare everywhere. Here included on the strength of a single male from Sikhim in the collection of the Indian Museum, Calcutta.

97. Discophora celinde, Stoll.

Occurs in the low valleys only throughout the warm weather. A freshly caught male is "a thing of beauty," but the splendid indigo-blue colour of the upperside soon greatly fades. The males of the Indian species of this genus as well as those of the genus *Enispe* have a very strong and unpleasant scent when first caught.

98. Discophora tullia, Cramer.

Commoner than *D. celinde*, Stoll, and occurs at the same seasons and in the same places. I have bred the larva; it feeds on bamboo. Dr. Staudinger has named the Indian form "Var. *indica*."

99. Discophora spiloptera, de Nicéville and Möller.

I am not at all happy about this species. Otto Möller believed it to be distinct, and wrote out a MS. description of it. This description I re-wrote and sent it to Mr. Elwes, who published it under our joint names. The species *looks* very distinct, but I greatly fear that it is only a spring (dry-season) form of *D. tullia*, Cramer. Lieutenant E. Y. Watson has similar specimens from Tilin in the Chin-Lushai Hills, also taken in the early spring. The Sikhim specimens came from Singla, 2,000 feet, and were taken in March.

100. Enispe euthymius, Doubleday.

Not uncommon at low elevations from April to October. On the wing it has the habits of a *Discophora*, and is often seen on ordure on roads at low elevations. *L. lunatus*, Leech, from Western China, is a closely allied species.

101. Enispe cycnus, Westwood.

Very rare in Sikhim, more common to the eastward in Bhutan. Occurs at 5,000 feet in Daling.

102. Æmona amathusia, Hewitson.

Mr. Otto Möller possessed a male, and Mr. A. V. Knyvett a male and two females of this rare species, all from Bhutan. The wet-season ocellated form has been named *Æ. pealii* by the late Mr. Wood-Mason; the dry-season form is the true *Æ. amathusia* according to Mr. W. Donerty.

103. THAUMANTIS DIORES, Doubleday.
A species of the heavy forests, occurring at low elevations only. Nearly always seen in couples or more in dense jungle flying short distances when disturbed and sitting with wings closed. It is probably seasonally dimorphic; the lighter, larger form, *T. ramdeo*, Moore, occurring in the dry-season, April to June; the smaller, darker form, true *T. diores*, in the rains, from August to October.

104. STICHOPHTHALMA CAMADEVA, Westwood.
This is one of the most lovely butterflies in the world. Fortunately, it is not rare, and occurs in forests at low elevations from May to September. It is probably single-brooded, the specimens taken late in the year being much worn and broken. Mr. Dudgeon has never seen it east of the Tista river, nor has he ever received specimens of it from Bhutan.

105. STICHOPHTHALMA NOURMAHAL, Westwood.
A very rare species. Mr. A. V. Knyvett has obtained through native collectors three males and a female in native Sikhim in two successive years in August.

106. STICHOPHTHALMA NURINISSA, de Nicéville.
Obtained annually in fair numbers by native collectors near Buxa in Bhutan.

107. CLEROME ARCESILAUS, Fabricius.
Very rare in Sikhim, but quite common in the adjoining country of Bhutan.

Subfamily ACRÆINÆ.

108. PAREBA VESTA, Fabricius.
Immensely common in Sikhim, and found from 2,000 to 7,000 feet elevation, and is certainly double, if not treble brooded. The black, spiny larvæ may be seen in hundreds in clusters by every road-side from October throughout the winter, at which time they are in a dormant state. Birds do not seem to eat them though they are most conspicuous; probably their compound spines are a sufficient protection. The larvæ appear to be polyphagous, eating any kind of weed. It is found in Western and Central China.

109. TELCHINIA VIOLÆ, Fabricius.
A butterfly of the plains rather than of the hills. I have seen only two or three properly authenticated Sikhim specimens. In the Western Duars at the foot of the hills it is quite common. Mr. Dudgeon has himself taken specimens in Daling at 3,000 feet.

Subfamily Nymphalinæ.

110. Ergolis merione, Cramer.

A common species at low elevations. The larva feeds on the castor-oil plant, *Ricinus communis*, Linn.

111. Ergolis ariadne, Linnæus.

Rarer than *E. merione*, but occurs like that species from March to November. The larva feeds on *Tragia involucrata*, Linn., a hairy, stinging, climbing plant.

112. Euripus consimilis, Westwood.

One of the rarest of the butterflies of Sikhim; a few specimens have been taken in the low outer valleys, in the Terai, and as far south as Jalpaiguri. The male is always rarer than the female.

113. Euripus halitherses, Doubleday and Hewitson.

The males are common, the females rarer. It occurs in the low valleys from March to November. The female, wherever the species is found, is a persistent mimic of the species of *Euplœa* (which are greatly protected butterflies) occurring with it. In Sikhim the first form of the female, which has been named *E. isa* by Moore, is a beautiful mimic of *E. diocletianus*, Fabricius (=*ramsayi*, Moore); while the second form of the female, which has been named *E. nyctelius* by Doubleday (=*cinnamomeus*, Wood-Mason) is a perfect mimic of a blue *Euplœa*, such as *E. linnæi*, Moore (=*midamus*, Linnæus, *auctorum*).

114. Cupha erymanthis, Drury.

Never common in Sikhim, but appears to occur at low elevations throughout the warmer months. I once captured a few specimens at Kalimpong in October. In Daling it is local at 3,000 feet.

115. Melitæa orientalis, Elwes.

Mr. H. J. Elwes and Otto Möller have obtained this species at high elevations on the Sikhim-Chumbi frontier. It is a local race of *M. sindura*, Moore.

116. Atella sinha, Kollar.

Not very common; found from 2,000 to 3,000 feet from May to October. I have never seen a female of this species, though hundreds of males have passed through my hands. Mr. Dudgeon reports it as occurring more commonly east of the Tista river at the same elevations. He has observed the female in June laying eggs at 2,500 feet.

117. Atella phalantha, Drury.

Much more common than the preceding, though by no means a common species in the hills. It is found throughout the warm months from the level of the Terai to about 5,000 feet. In Sikhim the pupa is dichroic; one form is green, red and golden; the other is white, black and golden; the latter is very beautiful.

118. ATELLA ALCIPPE, Cramer.

Appears to occur only in the outer valleys debouching on to the plains, such as Sivoke, from whence the natives bring it in considerable numbers. I have never seen it alive in Sikhim. It occurs almost throughout the year except in the winter.

119. CETHOSIA CYANE, Drury.

Common in Sikhim from April to December at 5,000 feet and below. The larvæ of this and the next two species feed in such numbers on the common white and blue passion-flower as to become a veritable nuisance.

120. CETHOSIA BIBLIS, Drury.

Also common, occurs up to 7,000 feet, and is found almost throughout the year. It is found in Western and Central China.

121. CYNTHIA EROTA, Fabricius.

Common from the Terai to 6,000 feet elevation almost all the year round. I have bred this species, *Cethosia biblis*, Drury, and *C. cyane*, Drury, from larvæ taken in numbers from the same passion-flower (*Passiflora* sp.), in October. The specimens of *C. erota* which emerge in the early spring from larvæ fed up in the late autumn are much smaller, and the females much lighter coloured, than the later broods of the year. In this species, as indeed in most tropical and subtropical species of butterflies, brood succeeds brood in regular succession throughout the year. These broods are more or less interrupted in the plains of Northern India where the rainfall is scanty, the intensely dry weather of the early summer acting like the cold winter of other regions in entirely stopping the further development of the species in any stage of its existence; but as soon as the rain falls at the burst of the monsoon, butterfly life resumes its activity, and fresh broods are rapidly developed. Single-brooded species are excessively rare in tropical and subtropical India, and my impression is that their occurrence at all arises from the fact that the larvæ have very weak jaws, and being able only to eat the youngest leaves of their respective food-plants. Single-brooded species in India, as far as I know, always occur in the early months of the year, when usually deciduous trees assume their new annual covering of leaves. The butterflies emerge from hibernated pupæ just before the young leaves are developed, lay their eggs on the leaf-buds or young twigs, the larvæ quickly emerge, feed up rapidly on the juicy and succulent young leaves, turn into pupæ in the course of a month, and so remain for 11 months till the following spring comes round, when they emerge as butterflies, and the cycle of their existence is completed.

122. Helcyra hemina, Hewitson.

A very rare butterfly, which occurs singly during the summer. It is less rare in the Daling division of Darjeeling, where it occurs at 4,000 feet. Mr. Dudgeon once took a specimen himself at 3,000 feet in Darjeeling, and found that it flies very swiftly, which may help to account for its scarcity in collections. Nearly all species of butterflies have their head-quarters somewhere where they are common, however rare they may be elsewhere, but *H. hemina* seems to be rare everywhere. Perhaps its day is over, or nearly so, and the species is gradually dying out. Or its head-quarters still have to be discovered. *H. superba*, Leech, from Western China, is an allied species.

123. Sephisa chandra, Moore.

The males of this species are not very common and are found at low elevations in the summer. The females are exceedingly rare and very variable, and appear to be in process of mimicking some species of *Danainæ*. The larva of the Western Himalayan species, *S. dichroa*, Kollar, feeds on oak. *S. princeps*, Fixsen, from Corea, is an allied species, a local race of which from Western and Central China has been described by Mr. Leech as *S. princeps*, var. *albimacula*.

124. Dilipa morgiana, Westwood.

Mr. A. V. Knyvett's collectors have obtained this species in Bhutan. I have not heard of its being captured in Sikhim, though it certainly occurs there. It has a very wide range, from the extreme end of the Himalayas to the west, through the Naga Hills and Shan Hills to the Black River in Upper Tonkin on the east. *D. fenestra*, Leech, from Western China (="*Apatura*" *chrysus*, Oberthür) is said to be allied to *D. morgiana*.

125. Apatura namouna, Doubleday.

Males not rare at low elevations throughout the summer; females very scarce, as is usual in this genus.

126. Apatura chevana, Moore.

A rare species at low elevations. It is a perfect mimic of some species of *Athyma*—say of *A. opalina*, Kollar; so much so, that it was originally described in the genus *Athyma*. I have specimens from Upper Burmah, and it is found in Western and Central China.

127. Apatura sordida, Moore.

Also rare, and occurs at low elevations only. It is one of the few species which appears to be found in Sikhim and nowhere else. Mr. Dudgeon has three males and three females from native Sikhim taken in October and November.

128. Apatura parvata, Moore.

Has been obtained by Mr. T. A. Hauxwell at about 4,000 feet in October below the station of Darjeeling, but it is very rare in Sikhim, far commoner at Daling at 5,000 feet and in Bhutan. The opposite sexes are very similarly coloured and marked, which is not the rule in this genus as represented in India.

129. Apatura (Rohana) parysatis, Westwood.

The males occur not uncommonly from 6,000 feet down to the bottom of the valleys, from April to November. The females are much rarer, and are splendid mimics of the two species of *Ergolis* occurring in Sikhim, these latter butterflies being, I believe, highly protected.

130. Hestina nama, Doubleday.

Occurs as high as 6,000 feet, but is more common from 2,000 to 4,000 feet. The females are much rarer than the males. It is, I think, a beautiful mimic of *Danais tytia*, Gray, but Mr. Elwes does not see the resemblance, as the flight is, he says, so different that he could distinguish it at once. The butterfly has a wide range, from Cashmere through the Himalayas to Siam, Western China, Burmah, the Malay Peninsula, and Sumatra.

131. Hestina persimilis, Westwood.

The males are rare, the females still more so. It probably occurs at low elevations, but little is known about it. Mr. Dudgeon reports that it is not uncommon at the foot of the hills in Daling. At Mussoorie the larva feeds on *Celtis australis*, Linn.

132. Herona marathus, Doubleday and Hewitson.

Not uncommon at low elevations. It has the habit, when disturbed, of settling head downwards with closed wings on the trunk of a tree, in which position it is particularly difficult to catch with a butterfly net. Like many other butterflies of this subfamily (*Euthalia* in its broadest sense, *Hestina*, &c.), it is very fond of over-ripe, strong-smelling fruit.

133. Precis iphita, Cramer.

This plain, sober-coloured butterfly is one of the commonest occurring in Sikhim, and is found up to about 8,000 feet almost throughout the year. The larva in Sikhim feeds on a species of *Strobilanthes*. The butterfly is found in Western and Central China.

134. Junonia almana, Linnæus.

I do not think there can be any doubt about *J. almana* being the dry-season and *J. asterie*, Linnæus, the wet-season form of one and the same species. In Sikhim it is found at low elevations throughout the year. It is, however, rarer west of the Tista river than it is on the eastern side, and it does not appear to occur in the inner valleys.

135. JUNONIA ATLITES, Linnæus.

A plains' rather than a hill butterfly, common in the Terai, rarer in the outer low hot valleys.

136. JUNONIA LEMONIAS, Linnæus.

Occurs up to 5,000 feet, and is not rare.

137. JUNONIA HIERTA, Fabricius.

Occurs somewhat rarely at low elevations west of the Tista river, but is very common at 1,500 feet to the east.

138. JUNONIA ORITHYIA, Linnæus.

The commonest species of the genus occurring in Sikhim, and is found from the level of the Terai up to 10,000 feet elevation. He is a lively little fellow, loves paths and roads, up and down which he continually flies.

139. NEPTIS (Rahinda) HORDONIA, Cramer.

A common species throughout the year at low elevations. It is seasonally dimorphic, true *N. hordonia* being the rains' form, *N. plagiosa*, Moore, occurring in the dry-season.

140. NEPTIS RADHA, Moore.

A very rare species in Sikhim, and I have only caught it once at about 4,000 feet elevation in October. Probably occurs throughout the warm months. Mr. Dudgeon has captured it several times at 5,000 feet, and finds that it is extremely fond of pitching on the same bush for several consecutive days. Its elevation extends to 7,000 and 8,000 feet, and he doubts its occurrence below 3,000 feet.

141. NEPTIS MIAH, Moore.

The males are very commonly met with sucking up the moisture from the sand in the beds of the hill streams at low elevations throughout the warm months. Found also in Western China.

142. NEPTIS ANANTA, Moore.

Very local in Sikhim, where I have never seen it on the wing. Mr. Elwes says it is found in the forests at 5,000 to 6,000 feet and at lower levels. He took it on the road to Pashok above Lopchu in June. Very common at 4,000 feet and upwards in Daling. It is found also in Western China both typically and as a local race which has been named var. *chinensis* by Leech.

143. NEPTIS VIRAJA, Moore.

Very rare, occurs in the Terai and low valleys, probably throughout the summer.

144. NEPTIS ZAIDA, Doubleday and Hewitson.

Rare. Mr. Elwes took it in June and July in the forest above Rangbi, at about 6,000 feet.

145. NEPTIS NANA, de Nicéville.

Occurs at Tonglo and in Bhutan in April and June, but is a very rare species. It is near to, but quite distinct from, *N. zaida.*

146. NEPTIS NYCTEUS, de Nicéville.

This is No. 131, *Neptis manasa,* Moore, of Mr. Elwes' list. He took a single male in the forest near the Rangbi jhora, on the road to Serail, at 6,000 feet, in June. The type specimens were obtained in June and July at Tonglo on the Singalela range at about 12,000 feet. Found by Mr. Dudgeon at 7,000 feet in Daling.

147. NEPTIS SANKARA, Kollar.

I have examined the type specimen of this species, which is a female, in the collection of the natural history museum at Vienna. Before it must fall *N. amba,* Moore, *N. carticoïdes,* Moore, and probably *N. amboïdes,* Moore. It is a rare species in Sikhim at 3,000 feet, but is far commoner in the Western Himalayas. Mr. Leech records it from Western and Central China as *N. amba,* but the Chinese form differs greatly from the Indian one in having all the bands and spots of the upperside yellow instead of white.

148. NEPTIS CARTICA, Moore.

Certainly not a common species in Sikhim, though it is more often met with than *N. sankara,* Kollar. It is found in the lower valleys throughout the warm weather.

149. NEPTIS VIKASI, Horsfield.

The commonest species of this group in Sikhim, and occurs at low elevations almost throughout the year.

150. NEPTIS LEUCOTHOË, Cramer.

Cramer figures this species well in his Pap. Ex., vol. iv, page 15, pl. ccxcvi, figs. E, F (1780), and records it from Java, China, and the Coromandel Coast of South India. It has received many names, *N. eurynome,* Westwood; *N. varmona,* Moore; *N. disrupta,* Moore (a "sport" or aberration); *N. adara,* Moore; *N. meetana,* Moore; *N. swinhoei,* Butler; *N. kamarupa,* Moore; *N. eurymene,* Butler; *N. andamana,* Moore; *N. nicobarica,* Moore; *N. mamaja,* Butler; *N. sangaica,* Moore, &c. My impression is that none of these will stand. If the European *N. aceris,* Lepechin, is admitted by the best entomologists to extend from Europe through Northern Asia to Corea and Japan, there can. I think, be little doubt that *N. leucothoë,* Cramer, has a similar extended range, being found throughout India (except in the desert tracts) from Bombay on the west, Ceylon on the south, through Burma, the Malay Peninsula, Siam, Cochin China, &c., South, Central, and Eastern China, and all the Malay Islands to the west of Wallace's line, and in Formosa and Hainan. In those portions of

India which have a well-marked dry- and wet-season, seasonal forms occur, the wet-season form being true *N. leucothoë*, and the dry-season *N. kamarupa*; the other names can be fairly evenly divided between these two forms. In Sikhim, as elsewhere, it is a very common species, and occurs everywhere at from 7,000 feet to the level of the plains throughout the warm months.

151. Neptis astola, Moore.

N. emodes, Moore, cannot I think be maintained as a species distinct from *N. astola*. It is perhaps hardly a less common species in Sikhim than *N. leucothoë*, Cramer, and occurs at the same time and in the same places.

152. Neptis nandina, Moore.

It has recently been discovered that the type specimens of *N. nandina* and *N. soma*, both described by Mr. Moore, represent one and the same species, the name *N. soma*, by which the species is generally known, having to fall before the older name, *N. nandina*. What has hitherto in India passed as *N. nandina*, has been named *N. yerburii*, by Butler. In Sikhim *N. nandina* occurs at low and medium elevations throughout the summer months. It is found also in Western China.

153. Neptis yerburii, Butler.

Generally known in India as *N. nandina*, Moore. Not uncommon in Sikhim up to 4,000 feet from April to December. In Mussoorie the larva feeds on *Celtis australis*, Linn.

154. Neptis adipala, Moore.

A somewhat rare species in Sikhim. Occurs in Western China also.

155. Neptis susruta, Moore.

A common species, occurring throughout the warm months up to 5,000 feet elevation. Found also in Western China.

156. Neptis ophiana, Moore.

Common at low elevations from March to December.

157. Cirrhochroa aoris, Doubleday and Hewitson.

Common up to about 6,000 feet from April to December. *C. abnormis*, Moore, and *C. jiraria*, Swinhoe, are both probably synonyms of *C. aoris*, though till these two species are figured it is impossible to say this with certainty.

158. Cirrhochroa mithila, Moore.

Much rarer than *C. aoris*; occurs in the same regions and in the same months as that species. It is not uncommon at Sivoke and east of the Tista river at low elevations. It has a very wide range, and has recently been obtained in the rains at Bankipur in Behar, by Mr. S. Robson.

159. Pseudergolis wedah, Kollar.

Not uncommon at the level of the Terai to about 6,000 feet, from March to November. In the Western Himalayas this species occurs almost entirely in the beds of hill streams, in Sikhim it is found there commonly, less frequently in forests. In Mussoorie the larva feeds on *Debregeasia bicolor*, Wedd. It is found also in Western and Central China.

160. Stibochiona nicea, Gray.

Occurs throughout the warm months at low elevations. It is found also in Western China.

161. Hypolimnas bolina, Linnæus.

A low-level butterfly occurring nearly all the year round commonly. It is found in Western China.

162. Hypolimnas misippus, Linnæus.

Very rare in Sikhim. The only females from thence that I have seen have been of the first form (named *diocippus* by Cramer).

163. Argynnis niphe, Linnæus.

Occurs almost in every month in the year, most usually at an elevation of 4,000 feet. I have bred the larva at Tukvar, where it was found feeding on wild violets amongst the tea bushes.

164. Argynnis childreni, Gray.

Occurs commonly at Tonglo at 9,000 to 12,000 feet, about midsummer. It is found also in the Khasi Hills, and in Western, Central and Eastern China.

165. Argynnis latona, Linnæus.

Very common in the interior, and has been taken as low as 5,000 feet in the station of Darjeeling during the winter. It occurs all along the road from Kalimpong to Pedong, and is found also in Western China.

166. Argynnis gemmata, Butler.

Apparently very common in July at high elevations in native Sikhim. Mr. Elwes has seen it on the high Chola Range.

167. Argynnis (Brenthis) clara, Blanchard.

Mr. J. Claude White obtained a single specimen at a high elevation in native Sikhim in 1891.

168. Argynnis (Brenthis) altissima, Elwes.

Very rare; has only, I believe, been obtained on two occasions by Mr. Elwes' native collectors in native Sikhim at an even higher elevation than that at which *A. gemmata* is found.

169. Argynnis (Brenthis) pales, Wiener Verzeichniss.

Mr. Elwes had three bad specimens brought him by natives from Chumbi and Bhutan, where it, doubtless, occurs at high elevations. I have never seen an example of this species from Sikhim.

170. Dichorragia nesimachus, Boisduval.

This species has a wide range, from Kulu, Kumaon, Nepal, Sikhim, Bhutan, Assam, Burmah, the Malay Peninsula, Sumatra, Java, Borneo, the Philippine Isles, Celebes, to China and Japan. In Sikhim it occurs somewhat rarely throughout the year at low elevations. Mr. Grose Smith has recently described an allied species from Western China as *D. nesseus.*

171. Calinaga buddha, Moore.

One of the rarest of the Sikhim butterflies, and has never, I believe, been caught by a European in that region. Mr. A. Grahame Young has, however, captured seven himself in the Western Himalayas; and seen at least fifty on the wing. It appears to be single-brooded and to occur in the spring in native Sikhim.

172. Penthema lisarda, Doubleday.

Occurs in thick forest. Major J. F. Malcolm Fawcett has taken it at 2,000 feet at Singla in May, and Mr. Dudgeon at 1,500 feet in Daling during May and June commonly. It is single-brooded. I possess specimens from Upper Burmah.

173. Neurosigma doubledaii, Westwood.

Rare in Sikhim and Bhutan at low elevations, and is apparently double-brooded, occurring in April and May and again in October. The species is better known perhaps as *N. siva*, Westwood.

174. Lebadea ismene, Doubleday and Hewitson.

Not rare up to the 3,000 feet throughout the warm weather.

175. Limenitis danava, Moore.

The male is rather rare, but is found from April to October from 1,500 to 7,000 feet. The female is excessively scarce. It occurs also in Western and Central China.

176. Limenitis daraxa, Doubleday and Hewitson.

Occurs from 1,000 to 8,000 feet, and throughout the warm months. The female is very rare, and does not differ from the male except in the green macular band on the upperside of both wings being somewhat broader, and the submarginal series of oval black spots (especially those on the hindwing) being more prominent. Found also in Sumatra.

177. Limenitis zayla, Doubleday and Hewitson.

Occurs not uncommonly in dense forests at 6,000 to 8,000 feet from June to August. It swarms on the Labah range in Daling.

178. LIMENITIS ZULEMA, Doubleday and Hewitson.

Very rare in Sikhim, less rarely found at Daling in May and June from 1,500 to 5,000 feet; also at Sivoke in April. It occurs also in Assam and Upper Burmah.

179. LIMENITIS DUDU, Westwood.

Found from 5,000 to 8,000 feet from June to August in dense forests. Flies round tops of trees on the highest points of ridges.

180. LIMENITIS (Moduza) PROCRIS, Cramer.

Common at low elevations from March to December.

181. ATHYMA PERIUS, Linnæus.

This species is found from Cashmere to Formosa and Hainan, and probably in most of the Indo-Malayan islands. It is common in Sikhim at low elevations, and flies all through the summer. The eastern Darjeeling and Bhutan form is unusually dark, the ground-colour of the underside being suffused with brownish.

182. ATHYMA JINA, Moore.

Rare, and confined to the zone of heavy forests between 6,000 and 8,000 feet, where Mr. Elwes has taken it in July. It also occurs in April. It is found in Western and Central China.

183. ATHYMA MAHESA, Moore.

Common in the low valleys from March to December. Mr. Leech has described a very dark local race of this species occurring in Western China as var. *serica.*

184. ATHYMA OPALINA, Kollar.

This species is at least double-brooded, and is found from 2,000 to 7,000 feet elevation from April to October. It is also seasonally dimorphic; the form which occurs in the dry-season (spring) is quite typical *A. opalina*, while that found in the wet-season is much darker, richer-coloured, and narrower-banded, and has been named *A. orientalis* by Mr. Elwes. Colonel Swinhoe says that the latter "appears to be a good constant form," which it certainly is not. He records *A. opalina* also from the Khasi Hills, but puts two other species of *Athyma* between it and *A. orientalis!* *A. opalina* occurs in Western and Central China, and Alphéraky has described a variety of it from Chouï-tchin-pou as *A. orientalis*, var. *constricta.*

185. ATHYMA SELENOPHORA, Kollar.

Males common, females rare at low elevations throughout the summer. The female was described as a distinct species by Mr. Moore under the name of *A. bahula.*

186. ATHYMA ZEROCA, Moore.

Males common, females rare. Occurs from the level of the Terai up to 4,000 feet from March to December.

187. Athyma cama, Moore.

Males common, females rare. Found at the same time of the year and at the same elevation as the two preceding species.

188. Athyma inara, Doubleday and Hewitson.

A. inarina, Butler, may be dropped, that species probably being a fictitious one. *A. inara* is common in Sikhim at low elevations all through the summer.

189. Abrota mirus, Fabricius.

Whether this species (= *A. ganga*, Moore) is really distinct from the next cannot, I fear, be conclusively determined until one or the other or both have been bred. In the male of *A. mirus* the four black bands on the upperside of the hindwing are at equal distances apart. Dr. J. G. Pilcher once had brought to him a pair of this species which had been caught *in copulâ*. The female was olive-green on the upperside. Both sexes are much rarer than *A. jumna*, Moore.

190. Abrota jumna, Moore.

In this species the male has the two median black bands on the upperside of the hindwing placed close together, the two outer bands far removed from them. Its female has the bands yellowish on the upperside. Both species occur together in Sikhim at low elevations from May to August, are by no means common, and appear to be confined to Sikhim. The only other known species in the genus is *A. pratti*, Leech, from Western China.

191. Euthalia (Symphædra) nais, Forster.

A butterfly found commonly in the plains, but very rarely in the hills. It occurs very sparingly in Sikhim, but Mr. G. C. Dudgeon has taken it on the outer spurs in Daling facing the Western Duars.

192. Euthalia (Lexias) dirtea, Fabricius.

Has been recorded from Nepal, and is common in Bhutan, but is very rare in Sikhim, which lies between the two. "*Symphædra*" *khasiana*, recently described by Colonel Swinhoe from the Khasi Hills, is an inconstant varietal form only of *E. dirtea*.

193. Euthalia (Dophla) iva, Moore.

This species was originally described from Sikhim. No specimen has of recent years been obtained in that well-worked region, except a single example in Mr. Dudgeon's collection from Daling, 6,000 feet, taken in August. I have lately purchased a pair from Manipur.

194. Euthalia (Dophla) nara, Moore.

This species was described from a female, its male being subsequently described as "*Adolias*" *anyte* by Hewitson. It is very rare in Sikhim, and is probably found only in the heavy forests. It is less rare east of the Tista river, where it occurs in July and September at 6,000 feet elevation.

195. EUTHALIA (Dophla) SAHADEVA, Moore.

Originally described from a male. I described its female for the first time in the Proceedings of the Asiatic Society of Bengal, 1892, p. 145. It is a very rare species in Sikhim, where it is found at 5,000 feet in August and September, but seems to be more common to the east in Bhutan and in the Khasi Hills, and occurs in Western China. Mr. Leech has described and figured the female as *E. pyrrha.*

196. EUTHALIA (Dophla) DURGA, Moore.

Of recent years owing to the great destruction of the forests for the cultivation of tea, this species has become very scarce in Sikhim. Otto Möller obtained it from June to August from 3,000 to 5,000 feet elevation. It is still fairly common in Bhutan. It is the largest known species in the subgenus.

197. EUTHALIA (Dophla) DUDA, Staudinger.

Probably the rarest species of the genus occurring in Sikhim. I possess a single pair only, the female from Bhutan, the male from the Khasi Hills. Dr. Staudinger described it from two males; Mr. Elwes also possesses two males, and Mr. Dudgeon one male—all from Sikhim.

198. EUTHALIA FRANCIÆ, Gray.

Common in Sikhim and Bhutan at 5,000 feet; it is found also in Nepal, the Naga, Khasi, Chin-Lushai, and Karen Hills. It probably flies about midsummer in the heavy forest zone in Sikhim.

199. EUTHALIA TELCHINIA, Ménétriés.

Occurs in the low valleys from 2,000 to 3,000 feet from April to October, rather rarely. The female was described as a distinct species under the name of "*Adolias*" *aphidas* by Hewitson.

200. EUTHALIA APPIADES, Ménétriés.

The commonest species of the genus occurring in Sikhim. It is found throughout the year at low elevations.

201. EUTHALIA JAHNU, Moore.

Rare at low elevations; probably found throughout the warm months. Its male was described by Mr. Moore as a distinct species under the name of "*Adolias*" *sananda.*

202. EUTHALIA GARUDA, Moore.

A common species in the low valleys and Terai, where it is to be found all the year round. It is a variable species, the dry-season forms being much lighter coloured than the wet, and the white spots on the forewing in both sexes differing greatly in different specimens in number and size. Colonel Swinhoe has recently described one of these varietal forms as *E. merilia* from the Khasi Hills. His *E. delmana* from Cheerapunji is the same species as my *E. eriphylæ*, which I possess from the Khasi Hills as well as from Tenasserim. My type specimen is very pale, and evidently belonged to the dry-season form, while *E. delmana* probably represents the rains' form. The species occurs in Sumatra also.

203. EUTHALIA PHEMIUS, Doubleday and Hewitson.

Not uncommon in Sikhim at low elevations from April to December. The female sex was described by Mr. Moore as a distinct species under the name of "*Adolias*" *sancara*.

204. EUTHALIA JAMA, Felder.

Very rare in Sikhim, probably found at low elevations throughout the summer.

205. EUTHALIA LUBENTINA, Cramer.

Rare (the female commoner than the male) at low elevations from April to October.

206. EUTHALIA ANOSIA, Moore.

Extremely rare ; has been obtained at Singla in April and October. It is found generally in river-beds, where it is fond of resting with outspread wings on the face of large boulders, from which it is then scarcely distinguishable.

207. EUTHALIA (Felderia) LEPIDEA, Butler.

I have taken this species in the hot valley below Badamtam in October; it is fairly common in the Terai and in Bhutan, and probably flies all through the summer.

208. EUTHALIA (Nora) KESAVA, Moore.

One of the commonest species at low elevations, 2,000 to 3,000 feet, and flies from April to December.

209. PYRAMEIS CARDUI, Linnæus.

At low elevations this cosmopolitan butterfly is found throughout the year, but more commonly in the winter, in the summer it is found up to 12,000 feet.

210. PYRAMEIS INDICA, Herbst.

Has the same times of appearance, and is found in the same places as *P. cardui*, Linnæus. It occurs also in China, Amurland, Corea, and Japan.

211. VANESSA CANACE, Linnæus.

Never common, but occurs up to 6,000 feet throughout the warm months. Found in Western and Central China.

212. VANESSA ANTIOPA, Linnæus.

Obtained by native collectors only in Chumbi or Bhutan in July and August. It occurs in Western China as well as in Japan.

213. VANESSA CASCHMIRENSIS, Kollar.

Occurs from 2,000 to 12,000 feet, and at low elevations flies in every month of the year. The larva as usual feeds on different species of nettle.

214. VANESSA RIZANA, Moore.

A few specimens have been obtained from time to time at very high elevations in native Sikhim by native collectors.

215. VANESSA LADAKENSIS, Moore.

Obtained by native collectors only, probably on the other side of the passes, in Tibet.

216. VANESSA XANTHOMELAS, Wiener Verzeichniss.

Recorded by Mr. Moore from Darjeeling, but confined in India as far as I know to the Western Himalayas.

217. VANESSA (Grapta) C-ALBUM, Linnæus, var. TIBETANA, Elwes.

Obtained only by native collectors in Chumbi and north-west Bhutan. Mr. Leech records this local race from Ta-chien-lu in Western China in July.

218. SYMBRENTHIA HIPPOCLUS, Cramer.

Common in Sikhim all through the warm months up to 6,000 feet elevation. The larva feeds on *Girardinia heterophylla*, Dcne. The butterfly is found in Western and Central China.

219. SYMBRENTHIA COTANDA, Moore.

More generally known as *S. hypselis*, Godart, but that species appears to be confined to Java. I have recently described the Indian, Burman and Malay Peninsula species as *S. sinis*, but *S. cotanda* is an older name. It is, next to *S. hippoclus*, Cramer, the commonest species in the genus occurring in Sikhim, and is found up to 4,000 feet almost throughout the year.

220. SYMBRENTHIA NIPHANDA, Moore.

A rather rare species, occurring up to 5,000 feet from March to October. Mr. Dudgeon has taken it several times at 3,500 feet on the Tukvar spur; it is also plentiful at Sivoke in March.

221. SYMBRENTHIA SILANA, de Nicéville.

Still rarer than *S. niphanda*, Moore, and has been found at low elevations only in March and May. It occurs in Bhutan also.

222. SYMBRENTHIA ASTHALA, Moore.

Has been brought in considerable numbers in April, May, and October from native Sikhim by native collectors. It is very plentiful at Sivoke in March. Found also in Western and Central China according to Mr. Leech, but the specimen he figures as *S. asthala* is a typical male of *S. hippoclus*, Cramer.

223. CYRESTIS THYODAMAS, Boisduval.

Occurs commonly from March to December up to about 6,000 feet. It is found in Western China, Japan, and in the Loochoo Islands. The larva is a queer object; it has two long horns on the head, a still larger one on the middle of the back (on the fifth segment), and a similar one on the twelfth segment. The pupa has two very long processes projecting forwards from the head and slightly upwardly curved containing the palpi, which remind one of the long "snout" of the imagines of the genus *Libythea*. The larva feeds on the leaves of various kinds of figs (*Ficus indica*, Linn., *F. nemoralis*, Wall., &c.)

224. CYRESTIS COCLES, Fabricius.

Extremely rare in Sikhim, which is probably the westernmost limit of its range. Single specimens have been taken at Singla and Sivoke, at low elevations, in the spring and autumn. The difference in coloration observed in this species may be due to seasonal causes. Mr. Dudgeon has observed that the green form occurs in March, and the brown one in August and September.

225. CYRESTIS (Chersonesia) RISA, Doubleday and Hewitson.

Occurs somewhat commonly at low elevations throughout the warm months of the year.

226. KALLIMA INACHUS, Boisduval.

Common at low elevations from March to November. It is found also in Western and Central China. When *frightened* it invariably settles, as far as I have noticed, with closed wings on a twig or branch. It sometimes, as Elwes points out, settles with open wings, but on these occasions it has, I feel sure, no thought of enemies. It is particularly fond of the juice from the bark of certain trees, and eagerly sips up the "sugar" of moth collectors. Stale beer, also old beer casks, are an irresistible attraction to these butterflies. Mr. G. C. Dudgeon has bred the larva in Bhutan on a common blue-flowered plant named *Strobilanthes capitatus*, T. Anderson. It may be interesting to note that while the Sumatran and Javan species of *Kallima* have yellow-banded males and bluish-white-banded females, the Bornean species is yellow-banded in both sexes like *K. inachus*.

227. KALLIMA KNYVETTII, de Nicéville.

Brought from near Buxa in Bhutan year after year, but never in large numbers, by native collectors. Mr. Elwes records it from the Naga Hills at about 5,000 feet.

228. DOLESCHALLIA POLIBETE, Cramer.

A common species up to 4,000 feet from April to December. The larva is said by Mr. G. C. Dudgeon to feed on various species of nettles, and is very conspicuous and common on the Tukvar spur at 3,500 feet.

229. CHARAXES (Eulepis) DOLON, Westwood.

Apparently single-brooded, and occurs at low elevations only in April and May. FEMALE. EXPANSE: 4·3 inches. DESCRIPTION: Larger than the male, but agreeing with it in every respect, except that the tails are about one-fourth longer, a little broader, especially at the tips, which are bluntly rounded instead of being gradually produced to a point. I have only seen one specimen of this sex, taken in Bhutan on 2nd May, 1892, and now in the collection of Mr. G. C. Dudgeon.

230. CHARAXES (Eulepis) EUDAMIPPUS, Doubleday.

A much commoner species in Sikhim in the spring than *C. dolon*, Westwood. Occurs from April to August according to Otto Möller. Found at low elevations only. The female has the anterior tail of the hindwing widest at its end, where it is obliquely truncated; the male has this tail quite narrow throughout, and ending in a point.

231. CHARAXES (Eulepis) ATHAMAS, Drury.

The commonest species of the genus occurring in Sikhim, and found from April to December from 6,000 feet to the level of the Terai. The larva feeds on a species of plant very like a prickly *Mimosa*. Colonel Swinhoe gives *C. bharata*, Felder, as a distinct species from the Khasi Hills, and places as a synonym *C. arja*, de Nicéville (*nec* Felder). He is altogether in error, and cannot have studied the descriptions of these two species carefully as I did when writing "The Butterflies of India, Burmah and Ceylon." Since the second volume of that work appeared dealing with the genus *Charaxes*, I have visited Vienna, and find that *C. bharata*, Felder, and *C. arja*, Felder, have been correctly identified by me, as proved by an examination of the types in Dr. C. Felder's collection.

232. CHARAXES (Eulepis) ARJA, Felder.

Common at low elevations in Sikhim throughout the year, though less so than *C. athamas*, Drury. It may be known from that species by the discal band of both wings and the subapical spot of the forewing on the upperside being white instead of green. The green colour of *C. athamas* is much brighter in freshly-caught specimens than in old cabinet ones, as it fades very quickly.

233. CHARAXES FABIUS, Fabricius.

A butterfly of the plains, but stragglers have been taken in Sikhim at low elevations from May to July. The larva feeds on the leaves of the tamarind tree.

234. CHARAXES (Haridra) MARMAX, Westwood.

Occurs from April to October at low elevations commonly. The female, as usual in the genus, is much rarer than the male.

235. CHARAXES (Haridra) LUNAWARA, Butler.

Much rarer than *C. marmax*, Westwood; occurs at the same seasons and elevations as that species.

236. CHARAXES (Haridra) ARISTOGITON, Felder.

Occurs with the two preceding species. I have examined the type specimen in Vienna, and find that I have correctly identified the species. I have had no difficulty in discriminating *C. aristogiton*, *C. lunawara*, and *C. marmax*.

237. CHARAXES (Haridra) HIERAX, Felder.

Distinctly rare in Sikhim, and occurs at low elevations only.

238. CHARAXES (Haridra) HIPPONAX, Felder.

Much commoner than *C. hierax*, Felder, with which it is found.

239. CHARAXES (Haridra) JALINDER, Butler.

Recorded by the describer from Darjeeling, but I have not been able to recognise the species from thence with certainly.

240. CHARAXES (Haridra) HINDIA, Butler.

Was originally described from Sikhim.

241. CHARAXES (Haridra) PLEISTOANAX, Felder.

Common in Sikhim throughout the summer months at low elevations. The five last-named species are very doubtfully distinct. The extreme forms can be instantly recognised, but numberless intermediate forms occur which connect the extreme forms together into one continuous chain. In the Khasi Hills even more named forms occur, Colonel Swinhoe citing eight in addition to the three first-named *Haridras* which I believe to be distinct, making eleven tawny *Charaxes* in all from one limited area.

Family LEMONIIDÆ.

Subfamily LIBYTHÆINÆ.

242. LIBYTHEA MYRRHA, Godart.

Found commonly at low elevations throughout the warm months. The first brood appears in June. Occurs also at Moupin in Western China.

243. LIBYTHEA LEPITA, Moore.

Much rarer than *L. myrrha*, Godart, and occurs at similar places and seasons. Found also in Western and Central China and in Japan.

Subfamily NEMEOBIINÆ.

244. ZEMEROS FLEGYAS, Cramer.

Excessively common from 1,000 to 6,000 feet almost throughout the year. The larva feeds on several species of *Mæsa*. It occurs right across China to near Ningpo on the east coast.

245. DODONA DIPŒA, Hewitson.

Common from 6,000 to 10,000 feet, from April to December, in forests.

246. DODONA OUIDA, Moore.

Occurs in Sikhim from 3,000 to 10,000 feet, and is not rare, flying throughout the warm months from March to September. Occurs in Western China.

247. DODONA ADONIRA, Hewitson.

A forest butterfly, found between 5,000 and 9,000 feet, never commonly east of the Tista river. I have caught it in October; it probably flies all through the summer. It is much less rare in Bhutan and Daling.

248. DODONA EGEON, Doubleday and Hewitson.

Recorded by Otto Möller at 1,000 feet in May. Very rare in Sikhim, commoner in Bhutan.

249. DODONA EUGENES, Bates.

Found at the same times and places with the much commoner *D. dipœa*, Hewitson. Mr. Leech has named a local race of this species from Western and Central China, *D. eugenes*, var. *maculosa*.

250. STIBOGES NYMPHIDIA, Butler.

Occurs, but not commonly, in Bhutan in the summer and autumn. As usual with this species, the males seem to be rarer than the females. It is found also in Western China commonly.

251. ABISARA FYLLA, Doubleday and Hewitson.

Occurs commonly at low elevations throughout the warm months. Found also in Western and Central China.

252. ABISARA NEOPHRON, Hewitson.

Met with at low elevations only from March to November.

253. ABISARA CHELA, de Nicéville.

Rarer than *A. neophron*, Hewitson; occurs at the same seasons and elevations, and perhaps at a little higher elevation.

254. ABISARA SUFFUSA, Moore.

Mr. Otto Möller obtained three specimens of this species in the Terai, and Mr. Dudgeon has taken it in Daling in May and September. It is a plains' rather than a hill butterfly.

Family LYCÆNIDÆ.

255. Gerydus boisduvali, Moore.

Not uncommon at low elevations from April to October. When flying it has the appearance of a sombre-coloured geometrid moth.

256. Paragerydus horsfieldi, Moore.

Recorded doubtfully from Sikhim by Elwes. The nearest point to Sikhim that I have received the species is Chittagong. I very much question its occurrence in the Eastern Himalayas.

257. Allotinus drumila, Moore.

Very rare; has been recorded at low elevations from March to May. Mr. Dudgeon has received a good many females from the Leesh river in Daling in March, but no males. Herr J. Röber has proposed the genus *Miletographa* for this species.

258. Allotinus multistrigatus, de Nicéville.

Even rarer than *A. drumila*, Moore, and occurs in the same localities with it. The males are more frequently obtained than the females. Both species occur in the Khasi Hills.

259. Poritia hewitsoni, Moore.

Occurs throughout the year up to 4,000 feet. I have never seen it alive. Mr. J. Gammie tells me that at Mongpoo in the middle of November it can be taken in thousands, both males and females, and occurs from the bottoms of the valleys up to nearly, if not quite, 4,000 feet. It is fond of settling on bamboo leaves, where it exhibits a flash of the most superb blue or green as it opens and shuts its wings.

260. Pithecops hylax, Fabricius.

Not uncommon at low elevations throughout the warm months. Its pupa resembles the face of an ape.

261. Neopithecops zalmora, Butler.

Common at low elevations from May to October.

262. Spalgis epius, Westwood.

Rare in the low villages from May to November. Its larva is carnivorous, and feeds on *Cocci* ("mealy-bugs"); its pupa, like that of *Pthecops*, resembles a monkey's face.

263. Taraka hamada, Druce.

Occurs from the level of the Terai up to 5,000 feet, and flies from April to October. It is not very common. It is found also in Western and Central China and in Sumatra.

264. Megisba malaya, Horsfield.

The tailed form is very common in Sikhim, but I have seen only two specimens from thence of the tailless form. It is a common species in Sikhim throughout the warm months at low elevations.

265. LYCÆNA LEHANA, Moore.

This species was originally described as *Polyommatus lehanus* from Ladak. The Sikhim form was named *Lycæna pheretes*, Hübner, var. *asiatica*, by Elwes. The Himalayan form of *L. pheretes* may be distinct from the European and Central Asian form, but the Ladak and Sikhim forms are practically identical. In Sikhim this species occurs only in the interior at very high elevations.

266. CHILADES LAIUS, Cramer.

Occurs only at the foot of the hills in the Terai, where the larva feeds on the wild citron. It is a common butterfly of the plains. It is highly seasonally dimorphic, the dry-season form being true *C. laius*, the wet-season form is *C. varunana*, Moore.

267. CHILADES TROCHILUS, Freyer.

Found only in the Terai.

268. CYANIRIS MARGINATA, de Nicéville.

A common species at about 7,000 feet elevation. Colonel Swinhoe says that in describing this species I unfortunately omitted to give Mr. Moore the credit for the MS. name he had proposed for it. If Colonel Swinhoe will refer to my original description of this species, he will find that Mr. Moore's MS. name is duly credited to him. It is needless to say that the law of priority has in this, as in all other cases, to be rigidly enforced, more especially in the present instance as there is no dispute about the dates on which the descriptions of this species by Mr. Moore and myself were published. Colonel Swinhoe gives Mr. Moore as the describer of this and some other species, while admitting that Mr. Moore's descriptions have not priority.

269. CYANIRIS ALBOCÆRULEUS, Moore.

Rare everywhere; occurs in Sikhim from 2,000 to 8,000 feet in nearly every month in the year. It is found also in Western China, Japan, and the Loochoo Islands.

270. CYANIRIS TRANSPECTUS, Moore.

A commom species, found from 1,000 to 9,000 feet elevation from April to November.

271. CYANIRIS LATIMARGO, Moore.

Mr. Moore says he has this species from Sikhim; I have so far failed to identify it. Colonel Swinhoe places it as a synonym of *C. transpectus*, Moore.

272. CYANIRIS PUSPA, Horsfield.

One of the commonest species of the genus wherever it is found (it has a very wide range, from Cashmere to Formosa, and occurs probably in all the Malay islands); in Sikhim it flies from the level of the Terai up to 10,000 feet, throughout the warm months.

273. Cyaniris placida, de Nicéville.

Common in Sikhim from 3,000 to 5,000 feet, probably at other elevations, throughout the warm months.

274. Cyaniris jynteana, de Nicéville.

Found from 2,000 to 9,000 feet. It is a common species throughout the year.

275. Cyaniris sikkima, Moore.

Described from Sikhim, but I have failed to recognise it.

276. Cyaniris dilectus, Moore.

A common species from the lower valleys up to 9,000 feet. It is found also in Western and Central China.

277. Zizera maha, Kollar.

Occurs throughout the year from 6,000 feet down to the level of the Terai, and is especially common on tea-garden paths at about 4,000 feet. The following new synonyms may be added to the already extensive synonymy of this species:—*Zizera oriens*, Butler, *Plebeius albocœruleus*, Röber, and *Lycœna opalina* and *L. marginata*, both of Poujade.

278. Zizera lysimon, Hübner.

A butterfly of the plains rather than of the hills. It occurs not uncommonly in the Terai. This little butterfly is found in Europe, Africa, Asia, Australia, and in many islands.

279. Zizera gaika, Trimen.

Occurs only in the Terai.

280. Zizera otis, Fabricius.

Common in the Terai, but stragglers are found at the foot of the hills and in the lower outer valleys. Mr. Leech records this species from Western China and the Loochoo Islands as *Z. sangra*, Moore. The "*Lycœna*" *thibetensis* of Poujade may be added to the synonymy of *Z. otis*.

281. Azanus uranus, Butler.

A rare species which Otto Möller took in the Terai only in July and August.

282. Orthomiella pontis, Elwes.

First discovered by Elwes on the bridge over the Rangbi Jhora, on the road from Darjeeling to Serail, at an elevation of 6,000 feet in May. Mr. J. Gammie informs me that in subsequent years in May it appeared on the Serail road for a few days in thousands. Mr. Leech gives the "*Chilades?*" *sinensis* of Elwes, from Central and Eastern China, as a synonym of *O. pontis*.

283. Lycænesthes emolus, Godart.

Very common at low elevations from March to October.

284. Lycænesthes lycænina, Felder.

Rarer than *L. emolus*, Godart, but found at the same elevation and season. Lieutenant E. Y. Watson has examined the type specimen of *L. lycambes*, Hewitson, which is recorded from Sikhim by Mr. Elwes, and informs me that it is without doubt identical with *L. lycænina*.

285. Niphanda cymbia, de Nicéville.

Common in the low valleys throughout the warm months; the males rarer than the females. The female of the dry-season form has the ground-colour white with a sprinkling of blue scales near the base on the upperside of both wings. This species occurs also in Upper Burmah.

286. Everes argiades, Pallas.

Not very rare at low elevations throughout the warm months.

287. Nacaduba macrophthalma, Felder.

I have seen the type of this species in the Vienna museum, and possess specimens of it from the Nicobar Isles. The type has the whitish lines on the underside much narrower and finer than specimens from India. In Sikhim it is a common species at low elevations throughout the summer months.

288. Nacaduba pavana, Horsfield.

May be known at once from the preceding species by all the whitish lines on the underside of both wings being much narrower. In Sikhim it is a somewhat rare species.

289. Nacaduba hermus, Felder.

N. viola, Moore, is a synonym of this species. It is rare in Sikhim at low elevations, and occurs from May to October.

290. Nacaduba atrata, Horsfield.

A rare species found at low elevations throughout the warmer months. I have recorded *N. prominens*, Moore, from Sikhim, but that species had, I think, better be dropped as a synonym of *N. atrata*, and it is highly probable that "*Lycæna*" *beroë*, Felder, is another synonym.

291. Nacaduba cœlestis, de Nicéville.

Very rare at low elevations only. I have recently received it from Upper Burmah.

292. Nacaduba bhutea, de Nicéville.

Not very rare, and occurs at low elevations, from 1,000 to 4,000 feet elevation, from April to October.

293. Nacaduba noreia, Felder.

I have seen the type of this species in the Vienna museum. It is a female, and was described from Ceylon. It is what I have called the tailless form of *N. ardates*, Moore. *N. noreia* being an older name, *N. ardates* has to be sunk as a synonym. *N. noreia* in both its tailed and tailless forms is very common in Sikhim at low elevations throughout the year.

294. NACADUBA DANA, de Nicéville.
Rare in Sikhim as elsewhere; males have been taken in the Terai and up to 7,000 feet elevation. The female is very rare.

295. JAMIDES BOCHUS, Cramer.
Occurs commonly at low elevations and up to the top of Senchal, 9,000 feet, throughout the rains from May to October. It is found also in Central China.

296. LAMPIDES ELPIS, Godart.
A common species from the level of the Terai to 4,000 feet, and is found even higher. Occurs all through the warm months. It is seasonally dimorphic. The larva feeds on the fruit of the cardamom.

297. LAMPIDES CELENO, Cramer.
This species is better known under its synonymic name of *L. œlianus*, Fabricius. In Sikhim it is found with the last, and occurs equally commonly. It is strongly seasonally dimorphic.

298. CATOCHRYSOPS STRABO, Fabricius.
Occurs from April to November, and from the level of the Terai up to 3,000 feet.

299. CATOCHRYSOPS CNEJUS, Fabricius.
Not so common as *C. strabo*, Fabricius, but occurs at the same times and places. It has been recently discovered in Western China.

300. CATOCHRYSOPS PANDAVA, Horsfield.
Strongly seasonally dimorphic; the wet-season form is true *C. pandava*, the dry-season form is *C. bengalia*, de Nicéville. Occurs at low elevations throughout the year.

301. TARUCUS THEOPHRASTUS, Fabricius.
Otto Möller has taken this species in the Terai only.

302. TARUCUS PLINIUS, Fabricius.
Occurs sparsely at low elevations and in the Terai. It is one of the earliest butterflies to emerge in the spring.

303. CASTALIUS ROSIMON, Fabricius.
Common in the Terai, and stragglers are found in the low valleys and outer hills throughout the year.

304. CASTALIUS ANANDA, de Nicéville.
Rare at low elevations from March to December. It is found as south as Sumatra.

305. CASTALIUS ELNA, Hewitson.

Common up to 4,000 or 5,000 feet from April to October. It is seasonally dimorphic, but the different forms have not been named. Mr. Elwes records *C. roxus*, Godart, from Sikhim, but it does not, I believe, occur further north than Burmah.

306. CASTALIUS DECIDIA, Hewitson.

Common at low elevations from April to October. It is seasonally dimorphic, the rains'-form being *C. hamatus*, Moore, an intermediate form is the true *C. decidia*, the dry-season form is *C. interruptus*, de Nicéville.

307. POLYOMMATUS BŒTICUS, Linnæus.

Found in Sikhim from the level of the Terai up to 10,000 feet, but never very commonly at the higher elevations.

308. AMBLYPODIA ANITA, Hewitson.

Mr. Elwes records a single specimen from Sikhim. It not at all improbably occurs in the Terai, but is not likely to be found in the hills.

309. IRAOTA TIMOLEON, Stoll.

Mr. Otto Möller obtained three males and six females of this species at low elevations and in the Terai, some taken in July, but it is a very rare species in Sikhim.

310. IRAOTA MÆCENAS, Fabricius.

Mr. Otto Möller had only three female specimens in his collection, all from the Terai, taken in April, November, and December, so it must be even rarer than *I. timoleon*, Stoll, from which as a species it is very doubtfully distinct, in which opinion Mr. Dudgeon concurs. He has received numerous specimens of both species taken together in Daling, all in May, and has seen the males flying round India-rubber and other trees of the genus *Ficus* at 1,500 feet.

311. SURENDRA QUERCETORUM, Moore.

Almost throughout the year, at low elevations. Both sexes common, but the female commoner than the male. The larva feeds on different species of *Acacia*.

312. ARRHOPALA CENTAURUS, Fabricius.

The local race of this species found in Sikhim, Bhutan, and Assam has been named *A. pirithous* by Mr. Moore. It is a very common species at low elevations in Sikhim, and occurs nearly all the year round. The larva feeds on the young leaves of the sál tree, and is carefully attended by the large and fierce red tree ant, *Œcophylla smaragdina*, Fabricius.

313. ARRHOPALA SILHETENSIS, Hewitson.

Excessively rare. I possess a single male example from Jalpaiguri, obtained by Mr. A. V. Knyvett and kindly given to me. The species is probably a straggler at Jalpaiguri, its head-quarters being almost certainly in the rich Terai forest at the foot of the hills.

314. ARRHOPALA ARAMA, de Nicéville.

I have a single male of this species from Sikhim in my collection, but do not know when it was captured or the exact locality. Major C. T. Bingham took a second specimen in May on the road from Kalimpong to Padong at 4,700 feet. Mr. Dudgeon possesses a single female taken at a low elevation in September. It must be very rare in the Eastern Himalayas, and is found also in Burmah.

315. ARRHOPALA AMANTES, Hewitson.

Occurs not uncommonly in the Terai and low on the hills.

316. ARRHOPALA ABSEUS, Hewitson.

Common up to 9,000 feet, and flies from June to December. The larva feeds on the leaves of the sál tree, and is attended by the ant, *Œcophylla smaragdina*, Fabricius.

317. ARRHOPALA ŒNEA, Hewitson.

A rare species in Sikhim; has been recorded from low elevations from October to December and again in February.

318. ARRHOPALA ATRAX, Hewitson.

A true plains' species, but occurs in the Sikhim Terai and low valleys up to 3,000 feet, from April to October.

319. ARRHOPALA SINGLA, de Nicéville.

A very rare species in Sikhim and found from 1,500 up to 5,000 feet in May and June. It seems not quite so scarce to the east of the Tista river, and has been taken in Upper Burmah.

320. ARRHOPALA TEESTA, de Nicéville.

Very similar to, though quite distinct from, *A. singla*, de Nicéville, and is much the more common species of the two in Sikhim, and occurs with it at low elevations. This species may be the same as *A. turbata*, Butler, described from Nikko in Japan, but I have not been able to compare males of the two species. *A. teesta* has a wide range, being found not only in Sikhim, Assam, and Burmah, but also in Sumatra and Java.

321. ARRHOPALA RAMA, Kollar.

Occurs in Sikhim at low elevations from April to October, and is rather rare. It is found also at Kiukiang in Central China.

322. ARRHOPALA ASOKA, de Nicéville.

A common species at low elevations from June to October.

323. ARRHOPALA ADRIANA, de Nicéville.

Occurs at the same elevations and seasons as *A. asoka*, de Nicéville, and is even more common. It is found also in the Chin-Lushai Hills.

324. Arrhopala fulgida, Hewitson.

Somewhat common from the level of the Terai up to 4,000 feet throughout the rains. I have taken it in the forest below Barnesbeg on the Lebong spur at about 3,000 feet elevation in October.

325. Arrhopala camdeo, Moore.

In Sikhim this species occurs only, as far as I am aware, in the Terai at the foot of the hills in July and August and as far south as Jalpaiguri. It is common at Sivoke in May. It is found also in Assam and Upper Burmah.

326. Arrhopala eumolphus, Cramer.

Rather common at low elevations from March to December. The female of this species is the *A. bupola* of Hewitson, recorded by Elwes from Sikhim as a separate species. *A. bazalus*, Hewitson, recorded by the writer from Sikhim, does not occur west of Assam. The specimens so recorded were wrongly identified.

327. Arrhopala moelleri, de Nicéville.

Never common; occurs in the rains from June to October at low elevations.

328. Arrhopala paramuta, de Nicéville.

Rather common at low elevations from April to October.

329. Arrhopala perimuta, Moore.

Very rare; found only in the low valleys from June to October.

330. Arrhopala areste, Hewitson.

Rare; has been taken at low elevations in February, and from July to November.

331. Arrhopala (Acesina) paraganesa, de Nicéville.

Rare; I have taken it at about 3,000 feet elevation. It flies in April, May, and October.

332. Curetis bulis, Doubleday and Hewitson.

Extremely common in Sikhim at low elevations at all seasons of the year, and as variable as common. The females in Sikhim appear to be always white (not ochreous) on the upperside. *C. discalis*, Moore, was described from Darjeeling, but is not separable from *C. bulis*. Mr. Elwes records *C. thetis*, Drury, from Sikhim, but I have never seen typical specimens of that species from thence.

333. Listeria dudgeonii, de Nicéville.

The type specimen is unique, and was captured at 2,500 feet elevation in Bhutan.

334. Zephyrus zoa, de Nicéville.

Described from a single example taken on Tiger Hill, above Darjeeling, at 8,000 feet elevation, in June. As no second specimen has been procured since the type was caught, I think it more than probable that it is an aberration or "sport" only of the next species.

335. Zephyrus duma, Hewitson.

Occurs in forests at 6,000 to 8,000 feet from June to August. The male is rather common, the female very rare.

336. Zephyrus ataxus, Doubleday and Hewitson.

Mr. Moore has recorded this species from Darjeeling, but I have never seen a specimen from thence. It occurs in the Western Himalayas and Western China, and is very rare there.

337. Zephyrus syla, Kollar.

Very rare in Sikhim (common in the Western Himalayas), and occurs from 8,000 to 10,000 feet elevation in the rains.

338. Zephyrus pavo, de Nicéville.

Excessively rare. I described the species from a single example taken near Buxa in Bhutan. Mr. W. Doherty obtained another specimen at Margherita in Upper Assam.

339. Chrysophanus phlæas, Linnæus.

Recorded by Mr. Moore from Darjeeling (which is certainly incorrect) and Bhutan. It is not improbable that this species does occur at high elevations in the interior, but, of recent years at any rate, no collector has caught it in Sikhim, Bhutan, or Western China.

340. Ilerda sena, Kollar.

Recorded by Mr. Moore from Darjeeling, but this is surely an error. It may perhaps occur in the interior of native Sikhim. It is a very common species in the Western Himalayas.

341. Ilerda epicles, Godart.

The commonest species of the genus in Sikhim, and found throughout the year at low elevations. The "*Thecla*" *phœnicoparyphus* of Holland, described from Hainan island off the China coast, is, as it deserves to be from the portentous length of its name, a synonym of this species. It occurs in Western China also.

342. Ilerda moorei, Hewitson.

Occurs at considerable elevations in native Sikhim, and has been recorded also from Bhutan under the name of *I. tamu*, Kollar.

343. Ilerda androcles, Doubleday and Hewitson.

Recorded by Mr. Moore from Darjeeling, but I think incorrectly. It is found in the Western Himalayas from Cashmere to Kumaon, and again in the Khasi Hills.

344. Ilerda viridipunctata, de Nicéville.

This species is confined in India (as far as I know) to Kumaon and Sikhim. It has been recorded in error from Sikhim by Mr. Elwes as

I. androcles, Doubleday and Hewitson. It is a common species from 6,000 to 9,000 feet, and flies throughout the warm months and as late as December. It is found also in Western China.

345. Ilerda brahma, Moore.

This is, in my opinion, one of the most lovely butterflies in the world, and the colouring of the upperside of the male is unique. Luckily in Sikhim it is a common species, especially so at an elevation of about 4,000 feet, but it is found from 3,000 to 6,000 feet, and from February to December. It occurs also in Kumaon, the Naga Hills, and at Bernardmyo and Momeit in Upper Burmah, and again in Western China.

346. Camena cippus, Fabricius.

Mr. Dudgeon has two males from Daling taken in August, and it has been found near Buxa in Bhutan. Recently Messrs. E. H. Aitken and J. Davidson have taken it quite commonly at Karwar, North Kanara, in the Bombay Presidency. Lieutenant E. Stokes Roberts, R.E., has taken it at Kolar in the Nilgiri hills in November. I have caught it in North-East Sumatra. It has been recorded from Borneo. It is an erratic species and appears in the most unexpected places.

347. Camena ctesia, Hewitson.

The males are quite common at low elevations from April to October. Mr. Elwes has figured a female taken as high as 6,000 feet. I possess another from the Khasi Hills received from the Revd. Walter A. Hamilton, which are the only specimens of that sex known to me. It is also found in Western China.

348. Camena deva, Moore.

Rare in Sikhim. Mr. Otto Möller possessed three males and four females taken in August and November. The male is found in the Terai and low valleys, but the female occurs rather plentifully on Rissoom in Daling at 6,000 feet.

349. Camena icetas, Hewitson.

Mr. A. V. Knyvett obtained three male specimens of this species near Darjeeling, and Mr. Dudgeon has two males from Rhenok, Sikhim, 6,000 feet, taken in May. It is common in the Western Himalayas, and is found in Upper Burmah, and in Western and Central China also. The *Iolaus contractus* of Leech is a synonym of this species.

350. Camena cotys, Hewitson.

Rare in Sikhim, and has been taken in the Rungeet Valley in May and August.

351. Maneca bhotea, Moore.

Very rare; has been taken on the Observatory Hill, 7,500 feet, in the station of Darjeeling, by Mr. A. V. Knyvett in May. It occurs also at Senchal in the same month.

352. MOTA MASSYLA, Hewitson.

Mr. Otto Möller obtained one female from Bhutan in May; in the Khasi Hills it has been obtained in fair numbers by Mr. Hamilton's native collectors. It occurs also in Upper Burmah.

353. APHNÆUS SYAMA, Horsfield.

Very common at low elevations throughout the year. Found in Western and Central China.

354. APHNÆUS LOHITA, Horsfield.

Quite as common as *A. syama*, Horsfield, occurring at the same places and seasons. Mr. Elwes records this species from Sikhim under its synonymic name, *A. himalayanus*, Moore. It is found also in Western and Central China.

355. APHNÆUS ICTIS, Hewitson.

Mr. Elwes records this species from Sikhim under the name of *A. elima*, Moore. As I do not consider that species to differ from *A. ictis*, I have used the latter name, as it is the older. *A. lunulifera*, Moore, was described from Darjeeling. I do not consider it to be specifically distinct from *A. ictis*. *A. ictis* is a fairly common species in Sikhim, occurring at low elevations.

356. APHNÆUS RUKMA, de Nicéville.

The type of this species still remains unique.

357. APHNÆUS NIPALICUS, Moore.

Described by Mr. Moore from Nepal and Sikhim, but unknown to me.

358. APHNÆUS SANI, de Nicéville.

Occurs rarely in Sikhim and Bhutan, and flies in April, May, July, and October.

359. APHNÆUS RUKMINI, de Nicéville.

Rare in Sikhim, where it has been taken in May.

360. TAJURIA INDRA, Moore.

Recorded by Elwes from Sikhim as "*Sithon*" *jalindra*, Horsfield, described from Java, which is the parent species. *T. indra* is rare in Sikhim, and occurs at low elevations from September to November.

361. TAJURIA MACULATUS, Hewitson.

Very rare, and occurs in May and June. It has never been taken in Sikhim except by native collectors. Mr. Harold S. Ferguson records it from the hills of Travancore, at Ponmudi, 1,000 feet. Occurs also at Sibsagar in Upper Assam, and in the Khasi Hills. It is not uncommon to the east of the Tista at 1,500 and again at 6,000 feet in May, where the varietal form figured in "The Butterflies of India, Burmah and Ceylon" is also fairly plentiful.

362. Tajuria illurgis, Hewitson.

Very rare. Occurs in Mussoorie, Sikhim (July, 5,000 feet), Bhutan (September), and in the Shan States and North Chin Hills.

363. Tajuria illurgioïdes, de Nicéville.

Recorded from Naini Tal in Kumaon; Kurseong near Darjeeling; and Senchal, near Darjeeling, 8,000 feet, August. Mr. Dudgeon has a male from Labah in Daling taken in April, and another from Bhutan in June. It is found from 5,000 to 8,000 feet. I possess one female from Upper Burmah. These localities are all that are known to me for the occurrence of this rare species.

364. Tajuria longinus, Fabricius.

Mr. Otto Möller obtained a few specimens in the Terai at the foot of the hills in July and September. It is a common species in the plains of India.

365. Tajuria diæus, Hewitson.

Extremely rare; has been taken in Sikhim in June, and in Bhutan in September.

366. Tajuria thyia, de Nicéville.

Mr. F. A. Möller obtained a single specimen of this species in Sikhim, and Mr. Dudgeon another from Daling taken in April. It was originally described from the Khasi Hills. The *T. luculentus* of Leech, from Central China, is a closely allied species.

367. Tajuria albiplaga, de Nicéville.

Described from two males and three females in Mr. Otto Möller's collection, which are all that are known to me.

368. Tajuria melastigma, de Nicéville.

Mr. Otto Möller had three males of this species in his collection, one taken in March.

369. Tajuria jangala, Horsfield.

The males of this species occur very commonly from April to October in the beds of streams running along the low valleys. The female is much rarer.

370. Tajuria istroidea, de Nicéville.

An excessively rare species, which was described from a single pair in Mr. Otto Möller's collection, the male captured in December. Mr. Dudgeon possesses a specimen from Bhutan taken in March.

371. Hypolycæna erylus, Godart.

A very common species at low elevations throughout the warm months.

372. Chliaria othona, Hewitson.

The males are common at low elevations from March to October; the female is much rarer. The larva feeds on orchids.

373. Chliaria kina, Hewitson.

Less common than *C. othona*, Hewitson, and has a much more restricted range in India. It is found in the low valleys up to about 3,000 feet, and from March to November. One form of the female is white.

374. Zeltus etolus, Fabricius.

Occurs commonly near water throughout the warm months at low elevations.

375. Charana mandarinus, Hewitson.

Very rare in Sikhim in May, September, and October. I have taken it on the Singla flat, at about 1,500 elevation, in October. It occurs also in the Terai and at Jalpaiguri, in Bhutan and in Assam. This species, like many of the genera *Camena* and *Tajuria*, is found at low elevations (1,500 feet), and again at from 5,000 to 6,000 feet, never being found in the intermediate zones.

376. Neocheritra fabronia, Hewitson.

Mr. G. C. Dudgeon obtained a male in the Tista Valley in October, and a female from Sivoke in May. These are the only known specimens of the species obtained in Sikhim.

377. Cheritrella truncipennis, de Nicéville.

Very rare in Sikhim, where it has been taken at low elevations in June. It is found also in the Khasi and Karen Hills.

378. Ticherra acte, Moore.

Probably found in every month in the year at low elevations. It is markedly seasonally dimorphic.

379. Ticherra symira, Hewitson.

The type specimen of this species, described from Sikhim, is the only one known. It is probably an aberration or "sport" of *T. acte*, Moore.

380. Cheritra freja, Fabricius.

Not uncommon in Bhutan; has not so far been recorded from Sikhim except by Mr. Elwes, but probably in error.

381. Horaga onyx, Moore.

Common at low elevations from April to October. It is seasonally dimorphic.

382. Horaga sikkima, Moore.

Much rarer than *H. onyx*, Moore. In Sikhim it has been taken at low elevations from July to October. It occurs in Bhutan and in the Khasi and North Chin Hills also.

383. Horaga viola, Moore.

The rarest species of the genus occurring in Sikhim. It is found at low elevations.

384. Catapœcilma elegans, Druce.
Common in the low valleys and up to 3,000 feet, and has been taken in March, April, and October.

385. Catapœcilma delicatum, de Nicéville.
Occurs only in Sikhim, and is very rare. It has been taken in April and May.

386. Biduanda melisa, Hewitson.
Originally described from Darjeeling and Maulmain. Mr. G. C. Dudgeon obtained a female in August in Bhutan. It has the costal margin of the hindwing on the upperside broadly orange-coloured like the male.

387. Biduanda cyara, Hewitson.
First described from Darjeeling and awaits rediscovery, as the type specimen is probably unique.

388. Loxura atymnus, Cramer.
Common almost throughout the year in the low valleys, and is found as high as 5,000 feet.

389. Yasoda tripunctata, Hewitson.
Occurs from the Terai up to 3,000 feet, from April to November. It is much rarer than *Loxura atymnus*, Cramer, and only comes to hand singly. Like that species it is seasonally dimorphic.

390. Lehera eryx, Linnæus.
Rare; the native collectors bring in a specimen now and again. It probably occurs at low elevations only.

391. Araotes lapithis, Moore.
I possess a single male from the late L. Mandelli's collection which probably came from Sikhim.

392. Deudorix epijarbas, Moore.
Occurs commonly at low elevations throughout the year. The larva feeds on the fruit of the pomegranate and horse-chestnut.

393. Zinaspa distorta, de Nicéville.
A very rare species, the male the rarer of the two sexes. It has been taken in Sikhim in March, May, July, and August at low elevations. It is also found in Western China.

394. Rapala tara, de Nicéville.
Mr. G. C. Dudgeon took a single specimen of this species in Bhutan at 1,500 feet in April; it is common in the Khasi Hills.

395. Rapala buxaria, de Nicéville.
Has been taken at Tonglo, Sikhim, at 10,000 feet, and elsewhere. Its range is probably from 4,000 feet upwards; it certainly

occurs at 5,000 feet. Also found in Bhutan in April, and in the Khasi Hills.

396. RAPALA SCHISTACEA, Moore.

Occurs in Sikhim at low elevations in April, June, and October, and also in Bhutan.

397. RAPALA SCINTILLA, de Nicéville.

Rare in Sikhim; occurs with *R. schistacea*, Moore.

398. RAPALA ORSEIS, Hewitson.

Common in Sikhim at low elevations from April to November.

399. RAPALA ROSACEA, de Nicéville.

Occurs rarely in Sikhim at elevations from 4,000 feet down to the level of the Terai, in March. It is found in the Khasi Hills also.

400. RAPALA NISSA, Kollar.

Occurs rather plentifully at low elevations in all but the four coldest months. It is found in Western and Central China, and has been named *R. subpurpurea* by Leech.

401. RAPALA PETOSIRIS, Hewitson.

Occurs almost throughout the year commonly at low elevations, the males assembling in little groups on the wet sandy margins of the streams to suck up the moisture. It is found in Siam and Java.

402. RAPALA JARBAS, Fabricius.

Common at low elevations all the summer and autumn.

403. BINDAHARA PHOCIDES, Fabricius.

Mr. Elwes took a single male of this species in Sikhim in July; Mr. Otto Möller possessed one male from Sikhim and another from near Buxa in Bhutan; and Mr. Dudgeon has a male from the Leesh river in Daling; these are all the specimens from the Eastern Himalayas known to me. Mr. W. H. Miskin has expressed the opinion that *B. phocides*, Fabricius, *B. sugriva*, Horsfield, *B. isabella*, Felder, and *B. jolcus*, Felder, "all represent one rather variable species." At present I am not prepared to accept this proposition, the three species admitted by me from the Indian region being quite distinct.

404. VIRACHOLA ISOCRATES, Fabricius.

Has been recorded by Mr. Moore from Darjeeling, but I have seen no specimens from thence.

405. VIRACHOLA PERSE, Hewitson.

I have a record of the appearance of the imago in Sikhim in January, February, March, May, October, November, and December. It probably flies throughout the year. Möller records it from the level of the Terai up to 9,000 feet.

406. SINTHUSA NASAKA, Horsfield.

Occurs from the level of the Terai up to 5,000 feet, from March to October, but is not common.

407. SINTHUSA CHANDRANA, Moore.

Rather common, but very local in Sikhim up to 5,000 feet, from March to October. It is found in Central China and at Foochau, and has been named "*Thecla*" *pratti* by Leech.

408. SINTHUSA VIRGO, Elwes.

Extremely rare. Mr. A. V. Knyvett has taken the male on Observatory Hill, 7,500 feet, in Darjeeling, in June; Mr. H. J. Elwes took a single female in May near the Rungbi bridge, at 6,000 feet.

409. LIPHYRA BRASSOLIS, Westwood.

One of the rarest of the Sikhim butterflies. Mr. Otto Möller's Lepcha collectors have brought in two or three specimens, but nothing definite is known as to the exact locality of capture. They have been taken in the height of the rains, in July and August. Mr. Dudgeon has it from Sivoke taken in April.

Family PAPILIONIDÆ.

Subfamily PIERINÆ.*

410. LEPTOSIA XIPHIA, Fabricius.

Occurs only at the lower elevations, where it flies from April to October.

411. DELIAS PYRAMUS, Wallace.

Common at low elevations from April to December.

412. DELIAS AGLAIA, Linnæus.

More commonly known as *D. pasithoë*, Linnæus. It occurs in the low hot valleys commonly throughout the year, except perhaps in the two coldest months.

413. DELIAS BELLADONNA, Fabricius.

Occurs from 1,000 to 11,000 feet in Sikhim, and flies all through the warm months. Heinrich Ritter von Mitis, who has recently monographed this genus, in addition to the parent form, true *D. belladonna*, gives seven "vars." of it. Of these, var. *a*, *ithiela*, Butler; and var. *g*, *amarantha*, Mitis, he records from Sikhim. Mr. H. J. Elwes includes var. *c*, *horsfieldii*, Gray. Von Mitis omits to

* There may hereafter be some rather considerable changes in the names of the *Pierinæ* from Sikhim when I have worked up the synonymy of the various species for the fourth volume of "The Butterflies of India, Burmah and Ceylon."

mention altogether *D. hearseyi* and *D. boyleæ*, both of Butler, the latter described from Darjeeling.

414. DELIAS SANACA, Moore.

Recorded from Darjeeling by Mr. Moore, but as far as I know confined wholly to the Western Himalayas. Some years it is common in Mussoorie, usually it is very rare, and often not seen at all. It is found in Western and Central China.

415. DELIAS DESCOMBESI, Boisduval.

Common from 1,000 to 3,000 feet elevation from March to December. It is an early riser, and commences to fly soon after sunrise.

416. DELIAS EUCHARIS, Drury.

Occurs very rarely at low elevations from April to October. It is a very common butterfly of the plains.

417. DELIAS HIERTE, Hübner.

Von Mitis records the parent form from Sikhim, and var. *c*, *indica*, Wallace (usually given as from Sikhim) from Burmah, Siam, Cochin China, and Malacca. It is a rare species in Sikhim, and occurs only in the low valleys and outer slopes of the hills.

418. DELIAS AGOSTINA, Hewitson.

Rather rare in the lower valleys from March to December.

419. PRIONERIS THESTYLIS, Doubleday.

A common species at elevations below 5,000 feet all through the warm weather. The females are very rare. It is strongly affected by the seasons; the dry-season form found early in the year has been named *P. watsonii* by Hewitson.

420. PRIONERIS CLEMANTHE, Doubleday.

Quite rare in Sikhim, and occurs from April to October at low elevations. In many years collecting, Mr. Otto Möller obtained two females only.

421. CATOPSILIA CROCALE, Cramer.

In India, Burmah and Ceylon two species of the genus alone occur according to my judgment, though Mr. Moore allows six from Ceylon alone, and Colonel Swinhoe would add still two more from India, *C. thisorella*, Boisduval, and *C. heera*, Swinhoe. *C. crocale* is the larger species of the two and the more common. It is not, I think, seasonally dimorphic, the innumerable varieties which are found in both sexes occurring at all times. In Sikhim it is a common species at low elevations almost throughout the year.

422. CATOPSILIA PYRANTHE, Linnæus.

This is the smaller and rarer of the two species. It is found at low elevations in Sikhim throughout the warm months. It may be seasonally dimorphic, the dry-season form being *C. gnoma*, Fabricius, the wet-season form being *C. chryseis*, Drury. Both forms are found in Sikhim with true *C. pyranthe*, which appears to be an intermediate form.

423. TERIAS HECABE, Linnæus.

Common in Sikhim as elsewhere, and flies all the year round at low elevations. Mr. Elwes records it from Tonglo, 10,000 feet, but it is only stragglers that extend their flights to so great an elevation.

424. TERIAS KANA, Moore.

A common species in Sikhim.

425. TERIAS SILHETANA, Wallace.

Lieutenant E. Y. Watson has recently shown that this species may be known by having three dark streaks or spots in the discoidal cell of the forewing on the underside in addition to the reniform spot defining the disco-cellular nervules, while *T. hecabe* never has more than two streaks or spots in addition to the reniform one. It also is a common species in Sikhim.

426. TERIAS LÆTA, Boisduval.

Rare in Sikhim, recorded from 7,000 to 9,000 feet from July to September.

427. TERIAS RAMA, Moore.

Also rare; occurs from 2,000 to 9,000 feet. This is probably the species which is recorded by Elwes as *T. venata*, Moore.

428. TERIAS LIBYTHEA, Fabricius.

Found at the foot of the hills only and is rare almost throughout tho year. It is recorded by Elwes under its synonymic name of *T. rubella*, Wallace.

429. TERIAS HARINA, Horsfield.

Occurs at low elevations only and is never common. Flies from April to December.

430. COLIAS FIELDII, Ménétriés.

Rare in Darjeeling itself, far more common in the interior at high elevations. It is found from 5,000 to 12,000 feet, and flies throughout the warm months according to the elevation. At the lowest elevation it is found almost throughout the cold weather. Occurs also in Western and Central China.

431. DERCAS VERHUELLII, van der Hoeven.

Local, but where it occurs abundant. Found at about 4,000 feet from May to October.

432. DERCAS WALLICHII, Doubleday.

Mr. Elwes records a single specimen from the interior. It is a common species in the Khasi Hills and in Western and Central China.

433. Gonepteryx nepalensis, Doubleday.

Mr. Moore records this species from Darjeeling, but I have not seen any specimens from thence. It is probably the same as the European "Brimstone Butterfly," *G. rhamni*, Linnæus.

434. Aporia soracta, Moore.

Recorded from Darjeeling by Mr. Moore, but confined as far as I am aware to the Western Himalayas.

435. Metaporia agathon, Gray.

Mr. Elwes records a single specimen obtained in 1883 by native collectors from the interior towards Bhutan, from whence Mr. Moore recorded it in 1857. In 1892 Mr. F. A. Möller received a single male from his Lepcha collectors, probably from the same locality.

436. Metaporia harrietæ, de Nicéville.

A single pair was obtained by Mr. F. A. Möller's collectors with the specimen of *M. agathon*, Gray, mentioned above.

437. Mancipium dubernardi, Oberthür.

Eight or nine males were obtained on the Tibet frontier by a native employed by Captain Harman, R.E. I have not seen the species, and of recent years it does not seem to have been obtained.

438. Mancipium canidia, Sparrman.

The "Small Cabbage White" of India. Flies throughout the year from 3,000 to 12,000 feet.

439. Mancipium brassicæ, Linnæus.

The "Large Cabbage White." Flies from March to December, and from 1,000 to 12,000 feet. The Eastern Himalayan form has been named "*Pieris*" *nepalensis* by Gray.

440. Mancipium melete, Ménétriés.

The "Green-veined White" of India. Occurs only in the interior, and is very rare.

441. Belenois mesentina, Cramer.

A common butterfly of the plains, rare in the hills. Occurs from April to October, and from 3,000 feet to the level of the Terai.

442. Huphina phryne, Fabricius.

A common species in the low valleys and up to 5,000 feet. It is subject to very great seasonal variability; the form flying in the spring is small and very pale, that in the rains is very large, dark, and richly-coloured.

443. Huphina nadina, Lucas.

Perhaps better known as *H. nama*, Moore. It is common at low elevations from March to December. The spring or dry-season form has been named *amba* by Wallace, and is much smaller and paler than the rains' form, having the underside pale greyish-brown instead of rich green.

444. CATOPHAGA PAULINA, Cramer.
Rare in Sikhim, where it occurs sporadically from April to October. It is found also in Western China.

445. APPIAS HIPPOÏDES, Moore.
One of the commonest butterflies at low elevations in Sikhim, and flies from March to December.

446. APPIAS VACANS, Butler.
Described from Darjeeling, but very doubtfully distinct from *A. hippoïdes*, Moore.

447. APPIAS LIBYTHEA, Fabricius.
Occurs rather rarely at 2,000 feet in May.

448. APPIAS NERO, Fabricius.
The Indian form of this wide-ranging species has been named *A. galba* by Wallace, but it seems to be barely distinct from the parent form. It is a mere straggler in Northern India. Mr. Otto Möller obtained one specimen from Sikhim, Mr. Wood-Mason obtained one in Cachar, and the Rev. Walter A. Hamilton a few in the Khasi Hills. It is fairly common in Upper Burmah. Messrs. Grose Smith and Kirby have recently described *A. nebo* from Upper Burmah, which is probably nothing but a dry-season form of *A. nero*.

449. HIPOSCRITIA LALAGE, Doubleday.
Occurs from the level of the Terai to over 10,000 feet, and flies from April to October. The females seem to be found chiefly at high elevations. This is also the case with *Delias belladonna*, Fabricius, and *Prioneris thestylis*, Doubleday.

450. HIPOSCRITIA PSEUDOLALAGE, Moore.
This species was described from Sikhim, but I know nothing regarding it. Colonel Swinhoe records it from the Khasi Hills. It is very doubtfully distinct.

451. HIPOSCRITIA INDRA, Moore.
The males are common at low elevations from April to October, the female, as usual in this genus, is excessively rare.

452. HIPOSCRITIA MAHANA, Moore.
I know nothing of this species, which was described from Darjeeling, and recorded from the Khasi Hills by Colonel Swinhoe. It is said to be allied to *H. indra*, Moore. It is possibly a seasonal form only of that species.

453. NEPHERONIA HIPPIA, Fabricius.

A true butterfly of the plains, occurring rarely in the Terai and in the low outer valleys.

454. NEPHERONIA AVATAR, Moore.

This very beautiful and distinct species occurs from 1,000 to 5,000 feet from April to November, and is not rare.

455. HEBOMOIA GLAUCIPPE, Linnæus.

Common from March to November from the Terai up to 5,000 feet.

456. IXIAS PYRENE, Linnæus.

Common throughout the warm months from 1,000 to 5,000 feet elevation. It is highly seasonally variable; the males of the dry-season forms flying early in the year are quite small and very lightly marked with black; the form flying in the rains is half as large again, and is very richly coloured, with a heavy black border to the hindwing.

Subfamily PAPILIONINÆ.

457. TEINOPALPUS IMPERIALIS, Hope.

In Sikhim this fine butterfly is known to occur on the tops of Birch Hill, Tiger Hill (Senchal), Tonglo, Tendong, and Rikisum, flying from April to August. It is found also in the Khasi and Naga Hills, and at Chang-yang in Central China. The female is far rarer than the male.

458. ORNITHOPTERA RHADAMANTHUS, Boisduval.

Common in the low valleys from May to October. It is found also in Western and Central China.

459. ORNITHOPTERA POMPEUS, Cramer.

Still more common than the preceding, occurring with it and at the same time of the year. The North Indian form has been described as a distinct species by Felder as *O. cerberus*, but cannot, I think, be separated from the typical form, which was described from Batavia in Java.

460. PAPILIO (Pangerana) ASTORION, Westwood.

Common from April to December and from the level of the Terai up to 7,000 feet.

461. PAPILIO (Pangerana) AIDONEUS, Doubleday.

Far rarer than *P. astorion*, Westwood, and found up to 3,000 feet, from April to November.

462. PAPILIO (Byasa) RAVANA, Moore.

A single pair of specimens of this species was recorded by Mr. Moore from Darjeeling in 1857. Mr. Elwes also possesses two specimens from old collections ticketed Sikhim. It is a species of the Western Himalayas, and it is very doubtful if it occurs in Sikhim at all.

463. Papilio (? Byasa) plutonius, Oberthür.

Two female examples were obtained in 1884 by native collectors from the interior, perhaps from Bhutan. None have been found since. It is found also in Western China.

464. Papilio (? Byasa) alcinous, Klug.

Recorded by Moore from Bhutan. Mr. Leech gives its distribution as Western and Central China, Corea, Japan, and the Loochoo Islands.

465. Papilio (Byasa) latreillii, Donovan.

Better known as *P. minereus*, Gray. It occurs in the thick, high forests from 7,000 to 9,000 feet, from March to August, and is not common in collections.

466. Papilio (Byasa) dasarada, Moore.

A common species, occurring from 1,000 to 8,000 feet from April till November. The butterfly has a very powerful and disagreeable odour, which is perceptible even years after the death of the insect.

467. Papilio (Byasa) philoxenus, Gray.

Common at the same elevations and times of year as *P. dasarada*, Moore. It occurs also in Siam, Western and Central China.

468. Papilio (Panosmiopsis) rhetenor, Westwood.

Occurs from April to October, and from the level of the Terai up to 6,000 feet. Both sexes are rare, the female, which is tailed, especially so. It is found in Western and Central China.

469. Papilio (Panosmiopsis) janaka, Moore.

Rare, found from 3,000 to 5,000 feet in May and June. Mr. Wood-Mason described this species under the name of *P. sikkimensis*.

470. Papilio (Menelaides) aristolochiæ, Fabricius.

An insect of the plains, but occurs commonly in the lower valleys throughout the warm months. It is widely distributed in China.

471. Papilio (Achillides) paris, Linnæus.

Very common from the Terai up to 5,000 feet, and flies all through the year except during the three coldest months. It is common in Western China.

472. Papilio (Achillides) krishna, Moore.

Occurs from May to August, from 3,000 to 9,000 feet. It is not uncommon on Senchal, and occurs in Western China.

473. Papilio (Achillides) arcturus, Westwood.

Found with *P. krishna*, Moore, and at the same seasons. By no means common in Sikhim. It occurs also in Western and Central China.

474. Papilio (Sarbaria) ganesa, Doubleday.

Occurs throughout the warm months at low elevations, and the male is very common. The female is, however, very rare, as are those of *P. paris*, *R. krishna*, and *P. arcturus*.

475. Papilio (Iliades) agenor, Linnæus.

The Indian form is more generally known as *P. androgeus*, Cramer. The female is polymorphic, but three distinct (though each is more or less variable) forms may be defined; the first is tailless, and is most like the male; the second is also tailless, but has a large white patch on the hindwing; the third is tailed, and is much marked with white spots on the disc of the hindwing. The species has received a vast number of names, but it is more than doubtful if the best of them represent anything but "local races." It is a very common species in Sikhim, and is found from April to December from the Terai to 5,000 feet. The second form of the female is alone rare, the third is the commonest of the three forms.

476. Papilio (Iliades) polymnestor, Cramer.

Mr. Otto Möller obtained a single specimen in Sikhim. It is purely a species of the plains.

477. Papilio (Sainia) protenor, Cramer.

Somewhat rare in Sikhim, and occurs from 2,000 to 5,000 feet throughout the warm months. It is common in China. The female is still rarer, and lacks the patch of modified buff-coloured scales on the costa of the hindwing on the upperside.

478. Papilio (Charus) helenus, Linnæus.

Found throughout the summer commonly at the lower elevations and as high as 6,000 feet. It is probably the commonest *Papilio* occurring in Sikhim. It is found right across China to Japan.

479. Papilio (Charus) chaon, Westwood.

A common species at low elevations from April to October.

480. Papilio (Tamera) castor, Westwood.

Flies from 1,000 to 3,000 feet from April to October, and is less common than *P. chaon*, Westwood, and *P. helenus*, Linnæus.

481. Papilio (Laertias) polytes, Linnæus.

A common species throughout the year, except in the three coldest months, at low elevations. The female is trimorphic; the first form is like the male; the second form mimics *P. aristolochiæ*, Fabricius; and the third form mimics *P. hector*, Linnæus. The latter form is extremely rare in Sikhim, as the butterfly it mimics does not occur there, the second form is the commonest of the three.

482. PAPILIO (Orpheides) ERICHTHONIUS, Cramer.

A butterfly of the plains, found only at low elevations sparingly. Mr. Dudgeon has found its larva at 1,500 feet feeding on wild citron.

483. PAPILIO (Menamopsis) SLATERI, Hewitson.

A single-brooded species, which flies in April and May in the low outer valleys only. It is common at Sivoke.

484. PAPILIO (Menamopsis) EPYCIDES, Hewitson.

Also single-brooded, occurring in April and May at low elevations, especially at Sivoke. It appears to be very local, but is not rare where found in river-beds at 1,000 feet. It occurs also in Bhutan, the Khasi Hills, and Upper Burmah ; also in Western China.

485. PAPILIO (Chilasa) CLYTIA, Linnæus.

Occurs from March to November commonly at low elevations.

486. PAPILIO (Chilasa) PANOPE, Linnæus.

Found with *P. clytia*, Linnæus, at the same elevations and seasons. I have no doubt that these two species are really one species, which is dimorphic in both sexes; but as this theory has never been proved, I have kept them distinct. Mr. Dudgeon has noticed the two species flying together, but has not succeeded in taking the opposite sexes *in copulâ*.

487. PAPILIO (Paranticopsis) MEGARUS, Westwood.

Mr. Elwes records this species from Sikhim on the strength of an old specimen so labelled. Its occurrence there is more than doubtful. It is found not uncommonly in the Khasi Hills and southwards.

488. PAPILIO (Paranticopsis) XENOCLES, Doubleday.

Flies in Sikhim from April to November from the level of the Terai up to about 3,000 feet. The males are fairly common, the females, as usual in the genus, are very rare.

489. PAPILIO (Paranticopsis) MACAREUS, Godart.

Single-brooded and rather rare in Sikhim, occurs in the low outer valleys only from April to June. The Sumatran form has been described as *P. macareus*, var. *xanthosoma* by Dr. Staudinger, the Bornean form as *P. macareus*, var. *macaristus* by Mr. Grose Smith (= *P. macareus*, var. *borneënsis*, Staudinger), and the Palawan form as *P. macareus*, var. *maccabæus*, also by Staudinger. I have figured a very curious aberration of *P. macareus* from Sikhim in the Journal of the Bombay Natural History Society, vol. vii, page 345, n. 18, pl. I, fig. 1, *male* (1892).

490. Papilio (Cadugoïdes) agestor, Gray.

Single-brooded and rather rare, flying from March to May from 5,000 to 7,000 feet. It is a beautiful mimic of *Danais tytia*, Gray, in both sexes. A local race named *restricta* by Leech occurs in Central China.

491. Papilio (Pazala) glycerion, Gray.

Probably single-brooded, and occurs at low elevations in May and June.

492. Papilio (Pathysa) paphus, de Nicéville.

Occurs from 3,000 to 7,000 feet from May to July. It was described by Mr. Charles Oberthür as *P. glycerion*, var. *mandarinus* before my description appeared; but as the species is a perfectly distinct one, and is not a "variety" of *P. glycerion*, that species not occurring in China, I think the name *P. paphus* should stand. It is common in Western China.

493. Papilio (Pathysa) agetes, Westwood.

Probably single-brooded. It occurs in the outer valleys, such as Sivoke, in April and May, and is rare. It occurs to the southwards as far as North-East Sumatra.

494. Papilio (Pathysa) antiphates, Cramer.

According to Mr. Otto Möller this species occurs from April till October in the lower valleys up to 3,000 feet. It is very common.

495. Papilio (Pathysa) anticrates, Doubleday.

Single-brooded, occurs in Sivoke in April and May only, when it is very common. It is also found along the Rungeet road in the same months, but elsewhere it seems scarce.

496. Papilio (Pathysa) nomius, Esper.

A species of the plains. A single straggler was obtained in Sikhim by Mr. Otto Möller.

497. Papilio (Dalchina) cloanthus, Westwood.

Flies from April to October from 2,000 to 4,000 feet. By no means common in Sikhim. A slight local race, *P. cloanthus*, var. *clymenus*, Leech, occurs in Western and Central China.

498. Papilio (Dalchina) sarpedon, Linnæus.

Common throughout the warm months from 1,000 to 7,000 feet elevation.

499. Papilio (Zetides) eurypylus, Linnæus.

Very common in the low valleys from April to October. It is very variable in Sikhim as elsewhere, the forms *P. telephus*, Felder, and *P. mecisteus*, Distant, occurring with the typical form at all seasons.

500. PAPILIO (Zetides) BATHYCLES, Zinken-Sommer.

Rather less common than *P. eurypylus*, Linnæus, but found at the same time and in the same places. It is equally variable and inconstant, these variations having received the names *P. chiron*, Wallace, *P. bathycloïdes*, Honrath, and *P. chironides*, Honrath. It occurs also in Central China.

501. PAPILIO (Zetides) AGAMEMNON, Linnæus.

Common at low elevations throughout the year.

502. PAPILIO (Dabasa) GYAS, Westwood.

Very rare in Sikhim, and occurs from 6,000 to 7,000 feet on Birch Hill, Senchal, and Rikisum, in July and August, but is more common on the Labah ridge in Daling at 7,000 feet. It is found in Western China under the name of *P. hercules*, Blanchard, = *P. sciron*, Leech, which seems to be a good local race.

503. PAPILIO (Meandrusa) EVAN, Doubleday.

Mr. G. C. Dudgeon possesses a male of this species taken at Sivoke on 15th March, 1890. To the eastwards in Bhutan and the Khasi Hills, it becomes somewhat common.

504. PAPILIO MACHAON, Linnæus.

The particular form of this species which occurs only at high elevations in the interior has been named *P. sikkimensis* by Mr. Moore. It flies in July and August.

505. PARNASSIUS HARDWICKII, Gray.

Common on the higher ranges in the interior. It is exceedingly variable; the blackest specimens of the species I have ever seen have come from Sikhim, others again are very light coloured.

506. PARNASSIUS EPAPHUS, Oberthür, var. SIKKIMENSIS, Elwes.

Appears to be excessively rare. Mr. H. J. Elwes took it once near the Donkia Pass, 18,000 feet, in native Sikhim in September, 1870, and in 1881 obtained fourteen specimens through a Bhutea plant collector from the Sikhim-Tibet frontier or in the Chumbi Valley. It does not appear to have been captured since.

507. PARNASSIUS ACCO, Gray.

Mr. H. J. Elwes records a single specimen received at the same time as the fourteen examples of *P. sikkimensis*, Elwes, above-mentioned.

508. ARMANDIA LIDDERDALII, Atkinson.

Both sexes occur not uncommonly during the summer on the top of a hill behind Buxa in Bhutan. Mr. W. Doherty has obtained the species in Assam.

Family HESPERIIDÆ.

509. Orthophœtus lidderdali, Elwes.

Described from a single male in the British Museum, the exact locality from which it came being unknown.

510. Capila jayadeva, Moore.

A rare species, recorded in Sikhim at low elevations from April to October. I possess five males and three females from Sikhim, and one female from the Khasi Hills. There are further specimens in the collection of the Indian Museum, Calcutta.

511. Calliana pieridoïdes, Moore.

I possess a single female example of this very rare species taken near Buxa in Bhutan. It is found also in Western China.

512. Pisola zennara, Moore.

Mr. Otto Möller records this species from the low valleys from April to August. I possess five males and three females, all from Sikhim, one of the former taken in October, but it is a rare species. I mention the number of specimens I possess of *C. jayadeva*, Moore, and *P. zennara*, Moore, as Colonel Swinhoe is desirous of knowing on what material I based my conclusions as to the correct sexing of these two species. I have seen no evidence of the existence of a third species in India in these two genera, as Colonel Swinhoe has suggested, though Lieutenant E. Y. Watson records a second species of the genus *Pisola*, the "*Chætocneme*" *cerinthus* of Felder, from Amboina, which, to judge from the figure, must have been described from a female, as the forewing has a broad oblique white band as have the females of *C. jayadeva* and *P. zennara*. Mr. Leech records *P. zennara* from Western China.

513. Satarupa gopala, Moore.

Rare in Sikhim; found at low elevations only from June to October. It is widely spread. I possess specimens from Assam, Burmah, and Sumatra.

514. Satarupa sambara, Moore.

Very common, and occurs at low elevations throughout the warm months.

515. Daimio bhagava, Moore.

Fairly common; occurs from 1,000 to 3,000 feet from April to October.

516. Daimio narada, Moore.

Rather rare; found at low elevations only throughout the year except in the winter. Mr. Leech has described a local race of this species from Western and Central China as var. *diversa*.

517. Daimio phisara, Moore.
Occurs as high as Mongpoo, 3,500 feet, and is not uncommon at low elevations from April to October.

518. Sarangesa dasahara, Moore.
Very common at low elevations throughout the warm months.

519. Coladenia indrani, Moore.
Common at low elevations throughout the year, but most common in the spring.

520. Coladenia tissa, Moore.
Mr. Otto Möller possessed a single example of this species, probably taken in the Terai. If *C. tissa* is a distinct species, of which I am by no means convinced, it would appear to be the form of *C. indrani*, Moore, occurring in the plains of India.

521. Coladenia dan, Fabricius.
Extremely common from 1,000 to 4,000 feet, from March to November. Mr. Moore records "*Hesperia*" *fatih*, Kollar, from Darjeeling, a Western Himalayan species, but probably *C. dan* is the species meant.

522. Celænorrhinus badia, Hewitson.
Excessively rare. There is one specimen in the Indian Museum, Calcutta, from Sikhim, obtained by Mr. Otto Möller; Mr. H. J. Elwes possesses a single specimen from Sikhim, Mr. G. C. Dudgeon one from Bhutan, taken in June, and the Rev. Walter A. Hamilton has obtained it on one occasion in the Khasi Hills, and has given me three specimens.

523. Celænorrhinus flavocincta, de Nicéville.
Has so far only been procured near Buxa in Bhutan, where it appears to be very rare.

524. Celænorrhinus chamunda, Moore.
Rather rare; recorded up to 4,000 feet from March to November.

525. Celænorrhinus sumitra, Moore.
Originally described from North-East Bengal. I have never been able to recognize it. Mr. Elwes states that he has "only three specimens taken in the forest near Rikisum in British Bhutan, at an elevation of 5,000 to 7,000 feet in August.". Mr. Leech records it from Western China, and figures the male.

526. Celænorrhinus leucocera, Kollar.
The commonest species of the genus in Sikhim as elsewhere, found from 1,000 to 4,000 feet from March to October.

527. CELÆNORRHINUS PULOMAYA, Moore.

Common in the virgin forest zone from 7,000 to 10,000 feet during the rains.

528. CELÆNORRHINUS PYRRHA, de Nicéville.

Found in Bhutan and the Khasi Hills. Nothing is known about its time of flight, as it has only been obtained by native collectors.

529. CELÆNORRHINUS PLAGIFERA, de Nicéville.

Not uncommon in Sikhim and Bhutan.

530. CELÆNORRHINUS PATULA, de Nicéville.

Described from a single pair only from Sikhim.

531. CELÆNORRHINUS FUSCA, Hampson.

Mr. G. C. Dudgeon has obtained a pair of this species in Sikhim, and I possess one female from thence. It was originally described from the Nilgiri Hills.

532. CELÆNORRHINUS NIGRICANS, de Nicéville.

Found at low elevations in Sikhim and Bhutan.

533. CELÆNORRHINUS DHANADA, Moore.

Rare in Sikhim, and found only at low elevations. Occurs in May to the east of the Teesta river.

534. TAGIADES RAVI, Moore.

A butterfly more of the plains than of the hills. Mr. Otto Möller obtained a few specimens of it in the Terai when he was manager of the Mohurgong Tea Estate.

535. TAGIADES GANA, Moore.

Occurs throughout the year at low elevations, but is not very common. The extent of the white area on the upperside of the hindwing is very variable.

536. TAGIADES ATTICUS, Fabricius.

A very variable species and excessively common in Sikhim, where it occurs at low elevations throughout the year. I have bred it; the larva feeds on bamboo. It occurs in Western China.

537. TAGIADES TABRICA, Hewitson.

Originally described from Darjeeling. The type specimen appears to be still unique.

538. TAGIADES PRALAYA, Moore.

Rare; occurs at low elevations during the rains.

539. DARPA HANRIA, Moore.

Rare; occurs at low elevations only in April and May. Found also in the Khasi Hills.

540. Ctenoptilum vasava, Moore.
Rare; found in April and May from 1,000 to 3,000 feet. It occurs also in Central and Eastern China.

541. Tapena agni, de Nicéville.
A rare species in Sikhim. I have taken it at Singla, at about 1,500 feet elevation, in October.

542. Tapena laxmi, de Nicéville.
Originally described from a female example from the Thaungyin forests in middle Tenasserim, Burma. Major J. F. Malcolm Fawcett obtained a single male example at Singla in May, at about 1,500 feet elevation.

543. Odontoptilum sura, Moore.
Common from 1,000 to 3,000 feet from April to October.

544. Caprona syrichthus, Felder.
Mr. Otto Möller obtained a few specimens of this species during the time he lived in the Terai. It does not appear to occur in the hills. Mr. Dudgeon records it from Bhutan at 1,500 feet, in May and July.

545. Hesperia galba, Fabricius.
Also obtained by Mr. Otto Möller during his residence in the Terai. Mr. Dudgeon notes its occurrence on the outer spurs at 1,500 feet.

546. Suastus gremius, Fabricius.
Very common at low elevations throughout the year. The larva feeds on palms, and the female butterfly in Calcutta often enters the houses to lay her eggs on the leaves of the ornamental palms so common in rooms in India.

547. Suastus aditus, Moore.
Very rare in Sikhim, as, indeed, it is everywhere, and is found in the low valleys only during the rains.

548. Suada swerga, de Nicéville.
Rare in the low valleys from June to October. It has a wide range. I possess specimens from Burmah, the Malay Peninsula, Sumatra, and Java.

549. Iambrix salsala, Moore.
Common at low elevations throughout the year.

550. Koruthaialos butleri, Wood-Mason and de Nicéville.
Rare in Sikhim, and found at low elevations probably throughout the year.

551. Aëromachus stigmata, Moore.
Not very rare; occurs from 1,000 to 4,000 feet throughout the warm months.

552. Aëromachus jhora, de Nicéville.
Found in the low valleys and up to 4,000 feet from April to November.

553. Aëromachus kali, de Nicéville.
Somewhat rare, and is found with *A. jhora*, de Nicéville. I have taken both in October in the Jebi Kola jhora close to the turbine house of the Tukvar Tea Estate at about 3,500 feet elevation.

554. Sebastonyma dolopia, Hewitson.
Occurs at low elevations from April to October, and is never very common.

555. Pedestes masuriensis, Moore.
Appears to occur only in native Sikhim from June to August at from 5,000 to 6,000 feet elevation.

556. Pedestes pandita, de Nicéville.
Native collectors bring this species in large numbers with *P. masuriensis*, Moore; the two species appear to fly together. Otto Möller records its occurrence from 2,000 to 3,000 feet elevation.

557. Arnetta atkinsoni, Moore.
A common species, occurring, I believe, at rather high elevations, from 6,000 to 8,000 feet. It is highly affected by the seasons, the dry-season form having been named "*Isoteinon*" *subtestaceus* and "*I.*" *khasianus* by Mr. Moore, the wet-season form being the true *A. atkinsoni*, Moore.

558. Hyarotis adrastus, Cramer.
Occurs from April to October from 4,000 feet to the level of the Terai, and is not rare.

559. Isma cephala, Hewitson.
Common at low elevations from April to October. Colonel Swinhoe has recently described the ordinary male of this variable species from a single example from "Shillong" as *Isma isota*.

560. Zographetus satwa, de Nicéville.
Occurs rather commonly from 1,000 to 3,000 feet from April to October.

561. Zographetus flavipennis, de Nicéville.
Very rare in Sikhim. I once took it at about 1,000 feet elevation in October on the Singla flat. It occurs in Bhutan, Burmah, and the Andamans, and not improbably the *Z. ogygia*, Hewitson, from Sumatra, is the same species, in which case the latter name has priority.

562. Matapa aria, Moore.

Obtained by Mr. Otto Möller in the Terai only. The species seems to be confined to the plains, is very common in Calcutta, and occurs as far south as Ceylon, the Andamans, Sumatra, Nias, and Java.

563. Matapa druna, Moore.

Not common; occurs from 1,000 to 3,000 feet from April to November.

564. Matapa sasivarna, Moore.

Rare; occurs throughout the year at low elevations.

565. Matapa shalgrama, de Nicéville.

Fairly common from 1,000 to 4,000 feet from April to November. Colonel Swinhoe records a specimen of this very local species from the Andaman Isles sent to him by the late Mr. R. Wimberley. *M. aria*, Moore, is very common at Port Blair, but I have never received *M. shalgrama* from thence. As I sent Mr. Wimberley many butterflies from Sikhim in exchange for local species, it is highly probable, I think, that a specimen of *M. shalgrama* from Sikhim became mixed up with his Andamanese butterflies.

566. Erionota thrax, Linnæus.

Brought in at times in considerable numbers from low elevations by the native collectors. Its larva feeds on the plantain, which is cultivated everywhere, and also grows wild in the jungle.

567. Erionota acroleuca, Wood-Mason and de Nicéville.

Very rare. I obtained one example, Mr. Otto Möller two only in Sikhim, after many years' assiduous collecting. It occurs also in Western and Central China, and has been named "*Hidari*" *grandis* by Leech. It has been named by six different writers since 1881.

568. Pudicitia pholus, de Nicéville.

Excessively rare. I possess the pair of type specimens taken near Buxa in Bhutan, and have received one more male from the Khasi Hills, generously presented to me by the Rev. Walter A. Hamilton.

569. Gangara thyrsis, Fabricius.

Rarer than *E. thrax*, Linnæus, found at low elevations only. The larva feeds on palms, especially on the date-palm.

570. Pamphila avanti, de Nicéville.

Described in 1886 from two specimens obtained by native collectors probably at high elevations near the passes, and not seen since.

571. Ochus subvittatus, Moore.

Not uncommon at low elevations from April to October.

572. Taractrocera mævius, Fabricius.

Obtained in the Terai only by Mr. Otto Möller.

573. TARACTROCERA DANNA, Moore.

Recorded by Mr. Moore from Bhutan, but found only in the Western Himalayas as far as I know.

574. AMPITTIA MARO, Fabricius.

Mr. Otto Möller took this species in the Terai only.

575. PADRAONA GOLA, Moore.

Not rare at low elevations throughout the warm months. It is found also in Central China.

576. PADRAONA DARA, Kollar.

Very common throughout the year from 1,000 to 5,000 feet.

577. PADRAONA MÆSOÏDES, Butler.

Occurs at the same times and seasons with the last-mentioned species.

578. TELICOTA AUGIAS, Linnæus.

Very rare in Sikhim. During many years collecting Mr. Otto Möller obtained one or two specimens only.

579. TELICOTA BAMBUSÆ, Moore.

Excessively common in Sikhim, occurring in all the warm months in abundance from 1,000 to 5,000 feet elevation. It is found also in Central China.

580. BAORIS (Chapra) MATHIAS, Fabricius.

Very common from 1,000 to 8,000 feet from March to December. Occurs thoughout China and Japan.

581. BAORIS (Chapra) AGNA, Moore.

Kept by Lieutenant E. Y. Watson distinct from *B. mathias*, Fabricius, and said by him to be the same species as *B. chaya*, Moore. Occurs in Sikhim with *B. mathias*, from which it may be known by its smaller spots in the forewing.

582. BAORIS (Chapra) SINENSIS, Mabille.

Better known as *Chapra prominens*, Moore, and of which *Pamphila similis*, Leech, is a synonym. Not very common. Occurs from 1,000 to 5,000 feet throughout the warm months. It is found also in Western and Central China.

583. BAORIS (Parnara) BADA, Moore.

Lieutenant E. Y. Watson retains this species as distinct from the next. It occurs rarely at low elevations.

584. BAORIS (Parnara) GUTTATUS, Bremer and Grey.

Also found at low elevations throughout the year.

585. BAORIS (Parnara) COLACA, Moore.

Not uncommon at low elevations from March to December. Occurs also in Western China.

586. BAORIS (Parnara) BEVANI, Moore.
Found at low elevations commonly during the rains.

587. BAORIS (Parnara) ASSAMENSIS, Wood-Mason and de Nicéville.
Occurs commonly at low elevations from March to December.

588. BAORIS (Parnara) PAGANA, de Nicéville.
Common; the native collectors sometimes bring it in considerable numbers. It occurs at Singla and at other places at a low elevation.

589. BAORIS (Parnara) PLEBEIA, de Nicéville.
When describing this species I carefully compared it with "*Parnara*" *kumara*, Moore, and also described the differences in the prehensores. Mr. Elwes says I do not allude to *P. kumara* in my description. *B. plebeia* is a common species at a low elevation in Sikhim.

590. BAORIS (Parnara) AUSTENI, Moore.
Not rare; occurs at low elevations throughout the year, and is found also in Western and Eastern China.

591. BAORIS (Parnara) TULSI, de Nicéville.
Rare in Sikhim and in the Khasi Hills, common in Upper Burmah, and is found in Java also. I caught the type specimen below Darjeeling at about 3,000 feet elevation in October.

592. BAORIS (Parnara) PELLUCIDA, Murray.
Better known as *Parnara toona*, Moore, of which the var. *quinquepuncta* of Mabille, from Japan, is a local race. Very common at low elevations throughout the year. It occurs as far south as Sumatra, and has been described and figured by Mr. W. L. Distant as *Baoris chaya*, Moore. It is found in Japan, Corea, the Kurile Islands, Amurland, Central and Western China.

593. BAORIS (Parnara) ELTOLA, Hewitson.
Common in Sikhim from 1,000 to 7,000 feet, all through the year.

594. BAORIS OCEIA, Hewitson.
Excessively common all through the warm months of the year, and is found from 1,000 to 5,000 feet. It is extremely variable, and has been called many bad names. It varies in the forewing being immaculate through every gradation of variation till the maximum number of eight hyaline spots is reached, and that in both sexes. Colonel Swinhoe in his paper on the Butterflies of the Khasi Hills tries to bolster up some of these inconstant forms which have been raised to specific rank, but his persistent efforts in this direction are not likely to be followed by serious lepidopterists. It is found also in Western, Central, and Eastern China.

595. HALPE MOOREI, Watson.

Better known in India as *H. beturia*, Hewitson. Recorded from Sikhim by Colonel Swinhoe, though Mr. Otto Möller does not seem to have ever obtained it there. It is a common butterfly of the plains, especially so in Calcutta, and may well be found in the Terai and on the outer slopes of the hills.

596. HALPE HOMOLEA, Hewitson.

Better known perhaps as *H. sikkima*, Moore. It is an excessively common species in Sikhim at low elevations throughout the warmer months. Colonel Swinhoe has recently described five new species of *Halpe*, all from "Shillong," though probably not one of them is to be found at that hill station, but many miles away from it in the low hot valleys at the foot of the hills. Four of these "new species" are from single specimens, one species from two examples. It is in the highest degree improbable that any of them will obtain currency; they are almost certainly bad species all of them.

597. HALPE SEPARATA, Moore.

Occurs in the forests about Senchal from 6,000 to 9,000 feet, especially in the rains.

598. HALPE KUMARA, de Nicéville.

A rare species, which occurs also in Bhutan.

599. HALPE HYRIE, de Nicéville.

Originally described from the Naga Hills. Mr. G. C. Dudgeon possesses a single female taken in Bhutan in May.

600. HALPE GUPTA, de Nicéville.

Apparently confined in India to Sikhim, and I believe it to occur only at the higher elevations from 6,000 to 9,000 feet. It is found also in Western China.

601. HALPE CERATA, Hewitson.

Found at low elevations commonly throughout the year.

602. HALPE ZEMA, Hewitson.

This species has a wide range and is found as far south as Nias island off the West coast of Sumatra. In Sikhim it is quite common, and is found from 1,000 to 3,000 feet from April to November.

603. HALPE AINA, de Nicéville.

A very rare species. I have no precise record of its time and place of appearance. Colonel Swinhoe records it from the Khasi Hills.

604. CUPITHA PURREEA, Moore.

Not common, occurs at low elevations only, and is found throughout the warm months.

605. Notocrypta feisthamelii, Boisduval.

Better known as *Plesioneura alysos*, Moore. Lieutenant Watson keeps the *N. curvifascia* of Felder, described from China, as a distinct species. I have seen the type specimen at Vienna, which is a female. As the white band on the underside of the forewing does not nearly reach the costa, it is probably distinct from *N. feisthamelii*, but is near to *N. restricta*, Moore. *N. feisthamelii* is one of the commonest species occurring in Sikhim, and is found in all the months of the year except the two or three coldest, and from 1,000 to 5,000 feet elevation. It is found also in Western China, and has been defined as a local race under the name of *rectifascia* by Leech.

606. Notocrypta restricta, Moore.

Colonel Swinhoe says this species is commoner in the Andaman Isles than *N. paralysos*, Wood-Mason and de Nicéville, and goes on to say that the latter appears to him to be identical with *N. feisthamelii*, omitting to notice the very distinctive white spotting of the hindwing on the underside which makes *N. paralysos* unique in the genus. *N. restricta* in Sikhim is a very common species at low elevations throughout the warm months. It is found also in Western and Central China and in the Loochoo Islands.

607. Udaspes folus, Cramer.

Occurs in the low valleys commonly throughout the year.

608. Baracus septentrionum, Wood-Mason and de Nicéville.

A very rare species in Sikhim and obtained only by Mr. Otto Möller in the Terai. Mr. Dudgeon has a male taken in March, and a female in August, both from a low elevation in Daling.

609. Astictopterus olivascens, Moore.

Also a Terai species, of which Mr. Otto Möller obtained a few specimens. The typical Sikhim form has the markings on the underside nearly obsolete. It occurs in Calcutta and is very common in Burmah. It is variable, and one of these slight and inconstant varieties has recently been named *A. kada* by Colonel Swinhoe. It occurs right across China to Hainan island, and the "*Cyclopides*" *chinensis* of Leech, *C. henrici* of Holland, and "*Steropis*" *nubilus* of Mabille, are synonyms.

610. Kerana diocles, Moore.

Very common at low elevations from March to December. It is widely spread, and is found in Sumatra and Java.

611. Pirdana rudolphii, Elwes and de Nicéville.

I know of only two specimens of this very rare species from Sikhim, both females, and one each in the collection of Colonel A. M. Lang, R.E., and myself, the latter taken by Mr. J. Gammie. I have both sexes from Java.

612. Plastingia noëmi, de Nicéville.

All the species of this genus appear to be rare, specimens being procured only one at a time and at distant intervals. *P. noëmi* is no exception to this rule. It is found in the low hot valleys from May to August.

613. Pithauria murdava, Moore.

Common throughout the warmer months at low elevations.

614. Pithauria stramineipennis, Wood-Mason and de Nicéville.

The females of both the species of *Pithauria* are very rare, though the males of both are so common. The present species occurs from April to November from 1,000 to 3,000 feet elevation. It is found in Western China.

615. Creteus cyrina, Hewitson.

Originally described by Hewitson from Darjeeling. I overlooked the description, and described it later on and figured it as *Parnara parca*. I possess a single example from Sikhim, taken in October. Mr. G. C. Dudgeon has obtained both sexes from the east of the Tista river in September and October. It is found also in the Khasi Hills.

616. Iton semamora, Moore.

Very rare in Sikhim, but I have taken it myself at about 3,000 feet in October. It occurs as far south as North-East Sumatra.

617. Ismene ataphus, Watson.

Lieutenant E. Y. Watson has recently shown that this species is distinct from the true *I. œdipodea*, Swainson, from Sumatra. It is rather rare in Sikhim, occurring at low elevations only.

618. Ismene jaina, Moore.

Not common, and found at low elevations only.

619. Ismene amara, Moore.

Rare; occurs from 1,000 to 3,000 feet during the warm months.

620. Ismene vasutana, Moore.

Rare; flies during the summer in the lower valleys.

621. Ismene anadi, de Nicéville.

Probably the rarest species of the genus occurring in Sikhim. It is found at a low elevation only, as far as is known.

622. Ismene harisa, Moore.

Somewhat common. I have on several occasions caught it myself in the low valleys in October. It occurs in Java.

623. Ismene gomata, Moore.

Very rare, especially the female. Found in the low hot valleys only from May to October. Mr. Leech describes a local race from Western China as var. *lara*.

624. Hasora badra, Moore.

A common species in both sexes from 1,000 to 4,000 feet from April to November.

625. Hasora anura, de Nicéville.

A rare species about which not much is known, though Mr. Dudgeon informs me that he has recently procured about twenty males and one female in March, April and May at 4,000 feet in Daling. It occurs also in the Khasi Hills, and in Western and Central China.

626. Hasora chabrona, Plötz.

Not uncommon in Sikhim, but hitherto overlooked. The male has no "male-mark," and both sexes possess a small subcostal yellow dot in the forewing which is never found in the next species.

627. Hasora (Parata) chromus, Cramer.

Fairly common during the rains at low elevations, otherwise rare in Sikhim. It is found also in Western China. Colonel Swinhoe records *Hasora vitta*, Butler, originally described from Borneo, from Sikhim, but I have failed to recognise the species from thence, unless it be *H. chabrona.*

628. Bibasis sena, Moore.

Occurs rarely in the low valleys only. It is found to the south as far as North-East Sumatra, from whence I possess specimens.

629. Badamia exclamationis, Fabricius.

One of the commonest of the "Skippers" found in Sikhim. It flies from April to October, and occurs from 1,000 to 6,000 feet elevation.

630. Rhopalocampta benjamini, Guérin.

Also common; flies throughout the year at from 1,000 to 7,000 feet elevation. It occurs right across China to Japan.

631. "Isoteinon" flavalum, de Nicéville.

The type specimen of this species is unique, and was obtained in native Sikhim. It is now in London in the possession of Mr. J. H. Leech, who bought Mr. Otto Möller's collection, so is not available for examination with a view to place it in its true position in accordance with Lieutenant E. Y. Watson's revision of the genera of the *Hesperiidæ.*

REPTILES.

NOTE.—The books consulted for this paper are Günther's "Reptiles of British India" and the "Reptilia and Batrachia of British India," by Boulenger.

I do not think there are either tortoises or turtles found in Independent Sikhim, although at least one tortoise is found in the Terai. If any are found in Independent Sikhim, they should precede the lizards in the order as above.

J. GAMMIE—30-8-91.

Lizards.

TEN species of lizards are recorded from Sikhim, five of which are skinks; one is a gecko or wall-lizard; one gho-samp; the common bloodsucker; *Japalura variegata*, which is popularly known by the European visitors as the chameleon on account of its rather showy colours, but does not belong to that family; and a beautiful glass-snake (*Ophisaurus gracilis*) which, as it is limbless, is often mistaken for a true snake, but can be readily recognized as belonging not to the snake but to the lizard family by the presence of eyelids. The gho-samp is the only large member of the family in Sikhim. It grows to a length of 4 feet. Its flesh is eaten by the natives and considered a delicacy.

The common cobra (*Naia tripudians*) is not uncommon. It keeps chiefly to the warmer slopes under 4,000 feet, but has been taken as high as 8,000. The ordinary length of an adult is five feet, but individuals of over six feet are occasionally killed. The species is variable in colour, but the Sikhim variety is usually of a uniform brownish-olive above, with a large ocellus, edged and centred with black, on the dilatable neck: beneath, for a few inches from the chin it is whitish crossed by a broad black band, and the rest of the lower parts black. *Naia bungarus* (the giant cobra) is also found in the lower valleys, but seldom ascends above 4,000 feet. It feeds mostly on other snakes, and grows to a length of 12 or 13 feet, of which the tail is 2½ feet. In colour the adult is of a uniform brownish-black with indistinct darker cross bands, but the young is much more gaily coloured, being jet black, beautifully ringed, from the snout to the tip of the tail, with white bands of about a quarter of an inch or more in breadth, the intervening black spaces being three or four times as broad. One of the pit-vipers (*Ancistrodon himalayanus*) is rare in Sikhim, and occurs between 5,000 and 10,000 feet. It is brown, spotted or banded with black, and grows to nearly 3 feet in length. The other three pit-vipers belong to the genus *Trimeresurus*, and are of repulsive aspect, having short tails and triangular shaped heads which are covered with numerous small scales instead of a few large shields as in most other snakes. *T. monticola* is thick bodied, and measures about 2 feet in length, of which the tail is only 3½ inches. It is reddish-brown with two rows of large, square, black spots along the upper parts of the back, and a row of smaller ones on each side. The under parts are marbled brown and white. *T. carinatus* is grass green with a yellowish tail and a white line running along the lower body scales. It is not so heavy as *T. monticola*, but is about a foot longer. *T. gramineus*, the third species, is also grass green, but the line along the outer scales is bright red, and the tail is reddish. Both of the green species keep to the hot valleys, ascending to about 4,000 feet, but *T. monticola* ascends to over 5,000. The Sikhim variety of the krait, *Bungarus cœruleus*, is of a uniform blackish-brown and is not common. *Bungarus bungaroides* is one of the rarest of snakes, and has been collected at 5,000 and 6,800 feet. It grows to over 2½ feet in length, and is not unlike the young of the giant cobra, being black, banded with white. *Callophis maclellandii*, the remaining venomous species, is red above and white below, with a very distinctly-defined black vertebral stripe running the whole length of the body, and irregularly-shaped broadish black bands crossing the sides and belly, but not meeting on the back by about half an inch, and between these black bands is a large ventral spot of the same colour. The head, which is small, is banded black and white. It is not uncommon between 5,000 and 7,000 feet. Considering the number of venomous species in Sikhim, the immunity of both man and beast in it from snake-bite is remarkable. Fatal cases are almost unknown, and even trivial cases are of rare occurrence.

Of the non-venomous species, three attain to considerable dimensions. The largest of them, by far, is *Python molurus*, whose usual length is 12 feet, but individuals of 16 to 20 feet are not very rare. It frequents low elevations, and feeds on small deer and other mammals which it kills by compression. The second in size is *Zaocys nigromarginatus*, a very beautiful snake of the cool forests between 4,000 and 6,000 feet. It is green (turning blue in spirits) with a broad black band on each side of the hinder half of the body and tail, and all the green scales are margined with black. It is rather thick bodied and grows to nine feet in length. It is peculiar among the Sikhim snakes in having an even number of rows of scales (14), all the others having odd numbers, viz., one vertebral row and an even number on each side. The third in size is *Zamenis mucosus*, the well-known rat-snake, which grows to seven feet in length. Of the other genera, *Tropidonotus* is the most numerous, being represented by five species. Several of them swim well, and one, *T. macrophthalmus*, has the misfortune to resemble the common cobra somewhat in colouration and in having a dilatable neck, and suffers accordingly, as it is often mistaken for it and mercilessly killed. There are four species each of *Coluber* and *Dipsas*; three of *Trachischium*; two each of *Simotes*, *Ablabes*, and *Typhlops*, and five genera are each represented in Sikhim by a single species only. Among them the more notable are *Dendrophis picta*, a prettily-coloured slender tree-snake, and *Dryophis prasinus*, a handsome green whip-snake, which grows to 7 feet in length, and is graceful in its movements. Both, although perfectly innocuous, are of ferocious and aggressive habits. *Amblycephalus monticola*, the only blunt-head in Sikhim, is alone among the Sikhim non-venomous snakes in being without the shield lying between the nasal and præocular shields, whilst it is (the loreal shield), with this solitary exception, present in all the harmless species, and is absent in every one of the venomous; so that in Sikhim the non-venomous species can at once be distinguished from the venomous, with the one exception mentioned, by the presence of the loreal shield which lies above the lip, and between the shield in contact with the front of the eye and the one in which the nostril is pierced. As already mentioned, *none* of the venomous sorts have this particular shield.

Frogs and toads, &c.

Of frogs and toads, there are about 16 species. Seven of them belong to the genus *Rana*; four to *Racophorous*; three to *Bufo*, and one each to *Cophophryne* and *Leptobrachium*. Amongst them are several prettily-coloured tree-frogs. The natives eat five species, and consider them tasty and wholesome food. They catch them at night by the light of bamboo torches, which so dazzles the creatures that they remain motionless and allow themselves to be caught. The Lepchas call the edible frog (*Rana liebigii*) of the Upper Forests "Lhak-pok-thalak," while the Nepali name is "Mhun-paha," and all natives agree that this kind is the best eating. It is even said that every kind of frog can be eaten, except the big toad with poisonous warts on his back. When the Lepchas make a bigger catch than they can eat fresh, they gut and smoke-dry the surplus for future use, when they will keep good for years, but get so hard and tough as to require much boiling. The edible frog named above is said to eat the young shoots of the "Malling" bamboo. Several of the species are recognized by their call. There is but one species of tailed-batrachian, a newt, (*Tylobotriton verrucosus*) and it is rare. There is also but one burrowing-batrachian, *Ichthyophis monochrous*, which is fairly common about 3—5,000 feet elevation. Were it not for its distinct head and eyes, it might easily be overlooked for one of the large earthworms.

BIRDS.

NOTE.—The books consulted for this paper are Jerdon's "Birds of India," Oates' "Birds of India," and Hume and Marshall's "Game Birds of India."

J. GAMMIE—22-8-91.

IN no part of the world of an equal area are birds more profusely represented in species than in Sikhim, where there are between 500 and 600. They vary in size from the gigantic lammergeyer, of about 4 feet in length and 9½ feet across the outstretched wings, down to a tiny flower-pecker, *Dicæum ignipectus*, barely exceeding 3 inches from the end of its beak to the tip of its tail. There are four species of kingfishers, but none are numerous in individuals; no doubt owing to the scarcity of fish, their natural food. They chiefly frequent the streams of the lower valleys and rarely are found above 4,000 feet. The smallest, and at the same time prettiest of them all, is *Ceyx tridactyla*, a lovely little creature of about 5 inches in length, and coloured with rufous, white, and different shades of glistening blue and violet. *Halcyon coromandelianus*, another beautiful species, is of a nearly uniform rich rufous colour overlaid with shining peach. The largest of all is crested, and spotted black and white. *Alcedo bengalensis*, the fourth species, closely resembles the English kingfisher, but is smaller. The other more conspicuous birds frequenting stream-sides are forktails, redstarts, a dipper, and a whistling-thrush. The forktails, of which there are four species, are quite characteristic of the darkly wooded mountain torrents of Sikhim. There they are at home on the rocks amidst the roar and the spray, but dash up the streams, with a weird sort of screaming noise, when suddenly disturbed. They are coloured black and white. In the winter season the white-capped redstart, *Chimarrhornis leucocephala*, is a conspicuous and common object of the lower stream beds, but goes high up to breed. It is chastely clad in a black coat and vest and a snow-white cap, and is rufous below. The dipper is of a uniform brown colour, and has the remarkable power of walking under the water where it finds its principal food. The whistling-thrush is a large handsome yellow-billed bird, over a foot long and of a black colour overlaid with glistening cobalt-blue. It is, perhaps, the most frequently noticed of the birds frequenting the stream-sides between 3,000 and 8,000 feet elevation.

Of woodpeckers there are about a dozen species. These readily attract attention by their showy colours and the habit, which their race have, of climbing on trees and tapping the stems in search of the larvæ of beetles, their favourite food. The species found in Sikhim vary in size from the black and white *Yungipicus rubricatus*, 5½ inches in length, to the yellow-naped *Chrysophlegma* of 14 inches. They are most numerous in the low, hot valleys, but several of the species are found at considerable elevations. There is but one permanent resident belonging to the parrot family, *Palæornis schisticeps*, and it is very abundant on the lower slopes from October till March, when it ascends to high elevations to breed. It is green, with a slaty-coloured head, and about 16 inches long. Occasionally, but rarely, stragglers of one or two of the plains' species are to be seen. About a dozen species of cuckoos visit Sikhim. Among them is the European cuckoo, whose call may be heard all day long, in the season, from about 3,500 feet upwards, but is commonest above 5,000 feet. By far the prettiest of them all is *Chrysococcyx Hodgsoni*, the emerald cuckoo. Above, it is of a brilliant emerald-green with a golden sheen, and below white, barred with shining green. It is a small bird, not being much more than half a foot in length. The fork-tailed cuckoo, *Surniculus dicruroides*, closely resembles the common king-crow, but its call, a whistling note five or six times repeated, betrays it.

The long-tailed honey-suckers or sun-birds are not excelled in beauty by any other of the Sikhim species. There are five of them, all belonging to the genus *Æthopyga*. The males of all of them are richly coloured on the head and long tail feathers, with lustrous metallic hues of different shades which change and flash in the sun with every movement. The prevailing colours of *Æ. ignicanda* are scarlet and violet; of *Æ. nipalensis* steel-green, maroon, and yellow, with flame-colour on the breast; and of *Æ. saturata* violet and black. Their curved bills are long and slender, and their bodies are elegantly shaped. They are found from the lowest valleys up to about 7,000 feet. There are several nuthatches, of which *Sitta formosa* is by far the handsomest. It is found about 6,000 feet, and like its cogeners, climbs about on trees in search of food after the manner of woodpeckers. The European hoopoo passes through Sikhim on its way to the plains in the autumn, and again in the spring on its return journey. There are three minivets, all of them remarkable for the gay plumage of both sexes, and for the extreme way the sexes of the same species differ from each other in colour. The male of the largest one, *Pericrocotus speciosus*, is a vermilion-red with black head, wings, and back, whilst its female is of the same pattern, but the colours are yellow and ashy-grey. It is abundant up to about 4,000 feet, and feeds in considerable parties. A flock of them seen flying in the bright sunshine is one of the sights of Sikhim not readily forgotten. There are two racket-tailed drongos, both of which have two of their tail feathers lengthened in a peculiar manner. From the end of the ordinary tail the outer feathers have a naked shaft of nearly a foot in length ending in a twisted barbed portion of some 3 inches long. When seen flying some distance off, the naked shafts are not readily perceptible, and the whole looks like a large bird chased by two small ones. Both species affect the dark jungles in the hot valleys below 3,000 feet. It is said that they can easily be taught to imitate other birds and noises. In the same places, but keeping still more to the deep shade of trees, is a lovely trogon, *Harpactes Hodgsoni*. Its prevailing colour is crimson.

Among the flycatchers, of which there are about 26 species in Sikhim, several being seasonal residents only, the fairy blue-chats are the most remarkable. There are several species, all common in the cool forests between 4,000 and 8,000 feet. The males of them all are brilliantly marked with different shades of glistening blue, but the females are demurely clothed in brown, with the blue of the male confined to a small spot on each side of the neck. *Nitidula Hodgsoni*, the pigmy blue flycatcher, which occurs about the same elevations, is one of the smallest and prettiest of the Sikhim birds. It is only $3\frac{3}{4}$ inches long. *Stoparola melanops*, the verditer-flycatcher, breeds in Sikhim at elevations over 5,000 feet, but is absent in winter. It is strikingly coloured, being of an almost uniform verditer-blue, and as it keeps to the road-sides, is one of the best known birds. A beautiful paradise flycatcher, *Terpsiphone affinis*, is found in the very lowest valleys. When in full plumage the male has the head and long-pointed crest black, and the rest of the plumage white with black shafts. Its tail grows to 14 inches in length. The white of the adult male is chiefly replaced in the female and young males with chestnut. There are eight or nine species of wrens, and they are mostly found creeping about among the undergrowth and fallen logs of the forests from 5,000 feet upwards, but the prettiest and rarest of them all, *Troglodytes punctatus*, is found as low as 2,000 feet. Of the true thrush family there are about a dozen representatives. One or two of them are fair songsters, the best being *Geocichla citrina*, a handsome blue and orange-coloured ground thrush of the hot valleys up to about 4,000 feet. The male of *Merula boulboul*, which is not unlike an English blackbird, but has a grey wing bar, is also a fair songster. It is found abundantly from 5,000 feet upwards. A fieldfare, *Planesticus atrogularis*, abounds in large flocks in the cold season, but goes further north to breed. A prettily marked mountain-thrush, *Oreocincla dauma*, may often be seen turning over the fallen leaves in the lower forests. It is of a brown colour spotted with white and the feathers fringed with black. It is of solitary habits, and rarely is more than one seen at a time. Laughing-thrushes and babblers are numerous both in species and individuals, and mostly occur in the forests and scrub over 5,000 feet elevation, but one or two species are found down to the bottoms of the hottest valleys They usually feed in small flocks, and many of them are noisy. The noisiest of them all is *Garrulax leucolophus*, the white-headed laughing-thrush, which frequents the jungles of the lower valleys up to about 4,000 feet. When disturbed the whole party unite in making most discordant noises resembling forced screaming laughter. On the other hand, the rufous-chinned laughing-thrush, *Janthocincla rufigularis*, large flocks of which are exceedingly common among the scrub jungle up to 4,000 feet, has a pleasant warbling note, which being kept up by the whole company constitutes a sweet song. There are five species of *Trochalopterum*, all pleasingly, although sombrely, plumaged; and the same number of scimitar-babblers, all with longish bills of a more or less scimitar shape. The bill of *Xiphoramphus supercilliaris*, the slender-billed scimitar-babbler, is remarkable, being very slender, much curved, and nearly 3 inches in length round the curve.

The bulbuls are also largely represented. The most abundant in numbers is *Molpestes bengalensis*, which is to be seen in large flocks among the scrub everywhere up to 4,000 feet. *Alcurus striatus*, the striated green bulbul, is almost as abundant, but keeps to the tree tops at elevations over 5,000 feet. The beautiful fairy blue bird, *Irena puella*, occurs rather low down, but is not common. The whole of the upper parts of the male are glistening cobalt-blue, and of the lower velvet-black. It is a large bird of 10 inches in length. There is only one oriole, *Oriolus Trailii*, and it is very unlike any of the plains orioles in appearance, being principally of an Indian-red colour, but it builds the same sort of nest and has a similarly marked egg. Of the stone-chat family the two most notable members are *Copsychus saularis*, the magpie-robin, and *Kittacincla macroura*, the shama, both famous songsters. The latter is usually found at the bottoms of the hot valleys only, but the former is commonest about 3,000 feet. The common and one or two other Indian tailor-birds are plentiful; and small warblers of many sorts abound. Wagtails are not numerous, and are mostly but seasonal visitors. Several species of pipits are abundant in the cold weather, and are sometimes known and used as ortolans. Two thrush-tits are among the most beautiful of the larger Sikhim birds. One of them, *Cochoa viridis*, is 15 inches long and of a bluish-green colour, with head, neck and tail cobalt-blue. It is not common. The second species, *C. purpurea*, is commoner and almost as beautiful, and of about the same size, but is coloured bluish-grey and purple. Both are found in the forests from about 6,000 feet upwards. Tits are numerous and varied. One of them, *Melanochlora sultanea*, which occurs up to 4,000 feet elevation, is remarkably coloured. Its body is altogether of a greenish-black with the forehead and a long prominent crest golden-yellow. The finch family is numerously represented in Sikhim, there being about 30 species. Among them are 3 grosbeaks, 3 bullfinches, 1 crossbill, 1 siskin,

8 rosefinches, 2 sparrows, 4 or 5 mountain-finches, and as many buntings. During the greater part of the year the majority of them are only to be found at very high elevations, but many descend as low as 6,000 feet in hard winters, and a few species are to be found at lower elevations the year round. The most conspicuously coloured of them all is *Hæmatospiza sipahi*, which is gorgeously arrayed in bright scarlet with brown wings and tail edged with scarlet. The female is brown with a bright yellow rump. It may be seen in considerable numbers as low as 5,000 feet so early in the year as October. At high elevations three or four larks are to be found.

The common swallow, *Hirundo rustica*, arrives about the end of January and leaves again in October. It begins breeding in March and brings up two or three broods in the year. The other species of swallow found in Sikhim, *Hirundo nipalensis*, is readily distinguished by its rusty-coloured rump. It builds a covered nest with a long tunnel for entrance, instead of the open cup-shaped nest of the common swallow. *Chelidon nipalensis*, Hodgson's martin, is abundant up to at least 5,000 feet, and remains the whole year, as does also the Indian edible-nest swiftlet, *Collocalia nidifica*. There are three goat suckers, of which *Caprimulgus albonotatus* is the commonest. In the breeding season its song is one of the most frequent sounds to be heard after dusk in the lower valleys up to nearly 4,000 feet. It is exactly the noise made by striking with a stone on a frozen pond. Of barbets there are four species. All breed in holes of trees and have monotonous calls. The largest one, *Megalaima grandis*, is very common. It grows to 13 inches in length, and is said to be excellent eating. *Psarisomus Dalhousiæ*, a broadbill, is a very showily-coloured bird, and is found in considerable flocks in the forests of the hot valleys. It is about the size of a blackbird and of a green colour marked with blue and yellow.

The European raven, *Corvus corax*, is found at high elevations, and a jungle crow, *Corvus macrorhynchus*, is frequent, although not in large numbers, from low elevations up to considerable heights. There is one jay, and there are also several magpies of sorts, the most conspicuous of which, *Cissa chinensis*, the hunting-jay, is crested and of a bluish-green colour with rufous wings. It is found up to about 4,000 feet elevation. Over 6,000 feet, usually in the big forests, are to be found two blue-magpies with tails half a yard in length. At elevations over 9,000 feet are to be found a nut-cracker and two choughs, one with a red and the other with a yellow bill. The great hornbill, *Homrains bicornis*, is a most remarkable bird. It is 4 feet long, and has a large yellow casque on the top of its bill. It affects the lower valleys up to 3,000 feet, but occasionally ascends higher. It goes in small flocks, and at times makes a loud unearthly-sounding noise, more like that of some large carnivorous mammal quarrelling over its prey than a bird. It breeds in hollows of lofty trees, and when the female enters to lay, she plasters herself in and remains in the hollow till the eggs are hatched, merely leaving a long slit wide enough to protrude her bill for the reception of the food which the male has to provide. The second and only other sort of hornbill in Sikhim is *Aceros nipalensis*, a hardly less remarkable bird. It is of similar habits, but of a rather smaller size and without the casque on the bill. It frequents higher elevations, and is considered good eating. The neck of the male is red and of the female black.

Amongst the birds of prey are vultures, eagles, falcons, hawks, owls, kestril, and kite. The lammergeyer is only found at high elevations, and other vultures are rather frequent visitors than permanent residents. The kestril is common in the cold weather, and the kite passes through, in immense numbers, towards the end of September, on its way to the plains, but a few remain permanently. The pigmy falcon, *Hierax entolmas*, a permanent resident of Sikhim, is an interesting little bird. It is prettily coloured on the upper parts being marked with black glossed with green, and streaked about the head and collared with white, and the lower parts reddish. It is only about half a foot in length, but has courage enough for ten times its size. It keeps mostly to the lowest valleys, but occasionally ascends to over 4,000 feet. Of all the birds of prey in Sikhim the black eagle, *Neopus malaiensis*, is oftenest seen, not that it is the commonest by any means, but because of its habit of continually soaring about, at no great height from the ground, the livelong day. Jerdon found that it fed chiefly on birds' eggs and nestlings. It also feeds on reptiles. The spotted hawk-eagle, *Spizactus nipalensis*, is a handsome bird of $2\frac{1}{2}$ feet long, and mostly found below 4,000 feet. The crested serpent eagle, *Spilornis cheela*, is common at low elevations. It is also a handsome bird, but its note, which it sometimes keeps calling for hours together, is a disagreeably loud and harsh squeal. The European sparrow-hawk and a crested goshawk are also fairly common. Of the owl tribe there are seven or eight species, varying in size from the brown wood-owl, *Syrnium nipalensis*, which measures 2 feet in length, to the pigmy owlet, *Glancidium brodiæi*, measuring but 6 inches. There are two *Scops* horned-owls.

There are nine or ten species of pigeons and doves. In the lower valleys, up to 4,000 feet, are to be found the Imperial pigeon, *Carpophaga insignis*; a pin-tailed green pigeon, *Spenocercus apicaudus*; a tree-dove, *Macropygia tusalia*; a spotted-dove, *Turtur suratensis*; and a bronze-winged dove, *Chalcophaps indicus*. At higher elevations are two wood-pigeons, *Alsocomus Hodgsonii* and *Palumbus pulchricollis*; a green-pigeon, *Spenocercus sphenurus*, which has the most musical note of all the Sikhim pigeons, and one or two others. The imperial pigeon is the largest, and grows to over a foot in length and 1½ lbs. in weight. It is quite a fruit-eater, and keeps to the forest-clad parts. The bronze-winged dove is a lovely creature. It is of shy, solitary habits, but may often be seen feeding on the road under deep shade on suddenly rounding a turn. Most of the pigeons are good eating.

Sikhim is but a poor country for sport, although at least 14 species of game birds are to be found in it by the patient and persevering sportsman, between the Rungeet river and the perpetual snows, but none of them can be called very abundant, and many are difficult to find. There are 4 pheasants, 3 quails, 2 hill-partridges, a jungle fowl, woodcock, a snow-cock, a snow-partridge, and a crake. The moonal, *Lophophorus impeyanus*, the largest and handsomest of the Sikhim pheasants, rarely descends below 10,000 feet. An adult male weighs up to 5¼ lbs. and is 28 inches long. It has a peacock-like crest, and its prevailing colour above is bronze-green glossed with gold; below is black, and the tail is cinnamon-red. The female is wholly brown, with a white chin and throat. The blood-pheasant, *Ithagenes cruentus*, frequents the same zone. It is a small bird, adult males of it usually weighing under 1¼ lbs. and measuring 18 inches in length. They are greyish coloured on the back and greenish below, with blood-red streaks on the breast, and the under-tail-coverts are also blood-red. The cere, legs, and spurs are crimson. The female is reddish-brown finely mottled with black. *Ceriornis satyra*, the Indian crimson tragopan, is usually found between 8,000 and 10,000 feet, but sometimes descends in winter to below 7,000 in search of the fruit of *Arisœma*, a large arum, its favourite food. The male is rich crimson below, with black-edged white ocelli on the breast and flanks. The most conspicuous marks about it when alive are the orbital regions, erectile horns, and dilatable skin about the throat, which are of a fine blue, but the colour fades after death. It weighs from 3½ to 4½ lbs. and measures 28 inches in length. The hen is brown, with a few of the feathers white-shafted. The kalij of the Nepalese, *Euplocamus albonotatus*, is the commonest of the Sikhim pheasants, and has the greatest range, being found from the lowest valleys up to 6,000 feet. The male is about 2 feet in length, and from 2¼ to 2¾ lbs. in weight. It is bluish-black above, with a long slender crest of the same colour and whitish below. The hen is brownish. *Gallus ferrugineus*, the red jungle-fowl, is also found from the bottoms of the lowest valleys, but rarely ascends higher than 4,500 feet. The male closely resembles the ordinary gamecock, and measures up to 28 inches in length and weighs from 1¾ to 2¼ lbs. The woodcock is a cold-weather visitor only, and is then to be found from about 3,000 feet upwards. The snow-cock and snow-partridge, as their names imply, frequent the snowy regions, and the quails and crake the zone lying between 3,000 and 6,000 feet.

A

LIST OF SIKHIM BIRDS,

SHOWING THEIR

GEOGRAPHICAL DISTRIBUTION.

No local lists published.

ALTHOUGH the avifauna of Sikhim is one of the richest in the world, and the country itself is a well-defined geographical unit, it is remarkable that no general list of Sikhim birds has hitherto been published.

The avifauna well collected, but further notes needed.

The fauna has been very fully explored and collected by Hodgson,[1] Hooker,[2] Jerdon,[3] W. T. Blanford,[4] Elwes,[4] Mandelli,[5] Gammie,[5] Brooks,[6] and others; but the records, with the exception of those of Jerdon and Blanford, consist mainly of detached notes on isolated species. Jerdon's general and systematic observations, which were confined to Darjeeling and the adjoining parts of British Sikhim,[7] were largely complemented by Blanford's account of his three months' tour in 1870 in Independent Sikhim, chiefly in the Alpine and Sub-alpine areas. And it is the writings of these two authorities, supplemented by the "Occasional Notes" from Sikhim, by Mr. Gammie in *Stray Feathers*, which afford most of the existing information on the extent and geographical distribution of Sikhim birds. Hodgson's British Museum Catalogue of his Sikhim skins gives practically no details of the habitats. And in regard to the necessity for further information Mr. Blanford has recently written,[8] "We require a large amount of additional information as to the range in height of Sikhim birds. Largely as they have been collected, there is, I think, less known about them on the whole than about the less numerous forms of the North-Western Himalayas."

---

[1] *Journal of the Asiatic Society of Bengal, The Bengal Sporting Magazine, Calcutta Jour. of Natural Hist., &c.*

[2] *Himalayan Journals*, I and II, London, 1854.

[3] *The Birds of India*, Calc., 1862.

[4] *Journal Asiatic Society, Bengal*, XLI, part ii (1872), page 30, *et seq.*

[5] *Stray Feathers*, Calcutta, 1873, *et seq.*

[6] *Stray Feathers*, VIII, page 464.

[7] Dr. Jerdon spent a year at Darjeeling about 1857.

[8] *In epist.* 1892.

Having traversed the greater part of both Independent[1] and British Sikhim, and collected over 2,000 specimens of the birds of this area, I find that the analysis of my material affords a considerable contribution towards a geographical distribution list for Sikhim, and also some additional notes on several of the species which aid in supplying the want referred to by Mr. Blanford.

My collection.

Sikhim owes its great variety of bird-life to its very varied natural features and its wide diversity of climate, ranging from the torrid heat of the *tarai*, skirting the base of its outer mountains, up to the arctic cold of its everlasting snows.

The richness of the Sikhim avifauna.

The climate of this country, in respect to its flora, has been roughly divided by Sir Joseph Hooker, as noted in a previous chapter, into the Tropical, Temperate, and Alpine zones. For our purposes, however, it is necessary to make a further subdivision of these zones, and also to recall briefly the geographical position and the leading physical features of Sikhim.

The climate.

Sikhim forms a narrow oblong tract in the South-Eastern Himalayas and Sub-Himalayas, with an area of over 4,000 square miles, wedged in between Nepal on the west, and Bhutan on the east, and bounded on the north by Tibet, and on the south by the plains of Bengal. Its position is peculiarly isolated, being separated from Nepal and Bhutan in great part by high wall-like ridges,[2] from Tibet by the snows and from Bengal by the dreaded *tarai*[3] jungle. The political division into "British Sikhim" or the Darjeeling district,[4] and "Independent Sikhim" cannot here be observed.

Geographical position.

Sikhim thus may be viewed as a stupendous stairway leading from the western border of the Tibetan plateau down to the plains of Bengal, with a fall of about 17,000 feet in 150 miles. The surface of this vast incline[5] is roughly cut up into an innumerable number of rugged peaks and tortuous valleys with deep gorges, adown which dash the glacial streams and torrents

Physical aspects.

[1] As an instance of the extent to which Sikhim has been neglected by European travellers, I may note that when Dr. D. D. Cunningham, F.R.S., and myself visited the Tangkar La Pass (16,500) in 1889, it was the second time only that it had been visited by Europeans, the first visitor having been Dr. (Sir Joseph) Hooker in 1849.

[2] The boundary on the western (Nepal) side includes Kangchendsönga, 28,156 feet high—the second highest mountain in the world, and its southern spur the "Single La" range.

[3] Hindi *tarai* = a swamp or marshy tract.

[4] The trans-Tista portion of Darjeeling district lately ceded by Bhutan, was formerly a part of the Sikhim State.

[5] Gneiss and mica schist are the chief formations; in the lowest ranges lime, sandstone, and shells are met with, and occasionally copper and iron ores. The surface soil is largely of a lateritic nature.

of water, precipitated by the excessive rainfall of this the rainiest section of the Himalayas. For, lying immediately opposite the top of the Bay of Bengal, and not being screened, like Bhutan, by intervening hills, Sikhim receives the full force of the monsoon storms from the south, thus acquiring the leading feature of its climate, viz., dampness—the steamy heat of the lower hills and *tarai*, and the cold dripping dampness of the upper forests of its outer ranges. The average rainfall of these latter is about 130 inches per annum, and they are cloud-capped for a great part of the year.

Tortuous rivers seam the face of the country in every direction.

River system.

The chief effluent river of Sikhim is the Tista, which flows in a generally southerly direction, and has for its headwaters the Lachhen and Lachhung, which unite at Tsünthang. The main branch of the Tista is the Great Rungeet, which joins it within the mountains. The depth of the gorge of the Tista and the Rungeet and other large tributaries is almost incredible. About thirty miles within the hills, the beds of the Tista and Rungeet are only about 600 feet above the sea level, and their banks thoroughly tropical. These great rivers carry a tropical and subtropical climate along their banks far into the interior of the country, till the semi-tropical vegetation becomes almost overhung by snow peaks.

Variety of climate.

Thus the ridges of the innumerable spurs form peninsulas and promontories of relatively temperate climate, running out into the sub-tropical areas of the deep ravines. In this way the gradations of climate are almost endless; and some of the inner and more land-locked valleys came to possess a relatively dry climate. In lower and outer Sikhim the even outline of the hills is seldom broken by cliffs or bluffs, and the valleys are usually ravine-like, with the rivers flowing in deep gorges. In Upper Sikhim the scenery becomes much bolder, cliffs are frequent, and the forest tends to be confined to the bottom of the valleys, which latter open out frequently into wide grassy meadows, such as at Lachhung and Yumthang. Throughout the greater part of Sikhim perennial streams and evergreen forest offer grateful resources to birds. There are few lakes, and those which do exist are mostly of very small size.

Climatic zones.

The climate of this country may be divided in respect to its fauna into the following zones:—

Zone			
I.—Tropical	Submontane or *Tarai.*	Outer grassy plain. Inner tangled forest and sál forest.	125—2,000 feet above the sea level.
	Hilly ...	... ...	
II.—Sub-tropical	... ...	... ...	2,000 to 5,000 feet.
III.—Temperate	... ...	... ...	5,000 to 9,000 „
IV.—Sub-Alpine	... ...	... ...	9,000 to 13,000 „
V.—Alpine	... ...	... ...	13,000 to 17,000 „

These zones are marked by characteristic changes in the vegetation. In the outer *tarai* the banks of the great rivers and adjoining depressions subject to inundation are clothed with giant grass. On the higher rolling land are stretches of *sál*[1] forest alternating with tangled jungle—much of it now cleared for cultivation. The Himalayas rise abruptly out of the *tarai* plain, and a tangled forest covers their sides up to about 5,000 feet.[2] The *temperate zone* coincides generally with "the oak forest" region, where the undergrowth becomes perceptibly less rank and dense. The oaks first appear about 4,500 feet, amongst the still luxuriant semi-tropical vegetation, as a few straggling large-leaved species, which gradually become more numerous towards 5,000 feet. The centre of the temperate zone has a mean temperature of about 50° Faht., that is very much the same as London; and in December and January frost, and sometimes snow, lies all day unthawed in situations with a northern exposure. The *Sub-Alpine zone* is practically the region of the rhododendron and pine forests. The pines appear about 9,000 feet and soon form open forests, alternating with stretches of rhododendron and dwarf bamboos, which at times form almost impenetrable matted scrub. The limit of trees is 13,000 to 14,000 feet, but in exposed situations it is much lower. Vegetation altogether disappears at about 15,000 feet, depending on exposure and proximity to snow peaks and glaciers. The line of perpetual snow ranges from about 16,000 to 17,000.

The zoological position of Sikhim.

In regard to *horizontal distribution*, Sikhim zoologically is situated on the border-land between the Palæarctic and Oriental regions[3] and, as we have seen, it connects with both these regions, viz., with Palæarctic Tibet and with several sections of the Oriental region. Thus its fauna is representative of both these regions—the Palæarctic forms entering from the north in the same way as the Oriental enter the mountains from the south; but a few Ethiopian forms also occur. As Sikhim stands at the junction of the Indian, Indo-Chinese, and Indo-Malayan subregions of the Oriental region, each of these regions is represented in its avifauna. The Oriental forms seem to ascend no higher than about 8,000 to 10,000 feet.

---

[1] *Shorea robusta.*

[2] In the upper sub-tropical section, the *Urticariæ*,—figs and nettles are very prominent.

[3] Wallace, following Sclater and other naturalists, divides the surface of the globe, zoologically, into six great regions, viz., (1) The *Palæarctic*, including Europe, Africa, north of the Sahara, and Asia north of the great wall of the Himalayas; (2) the *Ethiopian*, comprising the rest of Africa with South Arabia and Madagascar; (3) the *Oriental*, consisting of India, Southern China, Burma, Siam, and the Malay Peninsula and adjoining islands of the Archipelago; (4) the *Australian*, comprising Australia, New Zealand, and the remaining south-eastern islands of the Malay Archipelago, &c.; (5) the *Neartic*, and (6) *Neotropical*, approximately corresponding to North and South America.

The lists.

A few words are necessary regarding the list which is here presented in tabular form. The data therein given afford information regarding both the horizontal and vertical distribution. The order of enumeration is that of Oates' "Birds of India" in the new fauna series for British India. As, however, the 3rd volume of that work has not yet issued, the remaining birds are catalogued according to Jerdon's treatise. The figures therefore in column No. 1 of the table represents the serial number of Oates and Jerdon respectively: Jerdon having been first taken up, as he commences with the *Raptores* or Birds of Prey.

Vernacular names.

The Lepcha vernacular name are given as far as possible. Jerdon gave many of these, and they are very valuable, as being either the onomatopoetic reproductions of the call of the bird, or a descriptive title of some peculiarity in regard to its appearance or habits. The names were noted down by me direct from the Lepchas and occasionally they differ from those of Jerdon. It may be noted generally that the Lepcha prefix *dang* means "hot" and *'lho* means "cool hill" with reference to the habitat of the bird, *kanda* means crested, *nôk* = black, *dum* = white, *hĭr* = red, *paöyôr* = yellow, *fong* = green, *tī* = a contraction for *tīak* or head, *long* = stone, *küng* = wood, *bong* = tree-trunk, *fat* = earth, and *ung* = water, and after each name is added the word *fo* or "bird." The Pahāriyas, speaking a Sanskritic dialect—the *Pārbatiya*, and the Bhotiyas, including the Tibetans, are much less discriminating in their bird-names than the Lepchas, who are "born naturalists"; but some of their names also are given, especially in regard to those birds frequenting the zones below and above that inhabited by the Lepchas.

Rarity or otherwise.

The column showing "number of specimens" indicates in a general way the rarity or otherwise of the species. Where no number is entered, it means that though seen none were secured.

Inclusion of former records.

In order to render the list more complete, I have added such cases, as I could find, of the recorded presence of species, extra to those actually secured or seen by me; such species are put in brackets, and the names of the reporters are given.

Range.

In regard to vertical distribution it must be remembered that a given altitude in Upper Sikhim in proximity to the snows, represents a greater degree of cold than the same altitude in the outer ranges. It is remarkable how limited is the range of many of the species, notwithstanding their excellent means of locomotion.

Collecting stations.

To facilitate reference to the position of the collecting stations I here indicate roughly the *locale* of some of the chief of these, and where different altitudes are given for the same station it means that the specimens were obtained at varying altitudes on the flank of the particular mountain or valley—the altitude being approximately within about 500 feet of the actual elevation. The places in *Upper Sikhim* will be readily found on the map by their height and the sparsity of place names there—Tsungthāng (Chungtam), meaning in the vernacular "the Meadow of Marriage (of the Rivers)," is at the junction of the Lachhen and Lachhung, where they unite to form the Rangnyo or Tista. Thang-kar La is an exceptionally cold pass, as its name [viz., "The White (snow) plain"] implies, with many miles of landlocked snow all the year round. Poi La is almost within Chumbi-Tibetan territory and so is Byong Chhen—a shrub-fringed lake. In *Central Sikhim*, Lingcham, Yang-ong, and Dentam are below Pemiongchi in the Kulhait Valley. Namchi, Lingmo, Yang-gong, Temi, and Tingbi are on the flanks of Tendong and Mainom. Padom, Rang-guon, Mangzhim, and Neh Mendong are in the Tista Valley. Kitam, Seriyong, and Chakong are in the lower Rungeet-Ramam Valleys, and the Rathong is the chief feeder of the Rungeet—smaller feeders being the Little Rungeet, Ramam, and Ramith. Rhenok, Dolomchhen, Gangtok, Kabi, Rangpo, Phima, Fyumgang, Sathok, Dsekthang, Chomnaga, Takrang, and Phemtong are on ridges, leading up to the Eastern passes—the Chola and Jelep.

In *Lower Sikhim* or the Darjeeling District, Gokh, Singla, Lingtam, Takvar, and Kambal are in the Rungeet Valley. Pashok, Gielle, Matyouli, Rishap, Mangpu, and the Riang and Kul Jhora rivers are in the outer valley of the Tista which debouched into the plains at the Sivok Gorge. Lābah, Rishe La, Nambong, Gurubathan lead towards the Dichhu Valley and Bhutan. Mirik, Simana, and Jorpokri are on ridges leading down from the Nepal frontier to the Tarai.

As a postscript to the table I have added some notes regarding those specimens which differed from the descriptions published by Jerdon, Oates, and others.

The notes.

In conclusion, I have to acknowledge my indebtedness to Mr. Gammie—*the* naturalist of the district—for much kind assistance in the identification and question of residence of many of the species.

ORDER OF RAPTORES OR BIRDS OF PREY.

	1	2		3	4	5	6
	Number in Jerdon.	NAME.		Zone. Tr.= Tropic. STr.= Sub-trop. Te.= Temperate. SA.= Subalp. A.= Alpine.	Vertical range in feet.	Resident or not, or breeding. R.C.= Certainly permanent resident. R.P.= Probably resident. M.= Migratory. S.= Straggler. B.= Breeds.	REMARKS. * = *vide* 'Notes.'
		Scientific.	Vernacular. L.=Lepcha. P.=Pahăriya. B.=Bhotia or Tibetan.				
FAMILY VULTURIDÆ. Vultures.	1	*Vultur monachus*	L.—Gût pa-nom (or King of the Vultures).	Te.	4,000—	R.P.	
	2	*Otogyps calvus*	L.—Gût-a-nok...	Tr.—Te.	150—8,000		
	3 *bis.*	*Gyps fulvescens*	L.—Gût. P.—Gidh or (Scavenger).	Te.	...	......	*
	4	,, *tenuirostris*	B.—Gom-chhen, or The Hermit.	STr.			
	5	*Pseudogyps bengalensis*	......	Tr.—Te.	150—15,000		
	7	*Gypætus barbatus*	......	A.	14,000—18,000	R.P.	
FAMILY FALCONIDÆ. Falcons.	8	*Falco peregrinus*	......	Tr.—Te.	150—		
	11	,, *jugger*	......	Te.	...	R.P.	
	14	(*Hypotriorchis severus*)	......	Te.	...	R.	
	16	,, *chicquera*	......	Tr.	150—	M.	
	17	*Cerchneis tinnunculus*	L.—Ting-kyi	Te.—A.	150—10,000	M.	
	19	(*Erythropus vespertinus*)	......	Te.			
	20	*Hierax cærulescens*	L.—Ching-fin-nyel.	Tr.—STr.	200—4,000	R.C.	*
Hawks.	23	*Astur badius*	L.—Ting-kyi. B.—U-cham.	Tr.—Te.	150—	R.C.	
	24	*Accipiter nisus*	......	Te.	...	M.	
Eagles.	27	*Aquila nepalensis*	L.—Ong yău	Tr.—STr.	150—8,000	R.C.	*
	28	(,, *clanga*)	......	...	...	R.C.	
	32	*Neopus malayensis*	L.—Lak-nong-bong. B.—Hü-gong.	Te.	...	R.C.	
	33	*Nisætus fasciatus*	Ditto ditto ...	Te.			
	34	(*Limnætus niveus*)	......	...	150—	......	*
	36	,, *nepalensis*	L.—Kandă Panthi-ong or the crested Panthiong.	Tr.—Te.	200—3,500	......	*
	37	,, *kienierii*	Ditto ditto ...	Te.			
	39	*Spilornis cheela*	L.—Ung-panthi-ong, or O-ta-kyen.	Tr.—STr.	150—4,000	R.C.	
	40	(*Pandion haliaëtus*)	L.—Pan-ti-ong...	Te.			
	41	(*Poliætus ichthyætus*)	......	...	150		
Buzzards.	44	(*Buteo vulgaris*)	L.—Dang pang-ti-ong.	Tr.—Te.	150—9,000	R.P.	
	45	(,, *canescens*)	......	A.			
	47	,, *plumipes*	L.—Pang-thi-ong-nok.	...	7,000—14,000		
	49	(*Archibuteo strophiatus*).					
Harriers.	50	*Circus cyaneus*	......	STr.	...	M.	
	53	,, *melanoleucus*	P.—Pahatai	Tr.—Te.	150—4,000	M.	
	54	,, *æruginosus*	P.—Kutar	Tr.—Te.	150—	M.	
Kites.	55	*Haliastur indus*	P.—Brahmini chil.	Tr.	150—18,000	R.C.	*
	56	*Milvus govinda*	P.—Chil	Tr.—Te.	150—12,000	R.C.	
	56 *bis.*	,, *melanotis*	......	Tr.	150—	R.C.	
	56 *ter.*	,, *affinis*		Tr.—Te.	150—	R.C.	
	58	*Baza lophotes*	P.—Kohi	STr.			
	59	*Elanus melanopterus*	......	Tr.	150—.		

	1	2		3	4	5	6
	Number in Jerdon.	NAME. Scientific.	Vernacular. L.=Lepcha. P.=Pahāriya. B.=Bhotia or Tibetan.	Zone. Tr.=Tropic. STr.=Sub-trop. Te.=Temperate. SA.=Subalp. A.=Alpine.	Vertical range in feet.	Resident or not, or breeding. R.O.=Certainly permanent resident. R.P.=Probably resident. M.=Migratory. S.=Straggler. B.=Breeds.	REMARKS. * = *vide* 'Notes.'
RAPTORES, &c.—*concld.* FAMILY STRIGIDÆ OR OWLS. Hooting Owls.	64	*Syrnium newarense* ...	L.—Mik-dab-brū or 'short-eyed *brū* caller.'	Tr.—A. ...	200—13,000	......	*
	66	(,, *nivicolum*) ...	L.—Kashi-op tak-pum. B.—U-ko.	Te.—A. ...	7,000—16,000		
Horned Owls.	71	(*Huhua nepalensis*) ...	......	STr. ...	150—5,000	......	*
	72	*Ketupa ceylonensis* ...	......	STr. ...	150—5,000	......	*
	73	,, *flavipes* ...	L.—Lak-kyo-o mung (or 'the *kyo-o* calling devil').				
	74	*Scops pennatus* var. *rufus* .	......	Tr. ...	...	R.O.	*
	75	,, *lettia* ...	......	STr. ...	150—6,000	......	*
Owlets.	76	*Carine brama* ...	L.—Dang Tang-pum.	Tr. ...	150—		
	79	*Glaucidium cuculoides* ...	L.—Tang-pum...	STr.—Te	2,000—6,000		
	80	,, *brodii* ...	......	...	...	R.O.	
	81	*Ninox scutellatus* ...	L.—Tang-kyi per-chi-ok.	...	150—		
ORDER OF INCESSORES OR PERCHERS. TRIBE FISSIROSTRES. Fam. *Hirundinidæ.* Swifts.	82	....	......	...	...	M.—B.	
	85						
	94	... .	......	...	...	B.—R.P.	
	95	(*Acanthylis sylvatica*) ...	......	...	2,000—4,500	R.P.	
	97	(,, *caudacuta*) ...	L.—Sili-ang ti-phi-tim-bo.	...	...	B.	
	98	(*Cypselus melba*) ...	......	Te.—A. ...	150—		
	100	,, *affinis* ...	P.—Batasi or 'the windy.'	Tr.—STr. ...	1,000—12,000		
	103	*Collocalia fuciphaga* ...	......	Tr.—SA. ...	2,000—4,500	R.P.	
Fam. *Caprimulgidæ.* Night-jars.	106	*Otothrix hodgsoni* ...	......	STr.			
	107	*Caprimulgus indicus* ...	L.—Tá-mor ...	STr. ...	150—6,000	R.O.	*
	109	,, *albonotatus* ...	L.—Ding-pit ...	STr. ...	150—4,000	R.O.	
	114	(,, *monticolus*).					
Trogon.	116	*Harpactes hodgsoni* ...	L.—Sak-vôr ...	STr. ...	600—4,000	R.O.	
Bee-eaters.	117	*Merops viridis* ...	L.—Sang-rhyok or 'the copper colored.'	Tr. ...	150	R.P.	
	122	*Nyctiornis athertoni* ...	L.—Sang-rhyok	STr. ...	2,000—4,000	R.O.	
Rollers.	123	*Coracias indica* ...	P.—Nil-kant or 'bluethroat.'	Tr.			
	124	,, *affinis* ...	L.—Tak-rāl ...	Tr. ...	...	R.O.	
	126	*Eurystomus orientalis* ...	L.—Tak-rāl vong	Tr. ...	150—2,000		
Fam. *Halcyonidæ.* Kingfishers.	127	*Pelargopsis gurial* ...	L.—Fat-tym or 'the earthy headed.'	Tr., STr. ...	200—3,000		
	129	*Halcyon smyrnensis* ...	......	Tr. ...	150—1,000		
	131	,, *coromandelianus* ...	L.—Ter ...	STr. ...	300—1,500	R.O.	*
	133	*Ceyx tridactyla* ...	......	STr. ...	200—1,000	......	*

1	2		3	4	5	6
	Name.					
Number in Jerdon.	Scientific.	Vernacular. L.=Lepcha. P.=Pahāriya. B.=Bhotia or Tibetan.	Zone. Tr.=Tropic. STr.=Sub trop. Te.=Temperate. SA.=Subalp. A.=Alpine.	Vertical range in feet.	Resident or not, or breeding. R.C.=Certainly permanent resident. R.P.=Probably resident. M.=Migratory. S.=Straggler. B.=Breeds.	Remarks. * = *vide* 'Notes.'
Order Incessores—contd. Tribe Fissirostres—concld. Kingfishers—concld.						
134	*Alcedo bengalensis* ...	L.—Ung Chim, *i.e.*, 'The water Sasia,' *vide* No. 187.	Tr. ...	150—2,500	R.C.	The Lepcha name is founded on general resemblance to *Sasia* (No. 187).
135	„ *euryzona*					
135 *quat*	„ *meninting* ...	......	Tr. ...	150—2,000		
136	*Ceryle rudis* ...	L.—Ung ta-brik, *i.e.*, '*The brik brik* calling water-eater.'	Tr.			
137	„ *guttata* ...	L.—Ung ka-zhū or 'water dog,' with reference to its barking call.	Tr. ... STr. ...	150—500 300—4,000	 R.C.	
Fa. Eurylaimidæ. Broadbills.						
138	*Psarisomus dalhousiæ* ...	L.—Dang-mo mith.	Tr.—Te. ...	1,000—5,000	R.C.	
139	*Serilophus rubropygius* ...	L.—Rab kyūl ...	STr.—Te. ...	2,000—5,000	R.C.	*
Fa. Bucerotidæ. Hornbills.						
140	*Dichoceros cavatus* ...	......	STr. ...	300—3,000	R.C.	
142	*Hydrocissa albirostris* ...	......	Tr. ...	2,000—6,000	R.C.	
146	*Rhyticeros nepalensis* ...	......	STr. ...	2,000—6,000		
Tribe Scansores or Climbers. Fam. Psittacidæ. Parraquets.						
147	*Palæornis nepalensis* ...	L.—Né-tsô ...	STr.			
148	„ *torquatus* ...	......	Tr. ...	150		
149	„ *purpureus* ...	......	Tr.			
150	„ *schisticeps* ...	......	STr.—Te ...	2,000—5,000	M.	
152	„ *fasciatus* ...	......	STr. ...	—4,000	S.	
Fam. Picidæ. Woodpeckers.						
155	*Picus majoroides* ...	L.—Sa-dyer mong prek, or 'climbing tapper.'	Te.—SA. ...	3,000—12,000		
156	„ *cathpharius* ...	......	STr.—Te.			
157	„ *macei* ...	......	......	......	......	*
161	*Hypopicus hyperythrus* ...	......	Te.—SA. ...	9,000—12,000	......	*
162	*Yungipicus rubricatus* ...	......	Te. ...	3,000—9,000	R.C.	*
166	*Chrysocolaptes sultaneus* ...	L.—Tashi-on-bāu or 'The Glorious bāu.'	STr. ...	150—3,000	......	*
166 *bis.*	„ *delesserti*...	......	STr. ...	......	S.	*
168	(*Hulleripicus pulverulentus.*)	......	Tr.			

ORDER INCESSORES—*concld.* TRIBE SCANSORES—*concld.*

	1	2		3	4	5	6
	Number in Jerdon.	Name. Scientific.	Name. Vernacular. L.=Lepcha. P.=Pahāriya. B.=Bhotia or Tibetan.	Zone. Tr.=Tropic. STr.=Subtrop. Te.=Temperate. SA.=Subalp. A.=Alpine.	Vertical range in feet.	Resident or not, or breeding. R.C.=Certainly permanent resident. R.P.=Probably resident. M.=Migratory. S.=Straggler. B.=Breeds.	Remarks. *=*vide* 'Notes.'
Woodpeckers—*concld.*	172	*Gecinus occipitalis* ...	L.—Mong-chok	Tr.—Str. ...	150—5,000	......	*
	173	*Chrysophlegma flavinucha*	L.—Mong kli-ong	Tr.—Te. ...	150—7,000	......	*
	174	,, *chlorolopha*	......	Str.—Te. ...	150—10,000	......	*
	176	*Blythipicus pyrrhotis* ...	L.—Fi-ing (=its call).	STr. ...	...	......	*
	177	*Gecinulus grantius* ...	L.—Ka-ter ...	STr. ...	6,000—3,000	R.C.	*
	178	*Micropternus phaioceps* ...	L.—Fi-ing ...	STr. ...	600—4,000	R.C.	*
	180	*Brachypternus aurantius* ..	......	Tr. ...	150—	......	*
	181	,, *puncticollis*	......	Tr. ...	...	......	*
Piculets.	186	(*Vivia innominata*) ...	L.—Dang chim	STr. ...	3,000—6,000	R.C.	
	187	*Sasia ochracea* ...	L.—Chim ...	STr. ...	2,000—6,000	R.C.	*
	190	(*Indicator xanthonotus*) ...	......	...			
Fam. *Megalaimidæ.* Barbets.	191	*Megalæma marshallorum*...	L.—Kün-nyong	Te. ...	1,000—7,000	R.C.	Its call is "*nyong-ny-ong.*"
	192	,, *hodgsoni* ...	L.—Dang kün-nyong.	Tr. ... STr.	150 600—3,000	... R.C.	*
	195	,, *asiatica* ...	L.—Ktak (its call).	Tr.—Str. ...	150—6,000		
	196	,, *franklinii* ...	......	STr.—Te.	3,000—8,000,	R.C.	
	197	*Zantholæma hæmacephala*	'The copper-smith.'	Tr. ...	150		
Fam. *Cuculidæ.* Cuckoos.	199	*Cuculus canorus* ...	L.—Kuk-ku ...	Te. ...	3,000—8,000	M.	*
	200	(,, *striatus*) ...	L.—Tong-ting vyang.	Te. ...	...	M.	
	201	,, *poliocephalus* ...	L.—Dang-hlem. B.—Pi-chu-gya-po (= its call).	Te. ...	5,000—7,000	M.	
	202	,, *sonnerati* ...	......	...	...	M.	*
	203	,, *micropterus* ...	L.—Tak-po. B.—Kang-ka-tong (its call).	...	...	M.	*
	205	*Hierococcyx varius* ...	L.—Bim-pi-yul= its call. (The 'Brain-fever bird' of Europeans in India.)				
	206	(,, *nisicolor*) ...	L.—Ding-pit ...	...	...	M.	
	207	(,, *sparveroides*)	L.—Nimbin-pi-yul.	...	...	M.	
	210	(*Surniculus dicruroides*) ...	L.—Kar-rio-vyem.				
	211	(*Chrysceococcyx hodgsoni*) ...	L.—Ang-pha.				
	213	*Coccystes coromandus* ...	L.—Tse-ben ...	...	150		
	214	*Eudynamys honorata* ...	......	Tr. ...	150		* Very rare.
	214 *bis.*	,, *malayana* ...	......	Tr. ...	150		*
	215	*Rhopodytes tristis* ...	L.—Sang-ku (= the coppery or arrow-flight 'ku' caller.)	Str.—Te. ...	200—5,000	R.C.	
Crow-pheasants.	217	*Centrococcyx rufipennis* ...	......	...	150	......	*
	218	,, *bengalensis* ...	L—Nyong. B. Kyok-kyok.	Tr. ...	200—5,000 ... 150—15,000	......	*
	254	*Upupa epops* ...	L.—Rang-fun ...	...	...	At.	

N.B.—For continuation of *Incessores* according to Jerdon's numbers *see* Oates' Numerical List in this table which follows Jerdon's Series.

1	2		3	4	5	6
	Name.					
Number in Jerdon.	Scientific.	Vernacular. L.=Lepcha. P.=Pahāriya. B.=Bhotia or Tibetan.	Zone. Tr. =Tropic. STr.= Sub-trop. Te. = Temperate. SA. =Subalp. A. =Alpine.	Vertical range in feet.	Resident or not, or breeding. R.C. =Certainly permanent resident. R.P. =Probably resident. M. =Migratory. S. =Straggler. B. =Breeds.	Remarks. * = *vide* 'Notes.'
GEMITORES OR PIGEONS. — Fam. Columbidæ. — Pigeons.						
776	*Osmotreron phayrei* ...	......	Tr.			
778	*Sphenocercus sphenurus* ...	L.—Ku-hu ...	Te.			
779	,, *apicaudus* ...	L.—Sang-pong...	Str.—Tr. ...			
781	*Carpophaga insignis* ...	L.—Fo-mok ...	Str.—Te. ...	2,000— 6,000		
783	*Alsocomus hodgsonii* ...	......	Te.—Sa. ...	6,000—13,000		
785	*Palumbus pulchricollis* ...	L.—Ka-o.				
Doves.						
790	*Columba leuconota* ...	L.—'lho. peü-rintiep.	A. ...	10,000—13,000		
	......	B.—Bya-dén.				
791	*Macropygia tusalia* ...	L.—Ka-er ...	Te.	3,000—10,000		
793	*Turtur meena* ...	L.—Gu-gu ...	Tr.—Te. ...	150—10,000		
795	,, *suratensis* ...	......	Tr.—Te.			
797	,, *tranquebaricus* ...	......	Tr.			
798	*Chalcophaps indica* ...	.—Ka-er ...	STr. ...	150— 3,000		
ORDER RASORES OR SCRATCHERS (GAME BIRDS). — Fam. Phasianidæ. — Peafowl.						
803	*Pavo cristatus* ...	B.—Mab-ja. L.—Mongyung.	Tr. ...	150 2,000		
803 *quat.*	*Polyplectrum tibetanum* ...	......	Tr.—STr. ...	...	......	*
803 *sept.*	(*Crossoptilum* ,,) ...	B.—Lha-ja kong-mo, or The divine *kongmo*.	A. ...	...	......	*
Pheasants.						
804	*Lophophorus impeyanus* ...	L.—Fo-dong. B.—Chamdong.	SA.—A. ...	10,000—15,000	B. ...	"Dong" in Lepcha= *variegated* or "piebald," and in Burmese it is applied to peafowl and pheasants.
805	*Ceriornis satyra* ...	L.—Tar-rhyak. B.—Bap.	Te.—SA. ...	6,000—12,000		
807	*Ithagenes cruentes* ...	L.—Su-mong. B.—Se-mo.	SA.—A. ...	10,000—14,000		
811	*Gallophasis melanota* ...	L.—Kar-rhyak	STr.—Te. ...	1,000— 8,000	......	*
Jungle fowl.						
812	*Gallus ferrugineus* ...	L.—Tang-kling. B.—Nag-tse-ja or 'jungle-fowl.'	Tr.—STr. ...	150— 4,500		
Fam. Tetraonidæ. — Partridge.						
816 *bis.*	(*Tetraogallus tibetanus*) ...	B.—Hrak-pa ...	A. ...	15,000—18,000		
817	(*Lerwa nivicola*) ...	......	A.			
818	*Francolinus vulgaris* ...	......	Tr.—STr. ...	150— 4,000		
823	*Ortygornis gularis* ...	......	Tr.			
824	*Arboricola torqueola* ...	L.—Ko-hum-but	Te.—SA. ...	5,000—14,000		
825	,, *rufogularis* ...	......	STr.—Te. ...	1,000— 6,000	......	*
825 *bis.*	,, *mandellii* ...	......	Te. ...	...	......	*Rare—not previously reported from Sikhim.
Tinamidæ. — Quails.						
829	(*Coturnix communis*) ...	......	Tr. ...	150— 7,000	Br.	
	Turnix plumbipes ...	L.—Timok ...	Tr.—Te.			
ORDER GRALLATORES OR WADERS. — Tribe Pressirostres. Fam. Otidæ, &c. — Florikin.						
888	*Sypheotides bengalensis* ...	......	Tr.			
Plover.						
845	*Charadrius fulvus* ...	......	Tr.			
851	*Vanellus cristatus* ...	T.—Tshō-ja or 'Lake bird.'	Te. ...	...	......	*
857	*Hoplopterus ventralis* ...	......	STr. ...	...	Br.	
Cranes.						
863	*Grus antigone* ...	P.—Saras ...	Tr.			
865	,, *cinerea* ...	......	Tr.			

	1	2		3	4	5	6
		Name.					
	Number in Jerdon.	Scientific.	Vernacular. L.=Lepcha. P.=Pahāriya. B.=Bhotia or Tibetan.	Zone. STr.=Tropic. Tr.=Sub-trop. Te.=Temperate. SA.=Subalp. A.=Alpine.	Vertical range. in feet.	Resident or not, or breeding. R.C.=Certainly permanent resident. R.P.=Probably resident. M.=Migratory. S.=Straggler. B.=Breeds.	Remarks. * = *vide* 'Notes.'
Order Grallatores or Waders—*concld.* Tribe Longirostres. Snipe.	867	*Scolopax rusticola* ...	......	Te.—SA. ...	3,000—12,000	Br.	
	868	*Gallinago nemoricola* ...	L.—Ta-nok ...	STr.—Te.			
	869	" *solitaria* ...	......	STr.—Te. ...	2,000—6,000		
	870	" *sthenura* ...	......	Tr.			
	871	" *gallinaria* ...	......	Tr.			
	872	" *gallinula* ...	......	Tr.			
Sandpipers, &c.	875	*Limosa ægocephala* ...	......	Tr.			
	878	*Numenius phæopus* ...	......	Tr.			
	879	(*Ibidorhynchus struthersii*)	......	Tr.—A. ...	...	Br.	
	880	*Philomachus pugnax* ...	......	Tr.			
	885	*Tringa temminckii* ...	......	Tr.			
	891	*Actitis glareola* ...	......	Tr.			
	892	*Totanus ochropus* ...	......	Tr.			
	893	*Tringoides hypoleucus* ...	......	Tr.			
	894	*Totanus glottis* ...	......	Tr.			
Tribe Latitores. Rails, coots and water-hens.	900	*Metopidius indicus* ...	......	Tr.			
	903	(*Fulica atra*) ...	......	Tr.			
	905	*Gallinula chloropus* ...	......	Tr.			
	907	" *phœnicura* ...	......	Tr. ...	...		
	910	(*Porzana bailloni*) ...	......	Tr. ...	1,000—6,000	......	*
Tribe Cultirostres. Storks.	915	*Leptoptilus argala* ...	......	Tr.			
	920	*Dissura episcopa* ...	......	Tr.			
Herons.	922	(*Ardea sumatrana*) ...	......	Tr.			
	924	" *purpurea* ...	......	Tr.			
	925	*Herodias alba* ...	......	Tr.			
	927	" *garzetta* ...	......	Tr.			
	929	*Buphus coromandus* ...	......	Tr.			
	930	*Ardeola grayi* ...	......	Tr.			
	931	*Butorides javanica* ...	L.—Ung Fā-o nang.	Tr.—STr. ...	150—3,000	......	*
	933	*Ardetta cinnamomea* ...	......	Tr.			
	937	(*Nycticorax griseus*) ...	......	Tr. ...	...	Br.	
Ord. Natatores or Swimmers. Tr. Lamellirostres. Ducks.	954	*Casarca rutila* ...	......	Tr.— ...	150—15,000		
	972	(*Mergus castor*) ...	......	Tr.—A.			
Tr. Mergitores. Divers.	975	*Podiceps minor* ...	B.—Dô-dam-bya or 'Mud-stone bird.'	Tr.—SA. ...	150—10,000		
Tr. Vagatores. Terns.	982	*Sylochelidon caspia* ...	......	Tr.			
	984	*Hydrochelidon indica* ...	......	Tr.			
	985	*Sterna seena* ...	......	Tr. ...	...	......	*
	995	*Rhynchops albicollis* ...	......	Tr.			
Tr. Piscatores. Cormorants.	1005	*Phalacrocorax carbo* ...	......	Tr.			
	1007	" *pygmæus* ...	......	Tr.			
	1008	*Plotus melanogaster* ...	......	Tr.			

Group	1	2		3	4	5	6
	Number in Oates (Jerdon's Nos. are in brackets).	Name.		Zone. Tr.=Tropic. STr.=Sub-trop. Te.=Tem-perate. SA.=Subalp. A.=Alpine.	Vertical range in feet.	Resident or not, or breeding. RC.=Certainly perma-nent re-sident. RP.=Probably resident. M.=Migratory. S.=Straggler. B.=Breeds.	*Remarks. * = *vide* 'Notes.'
		Scientific.	Vernacular. L.=Lepcha. P.=Pahāriyā. B.=Bhotia or Tibetan.				
Order Passeres or Perchers. Family Corvidæ, Subfam. Corvinæ. Raven.	1 (J657)	*Corvus corax* ...	B.—U-lāk (=its call).	STr.—Te. ...	150—12,000	R.C.	
Crows.	4 (J660)	,, *macrorhynchus* ...	......	Tr. ...	150—	R.C.	
	7 (J663)	,, *splendens* ...	......	Tr. ...	150—	R.C.	
Magpies.	13 (J672)	*Urocissa flavirostris* ...	L.—'Lho-chab-ling. B.—Pya-nye-jubring, or 'The long-tailed mischiev-ous bird.'	Te.—A. ...	5,000—16,000	R.C.	
	14 (J673)	*Cissa chinensis* ...	L.—*Dang* chab-ling.	STr. ...	600—9,000	R.C.	
Tree-pies.	16 (J674)	*Dendrocitta rufa* ...	L.—Kar-rhyok (one of its calls).	Tr.—Str. ...	150—3,000	R.C.	
	18 (J676)	,, *himalayensis* ...	L.—'*Lho* kar-rhyok.	Te. ...	2,000—7,000	R.C.	
	19 (J677)	,, *frontalis* ...	......	Str. ...	500—3,000	R.C.	
Jay.	26 (J669)	*Garrulus bispecularis* ...	L.—'Lho kar-rhyūm.	A. ...	13,000—		
Nut-cracker.	27 (J666)	*Nucifraga hemispila* ...	L.—'Lho Tō-wa (=' brown.') B.—Ulak.	A. ...	10,000—15,000		
Chough.	29 (J679)	*Graculus eremita* ...	B.—Kyungkā ...	A. ...	12,000—18,000	...	Common; resident in all villages in Central Tibet.
Subfamily Parinæ or Tits. Uncrested tits.	31 (J645)	*Parus atriceps* ...	L.—Chin-chi tak-ka.	Tr. ...	150—		
	34 (J644)	,, *monticolus* ...	......	Te. ...	3,000—11,000		
	35 (J634)	*Ægithaliscus erythrocephalus.*	......	STr.—Te. ...	2,000—8,000		
	39 (J635)	,, *ioschistus* ...	......	Te.—SA ...	8,000—1,000		
	40 (J632)	*Sylviparus modestus.*					
Crested tits.	41 (J649)	*Machlolophus spilonotus.*					
	48 (J641)	*Lophophanes beavani* ...	L.—Tā-sō				
	49 (J637)	,, *dichrous* ...	L.—Chin-chin-ka				
Subfam. Paradoxornithinæ or Crow Tits. Crow tits.	50 (J381)	*Conostoma æmodium* ...	L.—Sok-ta-bon.				
	51 (J373)	*Paradoxornis flavirostris.*					
	53 (J376)	*Suthora unicolor* ...	L.—Chong-ta-fyep.				
	54 (J378)	,, *humii.*					
	58 (J377)	,, *ruficeps.*					
	60 (J375)	*Scæorhynchus ruficeps* ...	L.—Chong-ta-fyep.	Te. ...	1,800—7,000	R.C.	

ORDER PASSERES, FAMILY CRATEROPODIDÆ, OR BABBLERS, &c.

SUB-FAM. CRATEROPODINÆ.

	1	2		3	4	5	6
	Number in Oates (Jerdon's Nos. are in brackets).	Name. Scientific.	Name. Vernacular. L.=Lepcha. P.=Pahāriya. B.=Bhotia or Tibetan.	Zone. Tr.=Tropic. STr.=Sub-trop. Te.=Temperate. SA.=Subalp. A=Alpine.	Vertical range in feet.	Resident or not, or breeding. R.C.=Certainly permanent resident. R.P.=Probably resident. M.=Migratory. S.=Straggler. B.=Breeds.	REMARKS. * = *vide* 'Notes.'
Laughing thrushes.	61 (J374)	*Sceorhynchus gularis* ...	......	Te. ...	2,000—6,000	R.C.	
	62 (J410)	*Dryonastes ruficollis* ...	L.—Rab-chu ...	STr. ...	200—4,000	R.C.	
	65 (J408)	„ *cærulatus* ...	L.—Tak-ō-wal...	Te. ...	3,000—6,000	R.C.	
	69 (J407)	*Garrulax leucolophus* ...	L.—Kar-rio ...	STr.—Te. ...	200—11,000	R.C.	
	72 (J412)	„ *pectoralis* ...	L.—Kar-rha-ōm	STr. ...	200—4,000	R.C.	
	73 (J413)	„ *moniliger* ...	......	STr.—Te ...	150—7,000	R.C.	
	76 (J411)	„ *albigularis*.					
	78 (J414)	*Ianthocincla ocellata* ...	L.—*Lho-kar-rhyo.*				
	80 (J921)	„ *rufigularis* ...	......	STr. ...	2,000—7,000	R.C.	
	85 (J416)	*Trochalopterum nigrimentum.*	L.—Tar-zhi ...	Te.—SA. ...	5,000—11,000		
	87 (J422)	„ *phœniceum*	......	STr.—Te. ...	1,000—6,000	R.C.	
	88 (J417)	„ *subunicolor*	L.—Tar-zhi.				
	89 (J419)	„ *affine* ...	*Lho.*—Tar-zhi ...	SA.—A. ...	9,000—15,000		
	92 (J420)	„ *squamatum*	L.—Tar-zhi ...	STr. ...	2,500—5,000	R.C.	
		var. melanurum	......	STr.			
	100 (J426)	„ *imbricatum.*					
	101 (J383)	*Grammatoptila striata* ...	......	Te. ...	4,000—10,000	R.C.	
Babblers.	104 (J439)	*Argya earlii.*					
	110 (J434)	*Crateropus canorus.*					
	116 (J403)	*Pomatorhinus schisticeps*	L.—Phor-rhyum	STr. ...	200—7,000	R.C.	
	122 (J401)	„ *ferruginosus* ...	L.—Po-mong kaum-ut.				
	125 (J400)	„ *ruficollis* ...	L.—Yong-kaum-ut.				
	129 (J405)	„ *erythrogenys* ...	L.—Phor-rhyūm	STr. ...	2,000—5,000	R.C.	
	133 (J406)	*Xiphorhamphus superciliaris.*	......	Te. ...	3,500—7,000	R.C.	

ORDER PASSERES, &c.—*contd.*

Group	1	2		3	4	5	6
	Number in Oates (Jerdon's Nos. are in brackets).	NAME. Scientific.	Vernacular. L.=Lepcha. P.=Pahāriya. B.=Bhotia or Tibetan.	Zone. Tr.=Tropic. STr.=Sub-trop. Te.=Temperate. SA.=Subalp. A.=Alpine.	Vertical range in feet.	Resident or not, or breeding. R.C.=Certainly permanent resident. R.P.=Probably resident. M.=Migratory S.=Straggler. B.=Breeds.	REMARKS. * = *vide* 'Notes.'
SUB-FAM. TIMELIINÆ. Small babblers.	134 (J396)	*Timelia pileata.*					
	137 (J384)	*Gampsorhynchus rufulus* ...	L.—Po-tsung Yom -lŏp-shel.	STr. ...	150—3,500	R. C.	
	139 (J385)	*Pyctorhis sinensis.*					
	142	*Pellorneum mandellii* ...	L—Sing-gri-em.				
	160 (J387)	*Turdinus abotti.*					
	163 (J388)	*Alcippe nepalensis* ...	L.—Sang-riem.				
	169 (J391)	*Stachyrhidopsis nigriceps*	L.— Ditto ...	...	2,000—6,000	R.C.	
	172 (J393)	„ *ruficeps.*					
	182 (J619)	*Sittiparus castaneiceps* ...	......	Te.—SA. ...	4,000—12,000	R.C.	
	183 (J622)	*Proparus vinipectus.*					
	185 (J335)	*Rimator malacoptilus* ...	L.—Kar-rlok Tung-brek.	...	4,000—6,000	R.C.	
SUB-FAM. BRACHYPTERYGINÆ. Short-winged thrush-babblers.	187 (J343)	*Myiophonus temmincki* ...	L.—Chab-mong.				
	191 (J507)	*Larvivora brunnea.*					
	201 (J328)	*Tesia cyaniventris* ...	L.—Sam-tit Tam-mong.	STr. ...	2,000—5,000	R.C.	
	202 (J327)	*Oligura castanei-coronata*	L.—Sam-tit ...	STr. ...	2,000—5,000	R.C.	
SUB-FAM. SIBIINÆ. Sibias.	203 (J430)	*Sibia picaoides* ...	L.—Sam-bri-ak. B.—Tsi-Tsi gŏ-nam.	STr. ...	1,000—4,000	R.C.	
	204 (J489)	*Lioptila capistrata* ...	L.—Sim-bri-ak	Te. ...	3,000—9,000	R.C.	
	208 (J613)	„ *annectens* ...	......	STr. ...	1,000—4,000	R.C.	
Bar-wings.	211 (J427)	*Actinodura egertoni* ...	......	Te. ...	2,000—11,000	R.C.	
	213 (J428)	*Ixops nepalensis* ...	L.—Mung-shok	Te.—SA. ...	6,000—10,000	R.C.	
Flower-peckers.	217 (J625)	*Staphidia rufigenis* ...	......	Te.—SA. ...	2,060—12,000	R.C.	
	219 (J616)	*Siva strigula* ...	......	Te. ...	4,000—8,000	R.C.	

ORDER PASSERES, &c.—*contd.*

SUB-FAM. SIBUNÆ—*contd.* / SUB-FAM. LIOTRICHINÆ. — Flower-peckers—*contd.*

1	2		3	4	5	6
Number in Oates (Jerdon's Nos. are in brackets).	Name. Scientific.	Name. Vernacular. L. = Lepcha. P. = Pahäriya. B. = Bhotia or Tibetan.	Zone. Tr. = Tropic. STr. = Sub-trop. Te. = Temperate. SA. = Subalp. A. = Alpine.	Vertical range in feet.	Resident or not, or breeding. R.C. = Certainly permanent resident. R.P. = Probably resident. M. = Migratory. S. = Straggler. B. = Breeds.	Remarks. * = *vide* 'Notes.'
221 (J. 617)	*Siva cyanuroptera* ...	......	STr.—Te ...	2,000—7,000	R.C	
223 (J. 626)	*Yuhina gularis* ...	L.-Kundo chong-ge or To-gyi.				
224 (J. 627)	„ *occipitalis* ...	L.—Mong-grit.				
225 (J. 628)	„ *nigrimentum* ...	L.—Tw-ring-ging	...	2,000—3,000	R.C.	
228	*Zosterops simplex.*					
231 (J. 624)	*Ixulus occipitalis* ...	......	Te. ...	2,000—8,000	R.C.	
232 (J. 623)	„ *flavicollis* ...	......	Te. ...	3,000—8,000	R.C.	
234 (J. 630)	*Herpornis xantholeuca.*					
235 (J. 614)	*Liothrix lutea* ...	......	...	4,000—8,000	R.C.	
236 (J. 612)	*Cutia nepalensis* ...	......	STr.—Te ...	2,000—7,000	R.C.	
237 (J. 609)	*Pteruthius erythropterus*...	L.—Rab nön.				
246 (J. 629)	*Myzornis pyrrhura* ...	L.—'*Lho* sag-vyit				
247 (J. 465)	*Chloropsis aurifrons* ...	L.—Chak-lem. B.—Kar-thak-gyäm.				
249 (J. 466)	„ *hardwickii* ...	L.—Chak-lem ...	STr. ...	800—4,000		
254 (J. 469)	*Irena puella* ...	L.—Nä-ni-vik ...	Te. ...	800—8,000	......	I have only seen it about 2'000 in spring. *G.*
255 (J. 650)	*Melanochlora sultanea* ...	L.—Ta-sô ...	STr. ...	200—3,500	R.C.	
256 (J. 610)	*Hilarocichla rufiventris* ...	L.—Rüp-nön ...	Te. ...	3,000—10,000	R.C.	
257 (J. 615)	*Mesia argentauris* ...	L.—Dang rah-chil.	STr. ...	3,000—6,000	R.C.	
258 (J. 618)	*Minla ignei-tincta* ...	L.—Mang-lim ...	Te.—SA. ...	5,000—10,000		

SUB-FAM. BRACHYPODINÆ. — Bulbuls.

1	2		3	4	5	6
263 (J. 451)	*Criniger flaveolus* ...	L.—Si-nyim-plek. B.—Wö-kyi.				
269 (J. 444)	*Hypsipetes psaroides* ...	L.—Fa-kyi ...	STr. ...	2,000—5,000		
272 (J. 448)	*Hemixus flavalus* ...	L.—Shi-ma than-gong.				
275 (J. 447)	„ *macclellandi* ...	L.—Chin-chi-ok	STr. ...	1,000—3,000	R.C.	
277 (J. 449)	*Alcurus striatus* ...	L.—Si-nyim-plek	Te. ...	3,000—	R.C.	
282 (J. 461)	*Molpastes bengalensis* ...	......	STr. ...	200—5,000	R.C.	
284 (J. 461)	„ *leucogenys* ...	L.—Mang-kli-op	STr. ...	1,000—4,000	R.C.	
288 (J. 460)	*Otocompsa emeria* ...	......	STr. ...	150—2,000	R.C.	
290 (J. 456)	„ *flaviventris.*					

	1	2		3	4	5	6
	Number in Oates (Jerdon's Nos. are in brackets).	NAME.		Zone. Tr. = Tropic. STr. = Sub-trop. Te. = Temperate. SA. = Subalp. A. = Alpine.	Vertical range in feet.	Resident or not, or breeding. R.C. = Certainly permanent resident. R.P. = Probably resident. M. = Migratory. S. = Straggler. B. = Breeds.	REMARKS. * = *vide* 'Notes.'
		Scientific.	Vernacular. L. = Lepcha. P. = Pahāriya. B. = Bhotia or Tibetan.				
ORDER PASSERES—*contd.* FAM. SITTIDÆ. Nuthatches.	315 (J.248)	*Sitta himalayensis* ...	L.—Kung-hlān = wood and climber.	STr.			
	316 (J.251)	„ *cinnamoneiventris* ...	L.—Kung-hlān	Te.			
	324 (J.252)	„ *formosa* ...	L.—Tashi kuyi gumbo.	Te. ...	6,000—8,000	R.C.	
	325 (J.253)	„ *frontalis* ...	L.—Kung-hlān	STr. ...	200—3,000		
FAM. DICRURIDÆ. Drongos.	326 (J.279)	*Dicrurus annectens.*					
	327 (J.278)	„ *ater.*					
	328 (J.280)	„ *longicaudatus* ...	......	Tr.—STr. ...	150—5,000	M.?	
	330 (J.281)	„ *cærulescens.*					
	333	„ *cineraceus.*					
	334 (J.282)	*Chaptia ænea* ...	......	STr. ...	150—4,000	R.C.	
	335 (J.286)	*Chibia hottentota* ...	L.—Fo-vong ...	STr. ...	150—2,500		
	339 (J.283)	*Bhringa remifer* ...	......	STr. ...	200—3,000	R.C.	
	340 (J.284)	*Dissemurus paradiseus* ...	......	Tr. ...	200—1,000		
	353 (J.334)	*Elachura punctata* ...	L.—Mar-chok ...	STr.—Te. ...	2,000—	R.C.	
FAM. CERTHIIDÆ. Wrens.	355 (J.331)	*Urocichla caudata* ...	......	Te.—SA. ...	4,000—6,000	R.C.	
	356 (J.329)	*Pnœpyga squamata* ...	L.—Mar-chong-long.	SA.			
	357 (J.330)	„ *pusilla.*					
	358 (J.580)	*Regulus cristatus.*					
FAM. SYLVIIDÆ OR WARBLERS.	371 (J.519)	*Tribura thoracica* ...	......	STr. ...	5,000—	......	Taken its eggs at 5,000′ *G.*
	410 (J.523)	*Phylloscopus fuscatus.*					
Fly-catcher-warblers.	433 (J.569)	*Cryptolopha burkii.*					
	435 (J.572)	„ *jerdonii.*					
	436 (J.575)	„ *poliogenys.*					
	441 (J.571)	*Abrornis schisticeps.*					
	444 (J.579)	*Tickellia hodgsoni.*					
	448 (J.526)	*Horornis fortipes.*					
	454 (J.531)	*Phyllergates coronatus.*					
	455 (J.527)	*Horeites brunneifrons* ...	......	......	3,000—4,500		
Hill-warblers.	458 (J.547)	*Suya crinigera.*					
	459 (J.549)	„ *atrigularis.*					

ORDER PASSERES, &c.—*contd.*

Group	1	2		3	4	5	6
	Number in Oates (Jerdon's Nos. are in brackets).	NAME.		Zone. Tr.=Tropic. STr.=Sub-trop. Te.=Temperate. SA.=Subalp. A.=Alpine.	Vertical range in feet.	Resident or not, or breeding. R.C.=Certainly permanent resident. R.P.=Probably resident. M.=Migratory. S.=Straggler. B.=Breeds.	REMARKS. * =*vide* 'Notes.'
		Scientific.	Vernacular. L.=Lepcha. P.=Pahāriya. B.=Bhotia or Tibetan.				
FAM. LANIIDÆ. Shrikes.	475 (J.259)	*Lanius nigriceps* ...	L.—Sa-krik ...	STr. ...	150—5,000	R.C. ...	Ascends high to breed.
	476 (J.257)	" *erythronotus.*					
	477 (J.258)	" *tephronotus* ...	L.—Sa-thyét ...	...	1,000—11,000		
	484 (J.267)	*Hemipus picatus* ...	L.—Viagum ...	STr. ...	600—4,000	R.C.	
	486 (J.263)	*Tephrodornis pelvicus* ...	......	STr. ...	600—3,500		
Minivets or scarlet-shrikes.	490 (J.271)	*Pericrocotus speciosus* ...	L.—Sag-vyit ...	STr.—T. ...	500—7,000	R.C.	
	495 (J.273)	" *brevirostris*...	L.—Sag-vyitmé-dong (or the fire-tailed sag-vyit).	Te.—A. ...	500—15,000	......	In rainy season above 4,000′.
	498 (J.274)	" *solaris* ...	......	STr. ...	200—2,500		
	499 (J.275)	" *roseus.*					
Cuckoo-shrikes.	505 (J.269)	*Campophaga melanoschista.*					
	506	" *melanoptera.*					
Swallow shrikes.	510 (J.270)	*Graucalus macii* ...	L.—Talling ...	STr. ...	600—4,000	R.C.	
	512 (J.287)	*Artamus fuscus* ...	......	STr. ...	150—4,500	M.	
FAM. ORIOLIDÆ. Orioles.	518 (J.470)	*Oriolus kundoo* ...	L.—Melam-bok.				
	521 (J.472)	" *melanocephalus* ...	L.—Dang-melam-bok.				
	522 (J.474)	" *trailii* ...	L.—Malām-thim-bok.	Te. ...	1,000—7,000	R.C.	
FAM. EULABETIDÆ. Wattled myns.	524 (J.693)	*Eulabes intermedia.*					
FAM. STURNIDÆ. STARLINGS AND MYNAS. Mynas.	538 (J.688)	*Sturnia malabarica* ...	......	...	M.	......	Breeds at 3—4,000′. *G.*
	549 (J.684)	*Acridotheres tristis.*					
	551 (J.685)	" *ginginianus.*					
	555 (J.683)	*Sturnopastor contra.*					

1	2		3	4	5	6
Number in Oates (Jerdon's Nos. are in brackets).	Name.		Zone.		Resident or not, or breeding.	
	Scientific.	Vernacular. L=Lepcha. P.=Pahāriya. B.=Bhotia or Tibetan.	Tr.=Tropic. STr.=Sub-trop. Te.=Temperate. SA.=Subalp. A.=Alpine.	Vertical range in feet.	R.C.=Certainly permanent resident. R.P.=Probably resident. M.=Migratory. S.=Straggler. B.=Breeds.	Remarks. * = *vide* 'Notes.'
Order Passeres, &c.—*contd.* — Fam. Muscicapidæ or Fly-catchers — Fly-catchers.						
558 (J.296)	*Hemicheldon sibirica* ...	......	Te. ...	3,500—8,000	R.	
559 (J.299)	,, *ferruginea* ...	L.—Dangchimba	Te. ...	4,000—8,000	R.C.	
560	*Siphia strophiata* ...	L.—Siri-tik-tik (its call).				
562	,, *albicilla* ...	L.—Ribur.				
569 (J.326)	*Cyornis melanoleucus* ...	L.—Tunu-ti-ti ...	...	2,000—6,000	R.C.	
573 (J.309)	,, *pallidipes.*					
574 (J.303)	,, *unicolor* ...	......	Tr. ...	150—3,000		
575 (J.304)	,, *rubeculoides.*					
578 (J.313)	(*Nitidula hodgsoni*) ...	......	...	4,000	R.C.	
579 (J301).	*Stoparola melanops* ...	L.—Sib-yel ...	S.Tr.—Te.	2,000—8,000	B.M. (in Lower Sikhim).	Absent in winter (from Lower Sikhim). Breeds from 4,000' upwards. *G.*
589 (J.307)	*Alseonax ruficaudus.*					
590	,, *muttui.*					
592 (J.295)	*Culicicapa ceylonensis.*					
'Niltavas' or Fairy blue chats.						
593 (J.316)	*Niltava grandis* ...	L.—Nani-vikj ...	Te.—SA. ...	5,000—12,000	R.C.	
594 (J.314)	,, *sundara* ...	L.—Shima-tang-gong.	STr.—Te. ...	2,000—8,000	R.C.	
595 (J.315)	,, *macgrigoriæ* ...	Tat-tak-tak ...	STr.—Te. ...	,000—8,000	R.C.	
Fly-catchers.						
598 (J.288)	(*Terpsiphone paradisi*) ...	......	Tr.—STr. ...	200—2,000		
599	,, *affinis.*					
601 (J.290)	*Hypothymis azurea.*					
603 (J.294)	*Chelidorhynx hypoxanthum*					
605 (J.291)	*Rhipidura albicollis* ...	L.—Nm-dit-nong				
Fam. Turdidæ or Thrushes, &c. — Sub-fam. Saxicolinæ or Chats — Bush-Chats.						
610 (J.483)	*Pratincola maura* ...	......	Tr.—STr. ...	1,000—5,000	R.C.	
614 (J.487)	*Oreicola jerdonii.*					
615 (J.486)	(,, *ferrea*) ...	L.—Sarrak-chak	...	5,000	R.C.	

ORDER PASSERES, FAMILY TURDIDÆ—*contd.*

SUB-FAM. RUTICILLINÆ OR REDSTARTS, &c.

	1	2		3	4	5	6
	Number in Oates (Jerdon's Nos. are in brackets).	NAME.		Zone. Tr.=Tropic. STr.=Sub-trop. Te.=Temperate. SA.=Subalp. A.=Alpine.	Vertical range in feet.	Resident or not, or breeding. R.C.=Certainly permanent resident. R.P.=Probably resident. M.=Migratory. S.=Straggler. B.=Breeds.	REMARKS. *=*vide* 'Notes.'
		Scientific.	Vernacular. L.=epcha. P.=Pahāriya. B.=Bhotia or Tibetan.				
Fork-tails.	630 (J. 584)	*Henicurus maculatus* ...	L.—'Lho Sam-chin or mountain 'Sam-chin.'	Te ...	1,000—9,000	R. C.	
	631 (J. 584)	" *guttatus* ...	L.—Ung Sam-chin or water 'Sam-chin.'				
	632 (J. 586)	" *schistaceus* ...	......	STr. ...	150—3,000	R. C.	
	633 (J. 585)	" *immaculatus* ...	L.—Dang Sam-chim.	Tr. ...	150—		
	634	" *leschenaultii.*					
	637 (J. 587)	*Microcichla scouleri* ...	L.—Ung' Sam-chin fo kap or little water 'Sam-chin.'	STr. ...	1,000—5,000		
Redstarts.	638 (J. 506)	*Chimarrhornis leucocephalus.*	L.—Mar-ti-tap (=the butter-capped stone-settler).	Tr.—A. ...	3,000—15,000	R. C. M. in Lower Sikhim—cold weather only.	
	639 (J. 503)	*Ruticilla frontalis* ...	L.—Siri-tik-tik (=its call).	...	...	M.—cold weather only.	
	640 (J. 501)	" *schisticeps* ...	L.—'Lho ka-li-ik-tik.				
	641 (J. 500)	" *aurorea.*					
	643 (J. 498)	" *hodgsoni* ...	L.—Shib-tak.				
	644 (J. 497)	" *rufiventris.*					
	646 (J. 505)	*Rhyacornis fuliginosa.*					
Robins.	647 (J. 514)	*Cyanecula suecica.*					
	652	*Calliope tschebaiewi.*					
	653 (J. 511)	*Tarsiger chrysæus* ...	L.—Shib-trak-trak.	Te.—SA. ...	3,000—13,000		
	654 (J. 508)	*Ianthia rufilata.*					
	655 (J. 510)	" *indica* ...	L.—Ta-song ...	Te.—SA. ...	6,500—11,000		
	658 (J. 478)	*Grandala cœlicolor.*					
	659 (J. 477)	(*Notodela leucura*) ...	L.—Mangshia ...	Te. ...	4,000—		
	660 (J. 340)	*Callene frontalis.*					
	663 (J. 475)	*Copsychus saularis* ...	L.—Zo-nyong ...	STr. ...	...	150—4,000	
	664 (J. 476)	*Cittocincla macrura* ...	......	STr. ...	150—3,000		

Group	1	2		3	4	5	6
	Number in Oates (Jerdon's Nos. are in brackets).	Name. Scientific.	Name. Vernacular. L.=Lepcha. P.=Pahāriya. B.=Bhotia or Tibetan.	Zone. Tr.=Tropic. STr.=Sub-tropic. Te.=Temperate. SA.=Sub-Alpine. A.=Alpine.	Vertical range in feet.	Resident or not, or breedidg. R.C.=Certainly permanent resident. R.P.=Probably resident. M.=Migratoay. S.=Straggler. B.=Breeds.	Remarks. *=vide 'Notes.'
Order Passeres, Family Turdidæ—contd. Sub-fam. Turdinæ. Ouzels.	672 (J. 362)	*Merula albocincta* ...	L.—'Lhomong-rhyüm.				
	675 (J. 364)	,, *ruficollis* ...	......	A. ...	8,000—16,000	M.—winter only. *G.*	
	676 (J. 361)	,, *boulboul* ...	L.—Cha-mong...	Te. ...	4,000—12,000	R. C.	
	677 (J. 365)	,, *atrigularis* ...	L.—Mang-rhüm	A. ...	8,000—16,000	M.—winter only. *G.*	
Rock-thrushes.	686 (J. 355)	*Geocichla citrina* ...	L.—Mang-rhyüm or Kantu-na-yüm.	STr. ...	150—6,000	R. C.	
	690 (J. 352)	*Petrophila erythrogastra.*					
	692	,, *solitaria.*					
	693 (J. 351)	,, *cyana.*					
Mountain thrushes.	698 (J.371)	*Oreocincla dauma* ...	L.—Fat-nok-kyok (the earthy black 'kyok').	ST.—Te. ...	2,000—10,000		
	701 (J.370)	,, *mollissima* ...	L.—Mong-rhem.				
	702	,, *dixoni.*					
Brown thrushes.	704 (J. 350)	*Zoothera monticola* ...	L.—Fa-nok-kyok.				
	705	,, *marginata.*					
	706 (J.607)	*Cochoa purpurea* ...	L.—'Lho kar-rhyok.	Te. ...	2,500—10,000	......	Nest take at 6,000' *G.*
	707 (J.608)	,, *viridis* ...	......	STr.—Te. ...	500—8,000		
Sub-fam. Cinclinæ. Dippers.	708 (J.348)	*Cinclus kashmirensis* ...	L.—Nam-bong kar-rhyok				
	709 (J.347)	,, *asiaticus.*					
Sub-fam. Accentrinæ. Accentors.	712 (J. 652)	*Accentor nepalensis.*					
	718 (J. 654)	*Tharrhaleus strophiatus.*					
Fam. Ploceidæ. Weaver birds.	720 (J.694)	*Ploceus baya.*					
	721	,, *megarhynchus.*					
Munias.	727 (J.702)	*Uroloncha acuticauda* ...	......	Tr.—STr.	150—4,000	R. C.	
	735 (J.699)	,, *punctulata* ...	......	Tr.—STr.	150—4,000	R. C.	
Fam. Fringillidæ. Grosbeaks.	742 (J.726)	*Pycnorhamphus affinis.*					
	743 (J.728)	,, *carneipes.*					
Bulfinches.	746 (J.729)	*Pyrrhula erythrocephala...*	L.—'Lho Nam-prek				
	748 (J.731)	,, *nepalensis* ...	L.—Nam-prek.				

ORDER PASSERES, FAMILY TURDIDÆ—*contd.*

		1	2		3	4	5	6
		Number in Oates (Jerdon's Nos. are in brackets).	NAME.		Zone.		Resident or not, or breeding.	
			Scientific.	Vernacular. L. = Lepcha. P. = Pahāriya. B. = Bhotia or Tibetan.	Tr. = Tropic. STr. = Sub-trop. Te. = Temperate. SA. = Subalp. A. = Alpine.	Vertical range in feet.	R.C. = Certainly permanent resident. R.P. = Probably resident. M. = Migratory. S. = Straggler. B. = Breeds.	REMARKS. * = *vide* 'Notes.'
FAM. FRINGILLIDÆ.	Finches.	749 (J.733)	*Pyrrhoplectes epauletta.*					
		751 (J.735)	*Hæmatospiza sipahi* ...	L.—Fo-liu. B.—Ka-bya.				
	Rose finches.	754 (J.740)	*Propasser thura.*					
		755 (J.743)	" *pulcherrima.*					
		760	" *edwardsi* ...	L.—Folin. B.—Ka-bya.				
		761 (J.738)	*Carpodacus erythrius.*					
		765 (J.746)	*Procarduelis nepalensis.*					
	Buntings and sparrows.	770	*Acanthis brevirostris.*					
		773	*Chrysomitris tibetana* ...	L.—Tak-nyel nyŏn or 'the wormwood *nyŏn*.'				
		776 (J.706)	*Passer domestica.*					
		803 (J.724)	*Melophus melanicterus.*					
FAM. MOTACILLIDÆ OR WAGTAILS, &C.	Wagtails.	826	*Motacilla alba.*					
		827 (J.590)	" *leucopsis* ...	L.—Tang-zhen fleu.	...	...	Cold weather only.	
		829 (J.591)	" *personata.*					
		830	" *hodgsoni.*					
		831 (J.589)	" *maderaspatensis.*					
		837	" *citreola.*					
	Tree pipit.	841 (J.596)	*Anthus maculatus* ...	L.—Tong-zhim.				
		844 (J.604)	" *similis.*					
		846 (J.601)	" *striolatus* ...	......	...	...	Cold weather only.	
		848 (J.602)	" *campestris.*					

ORDER PASSERES, FAMILY TURDIDÆ—*concld.*

Group	1 Number in Oates (Jerdon's Nos. are in brackets).	2 Name. Scientific.	2 Name. Vernacular. L.=Lepcha. P.=Pahārya. B.=Bhotia or Tibetan.	3 Zone. Tr.=Tropic. STr.=Sub-trop. Tr.=Temperate. SA.=Subalp. A.=Alpine.	4 Vertical range in feet.	5 Resident or not, or breeding. R. C.=Certainly permanent resident. R.P.=Probably resident. M.=Migratory. S.=Straggler. B.=Breeds.	6 Remarks. *=*vide* 'Notes.'
FAM. NECTARINIDÆ. Sun-birds.	882 (J.225)	*Æthopygia seheriæ* ...	L.—Dang sag-vyet.	STr. ...	150—3,000		
	887 (J.228)	„ *ignicauda* ...	L.—'Lho sag-vyet.	Te. ...	...	......	At low elevations in winter and spring. Ascends high to breed. *G.*
	888 (J.227)	„ *gouldiæ* ...	......	...	4,000—6,000	R. C.	Have taken its eggs at 6,000'. *G.*
	890 (J.231)	„ *saturata* ...	L.—Dang sag-vyet.	STr. ...	1,000—5,000	R. C.	
	892 (J.229)	„ *nepalensis* ...	L.—Sag-vyet ...	...	3,000—9,000	R. C.	
Spider hunters.	906 (J.223)	*Arachnothera magna* ...	L.—Dang si-ri-ok	STr. ...	500—4,500	R. C.	
	909 (J.224)	„ *longirostris.*					
FAM. DICÆIDÆ. Pigmy flower-peckers.	912 (J.226)	*Dicæum cruentatum* ...	L.—Ti-pro.				
	914 (J.237)	„ *chrysorrhæum.*					
	915 (J.241)	„ *ignipectus.*					
FAM. PITTIDÆ. Pittas.	927 (J.344)	*Pitta nepalensis* ...	L.—Ta-ut ...	STr. ...	2,000—6,000	R. C.	
	935 (J.346)	„ *cucullata* ...	L.—Fat-tim.				

NOTES ON THE FOREGOING LIST OF SIKHIM BIRDS.

BY L. A. WADDELL, F.L.S.

3 bis. Gyps fulvescens (Hume).—This fine bird, a male, in October plumage, answers generally to the description of this species, but it differs in several details. The ruff is pale earthy-grey, more rufous on the mantle and interscapulars. Feathers of the back are not pale-centred. The rump is dark bronzy-brown, like the wings, only the lateral feathers being centred. No white patch on the back. Third primary is longest. Beneath, from the breast, darker, especially towards the vent and flanks, where the feathers have dark brown centres. The tail feathers have a subterminal broad whitish bar slightly mottled with brown. Length 36·5 inches, wings 24·7, tail 12·2, bill length (straight) from front of cere 2·05, breadth at gape 1·7, depth at cere 1·35, length of cere above 0·7, claw of midtoe (straight) 1·25.

17. Cerchneis tinnunculus.—Bill bluish-grey, greenish-yellow at base, and black at tip. Cere greenish-yellow. Feet ochrey. Claws blackish. Forehead greyish-rufous rather than yellowish.

20. Hierax cærulescens.—Bill horny-black with greenish-yellow base. Legs dark green. Claws black. Chin, vent, thigh, and under tail coverts dark ferruginous.

23. Astur badius.—The adults have the rufous demi-collar broad and well marked.

27. Aquila nepalensis.—A female in January. Length 31·3. Wing 23·2, and they reach to 2·6 from end of tail. The tail has no black subterminal band, nor have the shoulders, scapulars, wings, or under-surface any white spots or bars.

33. Nisætus fasciatus.—Young male in January. Length 24·4. It has the lower part of forehead almost pure white. Chin, throat, and breast are much darker than abdomen, owing to the feathers, which are white at their bases, having mesial dark brown streaks with fulvous centring which becomes larger and more rufous on the breast.

36. Limnætus nepalensis.—Male in January. Length 26·4. Crest 4·95. Claw of midtoe (straight) 1·1. Inner lining of wings light rufous-brown mostly with dark brown centres. The whitish spots on breast are in transverse series as interrupted bars. Rump uniform hair-brown except at flanks, which as well as the uppermost of the under tail coverts are barred whitish.

37. L. kienierii.—This extremely beautiful bird varies considerably from Jerdon's description. A male in April measures in length 26·4, wing 17·9, mid claw (straight) 1·1, central feathers of crest ·4—which latter is black with a white tip. Above the general colour is a very pale brown, lighter than in *L. nepalensis*. Head pale fulvous-white, becoming rufous on the hind neck, and all the feathers are white at the base with brown shafts and centres which become larger and duskier on the nape. Chin, throat, and breast white. The feathers of hind throat with brown shafts and centres like those along sides of breast and flanks. The secondary quills and the primary, greater, and median wing coverts are margined whitish towards their tips. Axillaries are rufous streaked with brown. Rump and upper tail coverts are margined with white. Tail has eight brown bands, and the tips of all the feathers are acuminate.

39. Spilornis cheela.—One of these, a male from Mathouli, on the east of the Tista, in March, with length of 28·5, has the undersurface from the throat to the breast an earthy-buff transversely barred with brownish. The chin, throat, cheeks, and ear coverts are pale bluish-grey. All the tail feathers are margined with white at their tips, and all have a subterminal band 2·7 broad of pure white very slightly mottled with pale brown at the lower border.

47. Buteo plumipes.—This bird, a young male, shot in October in the Poi La leading into Chumbi, corresponds with Blanford's description[1] except in the following details. The lores anteriorly are covered with albescent feathers with hair-like extremities; and posteriorly with radiating black hairs. The albescent feathers are prolonged upwards on either side of the forehead, giving a whitish streaky appearance in that region in front of the superciliary ridge. The ear coverts are paler than the general colour and mottled with some rufous-grey. Darkish moustachial stripe. On the nape a conspicuous demi-collar of pale fulvous bay streaks, due to feathers here being white with dark brown extremities margined proximately with pale fulvous-bay. The white spots on the scapulars are present, but require searching for by turning down the feathers. The whitish on the primary quills is mottled with buff along inner border of the inner webs. The pale dingy rufous bars on secondaries number from 5 to 3. Underwing coverts at shoulder are faintly margined with rufous. Throat and breast dark brown like back and thighs; a few of the feathers here with faintly rufous margins, and also on abdomen and flanks, but insufficient to give any general rufous tint. Tarsal plumes interspersed with thready tufts. Tarsal feathers mottled greyish-brown. The posterior tarsal large scutes number only four, above which are 8 bifid ones of hedra-, penta-, and sexagonal shapes. The anterior tarsal scales are hexagonal and pentagonal. The fourth primary is the longest, and the quills are emarginate on the inner and

[1] *loc cit.*, page 42.

outer webs as in Mr. Blanford's description. Length 19·2, wing 15·4, tail 9·35, tarsus 2·7, tarsus feathered in front for 1·7, midtoe without claw 1·2, claw round curve 0·78, inner toe 0·85, its claw 0·95. Bill straight from end of cereo ·68, round curveo ·85, from gape 1·4, depth at cere 0·6, breadth at gape 1·2.

53. Circus melanoleucus.—Greater wing coverts and tail silvery grey.

55. Haliastur indus.—Bill pale greenish-horny, yellowish at tip and commissure. Cere yellow. Irides: of male golden-yellow, of female bronzy-pink.

64. Syrnium newarense.—Adult male. Length 22·5, wing 15·3, tail 8·9, tarsus 2·5, bill at front (straight) 1·75, from gape 1·7. Anterior margin of cere to point of bill (straight) 1·0, width at gape 1·25, depth of closed bill at cere 0·8, closed wings short of tail 2·5.

Adult female. Length 20·0, wing 14·25, tail 8·7, tarsus 2·4, bill at front 1·6, from gape 1·55, anterior margin at cere to point of bill 0·9, width at gape 1·3, depth of closed bill at cere 0·8, closed wings short of tail 2·5.

These two birds are of identical appearance. The colour of the bands on the coverts and scapulars range from silvery-white to fulvous-buff. The tips of the quills are ashy. The pectoral band is present.

72. Ketupa ceylonensis.—Length of this female 23·5. Chin and upper throat ashy; lower throat white, some of the feathers having dark brown centrings and shaft streaks.

73. K. flavipes.—The lengths of these two birds are 25 and 22·6, and wing 18·2 and 18·1 respectively. The bill is horny-black with the lower mandible paler underneath. Claws dusky livid. The 'dashes of brown' on the under-surface are well-defined shaft streaks about 2·0 long by 0·2 in breadth. Its call is considered an omen of death; hence it is called by the Lepchas *mung*, which means 'devil.'

75. Scops lettia.—Mr. Gammie took the eggs of *E. surpigi* at 5,500′.

76. Carine brama.—Bill greenish-horny, darker at base. The feathers of hind neck are broadly margined at their tips with ashy-white, forming a demi-collar of that colour. In the disc a whitish supercilium in front. Chin, throat, and cheeks unsullied white.

81. Ninox scutellatus.—Head and nape a darker and more ashy-brown than rest of upper plumage. At sides of breast the spots are massed together, forming a dusky ferruginous patch. On abdomen and thigh-coverts the spots are cordate and of large size. Chin ashy-white. Throat mottled with fulvous.

107. Caprimulgus indicus.—Mr. Gammie took its eggs at 5,500′.

122. Nyctiornis athertoni.—Bill horny-blackish. Irides pale golden. Forehead greenish-cærulian.

123. Coracias indica.—Only the lower back is blue. The greater portion is dusky brown with a pale blue spot on the shoulder, which *C. affinis* has not got.

124. C. affinis.—Lores and ear-coverts light hair-brown. Cheeks, throat, and breast with purple shaft streaks, becoming cærulian on throat.

126. Eurystomus orientalis.—Bill deep coral red, except the tip of culmen which is dark horny; and none of the birds in May have any blue on the upper part of head-lores, cheeks or ear-coverts.

127. Pelargopsis gurial.—Side by side with the typical race exists a smaller race about 13·5 in length with a very much lighter cap of pale ashy-brown, and the chin is almost white; the buff under-plumage also is much less deep or rich. The kingfishers are confined to the lower and outer hills owing to the scarcity of fish in the higher glacier-fed streams.

129. Halcyon smyrnensis.—The tail feathers have black shafts, and all except the uppermost two have black margins to the inner webs.

131. H. coromandelianus.—Mr. Gammie gives its call as '*piccadilly-ooh-ooh-ooh.*'

134. Alcedo bengalensis.—One male from the Dichhu river shot in March, length 6·2. Irides dull crimson, differs from all the other specimens in having no rufous band posterior to the eye—the ear-coverts in their entire extent being cobalt with darkish streaks. Its chin and throat are pale buff—not pure white, and the rest of its lower surface is very deep ferruginous, almost chestnut.

138. Psarisomus dalhousiæ.—Bill dingy olive with culmen and mental ridge lemon-yellow; the commissure margins whitish-horny. No rictal bristles.

139. Serilophus rubropygius.—Has a somewhat shrike-like appearance with rictal bristly feathers and hairs. Irides dark slate. Orbital skin citrine. Bill dark plumbeous-olive with bony-yellow culmen and mental ridge; tip and commissure pale horny. Tarsus pale greenish-yellow. Metatarsus cobalt. Claws darkly livid with horny dorsal line and tips. An ill-defined supercilium of deep slaty-blue continued backwards to the margin of crest as dark hair-brown. The first primary quill without blue; the others, except the second, with a white streak on the inner border of the blue spot in outer web. The secondaries with a white subterminal streak bordering the bar of the slaty-blue tip. Beneath pale slaty-grey. The nuchal patch or demi-collar silvery-white in two specimens; in the third, December 29th, there is no trace of this white. Mr. Gammie has taken its nest at 3,800′.

147. Palæornis nepalensis.—Bill dusky cherry-red with yellowish tip; lower mandible paler. The demi-collar dull peach-rose. The glaucous blue is confined to the nape and does not extend to the cheeks. Feet dull ochrey. The wing-spot is dark crimson.

148. P. torquatus.—The blue wash on nape and sides of neck extends also to mantle and upper back, where it merges into the green. The nuchal ring of the females is emerald above and greenish-yellow below.

150. P. schisticeps.—Head dark slaty. The demi-collar of emerald-green has its posterior border ill-defined. The young male, January, length 13·2, has no wing-spot.

152. P. fasciatus.—Bill: upper mandible cherry-red, yellowish at tip; lower horny-black. Frontal band deep black. No supercilium. What seems a young male, in November, has bill entirely black, and the under-surface from the throat downwards uniform green. Mr. Gammie has shot it in spring at 3,300.'

155. Picus majoroides.—Bill: upper mandible blackish-slaty; lower pale bluish-grey in its anterior two-thirds. Average length 8 inches—none exceed 8·7. The general colour of the under-surface is a dingy isababelline, becoming dingy fulvous-buff on breast and abdomen, and merging into orange on the vent. No white spot on outer web of first primary. The three outer tail feathers are banded with yellowish. The lower forehead is dingy fulvous-grey. Neck patch is dull orange—in none is it silky golden-yellow, and it is not perceptibly duller in the adult females. A young male in September, length 7·7, has the crown feathers tipped with crimson, while there is no crimson on the nape; and its under-surface is almost as deeply streaked as in the adult; but its neck patches are pale tawny. It ranges up to the pine forests of Tankar La about 13,000 feet.

156. P. cathpharius.—These two birds agree well with Jerdon's description of this species except in size,—both are only 5·7 in length. One is a male from Gurubathan, 2,000 feet, in March, and has the full adult markings. The other, a young male from Single La 10,000, in November, and is also deeply marked with the exception of the crimson nuchal patches and gorget which are very pale crimson-buff.

157. P. macei.—Bill dusky plumbeous; anterior half of lower mandible livid, but not reddish. Irides dark brown. Lower forehead light fulvous-grey. Crest of male crimson mixed with ashy-black. The oval spots on side of breast are black, and the lower breast and abdomen are streaked with black or dusky, becoming irregular transverse bars on the loins. Thighs are fulvous-grey. Under tail coverts crimson.

161. Hypopicus hyperythrus.—Bill: upper mandible horny-black; lower pale bony-yellow, greenish at the base. Forehead greyish-white like chin, lores and cheeks. A rufous-bay demi-collar borders the crimson of the occiput and nape, and within this collar, in five specimens, is a short crimson bar, in the upper and hind part of neck, but in none is this bar continued to the undersides of the neck or breast. Wings black with white spots, generally in series with those of the back, forming transverse bars. Thighs whitish barred with black. Vent and under tail coverts crimson.

162. Yungipicus rubricatus.—Forehead greyish-white below, mottled dark fulvous above. Ear-coverts hair-brown. A female in February, length 5·1.

166. Chrysocolaptes sultaneus.—Bill dull greenish-horny, with the middle third of lower mandible paler. Claws darkly livid. The white band of nape is continued to upper back, where it ends in several large central drops of white.

166 bis. C. delesserti.—Bill as above; middle third of lower mandible paler. The dorsals, scapulars, and wing-coverts largely smeared with red. Forehead feathers with a few pale subterminal spots. A male in April at Simana on the Nepal frontier, elevation 7,000, measured—length 10·5, tail 3·7, wing 6·7, bill at front 1·8, at gape 2·15.

172. Gecinus occipitalis.—Bill horny-black. The males have the lower forehead ashy, each feather centred with black. Lores black mottled with grey. Black moustachial stripe along inferior border of mandible to below ear-coverts, where its extremity does not curve upwards. In none are the chin and part of the throat white. The chin is dusky ashy, becoming dingy olive on the upper throat. Two out of the four females have crimson on the head.

173. Chrysophlegma flavinucha.—Bill bluish-horny, becoming white towards the tip. Claws darkly livid. Nasal feathers in male greenish; in female reddish-brown. Feathers of forehead and crown have greenish tips, which become broader and more conspicuous on the occiput. The yellow of nape is silky golden. The female has the cheeks as well as the chin and throat reddish-brown and obscurely streaked with blackish. A young female in October has the cheeks unspotted ruddy-sulphureous, and the chin and throat faintly rufous with dusky streaks.

174. C. chlorolopha.—In the male the crimson supercilium is continued forwards to encircle the forehead, and backwards around the nape in front of the yellow, thus forming a continuous coronet. The dusky markings across the cheeks and throat have the form of irregular bars.

176. Blythipicus pyrrhotis.—Bill lemon-yellow, dusky olive at base, and pale horny at tip. Claws darkly livid. Forehead and chin pale vinous-grey, the midribs of the feathers of chin and upper throat being prolonged as black hairs.

177. Gecinulus grantius.—Forehead dingy fulvous. Chin and upper throat greenish-grey. Its usual call is "*terr-terr*," which is indicated by its Lepcha name. When it occasionally calls "*mī-mi*," this is regarded as an evil omen—*mī* being the negative particle in both the Lepcha and Bhotiya languages.

178. Micropternus phaioceps.—A slight crest. Irides dusky brown. Bill horny-black; the inferior border of lower mandible greenish-horny in its middle third. Three out of the seven females have the crimson mandibular stripe extending backwards to the ear-coverts. The colour of the breast ranges from light to dark chestnut-bay or ferruginous. In one female, without the crimson cheek stripes, the feathers of the chin and throat are darkly pigmented on either side of shaft, while the edges are unusually pale, almost like *M. gularis;* but the lower abdomen is barred. The feathers of crown and nape are smeared with the gum resin of some tree.

180. Brachypternus aurantius.—A male in March, length 11·6, generally answers to Jerdon's description. The feathers of the median and lesser wing coverts have subterminally a heart-shaped spot of fulvescent-white. The outer web of the primaries, excepting the first, have whitish spots corresponding with those on the inner, and these spots are three in number, excepting the second and third quills, which have one and two respectively. The tips of the primaries are greenish-brown.

181. B. puncticollis.—A female in February has the bill horny-black. Irides pale prune. Legs pale sap-green. Claws plumbeous. A conspicuous fringe of crimson-tipped feathers on the occiput. The median and lesser wing coverts are less spotted than in *B. aurantius.* The tertiary are unspotted; and the spots are of an acuminate ovoid shape. The primary quills have the whitish spots on their outer webs more defined and regular, so as to form two and-a-half interrupted whitish bars.

187. Sasia ochracea.—Bill: upper mandible horny-black; lower pale greenish underneath. Winglet margined with pale buff. Wing-lining and axillaries silvery-white. Rump and upper tail ochraceous—slightly lighter than breast. Legs fleshy-pink. Claws pale horny-grey.

192. Megalæma hodgsoni.—As there seems some doubt about the characters of this species, I give here some details of my seven specimens on the points in question:—

Males—

Length	9·7 — 8·8	inches.
Expanse	12·0 —11·6	„
Wing	5·3 — 5·2	„
Tail	3·4 — 3·15	„
Bill from gape	1·5 — 1·4	„
„ at front	1·15— 1·13	„

Females—

Length	10·1 — 8·6	inches.
Expanse	12·0 —11·3	„
Wing	5·4 — 5·3	„
Tail	3·3 — 2·8	„
Bill from gape	1·55— 1·45	„
„ at front	1·2 — 1·15	„

Bill livid yellowish-bony, less livid at base, and horny along commissure. Orbital skin deep yellow. In both sexes chin and throat greenish-white, with faint fulvous tinge on lower throat. The rib of each gular feather is prolonged into a black hair. The head, neck, breast, and upper abdomen are dingy fulvous-white, with pale brown edgings to each feather, which edgings, being broader on the forehead, crown, and neck, give to these parts a darker tint than the breast. First and second primaries free from green; they are black, with fulvous borders near the base of the inner web. Mr. Gammie has found it only in the Tarai.

195. M. asiatica.—The red rictal spot is margined posteriorly with green; and the band across crown is bordered anteriorly with golden-olive.

196. M. franklinii.—The first and second primaries have a pale edging on the inner web. The large rictal spot is orange. The narrow blue band fringing the black and crimson of nape extends also obsoletely along margin of throat patch, thus forming a complete ring.

199. Cuculus canorus.—The bill citrine at base, horny-black at tip and anterior part of culmen; the rest of the bill is sap-green. Gape and lining of mouth and throat rich deep orange. Legs ochrey. Claws dusky ochrey. Irides pale straw, with orange periphery. The breast bars average seventeen. The under tail coverts in one are almost free from markings. Its Lepcha name, viz., *kuk-ku*, is identical with the English one.

202. C. sonnerati.—A bird which does not seem to represent the hepatic stage of *C. canorus* differs somewhat from Jerdon's description of *C. sonnerati*. It is a female in May from Labah, 7,000 feet, and measures as follows:—Length 12·4, wing 8·2, bill from front 0·7, from gape 1·15. The colour of bill and gape is similar to *C. canorus*. The coverts of primaries are barred with rufous like the rest of the back, and all of the feathers on the upper surface, including the quills of wing and tail, and of the under-surface in front of the breast, are narrowly bordered with ashy at their tips. Under-surface from chin white with numerous transverse black bars, about $\frac{1}{12}$th of an inch broad. Rump more ashy than rest of upper plumage. Under tail coverts slightly fulvous, with arrow markings.

205. Hierococcyx varius.—Its Lepcha name "Bīm-pī-yul" is a good representation of its call. It is the "brain-fever" bird of many Europeans in India who thus interpret its call, and from its coming at the onset of the hot weather.

213. Coccystes coromandus.—Tail feathers, except uropygials and under tail coverts (which are black), are margined whitish at the tips. Two males in May measure in length 15·3, wings 6·4 and 6·5.

214. Eudynamys honorata.—Irides bright crimson in both sexes. Barring of tail in male almost imperceptible.

215. Rhopodytes tristis.—Bill unripe apple-green and orbital skin dull crimson.

217. Centrococcyx rufipennis.—Tail feathers margined with whitish at their tips.

218. C. bengalensis.—Tail feathers margined with rufous at their tips. Young in January, with bill fleshy-livid and culmen dark brown. Irides pale grey.

[For the intervening numbers comprising the rest of the *Passeres*, see the appended second series numbered according to OATES' new work on the *Birds of India.*]

776. Osmotreron phayrei.—This pretty pigeon seems very rare. Bill pale bluish-horny. Forehead and crown pale slate. Green of plumage dullish, lighter on chin and throat. Dusky orange buff patch on breast forming a semi-collar. Central tail feathers entirely olive-green. The tips of the lower tail feathers almost pure white. Length of males 10·7 to 10·3.

783. Alsocomus hodgsonii.—Only found in upper regions near the limits of forests. Is not common. Was not seen by Blanford.

785. Palumbus pulchricollis.—The isababelline-tipped feathers form a demi-collar and mantle.

790. Columba leuconota.—Only in upper regions. These formed for a time Hooker's sole animal food—*Himal. Jours.* II, page 72.

791. Macropygia tusalia.—Irides pale rosy-pink, legs and feet dull crimson-lake, claws greenish-horny. None of my four adult females have the crown barred—this barring is only found on one young male and one young female of December. The females are not more conspicuously barred than the males on the under-surface; but a one-year old female from Labah 7,000 in June, is finely barred all over under-surface from chin to under tail coverts, which latter have the superficial feathers also barred.

793. Turtur meena.—All of my specimens (6) are typical *T. meena* and cannot be classed as *T. rupicolus*. In none is the neck-spot black, nor has the tail a white tip, nor the under tail coverts any white—these are in all an almost uniform shade of dull ashy-grey.

795. T. suratensis.—Irides fleshy-purple like the orbital skin.

803 quat. Polyplectrum tibetanum.—Two males in April, length 25·0—26·2, tail 14·2—14·5, wing 8·6—8·8. These differ from Hume's plate in the *Game Birds of India*, &c., vol. I, page 105, in having the ground-colour pale ashy, without any rufous tint except at neck, where there is, in one of the birds, a dingy rufous tint over the ashy. The spots are much more numerous and minute than in the plate. The ocelli of the wings have a purply-green iridescence with deep lilac borders. The orbital skin is fleshy-pink. The chin and throat are fulvous-ashy, slightly paler on the cheeks, but much more fulvous than in the plate.

803 sept. Crossoptilum tibetanum.—Hume doubts whether this bird has been procured on this side of the Himalayas. Several Bhotiyas to whom I have shown Hume's plate (in *Game Birds*) state that it is found occasionally below the Kapap pass near the Jelep and also in the higher passes of Bhutan.

811. Gallophasis melanota.—These were all true *G. melanota*, and none approached *G. leucomelana.*

825. Arboricola torqueola.—The top of the head is olive like the back, with black shaft streaks.

825 bis. A. mandellii.—This seems to be the first record of these birds from Sikhim. Hume states (*Game Birds*, II, 84) that this species has only been found hitherto in the Bhutan Duars, and only about a dozen specimens. My two birds were got well within Sikhim—the first below Tendong, at an elevation of about 5,000, in December, and the second near Gangtok, about 4,000, in January. It may have escaped notice hitherto owing to its shyness.

851. Vanellus cristatus.—Jerdon states that this bird is found in India "only in the Panjab." My bird, from Maniphung, 7,000, near the Nepal frontier, in November, agrees with Jerdon's description generally; but it has the scapulars and the sooty-black feathers of the breast broadly margined with fulvous-white, and the mantle feathers more narrowly margined with the same.

891. Actitis glareola.—The outermost tail feather has a small black subterminal spot in the outer web.

907. Gallinula phœnicura.—A female in January has the lower forehead, lores, superciliary region, cheeks and ear-coverts white, very slightly mottled with brown.

931. Butorides javanica.—The blackish head and crest have a green gloss.

933. Ardetta cinnamomea.—Does not correspond well with Jerdon's description. The general tint above is a dusky cinnamon. It has a blackish chin and throat stripes, and all the under-surface broadly streaked longitudinally with dark brown.

955—970. Most of these migratory ducks pass over Sikhim without settling, but stragglers are occasionally shot.

985. Sterna seena.—The head, above, is mixed ashy-grey and black, the latter predominating over the hinder part of lores and ear coverts.

O. (1) **13. Urocissa flavirostris.**—Out of 14 specimens five have those portions of the lower plumage and tail, which are white in the ordinary specimens, of a more or less rich *fulvous* tint, and all of these came from the eastern side of the Tista and the Upper Lacchhen Valley, viz.—

1 male and 1 female from Samdong Lacchhen	...	November, 1891.
" " " Labah	... ...	June, 1892.
1 male from Fyumgang	... ...	April, 1891.

From Memphhuk, 13,000, below the Tangkar La, in October, was got an aged female with a horny-*black* bill.

O. **26. Garrulus bispecularis.**—Its range is very much higher than given by Oates. It does not seem to be known in Sikhim below 7,000, and is usually found in the pine forests—11,000 to 13,000.

O. **50. Conostoma æmodium.**—The English name is rather a misnomer as the bill is dull yellowish light orange, and Oates' woodcut is somewhat misleading as there is no dark colour post-orbitally.

O. **53. Suthora unicolor.**—Sides of head with pale streaks.

O. **54. S. humii.**—Bill is pale yellow.

O. **65. Dryonastes cærulatus.**—In all my eleven specimens the post-orbital region is lightly streaked. It extends up to below the Donkya to 16,000, and is therefore likely to be met with in Tibet.

O. **69. Garrulax leucolophus.**—Tail is obscurely barred.

O. **72. G. pectoralis.**—Two [1 male, Lingmo, November, and one female, Nimbong, (Br. Bhutan) January] have the chin and throat anterior to the gorget almost unsullied white, the rest have this region fulvous. One female from Rathong (4,000) had the upper back bordering the nachal collar fringed with white. Another (a female, Rungeet, April, 1891) had vinaceous-slaty instead of white on tail, under-surface, and supercilium, and no fulvous collar.

O. **73. G. moniliger.**—Have ear-coverts black with whitish centre.

O. **76. G. albigularis.**—In regard to the question of *location*, 2 are from Gurubathan, British Bhutan—with reference to Mr. Oates' note that he had not seen any from Bhutan. Not very common.

O. **80. Ianthocincla rufigularis.**—Not very common. My three specimens from (1) Tsunthang, *Tista* valley, 6,000; Singla, *Nepal* Frontier, 10,000, in April; and Phema, 7,000, in March, have not the exceptional colouring noted by Oates as characteristic of Nepal,

(1) O = *Oates'* serial number

Sikhim, and Bhutan birds—the chin and upper throat are deeply rufous. Ear coverts dingy rufous, and loreal patch light fulvous.

O. **85. Trochalopterum nigrimentum.**—Very common.

O. **92. T. squamatum.**—In regard to the two varieties noted by Oates, page 97, I note that three specimens, all *males*, in November, December, and January, have bronzed tails, and all have fulvous-brown lores. Seven specimens (1 male and 2 females in November, 1 female in each of the months of January, March, May, and December) have black tails and darker chin, the throat, under-surface, the vent, and upper tail coverts are very much darker, and in all these the females have grey lores and the males slightly fulvous ones, excepting two females which have slightly fulvous lores, and in one of these, an adult of May, the secondary and tertiary quills are white-tipped. None of the others have white-tipped quills except one male—also black-tailed—from Daling in March, which has faint traces of white tips in two of the secondaries. If would thus almost appear that the difference in colour of the tail was sexual, and that the 'one male' with black tail has been wrongly sexed.

O. **137. Gampsorhynchus rufulus.**—The chin and throat are also pure white.

O. **163. Alcippe nepalensis.**—Most of the specimens have the forehead feathers well covered and adhesive with pollen and resins.

O. **211. Actinodura egertoni.**—Each of the 17 birds has the median tail feathers barred throughout—Oates' key to the species of this genera is misleading and needs alterations.

O. **277. Alcurus striatus.**—Two are from 1,500 and 2,500. Oates puts lowest limit at 5,000.

O. **284. Molpastes leucogenys.**—Two females; margins of additional feathers faintly washed with sulphureous.

O. **288. Otocompsa emeria.**—The small size of Sikhim and Br. Bhutan specimens is notable. Adults in March, 1892, three (two 7″ length, one $7\frac{1}{10}$″ length), while my Assam specimens measured $8\frac{1}{2}$″ to $7\frac{3}{10}$″ length, but *mostly* $7\frac{3}{4}$″.

O. **490. Pericrocotus speciosus.**—In two females there is an extensive washing of scarlet on forehead, throat, breast, and thighs.

O. **498. P. solaris.**—Smaller one has a grey head.

O. **506. Campophaga melanoptera.**—All of the specimens have long grey hairs on nape and occiput. Oates does not give this species north of Arrakan, but this bird has a general coloration much lighter than *C. melanoschista*, and its additional coverts are white.

O. **630. Henicurus maculatus.**—Oates gives Nepal as the eastern limit of this species, but the Lepchas are quite familiar with this and the following species, as is also evident from their vernacular names for it.

O. **647. Cyanecula suecica.**—The outer tail feathers of the female have a large triangular white tip.

O. **672. Merula albocincta.**—"The white-collared ouzel" eight. My specimens support the view that these merge into one. The *males* (five) agree neither with *M. albocincta* nor with *M. castanea.* Four of the males are black, *except* forehead and crown, and in three also the occiput, which are ashy-grey with darker centres and very conspicuously lighter than back. None of them have chestnut anywhere—except one has obscure margin of the feathers of lower back and rump and under wing coverts dingy rufous. Scully, writing from Nepal, notes that all of his four specimens are typical *M. albocincta,* and he saw no *M. castanea.*

These do not agree well with Oates' description of male *M. albocincta,* yet they belong to this species rather than *M. castanea.* The crown and back of the males are not of the same colour. All of the males, especially those from January to May, have greyish foreheads and crown owing to the feathers being broadly edged with ashy. The back and rump are wholly black except in one, a September bird,—the feathers of these regions are narrowly margined with whitish-rufous, and in all the lower, most of the upper, tail coverts are edged with whitish, and in the females these feathers have whitish shafts.

O. **698. Oreocincla dauma.**—Seven specimens. One [Karung, Tista valley (below Yangang), May, 1891] has the ground-colour of lower plumage ochraceous-buff, and otherwise closely resembles *Oreocincla imbricata* of Ceylon, and other two *males* have chin, throat, breast, and under tail coverts ochraceous, while the femalas have these parts relatively whiter.

O. **704 and 705. Zoothera monticola, Z. marginata.** —One of each—1 male, Chowbanjan, April, 1891; 1 male, February, 1892.

In addition to the dark margination of the feathers and its shorter wing and smaller size, its lores and cheeks are pale mottled grey and ear coverts with conspicuously pale grey shafts, the blackish tips contrasting against the whitish subternal bands of the feathers of the side of the neck. Its greater and modium wing coverts are more conspicuously tipped with ochraceous than is *Z. monticola,* and in neither can the chin, throat, breast, and abdomen be said to be white—in *Z. marginata* the chin and throat are ashy grey and in *Z. monticola* ochraceous: on the breast and upper part of abdomen the dark brown tints predominate.

O. **831. Motacilla maderaspatensis.**—The chin, upper throat and an infra-mandibular streak, of a November male, are white, and the back is blackish-ashy.

O. **935. Pitta cucullata.**—Rare in Sikhim. Two specimens from Baxar, Bhutan, May, 2,000, young, but full grown (7 inches), have blackish wedge-shaped extremity to most of the feathers of the back, wings, and abdomen. The abdomen is pale bluish-green with a black spot on its lower area, bordering the crimson.

MAMMALS.

NOTE.—The works consulted for this paper are Jerdon's "Mammals of India" and the "Fauna of British India, Mammalia," Part I, by W. T. Blanford.

J. GAMMIE—6-10-91.

ACCORDING to Jerdon and Blanford, there are about 81 species of mammals in Sikhim. They may be roughly classified as follows, viz.:—3 monkeys, 8 of the true cat tribe, 2 civet-cats, 1 tree-cat, 2 mungooses, 2 of the dog tribe, 5 polecats and weasels, 1 ferret-badger, 3 otters, 1 cat-bear, 2 bears, 1 tree-shrew, 1 mole, 6 shrews, 2 water-shrews, 12 bats, 4 squirrels, 2 marmots, 8 rats and mice, 1 vole, 1 porcupine, 4 deer, 2 forest goats, 1 goat, 1 sheep, and 1 ant-eater; but the Lepchas consider there are more species of several of the larger animals than the above two European naturalists admit.

Blanford in the "Fauna of British India" series mentions 3 monkeys from Sikhim: the Bengal monkey (*Macacus rhesus*), which is found in large companies at low elevations, usually not exceeding 3,000 feet, has straight hair and is of a hair-brown colour, tinged greyish with rufescent hinder quarters; the Himalayan monkey (*Macacus ageamensis*) which is abundant from 3,000 up to 6,000 feet, is of similar habits and general appearance, but its hair is wavy and of a darker brown, and it wants the rufescent colour on the hinder quarters; and the Himalayan langūr (*Semnopithecus schistaceus*) which frequents the zone between 7,000 and 12,000 feet, and is said to differ in habits from the hanūmān only in inhabiting a much colder climate. The Lepchas say there are two species at those high altitudes: one of large size and going in pairs only; the other smaller and herding together in companies of 20 to 60 individuals, and often visiting the hot springs to lick the saline matter deposited round their edges.

The tiger is an occasional visitor only, but the leopard (*Felis pardus*) and the clouded-leopard (*Felis nebulosa*) are permanent residents and fairly common, the latter ascending to about 7,000 feet. The snow-leopard (*Felis uncia*), as its trivial name implies, inhabits high altitudes only. The marbled-cat (*Felis marmorata*) is an elegantly marked creature, attaining to a size of nearly 2 feet in length from nose to base of tail, which is 15 inches. It chiefly keeps to the warmer slopes, and is a miniature edition of the clouded-leopard, while the leopard-cat (*Felis bengalensis*), also of the warmer slopes, is the miniature of the common leopard. These two cats never become quite tame, however young they may be captured, and appear to be incapable of getting in the least attached to more than one person, but will stay about the house in which they have been brought up till they are about a year old, when they usually take to the jungles. They are wonderfully active in all their movements. The large Indian civet-cat (*Viverra tibetha*) is not uncommon up to at least 5,500 feet; and the spotted tiger-civet (*Prionodon pardicolor*) is a very beautiful and active but rare creature of the cooler forests about 5—6,000 feet; it is marked with large squarish black spots in longitudinal rows on a fulvous background. There is but one tree-cat (*Paradoxurus grayi*), and it is not uncommon in the warmer forests.

The small Indian mungoose (*Herpestes àuro-punctatus*) is occasionally found in the lower valleys, but the large crab-eating mungoose (*Herpestes urva*) is commoner and ascends to higher elevations. It is a creature of considerable size, its head and body measuring a foot and-a-half in length and its tail a foot.

The jackal is not uncommon. Jerdon and Blanford both say there is but one species of wild hog (*Cyon dukhunensis*) in Sikhim, but the natives are very positive about there being two, and that they differ both in size and habits as well as in colour. The large sort they call the *Hindu*, and say it goes in pairs only or in parties of three or four, and is of a brownish colour with a black muzzle; the other sort, which they call the *Mussalman*, is described as being considerably smaller, of a uniform reddish colour, and going in packs of ten or a dozen. They hunt in packs and kill wild pig, deer, goats, &c., and occasionally attack cattle. The *Hindu* sort is in great request among native cattle doctors, who consider every atom of its body, including the bones, but especially the stomach, an infallible remedy in rinderpest. It is smoke-dried and reduced to powder, and administered either dry or in water. Their faith in it is unbounded, notwithstanding that there does not appear to be a single authenticated instance on record of it ever having effected a cure. The belief in its efficacy may have originated with the idea when the disease first appeared in Sikhim, that the wild dog was in some mysterious manner the cause of it, and the wise men acted on the principle of giving the victim a "hair of the dog that bit him." The Nepalese also declare it to be a sure remedy in dysentery and other diseases mankind is subject to. The natives of the plains as well as of the hills believe in and use it, and there is a tradition that the Cabul traders have offered a hundred rupees for a living or freshly-killed wild dog of the *Hindu* variety. The *Mussalman* sort is not generally of so high repute as a medicine, and by some considered worthless.

The Indian marten (*Mustela flavigula*) is a common animal of a rather wide range, being found from the lower slopes up to about 7,000 feet, usually in pairs, but occasionally in parties of five or six. It feeds on birds, reptiles, and small mammals, and when opportunity offers is a robber of the fowl-house to an almost incredible extent. It is also a persistent robber of bee-hives. In colour it is of a dark brown above, and paler below, with a white chin and throat and yellow breast. It weighs from 4lbs. to 6lbs. The yellow-bellied weasel (*Putorius cathia*) is a pretty creature and not uncommon, about 3—4,000 feet. It is usually in parties of about half-a-dozen, and the leader is the very incarnation of courage and daring, and will attack anything, however large, in defence of its family. It is of a uniform dark brown colour above, yellow below, and weighs about 6 oz. Hodgson mentions that it "is exceedingly prized by the Nepalese for its service in ridding houses of rats," and that it is easily tamed, and is trained by the rich "to attack large fowls, geese, and even goats and sheep. So soon as it is loosed it rushes up the fowl's tail or the goat's leg, and seizes the great artery of the neck, nor ever quits its hold till the victim sinks under exhaustion from loss of blood." Others are common, but in the larger rivers only.

The cat-bear (*Aklurus fulgens*) occurs from about 7,000 feet upwards. It is a vegetable feeder and easily tamed. It is of a reddish colour above, darker below, and the greater part of the face is white and the tail is ringed. Full grown males weigh from 7lbs. to 9½lbs., and measure about 3½ feet from the snout to the tip of the tail, which is nearly half-a-yard. It is one of the most interesting of the Sikhim mammals. The brown bear (*Ursus arctus*) occurs at high altitudes, rarely below 11-12,000 feet, and the Himalayan black bear (*Ursus torquatus*) is common from there down to about 4,000 feet. It is an undesirable neighbour, as it destroys large quantities of the native crops, and at times kills cattle and occasionally the people themselves. In many places, but especially in isolated fields in the middle of jungle, the natives have to watch their crops when ripening to prevent their destruction by monkeys and bears. One way of frightening them is to have a clapper arrangement fixed in the middle of the field with a string of cane, often several hundred yards in length, led inside the dwelling-house from whence it is worked, and every time a member of the household wakes up he is expected to give the string a few lusty tugs to set the clapper going. These are the only two bears recorded from Sikhim, but the Lepchas are quite positive about there being a third species, resembling *torquatus* in appearance, but considerably smaller, and occurring at lower elevations; down in fact to the bottoms of the lowest valleys, but rarely ascending so high as 6,000 feet. It differs also in being arboreal in its habits, and it is dreaded much more than the larger one on account of its greater activity. It is probably *Ursus malayanus*, which is recorded from Java through to Chittagong and the Garo Hills, and may be found as far west as Sikhim.

There is one mole (*Talpa micrura*) of much the same habits as the European one, but does not throw up mole-hills as that species does, although it makes its runs near the surface of the ground in the same way. It is commonest about 4,000 feet, but is found as high as 8,000. The European mole is of doubtful occurrence in Sikhim. There are at least half-a-dozen species of shrews, including the "musk-rat," and eight sorts of rats and mice, two water-shrews, and a vole.

Two marmots are found at elevations exceeding 10,000 feet. They burrow in the ground and live in small colonies. One, if not both of them, barks like a dog, for which it was often mistaken by the European sentries at Gnatong and considered a nuisance in consequence, as they naturally thought it might be a dog along with a hostile Tibetan party for whom they had to keep a sharp look out. One porcupine (*Hystrix longicauda*) is common about 5—6,000 feet, where it is very destructive to the potato crop. Its flesh is much prized as an article of food.

The black hill squirrel (*Sciurus macrouroides*) is a large handsome animal of the lower forests, occasionally, but rarely, ascending as high as 5,000 feet. It measures 2½ feet from the nose to end of the tail, and is of a uniform dark brown on the back and sides, and yellowish below. Two small brown squirrels are not uncommon among the trees and bamboos of the lower and middle forests, and a pretty, small-striped species (*S. McClellandi*) occurs in the upper forests over 5,000 feet. A very handsome flying squirrel (*Pteromeys magnificus*) inhabits the forest between 5,000 and 10,000 feet. The head and body measure about 15 inches in length, and the tail over 20 inches. It is dark chestnut above and orange-coloured below. Even adults take not unkindly to confinement.

The *shon* or Sikhim stag (*Cervus affinis*) does not, perhaps, occur anywhere in Sikhim Proper, but inhabits the Chumbi Valley and country beyond. The *serow* or samber stag (*Rusa aristotelis*) is frequent at all elevations up to 9—10,000 feet. The commonest of the deer tribe in Sikhim is the barking-deer (*Cervulus aureus*), which is found from the lowest valleys up to 9,000 feet, and is really excellent eating when in good condition. Hodgson says:—"It has no powers of sustained speed and extensive leap, but is unmatched for flexibility and power of creeping through tangled underwood. They have indeed a weasel-like flexibility of spine and limbs, enabling them to wend on without kneeling, even when there is little perpendicular passage room; thus escaping their great enemy the wild dog." The natives hunt it greatly with dogs and bows, and they put bells on their dogs for the double purpose of frightening the deer out of their hidden refuges and indicating the whereabouts of the dogs. The

Lepchas believe that the fœtus dried and powdered is of great virtue in difficult confinements. The musk-deer (*Moschus moschiferus*) remains always at high elevations, rarely descending below 8,000 feet even in winter. The *serow* (*Nemorhœdus bubalina*) frequents the rockiest ravines over 6,000 feet, while the *goral* (*Nemorhœdus goral*) affects similar localities, but descends to 3,000 feet and is found up to 8,000. The *burhel* (*Ovis nahura*) is found in considerable flocks at high altitudes.

LAMAISM IN SIKHIM.

By L. A. WADDELL, M.B.

I.—HISTORIC SKETCH OF THE LAMAIC CHURCH IN SIKHIM.

Lāmaism the State religion of Sikhim.

Lāmaism or Tibetan Buddhism is the State religion of Sikhim, and professed by the majority of the people.[1] Indeed, the lāmas since entering the country about two and half centuries ago have retained the temporal power more or less directly in their hands; and the first of the present series of rulers was nominated by the pioneer lāmas.

No detailed account previously published.

No detailed account of Sikhim Lāmaism has hitherto been published.[2] In regard to the ritual also and general history of Lamaism, I have often differed from such authorities as Köppen[3] and Schlagintweit,[4] as I have enjoyed superior opportunities for studying the subject at first hand with living lāmas.

Described as a priestcraft.

As Lāmaism is essentially a priestcraft, I have dealt with it mainly in its sacerdotal aspects, and touch little upon its higher ethics and metaphysics of which most of the lāmas are wholly ignorant. And throughout this paper I use the term "lāma" in its popular sense, as a general term for all the clergy of the Tibetan Buddhist Church, and not in its special sense of the superior monk of a monastery or sect.

Sources of information.

My special sources of information have been notes taken during several visits to Sikhim and a prolonged residence at Darjeeling in the society of lāmas. For many of the local details I am especially indebted to the learned Sikhim Lāma Ugyén Gyātshô and the Tibetan Lāma Padma Chhö Phél, with whom I have consulted most of the indigenous and Tibetan books which contain references to the early history of Sikhim and Tibet.[5] These vernacular books contain no very systematic account either of the introduction of Lāmaism into Sikhim or of its origin in Tibet, and their contents are largely mixed with myth and legend; but by careful sifting and comparative treatment it is possible

[1] The Hinduized Nepalese lately settled in Eastern Sikhim are not natives of Sikhim.

[2] For general notes on Sikhim Lāma-ism after Schlagintweit, the chief writers are Sir John Edgar, Mr. A. W. Paul, C.I.E., who afforded me many facilities for acquiring information, Sir Joseph Hooker and Sir Richard Temple.

[3] KÖPPEN: *Die lamaische Hierarchie und Kirche*, Berlin, 1859

[4] E. SCHLAGINTWEIT: *Buddhism in Tibet*, London, 1863.

[5] I have also obtained valuable aid from the Mongol Lāma Sherap Gyātshô and Tungyik Wangdén of the Gelukpa monastery at Ghoom, and from Mr. Dorje Tshering of the Bhotiya school.

to get a residue which may be treated as fairly historical, seeing that the periods dealt with are so relatively recent.

Buddhism of purely Indian origin and growth.

Buddhism arose in India and flourished there for about fifteen centuries, until it was forcibly suppressed by the Muhammadan invaders in the latter end of the 12th century A.D.

Its origin.

According to the best authorities, Buddhism was founded at Benares about the 5th century B.C., when the newly-fledged Buddha preached his first sermon and made his first converts on the site now marked by the Sarnāth stupa.

Its spread in India.

Extension outside India.

The new religion soon spread over the North-Western Provinces and Oudh and extended down the Gangetic valley to Bihār. But its wide dissemination dates from the epoch of the Great Indian Emperor Aśoka, in the 3rd century B.C., who had his capital at the city of Pātna in Bihār. Aśoka made Buddhism the State religion; and, besides diligently promoting it in his own territories, he sent swarms of missionaries into neighbouring countries to preach the faith. From Aśoka's son, Mahendra, Ceylon claims to have obtained its Buddhism and the Pali alphabet; while the Aśoka missionaries Uttara and Sauna are similarly claimed by Burma.

To Ceylon.

Burma.

Cashmere, Afghanistan, and Mongolia.

China and Japan.

Buddhism spread through Afghanistan, Cashmere, and its adjoining principalities, into Mongolia and China, and through China to Japan, exercising on all the wilder tribes a marked civilizing influence. It was established in China about 61 A.D.

Its late extension to Tibet.

Up to the 7th century A.D. the people of Tibet were without a written language and were pure savages. Early in the 7th century A.D. was born Srong-tsan-gampo, whose ancestors since two or three generations had established their authority over Central Tibet, and had latterly harassed the western boundaries of China; so that the Chinese Emperor was glad to make peace with the young prince and gave him a princess of the Imperial house in marriage. Srong-tsan-gampo had two years previously married the daughter of the King of Nepal; and both these wives being bigoted Buddhists, they speedily converted Srong-tsan-gampo, who under their advice sent to India for Buddhist books and teachers; hence dates the introduction of Buddhism into Tibet.

Four great councils are reported to have been held for the suppression of heresy, viz.—

(1) The Council held at Rajagriha under the presidency of Mahā Kasyapa immediately after Buddha's death.

(2) The Council of Vaisāli held about 350 B.C. under Yashada.
(3) The Council of Pātaliputra (Pātna) held about 250 B.C. under Aśoka's orders, with Mogaliputra as president.
(4) The Council of Jalandhara held in the 1st century A.D. under the auspices of King Kanishka of Kashmir and the Panjab.

The great schisms.

The second Council dealt only with discipline. The third Council defined the Buddhist canon as now current in Ceylon and Burma and Siam. The fourth developed exorcism, and from it arose the *Dhārāni* formulæ for schism of the "Northern" and "Southern" schools.

The Southern school.

The Southern school is the more primitive and purer form; it includes the Burmese, Ceylonese, and Siamese forms of Buddhism. Its sacred language is Pali.

The Northern school.

The Northern school comprises the forms of Buddhism current in Kashmir, Mongolia, China, Manchuria, Japan, Nepal, Tibet, Bhutan, and Sikhim. Its sacred language is Sanskrit.

Its leader.

The schism was brought about by the Mahāyāna doctrine, a theistic and metaphysical form of Buddhism introduced by a monk named Asvagosha and specially advocated by *Nāgārjuna*, whose name is most intimately identified with it. Its chief work is the *Prajna pāramita* (Tib. *Sher-chin*) which recognises several grades of theoretical Buddhas and of numerous divine Bodhisatwas, or beings who have arrived at perfect wisdom (*Bodhi*), yet consent to remain a creature (*satwa*) for the good of men, and who must therefore be worshipped, and to whom prayers must be addressed.

Its nature.

Addition of mythology.

Mythology and mysticism followed necessarily from the growth of the Mahāyāna school, and its extension amongst races of devil worshippers. Like Hinduism, it admitted within the pale the gods and demons of the new nations it sought to convert. *Mysticism* reached its fullest expression in the *Tantrik* doctrines (a mixture of Siva-worship and magic) which spread throughout India about the 6th and 7th century of our era, affecting alike Buddhism and Hinduism. Arya Asañga, a Buddhist monk of Peshawar, who lived about 300 A.D., is supposed to have introduced Tantricism into Buddhism.

Mysticism.

Tantricism.

The Tantriks teach yogism and incantations addressed mostly to female energies, by which men may gain miraculous powers which may be used for purely selfish and secular objects. Just as they assigned female "energies"—the Hindu *Śaktis* or divine mothers—as companions to most of the gods, wives were allotted to the several Buddhas and Bodhisatwas.

Its numerous deities: female energies.

At an early date Buddhists worshipped the tree under which the Buddhahood was attained, and the monument which contained Buddha's relics, and the images of these two objects together with the Wheel as symbolic of the teaching.

Growth of image-worship by Buddhists.

Northern Buddhism had almost reached this impure stage when it was introduced into Tibet about the middle of the 7th century A.D. Hiuen Tsiang states that the Mahāyāna school then predominated in India, and tantrik and mystic doctrines were appearing.

State of Indian Buddhism at time of introduction to Tibet.

Lāmaism dates from over a century later than the first entry of Buddhism into Tibet, and in the meantime tantricism had greatly increased. About the same time the doctrine of the Kálachakra or supreme Deity, without beginning or end, the source of all things, [*Adi Buddha Samantabhadra* (Tib. *Kun-tu zang-po*)] was accepted by the Lāmas.

The Kālachakra.

Lāmaism was founded by the wizard-priest *Padma Sambhava* (Tib. *Pédma Jungné*),[1] *i.e.*, "The lotus born;" usually called by the Tibetans *Guru Rimbochhe*[2] or "The Precious Guru;" or simply "*Guru*," the Sanskrit for "teacher."

The founder of Lāmaism.

Lāmaism arose in the time of King Thī-Srong De-tsan, who reigned 740—786 A.D. The son of a Chinese princess, he inherited from his mother a strong prejudice in favour of Buddhism. He sent to India for books and teachers, and commenced a systematic translation from the Sanskrit and Chinese scriptures; and he built the first Buddhist monastery in Tibet, viz. Samyé (Sam-yas).

Lāmaism dates from a century later.

It was in connection with the building of this monastery that Padma Sambhava first came to Tibet. King Thī-Srong De-tsan's endeavours to build were all frustrated by earthquakes which were attributed to demons. On the advice of the Indian Buddhist monk Shantarakshita, the latter sent to the great Indian monastery of Nalanda for the wizard-priest Padma Sambhava of the Yogacharya School, who was a famous sorcerer.

Story of the visit to Tibet of its founder, Guru Rimpochhe.

Padma Sambhava, who was a native of Udyána, or Ghazni, a region famed for sorcery, promptly responded to the Tibetan king's request and arrived at Samyé, by way of Katmandu and Kyirong in Nepal, in the

His route to Tibet, and doings *en route*.

[1] Paḍma *ḃ*yung *g*naṣ.

[2] Gu-ru rin-po-chhe.

Plate I.

GENEALOGICAL TREE OF LĀMAIC SECTS.

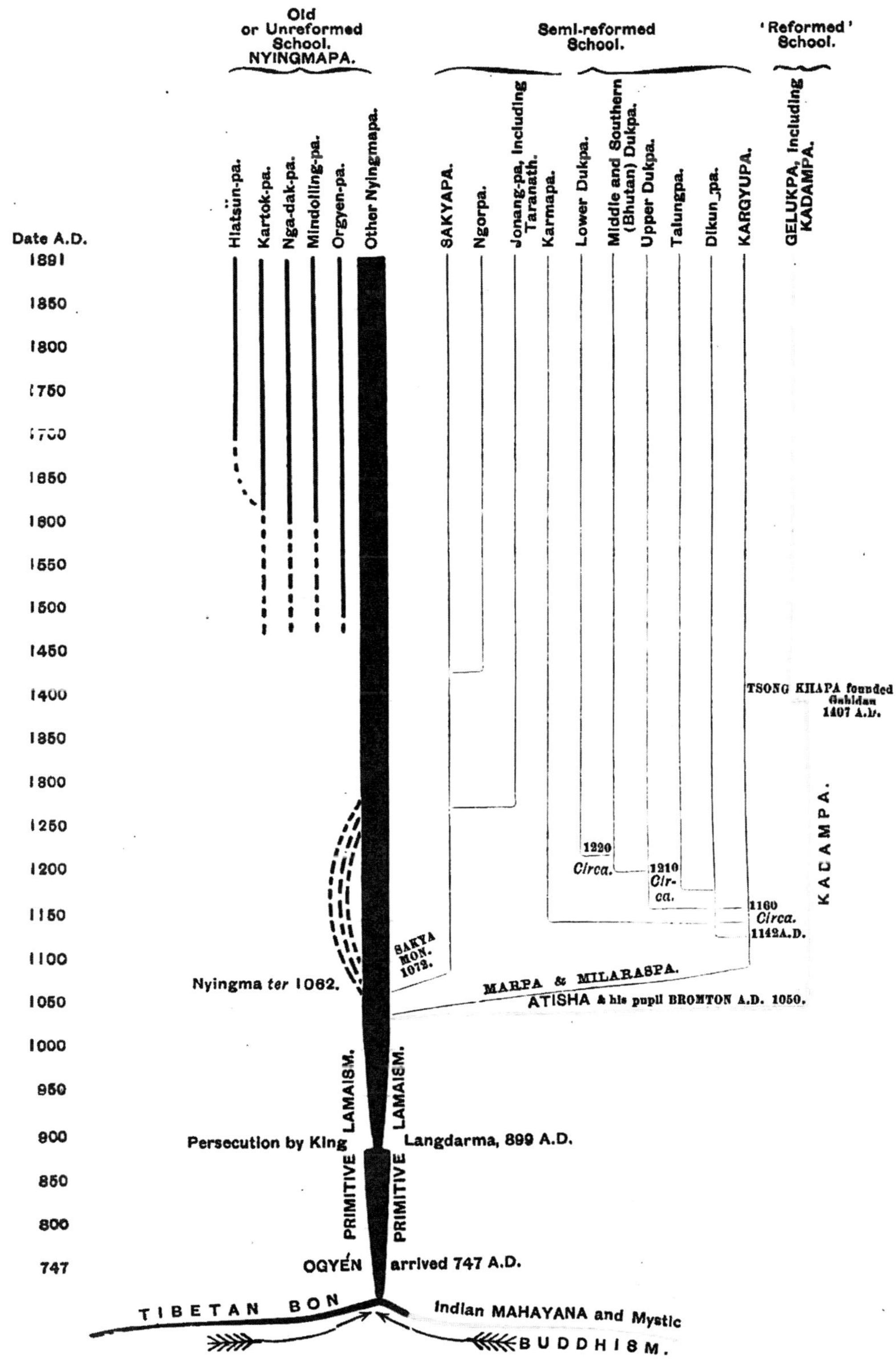

L. A. WADDELL, DEL.

year 747 A.D. With the *dorje* (Sansk. *Vajra*) or thunderbolt and spells from the Māhāyana he vanquished and converted the devils, built the monastery 749 A.D., and established the first community of lāmas.

"Lāmaism" defined.

Lāmaism may be defined as a mixture of Buddhism with a preponderating amount of mythology, mysticism, and magic: the doctrine of incarnate lāmas and the worship of canonized saints, now such prominent features of Lāmaism, are of recent origin. It was readily accepted as it protected the people from devils.

LAMAIC SECTS.

Atisha, the great reformer of Lāmaism.

The Lāmaic sects (PLATE I) date from the visit to Tibet of the Indian Buddhist monk Atisha (1038—1052 A.D.), who preached celibacy and moral abstinence, and deprecated the practice of the magic arts.

The *Kah-dam-pa* sect.

The *Ge-luk-pa*.

The reformed sect was called the *Kah-dam-pa*,[1] or "those bound by the orders," and three and-a-half centuries later, in Tsongkhāpa's hands, it became less ascetic and more ritualistic under the title of *Ge-luk-pa*, now the dominant sect in Tibet.

The unreformed, or *Nying-ma-pa*.

The unreformed residue were called the *Nying-ma-pa* or "the old sect."

THE GE-LUK-PA SECT.

Ge-luk-pa sect: its peculiarities. Tsongkhāpa.

Tsongkhāpa[2] gathered together the scattered members of the Kadampa and housed them in monasteries, under rigorous discipline. He made them carry a begging-bowl and wear a garment of a yellow colour after the fashion of Indian Buddhists. And he instituted a ritualistic service, in part, apparently, perhaps borrowed from the Nestorian Christian missionaries, who were settled at that time in Western China. The tutelary deities are Dorje-hjig-*b*yed, *b*De-mchhog and *g*Sang-wa-*h*duspa; and the guardian demons are "*m*Gonpo phyag-truk," or the six-armed protector, and Tam-chhen Chhos-gyal.

THE KARGYUPA SECT.

Kargyupa sect.

The Kargyupa sect was founded in the latter half of the eleventh century A.D. by Lāma Marpa, who had visited India and obtained special instruction from the Indian pandit Atisha and Atisha's teacher Naropa.

---

[1] *b*kah-dam-pa.

[2] *Tsongkhāpa* means "Of Tsongkhā or the Onion Country," the district of his birth in Western China near the eastern confines of Tibet. His proper name is *b*Lô-*b*zang-tak-pa; but he is best known to Europeans by his territorial title.

Its peculiarities.

The distinctive features of the Kargyupa sect are that they inhabit caves and profess meditation and the following doctrines:—

(*a*) Their guardian deity is "The Lord of the Black Cloak."[1]
(*b*) Their tutelary deity is Demchhok[2] (Skt. *Sambhara*), or "Chief of Happiness."
(*c*) Their mode of meditation or system of mystical insight is *Chhag-chhen*,[3] or in Sanskrit *Mahāmudra;* and their highest teacher is the mythical Dorje-Chhang[4] (Skt. *Bajra-dhara*), or "the holder of the Dorje."
(*d*) Their hat is called *gom-zha pü khyü*, or "the meditation hat with the crossed knees."

The *Kar-ma-pa.*

The diagram of Kar-gyupa sects (PLATE II) shows the relation of the sub-sects to the parent sect. The *Kar-ma-pa* adopted the Nyīngmapa *ter-ma* of Las-*h*prod-ling-pa.

The *Dī-kung-pa.*

The *Dī-kung-pa* take their title from the Dikung Monastery founded by Rinchhen-phün-tshog about the middle of the 12th century. Their Nyingmapa *ter-ma* is Padma ling-pa.

The *Ta-lung-pa.*

The *Ta-lung-pa* issued from the Dikungpa and take their title from the Talung Monastery founded by Ngag-dbang-chhos-gyalpo in 1179. They differ from their parent Dī-kung-pa in admitting also the *ter-ma* work adopted by the Kar-ma-pa.

The *Duk-pa.*

The *Duk-pa* are of three forms. The oldest is the *Upper Duk-pa*, which originated by *h*Gro-*m*gon-*r*tsang-pa-*r*gyal-ras (The patron of Animals, The Victory-clad Tsang-po) or *s*Prul *s*ku-*d*būng-*b*sam-wang-po of the Ralung Monastery in Gnam province of Tibet about the middle of tho 12th century. To emphasize the change the monastery was called *Duk*-Ralung, and a legend of the thunder-dragon *Duk* is related in connection therewith. It adopted the same *ter-ma* as the Dikungpa, but there seems some other distinctive tenet which I have not yet elicited. The *Middle Duk-pa* and the *Lower Duk-pa* arose very soon after.

The *Middle Duk-pa* took the *terma* book of Sangyas-ling-pa. This is the form of Kar-gyu-pa which now prevails in Bhutan under the name of *Duk-pa* or *Southern Duk-pa.* Its chief lāma is Zhab-drung Ngag-*d*bang-nam-gyal, a pupil of "Kun-*m*khyen padma *d*kar-po" or "The Omniscient White Lotus," who, in the 17th century A.D., settled at "*l*chags rit *r*ta *m*go" in Bhutan, and soon displaced the Karthok-pa and other forms of Nyingmapa Lamaism then existing in that country,

[1] *m*gon-po bar-nak.
[2] *b*de-mchhog.
[3] phyag-rgya-chhew-pa.
[4] *r*do-*r*je hchhang.

Plate II.

DIAGRAM SHOWING

THE AFFILIATION OF THE SUB-SECTS OF KAR-GYUPA.

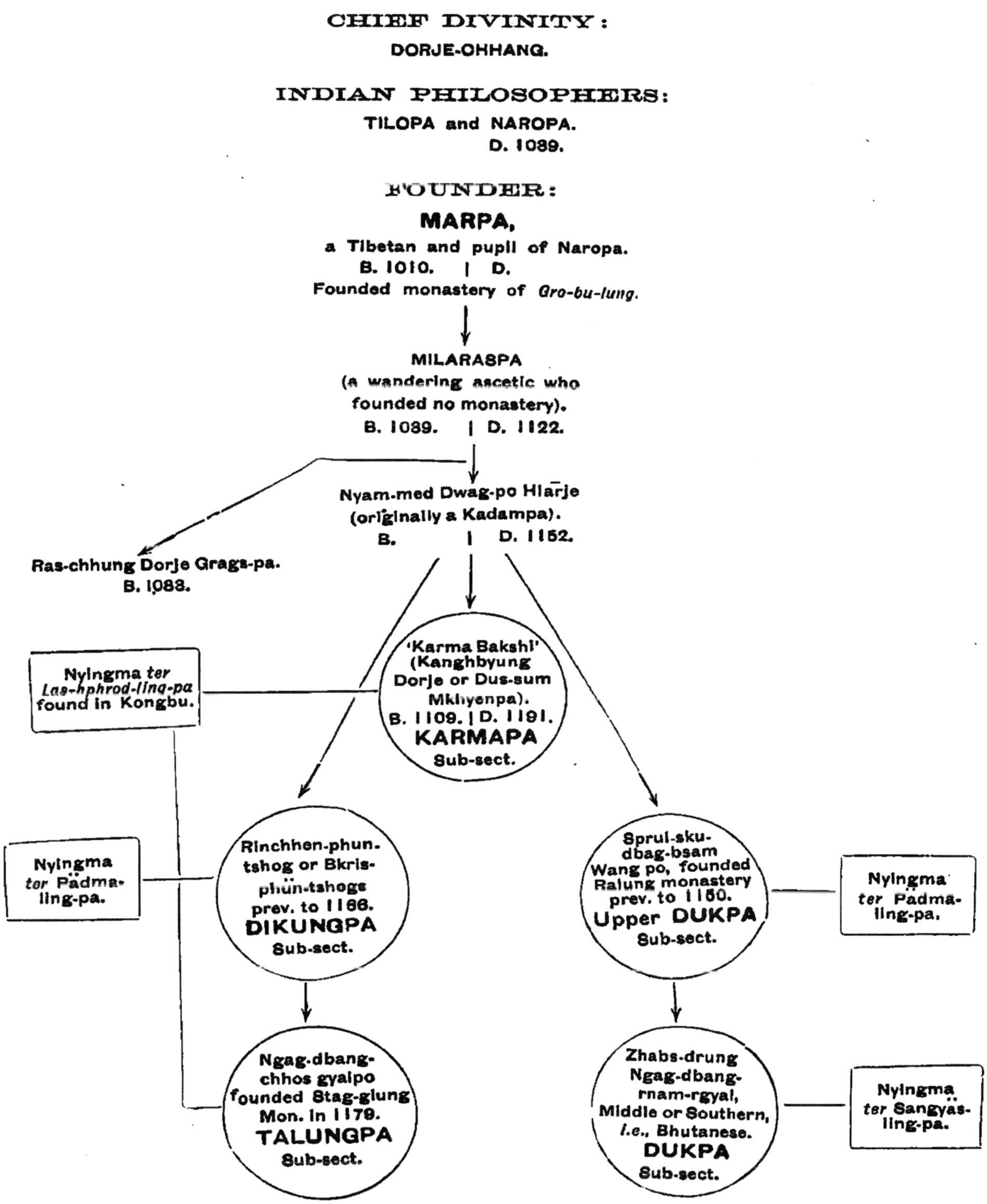

L. A. WADDELL, DEL.

and which are reputed to have been founded there directly by Lô-pön himself, who entered Bhutan *viâ* *g*Zhas-ma gang and left it by *m*Dung-tsang, and at *d*gon-tshal phu*k* are still shown his footprints on a rock.

THE SAKYA-PA SECT.

The *Sakya-pa* sect. Its title. Its specialities.

The *Sakya-pa* takes its name from the Sa-kya Monastery in Western Tibet, founded by *h*Khon-*d*kön-*m*chhog-*r*gyalpo. The name Sa-kya[1] refers to the light yellow colour of the scanty soil in that locality, which is rocky and almost bare of vegetation. The founder mixed together the "old" and "new" dispensations in regard to the *tantras*, calling his tantrik system gsang-*s*ngag*s*-*g*sar-nying, or "the new-old occult mystery." The Nyingmapa books adopted by the Sakya-pa are called *Dorje phurpai chhoga;* and from the newer school were taken Dem-chhok, Dorje-kando, Den-zhi, Maha-maha-ma-yab, Sangyé thöpa, and Dorje-dutsi. Its special meditative system is "Lam-*h*bras." Its guardian demons are *m*gon-po-gur or "The Guardian of the Tent" and *m*gon-po-zhal. Its hat is called Sā-zhu. Now, however, the Sakya sect is scarcely distinguishable from the Nyingmapa. Its sub-sects are as follow :—

Its sub-sects.

Ngor-pa.

The *Ngor-pa,* founded by Gun-gah Zang-po, issued from the Sakya-pa at the time of Tsongkhāpa. Its founder discarded the Nynimapa element in its tantrik system, retaining only the "new." It has many monasteries in Kham.

Jônang-po. *Tāranāth.*

The *Jônang-po,* issued from the Sakya-pa, in the person of Je-kun-gah-tol chhok, who was re-incarnated some centuries later as the great historian lāma Tāranāth, now the highest incarnate lāma of the Mongols and Chinese. This latter lāma built the monastery of Phüntsholing about a mile to the north of Jonang in Upper Tsang, which was one of the many seized by the great Dalai Lāma Lô-zang gyatsho and forcibly converted into a Gelukpa institution. This sect does not practically differ from the Ngor-pa. The distinction is only one of founders.

Nyingmapa entered Sikhim.

The *Nyingmapa* peculiarities have already been indicated in a general way. Further details will be found under the head of Sikhim Lāmaism. It was the Nyingma form of Lāmaism which first found its way into Sikhim about 250 years ago.

[1] Sa-*s*kya-pa.

INTRODUCTION OF LAMAISM INTO SIKHIM.

Legendary account of the Guru's visit to Sikhim.

It is believed in Sikhim that Guru Rimbochhe visited Sikhim during his travels in Tibet and its western border lands.

Lhatsün Chhembo first introduced Lāmaism to Sikhim.

The introduction of Lāmaism into Sikhim dates from the time of *Lhatsün Chhembo's* arrival there about the middle of the 17th century A.D. By this time Lāmaism had become a most powerful hierarchy in Tibet, and was extending its creed among the Himalayan and Central Asian tribes.

Lhatsün Chhembo "discovered" the holy sites of Sikhim.

His titles.

Lhatsün Chhembo was a native of Kongbu in the lower valley of the Tsangpo, which has a climate and physical appearance very similar to Sikhim. His name means "The great reverend God." His religious name is *Kun-zang nam-gyé*,[1] or "The entirely victorious Essence of Goodness." He is also known by the title of *Lhatsün nam-kha Jig-med*,[2] or "The Reverend God who fears not the sky," with reference to his alleged power of flying. He is also sometimes called *Kusho Dsog-chhen Chhembo*, or "The great Honourable Dsog-chhen"—*Dsog-chhen*, literally "The Great End," being the technical name for the system of mystical insight of the Nyingmapa, and *Kusho* means "the honourable."

His early history.

He was born in the fire-bird year of the tenth of the sixty-year cycles, corresponding to 1595 A.D., in the district of Kongbu in South-Eastern Tibet. Having spent many years in various monasteries and in travelling throughout Tibet and Sikhim, he ultimately in the year 1648 arrived in Lhassa and obtained such great repute by his learning as to attract the favourable notice of Gyalwa Ngak-Wang, the greatest of the Grand Lāmas, who shortly afterwards became the first Dalai Lāma.

At this time another lāma of the *Kartok-pa* sub-sect came by Kangla nangma searching for a path into Sikhim, and also tried without success the *sPreu-gyab-tak* (*i.e.*, "Monkey-back rock," with reference to its semblance to a monkey sitting with hands behind its back) and Dsong-ri, and the western shoulder of *sKam-pa Khab-rag*—a ridge of "*Kabru*" which runs down to the Rāthong river. He then arrived at the cave of "the very pleasant grove," and met the saint, who told him that as he was not destined to open the northern gate, he should go round and try the western.

Miraculous *reconnaissance* and entry.

Then Lhatsün Chhembo, traversing the Kangla nangma and finding no road beyond the cave of *Skam-pa Khabruk*, flew miraculously to the upper part of "Kabru" (24,000 feet), and there blew his kangling, and after

[1] Kun-*b*zang *r*nam-*r*gyal.

[2] lha-*br*tsun nam *m*khah *h*jigs med.

PLATE III.

an absence of two weeks flew down to where his servants were collected and guided them by a road *viâ* Dsongri to Norbugang in Sikhim.

He arrived in Sikhim with two other Nyingmapa lāmas. By "the western gate" of *Singlela* came a Kartok-pa lāma named Sempah Chhembo,[1] and a lāma of the Ngadakpa sub-sect, named Rigdsin Chhembo,[2] who had opened "the southern gate" by way of Darjeeling and Namchi respectively. The place where these three lāmas met was called by the Lepchas *Yok-sam*, which means "the three superior ones or noblemen," a literal translation of "the three lāmas."

Meeting two other lāmas.

The three lāmas held here a council at which Hlatsün Chhembo said, "Here are we three lāmas in a new and irreligious country. We must have a 'dispenser of gifts'[3] (*i.e.*, a king) to rule the country on our behalf." Then the *Nga-dak-pa* lāma said, "I am descended from the celebrated Tertön Nga-dak Nyang-rél, who was latterly a governor; I should therefore be the king." While the Kartok-pa lāma declared, "As I am of royal lineage I have the right to rule." Then *Hlatsün Chhembo* said, "In the prophesy of Guru Rimbochhe it is written that four noble brothers shall meet in Sikhim and arrange for its government. We are three of these come from the north, west, and south. Towards the east, it is written, there is at this epoch a man named *Phüntshog*,[4] a descendant of brave ancestors of *Kham* in Eastern Tibet. According, therefore, to the prophesy of the Guru we should invite him." Two messengers were then despatched to search for this Phüntshog. Going towards the extreme east near Gangtok they met a man churning milk and asked him his name. He without replying invited them to sit down and gave them milk to drink. After they were refreshed, he said his name was Phüntshog. He was then conducted to the lāmas, who crowned him by placing the holy water vase on his head and anointed him with the water; and exhorting him to rule the country religiously, gave him Hlatsün's own surname of Namgyé[5] and the title of *Chhö-gyal* (Skt. *Dharma-rājā*) or "religious king." Phüntshog Namgyé was at this time aged 38 years, and he became a lāma in the same year, which is said to have been 1641 A.D.

Their appointment and coronation of a king of Sikhim.

In appearance Lhatsün is usually represented as seated on a leopard-skin mat, with the right leg hanging down and his body almost naked—one of his titles is *He-ru-ka-pa*, which means "unclad." His complexion is dark blue. A chaplet of skulls encircles his brow. In his left hand is a skull cup filled with blood, and a trident topped with human heads

His appearance. (PLATE III.)

[1] Sems-*d*pah chhen-po.
[2] Rig-*h*dsin chhen-po, or 'the great Sage.'
[3] *s*byin-dak.
[4] Phun tshog*s*.
[5] *r*nam-*r*gyal.

rests in front of the left shoulder. The right hand is in a teaching attitude. He is believed to be the incarnation of the great Indian teacher Bhima Mitra.

His incarnation.

Development of Lāmaism in Sikhim, subsequent to the epoch of Lhatsün Chhembo.

The religions ousted by Lāmaism were the Pön (Bon), usually identified with Taouism, and the earlier demon and fairy worship of the Lepchas, which can scarcely be called a religion. Numerous traces of both of these primitive faiths are to be found embodied in Sikhim Lāmaism, which owes any special features it possesses to the preponderance of these two elements. Only two sects of lāmas exist in Sikhim, viz., the Nyingmapa and the Kargyupa as represented by the Karmapa. There are no Duk-pa monasteries in Sikhim, nor does there seem ever to have been any.

Its peculiarities.

Its sects.

The Nyingma-pa.

The Nyingma-pa[1] or "the old school" represents the primitive and unreformed style of Lāmaism. It is more largely tinged with the indigenous pre-Buddhist religious practices; and celibacy and abstinence are rarely practised.

The Nyingma-pa.

In Sikhim there are three sub-sects of Nyingma-pa, viz.—(1) the *Lhatsün-pa*, to which belong most of the monasteries with Pemiongchi at the head; (2) the *Kartok-pa* with the monasteries of Kartok and Dôling; and (3) the *Nga dak-pa* with the monasteries of Namchi, Tashiding, Sīnon, and Thang-môchhe.

Its sub-sects in Sikhim.

The Ter-ma of the *Lhatsün-pa* is the same as was adopted by the Karmapa, viz., the work *Lé-thö Ling-pa* discovered (*i.e.*, composed) by *Ja-tshön-pa* in Kongbu. But the Pemiongchi lāmas also follow the *Mindolling* monastery in giving pre-eminence to the *ter-ma* work of Dag-ling-pa as a form of ritual.

Lhatsün-pa.

The *Kartok-pa*,[2] taking their name from the title of their founder lāma *Kah-tok*, *i.e.*, "The Understander of the Precepts," give pre-eminence to the *tertön* work *Long-chhen rab chung.*[3] It has been suggested by Mr. Paul that Darjeeling, properly Dôrjeling, may owe its name to the tertön Dôrjelingpa, who visited the Kartok-pa Dô-ling (properly Dôrjeling) monastery in Sikhim, of which the old Darjeeling monastery was a branch.

Kartok-pa.

---

[1] *r*nying-ma-pa. | [2] *b*kah-*r*tog-pa. | [3] rig-hasin *r*god *l*dem.

The *Nga-dak-pa*, also taking their name from their founder "The owner of Sway or Dominion," who was of royal lineage, give pre-eminence to the *tertön* work of *Rig-dsin gö dem*[1] as a code of ritual.

Nga dak-pa.

Specialities of Nyingma-pa.

All sections of the Nyingma-pa agree in professing the creed called Dsog-chhen-bo, or "The Great End;" it is probable, however, that the Sanskrit *Maha-joga* is intended. This Dsog-chhen-bo doctrine is a purely theoretical distinction, in great part relating merely to the posture of the hands in meditation and little understood by the great majority of the members. The obvious and practical Nyingma-pa characteristics are (*a*) their special worship of Guru Rimbochhe; (*b*) their highest god is *Kuntu zang po* (Skt. *Samantabhadra*), "the Highest Goodness;" (*c*) their special tutelary deity is *Dub-pa kah gye;*[2] (*d*) their special guardian deity *Pal-gön de-nga;*[3] (*e*) and their peculiar red hat is named *Ugyén penzhu*, and (*f*) with these characteristics they exhibit, as a class, a greater laxity in living than any other sect of lāmas.

The worship of Guru Rimbochhe.

By the Nyingma-pa, the great wizard Guru Péma is worshipped as "a second Buddha," in spite of his uncelibate life, his semi-demoniac temper, and his being altogether void of any of the admirable traits of Buddha. It is just possible, however, that he is painted blacker than he really was, for most of the practices and rites which are credited to him were really the composition of the *tertöns* or "revealers of hidden scriptures" many centuries after his time. He is worshipped under eight forms, called *Guru Tsen-gye*, or "the eight worshipful names of the Teacher." These, together with their usual paraphrase, are here given:—

The Guru's eight forms.

I.—*Guru Pädma Jungné*,[4] "Born of a lotus" for the happiness of the three worlds.

II.—*Guru Pädma Sambhava*, "Saviour by the Religious Doctrine." (*N.B.*—This title is the pure Sanskrit equivalent of No. I.)

III.—*Guru Pädma Gyélpo*, "The King of the Three Collections of Scriptures" (*Skt.* "Tripitaka").

IV.—*Guru Dörje Dô-lö*,[5] "The *Dorje* or Diamond Comforter of all."

V.—*Guru Nyima Öd-zer*,[6] "The Enlightening Sun of Darkness."

VI.—*Guru Shakya Seng-ge*, "The Second Sakya—the Lion," who does the work of eight sages.

---

1 *k*long-chhen rab hbyani.
2 *s*grub-pa-*b*kah *b*rgyed.
3 *d*pal-*m*gon *s*de *l*nga.
4 gu-ru pad-ma *h*byung-*g*nas.
5 gu-ru *r*do-*r*je gro-lod.
6 gu-ru nyi-ma *h*od zer.

VII.—*Guru Seng-ge-dā dok*,[1] The propagator of religion in the six worlds—with "the roaring lion's voice."

VIII.—*Guru Lô-tén Chhog-Se*,[2] "The Conveyer of knowledge to all worlds."

Head monasteries of the Nyingma-pa sect.

The chief monastery of the Pemiongchi sect and its associated lāmas is at Mindolling in Central Tibet. The chief monastery of the Kartok-pa is at Der-ge in Kham (Eastern Tibet), celebrated for its excellent prints; and that of the Nga dak-pa at Dorje-tak, the greatest of the Nyingma-pa head-quarters, about two days' journey south-east of Lhassa. Until recently, Pemiongchi was in the habit of sending batches of its young lāmas to Mindolling for instruction in strict discipline and rites; but since some years this practice has been allowed to lapse.

The Karmapa sub-sect.

Karmapa in Sikhim.

The Karmapa, as we have already seen, was one of the earliest sub-sects of the Kargyupa. It differs from its parent Kargyupa in the adoption of the Nyingma "hidden revelation" found in Kongbo, and entitled Le-to Ling-pa or "the locally-revealed merit." And from the Duk-pa, another sub-sect of the Kargyupa, it differs in not having adopted the Nyingma tertön works Padma ling-pa and Sangyé ling-pa. The Karmapa sect was founded by Milaraspa's pupil Rangchug dorje. Their chief monastery is at Tö-lung tshur phu, founded in 1158 A.D. and about one day's journey to the north-west of Lhasa. They are Kargyupas who have retrograded towards the Nyingma-pa practices. Marpa, the nominal founder of the Kargyupa sect, was married, and few of the Karma-pa lāmas are celibate.

Tenets.

When established in Sikhim.

The first Karmapa monastery in Sikhim was built at Ralang about 1730 A.D. by the Sikhim ruler Gyur-med Namgyal at the special request of the Ninth Karmapa Grand Lāma—*d*Bang-chug-*r*dorje—in Tibet during a pilgrimage of the king in Tibet. Their other monasteries are at Ramtek and Phodang, and the "Phodang" monastery in the Bhotiya *basti* of Darjeeling which is a chapel of ease to Phodang.

Their temples.

The central image in a Karmapa temple is usually that of the founder of the sub-sect, viz., Karma "Bakshi," otherwise their temples do not differ from those of the Nyingma-pa sect.

[1] gu-ru Seng-ge *s*gra *s*grogs.

[2] gu-ru *b*lo-ldan mchhog Sred.

II.—GENERAL DESCRIPTION OF SIKHIM MONASTERIES.

Monasteries of three kinds.

Monasteries in Sikhim are of three kinds, viz.—(*a*) *Tak-phu*,[1] literally a "rock-cave" or cave-hermitage; (*b*) *Gömpa*,[2] literally "a solitary place" or monastery proper; and (*c*) the so-called "*gompas*" founded in or near villages. These latter are, as a rule, merely temples (*hla-khāng*) with one or more priests engaged in ministering to the religious wants of the villagers.

The four great caves of Sikhim.

The four great caves of Sikhim hallowed as the traditional abodes of Guru Rimbochhe and Lhatsün Chhembo, and now the objects of pilgrimage even to lāmas from Tibet, are distinguished according to the four cardinal points, viz.—

The NORTH *Lha-ri nying phu*, or "the old cave of God's hill." It is situated about three days' journey to the north of Tashiding, along a most difficult path. This is the most holy of the series.

The SOUTH *Kah-do Sang phu*,[3] or "cave of the occult fairies." Here it is said is a hot spring, and on the rock are many footprints ascribed to the fairies.

The EAST *Pé phu*,[4] or "secret cave." It lies between the Tendong and Mainom mountains, about five miles from Yangang. It is a vast cavern, reputed to extend by a bifurcation to both Tendong and Mainom. People go in with torches about a quarter of a mile. Its height varies from five feet to one hundred or two hundred feet.

The WEST *De-chhen phu*,[5] or "cave of Great Happiness." It is in the snow near Jongri, and only reachable in the autumn.

The *Gömpa*, or monastery proper.

"Gömpa," as has been noted, means "a solitary place," and most of the gömpas still are found in solitary places. Isolation from the world has always been a desideratum of Buddhist monks; not as an act of self-punishment, but merely to escape mundane temptations.

Its isolation.

The extreme isolation of some of the gömpas has its counterpart in Europe in the Alpine monasteries amid the everlasting snows. One of these gömpa is Tô-lung, which for the greater part of the year is quite cut off from the outer world, and at favourable times is only reachable from the south by a

[1] brag-phug. | [2] *d*yon-pa. | [3] *m*khah *h*gro *gs*ang. | [4] *s*bas. | [5] *b*de chhen.

path of flimsy rope and bamboo ladders leading across the face of precipices. Thus its solitude is seldom broken by visitors. The remote and almost inaccessible position of many of the Sikhim gömpas renders mendicancy impossible; but begging-with-bowl seems never to have been a feature of Lāmaism, even when the monastery adjoins a town or village.

Conditions necessary for its site.

The site occupied by the monastery is usually commanding and frequently picturesque. It should have a free outlook to the east to catch the first rays of the rising sun. The monastery buildings should be built in the long axis of the hill, and it is desirable to have a lake in front, even though it be several miles distant. These two conditions are expressed in the couplet:—

"Back to the hill-rock,
And front to the tarn."[1]

The door of the assembly room and temple is *cæteris paribus* built to face eastwards. The next best direction is south-east, and then south. If a stream directly drains the site or is visible a short way below, then the site is considered bad, as the virtue of the place escapes by the stream. In such a case the chief entrance is made in another direction. A waterfall, however, is of very good omen, and if one is visible in the neighbourhood, the entrance is made in that direction, should it not be too far removed from the east.

General plan of the buildings.

The monastic buildings cluster round the temple, which is also used as the Assembly Hall or *du-khang*, and corresponds to the *vihāra* of the earlier Buddhists. The temple building and its contents form the subject of the next chapter. Most of the outer detached buildings are dormitories for the monks, and have nothing to distinguish them from the ordinary houses of Sikhim, except, perhaps, that their surroundings are sometimes a trifle cleaner and more comfortable looking, and occasionally a few flowers are to be seen. One elderly monk and two or three novices usually occupy one house, and each house cooks its own meals independently, as there is no common refectory in the small monastic establishments of Sikhim. The menial lay servants are usually housed some distance off.

Its surroundings.

Lining the approaches to the monastery are rows of tall "prayer" flags, and several large lichen-clad chhortens and long mendong monuments.

[1] *r*gyab ri brag dang, *m*dun ri *m*tsho.

Chhortens.

The *chhortens*,[1] literally "receptacle for offerings" (Skt. *Da-garbha*, *Chaitya* or stupa[2]), are solid conical structures originally intended as relic-holders, but now are mostly erected as cenotaphs in memory of Buddha or canonized saints, and they have a suggestively funereal appearance. The original form of the stupa was a simple hemisphere with its convexity upwards and crowned by one or more umbrellas. Latterly they became more complex and elongated, especially in regard to their capitals. The details of many of the Lāmaic Chaityas are capable of an elemental interpretation, symbolic of the five elements into which a body is resolved on death. Thus, *vide* figure in margin modified from Remusat,[3] the lowest section, a solid rectangular block, typifies the solidity of the *earth*, above it *water* is represented by a globe, *fire* by a triangular tongue, *air* by a crescent—the inverted vault of the sky, and *ether* by an acuminated circle. The Chaityas of Sikhim are mainly of two forms. Each chhorten consists of a solid hemisphere—the true relic-holder—which stands on a plinth of several steps. The hemisphere is surmounted by a narrow neck bearing in a lotus-leaved basin a graded cone usually of 13 tiers, which are considered to represent umbrellas—the symbol of royalty; they are by others said to represent the 13 Bodhisatwa heavens of Nepalese Buddhist cosmography.[4] And the whole is topped by a horizontal disc bearing a smaller vertical disc set within a crescent, which popularly are said to typify the sun and moon, but which may have the elemental character already noted.

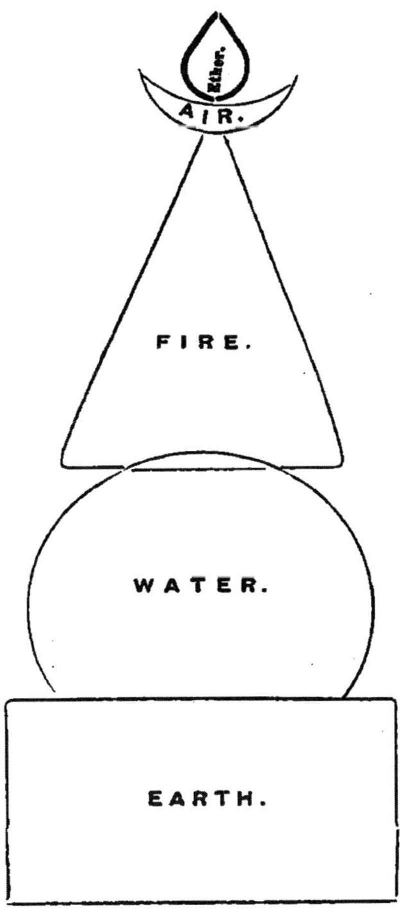

In the most common form, the hemisphere has its curved surface directed downwards. The second form especially common in Nepal,

[1] *mchhoḍ rten.*

[2] *Da-garbha* (Pali Da-goba) = relic receptacle. चैत्य *Chaitya* (= *chi* + styai = to heap together, a mound) came afterwards to be called *stupa* (स्तूप) and in Pali *Thupa* or vulgarly *Tope*, but was especially applied to a relic-holder in an Assembly Hall, while *stupa* denoted the larger one in the open air.

[3] *Foue Koue Ki*, Chap. XIII.

[4] HODGSON'S Essays on the Languages, &c., of Nepal and Tibet, Lond. 1874, page 80.

bears a closer resemblance to the older form of stupa, but its capital is more elongated, and it and the cone or pyramid is separated from the hemisphere by a square neck which bears on each face a pair of eyes which typify omniscience. In the wealthier monasteries the chhortens are occasionally whitewashed.

The great Tashiding chhorten.

The most holy chhorten in Sikhim is at Tashiding, the largest of the group figured by Hooker.[1] So sacred is it that the mere act of beholding it is supposed to cleanse from all sin, according to its name. Its full title is *Thong-wa rang tö*,[2] or "Saviour by mere sight." It owes its special sanctity to its reputedly containing some of the funereal granules[3] of the mythical Buddha antecedent to Shakya Muni, viz.—*O-sung*,[4] the relics having been deposited there by Jik-mi Pawo, the incarnation and successor of Lhatsün Chhembo. As a result of this repute it is a favourite object of pilgrimage.

Mendongs.

The *mendongs* are faced with blocks bearing in rudely cut characters the six-syllabled mystic sentence "*Om māni pädme hung*"—the same which is revolved in the "prayer-wheels." And occasionally it also bears coarsely outlined figures of the three favourite protecting divinities of Lāmaism, the *Ri-sum Gonpo*, or "the Three *Defensores Fidei*," viz.—the four-handed *Chérési* (Skt. *Avalokita*), *Jai-yang* (Skt. *Manjugosha*), and *Chākna Dorje* (Skt. *Bajrapāni*). As it is a pious act to add to these "*mani*" slabs, a mason is kept at the larger temples and places of special pilgrimage, who carves the necessary number of stones according to the order and at the expense of the donating pilgrim.

Pradakshina mode of passing religious buildings.

The above monuments must always be passed on the right hand, according to the ancient Hindu ceremonial of *pradakshina*, as a tribute of respect. And thus it is that the prayer cylinders must always be turned in a similar direction.

Lāma's throne.

In addition to the foregoing objects there is frequently found in the vicinity of the monastery a stone seat called a "throne" for the head lāma while giving *al-fresco* instruction to his pupils. One of the reputed thrones of Lhatsün Chhembo exists at the Pemiongchi chhorten, where the camp of visitors is usually pitched.

---

[1] *Himalayan Jours.*, Vol. I, page 320.

[2] *m*thong wa rang grol.

[3] It is believed by the lāmas that on the burning of the body of a Buddha no mere ash results, but two varieties of nodules which are named :—(*a*) *phe-dung*, small white seed-like granules; (*b*) *ring-srel*, yellowish larger nodules from the bones, and of these an enormous quantity are forthcoming. It is the former which are said to be preserved in the great Tashiding Chaitya.

[4] *h*oḍ srung.

There is no regular asylum for animals rescued from the butchers to save some person from pending death. Occasionally such ransomed cattle are to be found in the neighbourhood of monasteries where their pension-expenses have been covered by a donation from the party cured. The animals have their ears bored for a tuft of coloured rags as a distinctive mark.

Ransomed animals.

Not far from most monasteries are fertile fields of *murwa* (*Eleusine corocana*) from which is made the country beer, a beverage which the Sikhim monks do not deny themselves.

Murwa fields.

In the following table is given, what is described as, a complete list of monasteries in native Sikhim with the number of the monks in each, from official information supplied by Lama Ugyén Gyātsho:—

List of Sikhim monasteries.

List of Monasteries in Sikhim.

Serial No.	Map name.	Vernacular name.	Meaning of the name.	Date of building.	Number of monks.
1	Sanga Chelling	*g*sang *s*ngag*s* chhos gling.	The place of secret spells ...	1697	25
2	Dubdi ...	*s*grub-*s*de ...	The Hermit's cell ...	1701	30
3	Pemiongchi ...	pad-ma yang tse ...	The sublime perfect lotus ...	1705	108
4	Gantok ...	btsan-*m*khar ...	The Tsén's house ...	1716	3
5	Tashiding ...	*b*kra-shis-*l*ding ...	(*The large Tashiding temple* is the temple of the religious king or "*Dharma raja.*")	1716	20
6	Senan ...	*g*zil-*g*non ...	The suppressor of intense fear	1716	8
7	Rinchinpong ...	rin-chhen *s*pungs ...	The precious knoll ...	1730	8
8	Ralong ...	ra-*b*lang ...	......	1730	80
9	Mali ...	mad-lis ...	......	1740	15
10	Ram thek ...	Ram-tek ...	A Lepcha village name ...	1740	80
11	Fadung ...	pho-brang ...	The chapel royal ...	1740	100
12	Cheung tong ...	*b*tsun-thang ...	The Meadow of Marriage (of the two rivers), or of Dorje Phagmo.	1788	8
13	Ketsu perri ...	*m*khaḥ *s*pyoḍ *d*pal ri ...	The noble heaven-reaching mountain.	...	11
14	Lachung ...	thang-mô-chhen ...	The large plain ...	1788	5
15	Talung ...	*r*do lung ...	The stony valley ...	1789	90
16	Entchi ...	rab-*b*rten *g*ling ...	The high strong place ...	1840	15
17	Phensung ...	phan-*b*zang ...	The excellent banner or good bliss.	1840	100
18	Kartok ...	*b*kah-*r*tog ...	The Kartok (founder of a schism).	1840	20
19	Dalling ...	*r*do-*g*ling ...	"The stony site" or the place of the "Dorjeling" tertön.	1840	8
20	Yangong ...	*g*yang *s*gang ...	"The cliffy ridge" or "the lucky ridge."	1841	10
21	Labrong ...	*b*la-brang ...	The lāma's dwelling ...	1844	30

Serial No.	Map name.	Vernacular name.	Meaning of the name.	Date of building.	Number of monks.
22	Lachung ...	pon-po *s*gang ...	The Bon's ridge ...	1850	8
23	Lintse ...	lhun-*r*tse ...	The lofty summit ...	1850	15
24	Sinik ...	zî-mig ...	......	1850	30
25	Ringim ...	ri-*d*gon ...	Hermitage hill ...	1852	30
26	Lingthem ...	ling-tham ...	A Lepcha village name ...	1855	20
27	Changhe ...	*r*tsag-ngeṣ ...	......	...	...
28	Lachen ...	La-chhen ...	The big pass ...	1858	8
29	Giatong ...	zi-hdur ...	......	1860	8
30	Lingqui ...	ling-*b*kod ...	The uplifted limb ...	1860	20
31	Fadie ...	*h*phagô *r*gyạl ...	The sublime victor ...	1862	8
32	Nobling ...	nub-gling ...	The western place ...	1875	5
33	Namchi ...	*r*nam-*r*tse ...	The sky-top ...	1836	6
34	Pabia ...	*s*pa-*h*bi-*h*og ...	......	1875	20
35	Singtam ...	sing-ltam ...	A Lepcha village name ...	1884	6

In addition to the monasteries in this list are several religious buildings called by the people gömpas, but by the lamas only *hla-khang* or temples, such as Dé-thang, Ke-dum, &c.

The older monasteries.

The oldest monastery in Sikhim is Dub-de, founded by the pioneer lāma Lhatsün Chhembo. Soon afterwards shrines seem to have been erected at Tashiding, Pemiongchi, and Sang-nga-chhö-ling over spots consecrated to Guru Rimbochhe, and these ultimately became the nuclei of monasteries; Sangngachhöling and Pemiongchi being first built. As Sangngachhöling is open to members of all classes of Sikhim-Bhotiyas, Lepchas, Limbus, and also females and even deformed persons, it is said that Pemiongchi was designed, if not actually built, by Hlatsün Chhembo as a high-class monastery for *ṭa-sang* or "pure-monks" of pure Tibetan race, celibate and undeformed. Pemiongchi still retains this reputation for the professedly celibate character and good family of its monks; and its monks alone in Sikhim enjoy the title of *ṭa-sang*, and to its lāma is reserved the honour of anointing with holy-water the reigning sovereign.

Pemiongchi and its ṭa sang.

Monasteries according to sect.

The great majority of the monasteries belong to the Nyingmapa sub-sect of Lhatsün-pa, only Namchi, Tashiding, Sinön, and Thangmochhe belonging to the Ngadakpa sub-sect, and Kartok and Dô-ling to the Kartokpa sub-sect of Nyingmapa. All of these are practically subordinate to Pemiongchi, although Namchi and Kartok gömpas are nominally the heads of the Ngadakpa and Kartokpa respectively. Pemiongchi also exercises supervision over the Lepcha gömpas of Lingthem, Zimik, and Phaggye. Lepchas are admissible also to Rigön as well as Sangngachhöling. Nuns

Lepcha monasteries.

are admitted to a few monasteries, but their number is extremely small, and individually they are illiterate, old, and decrepit.

Nuns.

Only three monasteries belong to the Karmapa, viz., Ralang, Ramtek, and Phodang, and of these Phodang is now in reality the chief, although Ralang is the parent monastery.

At present the most flourishing monasteries in Sikhim are the Nyingmapa, Pemiongchi, and the Karmapa Phodang.

The names of the monasteries.

The names of the monasteries, as will be seen from the translations given in the second column of the table, are mostly Tibetan and of an ideal or mystic nature, but some are physically descriptive of the site, and a few are Lepcha place-names also of a descriptive character.

Proportion of lāmas to the Buddhist population.

The lāmas number nearly one thousand, and are very numerous in proportion to the Buddhist population of the country. In 1840, Dr. Campbell estimated[1] the Lepchas and Bhotiyas of Sikhim at 3,000 and 2,000 respectively; but Mr. White in his census of Sikhim in March 1891 gives the population roughly as—

Lepchas	...	...	...	5,800
Bhotiyas	...	...	...	4,700
Nepalese, &c.	...	...	...	19,500
				30,000

As the Nepalese are all professing Hindus, the lāmas are now dependent on the Bhotiyas and Lepchas for support, and we thus get a proportion of one lāmaic priest to every 10 or 11 of the indigenous population. But this does not represent the full priest-force of those two races, as it takes no count of the numerous devil-dancers and Lepcha priests patronized by both Bhotiyas and Lepchas.

III.—THE TEMPLE AND ITS CONTENTS.

The Temple.

The temple had no place in primitive Buddhism. It is the outcome of the worship of relics and images, and dates from the later and impurer stage of Buddhism.

Its names.

Its proper name is *Lhā-khāng* or "God's house;" but as it serves the purpose of an assembly room and school, it is also called respectively *Du-khāng*[2] (a meeting-room) and *Tsug-lak-khāng*[3] (an academy), although the former name is strictly applicable only to the hall in the lower flat in which the monks assemble for worship.

[1] *The Oriental*, page 13

[2] *h*du-khang.

[3] *g*tsug-lag-khang.

Exterior.

It is the chief and most conspicuous building in the monastery and isolated from the other buildings. It is usually surrounded by a paved path to allow of pious circumambulation, and it is sometimes shaded by a cypress tree. Built in the Sikhim style of architecture, it is a heavy ungainly building with squarish base, tapering whitewashed stone walls, and a huge projecting flattish roof of thatched bamboo. In the wealthier monasteries the thatch has lately been replaced by corrugated iron, which does not improve the appearance of the building. As the wide projecting eaves render the roof liable to be blown off, the latter is tied down to the ground at the four corners by long pendant ropes. The roof is surmounted by one or a pair of small bell-shaped domes of gilt copper: if a pair, they are placed one on either end of the ridge, and called *jira;*[1] if a solitary one in the middle of the ridge, it is called *gyal-tshén.*[2] They are emblematic of the umbrella-banner of victory and good fortune. The building is usually two stories in height with an outside stair on one flank, generally the right, leading to the upper flat. In front is an upper wooden balcony, the beams of which are rudely carved and its doors variously ornamented.[3] The necessary orientation of the building has already been noted.

In approaching the temple door the visitor must proceed with his right hand to the wall, in conformity with the Hindu ceremonial custom of *pradakshina* already noted. In niches along the base of the building, about three feet above the level of the path, are sometimes inserted rows of prayer-barrels which are turned by the visitor sweeping his hand over them as he proceeds.

Entrance.

The main door is entered by a short flight of steps. On ascending the steps, the entrance is at times screened by a large curtain of yak-hair hung from the upper balcony, which serves to keep out rain and snow from the frescoes in the vestibule.

Vestibule figures.

Entering the vestibule, we find its gateway guarded by several fiendish figures. These are—

I.—The Demon of the Locality, usually a *Tsén* or male demon of a red colour, but differing in name according to the locality.

[1] *kny*jira. | [2] *r*gyal-*m*tshan.

[3] At Pemiongchi the balcony doors contain painted representations of the seven precious things of a universal emperor (*Chakravarta rājā*), such as Shākyā was to have been had he not become a Buddha; viz.—(1) the precious wheel; (2) the precious white elephant; (3) the precious flying horse; (4) the precious gem; (5) the precious general; (6) the precious minister; and (7) the precious wife. These objects are frequently figured in the base of images and pictures of Buddha. *See* also Chapter V, page 323.

II.—Especially vicious demons of a more or less local character. Thus, at Pemiongchi is the *Gyalpo Shuk-dén* with a brown face and seated on a white elephant. He was formerly the learned lāma Panchhen Söd-nam*s* grak*s*-pa, who being falsely charged with licentious living and deposed, his spirit on his death took this actively malignant form and wreaks his wrath on all who do not worship him—inflicting disease and accident.

III.—A pair of hideous imps, one on either side, of a red and bluish-black colour, respectively, named *Ki-kang* or *Shemba Mar-nak*,[1] who butcher their victims.

IV.—Here also are sometimes portrayed the twelve *Täṇ-ma*,—aërial nymphs peculiar to Tibet, who sow disease and who were among the chief fiends subjugated by "The Guru."

The Guardian Kings of the Quarters.

Confronting the visitor in the vestibule are the four colossal images (frescoes) of the Kings of the Quarters, who guard the Universe and heavens against the outer demons. They are clad in full armour and of defiant mien. Two are placed on each side of the doorway. Their names are—

1. Yul-khor srung[2] (Skt. *Dhṛita-rāshṭra*), the white guardian of the east and King of the Gandharvas (Dri-za).
2. Phag-kye-pô[3] (Skt. *Virūḍhaka*), the yellow guardian of the south and King of the Kumbhāndas (Grul-bun).
3. Jé-mi-zang[4] (Skt. *Virūpāksha*), the red guardian of the west and King of the Nāgās (*k*Lu).
4. Nam-thö-sré[5] (Skt. *Vaisravana*), the green guardian of the north and King of the Yakshas (*g*Nod-*s*byin).

Sometimes the guardian of the north is given a yellow, and the guardian of the south a green, complexion, according to the later fashion of the gélukpa, thus making the complexion of the guardians to coincide with the mythic colours of the quarters.

Prayer-barrels.

In the smaller temples which possess no detached *Mani lhakhang*, one or more huge *Mani*[6] prayer-barrels are set at either end of the vestibule, and mechanically revolved by lay-devotees, each revolution being announced by an affixed lever striking a bell. As the bells are of different tones and are struck alternately, they form at times a not unpleasant chime.

[1] ki-kang *d*mar nag. | [2] yul *h*khor *b*srung. | [3] *h*phags *s*kyes-pa.
[4] *s*pyan mig *b*zang. | [5] *r*nam thos sra*s*.
[6] So called on account of their containing the "*Om mānī*" formula, *vide* page 289.

Door.

The door is of massive proportions, sometimes rudely carved and ornamented with brazen bosses. It opens in halves, giving entry directly to the temple.

Interior.

The temple is a large hall, with a double row of pillars separating it into a nave and two aisles, and the nave is terminated by the altar—*vide* diagram (PLATE IV). The whole of the interior, in whichever direction the eye turns, is a mass of rich colour, the walls to right and left being covered with frescoes of deities, saints, and demons, mostly of life-size, but in no regular order; and the beams are mostly painted red, picked out with lotus rosettes and other emblems. The brightest of colours are used, but the general effect is softened in the deep gloom of the temple, which is dimly lit only by the entrance door.

Central triad of images.

Above the altar are placed three colossal gilt images in a sitting attitude, "The Three Rarest Ones"[1] or trinity of the Lāmas. These three images should be *Shākya Muni* in the centre, with *Guru Rimbochhe* to the left (of the spectator) and *Ché-rési* to the right.

Shākya.

Shākya Muni is of a yellow colour with blue curly hair, and is occasionally attended by standing figures of his two chief disciples, Maugdalputra on his left and Shariputra on his right, each with an alarm-staff[2] and begging-bowl (Tib. *Hlun-sed*, Skt. *Patra*) in hand.

Guru Rimbochhe.

Guru Rimbochhe or *Pädma Jungné* (the Lotus-born) (PLATE V) usually sits in front of a screen of lotuses and wears his typical mitre-like hat shaped in the fashion of a lotus flower. He holds a *dorje* (the thunderbolt of Indra, the Hindu Jove) in his right hand and a human skull-cup of blood in his left, and resting on his left shoulder is a trident decorated with human heads.

His two wives.

He is almost always attended by his two ministering wives, viz., the Tibetan fairy *Khandō Ye-she Tsho-gyal*, holding a skull-cup of blood on his left, and the Indian *Lha-cham Mandarāwa*, holding a jar of wine for the Guru's use on his right.

Che-resi.

Ché-rési,[3] the patron god of Lāmaism and of Tibet, and incarnate in the Dalai Lāma, is represented white in colour, with four hands, the front pair of which are joined in devotion, while the upper right hand holds a crystal rosary, and the upper left a lotus flower.

---

[1] The title "Chief of Rarity" seems to have been the name of an indigenous Tibetan god.

[2] This is a staff (Tib. *Khar-sil*, Skt. *hi-ki-lo*) surmounted by 9 to 12 jingling rings, carried in the hand of the Indian Buddhist monk, to warn the villagers of his approach when he went a-begging, bowl in hand.

[3] *spyan-ras-gzigs*.

Plate IV.

DIAGRAMMATIC

GROUND PLAN OF A SIKHIM TEMPLE.

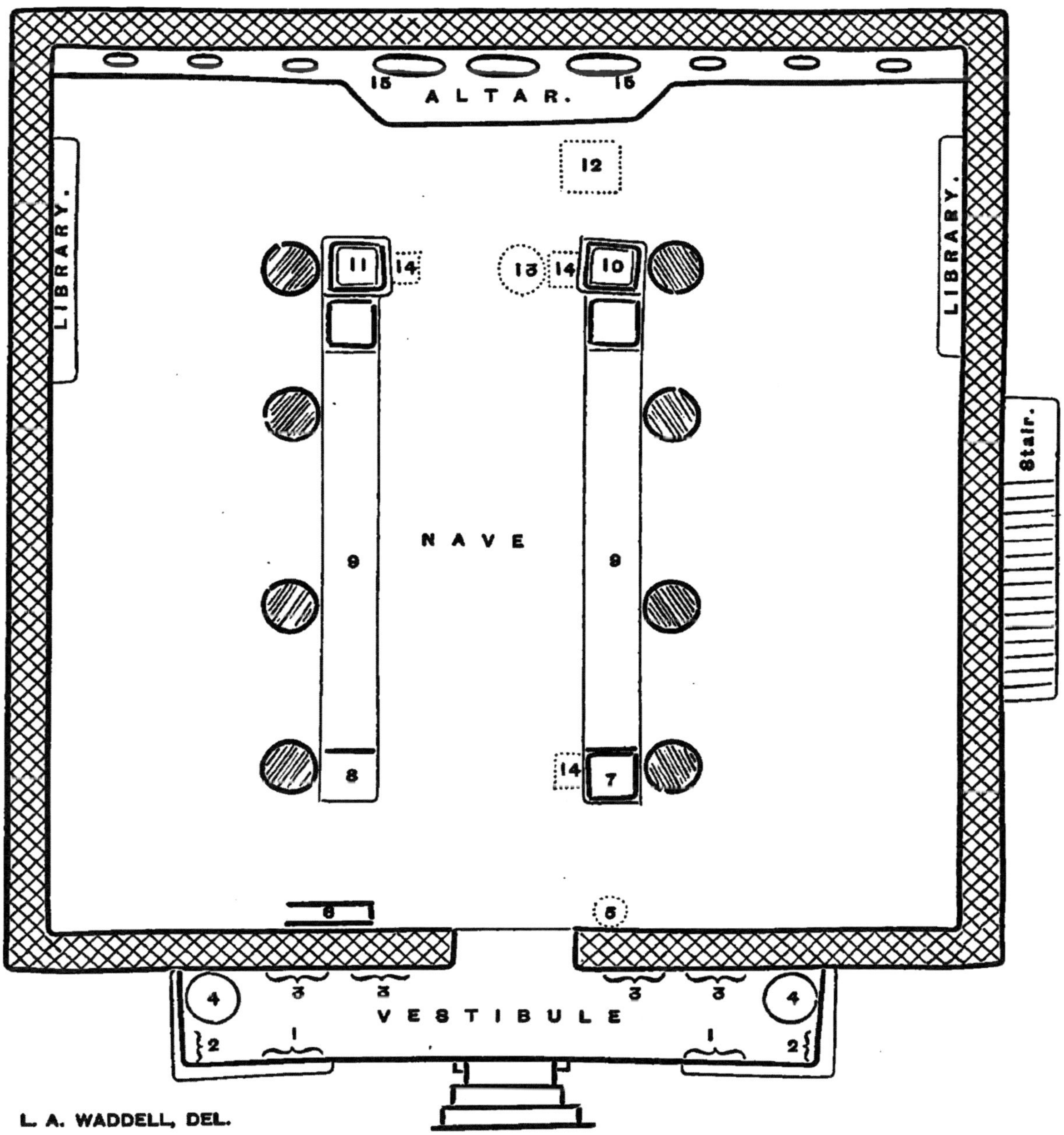

L. A. WADDELL, DEL.

1. Fresco of Locality demons.
2. " *Ki-kang Mar-nak* demons.
3. " Guardian Kings of Quarters.
4. Prayer-barrels.
5. Station of Chhö-timba or Provost Marshal.
6. Table for tea and soup.
7. Seat of Chhö-timba.
8. Seat of water-giver.
9. Seats of monks.
10. Seat of Dorje Lô-pön.
11. " Umdsé or Chief Celebrant.
12. " King or Abbot Visitant.
13. Site where lay-figure of corpse is laid.
14. Lamas' tables.
15. Idols.

Reg. No. 382. Bengal.—July 94.—500.

Zinco., S. I. O., Calcutta.

Reg. No. 362, Bengal.—July 94.—500.

Zinco., S. I. O., Calcutta.

This order of the images is, however, seldom observed. Most frequently in Nyingmapa temples the chief place is given to the *Guru*, and this is justified by his own statement that he was a second Buddha sent by Shākya Muni specially to Tibet and Sikhim, as Buddha himself had no leisure to go there. Sometimes Shākya's image is absent, the third image in such case being usually the fanciful Buddha Opā-meḍ (Skt. *Amitabha*, The Boundless Light) or Tse-pā-meḍ (Skt. *Amitāyus*, Unlimited Life), each with hands joined in the support of a begging-bowl (*hlun-ze*) or holy-water vase respectively. Tse-pā-meḍ, the god of long life, is always crowned. In Karmapa temples the chief place is given to the founder of the Karmapa sub-sect, namely, Karma Bakshi.

Other images.

Ranged on either side of this triad are the other large images of the temple. The following are especially common:—

Dorje-phāgmo (Skt. *Vajravarahī*)—"The Sow-faced Lady Dorje;" when with three heads, the left is that of a sow.

Döl-ma[1] (Skt. *Tāra*)—"The Unloosener" or Deliveress—the Virgin-mother, and in other aspects the wife, of the Buddhas and the Bodhisatwas. Further particulars regarding her and her worship are given in Chapter IV, page 313, *et seq.*

Chak-dor (Skt. *Vajrapāni*)—"The Wielder of the Thunderbolt" (*i.e.*, Jupiter), with uplifted bolt.

Jam-yang (Skt. *Manjughosa*)—"The god of Mystic Wisdom," with the flaming sword of light in his right hand and the lotus-supported book of wisdom in left.

Ché-rési (Skt. *Avalokita*)—"The Seer with keen eyes," in his usual four-handed form; or with eleven heads and a thousand arms, each with an eye in the palm. This is the great "God of Mercy," one of whose titles is "The Great Pitier"—his thousand eyes and arms graphically represent his being ever on the outlook to discover distress and to succour the troubled. This Bodhisatwa, together with the foregoing two, namely, Jam-yang and Chak-dor, are the especial *Defensores Fidei* of Lāmaism under the title of Rik-sum-gon-po or "The Triad Protectors."

Seng-dong-ma—"The Lion-faced Goddess."

Kang-chhen-dsö-nga—The chief "country-god of Sikhim," of red colour, carrying a gyaltshén or banner of victory, and mounted on a white lion. (PLATE VI).

His dwelling place is the mountain from which he takes his name—*Anglice* "Kanchinjingna." This graceful mountain, second in height only to Everest, was formerly in itself an object of worship, as

[1] *sgrol-ma.*

it towers high above every other object in the country, and is the first to receive the rays of the rising sun and the last to part with the setting sun. *Kangchhendsönga* literally means "the five repositories or ledges of the great snows," and is physically descriptive of its five peaks—the name having been given by the adjoining Tsangpa Tibetans, who also worshipped the mountain. But Lhatsün Chhembo gave the name a mythological meaning, and the mountain was made to become merely the habitation of the god of that name, and the five "repositories" were real store-houses of the god's treasure. The peak, which is most conspicuously gilded by the rising sun, is the treasury of gold, the peak which remains in cold grey shade is the silver treasury, and the other peaks are the stores of gems and grain of sorts and holy books. This idea of treasure naturally led to the god being physically represented somewhat after the style of "the god of *wealth*." He is on the whole a good-natured god, but rather impassive, and is therefore less worshipped than the more actively malignant deities. For further particulars of his worship, *see* Chapter VI on "Demonolatry," page 355.

Lhā-tsün Chhembo, the pioneer lāma of Sikhim; or other lāma-saint of Sikhim, or of the special sect to which the temple belongs.

The alleged existence, by Sir Monier Williams[1] and others[2] of images of Gorakhnāth in Tashiding, Tumlong, and other Sikhim temples is quite a mistake. No such image is known. The name evidently intended was Guru Rimbochhe.

Material of images.

The large images are generally of gilded clay, and the most artistic of these come from Pá-to or "Paro" in Bhutan. A few are of gilded copper and mostly made by Newaris in Nepal. All are consecrated by the introduction of pellets of paper inscribed with sacred texts.

Frescoes.

Amongst the frescoes on the walls are displayed the *Néden chu-ṭuk*, or the sixteen disciples of Buddha; and also numerous lāma-saints of Tibet.

Framed paintings.

There are also a few oil-paintings of divinities framed in silk of grotesque dragon pattern with a border, from within outwards, of "the primary" colours in their prismatic order of red, yellow, and blue. These pictures have mostly been brought from Tibet and Bhutan, and are sometimes creditable specimens of art.

Plan of interior.

The general plan of a temple interior is shown in the foregoing diagram. Along each side of the nave is a long low cushion about three inches high, the seat for the

[1] *Buddhism*, page 490.

[2] Campbell, *J. A. S. B.*, 1849; Hooker, Sir R. Temple, *Jour.*, page 212; *Him. Jours.* I, 323; II, page 195.

monks and novices. At the further end of the right-hand cushion on a throne about $2\frac{1}{2}$ feet high sits the *Dorje Lô-pön*,[1] the spiritual head of the monastery. Immediately below him, on a cushion about one foot high, is his assistant who plays the sī-nyen cymbals. Facing the Dorje Lô-pön, and seated on a similar throne at the further end of the left-hand cushion, is the *Um-dsé*[2] or chief chorister and celebrant and the temporal head of the monastery; and below him, on a cushion about one foot high, is the *Üchhung-pa* or Deputy Üm-dsé, who plays the large *tshö-rol* or assembly cymbals[3] at the command of the *Üm-dsé*, and officiates in the absence of the latter. At the door-end of the cushion on the right-hand side is a seat about one foot high for the *Chhö ṭim pa*,[4] a sort of provost-marshal who enforces discipline, and on the pillar behind his seat hangs his bamboo rod for corporal chastisement. During the entry and exit of the congregation he stands by the right side of the door. Facing him at the end of the left-hand cushion, but merely seated on a mat, is the *Chhab-dupa* or water-giver, who offers water to the monks and novices, for washing their hands and lips after each round of soup. To the left of the door is a table on which is set the tea and soup served out by the unpassed boy-probationers during the intervals of worship.

Seats of officers.

At the spot marked "13" on plan is placed the lay figure of the corpse whose spirit is to be withdrawn by the Dorje Lô-pön. At the point marked "12" is set the throne of the king or of the Labrang incarnate lama—the *Kyab-gon* or protector of religion—when either of them chances to visit the temple.

On each pillar is hung a small silk banner with five flaps, usually in vertical series of threes called *phén*,[5] and on each side of the altar is a large one of circular form called *chephur*.[6]

Decorations.

In some of the larger temples are side-chapels for the special shrine of Dorje-phagmo or other favourite divinity. The shrines of the deities and demons to whom flesh is offered are usually located in a detached building.

Side-chapels.

Upstairs are the images of secondary importance, and here among the frescoes covering the walls are usually found the *Gon-pos*, or demoniacal protectors of Lāmaism. These latter are of ferocious aspect, enveloped in flames and wielding various weapons. They are clothed in human and tiger skins, and adorned with snakes and human skulls and bones. Chief among

Upper flat.

[1] *r*do-rje *s*lob-*d*pon.
[2] *db*u-mdsad.
[3] tshog*s*-rol.
[4] chho*s* khrim*s*-pa.
[5] hphan.
[6] phye-phur.

these are (1) the blue-faced *Lhāmo*, the Kalī form of the Hindu Devi; (2) her consort *Māhakāla*, a destructive form of Shīva; (3) the horse-headed *Tamdin*, the Hāyagrīva of the Hindus and spouse of Dorje-phagmo.

"The Cycle of Existence."

Prominent among the frescoes is the *Sī-pa-ī khor-lô*[1] or "Cycle of existence," showing the regions of re-birth and the tortures of the damned. This picture is so very interesting and important that it demands more than passing notice.

The Pictorial Wheel of Life.

The *Sī-pa-ī-khor-lô* or "Cycle of Existence"—(*vide* Plate VII) for a copy of the Tashiding temple-picture[2]—is a graphic exposition of metempsychosis, one of the most fundamental laws of Buddhism—the secret of Buddha having consisted in the means he devised for escaping from this ceaseless round of re-births with its attendant sufferings.

This picture is one of the purest Buddhist emblems that the lāmas have preserved to us. And by its means I have been able to restore the fragment of a cycle in the verandah of Ajantā Cave No. XVII hitherto uninterpreted, and merely known as "the Zodiac." This picture portrays in symbolic and concrete form the three original sins and the recognized causes of re-birth (*Nidānas*), so as to ensure their being vividly perceived and avoided; while the evils of existence in its various forms and the tortures of the damned are intended to intimidate evil-doers. As the Sikhim copies of the picture misplace the order of the Nidānas, and are deficient in many details, I here describe the orthodox form of the picture as found in Tibet.

The picture consists of a large disc, the circular form of which symbolizes the ceaseless round of wordly existence. It is held in the clutches of a monster, whose head is seen overtopping the whole. This angry demon, who grips the disc with his claws and teeth, typifies the passionate clinging of the people to existence. In the centre of the disc are symbolized the three original sins, and around the margin the twelve linked chain of causes of re-birth; while the remainder of the disc is divided by radii into six compartments, which represent the six regions of re-birth.

These pictorial symbols of the abstract conceptions of the early Buddhists are extremely valuable as showing what is the traditional interpretation of the ambiguous Sanskrit and Pali metaphysical terms for the *Nidāna* found in the Indian Buddhist books, and the real

[1] Srid-pa-hi *h*khor-lô.

[2] Kindly supplied by Mr. White.

PLATE VII.

THE WHEEL OF LIFE.

From a tracing of the Tashiding Frescoe.

(Reduced to one-fourth.)

Plate VIII.

KEY TO PLATE VII.

THE WHEEL OF LIFE

From Tashiding Monastery.

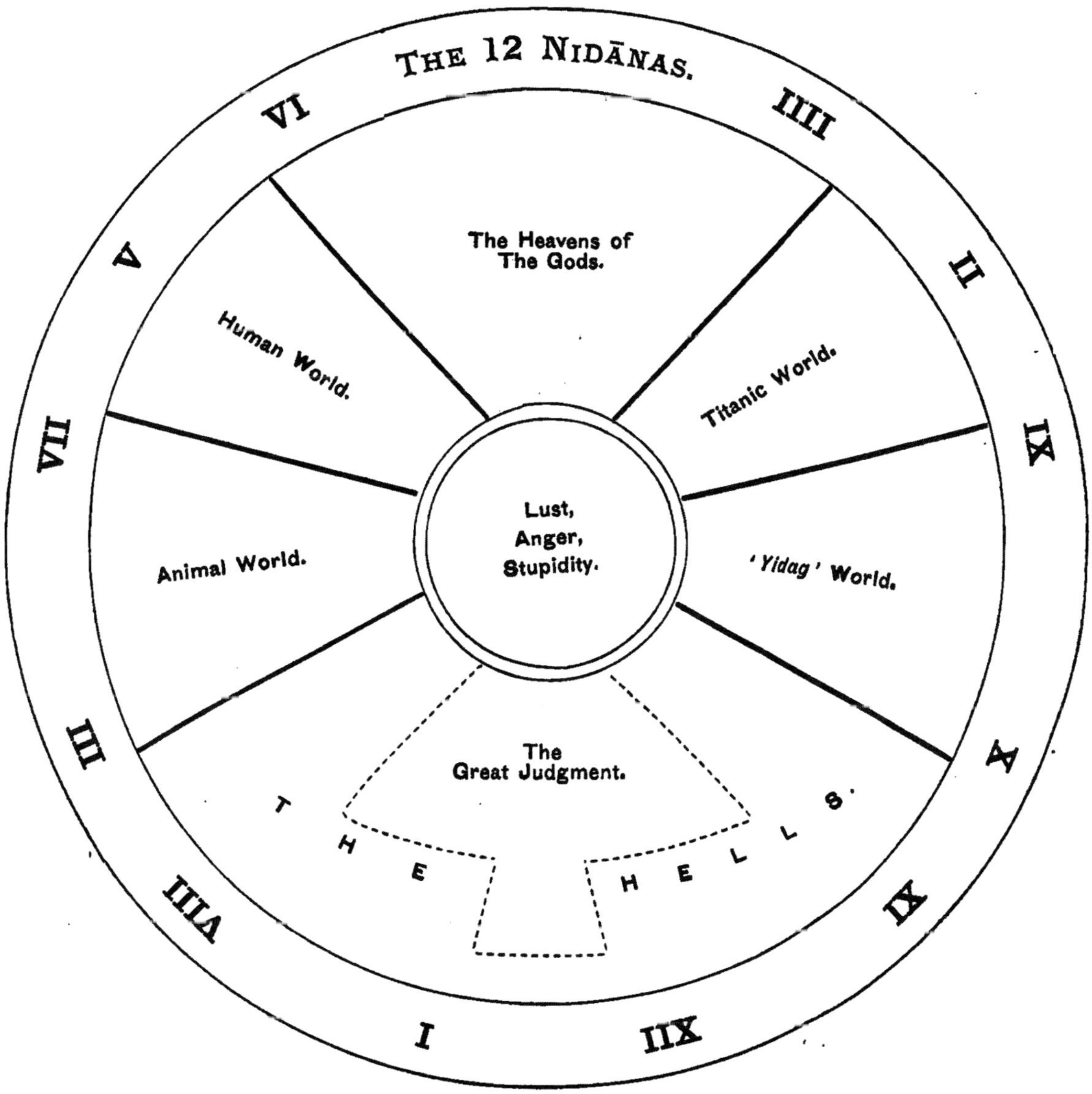

interpretation of which has formed a subject of much controversy amongst Western scholars.

The three original sins are depicted as (*a*) a *pig*, which has hold of the tail of (*b*) a *cock*, which has seized the tail of (*c*) a *snake*, which in its turn has hold of the pig's tail, thus forming a circle which revolves continuously around the world. The *pig* symbolizes the ignorance of stupidity; the cock, animal desire or lust; and the snake, anger.[1] If these three sins be avoided, then virtue results and merit is accumulated.

The causes of re-birth—the *Nidānas*—are categorically given as twelve in the form of a linked chain, the result of the first cause being the cause of the second, and so on; the ultimate result being suffering.[2] The illustrations with their lāmaic paraphrases are:—

I.—A blind old woman groping her way[3] = *marig-pa* (Skt. *Avidyā*) or "want of knowledge," which is the cardinal

---

[1] These sins are thus depicted by Sir E. ARNOLD in *The Light of Asia*, p. 164:—

"Patigha—*Hate*—
With serpents coiled about her waist, which suck
Poisonous milk from both her hanging dugs,
And with her curses mix their angry hiss.
Then followed Ruparaga—*Lust* of Days—
That sensual sin which out of greed for life
Forgets to live; and Lust of Fame * * * (and) Fiend of Pride
* * * * * * and—*Ignorance*—the Dam
Of Fear and Wrong, Avidya, hideous hag
Whose footsteps left the midnight darker."

[2] Sir E. ARNOLD (*loc. cit.*, p. 165) thus expresses the Nidānas:—

"Whirling on the Wheel,
* * * * * * * * * * *
Avidya—Delusion—Sets those snares,
Delusion breeds *Sankhāra*, Tendency
Perverse; Tendency Energy—*Vidnnān*—
Whereby comes *Nāmarūpa*, local form
And name and bodiment, bringing the man
With senses naked to the sensible,
A helpless mirror of all shows which pass
Across his heart, and so *Vedanā* grows
'Sense-life'—false in its gladness, fell in sadness;
But sad or glad, the Mother of Desire,
Trishna, that thirst which makes the living drink
Deeper and deeper of the false salt waves
Whereon they float, pleasures, ambitions, wealth,
Praise, fame, or domination, conquest, love;
Rich meats and robes and fair abodes and pride
Of ancient lines, and lust of days and strife
To live, and sins that flow from strife, some sweet,
Some bitter. Thus Life's thirst quenches itself
With draughts which double thirst."

[3] In the older pictures a man, who represents Buddha, is guiding the blind woman. But as the Ajanta painting gives for this a man leading a (blind) camel, it is evident that the Lamas constructed their picture from a written description, and interpreted the word *nga-mo* (rnga-mo), a camel—an animal practically unknown in Central Tibet—as *ga-mo* (rgad-mo) "an old woman."

cause of existence leading people to mistake for happiness the miseries of existence.

II.—A potter with his wheel making pots = *du-che* (Skt. *Sanskāra*) or *impressing*—literally "preparation or fashioning + action," showing the fruits of worldly labour are perishable objects—action being misdirected as a result of ignorance.

III.—A monkey eating fruit = *nam-she* (Skt. *Vijñāna*) or "entire knowledge" of good and evil fruits—tasting every fruit in the sense of a roving libertine without system; thus engendering *consciousness*.

IV.—A dying man with a physician feeling pulse[1] = *ming-zug* (Skt. *Nāma-rupa*) or "name and body," *i.e.*, individual being. Its fleeting character is shown by the man being about to lose his individuality and name in death.

V.—An empty house = *kye-chhe* (Skt. *Shadāyatana*) or "the five mortal sense organs and mind," illustrates the organs and the will which are the result of individual being—the hollowness of these is typified. The Ajanta painting depicts this by a mask, which is a much more appropriate symbol.

VI.—A pair of lovers kissing = *reg-pa* (Skt. *Sparsha*) or contact which results from the exercise of the sense organs and will.

VII.—An arrow entering a man's eye = *tshor-wa* (Skt. *Vedanā*) or "perception," the result of a contact. It includes joy and sorrow as well as pain.

VIII.—A man drinking wine[2] = *sre-pa* (Skt. *Trishṇā*) or "desire for more," including thirst and affection, which results from the exercise of the perceptive faculty.

IX.—A man gathering a large basketful of flowers = *len-pa* (Skt. *Upādāna*) "or taking": grasping indulgence in worldly matters—the result of desire.

X.—A pregnant woman = *srid-pa* (Skt. *Bhava*) or "continuity of existence," a desire for inheritance—the result of the clinging to worldly life and wealth.

XI.—A mother in childbirth = *kye-wa* (Skt. *Jati*) or birth as a result of No. X.

XII.—A human corpse being carried off = *ga-she* (Skt. *Jārāmarana*) or "decay and death" with all their sufferings, which are the result of birth.

---

[1] The newer style has a boat with human passengers being ferried across the ocean of life.

Another form is a pair of caressing lovers.

The six forms of re-birth—gro-baī rigs (Skt. *Gati*)—are shown in the inner circle. In the order of their superiority they are—

1. The gods or *lhā* (= Skt. *Sura* or *Deva*)—the highest form of existence.
2. The Titans, literally "ungodly spirits" or *lha-ma-yin* (= Skt. *Asura*).
3. Mankind or *mī* (Skt. *Nara*).
4. The Beasts or *du-dô* (Skt. *Tirjyak*).
5. The Tantalized ghosts—*yī-dag* (Skt. *Preta*).
6. Tho inhabitants of hell, *nyal-wa* (Skt. *Naraka*), the lowest of all.

The first three forms of existence are classed as good and the last three are bad; and all are under the immediate care of a Buddha, who stands in the centre of each compartment, and is a form of the Bodhisatwa Ché-ré-si (*Avalokita*), who is incarnate in the Dalai Grand Lāma at Lhasa.

The place of one's re-birth is dotormined solely by one's own deeds—although the lāmas now make faith and charms and ritual take the place of the good works of the earlier Buddhists. If the virtues are in excess of the sins, then the soul is re-born in one or other of the first three forms: as a god if the virtue be of the first degree, as an ungodly spirit if the virtue be of the second degree, and as a human being if the virtue is of the lowest order. While those whose sins preponderate are re-born in one or other of the last three forms, the most wicked going to hell, and the least wicked to the beasts.

The judgment is in every case meted out by the impartial "*Shinje chho gyal*" or "Religious King of the Dead," a form of *Yama*, the Hindu god of the dead, who holds a mirror in which the naked soul is reflected, while his servant *Shinje* weigh out in scales the good as opposed to the bad deeds; the former being represented by white pebbles, and the latter by black.—This incident usually occupies the upper portion of the hell-compartment of the *Sī-pa-ī khor-lô* picture.

The details of these several regions are briefly as follow:—

I. *The Gods.*—These are the gods of Indra's heaven of Hindu mythology rendered finite. Their life is the longest of all beings; but they, too, are within the operation of the law of continuous metamorphosis, and may be re-born in hell or in any other of the six regions. Their abode is the Mt. Meru (Tib. *Ri-rab*) of the Hindus, a mythical and invisible mountain-heaven[1] in the centre of the universe according to Hindu cosmogony.

The picture of the region of the gods shows a three-storied palace in the heavens of Indra, Desire occupying the lower, Brahma the middle, and the indigenous *Dā-lha*, the Tibetan war god, the

[1] "heaved up."

upper compartment. This curious perversion of the usual order of the heavens is notable, as the Lamas have placed the embodiment of passion—their war-god—above Brahma. These gods are surrounded by other gods, all with shining bodies and the special attributes of a god of this heaven, namely, (1) goddess-companions; (2) a lake of perfumed nectar (*amrita*), which is their *elixir vitæ* and source of their bodily lustre; (3) the *pag sam shing* or wish-granting tree, which bestows at once any fruit or food wished for; (4) the wish-granting cow, which yields instantly any drink wished for; (5) the horse of knowledge, which *Pegasus*-like carries his rider to the worlds of the present, past, and future; (6) his splendid dress and ornaments; (7) a fine palace; (8) a charming garden with flowers, which form his wreath, and pretty animals and singing birds. Along the border separating this world from that of the *lhamayin* (Asuras) are some of the gods armed with spears and other weapons under the direction of the war-god *Dā-lha* resisting the encroachments of the *lhamayin* of the lower world.

The human being who has been sufficiently charitable, virtuous, and pious during his earthly life may be re-born as a god and enjoy bliss for an almost incalculable time—one god's day being one hundred human years. And he is born into heaven in a full-grown state. But when his merit is exhausted, then his lake of nectar dries up, his wish-granting tree and cow and horse die, his splendid dress and ornaments disappear, his garden and flowers wither, his body, no longer bathed by nectar, loses its lustre, and his person becomes loathsome to his goddess companions and the other gods, who shun him, and he dies miserably. If he has led a virtuous life during his existence as a god, then he may be re-born in heaven, otherwise he goes to a lower region and may be even sent to hell.

II. *The Titans* (Lhamayin) *or ungodly spirits.*—These are the Titans or *Asuras* of Hindu mythology, and occupy the base of Mt. Meru, and are therefore intermediate between heaven and the earth. They have numerous joys and comforts; but are discontented, and envy the greater bliss of the gods, with whom they are continually fighting for some of the fruits of the heavenly wish-granting tree, which has its roots and trunk within their region.

This region is represented with a light yellow atmosphere, and contains a fortified house, with a lake and flowers and numerous animals. The people are all clad in full armour, and are engaged mostly in fighting with the gods across their frontier. Many of them are dead, or dying, or horribly mangled by the weapons of the gods, the most deadly of which is a wheel with teeth like a circular saw, which is thrown like the Sikh quoit. They always die in battle from their wounds, as they have no access to the nectar by which the gods obtain instant recovery when wounded.

As existence here is rather miserable, although it is above mankind, only the proud and envious are re-born here, but re-birth from this region mostly occurs in hell owing to the wicked life led during existence here.

III. *Mankind.*—The atmosphere of this region is blue or colourless. It shows the miseries of human existence which have to be endured by all alike, from prince to pauper: family troubles, striving after wealth, position, or necessaries of life, &c., &c.

The following phases of life are depicted amongst others:—

1. *Birth.*
2. *Old age.*—Decrepit old man and woman hobbling along.
3. *Disease.*—Sick man, with doctor feeling his pulse, or sick attempting to drink.
4. *Death.*—A dying man surrounded by weeping relatives, with a lāma doing worship near his head, and another monk ascertaining whether the breathing has ceased. Another scene depicts the dead body being carried off, preceded by a lāma, who carries the end of a scarf affixed to the corpse, and in the lāma's hand are a *damāru* (hand-drum) and a thigh-bone trumpet, while in the distance is the funereal pyre to cremate the body.

Other scenes illustrate worldly pleasure and business. A man sitting under a tree in front of his house, drinking tea or wine, and children at play, and hills in the distance. Traders bargaining, also a drunken man, a borrower, and a criminal being punished for crimes.

IV. *The Beasts.*—The atmosphore of this region is darker, but it has hills and trees and also some men, as it is merely a different aspect of the human world. Ruskin says "the fish is freer than the man;" but the lāmas think otherwise. They class all aquatic animals as "the Bonded Animals," and only terrestrial and flying animals are "The free." Hence the animal region is divided into an aquatic and a land-section, each peopled by characteristic animals. This is a state of greater misery than the human, as the animals prey on one another, and man also kills many of the animals and uses others as beasts of burden or for other utilitarian purposes.

The picture shows land animals of various kinds, some devouring others, and some human hunters killing game animals. In the water are fish and a variety of animals, also preying on one another.

V. *The Yidags or Tantalized Ghosts.*—The atmosphere of this region is also darkish. This is the special place of those who on earth were miserly, envious, and uncharitable. They have jewels and food and drink in plenty, but cannot enjoy them, and are always gnawed by hunger and thirst, as they are given huge bodies with microscopical mouths and gullets. And when any food is taken it is transformed to sharp knives and saws, which lacerate the bowels and come out externally, making large painful wounds. Others have fires constantly burning in their mouths.

VI. *The Hells.*—The atmosphere of the hells is black. Only eight hells are mentioned in the older Buddhist works, but the lāmas describe and figure eight cold and eight hot hells, and give two extra hells named *nyi-tshewa,* which includes the state of being flies and insects in the human world, and *nye-khorwa,* a milder hell filled with fiery ashes and rubbish and bodies in which those escaping from hell must dwell for a further period.

In the upper portion of this region is figured the King and Judge of the dead in the act of trying the spirits of the dead, with the good recording angel on his right hand, counting out the good deeds by white pebbles from his purse, and the incarnation of evil on his left hand displaying before the Judge the bad deeds as a pile of black pebbles. In front is the scale-holder, who weighs the good as against the bad deeds.

Those who have sinned in anger are sent to the hot hell, while those who have sinned through stupidity go to the cold hell, and each receives some appropriate punishment for misdeeds during life. To show the superiority of the lāmas to such tribunals, several are introduced walking serenely through the hells twirling their prayer wheels.

The hot hells are to the left (of spectator) and the cold to the right.

I. The hot hells—

1. *Yang-Sö* (Skt. *Samjiva*) = "again revived." Here the bodies are torn to pieces and then revived only to have the process repeated *ad libitum.*
2. *Thi-nag* (Skt. *Kālasutra*) = "black lines." Here the bodies are nailed down and 8 or 16 black lines marked along body, which is then sawn in sections along these lines by a burning hot saw. Another punishment here is the especial one of the slanderer or gossiper, who has his or her tongue enlarged and pegged out and constantly harrowed by spikes ploughing through it.
3. *Du-jom* (Skt. *Samghāta*) = "concentrated oppression." Here bodies are squeezed between animal-headed mountains or monster iron books (this is an especial punishment for monks, laymen, and infidels who have disregarded or profaned the scriptures). Others here are pounded in iron mortars.
4. *Ngu-bod* (Skt. *Rāurava*) = "weeping and screaming." The torture here is to be kept in glowing white iron houses and have melted iron poured down the throat.

5. *Ngu-bod Chhenpo* (Skt. *Mahārāurāva*) = "greater weeping and screaming." Here they are cooked in pots containing molten iron.
6. *Tshewa* (Skt. *Tāpana*) = "heat." The body is cast upon and transfixed by red-hot iron spikes.
7. *Rabtu-tshawa* (Skt. *Pratāpana*) = "highest heat." A three-spiked burning spear is thrust into body, and later rolled up within red-hot iron plates.
8. *Nar-med* (Skt. *Avichi*) = "endless torture." This is the most severe and longest punishment. The body is perpetually kept in flames, though never consumed.

II. The cold hells which have no place in the mythology of the Indian and Southern Buddhists are:—

1. *Chhu-bur chen* = "blistered and wrinkled." The torture here is constant immersion of the naked body in icy cold water, under which the body becomes covered with chilblains.
2. *Chhu-bur dolwa.*—The chilblains are forcibly cut and torn open, producing raw sores and deep chaps.
3. *A-cchu* = "achū!" an exclamation of anguish which vents itself in this expression and which resounds throughout this hell.
4. *Kyi-hüd.*—A worse degree of cold in which the tongue is paralysed and the exclamation "*kyi-hü!*" alone possible.
5. *So-tham-pa.*—The teeth and jaws are rigidly clenched through cold.
6. *Ut-pal tar-gé-pa.*—Livid sores which become everted like blue utpal flowers.
7. *Pé-ma tar gê-pa.*—The raw sores become red like lotus (*padma*) flowers.
8. *Pé-ma chhen-po tar-gé-pa.*—The flesh falls away from the bones like the petals of the great red lotus (*padma*), leaving raw sores which are continually gnawed and pecked by birds with iron beaks.

The duration of the stay in hell lasts until the great sins committed during the previous existence are expiated. This period may vary from a few years to thousands of years. From hell the usual course is back to earth, by the merit of good works done in a former existence. The lāmas explain this by saying that it is like the discharge of a criminal who has expiated his offence in jail: on release he gets back his clothes and any other personal properties he can justly lay claim to, and the benefit of any virtuous deeds he had formerly done.

The history of the *Sī-pa-ī khor-lô* as given by the lāmas is that Buddha on one occasion plucked a stalk of rice, and with its grains illustrated to his disciples his arguments on the 12 causes of existence and the continuous metamorphoses of animated beings in the six regions; and that later he personally directed the preparation of the picture in what is now known as the 'new' style which was specially intended for the conversion of the king of U-tra-ya-na (? Udhayana) and latterly introduced into Tibet in the 11th century A.D. by the Indian monk Atisha, who had received it from the followers of Phagpa Thog*s*-med or Arya Asaṅga. The "older" style, that is, as regards Tibet, is reported to have been the copy sanctioned by Lôpön Lu-ṭub or Guru Nagarjuna, the founder of the Mahāyāna system, and a copy of it was brought to Tibet by Bande Ye-shi in the 8th century A.D. in the reign of the Thi-srong-de-tsan, and reproduced in the monastery of Samyé. The present picture in the Samyé monastery is said to measure about 15 to 20 feet in diameter, and differs from the "newer" style chiefly in the absence of a figure of Buddha in the upper right-hand corner and of the Munis in each of the six regions.

The Altar and its Objects.

The altar.

The altar or *chhö-sham*[1] occupies the remote end of the nave of the temple. Above its middle is placed the chief image. A canopy, called *nam-yul* or "sky-country," on which are depicted the dragons of the sky, is stretched above the altar, and a large silken parasol, called *ḍuk* or umbrella—the oriental symbol of royalty—is suspended over the head of the central image. This umbrella slightly revolves in one or other direction by the ascending currents of warm air from the lamps.

Its tiers.

The altar should have at least two tiers. On the lower and narrow outer ledge are placed the offerings of water, rice, cake, flowers, and lamps. On the higher platform extending up to the images are placed the musical instruments and certain other utensils for worship.

Its accessories.

In front of the altar stands the spouted water-jug *chhab-pum*[2] for filling the smaller water vessels, a dish to hold grain for offerings *né-ze*,[3] an incense-holder *pö-dsin*,[4] and a pair of flower vases. And on the right (of the spectator) on a small stool or table is the rice *mandala* cone, with its three tiers, daily made up by the temple attendant, and symbolic of an offering of all the continents and associated islands of the world according to Hindu and Buddhist cosmography, with Mount Meru (Tibetan *Ri-rab*), the abode of the gods, as the culminating point: for detailed description, *see* Chapter V, page 320.

[1] *m*chhoḍ sham. | [2] chhab-bum. | [3] naṣ bzeḍ. | [4] spoṣ-*h*dsin.

The ordinary water and rice offerings are set in shallow brazen bowls, called *chhö-ting*,[1] composed of a brittle alloy of brass, silver, gold, and pounded precious stones. Their number is five or seven, usually the former. Two out of the five bowls should be filled with rice heaped up into a small cone; but as this must be daily renewed by fresh rice, which in Sikhim is somewhat expensive, fresh water is usually employed instead.

The offerings.

Another food-offering is a high, conical cake of dough, butter, and sugar, variously coloured, named *tormā* or *zhal-ze*, that is, "holy food." It is placed on a metal tray supported by a tripod. To save expense a painted dummy cake is usually employed.

Food offering.

The temple-lamp or *chhö-kong*[2] is a short pedestalled bowl, into a socket in the centre of which is thrust a cotton wick, and it is fed by melted butter. As the great mass of butter solidifies and remains mostly in this state, the lamp is practically a candle. The size varies according to the means and the number of the temple votaries, as it is an act of piety to add butter to the lamp. One is necessary, but two or more are desirable, and on special occasions 108 or 1,000 small lamps are offered.

Candles.

The "essential offerings," or *Nyer-chö chhö-pa*,[3] which are needed in every form of worship are seven in number, and must be placed in line and in a definite order, as shown in the following diagram:—

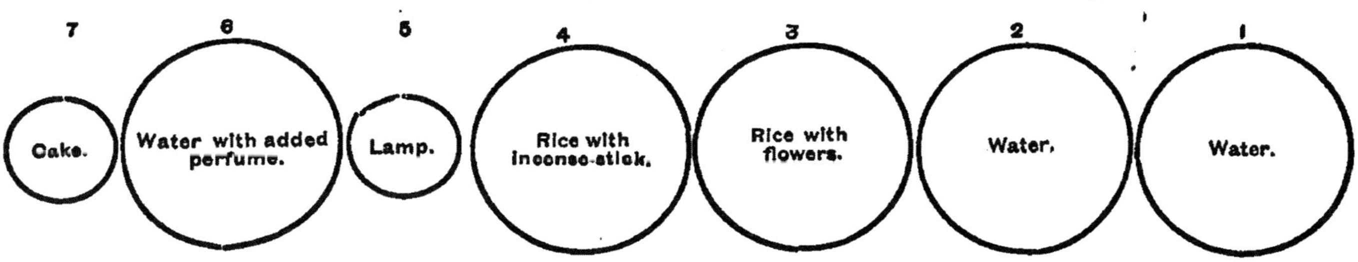

The cymbals are placed on the inner platform. On the top of the rice heaps of Nos. 3 and 4 should be placed respectively a flower, preferably the large-winged seed of the legume of the so-called *pag*-sam shing or "wish-granting tree," and a stick of incense. And in the bowl marked "No. 6" should be placed perfumed water; but these details are only observed on special occasions. Ordinarily the bowls are filled with plain water.

Order of offerings.

These offerings have each received a special Sanskritic name descriptive of their nature, viz.—

1. *Ār-gham* (or Ar-ganga), in Tibetan *chhö-yön*,[4] or excellent drinking river water.

[1] *m*chhoḍ ting. | [2] *m*chhoḍ *s*kong. | [3] nyer-*s*pyoḍ *m*chhoḍ-pa. | [4] mchhoḍ yon.

2. *Pā dyam*, in Tibetan *zhāb-sel*,[1] or the cool water for washing feet.
3. *Pukh-pe* (or Pushpe), in Tibetan *me-tok*,[2] flower.
4. *Dhu-pe*, in Tibetan *du-pö*,[3] incense fumes.
5. *A-loke*, in Tibetan *mar-me*,[4] lamp or light.
6. *Gan-dhe*, in Tibetan *ṭi-chhab*,[5] perfumed water for anointing body.
7. *Nai-wi-dya*, in Tibetan *zhāl-zé*,[6] sacred food.
8. *Shabta*, in Tibetan *rol-mo*,[7] cymbals.

This order is reversed in *Kargyupa* and *Gelukpa* temples when doing a certain kind of *yidam* or tutelary deity's worship. These eight offerings appear to be symbolic of the eight *Matris* or Divine mothers, *vide* Chapter V, page 323. And with them may also be compared the 16 stages of the Hindu worship of a deity which I append in a foot-note[8] for reference.

Accompanying worship.

On placing the above offerings in position in the order noted, the benefit of a full service of worship is obtained by merely chanting the following hymn:—

"*A-wa-tā-ya, A-wa-tā-ya. Om bajra! Ārgham, Pā-dyam, Pūkh-pe,* "*Dhū-pe, Ā-loke, Gan-dhe, Nāi-wi-dya, Shab-ta, Prāti-dsa-yī Swāhā!*" Which being interpreted is:—"Come! Come! *Om! Bajra* (the "thunderbolt)! Partake of these offerings! excellent drinking river "water, cool water for washing your feet, flowers for decking your "hair, pleasing incense fumes, lamp for lightening the darkness, "perfumed water for anointing your body, sacred food, the music of "cymbals! (here the cymbals are sounded.) Eat fully! *Swāhā!*"

Special banquet to the host of gods and demons.

A more elaborate arrangement of food offerings is seen in the banquet to the whole assembly of the gods and the demons, entitled Kön-chhok chī dü,[9] or "sacrifice to the whole assembly of the Rare Ones," which is

---

[1] zhabṣ sél. [2] me-tog. [3] pdug-spoṣ. [4] mar-me. [5] dri-chhab. [6] zhal-zaṣ. [7] rol-mo.

[8] In the Hindu worship of a deity there are 16 stages of ceremonial adoration following the Invocation to come (*āvāhan*), and the Invitation to be seated (*āsan*), and in each stage *mantras* are chanted. I have italicised those stages which are found in the above lāmaic ritual:—

1. *Pādya*, washing the idol's feet.
2. Azgha, washing the idol's hands.
3. Achmana, offering water to rinse mouth.
*4. Snāna, bathing the idol.
*5. Vastra, dressing the idol.
6. Chandan, offering sandal wood, saffron, or holi powder.
7. Akshat, offering rice.
8. *Pushpa*, offering flowers.
9. *Dhupa*, offering incense.
10. *Dipa*, offering lamp.
11. *Nuivedya*, offering food.
12. Achmana, second offering of water to rinse mouth.
13. Tāmbula, offering betel.
14. Supāri or puga, offering Areca nuts.
15. Dakshana, offering money.
16. Nizājan, waving lights or camphor.

[9] *d*kon mchhog *s*pyi *h*dus.

*The lāmas dress and bathe their idols only once or twice yearly.

frequently held in the temples. This feast is observed by all sects of lāmas, Nyingmapa, Gelukpa, &c., and is an interesting sample of devil-worship. The Nyingmapa fashion is here detailed, but it differs from the Gelukpa only in providing for a slightly larger party of demoniacal guests, the Gelukpa inviting only the following, viz., their chief Lāma, *i.e.*, Tsongkhapa, their tutelary deity Dorje-jik-che, Buddha, Chang-sem, the deified heroes, the fairies, the guardian demons of the Gelukpa creed, the god of wealth, the guardian demons of the caves where the *terma* (hidden revelations) are deposited, the five sister demons of Mount Everest, the twelve Tö-ma or aërial nymphs who sow disease, and the special "country" and "locality" gods.

When given.

This sacrifice should be done in the temples for the benefit of the lāmas on the 10th and 15th of every month. On behalf of laymen it must be done *once* annually at the expense of every individual layman who can afford it; and on extra occasions, as a thanksgiving for a successful undertaking, and as a propitiation in sickness, death, and disaster.

Its arrangement.

The arrangement of the banquet is shown in the following diagram:—

ARRANGEMENT OF
THE BANQUET TO THE WHOLE ASSEMBLY OF THE GODS AND DEMONS.

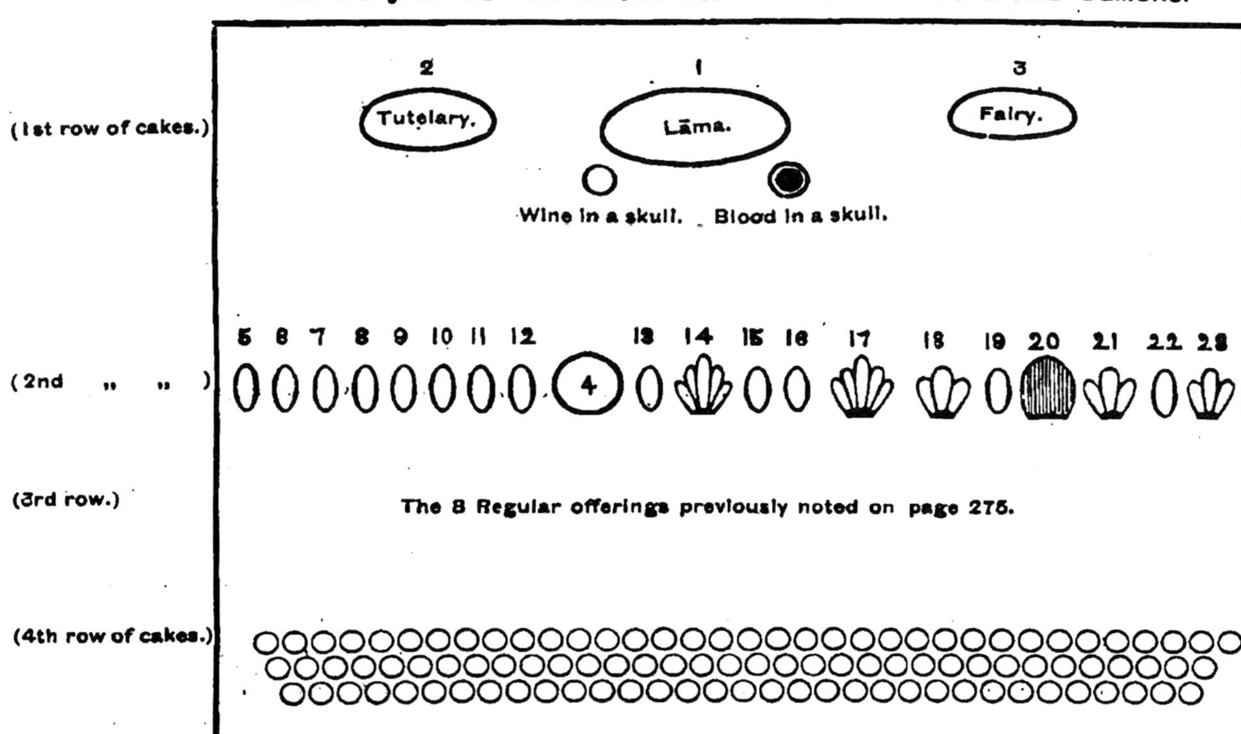

In the inmost row are the large coloured and ornamented *Baling* cakes for (1) the chief Lāma-Saint *Guru Rimbochhe*, (2) the tutelary deity, in this case *Guru ṭak-po*, a fierce demoniacal form of the Guru, and (3) the fairy with the lion face. For the Guru there is also placed on either side of his cake a skull-cup, the one to his right containing country wine, here called *Amrita* or "nectar" (in Tibetan—literally "devils' juice"), and the contents of the other are called *Rakta* or blood—infused tea is usually offered instead of blood. In the second row are the cakes for the guardians and protector of Lāmaism, usually with Buddha's cake (No. 4) in centre. The order of the cakes for these guardian demons is as follows—the attached figures relate to the foregoing diagram :—

No. 5. The Lion-faced demoness.
„ 6. The four-armed "Lord," a form of Mahakala.
„ 7. The god of wealth.
„ 8. The "Ruler" of Tibet's guardian (and in Sikhim the special guardian of the *Nga-dakpa* monasteries).
„ 9. The demon Blacksmith (red and black colour, rides a goat and carries an anvil and a bellows, was made a protector of lāmaism by Lô-pön).
„ 10. The Lord of the Rakshas.
„ 11. The Locality protector.
„ 12. The *Naga* demi-gods, white and black.
„ 13. The female fiend-nun of Di-kung monastery.
No. 14. The five everlasting Sisters of Mount Everest.
„ 15. The spirits of the Tank-drowned ones.
„ 16. The homestead demon-owner.
„ 17. The country god Kangchhend-sönga (mountain).
„ 18. The black devil, red devil and *Naga* of Darjeeling or special locality of temple.
„ 19. The demons who cause disease.
„ 20. The twelve aërial nymphs who cause disease.
„ 21. The demon owners of the "Ter" caves where the hidden revelations are deposited.
„ 22. The black and red devils and *Naga* of parent monastery of the priests of this temple.

In the third row are placed the "essential offerings" (*Nyer-chö chhö-pa*) already detailed on page 275, which are especially intended for the superior gods.

In the fourth and outmost row are an indefinite number of *tshok* (ཚོགས་) cakes which are especial dainties as an extra course for all. These cakes contain ordinary *torma* cake of cooked rice or barley, with the addition of some wine, and a mixture of cooked flesh and all sorts of eatables available.

The stages of the worship in this feast are as follows :—

1st.—Invitation to the deities and demons to come to the feast (Skt. *āvāhan*). This is accompanied by great clamour of drums, cymbals, horns and fifes, so as to attract the attention of the gods and demons.

2nd.—Requesting the guests to be seated (Skt. *āsan*).

3rd.—Begging them to partake of the food offered.

4th.—Praises the goodness and admirable qualities of the guests. This is done while the guests are partaking of the essence of the food.

5th.—Prayers for favours immediate and to come.

6th.—The especial delicacy *tshog* is then offered to all, on four plates, a plate for each row of guests, one plateful being reserved for the lāmas.

Then is done the ceremony of *Kang-so*,[1] or "expiation for religious duties left undone," which wipes off all arrears of religious duty. Here the *ku-nyer* or novice appointed for the occasion throws skywards, amid great noise of instruments, several of the *tshok* cakes to all the demi-gods and demons not specially included in the feast. One *tshok* cake is then given to each lāma in order of rank, from the highest to the lowest, as the food has been consecrated by the gods having eaten of it. They must, however, leave a portion, which is collected carefully, in a plate, in order, from the lowest to the head lāma. Above these collected fragments is placed a whole *torma* cake, and a worship entitled *Hlak-dor* is done, when the whole of these crumbs—the leavings of the lāmas—are contemptuously thrown down to the earth outside the temple door to those evil-spirits who have not yet been subjected by Lô-pön or subsequent lāmas.

Other articles on altar.

On the top of the altar are placed the following articles:—

(*i*) A miniature *chhorten* (= chaitya).[2]

(*ii*) One or more sacred books on each side of altar.

(*iii*) A *dor-je*, the lāmaic sceptre and type of the thunderbolt of Indra (Jupiter), and a bell *ṭilbu*.[3] The *dorje* is the counterpart of the bell, and when applied to the shoulder of the latter should be of exactly the same length as the bell-handle.

(*iv*) The holy-water vase—*thü-pum*[4]—and a metal mirror—*me-long*—hanging from its spout. The holy-water of the vase is tinged with saffron, and is sprinkled by means of a long stopper-rod, which is surmounted by a fan of peacock's feathers and the holy *kusa* grass.

(*v*) The divining arrow, bound with five coloured silks, called *dā-dar*.[5]

(*vi*) A large metal mirror—*me-long*—to reflect the image of the spirits.

(*vii*) Two pairs of cymbals. The pair used in the worship of Buddha and the higher divinities are called *sí-nyén*,[6] and

[1] *b*skang-*gso*.

[2] In the room in which worship is done there must be present these three essential objects representing the *s*ku-*g*sum (Skt. *Tri-kāya*) : (*a*) an image, (*b*) a chhorten, and (*c*) a holy book, which are symbolic of "The Three Holy Ones." In the early Indian Caves this Triad was represented by a *Chaitya* (= Buddha), *Wheel* (= Dharma), and a LION (= The Assembly).

[3] dril-bu. | [4] khru*s*-bum. | [5] *m*dah-dar. | [6] *s*il-*s*myan.

are of about 12 inches or more in diameter, with very small centre bosses. They are held vertically when in use, one above the other, and are manipulated gently. The pair of cymbals used in the worship of the inferior deities and demons are called *rol-mo*, and are of short diameter with very much broader bosses. They are held horizontally in the hands and forcibly clanged with great clamour.

(*viii*) Conch-shell trumpet—*tung*[1]—used with the sī-nyén cymbals.

(*ix*) Pair of copper hautboy-fifes—*gye-ling*.[2]

(*x*) Pair of long telescopic copper horns—*rā-dung*.[3]

(*xi*) Pair of human thigh-bone trumpets—*khāng-ling*.[4] These are sometimes encased in brass, with a wide copper flanged extremity on which are figured the three eyes and nose of the ogre-demon, the oval open extremity being the demon's mouth. In the preparation of these thigh-bone trumpets the bones of criminals or those who have died by violence are preferred, and an elaborate incantation is done, part of which consists in the lāma eating a portion of the skin of the bone, otherwise its blast would not be sufficiently powerful to summon the demons.

(*xii*) Pair of tiger thigh-bone trumpets—*tā-dung*.[5] These are not always present, and the last three instruments are only for the worship of the inferior gods and demons.

(*xiii*) Drums—

(*a*) A small hand-drum or *nga-chhung*[6] or *damāru*, like a large double egg-cup. Between its two faces are attached a pair of pendant leather knobs and a long-beaded flap for handle. When the drum is held by the upper part of the cloth handle and jerked alternately to right and left the knobs strike the faces of the drum. It is used daily to mark the pauses between different forms of worship.

(*b*) The big drum called *chhö-nga*,[7] or religious drum. These are of two kinds, one of which is suspended in a frame and beaten only occasionally and in Buddha's worship. The other is carried in the hand by means of a stem thrust through its curved border. These are beaten by drum-sticks with straight or curved handles.

(*c*) The human skull-drum made of *skull-caps* and of same style as the smaller drum (*a*) above described.

---

[1] dung.
[2] *r*gye-*g*ling
[3] ra*g*-dung.
[4] *r*kang-*g*ling.
[5] *s*tag-dung.
[6] *r*nga-chhung.
[7] chhos-*r*nga.

THE LĀMA'S TABLE.

Lāma's table.

To the right front of the altar stands the lāma's table, called *dün-chog*,[1] about 2½ feet in length and one foot in height. A cushion is placed behind it, and on this is spread a tiger or leopard-skin rug as a seat. The table should contain the following articles in the order and position shown in the diagram:—

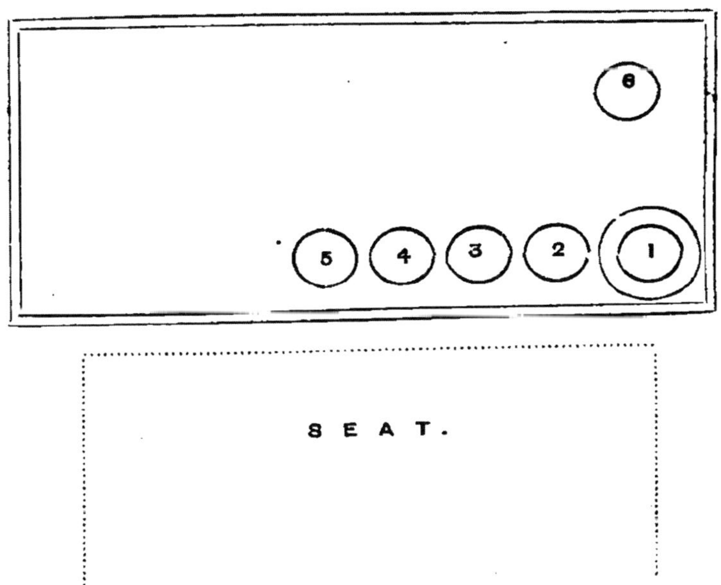

1. *Mandala*—rice cone.
2. *Chen-du* or *ne-sel*—saucer with loose rice for throwing in sacrifice.
3. Small *damāru* drum.
4. Bell.
5. *Dorje.*
6. *Lü-pum* vase.

Dorje Lô-pön's table.

The extensive arrangement here figured is properly that of the Dorje Lô-pön's table. Only three monks are allowed tables in the temple, viz.—

The *Dorje Lô-pön*, or abbot.
The *Um-dsé*, or chief celebrant.
The *Chho-ṭimba*, or provost-marshal.

Um-dsé's.

The Um-dsé's table faces that of the Dorje Lô-pön, and contains only a *tü-bum* or holy-water vase, bell, dorje and the large *tsho-rol* cymbals.

Chho-ṭimba's.

The table of the Chho-ṭimba stands in front of the latter's seat, near the door, and contains an incense goblet or *sang-bur*, bell and *dorje*.

[1] *m*dum-*l*chog.

Lāmaic Rosaries.

The rosary is an essential part of a lāma's dress. As a Buddhist article, the rosary is especially peculiar to the Northern school of Buddhists and the outcome of the esoteric teachings of the Mahāyāna school, instilling belief in the potency of muttering mystic spells and other strange formulas. In the very complicated rosaries of Japan[1] it has attained its highest development.

Its origin.

It is not enumerated in the Southern Scriptures among the articles necessary for a monk. But incidental mention is made by Shway Yoe[2] of a rosary with 108 beads; and several of the Burmese monks I have met possessed a rosary called "Bodhī," consisting of 72 black sub-cylindrical beads, which I understood were composed of slips of leaf inscribed with charmed words and rolled into pellets with the aid of lacquer or varnish.

The rosary is not conspicuous amongst Southern Buddhists, but among Tibetans it is everywhere visible.

It is also held in the hand of the image of the patron god of Tibet—Ché-ré-si (Skt. *Avalokita*), and its use is not confined to the lāmas. Nearly every layman and woman is possessed of a rosary on which at every opportunity they zealously store up merit; and they also use it for secular purposes, like the sliding balls of the Chinese, to assist in ordinary calculations: the beads to the right of the centre bead being called *ta-thang* and registering units, while those to the left are called *chu-dô* and record tens, which numbers suffice for their ordinary wants.

Its uses.

Description of the Rosary and its appendages.

The vernacular name for the rosary is "*phreng-ba*,"[3] pronounced *theng-wa* or vulgarly *theng-nga*, and literally means "a string of beads."

Vernacular name.

The rosary contains 108 beads of uniform size. The reason for this special number is alleged to be merely a provision to ensure the repetition of the sacred spell a full hundred times, and the extra beads are added to make up for any omission of beads through absent-mindedness during the telling process or for actual loss of beads by breakage; but the number is of mystic significance. Ché-ré-si and Döl-ma have each 108

The number 108.

[1] Note on Buddhist Rosaries in Japan. By J. M. James, Trans. Jap. As. Soc., page 173, 1881.

[2] *The Burman: His Life and Notions*, I., page 201.

[3] phreng-ba.

Plate IX.

LĀMAIC ROSARIES.

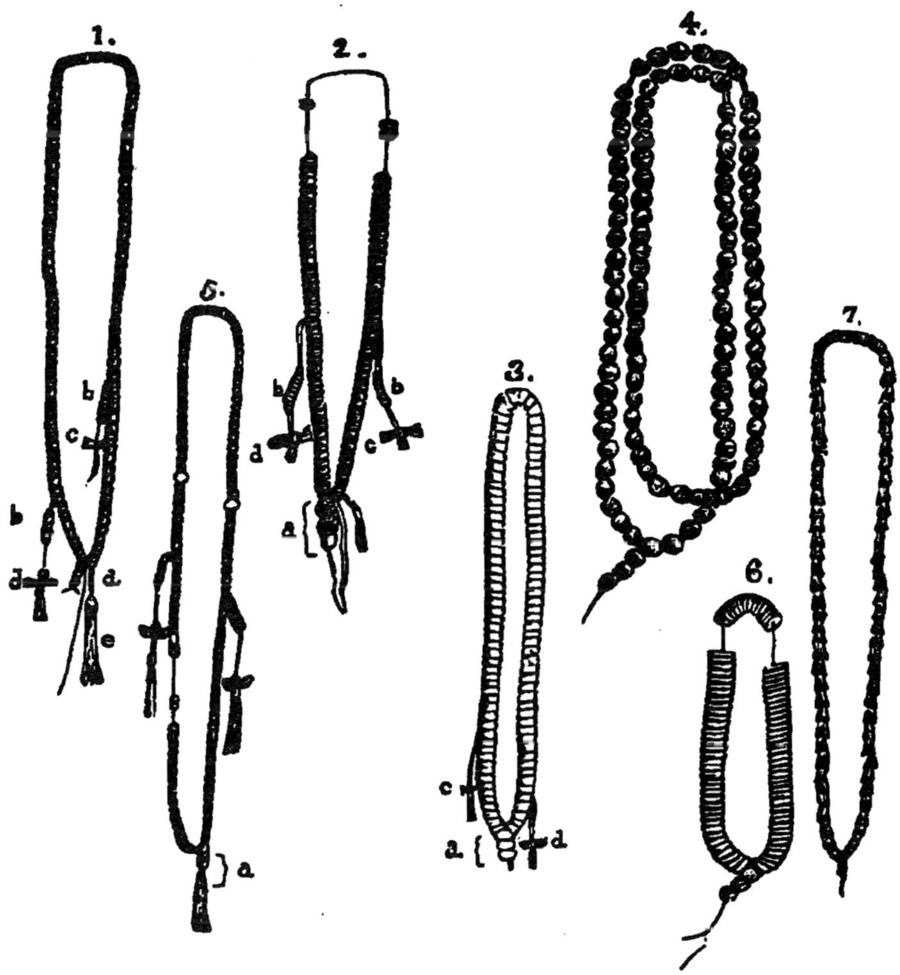

Fig. 1. The yellow wooden rosary of Geluk-pa sect.*
,, 2. ,, red sandal-wood ,, for Tamdin's worship.*
,, 3. ,, white conch-shell ,, ,, Chérési's do.*
,, 4. ,, *raksha* ,, ,, the Furies' do.
,, 5. A layman's rosary (beads of unequal size).*
,, 6. The human-skull (discs) rosary.
,, 7. ,, snake-spine do.

---

* *a* = *dô-dsin.*
b = counters.
c = bell-pendant.
d = *dorje*-pendant.
e = a tweezer and tooth-pick.

names; although it is not usual to tell these on the rosary. One hundred and eight is the usual number of lamps and cakes offered at great shrines; and in the later Kham editions of the lāmaic scriptures —the "*kah-gyur*"—the volumes have been extended from 100 to 108. The Southern scriptures state that 108 Brahmans were called by Gotama's father at the birth-feast to cast the embryo Buddha's horoscope, and the Burmese footprints of Buddha sometimes contain 108 subdivisions.[1] This mystic number is perhaps borrowed, like so many other lāmaic fashions, from the Hindus, of whom the Vaishnabs possess a rosary with 108 beads.

The head beads.

The two ends of the string of beads before being knotted are passed through three extra beads, the centre one of which is the largest. These are collectively called dok-dsin[2] or "retaining or seizing bead"—*vide* "a" in figures. The word is sometimes spelt *m*do-*h*dsin, and pronounced *dô-dsin*, which means "the union-holder." In either case the meaning is much the same. These beads keep the proper rosary beads in position, and indicate to the teller the completion of a cycle of beads.

This triad of beads symbolizes "the Three Holy Ones" of the Buddhist Trinity, viz., Buddha, Dharma (the Word), and Sangha (the Church, excluding the laity). The large central bead represents Buddha, while the smaller one intervening between it and the rosary beads represents the Church and is called "Our special Lāma-monitor,"[3] the personal Lāma-guide and confessor of the Tibetan Buddhist; and his symbolic presence on the rosary immediately at the end of the bead-cycle is to ensure becoming gravity and care in the act of telling the beads, as if he were actually present.

The ge-luk-pa or "reformed" sect of lāmas usually have only two beads as dok-dsin, in which case the terminal one is of much smaller size, and the pair are considered emblematic of a vase from which the beads spring.

The counters.

Attached to the rosary is a pair of strings of ten small pendant metallic rings as counters—*vide* "b" in the figures. One of these strings is terminated by a miniature *dorje* (the thunderbolt of Indra) and the other by a small bell—in tantric Buddhist figures the dorje is usually associated with a bell. The counters on the *dorje*-string register units of bead-cycles, while those on the bell-string mark tens of cycles. The counters and the ornaments of the strings are usually of silver, and inlaid with turquoise.

These two strings of counters are called ḍang-dsin[4] or "count-keepers," but vulgarly they are known as chub-shé[5] or "the ten

1 *The Burman: His Life and Notions*, I. page 201.

2 *r*dog-*h*dsin.

3 *r*tsa-wahi *b*la-ma.

4 grang-*h*dsin.

5 *l*chu-bshad.

markers." They may be attached at any part of the rosary string, but are usually affixed at the 8th and 21st bead on either side of the central bead.

Use of counters.

They are used in the following manner:—When about to tell the beads, the counters on each string are slid up the string. On completing a cycle of the beads the lowest counter on the dorje-string is slid down into contact with the dorje. And on each further cycle of beads being told a further counter is slipped down. When the ten have been exhausted, they are then slid up again and one counter is slipped down from the bell-string. The counters thus serve to register the utterance of $108 \times 10 \times 10 = 10{,}800$ prayers or mystic formulas. The number of formulas daily repeated in this way is enormous. The average daily number of repetitions may in the earlier stages of a lāma's career amount to 5,000 daily, but it depends somewhat on the zeal and leisure of the individual. A layman may repeat daily about five to twenty bead-cycles, but usually less. Old women are especially pious in this way, many telling over twenty bead-cycles daily. A middle-aged lāma friend of mine has repeated the spell of his tutelary deity alone over 2,000,000 times. It is not uncommon to find rosaries so worn away by the friction of so much handling that originally globular beads have become cylindrical.

Affixed to the rosary are small odds and ends, such as a metal tooth-pick, tweezer, small keys, &c.

Material of beads.

The materials of which the lāmaic rosaries are composed may to a certain extent vary in costliness according to the wealth of the wearer. The Khén-pos or abbots of large and wealthy monasteries have rosaries of pearl and other precious stones, and even of gold. Turner relates[1] that the Grand Tāshi Lāma possessed rosaries of pearls, emeralds, rubies, sapphires, coral, amber, crystal, and lapislazuli.

But the material of the rosary can only vary within rather narrow limits, its nature being determined by the particular sect to which the lāma belongs and the particular deity to whom worship is to be paid.

Yellow rosary.

The yellow rosary or *Se-theng*,[2] *vide* fig. 1, is the special rosary of the ge-luk-pa or "reformed school," also called "the yellow-hat sect" (shā-ser). The beads are formed from the ochrey-yellow wood of the *chang-chhub*,[3] literally "the Bodhi tree" or tree of supreme wisdom, which is said to grow in Central China. The wood is so deeply yellow that it is doubtful whether it be really that of the *pipal* (*Ficus religiosa*) which was the Bodhi tree under which Gautama attained his Buddhahood. These

[1] *Embassy to Tibet*, page 261, 1800. | [2] Ser-phreng. | [3] byang-chhub.

beads are manufactured wholesale by machinery at the temple called by Tibetans Rī-wo-tse-nga and by the Chinese *U-tha-Shan* or "The Five Peaks," about 200 miles south-west of Pekin. Huc gives a sketch[1] of this romantic place, but makes no mention of its rosaries. This rosary is of two kinds, viz., the usual form of spherical beads about the size of a pea, and a less common form of lozenge-shaped perforated discs about the size of a sixpence. This rosary is usable for all kinds of worship, including that of the furies.

The *Bo-dhi-tse*[2] rosary is the one chiefly in use among the nyingmapa, or "old (*i.e.*, unreformed) school" of lāmas. It is remarkable that its name also seeks to associate it with the Bodhi tree, but its beads are certainly not derived from the *Ficus* family. Its beads are the rough brown seeds of a tree which grows in the outer Himalayas. This rosary can be used for all kinds of worship, and may also be used by the ge-luk-pa in the worship of the fiercer deities.

White rosary.

The white rosary *ṭung-ṭheng*,[3] *vide* fig. 3, consists of cylindrical perforated discs of the conch shell (Tib. *ṭung*), and is especially used in the worship of Ché-ré-si—the usual form of whose image holds a white rosary in the upper right hand. This is the special rosary of nuns.

Crystal.

The rosary of plain crystal or uncoloured glass beads is also peculiar to Ché-ré-si.

Sandal.

The red sandal-wood rosary—*Tsén-den mar theng*,[4] *vide* fig. 2—consists of perforated discs of red sandal-wood (*Adenanthera pavonina*) or other wood of a similar appearance. It is used only in the worship of the fierce deity Tam-din (Skt. *Hayagriva*), a special protector of Lāmaism.

Coral.

The coral rosary *Chī-ru-theng*[5] is also used for Tam-din and by the nyingmapa sects for their wizard-saint Padma Sambhava's worship. Coral being so expensive, red beads of glass or composition are in general use instead. With this rosary it is usual to have the counters of turquoise or blue beads.

Human skull.

The rosary formed of discs of the human skull—the *thö-theng*,[6] *vide* fig. 6—is especially used for the worship of Dorje Jik-che (Skt. *Yāmā*), one of the forms of the King of the Dead. It frequently has its discs symmetrically divided by *raksha* beads into four series. There is no rosary formed of finger bones as has been sometimes stated.

Elephant-stone.

The "elephant-stone" rosary—*Lang-chhen-ḍö-pa*[7]—is prepared from a porous bony-like concretion which is sometimes found in the stomach of the elephant. It also

[1] *Travels in Tartary, Tibet and China*. By M. Huc and Gabet. Hazlitt's trans. I, page 79.
[2] po-dhi-tse.
[3] dung-phreng.
[4] tsanden.
[5] pyi-ru.
[6] thod-phreng.
[7] *g*lnag-chhen grod-pa.

being suggestive of bone, is used in worship of Yāmā. The real material, however, being extremely scarce and expensive, a substitute is usually had in beads made from the fibrous root of the bow-bambu (Zhu-shing) which has on section a structure very like the stomach-stone, and its name also means "stomach or digestion" as well as "bow."

"Rak-sha."

The *rak-sha* rosary,[1] *vide* fig. 4, formed of the large brown warty seeds of the *Elæocarpus Janitrus*, is specially used by the nyingmapa lāmas in the worship of the fierce deities and demons. The seeds of this tree are normally five-lobed, and it is interesting, from a botanical point of view, to find how relatively frequent is the occurrence of six lobes. Such abnormal seeds are highly prized by the Tibetans as being the offspring of the miraculous seeds of Padma Sambhava's rosary—the legend stating that the saint's rosary string broke while at his Halāshi hermitage, near the Kusi river in Nepal, and several of the detached beads remained unpicked up; and from these have resulted the six-lobed seeds. The demand for such uncommon seeds being great, it is astonishing how many of them are forthcoming to diligent search. This rosary is also commonly used by the indigenous Bon-po priests, and it is identical with the rosary of the Shivaic Hindus—the rudráksha (रुद्राक्ष = Rudra's [*i.e.*, fierce Shiva's] eyes), from which the Tibetan name of *rak·sha* is supposed to be derived.

Nan-ga pāni.

The *nang-ga pā-nī* rosary is only used for the worship of Nam-sé, the God of Wealth (Skt. *Kuvera*); and by the ngák-pa or wizards in their mystical incantations. It consists of glossy jet-black nuts about the size of a hazel, but of the shape of small horse-chestnuts. These are the seeds of the *lung-thang* tree, which grows in the sub-tropical forests of the south-eastern Himalayas. They are emblematic of the eyes of the Garuda bird, the chief assistant of Vajra-pāni (Jupiter) and the great enemy of snakes—hence is supposed to be derived the Sanskritic name of the beads, from *nága*, a serpent. Its use in the worship of the God of Wealth is noteworthy in the association of snakes—the mythological guardians of treasure—with the idea of wealth.

Snake-spines.

The rosary of *snake-spines* (vertebræ), *vide* fig. 7, is only used by the (ngāk·pa) sorcerers for purposes of sorcery and divination. The string contains about fifty vertebræ.

Rosaries and complexion.

The complexion of the god or goddess to be worshipped also determines sometimes the colour of the rosary-beads. Thus a turquoise rosary is occasionally used in the worship of the popular goddess Döl-ma, who

[1] rag·sha.

is of a bluish-green complexion. A red rosary with red Tam-din, a yellow with yellow Jam-yang; and Nam-sé, who is of a golden yellow colour, is worshipped with an amber rosary.

Lay rosaries.

The rosaries of the laity are composed of any sort of bead, according to the taste and wealth of the owner. They are mostly of glass beads of various colours, and the same rosary contains beads of a variety of sizes and colours interspersed with coral, amber, turquoise, &c.—*vide* fig. 5. The number of beads is the same as with the lāmas, but each of the counter strings are usually terminated by a *dorje*: both strings record only units of cycles, which suffice for the smaller amount of bead-telling done by the laity.

Mode of Telling the Beads.

Telling the beads.

When not in use the rosary is wound round the right wrist like a bracelet, or worn around the neck with the knotted end uppermost.

How called.

The act of telling the beads is called *tang-che*, which literally means "to purr" like a cat, and the muttering of the prayers is rather suggestive of this sound.

Mode of.

In telling the beads the right hand is passed through the rosary, which is allowed to hang freely down with the knotted end upwards. The hand with the thumb upwards is then usually carried to the breast and held there stationary during the recital. On pronouncing the initial word "Om," the first bead resting on the knuckle is grasped by raising the thumb and quickly depressing its tip to seize the bead against the outer part of the second joint of the index finger. During the rest of the sentence the bead, still grasped between the thumb and index finger, is gently revolved to the right, and on conclusion of the sentence is dropped down the palm-side of the string. Then with another "Om" the next bead is seized and treated in like manner, and so on throughout the cycle.

On concluding each cycle of the beads, it is usual to finger each of the three "keeper-beads," saying respectively "Om! Ah! Hung!" the mystic symbols of the lāmaic trinity.

The Mystic Formulas for the Beads.

The mystic formulas.

The mystic formulas for the beads follow the prayer properly so called, and are believed to contain the essence of the formal prayer, and to act as powerful spells. They are of a Sanskritic nature, usually containing the name of the deity addressed, but are more or less wholly unintelligible to the worshipper.

The formula used at any particular time varies according to the particular deity being worshipped. But the one most frequently used by the individual lāma is that of his own *yī-dam* or tutelary deity, which varies according to the sect to which the lāma belongs.

The formulas most frequently used are shown in the following table:—

Name of Deity.	The Spell.	Special kind of rosary used.
1. Dor-je jik-che.[1] Skt. *Yāma (antaka)*.	Om! Ya-mān-ta-taka hung phäṭ!	Human skull or "stomach-stone."
2. Chā-na dorje.[2] Skt. *Vajrapani*.	{ Om! Bäjrapāṇi hung phäṭ! Om! Bäjra dsan-da maha ro-khana hung!	Raksha. Do.
3. Tam-ḍin.[3] Skt. *Hayagriva*.	Om! päḍ-ma ta krid hung phäṭ!	Red sandal or coral.
4. Ché-ré-si or Thuk-je-chhenbo.[4] Skt. *Avalokita*.	Om! māni päḍ-me hung!	Conch shell or crystal.
5. Döl-ma jang-khu.[5] Skt. *Tāra*.	Om! Tā-re tut-tā-re ture swā-hā!	Bodhitse or turquoise.
6. Döl-kar.[6] Skt. *Sitatāra*.	Om! Tā-re tut-tā-re mama ā-yur puṇye-dsanyana pusphpi-ṭa ku-ru swā-hā!	Bodhitse.
7. Dor-je phak-mo.[7] Skt. *Vajra varahi*.	Om! sar-ba Bud-ha ḍakkin-ni hung phäṭ!	Ditto.
8. Ozer-chén-ma.[8] Skt. *Marici*.	Om! Ma-ri-tsye mam swā-hā!	Ditto.
9. Gön-po nag-po.[9] Skt. *Kālānātha*.	Om! Srî Ma-hā-kā-la hung phäṭ swā-hā!	Raksha.
10. Nam-sé.[10] Skt. *Kuvera*.	Om! Baī-śrā-ma-na ye swā-hā!	Nangapāni.
11. Dsam bha-la.[11] Skt. *Jambhala*.	Om! Dsam-bha-la dsalen-dra ye swā-hā!	Ditto.
12. Seng-ge-ḍa.[12] Skt. *Singhānāda*.	Om! ā-hrīh Sing-ha-nāda hung phäṭ!	Conch shell or crystal.
13. Jam-yang.[13] Skt. *Manjughosa*.	Om! a-ra-pa-tsa-na-ḍhi!	Yellow rosary.
14. Dem-chhok.[14] Skt. *Samvara*.	Om! hrih ha-ha hung hung phäṭ	Bodhitse.
15. Päḍ-ma jung-né.[15] Skt. *Padma sambhava*.	Om! bäjra gu-ru päḍma sid-dhī hung!	Coral or bodhitse.

[1] *r*do-rje-*h*jigs-byeḍ.
[2] phyag-na *r*do-rje.
[3] *r*ta-mgrin.
[4] grugs-*r*je chhen-po.
[5] *s*grol-ma *l*jang-khu.
[6] *s*grol-*d*kar.
[7] do-rje phag-mo.
[8] *h*od-zer-chan-ma.
[9] *m*gon-po nag-po.
[10] *r*nam-sras.
[11] dsam-bha-la.
[12] seng-ge-*s*gra.
[13] *h*jam-*d*byangs.
[14] *b*de-mchhog.
[15] pad-ma *h*byung-*g*naṣ.

The concluding word *phăț* which follows the mystic *hung* in many of these spells is cognate with the current Hindustani word *phat*, and means "may the enemy be *destroyed utterly*."

Origin of the formula "Om mâni."

The laity through want of knowledge seldom use with their rosaries other than the well-known lamaic formula "*Om! mā-ṇī pad-me Hung*," *i.e.*, "Hail! to the Jewel in the lotus! *Hung*." This refers to the Bōdhisatwa Chérési (Skt. *Padmapāni*), the patron-god of Tibet, who, like Buddha, is usually represented as seated or standing within a lotus flower, and who is believed to have been born from such a flower. It has, however, many mystic meanings. And no wonder this formula is so popular and constantly being repeated by both laity and lāmas, for its mere enunciation is credited with stopping the cycle of re-birth, and reaching directly to Nirvana. Thus, it is stated in the Māni-kah-bum with extravagant rhapsody that this formula "is the essence of all happiness, prosperity, and knowledge, and the great means of deliverance," and that the *om* closes re-birth amongst the gods, *ma* among the Titans, *ni* as a man, *pad* as a beast, *me* as a "yidag," and *hung* as an inhabitant of hell. And in keeping with this view each of these six syllables is given the distinctive colour of these six states of re-birth, viz. *om*, the godly *white*; *ma*, the titanic *blue*; *ni*, the human *yellow*; *pad*, the animal *green*; *me*, the "yidag" *red*; *hung*, the hellish *black*. This formula is of comparatively modern origin; its first appearance seems to be in the legendary history (*b*kah bum) of King Srong-tsan-gam-bo, which was one of the so-called "hidden" treatises, and probably written about the 14th or 16th century A.D.[1] With this formula, which is peculiar to Tibet, may be compared the Chinese and Japanese spells "*Nāmo Butsu*" (= Skt. *Nāmo Buddhaya*, *i.e.*, salutation to Buddha!) and *Nāmo O-mi-to-Fu* (= Skt. *Nāmo Amitābha*, *i.e.*, salutation to the Boundless Light!—a fanciful form of Buddha). The Burmese, so far as I have seen, seem to use their rosary merely for repeating the names of the Buddhist Trinity, viz., "Phrā" or Buddha, "Tara" or Dharma, and Sangha. And the number of beads in their rosary is a multiple of 3 × 3 as with the lāmas. On completing the cycle the central bead is fingered with the pessimistic formula "*Anitsa, Dukha, Anātha.*"—all is transitory, painful, and unreal.

[1] Since the above was in type, I find that ROCKHILL in *The Land of the Lamas*, London, 1891, page 326, notes that Wilhelm de Rubruk, writing in the second half of the 13th century, A.D. (Soc. de Geog. de Paris, IV, page 283) states regarding the Buddhist monks of Karakorum: "Habent etiam quocumque vadunt semper in manibus quandaun testem centum vel ducentorum nucleorum sicut nos portamus paternoster et dicunt semper hec verba *on man baccam* hoc est *Deus, tu nosti*, secundum quod quidam eorum interpretatus est michi, et totiens exspectat, remunerationem a Deo quotiens hoc dicendo memoratur." Mr. Rockhill also independently arrives at a similar conclusion to that noted by me above, as to the relatively modern composition of the Mani *b*kāh *h*bum.

List of the Masks.

In the vernacular a mask is called *bak.*[1] The masks for the religious dances in Sikhim are carved out of the tough light wood of the giant climber called *zar*; while in Tibet, where wood is scarce, they are composed of mashed paper and cloth. In all cases they are fantastically painted and varnished, and usually provided with a yak-tail wig.

The masks.

The masks found in Sikhim temples are the following:—

I.—King of the Ogre deities *Ku.*[2]	1. *Yeshe gon-po*[3] or Mahākāla. Colour red. 2. *Guru ḍak-mar*, a fierce form of Guru Rimbochhe. Colour red.
II.—The angry Ogre deities *To-wo.*[4]	3. *Lhāmo Mak-zor ma*, or Mahārāni, the *Kāli* form of Devi. Colour blue. 4. *Lang*,[5] the Bull. Colour black. 5. *Tāg*,[6] the Tiger. Colour brown. 6. *Sengge*, the Lion. Colour white. 7. *Khyung*, the Garuda-bird. Colour green. 8. *Teu*,[7] the Monkey. Colour ruddy brown. 9. *Sha-wa*, the Stag. Colour fawn. 10. *Yāk*, the Yak. Colour black.

The above are all of hideous appearance and huge size, having a vertical diameter of at least twice the length of an ordinary human face, and a breadth in proportion. Each has projecting tusks and three eyes, the central eye being the eye of fore-knowledge. Those of an anthropoid form have a chaplet of five skulls, with pendant bead ornaments of human bones.

III.—The Ghouls ...	11. *Tur* or Grave-yard ghosts. A monster human skull of yellowish colour. A pair of these are needed.
IV.—The Earth demons—servants of above.	12. *Sa-chak pa.* Large hideous masks with only two eyes.
V.—The Indian Teacher—buffoons.	13. *A-tsa-ra* (Skt. *acharya* = teacher). These are of ordinary human size, white in colour, with moustaches and hair done up into a coil. Their wives are red or yellow complexioned.

---

[1] *ḥ*bag.
[2] *s*ku.
[3] Ye-she *m*gon-po.
[4] *g*lang.
[5] *s*tag.
[6] *s*pre-u.
[7] khro-bo, from Skt. *khroda.*

The dresses accompanying the first two classes of masks are ample robes of rich brocade and satin, with gilt embroidery. The dress of the skeletons is tight fitting white calico with red bands to imitate the ribs and limb bones.

Dress of masquers.

The weapons carried by the maskers are made of wood carved with dorje patterns. The staves of the skeletons are topped by a death's-head.

The object and meaning of the masked play are described under the heading of Lāmaic Festivals.

The Lāmaic Library.

The larger monasteries in Sikhim all try to possess a copy of the two great lāmaic encyclopædias, (*a*) the *Kah-gyur* or vulgarly *Kān-gyur*,[1] *i.e.*, "The translated Commandments," and (*b*) the *Téngyur*[2] or "Translated doctrinal Commentaries" by reputed saints. All of the treatises contained in the Kah-gyur and most of those in the Téngyur were translated from the Sanskrit of the later Buddhist Church in India and Kashmir, and a few from the Chinese, mostly in the 9th and 12th centuries; but the Téngyur contains also much later works. The translations were done by the Indian Pandits and Tibetan translators (*lótsāvas*) and Chinese priests. They were collected in their present form only about the beginning of the last (18th) century of our era.

Lāmaic encyclopædias.

Kān-gyur.

The common edition of the Kah-gyur is printed from wooden blocks at Narthang, about six miles from Tashelhunpo,[3] and fills 100 bulky volumes of about 1,000 pages each. A later edition, printed at Der-ge in Eastern Tibet (Kham), contains the same matter distributed in volumes so as to reach the mystic number of 108. The Téngyur contains 225 or more volumes, and has treatises on the Indian philosophic schools, grammar, logic, astrology, medicine, &c. The cost at the printing establishment is about ten rupees *per* volume.

Téngyur.

The expense of such a library being so great, Pemiongchi and Labrang are the only monasteries in Sikhim which possess a complete set of both encyclopædias. But several monasteries possess a full set of the Kah-gyur scriptures.

Divisions of Kah-gyur.

The *Kah-gyur* as regards its contents is divided into three great sections, viz.—

I.—The *Dulva* (Skt. *Vinaya*) or Discipline, in 13 volumes.

[1] *b*kah-*h*gyur. | [2] *b*stan-*h*gyur.

[3] The capital of Western Tibet (Tsāng), and head-quarters of the Panchhen (= great teacher) Grand Lāma, the incarnation of the mythical Buddha Amitabha.

II.—The *Dô* (Skt. *Sutra*) or Sermons of the Buddhas, in 66 volumes.

III.—The *Sher-chin* with its divisions (Skt. *Abi-dharmma*) or Transcendental Wisdom, in 21 volumes.

These divisions broadly correspond to the classification of the Southern Buddhist Canon into the Tripitakā or 'three baskets or collections;' but the lāmaic versions are all of a highly inflated and tantrik type, and the *Gyut* or tantrik charms and incantations to the number of 22 volumes, which has no counterpart in the Southern scriptures, has been introduced into the *Dô* class of the Kah-gyur.

As might be supposed from the leading part which mysticism plays in the lāmaic creed, the sections of the Kah-gyur which are most highly prized are the *Dô* and the *Sher-chin* or Transcendental Wisdom of the tantrik kind.

"Bum."

"Nyi-ṭhi."

"Gyé-tong-ba."

"Dorje-chöpa."

The monasteries which cannot afford to buy the full Kah-gyur —and these in Sikhim form the majority—possess the following parts of the Sher-chin, viz., the 12 volumes called *Bum*, literally "100,000" precepts of Transcendental Wisdom, forming the main body of the Sher-chin. Also the abridged edition of the same in three volumes called *Nyi-ṭhi*, literally "the 20,000" precepts, adapted forthose individuals who are unable to peruse the full text. And for the common use of the junior clergy a still smaller abstract in one volume exists under the name of *Gyé-tong-ba*—literally, "the 8,000" precepts of Transcendental Wisdom. This is the volume which is carried on the lotus of Jam-pal, the God of Wisdom. The *Dorje-chöpa* or the "Diamond cutter" is a sloka which is commonly printed in separate form. And for the youngest boy-novices is prepared a tract of about six leaves containing the most popular portions of the Sherchin.

Dô-mang.

From the Dô division of the Kah-gyur are culled out those mystic formulas, mostly in unintelligible Sanskrit, which are deemed most potent as charms, and these form the volume named *mDo*-mang *gzung*[1] *bs*dus or curtly *Dô-mang* or "assorted aphorisms"—literally "many *sutras*." These formulas are not used in the worship of the Buddhas and superior gods, but only as priestly incantations in the treatment of disease and ill-fortune. Being thus the forms of worship of which the laity have most experience, small pocket editions of one or other *Sutra* are to be found in the possession of all literate laymen, as the mere act of reading these charms suffices to ward off the demon-bred disease and misfortune.

[1] *gzungs* = Skt. *dharani*, which is a mystic spell like the Hindu *mantra*.

The books of ordinary worship and ritual, and the school-text books for the boy-probationers and novices, are also an essential part of the monastic library. And they must be daily repeated till their contents are fully learned by heart.

Each monastery also possesses one or more of the legendary accounts of the great wizard-saint of the Nyingmapa lāmas, viz., Lô-pön Rimbochhe, or Pédmajungné, who is believed to have visited Sikhim. These are entitled *Pédma kah-thang* (The displayed orders of the Lotus-born One) or *Tang-yik Sertheng* (The golden Rosary of plain Epistles); also more or less fragmentary bits of the works of the pioneer lāma of Sikhim—Lha-tsün Chhembo, especially his *Né-yik* or "Story of the Sacred Sites of Sikhim," and his manual of worship of the great mountain god Kangchhendsönga (Ang. *Kanchinjingna*). Monasteries of the Karmapa and Dukpa sects contain the "Kargyupa Golden Rosary" and the *namthars* or biographies of the special lāma-saints of the Karmapa or of the Bhutan lāma-saints. And each monastery possesses a manuscript account of its own history (*deb-ther*), although this is kept out of sight.

Pédma kah-thang, &c.

"Namthars."

A few Lepcha sacred books are to be found in the Lepcha monasteries and in the possession of a few Lepcha laymen. They are mostly translations from the Tibetan. The titles of the chief ones are (1) *Tāshi Sung*, a fabulous history of Guru Rimbochhe; (2) *Guru Chhö Wang*, a tertön work of Tibet; (3) *Sākun de-lok*, the narrative of a visit to Hades by a resuscitated man named Sākun; (4) *Ek-doshi manlom*—forms of worship.

Lepcha scriptures.

Individual lāmas possess special books according to their private means and inclinations, such as the *Manikāhbum*, a legendary history of Ché-ré-si, the patron god of Tibet, and of the origin of the mystic sentence "Om Mani," &c.; the songs of the great mendicant sage *Milarépa*, books on the worship of Dölma and other favourite and tutelary deities. The specialist in medicine has one or more fantastic medical works, and the *Tsi-pa*[1] or astrologer has the *Baidyur karpo* and other books on astrological calculations.

Miscellaneous books.

The books are deposited in an open pigeon-holed rack-work. Each book consists of several hundred leaves, and each leaf is of tough unglazed country paper, about two feet long by half a foot broad. The leaves forming the volume are wrapped in a napkin; and the package then placed between two heavy wooden blocks, as covers, which bear on their front border the name of the book in letters graved in relief and gilt. The whole parcel is firmly bound by

[1] This is the "*Chebu* Lama" of Hooker's *Himalayan Journals*.

a broad tape and buckle tied across its middle. These ponderous tomes are very unwieldy and not easy of reference. When being read the book is held across the knees, and the upper board and the leaves as read are lifted towards the reader and repiled in order in his lap. Before opening its fastenings, and also on retying the parcel, the monk places the book reverently on his head, saying, "may I obtain the blessing of Thy Holy Word."

IV.—THE MONKHOOD.

Under this heading are detailed the Curriculum for the Monkhood, the Lāmaic Grades and Discipline, and the Daily Routine of a lāma's life in Sikhim.

I.—THE CURRICULUM.

Popularity of the Church.

In nearly every Bhotiya[1] family in Sikhim, one son is devoted to the Church. This practice is fostered by the deep religious habit of the people and the attractions offered by the high social position and privileges enjoyed by the lāmas, rendering them superior to the highest lay official and free from ordinary tribunals. A certain amount of reflected honour also attaches to the family which has afforded the lāma.

In the family.

The rule is for the second son to become a lāma, while the eldest son marries in order to continue the family name and property, and be the bread-winner.

Course of training.

The course of training which I now detail is that which obtains at Pemiongchi, as that monastery is regarded as a standard one which the other monasteries try to live up to.

Age.

Preliminary Examination—Physical.—The boy-candidate for admission is usually brought to the monastery between the age of eight and ten years, and very seldom over twelve years.

Parentage.

The parentage of the boy is enquired into (and at Pemiongchi only those candidates who are of relatively pure Tibetan descent are ordinarily admitted to that monastery).

Physical examination.

The boy is then physically examined to ascertain that he is free from deformity or defect in his limbs and faculties. If he stammers or is a cripple in any way or bent in body, he is rejected. When he

[1] "Bhotiya" means an inhabitant of "Bhot" or Tibet, and is thus synonymous with "Tibetan." It includes those residents of Sikhim who are of Tibetan ancestry, and who, though largely mixed with Lepcha blood, retain Tibetan speech and manners. These only are professing Lāmaists and eligible to become orthodox lāmas. Lepchas are not eligible.

has passed this physical examination he is made over by his father or guardian to any senior relative he may have amongst the monks. Should he have no relative in the monastery, then by consulting his horoscope one of the monks is fixed upon as being his most suitable tutor; and this tutor receives from the boy's father a present of tea, eatables, and beer. The tutor then takes the boy inside the great hall where the monks are assembled, and publicly stating the parentage of the boy and the other details, and offering presents of beer, he asks the permission of the *db*U-chhos, or elder monks, to take the boy as a pupil. When approved, the boy becomes a probationer.

Tutor.

Probation.—As a probationer he is little more than a private schoolboy under the care of his tutor. His hair is cropped without any ceremony, and he wears his ordinary lay dress. He is taught by his tutor the alphabet (the "Ka, Kha, Ga," as it is called), and afterwards to read and recite by heart the following small booklets of about six or seven leaves each[1] :—

His position.

Tuition and list of text-books.

Leū *b*dun ma or "The Seven Chapters"—A prayer-book of Guru Rimpochhe.
Bar-chhad lam *g*sel or "Charms to clear the way from Danger and Injury"—a prayer to "The Guru" in twelve stanzas.
Sher-phyin—An Abstract of Transcendental Wisdom in six leaves.
*s*Ku-rim—a sacrificial service for averting a calamity.
Mon-lam—Prayers for general welfare.
*s*Dig shags or "The Confession of Sins."[2] The mere act of reading this holy booklet even as a school exercise cleanses from sin. Most of the monasteries possess their own blocks for printing this pamphlet. Both the text and its translation have been given by Schlagintweit.[3]
*r*Dor *g*chod,—a *Sutra* from the Book of Transcendental Wisdom.

Phyogs-*b*chui-phyogs-dra*l* or "Description of the Ten Directions"	6 pages.
Namo Guru—"Salutation to The Guru"	5 ,,
*m*Chhod-*h*bul—To give offerings	6 ,,
*g*Torma—Sacred cake	8 ,,
*b*Sangs *b*sur—Incense and butter-incense	5 ,,
*l*To-mchhod—Rice offering	4 ,,
Rig-*h*dsin *s*ngön-*h*gro—The First essay of the Sage ...	4 ,,
*d*rag-*d*mar *s*ngon-*h*gro—The Primer of the Red Fierce Deity	4 ,,
*b*Kah *b*rgye*d*—"The Eight Commands" or precepts ...	4 ,,
*b*De *g*shegs kun *h*dus—The Collection of the Tathagathas ...	4 ,,
Yeshe*s* *s*ku *m*chho*g*—The best Fore-knowledge	5 ,,
*r*Tsa-*g*dung *b*shag-*g*sal—The root-pillar of Clear Confession...	4 ,,

[1] Such small manuals are about eight or ten inches long by two to three inches broad and usually have the leaves stitched together.
[2] The word for *sin* is "scorpion," thus conveying the idea of a vile, venomous, clawing, acrid thing.
[3] *Op. cit.*, pages 122 to 142.

The young probationer is also instructed in certain golden maxims of a moral kind, of which the following are examples:—

Some precious maxims.

" *The four Precipices in Speech.*—If speech be too long, it is tedious; "if too short, its meaning is not appreciated; if "rough, it ruffles the temper of the hearers; if soft, "it is unsatisfying.

On speech.

" *The Requirements of Speech.*—Speech must possess vigour or it "will not interest; it must be bright or it will not "enlighten; it must be suitably ended, otherwise "its effect will be lost.

" *The Qualities of Speech.*—Speech must be bold as a lion, gentle "and soft as a hare, impressive as a serpent, pointed as an arrow, "and evenly balanced as a *dorje* held by its middle (literally '*waist*').

" *The four Relations of Speech.*—The necessary question should first "be stated. The later arguments should be connected with the "former. Essentials should be repeated. The meanings should be "illustrated by examples.

"The great religious king Srong-*b*tsan-*s*gam-po has said,[1] 'speech "should float forth freely like a bird into the sky, and be clothed in "charming dress like a goddess. At the outset the object of the "speech should be made clear like an unclouded sky. The speech "should proceed like the excavation of treasure. The arguments "should be agile like a deer chased by fresh hounds, without hesita-"tion or pause.'

Human gatherings.

" *Collections of human beings* occur for three purposes, namely, (I) "happiness, (II) sorrow, and (III) worldly gossip. "The gatherings for happiness are three, namely, "(1) for doing virtuous acts, (2) for worship in the temples, and "(3) for erecting houses and for feasts. The gatherings for virtuous "acts are four, viz., the gathering of the monks, the gathering of "the laity for worship, writing and copying holy books, and giving "away wealth in charity. There are six kinds of gatherings for "worship, namely, the gathering of the rich, the gathering in a "separate place of the common men, the gathering for thanksgiving "of those who have escaped from their enemy's grasp, traders "who have escaped returned safely and successfully, sick men "from the devouring jaws of death, and youths on gaining a "victory.

Low conduct.

" *The eight acts of Low-born persons.*—Using coarse language, im-"politeness, talking with pride, want of foresight, "harsh manners, staring, immoral conduct, and "stealing.

[1] In the Mani *b*kah-*h*bum, *vide* page 293.

"*The ten Faults.*—Unbelief in books, disrespect of teachers, "making one's self unpleasant, covetousness, speak- "ing too much, ridiculing another's misfortune, using "abusive language, being angry with old men or with women, "borrowing what cannot be repaid, and stealing.

The ten Faults.

"*The three Improper Acts.*—To speak of a "subject of which one is ignorant, to take an oath, "to give poison to any one."

The three Improper Acts.

After two or three years spent in this training, during which corporal chastisement is freely inflicted, if the boy is then found to be hopelessly stupid, he is dismissed; while should he prove to be fairly intelligent, he is admitted to the regular noviciate. The object of this probationary stage is to weed out unpromising individuals.

Test of results.

THE NOVICIATE.

The novice or "Grā-pa," pronounced "Ṭá-pa," [literally "student" or "learner," and seldom called *d*gen-yen or *d*ge-thsul (*Skt.* Śrāmaṇa)] is, now for the first time brought under monastic rules. He is ceremoniously shaved, takes the vows, assumes the dress of a monk, and receives a religious name.

Its general character.

The candidate for the noviciate is searchingly interrogated by the *db*U-chhos (or elder lāmas) regarding his descent, his entrance donation and presents being proportionate to the impurity of his descent. If he has a good strain of Tibetan blood, he is let off cheaply and *vice versâ;* but it is the paternal descent which is most regarded: mixed blood on the mother's side being tolerated to a considerable extent.[1]

Appraising of descent.

When the boy's descent is satisfactorily appraised, the *db*U-chho*s* of the Great Assembly Hall are requested to place the boy under the "*s*gris" or General Rules. And on permission being accorded, the parent or guardian of the boy prepares a feast of food and beer for the monks. After a few months another present of food and beer, accompanied by a flesh gift of a pig or bullock, must be made, with the request for a *g*tor-*b*zing*s* in the temple. A suitable date for this is fixed by astrology.

Preliminary presents, &c.

[1] The alleged reason for this being the pre-eminence of the father, from whom comes the bone and structure of the child, while from the mother only came "the flesh." It is notable that the Tibetans habitually say "apo-ame," *i.e.*, father and mother, and not like the Indians "*ma-bap,*" *i.e.*, mother and father.

Formal acceptance of candidate.

Then a magic circle or *mandal*[1] is prepared. And on the following morning all the monks (*d*ge-dun) before early mass drink tea at the expense of the candidate. And after early mass, when all the monks have departed except the elders (*db*U-chho*s*), the parent or guardian of the boy with his relatives, who has been waiting outside, now requests an interview with the elders (*db*U-chho*s*), and accompanies his request with a present of a slaughtered pig and a load of beer, a load of parched gram (zib-*h*bra*s*), and about half a maund of rice. On these being accepted, the boy is brought in and is made to recite some of the books he has learned, especially "the Eight Precepts," "the Refuge formula," "the performance of religious kindness," and the celebration ritual of "*s*Ku-rim" and "Mon-lam." Then is done the ceremony of *b*Ge*s*-*s*prad and the proclamation *b*Kab-*bs*go.

Tonsuring, baptism, &c.

The boy is then tonsured (in Pemiongchi this is done with the identical razor used by the pioneer lama Lhatsun Chhembo). He then is given a religious name, and takes the usual vows of poverty, celibacy, &c., followed by the declaration that "From to-day I have entered on a religious life." The ceremony concludes with a present to the "*g*na*s* zhag," of two bricks of Chinese tea: when these are not procurable the sum of seven rupees is paid.

Introduction to Assembly as a bride.

At the midday mass, the boy is brought into the Great Assembly Hall dressed in the three pieces of monkish vestment (chhö*s*-gö*s*) and carrying a bundle of incense sticks; and he is chaperoned by a monk (gonpa) named the "bride-companion" (ba-grag*s*), as this ceremony is regarded as a marriage with the Church. He sits down on an appointed seat by the side of the bride-companion, who instructs him in the rules and etiquette (*s*gri*s*) of the monkish manner of sitting, walking, &c.

Confirmation of noviciate.

Then mass is begun, and on its conclusion beer is brought inside in a skull-cup, and distributed to the assembled monks under the name of *g*zo-chhang. (It is considered improper to bring the ordinary bamboo jugs of beer into the Assembly Hall.) Then a pig and a bullock are given by the boy's people, as well as a money present. If the boy's relatives are wealthy, this sum should amount to two rupees for each of the two *db*U-chho*s* and one rupee to each of the 108 monks. But if the boy's relatives are poor, the total amount may be limited to sixty rupees. Should, however, this money and "flesh" presents not be forthcoming, the boy's admission cannot be confirmed.

On the third day, that particular one of the boy's relatives who is the "dispenser of gifts" (*s*byin *b*dag*s*) must visit each of the two

[1] For description, *vide* Chapter V, page 320.

*db*U-chhos at their respective chambers, taking an offering of rice, beer, and flour. And each *db*U-chhos gives about ten rupees as a return present for the articles received. Then the boy's relatives return to their homes.

His life as a novice.

The boy is now subject to the monastery rules and discipline; and must practise and learn by heart the books of the magic circles (dKyil-*h*kor). And he shares in most of the privileges of the other monks, getting his share of meat and lay offerings of money and gifts of alms—these latter two are, however, appropriated by his lāma-tutor. And he resides in the monastery, getting occasionally leave of absence for a month or so to re-visit his home. He must implicitly obey his tutor, and the relatives of the boy must come frequently to pay their respects to the tutor, bringing presents of cooked food, &c.

First professional examination.

Examinations.—Within a year of his admission to the order he should attempt to pass the first professional examination, and in the following year or two the second examination for promotion. And until he passes these examinations he must perform the menial office of serving out tea and beer to the elder monks in the Great Assembly Hall.

How conducted.

The examinations are conducted in the presence of the assembled monks, who observe a solemn silence, and the test is for the candidate to stand up in the assembly and recite by heart all the prescribed books. The ordeal is a very trying one, so that the candidate is given a companion to prompt and encourage him. The first examination lasts for three days; and nine intervals are allowed daily during the examination, and these intervals are utilized by the candidates in revising the next exercise, in company with their teacher.

The text-books for First Examination.

The books for the First Examination comprise the worship necessary for three "magic circles," viz.—The *first* is the magic circle of *d*Kon-*m*chhog *s*pyi *h*dus Rig-*h*dsin *h*dsah *m*tshan *s*nying-poī chhos *h*khor.[1] This book contains about sixty pages, and its recitation takes nearly one whole day. It comprises the chapters:—

(1) Tshe-*s*grub or The obtaining of long life.
(2) Zhi-khro—The mild and angry deities.
(3) Guru-drag—The fierce form of Padma Sambhava.
(4) Seng-*g*dongma—The lion-faced demoness.
(5) Chhos *s*kyong-Mahakala Yeshes *m*gonpo.
(6) Thang-lha,[2] *m*Dsöd-*l*nga, Lha-chhen and *s*Man *b*stün—Local and mountain deities.
(7) *bs*Kang *bs*hags, tshogs and Tashi *s*mon-lam.

[1] Or "Banquet to the whole assembly of the Gods and Demons"—*vide* page 276.
[2] Mt. Thang-lha with its spirit "Kiting" is a northern guardian of Sikhim.

The *second* comprises the magic circle of the collection of the Tathagathas and "the powerful great pitiful one" (Avalokita)—*b*De-*g*shegs-kün *h*dus-gar-*db*ang, Thugs-rje chhen-po, of about 40 pages.

Then follow the magic circles of the fierce and demoniacal deities Guru-drag-*d*mar, Khrowo-rol waī *g*tor-zlog and Drag-poī-las Guruī-*g*sol-*h*debs len-*b*dunma, Kha *h*don chhos spyo*d*.

Penalties of failure to pass.

Those who disgracefully fail to pass this examination are taken outside and beaten by the Chhos-khrims-pa. And repeated failure up to a limit of three years necessitates the rejection of members from the Order. Should, however, the boy be rich and wish re-entry, he may be re-admitted on paying presents and money on a higher scale than formerly, without which no re-admission is possible. If the rejected candidate be poor and he wishes to continue a religious life, he can only do so as a lay-devotee doing drudgery about the monastery buildings. Or he may set up in some village as an unorthodox lāma-priest.

The majority fail to pass at the first attempt. And failure on the part of the candidate attaches a stigma to his teacher, while in the event of the boy chanting the exercises correctly and with pleasing voice in the orthodox oratorical manner, his teacher is highly complimented.

The Second Examination is conducted like the first one, and lasts for two days, but at this examination "the iron letter" (*i.e.*, inflexible rule) *l*chag-yig is solemnly read out before the examination.

The text-books for Second Examination.

The books to be recited by heart at the Second Examination are the following:—

(1) The worship of "The Lake-born *Vajra*" (*m*Tsho-skyes-*r*dorje), *i.e.*, Padma Sambhava and the *Guru*-Sage who has obtained understanding (Rig-*h*dsin *r*tog *s*grub-guru).

(2) The three roots of sagedom (Rig *h*dsin *r*tsa-*g*sum)—

(*a*) Rig *h*dsin lhamaī-las.

(*b*) Tshe-*s*grub khog *db*ugs.

(*c*) *g*Sang *s*grub dongyi *s*nying-po.

(3) The deeds of Dorje Phāgmo (*r*Dorje phagmoī-las), the great happiness of zag-med (zag-med *b*de-chhen), and the four classes of the Fierce Guardians—chhos srung drag-po *s*de *b*zhi. The names of these demons are—on the east, *k*Lu-*b*dud Munpa nagpo; on the south, Srinpo Lanka-*m*grim-*b*chu; on the west, Mamo Sha-za phra-gral nag-po; on the north, *g*Shenpa *s*Pu-gri-*d*marpo.

(4) The subjugation of the host of demons—The offering to the Dhyāni Budhas *b*dud *d*pung zil non, Kun-*b*zang, *m*chho*d*-*s*prin.

(5) The sacrificial ceremony *b*skang *b*shāgs, viz., Rig-dsin *b*skang-*b*shags, Phagmai *b*skang *b*shags.

(6) The prayer of the glorious "Tāshi"—the Lepcha name for Padma Sambhava—Tāshi-*s*mon-lam.

The above books reach to about fifty-five pages.

(7) The circle of the eight Commanders of the collected Buddhas. *b*Kah *b*gyad *b*de *g*shegs *h*duspai *d*kyil-*h*khor kyi las and Khrowo-rol waī *g*tor-zlog gyi *s*korī *b*kah *b*rgyad. This has about 40 pages. [The names of the eight Commanders, *b*Kah-*b*gyads, are—(1) Chhe-*m*chhog, (2) Yang-dag, (3) *g*Shin-*r*je, (4) *r*Ta-mgrin, (5) Phurpa, (6) Mamo, (7) *h*Gad *s*tong, (8) Rig-*h*dsin).]

When the young monk recites by heart all these books satisfactorily, and so passes this examination, he is not subject to any further ordeal of examination: this being the final one.

Ordinary practice.

It should be noted, however, that outside Pemiongchi practically no examination obtains. All that is done is merely to insist on the young monks endeavouring to commit to memory as many of these books as possible.

His position and privileges.

The Monkhood.—On passing these two examinations, the successful candidate becomes a junior monk, and is supposed to keep "The Ten Precepts,"[1] but he is still called a grā-pa or "learner." [The term *d*ge-*s*long or "the virtuous beggar," which may be considered as representing the *Bhikhu* of Indian Buddhism, is not in use in Sikhim; and in Tibet it is restricted to those lāmas who profess the strict observation of the 253 obligations.] He is presented with a scarf of honour by the monks, and is considered a member of the Order—even although he be under 20 years of age. And from that date he is relieved of the menial office of serving out tea and beer, and he takes a higher seat in the Assembly Hall. And he now directly receives his share of the money and other lay gifts which had hitherto been the perquisite of his tutor. And he has the privilege of drinking beer which he should not previously have tasted—although abstinence from intoxicating drinks is one of "the eight precepts." And he may even drink the beer off the same table as his teacher. But he may not yet discuss any great subject with his master, as this would be disrespectful. He is taught to pay his teacher the deepest respect and to place implicit reliance on all his sayings.

[1] The Ten Precepts (Skt. *Dasasila*) Mi-*d*gé-*b*chu—literally "The Ten Unvirtuous Deeds," according to the Lāmas, are (1) Not to kill any living being, (2) Not to steal, (3) Not to commit adultery, (4) Not to lie, (5) Not to drink wine (this is not observed), (6) Not to sit on a lofty seat or have a large bed, (7) Not to wear flowers or ribbons, (8) Not to be fond of songs or dances, (9) Not to wear ornaments of gold or silver, (10) Not to eat flesh food after noon.

He now is instructed in the preparation and adornment of *torma*, or sacred food for the gods and demons; and in the blowing of the copper trumpets, in the manipulation of the cymbals, and in dancing and rhetoric, and in any science which he fancies. And he is now at liberty to choose for himself a teacher. The "sciences" usually taken up are astrology, medicine, and painting, but the majority of the newly-fledged monks are content with the position of an ordinary monk.

His further academic instruction.

Until, however, he commits to memory the following books, he will never become a successful chaplain or family priest (*m*chhod-*g*nas), which is a paying business and the goal of most of the monks. For those lāmas who can recite by heart all the Litanies and other sacerdotal ritual, without consulting their books, are much more popular and sought after than those who read their ritual service. He therefore tries to learn by heart—"The real story of animal beings by Sagon, who had returned from the dead" (Sagon *h*gro *d*ngos zhi), and the Litany of Avalokita—The Powerful Great Pitier (gar-*db*ang Thug-*r*je chhenpo), and "The exhorting Mani," which are used on the occasion of a death. Also "The ripe (magic) circle which draws to the best and most pleasing dwelling" (*s*min-byed-*db*yang gi-*d*kyil-*h*kor *db*ang *m*chhog-*g*nas *h*dren).

His sacerdotal functions.

I have already noted that the majority of the lāmas exercise sacerdotal functions, and are priests rather than monks. Many of the lāmas are permitted to reside in their villages for the greater part of the year, ostensibly as village-priests for the convenience of the people. They must, however, return at definite intervals to their parent-monastery, which keeps a roll of all its members and punishes those individuals who absent themselves for unduly long periods.

The regulation which is most frequently violated is that of celibacy; but in most of the institutions other than Pemiongchi celibacy is not observed. Should it be proved that a Pemiongchi monk consorts with women, he will be expelled by a chapter, unless it be his first offence and he prays publicly for forgiveness, and then is awarded some penance and pays a fine of 180 rupees according to the rules of the *l*Chags-yig. He must also pay over again the entrance fees and presents as before.

Penalty for violation of celibacy.

II.—LĀMAIC GRADES AND DISCIPLINE.

The consecutive offices through which the young lāma must pass to reach the highest grades are the following:—

Lower offices.

I.—Conch-shell Blower—for about one year. These go in pairs.

II.—Pourer of holy water, or Chhab-*h*dren—for one year.

III.—Image care-taker or *s*Ku-*g*nyer—for three years.

The *Ku-nyer* is also charged with the duty of dusting and arranging the objects on the altar and making the offerings of water, lamps, sacred food, &c., and the removal of the same.

Higher offices.

On completing his service in this last office he passes out of the stage of *g*rā-pa (pronounced *tā-pa*) or learner, and becomes an *db*U-chhos (pronounced "u-chhö") or "Head of Religion." And by the laity he now is called *Yā-pa* or "Reverend Father." From this class of *db*U-chhos are selected the officials to fill the special offices of IV and V, and one from the Pemiongchi monastery acts for a term of a few years as family priest to the Sikhim Raja, doing especially the *s*Kang-*g*so worship.

U-chhö or *Yā-pa.*

IV.—The Commissariat Manager or *s*pyi-*g*nyer (pronounced *Chi-nyer*) tenable for three years. There are two of these, and they are in charge of the lay menials of the monastery. When the menials have any complaint it must be made through the Commissariat Manager, who privately informs one of the *db*U-chhos of the details, and afterwards it is laid before the assembly of *db*U-chhos under the presidency of the U-mdse and Dorje *s*Lob-*d*pon. The orders which are then passed are communicated by the two Commissariat Managers to the menials concerned.

The Commissariat officer—*Chi-nyer.*

V.—Provost Marshal or Chhos khrims-pa (pronounced *Chhö-ṭim-ba*), an appointment tenable for one year. This office requires qualities of pre-eminent learning, popularity, tact, and the ability to enforce discipline and respect. The Provost Marshal is appointed by the vote of the monks (*ṭāpa*). These select one of the yāpas or superior monks, and recommend him to the Sikhim Raja in a memorial, which they all sign. The Raja's minister then informs the nominee that he has been appointed Provost Marshal for the current year, and that into his charge have been placed all the books of the Library, including the *l*Chags-yig Rules, and certain advice is given him, accompanied by the presentation of an exceptionally long and honourable scarf; a refreshment of tea and beer is given.

The Provost Marshal—*Chhö-ṭim-ba.*

One of his duties is to read the *l*Chags-yig Rules to the assembled monks, and also lecture to them occasionally on religious and civil history and discipline.

He is the recognised head of the monks and their spokesman. When any person requests that the "Banquet to the whole assembly of the Gods and Demons" (Tshogs-*h*khor)—*vide* page 276—be performed, all the monks assemble and do the necessary worship and make the magic circles. It is the *Chhö-ṭim-ba* who declares the object of the sacrifice, viz., for one or other of the four conditions—birth, old age, sickness or death.

He is usually re-appointed for one or more terms, as there is difficulty in finding suitable men for this appointment.

After filling the above office he is eligible for the two highest appointments in the monastery, viz.—

VI.—Principal and *Chief Celebrant* or *db*U-*m*dsad (pronounced *Um-dsé*); and

VII.—Patriarch or *r*Do-rje *s*Lob-*d*pon (pronounced Dorje Lô-pön).

These two offices are held for life, and the holders enjoy equal rank and receive the same stipend and perquisites, and, as we have seen, sit opposite each other in the assembly room. But the Um-dsé is always the more learned of the two, and is necessarily something of a man of the world. He supervises the whole establishment and controls the discussions, and it is to him that the peasantry resort for advice and settlement of their disputes. The Dorje Lô-pön upholds the dignity of religion by taking no part in secular matters and doing the mechanical work of meditation and some of the higher ritual, one of his chief duties being to abstract the soul of the dead and despatch it on the right path to heaven or for a new rebirth.

The Um-dsé.

The *Dorje Lö-pön.*

The Incarnate Lāma of *bLa*-brang monastery is supposed to exercise the functions of a Bishop of Sikhim; but he has only the title of Protector of Religion—the titles of *Do-dam-pa* or "bishop," *Khénpo* (*m*khan-po) or "abbot" are not used in Sikhim.

Bishop.

III.—MONASTIC ROUTINE.

The daily routine of the Sikhim monk differs somewhat, according to whether (*a*) he be living apart from his monastery, say, as a village priest, or (*b*) as a resident in a monastery, or (*c*) as a solitary hermit. I will describe the practices in this order.

As a Village Priest.

The monk immediately on waking must arise from his couch, even though it be midnight, and commence to chant the mi-*r*tak-*r*gyu*d*-*bs*kul, taking care to pronounce all the words fully and distinctly. This contains the instructions of his special Lāma-preceptor (*r*tsa-wa-*b*lama), and in the recital the monk must call vividly to mind his spiritual guide. This is followed by a prayer for a number of requests by the monk himself.

Night devotion.

Then he assumes the meditative posture of "the seven attitudes," in order to subjugate the five senses. These attitudes are—(1) sitting with legs flexed in the well-known attitude of Buddha; (2) the hands resting one above the other in the lap; (3) head slightly bent forwards; (4) eyes fixed on the tip of the nose; (5) shoulders "floating like the wings of a vulture;" (6) spine erect and "straight like an arrow;" (7) tongue arched upwards to palate like the curving petals of the eight-leaved lotus. While in this posture he must think that he is alone in a wilderness.

"Meditative" postures.

The three original sins of the body are then got rid of according to the humoural physiology of the ancients in the three series of *db*uma, roma, and *r*kyang-ma. After taking a deep inspiration, the air of the *roma* veins is expelled three times, and thus "the white wind" is let out from the right nostril three times in short and forcible expiratory gusts. This expels all Anger. Then from the left nostril is thrice expelled in a similar way "the red air," which rids from Lust. The colourless central air is thrice expelled, which frees from Ignorance. On concluding these processes, the monk must mentally realize that all ignorance, lust, and anger—the three Original Sins—have disappeared like frost before a scorching sun.

Expulsion of the three Original Sins.

He then says the "a-lia-ki," keeping his tongue curved like a lotus petal. This is followed by his chanting the *b*lamaī *r*nal-*h*byor or "the Yoga of the Lāma," during which he must mentally conceive his Lāma-guide as sitting overhead upon a lotus flower.

Mummery.

Then, assuming the spiritual guise of his *Yidam* or tutelary deity, he chants the Four Preliminary Services—the *s*ngon-gro *b*zi-*h*byor. These are the Refuge formula or *s*kyab*s*-*h*gro—*vide* page 308—which cleanses the darkness of the Body, the Hundred Letters or Yige-*br*gyapa, which cleanses all obscurity in Speech; and the magic circle of rice—the *Mandala*, see page 324—which cleanses the Mind; and the prayer *g*sol-*h*deb*s*, classifying the lāmas up to the most perfect one, confers Perfection on the monk himself.

Ritual.

This is followed by the chanting of *b*la-grub, "the obtaining of the Lāma," and "the obtaining of the ornaments *s*nyen-grub."

The mild deity in this worship is called "The Agreeable One" (*m*thun) and the demon (drag-po) is called "The Repulsive" (*b*zle-pa). The demoniacal form must be recited that full number of times which the lāma bound himself to do by vow before his spiritual tutor, viz., 100, 1,000, or 10,000 times daily. Those not bound in this way by vows repeat the charm as many times as they conveniently can.

Repetition of *mantras.*

Having done this, he may retire again to sleep, if the night be not very far advanced. But if the dawn is near, he must not go to sleep, but should employ the interval in several sorts of prayer (*s*mon-lam).

Further devotion.

As soon as day dawns, he must wash his face and rinse his mouth and do the worship above noted, should he not have already done so; also the following rites:—

At dawn.

1*st.*—Prepare sacred food for the six sorts of beings (Rigs-strug-gi-*g*torma) and send it to Ngo-wo-yidag—The Tantalized Ghosts.

Offerings.

2*nd.*—Offer incense, butter-incense, and wine-oblation (*g*ser-*s*kyem). The incense is offered to the good spirits—firstly, to the chief god and the lāma; secondly, to the class of "king" gods; and thirdly, to the mountain god Kang-chhen dsönga (*Ang.* Kanchinjingna). Then offerings are made to the spirits of caves (who guarded and still guard the hidden revelations therein deposited), the *d*gra-lha or "gods of Battle," the Yul-lha or country gods, the *g*zi-*b*dag or local gods, and the *s*de-*b*rgya*d*, "the eight classes of deities."[1] The butter-incense is only given to the most malignant class of the demons and evil spirits.

Some breakfast is now taken, consisting of *thugpa* or weak soup, followed by tea with parched grain. Any especial work which has to be done will now be attended to, failing which some *d*ge-*s*byor or other service will be chanted. And if any temple or chaitya (chhorten) be at hand, these will be circumambulated with "prayer-wheel" revolving in hand and chanting *mantras.* Then is done any priestly service required by the villagers.

Morning's occupation.

About two o'clock in the afternoon a meal of rice is taken, followed by beer by those who take it, or by tea for non-beer drinkers.

About six o'clock P.M. is done the *g*tor-*bs*ngös service, in which, after assuming his tutelary deity, he chants the *s*ngon-gro and the *s*kyab-gro.[2] Then is done a chhoga (a form of celebration-worship) with bell and small drum in hands, followed by an invocation to all the host of Lāmas, yidams and Chhos-*s*kyong (*Defensores Fidei*), on the assembly of all of whom there is done the worship of the magic-circle of a tutelary deity (*Yidam*).

Evening service.

At 9 or 10 P.M. he retires to sleep.

IN MONASTIC RESIDENCE.

In monastic residence the worship is conducted with much more ceremony, especially on feast days.

Monastery routine.

[1] For list of these, *vide* Chapter VI, page 356. [2] *Vide* page 305.

In the morning, after offering the sacred food, incense, and butter-incense, a conch-shell is blown, on which all the monks must come out of their chambers (gra-shag). On the second blast all collect in the Great Assembly Hall, and during this entry into the hall the Provost Marshal (chhos-*k*hrimba) stands beside the door with his rod in hand. All the monks seat themselves in Buddha fashion, each on his own mat. The monk's feet must not project and his clothes must not hang down or rest upon the mat. Each must face straight to his front with eyes fixed on the tip of his nose. And the most solemn silence must be observed. The slightest breach of these rules is promptly punished by the rod of the Provost Marshal or, in the case of the younger novices, by the *s*Ku-*g*nyer.

Morning muster for mass.

When all have been properly seated, then two or three of the most inferior novices who have not passed their examination and who occupy back seats, rise up and serve out tea to the assembly,[1] each monk producing from his breast pocket his own cup and having it filled up by these novices. Before drinking it all must wait for the Um-dsé to say the Grace, in which all the assembly joins.

Service of tea.

Grace before drinking.

A usual grace is—

"We humbly beseech Thee! that we and our relatives throughout all of our life-cycles may never be separated from the Three Holy Ones! May the blessing of The Trinity enter into this drink!"

Then sprinkling a few drops on the ground with the tips of the fore and middle fingers:—

"To all the dread locality demons of this country, we offer this good Chinese tea! Let us obtain our wishes! And may the doctrines of Buddha be extended!"

The tea is then drunk and the cup is refilled two or three times.

The service of tea is succeeded by soup named "*g*sol-jam thugpa," and served by a new set of the novice underlings. When the cups are filled the Um-dsé, joined by all the monks, chants the "thug-pai *m*chhod-pa," or "the Sacrificial Offering of the Soup." Three or four cups of soup are supplied to each monk. The hall is then swept by junior monks.

Service of soup.

The Um-dsé then inspects the magic circle (*d*Kyil-*k*khor)[2] to see that it is correct, and this ascertained he commences the celebration. He always heads the service, the rest of the congregration repeating it word by word closely after him and using a *Psalter*. This service consists of the

Celebration of Mass.

[1] No layman is allowed to serve out the monks' food. The lay servants bring it to the outside door of the building and there deposit it.

[2] For its description, *vide* Chapter V, page 320.

*s*ngön-*h*gro, *s*kyab*s*-*h*gro and las-*s*byang, on the conclusion of which the assembly disperses. As a sample of this part of the worship, I here translate a short version of the *s*Kyab*s*-*h*gro (vulgarly "*KYAM-DÔ*"), or

THE REFUGE FORMULA.

The Refuge formula.

This service well illustrates the very depraved form of Buddhism which is professed by the lāmas. For here we find that the original *Triple* Refuge formula for Buddha, The Word and The Assembly has been extended by the lāmas to include within its bounds the vast host of deities, demons and deified saints of Tibet as well as many of the Indian Mahayana and Yogacharya saints. Its text is as follows:—

"We—all beings—through the intercession of the Lāma, go for refuge to Buddha!

"We go for refuge to Buddha's Books (Dharma)!

"We go for refuge to The Assembly of the Lāmas (Sanghha)!

"We go for refuge to the host of the Gods and their retinue of the Yidam (tantalized ghosts), *m*Khah-*h*gros (fairies), and the Defenders of THE Religion who people the sky!

"We go for refuge to the victorious Lāmas who have descended from the Sky (*i.e.*, all inspired Lāmas)!

"We go for refuge to The Lāma who is the holder of Wisdom and the Tantra! (*i.e.*, The holder of *Padma Jungre* as personified by Wisdom and Tantra.)

"We go for refuge to the All-Good Father-Mother, *Samanta-bhadra*—Yab-yum Kun tu-*b*zang-po! (The primordial Buddha-God.)

"We go for refuge to the divinely adorned Mild and Angry Loving Ones—Long*s*-sku-zhi-khro-rab-*h*byam!

"We go for refuge to the *Maha Vajradhara* Incarnation (of Shakyámuni)—*s*prul-*s*ku-Dorje-*h*chhang-chhen!

"We go for refuge to The Diamond Sworded Guide '*Vajrasatwa*' —*s*Ton-pa-Dorje-Sems-pa!

"We go for refuge to the victorious *Shakya Muni*—*r*Gyal-wa Shakya-Thub-pa!

"We go for refuge to the Fierce *Vajrapani*—Phyag-na-Dorjé-*g*tum-po!

"We go for refuge to the Converted Mother *Devi Marici*—Yum-*h*gyur-lha-mo öd-zer-chan ma!

"We go for refuge to the Learned *Acharji Manjusri*—*s*Lob-*d*pon *h*Jam *d*pal *b*shes-*b*snyen!

"We go for refuge to the *Pandita Sri Singha*—Pan-chhen-Shri-Singha!

"We go for refuge to the *Jina Jñyana Suda*—*r*Gyal-wa-*g*yang-na-su-da!

"We go for refuge to the *Pandita Bimala Mitra*—Panchhen Bhi-ma-la-ri-tma!

"We go for refuge to the Incarnate Lotus-born *Padma Sambhava*—*s*prul-*s*ku-Pad-ma-*h*byung-*g*na*s*!

"We go for refuge to (his wife) the *Dakini* of the Ocean of Fore-knowledge—*m*Khah-*h*gro-ye-*s*hes-*m*tsho-*r*gyal!

"We go for refuge to The Religious King *Dharma raja* Thi-srong-de-tsén—Chhös-*r*gyal-Khri-srong-*l*deū-*b*tsan!

"We go for refuge to The Apocalyse Finder—Tertön Myang-ban-ting-*h*dsin-*b*zang-po!

"We go for refuge to The Guru's disciple, the Victor *Sthavira* Dang-ma—*g*nas-*br*tan-*l*dang-ma-hlun-*r*gyal!

"We go for refuge to the Reverend Sister, the powerful Lioness Lady *Singeshwara*—*l*che-*b*tsun Seng-ge-*d*bang-phyug!

"We go for refuge to the Incarnate *Jina* Zhang—tön *s*prul-*s*ku-*r*gyal-wa-zhang-*r*tön!

"We go for refuge to The Gu-ru, clever above thousands—*m*Khas-pa-nyid-*h*bum!

"We go for refuge to *Dharma Gurunath Ber*-nag—Chho*s*-*b*dag-gu-ru-jo-*h*ber-nak *m*gon-po!

"We go for refuge to The Illusive Lion *Gyábá*—Khrul-zhig-seng-ge-*r*gyab-ba!

"We go for refuge to the Great Devotee 'The Clearer of the misty moon'—Grub-chhen-zla-wa mün sel!

"We go for refuge to the Indian Sage *Kumaraja*—Rig-*h*dsin-ku-ma-ra-dsa!

"We go for refuge to the *Jina* Prince of the Scentless Rays—*r*Gyal-*s*re*s*-Dri-me*d*-*h*o*d*-zer!

"We go for refuge to the Incarnate 'Noble Banner of Victory'—*s*prul-*s*ku-*d*Pal-*h*byor-*r*gyal-*m*tshan!

"We go for refuge to the Omniscient renowned *Chandrakirti*—Kun-*m*khyen-Zla-wa-grag*s*-pa!

"We go for refuge to The Three Incarnate Kind brothers—Drin-chhen-*s*prul-*s*ku-*m*chhed-*g*sum!

"We go for refuge to the Bodhisatwa, The Noble Ocean—Byang-sem*s*-*d*Pal-*h*byor-*r*gya *m*tsho!

"We go for refuge to the Incarnate Sage, the religious Vajra—*s*prul-*s*ku-Rig-*h*dsin-chho*s*-*r*dor!

"We go for refuge to The Entirely accomplished and renowned Speaker—Yong*s*-*h*dsin-ngag-*db*ang-grags-pa!

"We go for refuge to *Mahāguru Dharmarāja*—*b*La-chhen-Chho*s* kyi-*r*gyal-po!

"We go for refuge to the Revelation Finder Zhigpoling—*g*ter-*b*ton-zhig-po-*g*ling-pa!

"We go for refuge to the Religious king of accomplished knowledge[1]—Chhos-*r*gyal-yon-ten-Phuntshog*s* !

"We go for refuge to The Banner of obtained Wisdom—*m*Khas-grub-*b*Lo-gro*s*-*r*gyal-*m*tshan !

"We go for refuge to The Unequalled useful Vajra—Tshung med-*g*zhan-phan-Dorje !

"We go for refuge to the Radical (*Mula*) Lāma Aśoka—Myangan-med-*r*Tsa-wai-*b*La-ma ![2]

"We go for refuge to the Lāma of the Three collections of the Mula Tantra—*r*Tsa *r*Gyud-düs-*g*sum-*b*La-ma !

"We go for refuge to the accomplished Sage *Satwa* Phuntshogs—Sems-*d*pah Phun-tshogs-rig-*h*dsin !

"We go for refuge to The Beloved Religious King *hsTan-h*dsin,[3] the holder of the doctrines—Chho*s*-*r*gyal-Byam*s*-pa-*bsTan-h*dsin !

"We go for refuge to the Reverend Sky *Vajra*—*m*Khas-*b*tsun-Nam-*m*khah-Dorje !

"We go for refuge to the *Shri-Ratna-Bhadra-Satwa*—Sems-*d*pah-Rin-chhen-*d*Pal-*b*zang !

"We go for refuge to the collection of mild and angry Yidams (Tutelary gods) !

"We go for refuge to the holy doctrine of *Maha Anta* or the Great End—*r*Dsog*s*pa-chhen-po !

"We go for refuge to The male and female Saints of the Country !

"We go for refuge to The Fairies (*m*Khah hgro), Defenders of Religion (Chhös-*s*kyongs), and Guardians (*b*Srung*s* ma) !

"Oh ! Lāma ! Bless us as you have been blessed ; Bless us with the blessing of the Tantras !

"We beg you to bless us with *OM*, which is the BODY. We beg you to purify our sins and pollutions of the body. We beg you to increase happiness without any sickness. We beg you to give us the real undying gift of life !

"We beg you to bless us with *AH*, which is the COMMAND. We beg you to purify the sins and pollution of speech. We beg you to give us the power of speech. We beg you to confer on us the gift of perfect speech !

"We beg you to bless us with the *HUM* (pr. *Hung*), which is the MIND ! We beg you to purify the pollution and sins of the mind ! We beg you to give us the real gift of pure heart. We beg you to empower us with the four powers !

"We pray you to give us the gifts of the True Body, Command and Mind !

---

[1] The first Bhotiya King of Sikhim, *vide* page 249.

[2] This may be a reference to the great Emperor Aśoka or his confessor—Upagupta, the Thirteenth Patriarch of the early Buddhist Church in India.

[3] The sixth Bhotiya King of Sikhim, *circa* 1770—90.

" —*OM—AH—HUNG!*—

"Give us such blessing as will clear away the sins and pollution of bad deeds!

"We beg you to soften the evils of bad causes!

"We beg you to bless us with the prosperity of our body, *i.e.*, health.

"Bless us with mental guidance.

"Bless us with Buddhahood soon.

"Bless us by cutting us off from (worldly) illusions.

"Bless us by putting us into The Right Path.

"Bless us by making us understand all religious things.

"Bless us to be useful to each other with kindliness.

"Bless us with the ability of doing good and delivering the animal beings from misery.

"Bless us to know ourselves thoroughly.

"Bless us to be mild from the depths of our heart.

"Bless us to be brave as Yourself.

"Bless us with the Tantras as Yourself!

"Now, we, the innumerable animal beings, conceive that we have "become pure in thought like Buddha, and we conceive that we are "working for the welfare of the other animal beings. We, now having "obtained the qualities of the collection of the gods and the roots of the "Tantras, and the zhi-wa, *r*gya*s*-pa, *d*bang and Phrin-las, pray that all "the animal beings be possessed of happiness and be freed from misery. "Let us all animals be freed from lust, anger, and attachment to worldly "affairs, and let us perfectly understand the true nature of religion!

"Now, O! Father-Mother! The unadorned Dharma Kāya *Samanta* "*bhadra*—Yab-yum Chhos-*s*ku-Kun-*b*zang! The richly adorned Mild "and Angry Loving Ones—Long*s*-*s*ku-zhi-khro-rab-*h*byam*s!* The "incarnate sages of the Skull Rosary—*s*prul-*s*ku-rigs-*h*dsin-thöd-"*h*phreng-*bs*tsal! and the Mula Tantra Lama—Tsa-*r*gyu*d*-*b*la-ma! "I now beg You to depart!

"O! Ghosts of heroes, *d*Pa-o! Female fiends, Dakkini Demo-"niacal Defenders of the faith, Chho*s*-*s*kyong*s!* The Holy Guardians "of the Commandments—Dam-chan-*b*kah-i-*b*srung-ma! And all those "that we invited to this place! I beg You All now to depart!

"O! The powerful King of the Angry Deities, Khro-wo-i-*r*gyal-"po-*s*tob-po-chhe! The powerful Ishwara and the host of the Country "Guardian Gods—*m*thu-*s*tob*s*-*d*bang-phyug-yul-*h*khor-srung! And "all those others that were invited to this place with all their retinue! "I beg You All now to depart!

"MAY GLORY COME! *Tashi-shok!*

"LET VIRTUE COME! *dGé-o!*"

[Here endeth The Refuge Service.]

About 8 A.M. the conch-shell blast again summons the monks to the Assembly Hall, where, after partaking of refreshments of tea and parched grain in the manner already described, a full celebration (chhoga) is done. And on its conclusion the monks disperse.

Other services.

About 10 A.M. a Chinese drum is beaten to muster the monks in the Assembly Hall. At this meeting rice and meat and vegetables are served out as before, and with this is also served beer called *g*sos-*r*gyab, the *l*to-*m*chhod being done as formerly. A full celebration is then performed and the meeting dissolves.

In the afternoon a conch shell is blown for tea and a Chinese drum beaten for beer, the monks assembling as before and doing a full celebration of the worship of Mahakala Natha (*m*gonpo) and the Guardians of Religion respectively.

When sacerdotal celebrations on behalf of lay individuals have to be done, they are introduced within the latter celebration, which is interrupted for this purpose. And after each of these extra celebrations the monks remain outside the Assembly Hall for a very short time and then re-assemble. On finishing the extra chhogas, the chhoga of the Religious Guardians is then resumed and concluded.

In the evening another assembly, preceded by tea as refreshment, conducts the celebration of *s*kang-shags with 108 lamps.

Another and final assembly for the day is made by beat of drum, and rice and flesh-meat is served out.

The refreshments and meals usually number nine daily.

In Hermitage.

In the case of the hermit-lāma (or *m*tshams-pa), of which there are very few in Sikhim, he is engaged all day long in mortifying his passions and worldly desires, repeating mantras and practising those postures and magic rites which, according to the Tantrik school, give miraculous powers and a short cut to Nirvana.

Hermits.

The order of these exercises, according to the book entitled, "The complete Esoteric Tantra,"[1] the reputed work of Padma Sambhava, is as follows:—

Their meditation, &c.

1*st.*—The mode of placing the three mystic words (*i.e.*, *ku*, *sung*, and *tuk*).

2*nd.*—The Nectar-replying rosary.

3*rd.*—The jewelled rosary-guide for Ascending.

4*th.*—Secret counsels of the four Yogas.

5*th.*—The great Root of the Heart.

[1] *g*sang-*s*ngags *l*pyi *r*gyud.

6*th*.—The Lamp of The Three Dwellings.
7*th*.—The bright Loosener of the Illusion.
8*th*.—The water-drawing "dorje."
9*th*.—The secret guide to the fierce Dakini.
10*th*.—The drawing of the Essence of the stony nectar.
11*th*.—Counsel on the Dakinis' habits.
12*th*.—Fathoming the mystery of the Dakinis.
13*th*.—Counsel for the Khandoma—Fairies' heart-root.
14*th*.—The Four Words for the path of Pardo.[1]
15*th*.—The Pardo of the angry demons.
16*th*.—To recognise the Gyalwa Rig-na or The Five Former Buddhas. Then Nirvana is reached.

The hermit-lāmas of Sikhim usually leave their hermitage for some months annually to visit villages and places of pilgrimage. A true hermit who has cut off all connection with the world is called *s*gom-chhen or "great devotee."

Temporary hermitage and its exercises.

Theoretically it ought to be part of the training of every young lāma to spend in hermitage a period of three years, three months, and three days, in order to accustom himself to ascetic rites. But this practice is very rarely observed in Sikhim for any period, and when it is done, a period of three months and three days is considered sufficient. During this seclusion he repeats the mantra of his tutelary deity an incredible number of times. *s*Ngon-gro-*b*zi-*h*byor, complete in all its four sections, must be repeated 100,000 times. In the "Kyab-do" portion he must prostrate himself to the ground 100,000 times. The repetition of the Yige-*br*gya-pa itself takes about two months; and in addition must be chanted the following voluminous services:—

Phyi-*h*grub, nang-*h*grub, *g*sang-*h*grub, *b*la-*h*grub, *s*nyen-grub, *h*phrin-las, and *b*zi-*h*grub.

As a sample of the form of lāmaic ritual employed in the worship of a special divinity, I give here a translation of the manual entitled—

The Worship of Dölma,[2] The Deliveress.

Her popularity.

Dölma is one of the most popular of the deities, and a large proportion of the laity can repeat her services by heart. She is known to Northern Buddhism by the Sanskrit name of Tārā of which Dölma is a literal Tibetan translation, meaning "The Unloosener (of difficulties)" or "The Saviouress." And it is to this attribute of being ever ready to help and easily

[1] *Pardo*, the ghostly interval between death and judgment—*vide* article "Wheel of Life," in chapter on "Temple," page 266.
[2] *s*grol-ma, vulgarly *Dö-ma*.

approachable that she owes her popularity. Most of the other deities cannot be approached without the mediation of a lāma; but the poorest layman or woman may secure the immediate attention of Dölma by simply appealing to her direct.

Semblance to The Virgin Mary.

The striking similarity between Dölma and "The Virgin Mary" of Roman Catholicism has excited comment. Dölma, like The Virgin Mary, occupies a maternal relation to the Buddhas, and is an intercessor, a ready hearer of prayers, easily approachable, and able and willing to relieve or soothe petty troubles, and her name is a favourite personal name for women.

Origin of her worship.

Her worship seems to date from about the 7th century A.D., when Tantric ideas began to tinge Indian Buddhism. It seems to me that the name was evidently suggested by the Hindu myth of *Budha*, or the planet Mercury, whose mother was Tārā; and either by wilful or accidental confusion the idea got transferred to *Buddha*, who about this time also received a place in the Hindu Pantheon.

Her forms.

There are now two recognized classes of the goddess Dölma, viz.—

(*a*) The *Green* Dölma—"*The* Dölma" of the Tibetans, of which King Srongtsan-gampo's *Nepalese* wife was an incarnation, and

(*b*) The *White* Dölma—who is especially worshipped in China and Mongolia and very seldom in Tibet. King Srongtsan-gampo's *Chinese* wife is believed to be an incarnation of this form.

The white form.

The white form is seated like a Buddha, and has seven eyes, one being in the forehead in addition to the ordinary facial pair, and one in each palm and in the sole of each foot.

The green form.

The green form—"*The* Dölma" of the Tibetans—is usually represented in the form of a bejewelled young Indian woman of a green complexion seated on a lotus, with her left leg hanging down and holding a long-stemmed lotus flower. She is, however, given a variety of other forms, mild and demoniacal, to the number of twenty-one or more. The demoniacal forms[1] are very similar to those of the Hindu Durga. These several forms are evidently the objective representations in concrete fashion of the numerous titles of the goddess:—thus Locanā, Māmaki, Vajradhatviswari, Pandara, Ugratārā, Ratnatārā, Bhrikutitārā, Visvatārā, &c. And latterly her names have been extended to reach the mystic number of 108.

[1] Khrô-*g*nyer chan (pr. *To-nyer chén*), "She with frowning brows," &c.

Her Manual of Worship.

Her Manual of Worship is alleged internally to have been composed by the first of the seven mythical Dhyani Buddhas, *viz.*, Vipashyi. The appendix, however, is signed by Gedun Dub, the Grand Lāma, who built Tashi-lhunpo monastery *circa* 1445 A.D., so that it is possible he composed this version.

The Manual is here translated:—

"EXHORTATION TO DÖLMA'S WORSHIP.

"If we worship this high and pure-souled goddess when we "retire in the dusk and get up in the morning, then all our fears and "worldly anxieties will 'give way,' and our sins be forgiven. SHE— "The conqueror of myriad hosts, will strengthen us. She will do more "than this! She will reach us directly to the end of our transmigra-"tion to Buddha and Nirvana!

"She will expel the direst poisons and relieve us from all anxieties "as to food and drink, and all our wants will be satisfied; and all devils "and plagues and poisons will be annihilated utterly; and the burdens "of all animals will be lightened! If you chant her hymn two or three "or six or seven times, your desire for a son will be realized! Or, "should you wish wealth, you will obtain it, and all other wishes will "be gratified and every sort of demon will be wholly overcome!"

HER WORSHIP.

Her worship is divided into seven stages, viz.—

(1) Invocation—Calling her to come.
(2) Presentation of offerings of sacred food, water, flowers and rice, and occasionally a *mandala* or magic circle offering.
(3) Hymn in her praise.
(4) Repetition of her spell or *mantra*.
(5) (6) Prayers for benefits present and to come.
(7) Benediction.

I.

INVOCATION.

"Hail! O! emeraldine Dölma!
Who art the Saviour of all beings!
I pray Thee descend from Thy heavenly mansion, at Potala,
Together with all Thy retinue of gods, titans, and deliverers!
I humbly prostrate myself at Thy lotus feet!
Deliver us from all distress!
Hail to Thee, Our Holy Mother!"

II.

Presentation of Offerings (Sacrificial).

"We hail Thee! O Rever'd and Sublime Dölma!
Who art adored by all the kings and princes
Of the ten directions and of the present, past and future.
We pray Thee to accept these offerings
Of flowers, incense, perfumed lamps,
Precious food, the music of cymbals,
And the other offerings!
We sincerely beg Thee in all of Thy divine Forms[1]
To partake of the food now offered!
On confessing to Thee penitently their sins
The most sinful hearts, yea! even the committers of the
Ten vices and the five boundless sins,
Will obtain forgiveness and reach
Perfection of soul—through Thee!
If we (human beings) have amassed any merit
In the three periods, the present, past and future,
We rejoice in this good fortune, when we consider
The unfortunate lot of the poor (lower) animals
Piteously engulphed in the ocean of misery.
On their behalf, we now beg to turn the wheel of religion!
We beseech Thee by whatever merit we've accumulated
To kindly regard all the animals.
And for ourselves!
When our merit has reached perfection
Let us not we pray Thee
Linger longer in this world!"

III.

Hymns in praise of Dölma.

(*In her Twenty-one Forms.*[1])

"Adoration to Arya Tārā!
And Avalokita (her spiritual father),
Rich in power and the store-house of pity!

Hail! rever'd and sublime Dölma!
We adore Thee!

---

[1] Each stanza refers to a different form of the goddess as noted in the foregoing text.

"Hail! Dölma! Thou ever ready heroine!
Born, like a lightning-flash, from the pitying tear[1]
Shed for humanity by The Lord of the three worlds
The Lotus-born!

Hail! to Thee whose face is shining
As a hundred harvest moons
Lit by the splendid light of
A full thousand fulgent stars!

Hail! O! Thou whose hand is decked with
The Blue and Golden water-lotus!
Thou beneficent and zealous Soother of difficulties,
Thou monopoliseth the realms of woe, as well as action.

Hail! O! Thou with head adorned by Tathagatha[2]
Conqueror of the Universe!
Thou hast overcome Thine enemies without exception
And shown Thyself a saintly Victor.

Hail! By Thy mystic '*Tut-ta-ra-hung.*'[3]
Thou possesseth the realms of earth and sky.
Thou treadest under foot the seven worlds
And makest one and all to bend!

Hail! The mighty gods adore Thee—
Indra, Agni, Brahma and the Lord of the Winds;
The risen ghosts and the dread 'Ti-za';
The horde of harmful spirits praise Thee!

Hail! By Thy mystic '*tré*' and '*phät*'
Thou destroyest the cunning schemes of Thy opponents.
With Thy right leg flexed and the left extended,
Thou consumest Thine enemies with devouring fire!

Hail! With Thy awful word '*tu-re*'[4]
Thou banishest the bravest of devils!
With the mere frown of Thy tear-born face
Thou completely routeth enemies!

[1] The allusion here is that Avalokita—"The Storehouse of Pity"—on looking down upon the world shed tears out of pity for the misery of humanity. The tear from the left eye on falling to the earth formed a lake, on which instantly, like a lightning-flash, appeared, floating on a lotus flower, the goddess Dölma, who was then commissioned by Avalokita to soothe human suffering.

[2] In this form of Dölma's image a figure of Tathagatha Amitabhā Buddha is seated on her hair.

[3] & [4] Part of Dölma's spell or *mantra* already given under head of "Rosaries," *vide* page 288.

"Hail! Thou emblem of The Three Holies!
With lovely hand posed on Thy breast
And shining within a glorious halo
Thou confoundeth Thy enemies with dazzling light!

Hail! In Thy placid mood
Thy glory gains brilliancy from Thy gems
And laughing in Thy '*Tutu-ra tutu-ra*'[1]
Thou enslaveth the hearts of man and fiend!

Hail! Oh! Owner of all the earth.
Thou maketh the mighty bend their head
And quake beneath Thy angry frown
While all the poor Thou cherisheth!

Hail! With crescent moon as a diadem,
And adorned with every jewel,
And O-pag-med in Thy plaited hair
Thou sheddeth excessive light!

Hail! Thy necklace[2] glows
Like the fire of the last *kalpa*[3]
And wreathed in smiles and with right foot extended
Thou wholly vanquisheth Thy enemies.

Hail! Happy virtuous Soother!
Thou actively sootheth our every woe
By '*Swa-ha, Om!*' and Thy immaculateness
Thou cleanseth from foulest sin!

Hail! With glorious dazzling halo,
Thou overpowereth all Thine enemies.
Thou coined for us the ten mystic words
And by '*Hung*' Thou solved all knowledge!

Hail! With bent foot and Thy '*Tu-re*'
Thou possesseth the realms of 'Hung'
O! Omniscient One!
And Thou shaketh the three worlds!

Hail! holding in uplifted hand
The marked beast of the heavenly lakes,
With Thy '*Tara*' and '*Phat*'
Thou purgeth from all poison!

Hail! Thou teacher of Indra,
The King of Gods, and the goddesses,
With Thy wealth of charming armour
Thou saveth from evil dreams and strife!

[1] Part of her *mantra*.
[2] Or rosary.
[3] At the end of each *kalpa* the world is consumed by fire.

"Hail! Thou cleanseth the mist
From off the eyes of sun and moon!
By saying '*Tā-ra*' and '*Tu ta-ra*'
Thou savest from the most fearful plague!
Hail! Thou forceth the three worlds to admit
Thy benign use of godly power,
With Thy potent '*Tu-re*'
Thou routest the host of ghosts and devils!
We proclaim the might of Thy mystic spells.
All Hail to these—
Thy one-and-twenty forms!"

IV.

[Here is repeated on the rosary 108 times the mantra of Dölma, viz.—

"*Om! Tāre tut-ta-re ture swā-ha!*"]

V & VI.

PRAYER FOR BLESSINGS.

"I beg thee O! Revered Victorious and Merciful One! to purify "me and all other beings of the universe thoroughly from the two evil "thoughts; and make us quickly obtain the perfection of Buddha. If "we cannot attain this perfection within a few generations, then grant "us the highest earthly and heavenly happiness and all knowledge. "And relieve us, we beseech Thee, from evil spirits, plague, disease, "untimely death, bad dreams, bad omens and all the eight fears and "accidents. And in our passage through this world grant unto us the "most perfect bliss—without possibility of increase—and may all our "desires be realized without exertion.

"Let the holy religion prosper, and in whatever place we dwell, "we beg Thee to soothe there disease and poverty, fighting and "disputes, and to increase the holy religion.

"And may Thy good[1] face always beam on me and appear large "like the moon in forwarding my heart's object of admission to the "heavenly circle and Nirvana.

"Let me obtain the favourite god of my former life, and let me "gain entry into the prophesied paradise of the Three Buddhas of "the past, present, and future.

"Now! O! Thou! The Great Worker!
Thou quick Soother and gracious Mother,
Holding the *utpal* flower!
Let thy glory come!
"*TASHI SHOK!*"

[1] In contradistinction to *fury-face*.

V.—SOME MAGIC RITES AND CHARMS.

Tibetan Superstitions.

Magic and mysticism enter largely into lāmaic ritual, and especially into the priestly ministrations for the laity. Under this head I describe a few of the more prominent magic rites, viz., the "*Mandala*" offering in effigy of the Universe, &c., &c., which forms part of the daily worship of every lāma; the casting of lots for soothsaying purposes, charms against sickness and accidents of sorts, ill-luck, &c., and the printed charms for luck which form the "prayer-flags" and tufts of rags affixed to trees, bridges, &c.

Magic and mystic rites here described.

The "Mandala" or Magic Circle-offering of the Universe.

It is a matter of history how Aśoka, the greatest of Indian Emperors, thrice offered India to the Buddhist church and thrice redeemed it with his treasure and jewels. The lāmas, however, are much more magnificently generous than Aśoka, for every day each lāma offers to the Buddhas and other saints and demons not only the whole of India, but the entire universe, including the heavens and their inhabitants. This is done in effigy, but the offering is considered to be none the less effective than were it actually made in reality. To render this ceremony intelligible we must refer to the lāmaic ideas on the cosmogony of the universe.

The daily offering of the Universe.

The UNIVERSE according to the LĀMAS.

The universe according to the lāmas—and they closely follow Hindu notions on the subject—is graphically depicted in the chart facing this page (Plate X).

"The Universe" of the Lāmas.

The system of worlds forming one universe (*sakwal*), of which there are many, consists of a series of fabulous continents circularly disposed around the great central mass *Ri-rab* (Mt. Meru) which supports the heavens, and which is separated from the circle of continents by seven concentric oceans alternating with seven concentric whorls of golden mountains, and the whole system

General description.

PLATE X.

CHART OF
THE UNIVERSE ACCORDING TO THE LAMAS
TO ILLUSTRATE THEIR DAILY MANDALA OFFERING.

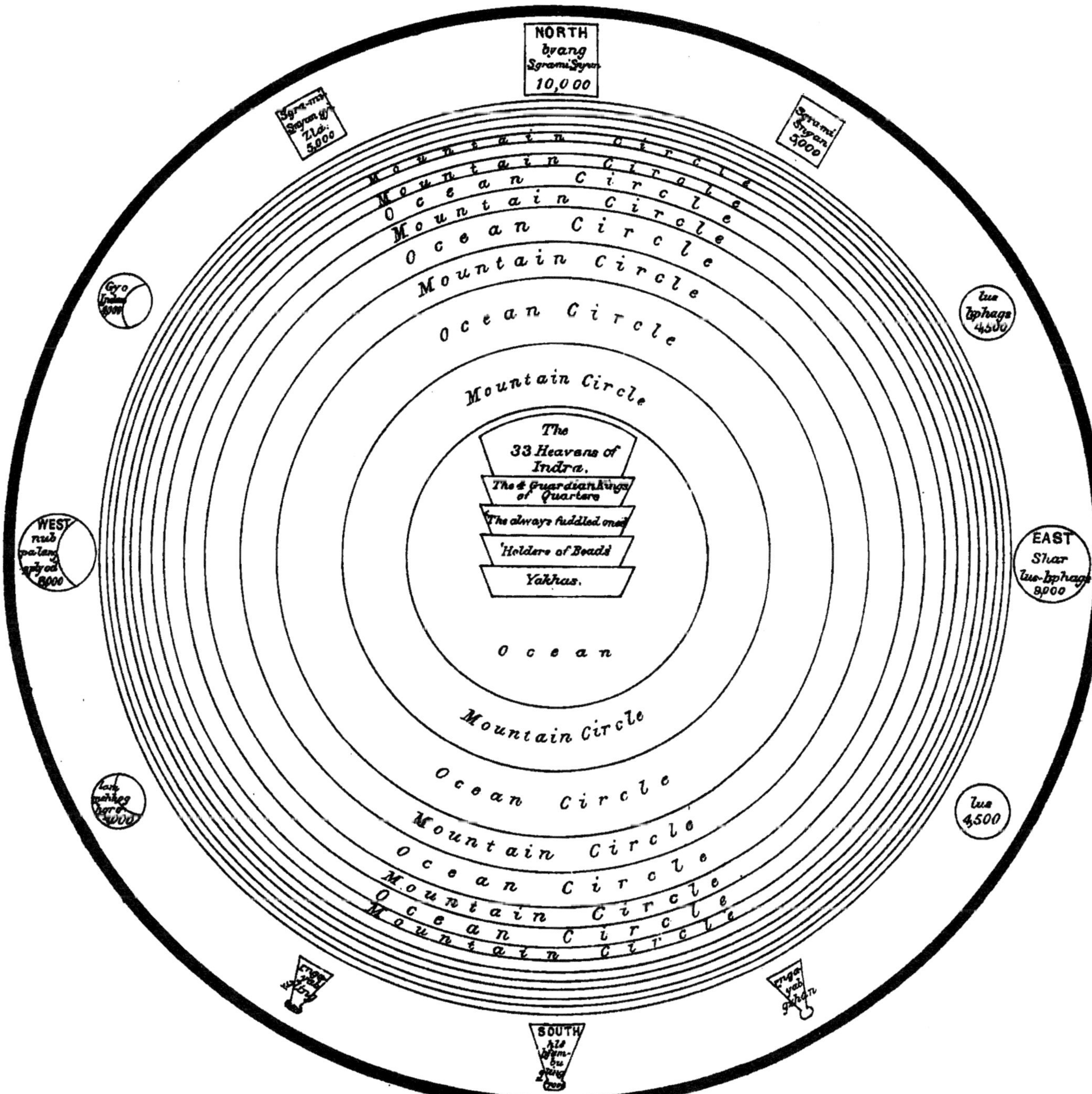

Reg. No. 375, Bengal.—July 94.—500.

Litho S I. O. Calcutta.

is girdled externally by an iron wall, 312½ miles[1] high and 3,602,625 miles in circumference, which shuts in the light of the sun, moon, and stars; outside this wall is perpetual darkness until another universe is reached. The primary support of each universe is a "warp and woof" of blue air like crossed *dorjes*, upon which rests "the body of the waters" and in this latter ocean are set the "continents" with bases of "solid gold," and underneath the central Mount Meru are the Hells.

Dimensions.

The dimensions are as follow:—Mount Meru towers 80,000 miles above the ocean, and it extends for the same distance below the waters. Enveloping it is an "enchanted ocean" (rolwai *m*tsho) 80,000 miles in width and the same in depth. To this succeeds a wall of golden mountains named the "Track of the Neck-Yoke," 40,000 miles high and the same in width, and beyond this is an enchanted ocean of the same dimensions. Externally to these are consecutive circles of alternating pairs of golden mountains and enchanted oceans of gradually diminishing dimensions as to width, depth, and height, viz. of 20,000, 10,000, 5,000, 2,500, 1,250, and 625 respectively, which brings us to the so-called "continents" in the outer ocean.

The continents.

These "continents" are really worlds, for under the heading of *Jambuling* (Skt. *Jambudwip*) is included the whole known world, both oriental and occidental. All the other "continents" specified by the lāmas are therefore purely fabulous, as in Hindu mythology. The chief continents are four in number, one being situated exactly in each of the four directions, and each continent has a smaller satellite on either side, thus bringing the total up to twelve.

The description of these continents briefly is:—

On the *East* is "Lus-*h*pags" (Skt. *Videha*), or "vast body." This is shaped like the crescent moon, and is white in colour. It is 9,000 miles in diameter, and the inhabitants are described as tranquil and mild, and of excellent conduct, and with faces of same shape as this continent, *i.e.*, crescentic like the moon.

On the *South* is "Jambuling" (Skt. *Jambudwip*), or our own world. It is shaped like the shoulder-blade of a sheep, and is blue in colour. It is the smallest of all, being only 7,000 miles in diameter. Here are found riches and plenty, but also acts of sin as well as virtue. The inhabitants have faces of the same shape as the continent, *i.e.*, sub-triangular.

[1] The Tibetan measure is a "*d*pag-tshad" which, according to Csoma deKörös, equals 4,000 fathoms, and hence a geographical mile. But it seems to correspond to the same Indian unit of measure which is translated in the Ceylonese scriptures as a Yojana, *i.e.*, a unit of about 4 *kos*, and therefore over five or six geographical miles.

On the *West* is "ba-*g*lang *s*pyöd" (Skt. *Godhanya* or "Wealth of Oxen"), which in shape is like the sun and red in colour. It is 8,000 miles in diameter. Its inhabitants are extremely powerful, and (as the name literally means, *cow* + *ox* + *action*) they are believed to be specially addicted to eating cattle, and their faces are round like the sun.

On the *North* is "*s*gra-mi-*s*nyan" (Skt. *Uttara Kuru* or "Elevated *Kuru*"-tribe) of square shape and green in colour, and the largest of all the continents, being 10,000 miles in diameter. Its inhabitants are extremely fierce and noisy. They have square faces "like horses"; and live on trees, which supply all their wants. They become tree-spirits on their death; and these trees afterwards emit "bad sounds" (this is evidently, like many of the other legends, due to a puerile and false interpretation of the etymology of the word).

The satellite continents resemble their parent one in shape and are half its size. The left satellite of Jambuling, viz. Ngāyabling, is the fabulous country of the Rakshas, to which Padma Sambhava is believed to have gone and be still there reigning. And each of the latter presents towards Mount Meru one of the following objects respectively, viz., The Mountain of Jewels, The wish-granting tree (*d*pag-*b*sam kyi shing), The wish-granting cow ("*h*dod-*h*zo-ī-ba"), and "The self-sprung crops" (ma-*s*mos-pi lo-thog) already referred to as divine objects in the description of "The Cycle of Existence."

Mount Ri-rab (Meru).

In the very centre of this system "The King of Mountains, Mount Ri-rab" (Meru), towers erect "like the handle of a hand millstone," and underneath it are the hells. It is composed of jewels: its eastern face is of silver, the south of jasper (Baidhuriya) stone, the west of ruby, and the north of gold. It has four lower compartments before the heavens are reached. The lowest of these compartments is inhabited by the "*g*nod *s*byin,"

Its compartments.

usually interpreted as Yaksha, but really "givers of *injury*," and therefore bad genii—and these hold wooden plates. Above this is "the bead or wreath-holder's" region [phreng thog (Skt. *Śragdharā*), which seems to be a title of the Garuḍas]. Above this is the region of the Nāgas, above whom are "the eternally fuddled ones" (*r*tak myos). Above whom are the four Great Guardian Kings of the Quarters.[1] And above Mount Meru,

[1] *Vide* page 261 for particulars of the Four Guardian Kings of the Quarters. Another arrangement gives guardian deities for each of "the ten directions," viz., Indra on the East; Agni (the fire god) on the South-East; Yama (the death god) on the South; Rakshas (? Sura) on the South-West; Varuṅa (the water god) on the West; Vāyu (the wind god) on the North-West; Yakhas on the North; Soma (the moon) on the North-East; Brāhma, above; Bhupati (sa-*b*dag or Earth Spirit) below.

at an elevation of 160,000 miles from the base, are the heavens of the gods, amongst the lower of which are the 33 sensuous heavens of Indra. Above Indra's and Māra's heavens of desire are the less sensuous heavens of Brahma's *d*gah-*l*dan "Paradise," *h*phrul-*d*gah, and *g*zhan *h*phrul *d*wang byed, and above all these is The God of Gods, The Primordial Buddha—*Kuntu-zang-po* (Skt. *Samanta-bhadra*) or "The Best of All" in the highest Brahmalôka called *h*g-min (Skt. *Akanista*), (pronounced "O-min") or "The Supreme."

The Heavens.

Inhabiting the air, on a level with Indra's heaven, is the circle of The Eight Goddesses—(or *Hlāmo*) the *Mātris* of the earlier Hindus. These goddesses are all of beautiful appearance, and are thus named and described:—

The eight "*Matri*" goddesses.

1. "*s*Geg-mo-ma" (Skt. *Lāsyā*) of white complexion, holding a mirror and in a coquettish (*sgeg-pa*) attitude.
2. "*h*Phreng-ba-ma" (Skt. *Mālā*) of yellow colour, holding a rosary (*h*phreng-ba).
3. "*g*Lu-ma" (Skt. *Gītā*) of red colour, holding a lyre symbolizing music (*g*lu).
4. "Gar-ma" of green colour in a dancing attitude.
5. "Me-tog-ma" (Skt. *Pushpā*) of white colour, holding a flower (me-tog).
6. "*b*Dug-*s*pös ma" (Skt. *Dhupa*) of yellow colour, holding an incense (*b*Dug-*s*pös) vase.
7. "*s*Nang-*g*sal-ma" (? Skt. *Dipa*) of red colour, holding a lamp.
8. "Dri-chha-ma" (Skt. *Gandha*) of green colour, holding a shell-vase of perfume (dri).

Immediately outside these goddesses, and also suspended in the air, in fixed positions, are "*The Seven Precious Things*"[1] of a Chakravartin-rāja, or universal monarch, viz.—

"The Seven Precious Things" of an Emperor.

(1) hK*horlo rin-po-chhe* (Skt. *Chakra ratna*), or the victorious *Wheel* of a thousand spokes.
(2) *Nor-bu rin-po-chhe* (Skt. *Mani ratna*), The mother of *Jewels*.
(3) *Tsün-mo rin-po-chhe* (Skt. *Stri ratna*), The jewel of a *Wife*.
(4) *bLön-po rin-po-chhe* (Skt. *Mahajan ratna*), The good *Minister*.
(5) g*Lang-po rin-po-chhe* (Skt. *Hasti ratna*), The jewel of a white *Elephant*.
(6) r*Ta-mchhog rin-po-chhe* (Skt. *Ashwa ratna*), The best *Horse* jewel.

[1] rin-po-chhe *s*na *b*dun.

(7) d*Mag-pön rin-po-chhe* (Skt. *Sena-pati ratna*), The jewel of a *General*.

And to these have been added an eighth, viz.—

(8) *Bum-pa-ter*—the *Vase* for storing all the riches of the three worlds.

In the inmost circle immediately around Ri-rab are :—

Nyima or The Sun, consisting of "glazed fire," with its chariot drawn by ten horses.

Da-wa or the Moon, composed of "glazed water," with its chariot and seven horses.

Rin-po-chhe Duk or the Jewelled Umbrella of Sovereignty.

Gyal-tshén (Skt. *Dhwaja*) or Banner of Victory.

And in the centre of all, in the heavens of Indra, is the store of the entire treasure of the gods.

THE MODE OF OFFERING THE MANḌALA.

The mode of offering the Universe in effigy is as follows:—

The ceremony of making the *manḍala*.

Having wiped the 'manḍal' tray with the right arm or sleeve, take a fistful of rice in either hand, and sprinkle some on the tray to lay the Foundation of the Universe of mighty Gold. Then set down the large ring, which is the Iron Girdle of the Universe. Then in the middle set down a dole of rice as Ri-rab (Mount Meru). Then in the order given in the attached diagram (PLATE XI) are set down a few grains of rice representing the 38 component portions of the Universe, each of which is named at the time of depositing its representative rice. The ritual for all sects of lāmas during this ceremony is practically the same. I here append the text as used by the Kargyupa of the Bhotiya *Basti* Gompa at Darjeeling.

The mental part of the process.

During this ceremony it is specially insisted on that the performer must mentally conceive that he is actually bestowing all this wealth of continents, gods, &c., &c., upon his lāmaic deities, who themselves are quite outside the system of the Universe.

THE MANḌALA SERVICE.

The words employed during the offering of the Manḍala are the following.

N.B.—The figures in brackets correspond to those in the diagram and indicate the several points in the magic circle where the doles of rice are deposited during this celebration service.

DIAGRAM
showing
THE COMPOSITION OF THE MANDALA
OFFERING OF THE UNIVERSE.

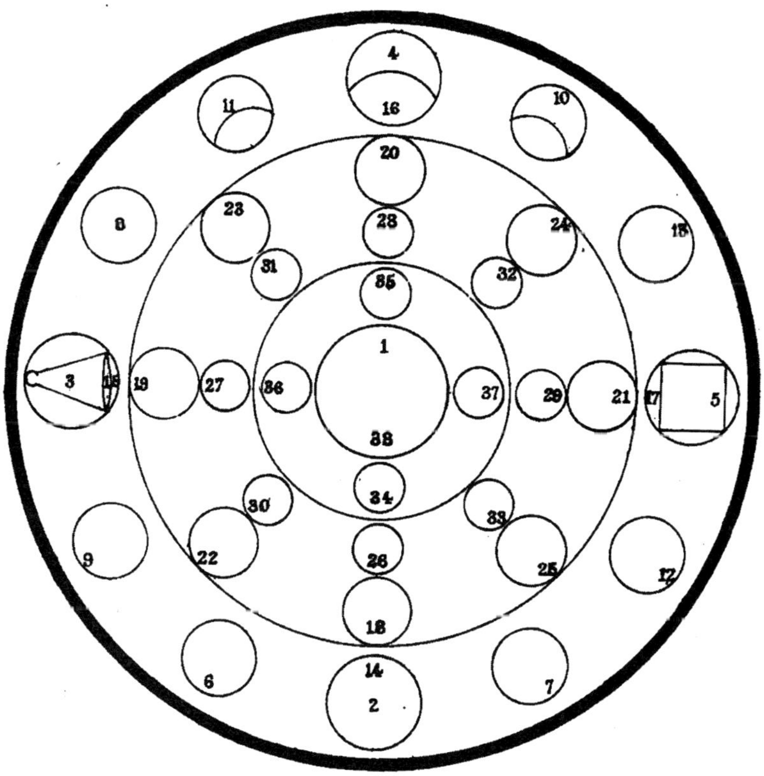

FRONT.

REFERENCES.

The numbers are in the order of the procedure.

1. Ri Gyalpo Ri-rabs.

THE GREAT CONTINENTS.

2. Shar lü Phag-po.
3. Hlô Jam-bu-ling.
4. Nub Pa-lang Jö.
5. Chang da-mi nyen.

THE SATELLITE CONTINENTS.

6. Lü tang.
7. Lü phag.
8. Nga-yab tang.
9. Nga-yab zhén.
10. Yô-dén tang.
11. Lam-chhog dô.
12. Da-mi nyen tang.
13. Da-mi nyen kyi da.

THE 4 WORLDLY TREASURES.

14. Rin-pochhe-ï ri-wô.
15. Pag-sam Kyi Shing.
16. Dod jô-ï-loo.
17. Ma-mō pa-ï lô thog.

THE SEVEN PRECIOUS THINGS.

18. Khor-lo.
19. Nar-bu.
20. Tsün-mo.
21. Lön-po.
22. Lang-po.
23. Tam-chhog.
24. Mag-pön.

25. Ter chhen-po-ï Bum-pa.

THE 8 MATRI GODDESSES.

26. Gog-mo-ma.
27. Theng-wa ma.
28. Lu-ma.
29. Gar-ma.
30. Me-tog ma.
31. Dug-pö ma.
32. Nang sol-ma.
33. Di chhab ma.

SUN AND MOON.

34. Nyi-ma
35. Da-wa

36. Rinpo-chhe-ï dug.
37. Chhog-lé nam-par Gyal-wa-ï Gyat-tohén.
38. Nam-par Gyal-wā-ï Khang zang.

Reg. No. 175, Bengal.—July, 94.—500.

Litho., S. I. O., Calcutta.

"*Om! Bajra bhrummi ah Hum!*

"On the entirely clear foundation of solid gold is *Om! bajra-* "*rekhe-ah Hum.*

"On the middle of the outer iron wall is *Hum* and Ri-rab (Meru), "the King of Mountains. (1)

"On the East is Lüs-*h*phags-po, (2)

"On the South *h*Jam-bu-*g*ling, (3)

"On the West Ba-lang-*s*pyöd, (4) and

"On the North *s*Gra-mi-*s*nyan. (5)

"On either side of the Eastern continent Lüs-*h*phags are Lüs (6) "and Lüs-*h*phags. (7)

"On either side of the Southern continent are *r*Nga-yab (8) and "*r*Nga-yab-*g*zhan. (9)

"On either side of the Western continent are Yonten (10) and "Lam-*m*chhog-*h*gra. (11)

"And on either side of the Northern continent are *s*Gra-mi- "*s*nyan (12) and *s*Gra-mi-*s*nyan-gyi-*m*dah. (13)

"There are mountains of jewels (14), wish-granting trees (15), "wish-granting cows (16), unploughed crops (17), the precious "Wheel (18), the precious *Norbu* jewel (19), the precious Queen (20), "the precious Minister (21), the precious Elephant (22), the precious "Horse (23), the precious Battle-chief (24), the Bumpa of the great "treasure (25), the Goddesses *s*geg-pa-ma (26), *h*Phreng-wa-ma (27), "*g*Lu-ma (28), Gar-ma (29), Me-tog-ma (30), *b*Dug-spös-ma (31), "sNang-*g*sal-ma (32), Dri-chhal-ma (33), the sun (34), moon (35), "jewelled umbrella (35), the ensign of victory (37), which is entirely "victorious from all directions, and in the middle are the gods (38), "the most accomplished and wealthy of the beings!

"I offer you all these constituent parts of the Universe all com- "plete! O! noble, kind, and holy Lāma! O! tutelary *Yidam* gods of "the magic circle, and all the Collections of Buddhas and Bodhisatwas!

"I beg you all to receive these offerings for the benefit of the "Animal beings!

"I offer you O! Buddhas! the four continents and Ri-rab (Meru) "adorned with the sun and moon on a foundation of incense and "flowers. Let all the Animal beings enjoy happiness!

"I offer you O! You whole assembly of accomplished Supreme "Beings of the outside, inside, and hidden regions, the entire wealth "and body of all these mythical regions. I beg you all to give us the "best of all real gifts, and also the real gift of *r*Dsogs-pa-chhen-po "(the mystic insight sought by the Nyingmapa)!

"I offer up this fresh magic circle, through the virtue of which "let no injury beset the path of purity, but let us have the grace of "the Jinas of the three times, and let us, the innumerable Animal "beings, be delivered from this illusive world!

"I offer up salutations, offerings, confessions of sins, and repent- "ance. What virtue has been accumulated by myself and others, "let it go to the attainment of our great end. *Idam-ratna manḍala "kamniryah teyāmi!*

"I humbly prostrate myself three times to all who are worthy "of worship, with my whole heart and body.

"TASHI SHOK!—LET GLORY COME!"

In order to complete the view of this Daily Service of Offerings called—

THE PRESENTATION OF OFFERINGS OR *m*CHHÖ*d*-*h*BUL.

The daily service of "Presentation of Offerings."

I here give that portion of the celebration which preceded the *Manḍala*, as the *Manḍala* is only its concluding portion:—

"*OM! swabhawashudha sarba dharma swabha- "washudha-hang!* The dwelling-place of the sphere of the supreme "ok-min-*s*tug-po-*b*kod is well furnished with good foundations and "adorned on every side with lotuses and jewels.

"By enunciating the word HUNG! there flow out these offerings, "viz., excellent sacrifice (*m*chhöd-yön), cool water (zhabs-*g*sil), flowers "(me-tok), incense (*b*dug-spös), lamps (mar-me), perfumed water (dri- "chhab), holy food (zhal-zas), music of cymbals (rol-mo), the five "sensuous gifts (*h*död-yön-lnga), the seven kinds of jewels (rin-po-chhe- "*s*na-*b*dun), the eight glorious symbols, A-dah-na of Dorje-hla-mo-bchu- "trug-mchhog, *r*du-*r*di-ra of various sorts, and many other offerings "of endless variety, which are pleasing to the senses, sufficient to "fill all the celestial regions."

(Then here with melodious voice and hands in proper attitude make the offering up of—

I.—The EIGHT ESSENTIAL OFFERINGS,

The "Essential" offerings.

Nyer-*m*chhod—*vide* page 275—and chant—"All the excellent offer- "ings of every variety that are available in the three "empty regions and others, I arrange with great "reverence, and offer up to all the Jinas (*r*Gyal-was) "with their princes. O! I beg you to take them for the benefit "of the Animal beings. *Om! sarba Tathagatha Arghang-pra- ti- tsa "swa-hah!*

"All the cool Foot-bathing water (zhabs-*g*sel) of every variety that "is available in the three worlds and others, I arrange with great "reverence, and offer up to all the Jinas and their princes. O! I beg "you to take them for the benefit of the Animal beings. *Om! sarba* "*Tathagatha-Padyam-pratitsa swa-hah!*

"All the Flowers (me-tog) of every variety that are available in "the three empty (worlds) and others, I arrange with great reverence, "and offer up to all the Jinas and their princes. O! I beg you to "take them for the benefit of the Animal beings. *Om! sarba Tathagata-* "*Puh-pe-pratitsa swa-hah!*

"All the Incense (*b*dug-*s*pös) of every variety that are availablo "in the three empty (worlds) and others, I arrange with great reverence, "and offer up to all the Jinas and their princes. O! I beg you to "take them for the benefit of the Animal beings. *Om! sarba Tathagata* "*Dhuh-pe pratitsa swa-hah!*

"All the Lamps (*s*nang-*s*sal) of every variety that are available "in the three empty (worlds) and others, I arrange with great reverence, "and offer up to the victors and the princes. O! I beg you to take "tthem for he benefit of the Animal beings. *Om! sarba Tathagata* "*A-lo-ke pratitsa swa-hah!*

"All the Scented water (dri-chhab) of every variety that are "available in the three empty (worlds) and others, I arrange with great "reverence, and offer up to all the victors and the princes. O! I beg "you to take them for the benefit of the Animal beings. *Om! sarba* "*Tathagata Gandhe pratitsa swa-hah!*

"All the holy Food (zhal-za*s*) of every variety that are available "in the three empty (worlds), I arrange with great reverence, and "offer up to all the victors and princes. O! I beg you to take them "for the benefit of the Animal beings. *Om! sarba Tathagate Ne-waide* "*pratitsa swa-hah!*

"All the Music (*s*sil-*s*nyen) of every variety that are available in "the three empty (worlds) and others, I arrange with great reverence, "and offer up to all the victors and the princes. O! I beg you to "take them for the benefit of the Animal beings. *Om! sarba Tathagata* "*shapta pratitsa swa-hah!*"

II.—The OFFERING of the FIVE SENSUOUS EXCELLENT THINGS.

The five Sensuous Excellent Things.

(*h*Död-yön).—"I here offer the best things of every variety "which are most pleasing to the senses in shape "and colours, to the circle of the gods with all "my heart and reverence. O! please receive them "and (in return) I beg you to give me the best and the highest attain-"ment (*i.e.*, Nirvana). *Om! sarba Tathagata Rupa kama guna badsara-* "*pu-dsi-te-ah Hum!*

"I offer the rarest things of all the directions with pleasing voice "and chaste words to the circle of the gods with all heart and reverence. O! I beg you to receive them, and I pray you to confer on "me the best and highest attainment. *Om! sarba Tathagata Shapta "kama guna badsara-pu-dsi-te-ah Hum!*

"I offer you the old grains of sandal wood, spice (*bd*kar), &c., of "the best scent of every variety to the circle of the gods with all heart "and reverence. O! I beg you to receive it, and I pray you to confer "on me the best and highest attainment. *Om! sarba Tathagata Gandhe "karma guna badsara-pu-dsi-te-ah Hum!*

"I offer all the things with moisture and taste, and all the best "tastes suitable to the body and mind, to the circle of the gods with "great respect and reverence. O! I beg you to receive it and I pray "you to confer on me the best and highest attainment. *Om! sarba "Tathagata Nai-we-te-dkar-ma guna badsara-pu-dsi-te-ah Hum!*

"I offer all that is pleasing and soft to the touch, and which makes "the body and the mind happy, with great respect and reverence. O! "I beg you to receive them, and I pray you to confer on me the best "and highest attainment. *Om! sarba Tathagata Parsha kama guna bad-"sara-pu-dsi-te-ah Hum!*"

III.—The OFFERING of the SEVEN PRECIOUS THINGS.

[(Rinchhen *sna-b*dun) NOTE.—"These are to be distinguished "from 'The Seven Banners' (Gyaltshen *sna* dün) which are detailed "in foot-note.[1]]

The Seven Precious Things.

"I offer this precious Wheel to all those that have gone to happi-"ness, *i.e.*, the Buddhas. Let us be stopped from "further rebirths in this world; and let us be able to "turn the wheel of religion. *Om! sarba Tathagata "Chakra ratna pu-dsi-te-ah Hum!*

"I offer this precious *Norbu* jewel to all the Buddhas. O! let us "be separated from hunger and poverty, and let us be possessed of "accomplished wealth. *Om! sarba Tathagata Mani ratna pu-dsi-te-ah Hum!*

---

[1] *The Seven Banners*—"Gyaltshen *sna b*dun"—are:—

1. Kangsang	Rimpochhe or	The precious		House.
2. Gös	"	"	"	Royal Vestments.
3. Hlam	"	"	"	Boot.
4. Langchhen chem	"	"	"	Elephant's tusk.
5. Tsunmo na-ja	"	"	"	Queen's Ear-ring.
6. Gyalpo "	"	"	"	King's "
7. Norbu Rimpochh	"	"	"	Jewel.

"I offer the precious Queen-Wife to all the Buddhas. O! let us "understand the meaning of wisdom, and let us be connected with "means and wisdom. *Om! sarba Tathagata Stīratna pu-dsi-te-ah* "*Hum!*

"I offer the precious Minister to all Buddhas. O! let our thoughts "be firm and good, and let us be acquainted with all the branches of "knowledge. *Om! sarba Tathagata 'Girti' ratna pu-dsi-te-ah Hum!*

"I offer the precious *Elephant* to the Buddhas. O! let us have the "highest and supreme *yana* as our vehicle, and let us become acquainted "with the All-knowing one. *Om! sarba Tathagata Hasti ratna pu-dsi-te-*"*ah Hum!*

"I offer the precious '*best Horse*' to all the Buddhas. Oh! let us "be delivered from the rebirths of this world, and let us be possessed of "miracles, power, and Buddhahood. *Om! sarba Tathagata Ashwa ratna* "*pu-dsi-te-ah Hum!*

"I offer the precious *General* to all the Buddhas. Oh! let us be "separated from the noisy din, and let us attain the most pleasing of "sounds. *Om! sarba Tathagata Khatri-ka ratna pu-dsi-te-ah Hum!*"

IV.—The OFFERING of the EIGHT GLORIOUS SYMBOLS.

The Eight Glorious Symbols.

(*Tashi-ṭa gyé*).—"*Hum!* I offer to The Three supreme Holy "Ones the precious glory of the glorious *golden* "*umbrella* which shines over the heads of the Bud-"dhas according to their signs and accomplishments. "Let the glorious umbrella come over the heads of all the Animal "beings!

"I offer to the Three supreme Holy Ones the glorious *Banner of* "*Victory* (rgyal-mtshan) which shines over the heads of the Buddhas. "Let the Animal beings gain glorious victory over the devils!

"I offer to the Three supreme Holy Ones the glorious *Golden Fish* "which shines in the eyes of Buddhas. Let the glory of the Animal "beings possessed of the five eyes come!

"I offer to the Three supreme Holy Ones the glorious *conch-shell* "which shines over the commands of the Buddhas. Let Animal "beings be possessed of the melodious commands of the glorious "Religion!

"I offer to the Three supreme Holy Ones the glorious *vase* of "treasure which shines over the neck of the Buddhas. Let the Animal "beings be possessed of the undying treasure of the glorious life to "come!

"I offer to the Three supreme Holy Ones the precious *lotus* which "shines over the tongue of the Buddhas. Let the Animal beings be "possessed of glorious knowledge!

"I offer to the Three supreme Holy Ones glorious symbol *Sri-* "'*bi-u*' which shines over the heart of the Buddhas. Let the Animal "beings be possessed of unchangeable piety!

"I offer to the Three supreme Holy Ones the precious glory of "the precious *wheel* which shines over the feet of the Buddhas. Let "the Animal beings obtain the true path to good conduct!"

(Here follows the *Mandala* service already detailed above.)

Divination by Lots.

Lucky and unlucky days and times.

Omens.

The elements of luck and chance are allowed to influence nearly every action of both lāmas and laity. Each hour and day of the week possesses a lucky or unlucky character, and the days of the month according to their order introduce another set of lucky and unlucky combinations. And omens are eagerly watched for and noted.

Divination.

And in addition to the consideration of the foregoing influences it is an almost universal practice to take a special Divination by lot for even ordinary and most trivial affairs. Divination is done by both lāmas and laity. Most laymen as well as lāmas possess small divining manuals called *mô* or "mô-pe," *i.e.*, short for "mô-pecha," or "The *mô* book." These books show the portent attached to the particular number which is elicited and also the initiatory spells. Divination is commonly made by lāmaic cards, by the rosary, by seeds or pebble counters; less commonly by dice, and rarely by sheep's shoulder-blades.

By Cards.

The cards used for divination purposes are small oblong strips of card-board, each representing several degrees of lucky and unlucky portents suitably inscribed and pictorially illustrated, and to each of these is attached a small thread. In consulting this oracle, an invocation to a favourite deity is made, frequently the goddess Dölma, and the packet is held by the left hand on a level with the face, when, with eyes closed, one of the threads is grasped, and its attached card is drawn out, and in accordance with the average of three draws is considered the luck of the proposed undertaking, or the ultimate result of the sickness or the other question of fortune sought for.

Divination by the Rosary. Preliminary spell.

Divination by the Rosary is especially practised by the more illiterate people, and by the Bon priests. The preliminary spell is:—"*gsol! ye-dhar-ma! Om-sha-sha mu-ne-ye-swa-hah! Kra-mu-ne-ye swa-hah! madah-shu-mu-ne ye-swa-hah!*" After having repeated this, breathe upon the Rosary and say "*Namo-Guru!* I bow down before the kind, merciful, and "noble Lāma, the three Holy Ones, the *yidam* (tutelary deity), and "before all the collections of Dakinis, Religion protectors and "Guardians of the Magic Circle, and I beg that you will cause the "truth to descend on this lot. I also beg you, O! Religious Protectors "and Guardians, Brahma, Indra, the ten religious protectors, Nanda "and Takshaka, the Nāga Kings, including the eight great Nāgas, "the sun, the eight planets, the twenty-eight constellations of stars, "the twelve great Chiefs of the Injurers, and the great owners of "the localities, let the true light descend on my lot and let the truth "and reality appear in it."

Manipulation of Rosary.

After having repeated the above, the rosary is taken in the palm and well mixed between the two revolving palms and the hands clapped thrice. Then, closing the eyes, a portion of the rosary is seized between the thumb and finger of each hand, and opening the eyes the intervening beads are counted from each end in threes. And according to the remainder being 1, 2, or 3 in successive countings depends the result. Thus:—

Results.

(1) *If One as a remainder comes after One* as the previous remainder, everything is favourable in life, in friendship, in trade, &c.

(2) *If Two comes after Two* it is bad:—"The cloudless sky will be suddenly darkened and there will be loss of wealth. So Rim-*h*gro must be done repeatedly and the gods must be worshipped, which are the only preventions."

(3) *If Three comes after Three* it is very good:—"Prosperity is at hand in trade and everything."

(4) *If Three comes after One* it is good:—"Rice plants will grow on sandy hills, widows will obtain husbands, and poor men will obtain riches."

(5) *If One comes after Two* it is good:—"Every wish will be fulfilled and riches will be found; if one travels to a dangerous place one will escape every danger."

(6) *If One comes after Three* it is good:—"God's help will always be at hand, therefore worship the gods."

(7) *If Two comes after Three* it is not very good, it is middling:—"Legal proceedings will come."

(8) *If Three comes after Two* it is good:—"Turquoise fountains will spring out and fertilize the grounds, unexpected food will be obtained, and escape is at hand from any danger."

(9) *If Two comes after One* it is bad:—"Contagious disease will come. But if the gods be worshipped and the devils be propitiated, then it will be prevented."

The most ordinary mode of divination is by counters of seeds or pebbles in sets of 15 or 21, which may be used with or without a dice-board. If a dice-board be used, it consists of small squares drawn on paper to the number of 15 or of 21, and each square has got a number within a circle corresponding to a number in the *mô-pe* or divination book. The counters are white and black pebbles or seeds, only one black one to each series. And after the invocation to the special deity and shaking up and mixing all the seeds in the closed palm they are then told out between the forefinger and thumb of the still closed palm on to the squares in the numerical order of the latter, and the number on which the black seed comes out determines by means of the *mô-pe* book the divination result of the particular fortune sought for.

By seeds or pebbles.

The set of fifteen squares is called "Gya-nak-*s*man-chhu," or "The Chinese medicinal water."

In Fifteen.

15	14	13	12	11
6	7	8	9	10
5	4	3	2	1

It consists of a triple series of five squares, with the numbers arranged as in the above sketch. But properly, as its name implies, the seeds should be dropped into a vessel of water and no dice-board is thus needed. This divination is used especially in sickness, hence it is called "medicinal." But the manual most commonly consulted for the prognosis and treatment of sickness is the "Hlamo-*b*rgy*a*d-*r*tsi*s*," or "The Account of the Eight Goddesses." This book gives a fixed prognosis and prescription of remedial worship for each of the 30 days of the month in series of fours. Thus for its reference only the day of the month is needed and no dice or seeds are necessary. Another manual named du*s*-tshod-*r*tsi*s* gives similar information in regard to the particular time of the day of the occurrence in question. These two manuals are, however, considered only "Astrological" books and not "*mo*" or divination manuals.

The set of twenty-one squares is called "The Twenty-one Dölmas," after the twenty-one forms of that obliging goddess.

In Twenty-one.

Image of Dölma.

17	18	19	20	21
16	15	14	13	12
7	8	9	10	11
6	5	4	3	2 / 1

Above the centre of the diagram is a figure of the goddess, who is specially invoked in this divination. The numbers run as in the diagram here given. As a sample of the oracles I give here a few of the divination-results from Dölma's series. If the black seed falls on 1, 2, 8 or 9, the divination is as follows:—

No. 1. *The Jewel.*—If you do not go to sea then you will get the jewel. For merchants' and thieves' adventures it is good. For your own house and soul it is excellent.

But if you are sick it is somewhat bad. For travelling you should first feed people and dogs. You will obtain a son and get temporal power. Your wishes will ultimately be obtained. You have as an enemy a thief.

No. 2. *The Turquoise Spring.*—The dried valley will yield springs and plants will become verdant, and timely rain will fall. The absent will soon return. Do the *d*pang-*b*sto*d* worship of the Enemy God (sgra-lha) and the worship of your special god (*m*chhod lha). It is good for marriage.

No. 8. *The Conch Chaitya.*—In the supreme *Ok-min* heavens it is good for the lower animals. In the three worlds of existence is long life and auspicious time. Your desires will be realized. Life is good. If you are ill, whitewash the Chaitya and worship in the Temple. The enemy is somewhat present. For merchants the time is rather late, but no serious loss will happen. For health it is good.

No. 9. *The Invalid.*—If an actual invalid it is due to the demon of the grand-parents. Agriculture will be bad. Cattle will suffer. To prevent this, offer the "black" cake of the three heads (*g*tor nag *m*gô sum) and do Yang-kuk or "calling for Luck." For your wishes, business, and credit it is a bad outlook. For sickness do "Tse-dub" or "Obtaining Long Life." Mend the road and repaint the "*Mani*" stones. Household things and Life are bad. For these read the "dô-mang" (*vide* page 292), also Du-Kar and Dok. The ancestral devil is to be suppressed by Sri-*g*non. Avoid conflict with the enemy and new schemes and long journeys.

The titles of the other numbers somewhat indicate the nature of their contents, viz.—

3. Golden *Dorje*.
4. Painted vase.
5. Turquoise parrot.
6. Verdant plants.
7. Lady carrying child.
10. White Lion.
11. Golden vase.
12. Turquoise Dragon.
13. Garuda.
14. Tigress.
15. Sun and Moon.
16. Enemy with bow and arrows.
17. Fiendess with red mouth.
18. *h*gong king-devil.
19. Peacock.
20. Glorious white conch.
21. The great king.

In Twenty-eight.

The above are the forms of dice-boards used by the laity and the lower clergy. The more respectable lāmas use a circular disc with twenty-eight divisions in the form of three concentric lotus flowers, each of the petals of the two outer whorls bearing a number which corresponds to a number in the divining manual which is called "Las-bye*d m*thong-ba kun-*l*dan," or "The one who sees all actions." The margin of the disc is surrounded by flames. This more artistic arrangement is shown in PLATE XII. As a sample of this oracle I give here the detail of No. 1 and list of the presiding divinities of the other number.

No. 1, *Bhagawan* (a title of Buddha). "You are of the wise class, "or if not, you will get a wise son. Your god needs to be worshipped "fully, and what you desire will be realized, and you will obtain "long life and freedom from sickness. And if you are a male this "blessing will last for nine years. If you are a female then nine "monks must be engaged to read the nyīṭhi (*vide* page 292), and four "monks must do the *d̆ok-pa*, clapping of hands to drive away the evil "spirits; for in the south is a King Demon who is angry with you "and your heart is disturbed and your temper bad. On this account "do the worship of the King Demon and wear his charm. In your "house children will be unsafe, but they will not die. Your valuable "goods are likely to go, therefore do the worship of *Nor-thub* or 'the "obtaining of wealth.'"

The names of the divinities of the other numbers, which give some indication of the nature of the divination, are:—

2. Cherési.
3. Ugyen Rimbochhe.
4. Dŏlma.
5. Chakna Dorje.
6. Yeshe Norbu.
7. Chandan.
8. Indra.
9. Manjusri.
10. Dorje leg-pa.
11. Sirge Shāshi.
12. Dorje Gyatham.
13. Yuduk Ngonmo.
14. Tongngan Lhamo.
15. Tamchhen Naypo.
16. Lungpa Kyithik.
17. Durpag Nag.
18. Garwa Bishu.
19. Gyacha kua.
20. Nad-*b*dak Remati, God of sickness.
21. Tsunpa.
22. Chhui Lhamo.
23. Tuk-zig-pa.
24. Sipi Kukhor.
25. Damcha Dzema.
26. Dreo Dagyak.
27. Purnang Ukpu.
28. Ngāg-nag.

By Dice.

The Dice used in divination and fortune-telling are of two sorts, viz., (*a*) ordinary ivory or bone dice marked with black dots from 1 to 6 as in European dice, and (*b*) a solitary wooden cube, on each of the six sides of which is carved a letter corresponding to a similar letter in the manual.

Ordinary Ivory dice.

The ordinary ivory dice are used in a set of three with the *Hlamo Mô* or "The Goddess Divination Manual," which provides for results from 3 to 18. These three dice are usually thrown on the book itself from the bare hand after having been shaken up in the closed palm. More luxurious people have a small wooden bowl from which to throw the dice, and a pad on which

Reg No. 375, Bengal.—July 94.—600.

Litho . S. I. O., Calcutta.

to throw them. Such dice with pad and bowl are also used in the gambling games called Shô-pāra.[1]

Wooden dice.

The solitary wooden dice is used for divination by the manual of Manjusri (Jam-*d*pal). It contains on its six sides the six letters, compound or otherwise, of Manjusri's spell, viz.—

A	RA	PA	TSA	NA	ḌI

The wood of this dice should be made of either Manjusri's sacred "bla" tree, or *chandan*, or rose-wood, or if none of these woods are available, then the dice should be made of conch-shell or glass.

In the manual key to this dice the portent of each letter is divided into the following sections, viz.—House, Favours, Life, Medical, Enemy, Visitors, Business, Travel, Lost property, Wealth, Sickness, &c., which cover all the ordinary objects for which the oracle is consulted. As an example I here extract the portents of A:—

"'A' is the best of all for great lāmas and for lay officers, and "what you will perform will have a good result. For low people it "means a little sadness; therefore worship your favourite god.

[1] Another common game of chance is called "The pushing of the Tiger" (*S*tām-küs-bo), and by the Lepchas "The Drawing of the Tiger" (Sathông kü), and by the Pahariahs (*i.e.*, the professing Hindu hillmen) "The handling of the Tiger" (bagh-tsal). It is played by two persons or by two companies on a board of the figure here shown in the margin. Four pieces of charcoal at the four corners represent four tigers, and 19 grains of Indian-corn in rows represent cows or goats. The object of the leader of the tigers is to kill all the cows or goats, while the leader of the cows endeavours to keep the tigers at bay. All the moves are made according to rule.

"*House section.*—All your household will be happy and lucky, and "for a time your house will be safe; but where the cattle dwell, there "a thief and rogue will perhaps come. To avoid this repeat, or get "repeated (by lāmas), 10,000 times the spell (*g*zung) of Arya Marici "Phagpa-hod-zer-chan-ma—(*vide* page 288).

"*Favours section.*—The favours you wish will be got gradually. To "remove the difficulty in the way of getting these repeat, or get repeated, "100,000 times the *g*zung of gra-lnga, and also of Devi lô-gyön-ma "(this latter is *Om! pisha-tsi par-na-sha-wa-ri sarba dsô-la-ta-sha-ma-na-ye "swa-hā!*), and do the *Dug-kar* with its contained *b*zlog-*b*sgyur (clapping "of hands) celebration.

"*Life* (*Srog*).—This is good. But the *g*dön demon from the east "and south came with a blue and black article you got. To clear "away this cloud do, or get done, 100,000 grib-sel and do the Nāga "worship and read, or get read, 1,000 times Sherab-Nyingpo.

"*Medical*—Taking the medicine prescribed for you for a long "time secretly you will recover. Also burn a lamp nightly from "sunset to sunrise as an offering to the gods.

"*Enemy.*—You will not suffer, as your god is strong and will "protect you.

"*Visitors*—probable.—They are coming, or news of their visit will "soon be received.

"*Business.*—If you quickly do business it will be profitable—"delay will be unprofitable.

"*Travel.*—The actual leaving of your house will be difficult, but "if you persevere you will travel safely.

"*Lost property.*—If you go to the north-west you will get the lost "property, or news of it."

The gamble of Rebirth.

A peculiar application of the dice is that for determining the successive regions and grades of one's future rebirths. Fifty-six or more squares of about 2 inches a side are painted side by side in contrasting colours on a large sheet of cloth, thus giving a chequered area like an ordinary draught or chess board. Each of these squares represents a certain phase of existence in one or other of the six regions of rebirth (*vide* page 269), and on it is graphically depicted a figure or scene expressive of the particular state of existence in the world of man, or beast, or god, or in hell, etc. Each square bears in its centre the name of its particular form of existence, and it also contains the names of six other possible states of rebirth from this particular existence, the names of each of these grades of rebirth being preceded by one or other of the following six letters:—A, S, R, G, D, Y, which are also borne on the six faces of the wooden cube which forms the solitary dice for this gamble.

Starting from the world of human existence the dice is thrown, and the letter which turns up determines the region of the next rebirth (*see* the list in next paragraph). Then proceeding from it the dice is again thrown and the turned-up letter indicates the next state of rebirth from this new existence, and so on from square to square *ad infinitum*.

For the lāmaic layman there thus appear only six states of rebirth ordinarily possible, viz.—

A. *s*ngags-lam *h*gro, *i.e.*, the path of the sorcerer.
S. Nyin tshog*s* lam.
R. dud *h*gro or the "bent goer's," *i.e.*, the beasts.
G. Bonpo lok chhö*s*, *i.e.*, a follower of the Bön or pre-lāmaic form of religion in Tibet. It is called Lok chhö*s* or "the reverse religion," because much of their ritual is the reverse of the lāmaic form; thus chaityas are circumambulated in the reverse direction, and prayer-wheels are turned in the reverse way and the "*om mani*" is repeated backward, and the swastika has its ends turned in the reverse fashion.
D. Mutegpa, *i.e.*, as an Indian heretic.
Y. Sridpaī-bar-do—a ghostly state.

The dice accompanying my copy of this board seems to have been loaded so as to show up the letter Y, which gives a ghostly existence, and thus necessitates the performance of many expensive rites to counteract so undesirable a fate.

The grand *coup*.

Extra to the ordinary six states of possible rebirth are the extraordinary states of rebirth to be obtained by the grand *coup* of turning up the *A* five times in succession or the *S* 13 times in succession. The former event means direct rebirth in the paradise of Padma Sambhava and his mythical Buddha *Kuntu zangpo* (Skt. *Samanta bhadra*), while the latter event is rebirth immediately into the grander paradise of the coming Buddha *Champa* (Skt. *Maitreya*).

The Lāmaic Zadkiel.

Every year has its general character for good or evil foretold in the astrological books, but like most oracular utterances, these prophecies are couched in rather ambiguous terms, and as there are four or five versions of these forecasts for each year of the twelve-year cycle in addition to a separate set for each year of the sixty-year cycle, there is thus considerable latitude allowed for accounting for most phenomena. In 1890, during that great visitation of locusts which swarmed over India and into Sikhim as well, the local lāmas were in great glee on finding that the plague of locusts was down in the lāmaic forecast for that year. I examined the old printed books and found that in one of the more common versions of the twelve-year cycle a plague of *chhaga* was foretold for that year, and *chhaga* is a short form of the word for "locust." And it seemed that it could not come out in the forecast oftener than about once in six to twelve years.

Talismans and Amulet-Charms.

Talismans as curative medicine.

Talismans, and especially amulet-charms, are innumerable. There are special sorts for nearly every kind of disease, accident, or misfortune, and the eating of the paper on which a charm has been written is an ordinary form of combatting disease. The letters used in such cases are called *za-zig* or "Eatable letters," and are magic sentences printed or written on paper in what is called the "Fairy" character—an old form of Devanagari. But in other cases merely the washings of the reflection of the writing in a mirror constitutes the physic. Thus to cure the evil eye as shown by symptoms of mind wandering and demented condition—called "*b*yad-*h*grol"—it is ordered as follows:—Write with Chinese ink on a piece of wood the particular letters, and smear the writing over with myrobalams and saffron as varnish, and every 29 days reflect this inscribed wood in a mirror, and during reflection wash the face of the mirror with beer and collect a cupful of such beer and drink it in nine sips.

Amulets.

Every individual has always one or more of these charms, usually folded up into little cloth-covered packets tied around with coloured threads in geometrical pattern and worn around the neck. Others are kept in small metallic cases called "ka-o," fastened to the girdle or sash, and others are affixed overhead in the house or tent to ward off lightning, hail, &c., and for cattle special charms are read and sometimes pasted on the walls of the stalls, &c.

General form of Charm.

Most of these charms against accident, disease, and ill-fortune are in the form shown in Plate XIII, which is called the bLa-ma *d*gongs-*h*dus, or "The Assembly of the Hearts of the Lāmas," as it is believed to contain the essence of the most powerful religious aphorisms. It consists of a series of concentric circles of spells surrounded by flames, amid which in the four corners are the symbols of (*a*) a *dorje* or thunderbolt's sceptre; (*b*) the precious trifid jewel; (*c*) a lotus flower, and (*d*) a flaming dagger with a *dorje* hilt. And in the interior is an eight-petalled lotus-flower, each petal bearing mystic syllables, and in its centre is a circular space of about an inch in diameter, in which is

THE GENERAL CHARM PRINT
ENTITLED "THE ASSEMBLY OF LAMA'S HEARTS".

Reg. No. 444, Fin.—July 94.—500.

Photo., S. I. O., Calcutta

placed the especial mystic charm in the form of one or more letters in the Old Indian character of the 4th or 5th century A.D., inscribed in a cabalistic manner with special materials, as detailed in the Manual on the subject. The translation of the inscribed aphorisms is here given:—

Of the nature of Sympathetic Magic.

In the Outmost Circle.—"Guard the Body, Mind and Speech of this charm-holder! *Rakhya, rakhya, kuruye swaha! Angtadyatha! Om muni muni mahamuniye swaha,*" (Here follows "The Buddhist Creed":—)

"OM! Ye dharmā hetu prabhavā
Hetum teshān Tathāgato
Hyatha data teshān chayo nirodha
Evam vādi Mahā Śramaṅa.[1]"

(Here follows the Dhyāni Buddhas:—) "*Birotsana Om bajra Akshobha Hung, Ratna Sambhava Hri, Bargudhara Hri, Amoga Siddha Ah!*"

In Second Circle.—"Om! nama Samanta Buddhanam, Wama Samanta Dharmanam, nama Samanta Sangghanam. Om Sititabatrai. Om Bimala, Om Shadkara, Om Brahyarigar bajra ustsikhatsa krawarti Sarbayana manta mūla barma hana dhanamhā. Namkilanibā makriayena keni chatkramtamtata sarban rātsin rātsin dakhinda bhinda tsiri tsiri giri giri mada mada hung hung phat phat."

In Third Circle.—"Guard the Body, Mind and Speech of this charm-holder! *Mama* rakya rakhya kuruye swahā. (Here follow the letters of the alphabet:—) Ang, a, ā, i, ī, u, ū, ri, rī, li, lī, e, ai, o, au, ang, a, ka, kh, g, gh, ng, ts, tsh, ds, dsā,-ny, ta, th, d, dā, na, ṭ, ṭh, ḍ, ḍh, ṇ, p, ph, b, bh, m, y, r, l, w, sh, ṣh, s, h, khy!"

In Fourth Circle.—"Hung, Hung," &c.

In Fifth Circle.—"Hri, Hri," &c.

In Sixth Circle.—"*Om! Ā! Hung! Hri! Guru! Deva! Dakkini! Sarbasiddhipala Hung! Ā!*"

[1] This "Buddhist Creed," which is carved on most of the later Buddhist votive images in India, HODGSON translates (J. A. S. No. 40, 1835):—"The cause or causes of all sentient existence in the versatile world the Tathagata has explained. The Great Sramaṇa (*i.e.*, Buddha) hath likewise explained the cause or causes of the cessation of all such existence." This stanza is complete in itself, but a second is occasionally added, namely:—

"Sarba pāpasya akaranam
Kuśalasyopasapradām
Swachittam pariyodapanam
Otan Buddhānuśāsanam,"

which Csoma deKōrōs has translated:—

"No vice is to be committed;
Every virtue must be perfectly practised;
The mind must be brought under entire subjection;
This is the commandment of Buddha."

As most of these specific charms are evidently derived from ancient Indian sources, and are of the nature of Sympathetic Magic, probably dating back to Vedic times, I here give several examples:—

Thus to make the

Charm protective against Bullets and Weapons,

The directions are as these:—With the blood of a wounded man draw the annexed monogram (*D̥°ḁ*) and insert in the vacant space in the centre of the aforesaid print of "The Assembly of the Hearts of the Lāmas." The sheet should then be folded and wrapped in a piece of *red* silk, and, tied with a piece of string, be worn around the neck or an unexposed part of your breast immediately next the skin, and never removed.

Charm against wounds.

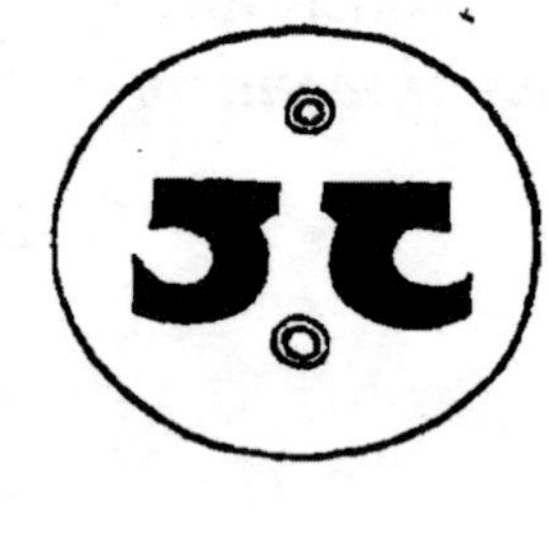

Charm for Leprosy.—On a piece of paper made from the bark of the poisonous laurel write with a mixture of the blood of the individual and the ulcerous discharge and urine of a leper the monogram (? CHCH) and insert into the centre of the print, and fold up and wear around neck.

Charm for Clawing Animals (*i.e.*, Tiger, Cats, Bear).—On a miniature knife write with a mixture of *myrobalams* and musk water the monogram (? ZAH) and tie up in the print, &c. (Here the knife seems to represent the animal's claw.)

For Dog-bite.—With the blood of a leopard write the monogram HRI and insert into the print, and fold up and enclose within a piece of leopard skin and wear around neck. (The leopard preys on dogs.)

For Cholera (or "vomiting, purging, and cramps").—With the dung of a black horse and black sulphur and musk water write the monogram (? ZA) and insert in the print and fold up in a piece of snake's skin and wear. (The dung may represent the purging, the black colour the deadly character, and the snake-skin the virulence of the disease.)

For Small-pox.—With the juice of the Som (? pine) tree write the monogram (? OM), and sprinkle over it some pulverised bone of a man who has died from small-pox, and insert, &c.

For Domestic Bickering.—Write the monogram (? RE) and insert in the print and fold up and bind with a thread made of the mixed hairs of a dog, goat, and sheep, and enclose in a mouse's skin. (This seems to represent union of domestic elements.)

For External Quarrels.—With the blood of a bearded goat write the monogram (? TAṀGI) and insert in print and wrap in a piece of a horse's skin and enclose in an otter's skin.

For Poison.—With blood of a peacock write the monogram (? GRA) with the moustache of a hare and insert in print and fold up with the feathers of the eagle, and enclose in the stomach of a monkey.

For Slander and Scandal.—With earth taken from the travellers' *sarai* (halting place) fire, or if this is not procurable, with some of the menses of a courtesan, write the monogram (? ZOMA) and insert in print and fold up, &c. (Travellers' *sarai* fires and courtesans are regarded as especial places of gossip and scandalmongers respectively.)

To cleanse from Sin of Perjury.—Write the monogram (? SA) and insert in print and fold up with the ear of a hare, the tongue of a hyæna, and the ear of a sow, and wrap in a piece of the robe of an unburied corpse, and wear it below the waist or in the shoe.

For Bad Dreams.—With the tears or with the urine of a person possessed of second-sight write the monogram (ZI) and insert in print and bind up in piece of the wearer's own cloth with one of his own eyelashes, and pass the parcel through the hands of persons of nine different castes.

For Bad Omens.—With blood of an owl write the monogram (? AMRA) and insert in print along with monkey's hair, and bind in a piece of fox's skin.

For Fever.—With cold camphor and musk water write the monogram (? LO) and insert, &c.

For Cold.—With the three hot spices (black pepper, long pepper, and ginger) and water write monogram and insert, &c.

For Lightning and Hail.—With human menstrual blood write the monogram (? GA or CHA) and insert in print and bind in a piece of the skirt of a widow.

For the Nāgas.—On a piece of birch-bark,[1] with a paste of musk and sweet marsh flag and incense, write the monogram (S) and insert in print and bind in a frog's skin and wear. (Note here the use of a water-plant and frog's skin in relation to the deities of water—the Nāgas.)

For the Yakshas.—On a piece of red silk write the monogram (? TI) and insert in print and wrap up with filings of the five precious things and a small dough image of your enemy, and wear (the Yakshas are associated with wealth and also guardianship).

For Seminal Emissions.—With a ruby write the monogram DA and insert in print, and bind it with a blue and red thread spun by a virgin maid and wear round neck.

For Bad Planets.—With the ashes of a cremated human body which had died on an unlucky day (*e.g.*, died on a Sunday or a Saturday) made into paste with water, write the monogram and place on a small sheet of copper which has been perforated in nine spots, and wrap up with a small wooden image of a penis and wear. (The nine perforations

[1] Birch-bark, though not used in Tibet, was used in ancient India and Persia as a writing material. The rituals of the Magi in the most ancient Persian were written on birch-bark. See also Q. Curtius, VIII, 9, § 15, *Ariana Antiqua*, pp. 60, 84; PRINSEP'S *Essays*. *H. Tsiang's Life*, p. 153.

represent the nine planets of Hindu astronomy. The use of this charm is very common in the Tsang province of Tibet, where the wooden image is worn externally.)

For Theft.—With the blood of a thief or a black dog write the monogram (? LI) and insert in print and wrap inside a mouse-skin and tie to a post in the house. (The mouse is a thief, and the charm seems to be on the principle of setting a thief to catch a thief.)

For Foul Smells.—On white silk, with a paste of the six perfumes, write the monogram SAM and insert in print and fold up and bind on crown of head. Then the *Jinas* of the ten directions will assist, and the bad smells will disappear and prove innocuous.

For Fire-side Cooking Smells offensive to House Gods.—With the blood of a hybrid bull-calf write the monogram GAU and insert in the print and fold up in a piece of the skin of a hedge-hog.

GARUDA CHARM AGAINST PLAGUE AND OTHER DISEASES.

Charm against plagues.

This charm consists of a monster figure of the Garuda, The King of Birds, with a snake in its mouth, and each of its outstretched plumes bears a text (PLATE XIV). This charm also contains the "Buddhist Creed." The charm-inscription runs:—

"*Om! Bhrum satrirbad namkhamjamram.*
Om! bisakhrilimili hala swaha!
Om! bisakhrilimilihalayā skachig!
Guard the holder (*i.e.*, the wearer) of this from all the host of diseases, of evil spirits and injuries, including contagious diseases, sore-throat, cough, rheumatism, the black 'rgyughgyel,' *h*brum-bu, and all kinds of plague of the body, speech, and mind!
Ye dharmā hetu prabhavā.
Hetum teshān Tathāgato.
Hyatha-data teshāntsayo nirodha.
Evam vādi Mahā Śramana.

Habatse habatse hum sod.
Suru suru hum sod.
Sukarjuka hum sod.
Sati karur hum sod.
Kularakhyi hum sod.
Merumthuntse hum sod.
Mahakurunhaguru triga gurunam naga shara ramram duldul nagatsita pho naga chunglinga shag thumamnyogs sos.
Guard the holder.
Om! thamitharati sadunte dswaramghaye swaha!"

GARUDA-CHARM
AGAINST PLAGUES & OTHER DISEASES.

Reg. No. 444, Fin.—July 94.—500

Photo., S. I. O., Calcutta.

Fig. 1.

CHARM AGAINST DOG-BITE.

Fig. 2.

CHARM AGAINST EAGLES & BIRDS OF PREY.

Reg. No 376, Fin.—July 94.—500

Photo., S. I. O., Calcutta.

SCORPION-CHARM
AGAINST INJURY BY DEMONS.

1. *Klu or Naga*
2. *Sa-bdak or Bhupati*
3. *Dri-mo fiendess*
4. *Rgyal-po demon*

Reg. No 376, Fin.—July 94.—500

Photo., S I O., Calcutta.

TAMDIN CHARM
AGAINST DISEASE, &c

Another charm for disease is given in PLATE XV, where the fierce demon Tamdin, clad in human and animal skins, bears on his front a disc with concentric circles of spells.

SCORPION CHARM AGAINST INJURY BY DEMONS.

Charm against injury by Demons.

This charm is in the form of a scorpion, whose mouth, tipped by flames, forms the apex of the picture. On its shoulder are seated the especial demons to be protected against—*vide* illustration in PLATE XVI, for details. The inscription runs:—

"*Āyama durur tsa shana zhamaya.*
Hum! Om! Ā! Hung! Ārtsignirtsig!
Namo Bhagawati Hum! Hum! Phat!"

"A guard against all the injuries of '*r*gyalpo,' 'drimo' (a malignant demon specially injuring women), '*b*tsan' (or red demons), 'sa-dag' (or earth-demons), *k*lu (or *nāga*), including '*g*nyan' (a plague-causing subordinate of the *nāga*).

"Against injury by these preserve!"

And the figures are hemmed in by the mystic syllables:—"*Jsa! Hung! Hung! Bam! Hō!*"

CHARM AGAINST DOG-BITE.

Charm against dog-bite.

The huge Tibetan mastiffs are let loose at night as watch-dogs, and roaming about in a ferocious state are a source of much alarm to travellers, who therefore carry the following charm against dog-bite. It consists of a picture of a dog fettered and muzzled by a chain, terminated by the mystic and all-powerful *dorje*. See PLATE XVII, fig. 1. And it contains the following inscribed Sanskrit *mantras* and statements:—"The mouth of the blue[1] dog is bound beforehand! *Om-riti sri-ti swahah! Om-riti sri-ti swahah!*" (and this is again written twice along the body of the dog)

"*Om! badsara ghanana kara kukuratsa sal sal nan marya smugs smugs kukuratsa khaihamtsa le tsa le mun mun sar sar rgyug kha tha mu chhu chhing hchhang ma raya rakkhya rakkhya!* (It is) fixed! fixed!"

CHARM AGAINST EAGLES AND BIRDS OF PREY.

Against Eagles.

Eagles play havoc with the young herds of the pastoral Bhotiyas of the Sikhim uplands and Tibet. For this the people use the charm, *vide* fig. 2 of PLATE XVII, which they tie up near their huts. The central figure is a manacled

[1] *Blue* is the contemptuous colour in which any offensive dog is to be regarded.

bird, representation of the eagle or other bird of prey; and around it is the following text:—

"A guard against all injuries of the covetous, sky-soaring Monarch Bird. (It is) fixed! fixed! *Om smege smege bhumbhum ngu!*"

CHARM FOR KILLING ONE'S ENEMY.

The full details are here translated:—

"*Om!* Salutation to the revered Manjusri!"

Charm for killing one's Enemy.

The necessary materials for the killing of one's enemy are the following:—

1. An axe with three heads, the right of which is bull-headed, the left snake-headed, and the middle one pig-headed.
2. On the middle head a lamp is to be kept.
3. In the pig's mouth an image of a human being made of wheaten flour (a *linga*). The upper part of the body is black and the lower part red. On the side of the upper part of the body draw the figure of the eight great planets, and on the lower part of the body the twenty-eight constellations of stars. Write also the eight parkha, the nine mewa, the claws of the Garuda in the hands, the wing of the eagles and the snake tail.
4. Hang a bow and an arrow on the left and load him with provisions on the back. Hang an owl's feather on right and a rook's feather on left; stick a piece of the poison tree on the upper part of the body, and surround him with red swords on all sides. Then a red Rgyangbu wood on the right, a yellow one on the left, a black one in the middle, and many blue ones on several places.
5. Then sitting in quiet meditation recite the following:—

"*Hung!* This axe with a bull's head on the right will repel all the "injuries of the *s*ngagpas and Bonpos—sorcerers; the snake on the left "will repel all the classes of plagues; the pig head in the middle will "repel the *sa-dag* and other earth-demons; the *linga* image in the mouth "will repel all the evil spirits without remainder, and the lamp on the "head will repel the evil spirits of the upper regions. O! the axe will "pierce the heart of the angry enemy and also of the hosts of evil "spirits!!!

"*Hung!* The axe having its upper body black will repel the "hosts of *b*düd demons; the lower part of the body which is red will "repel the mamos, she-fiends, and diseases; the eagle-winged part of "the body will repel the eight classes of demons; the snake-tailed body "will repel the sa-dag, nāga and the *g*nyan demons; the Guruda-clawed "hands will repel the hosts of she-demons; the arrow on the right will "repel all the inauspicious cases, and the bow in the left will repel all "the hosts of the The-u-brang demon. O! the axe will cleave the "angry enemy and all the hosts of the injuring demons!!!

"*Hung!* the red nam-kha on the right will repel all the hosts of "*b*tsan; the yellow one on the left will repel the injuries of the "*H*byungpo demons; the *m*dah on the right will repel the injuries "of the *b*düd demons; the khram-shing on the back will repel the "injuries of mamo she-demons, and the *H*phang on the left the *b*düd "she-demons. O! the axe will cleave the angry enemy and all the "hosts of the injuring demons!!!

"*Hung!* the owl's feather on the right will repel the eighty unlucky "signs; the rook's feather on the left will repel the drowning misery; "the stick on the waist will repel the former enemies; the surroundings "of swords will overcome the future enemies, and the provisions on "the back will expel all desires and lusts.

"*Hung!* O! the axe adorned with the figures of the eight planets "will repel the *G*zah-*b*dud, the planet demon, and the twenty-eight "constellations of stars will repel the injuries of the bad stars.

"*Hung!* the axe with the nine mewa repel as follows:—(1) The "white mewa repel the The-u-brang demon; (2) the black one repel "the Ro-*h*dod demon; (3) the indigo-coloured one repel the blackest "misery; (4) the green repel the Nāgas and the evil spirits; (5) the "yellow repel the *r*gyal-po; (6) the white repel the Gongpo; (7) "the red repel the Yugdor; (8) the red repel the Gyang-gral, and (9) "the white repel the Hlag-chhad demon. O! the axe will smash the "enemies and the hosts of injuring and eating demons.

"*Hung!* Kye! Kye! the eight parkha which surround the axe "repel in this way:—The Li-*d*mar riding on a fowl will repel the "injuries of mamo she demons, the khön-*l*chag*s* riding on a *s*dig-*s*brul "snake will repel the sa-*b*dag, Nāga and *g*Nyan; the Da-*d*kar riding "on a fowl will repel the injuries of swords and other cutting tools; "the khen-*r*gan riding on a dragon will repel the hosts of *r*Gyalpos; "the kham-nag riding on a crocodile will repel the hosts of nāga; the "Gyan-ri-riding on a bull will repel the injuries of *s*Ngag*s*pa sorcerers; "the zin-shing riding on an ass will repel the hosts of evil spirits, and "the zon-*r*lung riding on a mule will repel all the demons of the "cemetery. O! the axe will smash the enemies and the hosts of the "injuring and eating demons.

"*Hung!* oh! you tiger and vulture-headed of the shing-kham*s* "(tree-region)[1]! I beg you to repel the enemies.

"O! you snake and horse-headed of the southern me-kham*s* (fire- "regions)! I beg you to repel the enemies

"O! you bird and monkey-headed of the western *l*chag*s*-kham*s* "(iron-region)! I beg you to repel the enemies.

[1] This is a reference to "the elements."

"O! you pig and rat-headed of the northern sa-khams (earth-"region)! I beg you to repel the enemies.

"O! you four gshed with the heads of bull, sheep, dog, and "dragon! I beg you to repel the enemies.

"O! Axe! cleave the heads of the enemies and all the hosts of "the injuring evil spirits.

"This most powerful axe will split the hardest caves, dry up the "mightiest oceans, break down the tallest trees, flatten the powerful "iron, knock down the strongest man, kill the biggest cattle, and "destroy all the most gigantic evil spirits. Now, overtake the injur-"ing evil spirits and the enemies.

"This all-powerful axe will bring everything to complete exter-"mination and defeat whoever challenges. Now, go on to them, "destroying whatsoever comes in your way!

"May you cause this dispenser of gifts to be separated from lust; "may you not break the true commands of the '*s*ngag*s*-*h*chhang,' "or the mantra-holder, and the holy orders of the three Holy Ones. "Separate all injuries of enemies from the dispenser of gifts. Let my "(yoga or *r*nal-*h*byorpa) desires be fulfilled. Pray carry out all the "works that are here entrusted to you.

"O! you three-headed one with a black body! now promise that "you will comply with the orders.

"Upset all the bad dreams and unlucky signs;
" ,, ,, 80,000 kinds of evil spirits;
" ,, ,, 424 ,, bad deeds;
" ,, ,, 720 ,, diseases;
" ,, ,, 360 ,, mind-distractions;
" ,, ,, 8 ,, untimely deaths.

"Let glory come! *Tashi-shok!*
"*Sarba-mangalam!*"

Other contrivances for the same.

During the Sikhim expedition of 1888, near Mt. Paul on the Tukola ridge, where the final attack of the Tibetans was made, there was found one of the mystic contrivances for the destruction of the enemy. It consisted of an obliquely carved piece of wood, about 14 inches long, like a miniature screw-propeller of a steamer, and acted like the tan of a wind-mill. It was admittedly a charm for the destruction of the enemy. And on it was written a long, unintelligible Bon *Mantra* of the kind called *zhang-zhung*, followed by a call for the assistance of the fierce deities Tam-din, Vajra-pani and the Garuda, and concluding with "*phut! phat*"—Break! Destroy! It may also be mentioned here that the bodies of all the Tibetans slain in these encounters were found to have one or more charms against wounds, most of them being quite new, and some of the more elaborate ones, which contained in their centre figures of the weapons charmed against, viz., swords, muskets, &c., had cost their wearers as much as twenty-five rupees apiece.

And for torturing one's enemy short of death there is the same popular practice as obtains amongst occidentals, namely, of making a little clay image of the enemy and thrusting pins into it.

The "Prayer-flags."

The Luck-flags.

The most extensively used of all the so-called "prayer-flags," or *Dā-cho*,[1] is that for Luck, and called *Lung-ta*,[2] literally "*the airy horse*," which, Pegasus-like, is supposed to carry the luck of the individual through the air in every direction wished for. This practice has something in common with the ancient Hindu rite of "The raising of Indra's Banner" (*Dhwaja*),[3] and it seems to be like "the prayer-wheel," a mystic perversion of one of the earlier symbols of Buddhist mythology. In the Buddhist scriptures there constantly occurs the metaphor of "turning the Wheel of the Law" with reference to Buddha's preaching, and this figure of speech seems to have suggested to the lāmas, who are ever ready to symbolise trifles realistically, their materialistic invention of the prayer-wheel, whereby every individual may "turn the Wheel of the Law" conveniently. In like manner the "Airy Horse of Luck" seems to me to have its origin in the Jewel-Horse of the Universal Monarch, such as Buddha was to have been had he cared for worldly grandeur. The Jewel-Horse carries its rider, Pegasus-like, through the air in whatever direction wished for, and thus it seems to have become associated with the idea of realization of material wishes, and especially wealth and jewels. This horse also forms the *Vahan* or throne-support of the mythical Dhyani Buddha named *Ratna Sambhava*, or "the *Jewel*-born One," who is often represented symbolically by a jewel. And as evidence of this identity we find in many of the *Lung-ta* flags that the picture of a jewel takes the place of the horse which is not figured. It is also notable that the mythic people of the northern continent, over whom presides Kuvera, or Vaisravana, the God of *Wealth*, are "horse-faced." The flags are printed ont he unglazed tough country paper, and are obtainable on purchase from the lāmas, but no lāma is necessarily needed for the actual planting of the flag and its attendant rites. When the *Lung-ta*-flag is expended it is said to be *dar-ba*.

Origin of Luck-flag.

[1] Dar-*l*chog. | [2] *r*Lung-*r*ta.

[3] And the votive pillars of the earlier Buddhists offered for railings to stupas were called *Dhwája*.

These flags are of four sorts, viz.—

I. The *Lung-ta* proper (*vide* PLATE XVIII[1]), which is of almost square form, about 4 to 6 inches long, and contains in the centre the figure of a horse with the mystic jewel *Norbu* on its back. It is hung upon the ridges of the houses and in the vicinity of dwellings. The printed contents of this sort of flag vary somewhat in the order in which the deified lāmas are addressed, some giving the first place to Guru-Rinpochhe, while others give it to Manjusri, but all have the same general form, with the horse bearing the Norbu jewel in the centre and in the four corners the names of the tiger, lion, garuda, and dragon. A translation of one of these is here given:—

Lung-ta.

TIGER. LION.

"Hail! *Wagishwari mum!* (*i.e.*, yellow Manjusri's spell).
Hail! to the jewel in the lotus! Hung! (*i.e.*, Avalokita's spell).
Hail! to the holder of the Dorje (or thunderbolt)! Hung! (*i.e.*, Vajrapani's spell).
Hail! to Vajra-satwa (The Diamond Souled one!)
Hail! *Amarahnihdsiwantiye swahâh.*
(The above is in Sanskrit. Here follows in Tibetan.)
Here! Let the above entire collection (of deities whose spells have been given) prosper . . . . . . (here is inserted the year of birth of the individual), and also prosper—
the *Body* (*i.e.*, to save from sickness),
the *Speech* (*i.e.*, to give victory in disputations),
and the *Mind* (*i.e.*, to obtain all desires);
of this year holder (above specified)
and may Buddha's doctrine prosper!"

GARUDA. DRAGON.

It is to be noted that herein are invoked through their spells the Rigs-*g*sum *m*gönpo or the three great spiritual protectors (*defensores fidei*) of lāmaism, viz.—

The Defensores Fidei of Lāmaism.

1. *Manjusri*, who conveys wisdom.
2. *Avalokita*, who saves from hell and all fears.
3. *Vajrapani*, who saves from accident and all bodily injuries,

and in addition to the above are given the spells of—

4. *Vajra Satwa*, who purifies the soul from sin; and
5. *Amitayus*, who confers long life.

[1] SCHLAGINTWEIT's figure, in addition to being printed in reversed fashion, is so mutilated and indistinct that I give another illustration.

THE PEGASUS-HORSE OF LUCK

THE LUNG-TA FLAG.

Reg. No 376, Fin.—July 94.—500

Photo., S. I. O., Calcutta.

PLATE XIX.

Reg. No. 376. Fin.—July 94.—500

Photo., S. I. O., Calcutta.

II. The second form is called *chö-pén.*[1] It is of a long, narrow, oblong shape, about 8 to 10 inches in length. This sort of *lung-ta* is for tying to twigs of trees or to bridges, or to sticks for planting on the tops of hills. Its text has generally the same arrangement as form No. I, but it wants the horse-picture in the centre. Its Tibetan portion usually closes with "May the entire collection (of the foregoing deities) prosper the power, airy horse, age and life of this pear holder, and make them increase like the growing new moon."

The *ché-pön.*

Very poor people, who cannot afford the expense of the printed charms, merely write on a short slip of paper the name of the birth-year of the individual, and add "May his *lung-ta* prosper."

One Lung-ta for each member of a household must be planted on the 3rd day of every month (lunar) on the top of any hill near at hand, or on the branch of a tree near a spring, or tied to the sides of a bridge; and on affixing the flag a stick of incense is burned. And a small quantity of flour, grain, flesh, and beer are offered to the earth-demon (sa-dag) of the hill-top by sprinkling them around, saying "*So! So!* Take! Take!"

III. A more expanded form of the Luck-flag is the *Gyal-tsén dse-mo* or "Victorious banner," which is generally of the same form as No. 1, but containing a much larger amount of holy texts, and also usually the eight glorious symbols of which the lotus forms the base of the print. It prospers not only Luck in wealth, but also the Life, Body and Power of the individual.

IV. THE VAST LUCK-CHARM (PLATE XIX).—This fourth form of Lung-ta is named "*g*lang-po stob *r*gyas," or "That which makes vast, like the Elephant."[2] It is pasted to the walls of the houses, or folded up and worn around the neck as a charm for good luck. It consists of a cross Dorje in the centre with a Garuda and a Peacock, the jewelled Elephant and the jewelled Horse, each bearing an eight-leaved lotus disc on which are inscribed the following Sanskrit and Tibetan texts. The other symbols are "the eight glorious Symbols,"[1] already described, *vide* page 329; viz., the umbrella, golden fish, vase of treasure, lotus flower, conch shell, banner of victory, wheel, and the sri "*beu*" or cabalistic figure of an intertwined coil of rope.

The Vast Luck-flag.

And around the margin is "the Buddhist creed" repeated several times, also the letters of the alphabet, together with the words "May "the life, body, power and the 'airy horse' of the holder of this "charm prosper his body, speech, and wishes, and cause them to

[1] Chod-pan or *s*byod-pan.

[2] *b*kra shi-*r*tag*s*-*b*rgyad.

"increase like the growing new moon; may he be possessed of all "wealth and riches, and be guarded against all kinds of injury."

In the upper left-hand disc:—"May the *life* of this charm-"holder be raised sublimely (like the flight of the garuda here re-"presented). *Om! sal sal hobana sal sal ye swahā! Om! Om! sarba* "*kata kata sata kata sala ya nata sah wa ye swaha! Om! kili kili mili mili* "*kuru kuru huna huna ye swaha!* O! May the life of this charm-"holder be raised on high!"

In the upper right-hand disc:—"May the *body* of this charm-"holder be raised sublimely (like the flight of the peacock here re-"presented). *Om! yer yer hobana yer yer ye swaha! Om! sarba* "*Tathagata bhiri bhiri bata bata miri miri mili mili ae bata sarba gata-*"*gata shramana sarba gata-gata shramana sarba!* O! May the body "of this charm-holder be raised on high."

In lower left-hand disc:—"May the power of this charm-"holder be raised sublimely (like the precious elephant here repre-"sented). *Om! Mer mer hobana mer mer ye swaha! Om sarba dhara* "*dhara bara dhara ghi kha ye swaha! Sarba kili kili na hah kang* "*li sarba bhara bhara sambhara sambhara!* O! May the power and "wealth of this charm-holder be increased and all the injuries be "guarded against."

In lower right-hand circle:—"May the 'Airy Horse' of this "charm-holder be raised sublimely (with the celerity of 'the precious "horse' here represented). *Om! lam lam hobana lam lam lam swaha!* "*Om! Sarba kara kara phat! Sarbha dhuru dhuru na phat! Sarba* "*kata kata kata na phat! Sarba kili kili na phat! Sarbha mala mala* "*swaha!* O! May the 'Airy Horse' of the charm-holder be raised "on high and guarded against all injury."

In the central disc over the junction of the cross *Dorje* is written:— "*Om! neh ya rani jiwenti ye swaha!* O! May this charm-holder be "given the undying gift of soul everlasting (as the adamantine cross "Dorje herein pictured)."

The Worship for the Planting of the Luck-Flags.

Worship for Luck-Flag.

There is a regular form of lāmaic worship for the planting of the Luck-flags. And it is advised to be done whenever one feels unhappy and down in luck through injury by the earth-demons, &c. It is called "The great statue of Lungta," and is as follows:—

First of all make a *mandala* offering of Ri-rab (Mt. Meru), consisting of three series on a cushion with a sky canopy (namkha) of a yellow colour, above a blue one towards the east, a red one towards the south, a white one towards the west, and a black one towards the north. The canopies are to be fixed in the ends of a perfect square set in the four directions, around which are the twelve-year cycle, the nine *g*torma-cakes (*b*shös) representing the nine Mewas, eight lamps representing the eight parkha, eight planets, twenty-eight constellations of stars, five *g*tormas, five glüd (small balls of wheaten flour offered to demons as ransom), five arrows with silk streamers (*m*dah-dar) of the five different colours, and many more *m*dah *r*gyang-bu and *h*phang. The above must be arranged by a practical man, and then the ceremony begins with the fingers in the proper attitude of the twelve cycle of years, and recitation of the following in a raised and melodious voice:—

"*Kye! Kye!* In the eastern horizon from where the sun rises, "there is a region of tigers, hares, and trees. The enemy of the "trees is the Iron which is to be found in the western horizon, and "where the enemy, the life-cutting *b*düd demon, is also to be "found. In that place are the demons who injure the life, body, "power and the 'Airy Horse.' The devil *b*düd who commands them "also lives in the occidental region: he is a white man with the heads "of a bird and a monkey, and holds a white hawk on the right "and a black demon-rod on the left. O! Bird and monkey-headed "demon! Accept this ransom and call back all the injuring demons.

"*Kye! Kye!* In the southern horizon there is a region of horses, "snakes and fire. The enemy of the fire is the water, which is to "be found in the northern horizon and where the enemy, the life-"cutting *b*düd, is also to be found. In that place are the demons who "injure the life, body, power and the airy horse. The *b*düd who "commands them also lives in the northern region; he is a blue man "with the heads of a rat and a pig, holding water-snare on his right "and a demon-king on his left. O! Rat and pig-headed demon! "Accept this ransom and call back all the injuring demons.

"*Kye! Kye!* In the occidental horizon there is a region of "birds, monkeys and Iron. The enemy of the Iron is the fire which "is to be found in the eastern horizon, where also is the enemy, the "life-cutting *b*düd. In that place are the demons who injure the life, "body, power and the airy horse. The *b*düd who commands them "also lives in the occidental region; he is a green man with the "heads of a tiger and a vulture, holding a purse of disease on his "right and left. O! Tiger and vulture-headed demon! Accept this "ransom and call back all the injuring demons.

"*Kye! Kye!* In the northern horizon there is a region of "pigs, rats and water. The enemy of the water is fire which is to be "found in the southern horizon, where is the enemy, the life-"cutting *b*düd. In that place are the demons who injure the life, "body, power and the airy horse. The *b*düd who commands them "lives in the northern region; he is a yellow man with heads of solid "gold, holding a yellow tapestry (ba-den) on his right and a demon's "rope on his left. O! Golden-headed demon! Accept this ransom "and call back all the injuring demons.

"*Kye! Kye!* In the boundary of the south-eastern horizon there "is a yellow dragon-headed man; he is the injuring demon, to whom "I offer this ransom. O! Dragon-headed demon! Accept this ransom "and call back all the injuring demons.

"*Kye! Kye!* In the boundary of the south-western horizon "there is a yellow sheep-headed woman; she is the injuring de-"moness to whom I offer this ransom. O! Sheep-headed demon! "Accept this ransom and call back all the injuring demons.

"*Kye! Kye!* In the boundary of the north-western horizon "there is a yellow dog-headed man; he is the injuring demon to "whom I offer this ransom. O! Dog-headed demon! Accept this "ransom and call back all the injuring demons.

"*Kye! Kye!* In the boundary of the north-eastern horizon there "is a yellow bull-headed woman; she is the injuring demoness to "whom I offer this ransom. O! Bull-headed demoness! Accept "this ransom and call back all the injuring demons!

"O! Upset all the injuring evil spirits!
"O! ,, ,, disagreeable demons!
"O! ,, ,, demons who injure the life, body, power and the airy horse!
"O! ,, ,, wandering demons!
"O! ,, ,, ill-luck of bad 'airy-horses'!
"O! ,, ,, bad and frightful goblins!
"O! ,, ,, unfavourable circumstances!
"O! ,, ,, openings of the sky!
"O! ,, ,, ,, ,, earth!
"O! ,, ,, injuries of bad demons!

"O! May we be separated from all kinds of injuries and be "favoured with the real gift, which we earnestly seek!"

"'May virtue increase!' '*Ge-leg-phel!*'
"'Glory!' '*Tashi!*' '*Swaha!*'"

The magic of lāmaist Astrology is detailed in the following chapter on Demonolatry, as it is always associated with the prescription of demon worship.

VI.—DEMONOLATRY.

Like most mountaineers, the Sikhimites and Tibetans are thorough-going demon-worshippers. In every nook, path, big tree, rock, spring, waterfall, and lake there lurks a devil; hence there are few persons who will venture out alone after dark. The sky, the ground, the house, the field, the country, have each their special demons, and sickness is always due to malign demoniacal influence.

Personal demons.

The body also of each individual is beset by a burden of spirits namod the "*h*go-wa-lha," or "the personal chief gods," who are in a sense the guardians of his body. These are not only worshipped by the laity, but the lāmas regularly invoke them in their oblations in the "Ser-khyem" and "Né-sal" worship. These personal gods, some of which are of an ancestral nature, are five in number, viz.—

1. *The Male Ancestral god* (Phô-lha). This god sits under the armpits. Worship of him procures long life and preservation from harm.

2. *The Mother-god* (mo-lha) or maternal uncle god (*zhang-lha*). It is said to obtain the latter synonym on account of the custom by which a child, shortly after birth, is taken to the mother's house, which usually is "the uncle's house." I doubt, however, this being the true maternal interpretation.[1] The worship of this god secures strength.

3. *The Life god* (Srog-lha), which resides over the heart Instead of this god is frequently enumerated the *Nor-lha*. who sits in the left armpit and whose worship brings wealth.

[1] Zhang-lha is usually interpreted "maternal uncle god," but it may also mean "uterine god."

4. *The Birthplace god* (Yul-lha, literally "country-god"), which resides on the crown of the head, and whose worship secures dominion and fame.

5. *The Enemy god* (*d*gra-lha), pronounced vulgarly "*dab-lha*," which sits on the right shoulder. In this connection it is notable that no one willingly will allow any object to rest on his right shoulder, for the reason that it injures the "*dab-lha*," and no friend will familiarly lay his hand on his friend's right shoulder for the same reason.

The "dá-lha" or enemy god.

This latter god, who is figured in "the Wheel of Life," *vide* page 266, is especially worshipped by soldiers, as he defends against the enemy. But he is also worshipped by all the laity once at least during the year for overcoming their individual enemies. Usually the whole village in concert celebrates this worship: the men carrying swords and shields, and they dance and leap about, concluding with a great shout of victory.[1]

In addition to these so-called "personal gods" proper are the good and bad spirits already mentioned, in connection with "the Wheel of Life," who sit on the individual's shoulders and prompt him to good and evil deeds respectively, and leave him only on his arrival before the Great Judge of the dead. These are practically identical with the good and evil genius of the Romans—the *Genium Album et Nigrum* of Horace.[2]

Those demons which are worshipped when the individual is happy and in health are called "the pleasing spirits;" but they also may be worshipped in sickness or other affliction. Each class of spirits or "gods" has a particular season for worship. Thus:—

Worship according to Season.

The Earth gods (sa-gzhi mi-rig-gi-*lha*) are worshipped in the spring.

The Ancestral gods (*s*mra zhang chhung-gi-lha) are worshipped in the summer season.

The "Three Upper Gods" (*s*tod-sum paū-lha) in the autumn.

[1] The story of his acquiring from the *sea* the banner of victory is suggestive of Indra's victorious banner, also procured from the sea.—*Brihat Sanhita*, translated by Dr. Kern, *J. Roy. As. Socy.* (new series), VI, page 44.

[2] *Horat.* 2. *Epist.*

The Royal Ancestor of the Sikhim King—the divine *Minyak King* (*s*tong mi-nyag-gi-lha) in the winter.[1]

Country gods.

"The Country gods" or *Yul-lha* of Sikhim are, like the analogous Penates of the Romans, innumerable, but the chief two are the mountain-god Kang-chhen-dsö-nga (*Ang.* Kanchinjingna), who is of a mild, inactive disposition, and styled a "Protector of religion," and his subordinate Yab-*b*dud, or "the Black Father Devil." This latter is of an actively malignant disposition, and rides on the south wind. His especial shrine is in the Tista valley near Sivok, where he is worshipped with bloody sacrifice. His respectful name as given by Lhatsün Chhembo, who composed for both him and Kang-chhen-dsö-nga special manuals of service, is "ma-*m*gon *l*cham-bras." And for him is prescribed actual sacrifice of life: a black ox is to be killed, and the entrails, brain, heart, &c., of it are ordered to be set upon the skinned hide, while the flesh is consumed by the votaries. For very poor people the sacrifice of a cock, as with the ancient Greeks to the destructive Nox and his counterpart Erebus, is considered sufficient.[2] The offering of the sacrifice is in the nature of a bargain, and is indeed actually termed such, viz. "ngo-len," the demon being asked to accept the offering of flesh, &c., and in return for this gift not to trouble the donors.

The "Black Father Devil."

The mountain-god Kang-chhen-dsö-nga.

In Kang-chhen-dsö-nga's worship also flesh meat needs to be given. And although the flesh of cows and other cattle is now offered on such occasions, there is a tradition that formerly human flesh was offered. And the most acceptable flesh was the human flesh of "the infidel destroyers of the religion." Kang-chhen-dsö-nga was never the tutor of Sakya Muni, as has been alleged—he is only a *zhi-dak* demon. Kang-chhen-dsö-nga's personality has already been referred to.[3] One of his titles is "Head Tiger," as each of the five peaks is believed to be crowned by an animal—the highest peak by a tiger, and the other peaks by a lion, elephant, horse, and a *garuda*—a bird like the fabled "roc."[4]

In every village there is a recognized *zhi-dak*,[5] or "Foundation-owner demon," who is ordinarily either a "black devil" (*b*dud), a

[1] The Sikhim King is descended from the Mi-nyak dynasty of Kham in Eastern Tibet—a dynasty which once held sway over Western China, and regarded as semi-divine by the Tibetans. It is said to have been founded by a son of Thi-srong-de-tsan, the Tibetan King who was associated with Padma-Sambhava in the foundation of Lāmaism.

[2] Most Sikhimites before sowing a field sacrifice a cock to the demons.

[3] *Vide* page 263.

[4] *Vide* also page 342.

[5] *g*zhi-*b*dag, literally "foundation-owner."

red devil (tsan) or a Nāga (*k*lu), or some other form as detailed below.[1]

Local gods.

The *red* demons.

The *zhi-dak* demons of the monasteries and temples are always *tsén* (tsan) or red demons, who usually are the spirits of deceased novices or ill-natured lāmas. And they are especially worshipped with bloody sacrifice and *red* coloured substances:—

"Rowan tree and *red* threid.
Gars the witches tyne their speid."

The Pemiongchi *tsén* is named *Da-wa senge* (zla-ba sengze) or "the Moon Lion." The Yangong Gompa *tsén* is named *Lha tsen-pa* or "the Tsén god." The Darjeeling *tsén* is named *Chho-leg nam-gyal* or "the Victorious good religion." The shrine of this latter is on Observatory Hill, and it is worshipped under the name of Mahākala by the professing Hindu hillmen with the same bloody rites as the Bhotiyas and Lepchas. For the worship of each of the Monastery or Temple *tséns* there exist special manuals of ritual.

The owner-demons of ridges and passes.

It is to the *zhi-dak* that travellers offer a rag torn from their clothes and tied to a stick on gaining the summit of a hill or pass. While planting this offering on the cairn, which is called "*lap-che*," the traveller in a meek voice calls the demon by uttering the mystic "*kī-ki ! kī-kī !*," then he adds "*sô-sô ! sô-sô !*" which means presentation or "offering."[2] Then he exclaims in a loud triumphant strain "*Lhā-gyal-ō ! Lhā-gyal-ō !*" "God has won! God has won!"

Soothsaying and Necromancy.

Exorcising of devils in cases of sickness and misfortune is done by the regular devil-dancers—"Pā-wo" and "Nyén-jorma," and oracular deliverances are most extensively made by the professional *lha-pa*, of whom

[1] If a man's sins are insufficient to procure rebirth even in the hells, he is reborn as a zhi-dak—say the Sikhim Lāmas. The zhi-dak may be one or other of the eight classes, viz.—

(1) "lha" or "spirits" (all male) of a white colour and a fairly good disposition; but they must suffer many indignities in order to procure a higher rebirth.
(2) "*k*lu," or Nāgas, mostly green in colour and frequenting lakes or springs.
(3) *g*nad-*s*byan, or "disease-givers," are also red in colour.
(4) *b*dud (or black devils). All are male and are extremely wicked. They are the spirits of those who opposed in life the true religion. They eat flesh and are not to be appeased without a pig—the most luscious morsel to a hillman's palate. Their wives are called *b*dud-mo.
(5) "tsan," or red demons (all male). They are usually the spirits of deceased novices, and are therefore especially associated with Gompas.
(6) "*r*gyal-po," or "Victors," are white in colour, and are spirits of kings and deceased lāmas who fail to reach Nirvana.
(7) "ma-mo" are all female, and black in colour. It includes *Mak-sor rgyal ma*, called also *Mahārāni*, or "the Great Queen," the disease-producing form of the Hindu Durgá.
(8) "*gzah*" or "planets"—Rahula, &c.

[2] This exclamation *gsol-gsol* may also mean "worship" or "entreaty."

I have not space to speak here. I can only give here a few of the more conspicuous instances of orthodox lāmaic devil-worship.

The Lāmas and devil-worship.

The portending machinations of most of the devils are only to be foreseen, discerned, and counteracted by the lāmas, who especially lay themselves out for this sort of work and provide certain remedies for the pacification or coercion of the demons of the air, the earth, the locality, house, the death-demon, &c.

Lāmas are the prescribers of the devil-worship.

Indeed, the lāmas are the prescribers of most of the demon-worship, and derive their chief means of livelihood from their conduct of this demon-worship, rendered on account of, and at the expense of, the laity, who offer it on the especial recommendation of the lāmas themselves. A few of the most intelligent of the lāmas become *Tsi-pa*[1] lāmas or astrologers. And all the laity have been led to understand that it is absolutely necessary for each individual to have recourse to the *Tsi-pa* lāma on each of the three great epochs of life, viz., birth, marriage, and death; and also at the beginning of each year to have a forecast of the year's ill-fortune and its remedies drawn out for them.[2] The astrologer-lāmas therefore have a constant stream of persons flocking to them for prescriptions as to what deities and demons require appeasing and the remedies necessary to neutralize these portending evils.

The prescriptions are based on Chinese astrology.

The nature of these prescriptions of worship will best be illustrated by a concrete example. But to render this intelligible it is necessary to refer, first of all, to the chronological nomenclature current in Sikhim and Tibet.

Nomenclature of the Chinese system of chronology.

The Tibetan system of reckoning time is by the twelve-year and sixty-year cycles of Jupiter. The twelve-year cycle is used for short periods, and the particular year, as in the Chinese style, bears the name of one or other of the following twelve animals:—

1. Mouse.	5. Dragon.	9. Monkey.
2. Ox.	6. Serpent.	10. Bird.
3. Tiger.	7. Horse.	11. Dog.
4. Hare.	8. Sheep.	12. Hog.

And in the case of the sixty-year cycle these animals are combined with the five elements, viz.—1. Wood (*shing*), 2. Fire (*me*), 3. Earth (*sa*), 4. Iron (*chak*), and 5. Water (*chhu*); and each element is given

[1] *r*tsis-pa—the *Chebu* of *Hooker's Himalayan Jours.*

[2] The horoscope for birth is named *s*kye*s*-rtsis, that for the whole life is tshe-rabs la*s* *r*tsis. The annual horoscope is *s*kag-rtsis, that for marriage is pag-*r*tsi*s*, and for death *g*shin-*r*tsi*s*.

a pair of animals, the first being considered a male and the second a female. I append as a footnote[1] a detailed list of the years of the current cycle as an illustration and for reference in regard to the horoscopes which I will translate presently.

The conflict of the animals.

It is by giving a realistic meaning to these several animals and elements, after which the years are named, that the lāma astrologers arrive at their endless variety of combinations of attraction and repulsion in regard to their casting of horoscopes and their prescriptions of the requisite worship and offerings necessary to counteract

[1] THE TIBETAN CHRONOLOGICAL TABLE here given differs from that of Schlagintweit (*op. cit.*, p. 282) in making the initial year of the current sixty-year cycle, viz., the fifteenth *Rabjung*, coincide with the year 1867 A.D., as this is alleged by the learned *Tsipa* Lāma of Darjeeling to be the true epoch, and not the year 1866 as given by Schlagintweit.

Year A.D.	Tibetan Era.			Year A.D.	Tibetan Era.		
	Cycle No.	Cyclical year.	Year-name.		Cycle No.	Cyclical year.	Year-name.
1858	XIV	52	Earth-Horse.	1890	XV	24	Iron-Tiger.
1859	,,	53	,, -Sheep.	1891	,,	25	,, -Hare.
1860	,,	54	Iron-Ape.	1892	,,	26	Water-Dragon.
1861	,,	55	,, -Bird.	1893	,,	27	,, -Serpent.
1862	,,	56	Water-Dog.	1894	,,	28	Wood-Horse.
1863	,,	57	,, -Hog.	1895	,,	29	,, -Sheep.
1864	,,	58	Wood-Mouse.	1896	,,	30	Fire-Ape.
1865	,,	59	,, -Ox.	1897	,,	31	,, -Bird.
1866	,,	60	Fire-Tiger.	1898	,,	32	Earth-Dog.
1867	XV	1	,, -Hare.	1899	,,	33	,, -Hog.
1868	,,	2	Earth-Dragon.	1900	,,	34	Iron-Mouse.
1869	,,	3	,, -Serpent.	1901	,,	35	,, -Ox.
1870	,,	4	Iron-Horse.	1902	,,	36	Water-Tiger.
1871	,,	5	,, -Sheep.	1903	,,	37	,, -Hare.
1872	,,	6	Water-Ape.	1904	,,	38	Wood-Dragon.
1873	,,	7	,, -Bird.	1905	,,	39	,, -Serpent.
1874	,,	8	Wood-Dog.	1906	,,	40	Fire-Horse.
1875	,,	9	,, -Hog.	1907	,,	41	,, -Sheep.
1876	,,	10	Fire-Mouse.	1908	,,	42	Earth-Ape.
1877	,,	11	,, -Ox.	1909	,,	43	,, -Bird.
1878	,,	12	Earth-Tiger.	1910	,,	44	Iron-Dog.
1879	,,	13	,, -Hare.	1911	,,	45	,, -Hog.
1880	,,	14	Iron-Dragon.	1912	,,	46	Water-Mouse.
1881	,,	15	,, -Serpent.	1913	,,	47	,, -Ox.
1882	,,	16	Water-Horse.	1914	,,	48	Wood-Tiger.
1883	,,	17	,, -Sheep.	1915	,,	49	,, -Hare.
1884	,,	18	Wood-Ape.	1916	,,	50	Fire-Dragon.
1885	,,	19	,, -Bird.	1917	,,	51	,, -Serpent.
1886	,,	20	Fire-Dog.	1918	,,	52	Earth-Horse.
1887	,,	21	,, -Hog.	1919	,,	53	,, -Sheep.
1888	,,	22	Earth-Mouse.	1920	,,	54	Iron-Ape.
1889	,,	23	,, -Ox.	1921	,,	55	,, -Bird.

the evils thus brought to light. The animals are more or less antagonistic to each other, and their most unlucky combinations are as follows :—

Mouse and Horse.
Ox and Sheep.
Tiger and Monkey.
Hare and Bird.
Dragon and Dog.
Serpent and Hog.

Relationships of the elements.

But it is with the five elements that the degrees of affinity and antagonism are most fully defined, according to certain more or less obvious inter-relations of the elements. The recognised degrees of relationship are (1) *mother* or greatest affection, (2) *son* or neutrality, (3) *friend* or mediocre affection, and (4) *enemy* or repulsion. The relationships of the elements are thus stated to be the following:—

MATERNAL :—

Wood's *mother* is Water (for wood cannot grow without water).
Water's ,, is Iron (for water-channels for irrigation cannot be made, and therefore water cannot come, without iron).
Iron's ,, is Earth (for earth is the matrix in which iron is found).
Earth's ,, is Fire (for earth is the ash-product of fire).
Fire's ,, is Wood [for without wood (carbon) fire is not].

FILIAL :—

Wood's *son* is Fire
Fire's ,, is Earth
Earth's ,, is Iron
Iron's ,, is Water
Water's ,, is Wood

} This is merely a reverse way of presenting the above details.

HOSTILE :—

Wood's *enemy* is Iron (as iron instruments cut down wood).
Iron's ,, is Fire (as fire melts iron and alters its shape).
Fire's ,, is Water (as water extinguishes fire).
Water's ,, is Earth (as earth hems in water).
Earth's ,, is Wood (as wood grows at the expense of and impoverishes earth).

AMICABLE :—

Wood's *friend* (benefactor) is Earth (as it cannot grow without earth).
Water's ,, ,, is Fire (as it heats water for cooking).
Fire's ,, ,, is Iron (as it absorbs heat and thus assists the continuance of fire).
Iron's ,, ,, is Wood (as it supplies the handle to iron weapons and is its non-conductor).

General nature of the horoscope.

Each of the various kinds of horoscopes[1] takes into account the conflict or otherwise of the elemental and astral influences which were in authority at the time of the person's birth, as compared with the existing influences operative at the times consulted. The ordinary horoscope is usually arranged under the following six heads, viz.—

1. The year of birth of the individual in its auspicious or inauspicious bearings.
2. His *Parkha* (in Chinese "*pah-kwah*"), one or other of the eight celestial figures.
3. His *Log-men* or "Reversed calculation" of age. This is evidently introduced in order to afford a further variety of conflicts—see note, page 363.
4. "The Seizing-Rope of the Sky."—This seems to refer to a popular idea of ultimate ascent to the celestial regions by means of an invisible rope.
5. The Earth-dagger.—This is an invisible dagger, and is for the individual the emblem of stability and safety so long as it is reported to be fixed firmly in the earth.
6. The *Mewa* or "blots."—One or other of the nine geomantic figures, evidently of Chinese origin.

And each of these several heads is separately considered in detail with reference to its conflicts in regard to—

(*a*) the life or "srog"—pronounced *sok ;*
(*b*) the body or *lüs ;*
(*c*) the power orcapability, "*d*hang-thang"—pronounced "*wang-thang ;*"
(*d*) the luck ("wind horse") or "*r*lung-*r*ta"—pronounced *lungta ;*
(*e*) the intelligence or *b*la.

[1] The horoscope for birth is named *s*kye*s*-rtsis, that for the whole life is tshe-rabs la*s* *r*tsis. The annual horoscope is *s*kag-rtsis, that for marriage is pag-*r*tsi*s*, and for death *g*shin-*r*tsi*s*.

The particular Parkha and Mewa for the several times are found by reference to the almanac; but the other details are elicited by divers calculations made upon the astrologer's board, and in consultation with the various manuals on the subject.

The Astrologer's board.

The astrologer's board consists of a large napkin on which are drawn squares and the other necessary geomantic figures, all in a definite and convenient relation to each other. This napkin is spread on a table, and the calculations are made with coloured buttons as counters which are kept in a bag—the several elements having each a recognized colour: thus wood is *green*, fire is *red*, earth is *yellow*, iron is *white*, and water is *blue*. These counters are placed on the coloured squares as in a chess board, and are moved according to rule, either transversely from right to left or *vice versâ*, or longitudinally over the requisite number of squares; and in addition are kept handy a heap of numerous small white and black counters to register the total results. In the top row of the board are the 60 squares of the 60-year cycle, all named and in the proper colour of their elements. And the succeeding rows of squares are those of the sok, lüs, wang-thang, lungta, and *b*la series, each with its appropriate succession of coloured elements. The other divisions relate to the Parkhas and Mewas.

The calculations.

The calculations are made according to rule backwards or forwards a certain number of years in the row of the 60-year cycle squares, and the secondary results come out of the vertical columns of the sok, lüs, &c., series according to the conflict of their respective elements as therein found; the results being noted by white or black seeds or buttons, which have the following values:—

Symbols of degrees of relationship.

The seven recognized degrees of affinity or repulsion are expressed in the astrological accounts by the following signs of circles and crosses, and during the calculation the circles are represented by white buttons and the crosses by black buttons or seeds:—

When the conflict of the elements comes out—		*Mother*, *i.e.*, the *best* degree	= ooo
Ditto	ditto	*Friend*, *i.e.*, the *better* ,,	= oo
Ditto	ditto	{ *Water* + *Water* / *Earth* + *Earth* } *i.e.*, *a harmless mixture & ∴ good*	= o
Ditto	ditto	*Son*, *i.e.*, *neutral*	= o×
Ditto	ditto	{ *Wood* + *Wood* / *Fire* + *Fire* / *Iron* + *Iron* } *i.e.*, *unmiscibility & ∴ opposition & bad*	= ×
Ditto	ditto	*Enemy*, *i.e.*, *worse*	= ××
Ditto	ditto	*deadly hate*, *i.e.*, *worst*	= ×××

For example, water meeting iron, *i.e.*, its "*mother*," is the very best and ∴ = ooo, and the same would be true of fire meeting wood. But wood meeting earth would = "*friend*," and therefore = oo; but should earth meet wood, then it would be "*enemy*," and therefore = ×× ; and water meeting wood = "*neutrality*" or o×. While fire meeting water = "*deadly hate*," and therefore = ×××. Then the average of the total is taken as the average result of the conflict. And the several remedies necessary to avoid each and all of the calamities thus foretold are specified categorically in the astrologer's books.

Prescription for worship on account of One Year's ill-luck. An Annual Horoscope.

With this explanation I now give here a sample copy of the prescription of worship, demoniacal and otherwise, for one family for one year's ill-luck, in which the prescribed worship is italicised. I have added in foot-notes some further explanations which may be consulted by those interested in knowing in more detail the methods by which the lāma-astrologer makes his calculations.

"*The MISFORTUNE ACCOUNT of the Family of* ——— *for The EARTH-MOUSE YEAR* (i.e., 1888 A.D.)

Salutation to Manju Sri![1]

A.—For the Father of the family.

I.—According to the BIRTH CONFLICT—

This male, aged 26 years, being born in the Water-Hog year, that year conflicts with the Earth-Mouse year (the present year) as follows:—

srok or life	= o,	or *good.*[2]
lus or body	= oo,	or *better.*[3]
wang thang or power	= ××,	or *worse.*
lung-ta or wind-horse	= ooo,	or *best.*
la or intelligence	= ×,	or *bad.*

[1] The Bodhisat Manjusri is the presiding divinity of the astrologers, and he is always invoked at the head of astrologic prescriptions.

[2] The year of his birth being the Water-Hog gives, according to the astrologic table, Water as the *srog* for that year, and the present year being the Earth-Mouse year its *srog* according to the table, is also Water. Therefore Water meeting Water = O, *i.e.*, "good."

[3] The *lus* of these two years are found by the table to give the elements respectively of Water and Fire. Therefore Water meeting its friend Fire = OO or "better," *i.e.*, good of the second degree.

"1. *As modified by 'Parkha.'*—His *Parkha* for the year is *Khon*, which gives the Earth-Sheep year and the following conflict.

life	=	worse.
body	=	better.
power	=	worse than bad.
wind-horse	=	bad.
intelligence	=	worse.

2. *As modified by 'Reversed Age Calculation.'*—This gives a 'good' result,[1] therefore = o.

3. *As modified by 'The Seizing-Rope of the Sky.'*—This gives a 'good' result,[2] therefore = o. [If it were bad, '*Nam-go*' is prescribed 'to close the door of the sky' (spirits).][3]

4. *As modified by 'The Earth dagger.'*—This gives a medium average. [If it were bad would have to do '*Sā-gô*' or closure of the door of the earth (spirits).][4]

The Summary of the year's conflict as to birth together with its prescribed remedies are therefore :—

'Life' has black in excess; therefore to procure long life *have read very much the 'Tshe-dô' and Tshe zung* or *The Sutra and Dharanis for Long Life.*

'Body' has white in excess; therefore the body will be free from sickness (*i.e.*, only as regards this one head of calculation).

[1] This *Log-men* or "Reversed + downwards" is a more abstruse calculation according to the saying :—

"skyes-pa pu-yi stag thog nas lo grangs thur,
"bud-med ma-yi sprel-thog nas lo grangs gyen."
For *males*—the *sons* of elements—begin from *Tiger* and count age *downwards.*
For *females*—the *mothers*—begin from *Ape* and count age *upwards.*

Thus the birth year of this individual being Water-Hog, and he being a male, and the *son* of Water being Wood, gives us for his *Log-men* the Wood-Tiger year (which = 1854 A.D.) And as he is a male, on counting *downwards* from the Wood-Tiger the number of years of his age (*i.e.* 26), we get the year Earth-Hare (*i.e.*, 1879 A.D.). And according to the Log-men Manual, the Earth-Hare year is "*h*byor-pa," or *Riches*, which is given the value of "good," *ie.*= O.

[2] This is calculated on the *srog* of the *Log-men* year, minus five years. In this case we have seen the *Log-men* year is the Earth-Hare year. Counting back to the fifth year gives the Wood-Hog, which has as its *srog* the element water, and the *srog* of the present 1888 A.D. year, viz., Earth-Mouse, being also Water, therefore = O or good for the "sky-seizing Rope."

[3] *Vide* page 373.

[4] *Vide* page 371.

"'Power' has black in excess; therefore food will be scanty: therefore crops will suffer, and cattle will die or be lost.

For this—

(*a*) *have read very much* 'Yang-gug' *or the Luck-Bestowing and* 'Nor-zang' (*the Best Wealth*);
(*b*) *offer Torma or holy food;*
(*c*) *also give food and sweets to monks and children.*

'Luck' has black in excess; therefore be careful not to provoke a law suit or go on a long journey.

For this—

(*a*) *do 'Du-kar'* 100 *times;*
(*b*) *plant as many 'Lung-ta' flags*[1] *as years of your age;*
(*c*) *offer in the temple* 13 *lamps with incense, &c.;*
(*d*) *have read the 'mDo-mang' very much;*
(*e*) *make an image of yourself* (*of cooked barley or rice*) *and throw it towards your enemy;*
(*f*) *also make an earthen chaitya.*

'Intelligence' has black in excess; therefore *have read the 'La-guk' or worship for recalling the intelligence.*

II.—According to PARKHA—

His parkha for the year being '*khon*,' he cannot during the year excavate earth or remove stones. The Nāgas and the Earth-owning demons are opposed to him. He is especially liable to the diseases of stiffened joints and skin disorders. In the second month he is especially subject to danger. The N. and E. and S. directions are bad for him; he must not go there. *For removing these evils* (*a*) *have read the 'Gyétong-ba' and* (*b*) *do the worship of 'Gya-zhi-tong'* [= 'The 400,' i.e., 100 *torma* or holy cakes, 100 *lamps and* 100 *rice and* 100 *water offerings*] *and* (*c*) *offer a lamp daily in worship.*

III.—According to MEWA—

His mewa is *Dün-mar* (= the 7 reds); therefore the Tsen and Gyalpo demons give trouble. Dreams will be bad. The gods are

[1] *Vide ante*, page 348.

"displeased. Head, Liver, and Heart will give pain, and Boils will "ensue. To prevent these evils—

(*a*) *make a 'Tsen mdos' and a 'Gyal mdos' (This is somewhat like the Sā-gô,*[1] *but without the Ram's head)* ;

(*b*) *The favourite gods and guardians (srung-ma) of individual : Do their worship energetically ;* and

(*c*) *ransom a sheep from the butchers.*

B.—For the Wife.

I.—According to Birth conflict—

This female born in Iron-Monkey year (*i.e.*, 29 years ago). That year compared with the Earth-Mouse year (*i.e.*, 1888 A.D.) gives :—

sok	= o ×
lü	= o ×
wang-thang	= o o o
lungta	= ×
lā	= o ×

1. *As modified by her Parkha,* which is *Li*—

sok	= × ×
lü	= o o
wang-thang	= × ×
lungta	= o
lā	= × ×

2. *As modified by 'Reversed Age Calculation'* = ×
3. *As modified by 'The Sky-rope'* = o ×
4. *As modified by 'The Earth-dagger'* = o o o

The Total of the year's conflict is therefore :—

Sok and *Lü* are *bad* like No. 1, and must be treated accordingly in addition to No. 1.

Lus and *Wang-thang* are good.

Lungta is neutral ; therefore the good people will be kind to you ; and the bad people will trouble ; therefore it is necessary *to do very much 'Mikha ṭa ḍok,' literally to drive away scandal* (literally = *men's mouth*).

The Sky-seizing Rope is interrupted (*i.e.* cut) ; therefore—

(1) *do very much 'te-gyed,' and 'ser-khyem'* (or oblation of wine to the gods);

(2) *prepare a 'nam-gô' to close breach in the sky-connection.*

[1] *Vide* page 363.

"The conjunction of her year (Monkey with Mouse) is not good; therefore she cannot journey far. And if she does any business she will suffer; therefore *have read 'Tâshi tsig-pa.'*

II.—According to PARKHA—

The Parkha being *Li*, she must not try to build or repair a house or allow any marriage in her house or spill any water on the hearth. The devil-spirit of a dead person is offended with her. Headache and eyeache will occur; therefore—

(*a*) do not look at fresh flesh meat or blood;
(*b*) in the 8th month will be especially bad;
(*c*) must not go W. or N.W.;
(*d*) *have read the 'Dô-mang' and 'Gye-tong;'*
(*e*) be careful not to provoke quarrels.

III.—According to MEWA—

Her Mewa is *'some thing;'* therefore will occur sudden domestic quarrels of great seriousness, lying reports of infidelity, also grief among relatives, and dropsy. To prevent these do—

(*a*) *Gya zhi* (i.e., 100 *lamps*, 100 *rice*, 100 *water*, *and* 100 *torma*).
(*b*) *Lu-ṭor*, or offering of cake to the *Nāgas* and *Dug-kar* (= white umbrella god with 1,000 heads).
(*c*) *Also ransom a goat.*

C.—FOR THE DAUGHTER, AGED 7.

I.—According to BIRTH CONFLICT—

This female, born in the Water-Horse year, 7 years ago. That year conflicted with the Earth-Mouse year as follows:—

sok	= × ×
lü	= ○ ×
wang-thang	= × ×
lungta	= ○ ○
lā	= × ×

1. *As modified by her 'Parkha,'* which is *zin.* Its—

sok	= ○ ○ ○
lü	= ○ ○ ○
wang-thang	= ○ ×
lungta	= × ×
lā	= ○ ○ ○

2. *As modified by her 'Reversed Age Calculation'* = ○
3. *As* per *'Sky-rope'* = ○ ×
4. *As* per *'The Earth dagger'* = ○ ×

"The Total of the year's conflict therefore is—

Sok, Lā, Lü, and *Lung-ta* are good of 2nd degree, *Wang-thang* is bad; therefore *do as for her father No.* 1, *above noted.*

'Sky-seizing Rope' and 'Earth-dagger' are neutral. For evil Sky-seizing Rope, *have read the Sutra* '*Nam-mkha-ī snying-poī mdo.*'
And for Earth-dagger have read '*Sa-yi snying-po-ī mdo,*'
and repeat as frequently as years of age, i.e., 7 *times.*

The conjunction of her birth year, the Horse, with that of the present year, the Mouse, is very bad, as these two are enemies; *for this have read* rgya nag sky zlong-gangmang.

II.—According to PARKHA—

Her Parkha is *zin.* Be careful not to break a twig or demolish any tree sacred to the Nāgas or other deities (*g*nyan), and don't handle a carpenter's tool for the same reason. In 2nd month when buds come out, it is somewhat bad for you, as the Nāgas are then pre-eminent. The West and N.W. directions are bad and have to be avoided. *For these evils have read the* '*Dô-mang.*'

III.—According to MEWA—

Her Mewa is *like her father's* (*No.* 1), *and therefore do accordingly.*

D.—FOR THE SON, AGED 5.

I.—According to BIRTH CONFLICT—

This male (son), born in the Wood-Ape year, 5 years ago. That year compared with the Earth-Mouse year gives—

sok = o ×
lü = o o
w. = o o
l. = ×
lā = o ×

1. *As modified by his* '*Parkha,*' which is *kham.* Its—

sok = o ×
lü = o
w. = o o o
l. = o o o
lā = o o o

2. *As* per '*Reversed Age Calculation*' = ×
3. *As* per '*Sky-rope*' = o o
4. *As* per '*Earth-dagger*' = × ×

"The Total of the year's conflict therefore is—

Lü, Wang-thang, and Lung-ta are good.
Lā and Sok are neutral or middling.
The Sky-rope is *not broken*, and therefore good.
The Earth-dagger is withdrawn, and therefore bad.

For the latter—

(*a*) *make as many clay Chaityas as possible ;*
(*b*) *the torma-cake of the earth-goddess* (*Sa-yi-lha-mo*) *; and*
(*c*) *give also torma-cake to the Lu* (*Nāga*).

II.—According to ' PARKHA '—

His parkha being *kham*, don't go to a large river, and to pools and other waters reputed to be the abode of water-spirits. Don't stir or *disturb* the water. Don't go out at night. Don't eat fish. The *tsén* kind of Nāgas are ill disposed to you. These spirits are especially malevolent to you in the 6th month; therefore be careful. Don't go in a S.W. and N.E. direction. *Have read* (1) *klu hbum and* (2) *Ser-hod dampa hdon.*

III.—According to MEWA—

This Mewa is *ku-mar* (or 'the red 9'). The Mamo and Tsén are ill disposed to you.

For these two—

(*a*) *make* ' *de-gnyis kyi mdos gtong,*' which is like the *Sa-gô* and 'Sky-door' with threads and masts, and
(*b*) *have read well* ' *gser-hod gyang skyabs.*'

General Note on the Grand Average of the above.

The *Mewa* is excessively red. It thus betokens shedding of blood by accident.

Therefore must make ' *Tsan mdos* ' *and* ' *Mamo* bloody *mdos.*' } Are like the ' *Sa-gô* ' mast.

And have read as much as possible—(1) *stobs po-chhe-ī-gzungs*, (2) *gzak-i yum*, (3) *nor-rgyun-ma-ī gzungs gang-mang sgrogs.*"

The enormous amount of lāmaic worship prescribed.

The above is a fair sample of a prescription of worship to be done by one family on account of the current year's demoniacal influences. In addition to the worship therein prescribed there also needs to be done the special worship for *each* individual according to his or her own life's horoscope as taken at birth ; and in the case of husband and wife, their additional burden of new worship which

THE TIBETAN HOUSE-GOD.

Reg. No. 398, Fin.—July 94.—500.

Photo., S. I. O., Calcutta

accrued to their life horoscope on marriage, due to the new set of conflicts introduced by the conjunction of their respective years and their noxious influences. And the actual occurrence of sickness, notwithstanding the execution of all this costly worship, necessitates the further employment of lāmas, and the recourse by the more wealthy to a devil-dancer or to a special additional horoscope by the *Tsi-pa* lāma. So that one family alone is prescribed a sufficient number of sacerdotal tasks to engage a couple of lāmas fairly fully for several months of the year. To get through the prescribed reading of the several bulky scriptures within reasonable time, it is the practice to call in several lāmas, and each at the same time reads a different book for the benefit of the lay individual concerned.

The House Demon.

His appearance is best shown by his picture given in Plate XX.

The house demon.

He is called the "Nang-lha,"[1] or Inside God, and is of the nature of a Sa-dag or "Earth-owner demon." And as he is of a roving disposition, occupying during the several seasons quite different parts of the house, his presence is a constant source of anxiety to the householders, as no objects can be deposited in the place where he has taken up his position for the time being; nor can it be even swept or disturbed in any way without incurring his deadly wrath. It is somewhat satisfactory, however, that all the house-gods of the country regulate their movements in a definite and known order.

His movements.

In the 1st and 2nd month he occupies the centre of the house, and is then called "Khyim-lha-gel-thung."

In the 3rd and 4th month stands in the doorway, and is called "Sgo-lha-*r*ta-*g*yag," "the door-God of the horse and yak."

,, 5th	,,	stands under the eaves, and is called "*y*ngas-pa."
,, 6th	,,	stands at the south-west corner of the house.
,, 7th and 8th	,,	stands under the eaves.
,, 9th and 10th	,,	stands in the portable fire-tripod or grate.
,, 11th and 12th	,,	stands at the kitchen fireside, where a place is reserved for him. He is then called the "thab-lha" or "Kitchen God."

[1] In Chinese he is said to be named "*Zug-je.*" The "House-God" of the Hindus appears to be a totally different personage—*vide* The *Brihat Sanhita,* liii, translated by Dr. Kern in *Jour. Royal As. Soc.*, New series, VI, page 279.

His movements thus bear a certain relation to the season, as he is outside in the hottest weather and at the fire in the coldest.

Old fashion.

Formerly his movements were somewhat different. According to the ancient tradition he used to circulate much more extensively and frequently as follows:—

In 1st month he dwelt on the roof for the first half of the month and for latter half on the floor. To repair the roof at such a time means the death of the head of the family.

In 2nd ,, ,, at top of stairway. The stair during this month cannot be mended, otherwise one of the family will die.

In 3rd ,, ,, in the granary. Cannot make any alterations there during this month, otherwise all the grain will be bewitched and spoiled.

In 4th ,, ,, on the doorway. Then cannot mend doorway, otherwise that member of the family absent on a journey will die.

In 5th ,, ,, in the hand corn-mill and the water-mill. Then cannot mend these, otherwise all luck will depart.

In 6th ,, ,, in any foxes' or rats' holes near the house. Then cannot interfere with these holes, otherwise a child will die.

In 7th ,, ,, on roof. Then cannot repair, otherwise the husband will die.

In 8th ,, ,, in the wall foundation. Then cannot repair, otherwise a child will die.

In 9th ,, ,, up the chimney. Then must not repair, otherwise house will be transferred to a new owner.

In 10th ,, ,, in the beams or standard posts. Then cannot repair, otherwise the house will collapse.

In 11th ,, ,, underneath fire-place. Then cannot repair, otherwise the housewife will die of hiccup or vomitting.

In 12th ,, ,, in the stable. Then cannot repair or disturb it, otherwise the cattle will die or be lost.

His prohibitions inflicted.

The other precautions in regard to his presence and the penalties for disturbing him are as follows:—In the 1st and 2nd month when the god is in the middle of the house, the fire-grate must not be placed there, but in a corner of the house, and no dead body must be placed there.

When at the door no bride or bridegroom can come or go, nor any corpse. Should there, however, be no other way of exit by a window or otherwise, and there be urgency in the matter of the passage of a bride, bridegroom, or corpse, then must be made with wheaten flour the images of a horse and a yak, placing on each image respectively some skin and hair of each of these animals. Then tea and beer are also offered to the spirit, who is then invited to sit on these images. Then the door is removed from its hinges and carried outside, and the bride, bridegroom, or corpse is taken out or enters, and the door is again restored to its place.

When at the kitchen fire. No part of the fire-place can be removed or mended at that time, and no corpse can go there, nor must any marriage then take place. And should any visitor arrive, he must be screened off from the fire-place by a blanket and the "chhös-mge-khri" scripture read.

When in the verandah, there is a little trouble; only the outside of the house must not be whitewashed nor repaired or disturbed in any way.

Should it be thought that he has been slightly offended, and in every case so as to err on the safe side, it is recommended that the worship of "*s*pang-kong-*s*nang-*br*gyad chhab-*g*tor-*b*chos," or "the water sacrifice of the 8 Injurers," should be done.

The Demons of the Earth.

Earth demons.

The local earth demons are named *Sab-dak* or *Sa-dak-po* (sa-*b*dag-po) or "Earth owners." The most malignant are the "*g*nyan." These infest certain trees and rocks which are always studiously shunned and respected, and usually daubed with paint in adoration. The earth demons are very numerous, but they are all under the authority of "Old mother *Khönma*." She rides upon a ram, and is dressed in golden-yellow robes, and her personal attendant is "sa-thel-ngag-po." In her hand she holds a golden noose, and her face contains 80 wrinkles.

Their worship.

The ceremony of *Sa-gô*, so frequently referred to in the lāmaic prescriptions, is addressed to her. It literally means "the closing of the open doors of the earth" to the earth spirits, and it is very similar to the worship of the *Lares* by the Romans.

In this rite is prepared the magical emblem consisting of an elaborate arrangement of masts and strings and a variety of mystic objects; most prominent among which is a ram's skull with attached horns, which is directed *downwards* towards the earth.

Inside the ram's skull is put some gold leaf, silver, turquoise, and portions of every precious object available, as well as portions of dry eatables, rice, wheat, pulses, &c.

On the forehead is painted in ochre-colour[1] the mystic celestial (Parkha) sign of Khön, and on the right jaw the sun, and on the left jaw the moon, and above it is adorned with (1) "namka" masts, *i.e.*, masts to which are attached diamond-shaped and square figures made by winding coloured threads in geometric patterns; (2) *tar-zab* or pieces of silk rag, and (3) *tong-tse* or Chinese pice (Ang. "cash") and several wool-knobbed sticks of *phang-khra*.

Along the base are inserted on separate slips of wood the following images, &c. :—

1. A man's picture (*pho-dong*).
2. A woman's do. (*mo-dong*) with a spindle in her hand.
3. A house do.
4. A tree do. [*tam-shing* (khram-shing)].
5. Figures of the mystic 8 *Parkha* and the 9 Mewa.

The whole arrangement is now fixed to the outside of the house above the door; the object of these figures of a man, wife, and house is to deceive the demons should they still come in spite of this offering, and to mislead them into the belief that the foregoing pictures are the inmates of the house, so that they may wreak their wrath on these bits of wood and so save the real human occupants.

Then when all is ready and fixed, the lāma turns to the south-west and chants—

"O! O! *ke! ke!* Through the nine series of earths you are known as "Old Mother Khön-ma, the mother of all the Sa-dak-po. You are the "guardian of the earth's doors. The dainty things which you especi- "ally desire we herewith offer, *viz.*, a couch-white skull of a ram, on "whose right cheek the sun is shining like burnished gold, and on the "left cheek the moon gleams dimly like a conch-shell. The forehead "bears the sign of Khön, and the whole is adorned with every sort of "silk, wool and colour and precious substances, and it is also given the "spell of Khön (here the lāma breathes upon it). All these good "things are here offered to you, so please close the open doors of the "earth to the family who here has offered you these things, and do not "let your servant Sa-thel ngag-po and the rest of the earth spirits "do harm to this family. By this offering let all the doors of the earth "be shut. O! O! *ke! ke!* Do not let your servants injure us when "we build a house or repair this one, nor when we are engaged in

[1] The symbolic colour of the earth.

"marriage matters, and let everything happen to this family according "to their wishes. Do not be angry with us, but do us the favours we "ask.

"*Om kharal dok!*[1] (here clap hands)
Om khamrhil dok! (do. do.)
Benneu swāhā!"

THE DEMONS OF THE SKY.

Sky demons.

The local demons of the sky are under the control of the grandfather of the three worlds—Old Father Khen-pa, who is an old man with snow-white hair, dressed in white, and riding on the white dog of the sky, and in his hand he carries a crystal wand. He is the owner of the sky.

Their worship.

The ceremony called *nam-gô*, or "the closing of the doors of the sky," so frequently prescribed by the *tsi-pa* lāmas, is addressed to him. An arrangement of masts, threads, images, &c., exactly similar to that used in the above-noted *sa-gô* ceremony, is constructed, the only difference being that in this case a dog's skull is used (the Dog was especially associated with the analogous Lares worship of the Romans, *vide* foot-note[2]), and it is directed upwards, pointing to the sky; and the sign of the *parkha* painted on the forehead is that of *Khen*, and is in blue colours. And the ceremony is the same except in its introduction and in the name of the chief servants:—

"O! O! we turn towards the Western sun, to the celestial mansion "where the sky is of turquoise, to the grandfather of the three worlds— "Old Khen-pa, the owner of the sky. Pray cause your servant, the "white Nam-tel, to work for our benefit, and send the great planet "Pemba (Saturn) as a friendly messenger, &c. &c."

PREVENTION FROM INJURY BY THE EIGHT CLASSES (OF DEMONS).

Om-swa-ti! The means of preventing the injuries of the eight classes (of demons).

[1] The meaning of the "*dok*" is "let all evils be annihilated!"

[2] "The images of men and women made of wool were hung in the streets, and so many balls made of wool as there were servants in the family, and so many complete images as there were children (*Festus apud Lil. Gyr*). The meaning of which custom was this: These feasts were dedicated to the Lares, who were esteemed infernal gods; the people desiring hereby that these gods would be contented with these woollen images and spare the persons represented by them. These Lares sometimes were clothed in the skins of *dogs* (*Plutarch. in Prob.*) and were sometimes fashioned in the shape of dogs (*Plautus*), whence that creature was consecrated to them."—*Tooke's Pantheon*, page 280.

First of all prepare offerings of blood, milk, curdled milk, tea, beer, and clean water, which must be arranged properly, and the *mantras* or spells of "The Vast Sky-like Treasury" or *Om-ā hung-bajra-sparnakham* must be repeated. Then chant:—

The offerings.

"I beg you O! all guardians and evil spirits (of the under-noted "places) to attend to this invitation, *viz.*, the dwellers "of the vast extending ocean of the Upper-Ngari "khorsum (*s*töd-*m*ngah-ri-*s*kor-*g*sum), the Intermediate, Central West- "ern—the four divisions of Tibet (bar-*d*bus *g*tsang-ru-*b*zhi), Amdo "Kham and Gango of Eastern Tibet and Bhotan (*s*mad-*m*do-khams- "*s*gang-drug),[1] India (the white plain), China (the black plain), Li-bal[2] "Mongolia (the yellow plain), Upper and Lower Turkistan, and all the "kingdom of this continent (*h*jsambu-*g*ling), the other three great con- "tinents and the eight islands (*vide* Chart of Lāmaic Universe, page "320), and also the spirits of all retired nooks, deserts, rocky places, "caves, cemetery, fire-hearths, fortresses, streams, oceans, ponds, foun- "tains, forests, roads, empty and uninhabited places, farms and other "important places; and also those who always attend the congregation "of priests, parties of women, festivals of births, singing parties and "the learners of arts, and also all the dwellers from the highest to the "lowest regions of hell.

The Prayer.

"I beg you, O! ye guardians of the different kinds of *r*gyüd, to "attend this invitation.

"I beg you, O! Pho-hla, mo-lha, zhang-lha, srog-lha, and yul-lha, "to attend this invitation.

"I beg you, O! *d*gra-lha of noble and ancient generations, to "attend this invitation.

"I beg you, O! all ye gods of the white party who give refuge, to "attend this invitation.

"I beg you, O! all ye demons of the black party who are averse to "the true path, to attend this invitation.

"I beg you, O! all ye goblins and demons from the highest "order to the lowest, counting from *btsan* down to shin-*h*dre (life-taking "demon), *g*sön-*h*dre (the demon-eater of living animals), and all the "inferior classes of divinities, to attend this invitation; *viz.*, lha "(gods), nága, *b*düd, *b*tsan, yamantaka (*g*shin-*r*je), mamo, *g*zah (plan- "ets), *r*gyal-po *d*Mu, the-u-rang, sa-*b*dag, *g*nyan, srin-po and the "injurers of all the regions.

[1] *i. e.*, the Lower Dô (or Amdô), Kham, and "The Six Ridges"—provinces of Eastern Tibet.

[2] *Li*-yul or Khoten, and *Pal*-yul or Nepal.

"O! I give to you all these offerings of red blood, of sweet tea, "of clean water, of intoxicating drink, and of white butter. I make "these offerings to you all. Pray accept them:

Those who prefer beer, please take beer!
,, ,, tea ,, ,, tea!
,, ,, blood ,, ,, blood!
,, ,, water ,, ,, water!
,, ,, milk ,, ,, milk!

Pray accept these food offerings and do us no further injury!
Pray do not injure the human beings of the upper regions!
,, ,, lower animals of the lower regions!
,, ,, crops of the fields!
,, ,, moisture of the plants!
,, ,, essence of wealth!
,, ,, good qualities of the kingdom!
,, ,, wealth and riches!
,, ,, good repute and influence!
,, ,, life and soul!
,, ,, breath and prosperity!

O! may we all be possessed of perfect minds!
O! may we all be happy and useful to each other!
O! may we all obtain the highest power of Tathagatas!
O! may we all obtain the sphere of piety, and having obtained it, may all our wishes be fulfilled and reach the supreme end!

Bajra mu! Now I beg you all to depart to your respective dwellings!

"Let Glory como!" "*Tashi shok!*"
"Virtue!" "*dGe-o!*"

EXORCISING THE DISEASE-PRODUCING DEMONS—THE "SHE."

The Disease-demon is exorcised by threats.

The demons who produce disease, short of actual death, are called *g*shed (pronounced *she*). These are exorcised by an elaborate ceremony in which a variety of images and offerings are made. And the officiating lāma invoking his tutelary demon thereby assumes spiritually the dread guise of his favourite demon, and orders out the disease-demon under threat of being himself eaten up by the awful tutelary demon which now possesses the lāma.

The directions for this exorcism are the following:—

The offerings, and effigies.

On the five terraces of the magic circle of Rirab (*vide* Mandala or Magic Circle, page 320) make the image of a yellow frog with a nam-kha, having its belly and face yellow, and on the east, a two-headed figure with heads of a tiger and a vulture, riding on an ass and holding the eight *parkhas;* on the south a two-headed figure with heads of a horse and a snake, riding on a red horse and holding a lamp; on the west a two-headed figure with heads of a bird and a monkey, holding a sword and riding on a goat; and on the north a two-headed youth with heads of a rat and a pig, riding on a blue pig and holding a water-bag. On the south-east, a dragon-headed woman riding on a *m*dsô (half-breed yak); on the south-west a sheep-headed woman riding on a bull; on the north-west a dog-headed woman riding on a wolf; and on the north-east a bull-headed woman riding on a buffalo. Thirteen *h*phang,[1] *m*dah, *r*gyang-bu, and nam-kha. Iron on the east, water on the south, fire on the west, and gold on the north with a *s*lüd, literally "*ransom*" of dough-cake of wheaten flour, in their front, and a lamp and a piece of flesh on each corner. Then bless it with the six mantras and the six mudras.

The exorcism.

Then assuming the guise of one's own tutelary deity or *yidam*, chant the following :—

"Salutation to (the Chinese King) Kong-*r*tse-*h*phrul-*r*gyal, an "incarnation of Manjusri!

"*Hung!* Hear me, O! you collection of *g*she*d* demons! Hear me, "O! all you *g*she*d* that cause injury! Listen to my orders and come "to receive my presents with great reverence!

"I am the representative of the King of the Angry Demons "(Khro*r*gyal)!

"I am a great demon-eater!!!

"I am The All-terrifying and Injuring One! There is no one who "dare disobey my commands!

"There is nothing which is not composed of the five elements, and "there is nothing to obstruct the communication of my words to your "ear. So then, come to receive this ransom!

"O! all you evil spirits and the ghosts of the dead! listen to me "and come to receive this present. Through the power of the element "of Iron, O! eating-demons, ghosts and evil spirits! come to receive "this present with mild hearts. O! you *g*she*d* of the four directions, "eating-demons, ghosts and evil spirits! come and receive it with mild "hearts. *Ja-hung-bi-hô!*

"*Hung!* The *g*she*d* of the eastern direction is the woman with the "heads of a tiger and vulture, riding on a red ass. She is surrounded "by a thousand attendant *g*she*d*. O! you! having received this ransom, "do not injure the dispenser of gifts, and expel all the eating-demons, "ghosts and evil spirits of the east. I here drive away all the "*g*she*d* by this burning thunderbolt through the force of truth. O!

[1] *Vide ante* articlo "Nam-gô."

"eating-demons, life-cutters, breath-takers, death-causers, and all the "evil spirits! I drive you all away. If you remain here any longer, "I, 'Yeshes-khro-wo-chhen-po,' or 'the Great Angry One of Fore- "knowledge,' will break your heads into a hundred bits and cut "up your body into a thousand pieces. Therefore, without disobey- "ing my commands, begone instantly. *Om mama khamkham chhuye* "*swahah!*

"*Hung!* The *g*she*d* of the southern direction has the heads of a "horse and a snake, and rides on a red horse, and he is surrounded by "a thousand attendant *g*she*d*. O! you! having received this ransom, "do not injure the dispenser of these gifts, and expel all the eating- "demons, ghosts and evil spirits of the south. I here drive away all "you *g*she*d* by this burning brand through the force of truth. O! you "injurers of me and the dispenser of these gifts, you eating-demons, "life-cutters, breath-takers, death-causers, and all you evil spirits! I "drive you all away. If you do not depart instantly, I, 'the Great "Angry Ono of Foreknowledge,' will smash your head into a hundred "bits and cut up your body into a thousand pieces. Begone imme- "diately and do not disobey my commands. *Om mama ramramye* "*hung phat!*

"*Hung!* The *g*she*d* of the western direction has two heads of a "bird and a monkey, and rides on a grey goat, and he is surrounded by "a thousand attendant *g*she*d*. O! you! having received this ransom, "do not approach the dispenser of these gifts, and expel all the eating- "demons, ghosts and the evil spirits of the west. I here drive away "all these *g*she*d* by the burning sword through the force of truth. O! "you injurers of me and this dispenser of gifts, you eating-demons, life- "cutters, breath-takers, death-causers, and all you evil spirits! I drive "you all away. If you stay without, I, 'the Great Angry One of Fore- "knowledge,' will smash your head into a hundred bits and cut up "your body into a thousand pieces. Begone immediately and obey "my commands. *Om mama karakaraye hung phat!*

"*Hung!* The *g*she*d* of the northern direction has the heads of "a rat and a pig, and rides on a blue pig, and he is surrounded by a "thousand attendant *g*she*d*. O! you! having received this ransom, do "not injure the dispenser of these gifts, and expel all the eating-demons, "ghosts and the evil spirits of the north. I here drive away all you "*g*she*d* by the golden rod through the force of truth. O! you injurers of "me and this dispenser of gifts, you eating-demons, life-cutters, breath- "takers, death-causers, and all you evil spirits! I drive you all away. "If you remain here, I, 'the Great Angry One of Foreknowledge,' "will smash your heads into a hundred bits and cut up your body into "a thousand pieces. So depart instantly and obey my commands. "*Om mama khamkham chhueye swahah!*

"*Hung!* The *g*she*d* of the south-east is the dragon-headed woman, "riding on a *m*dsô-yak. She is surrounded by thousands of *g*she*d* as "her attendants. O! you! having received this ransom, do not injure "the dispenser of these gifts, and expel all the eating-demons, ghosts "of the dead, and all the evil spirits towards the boundary of the "south-east.

"*Hung!* The *g*she*d* of the south-west is the sheep-headed "woman, riding on a bull. She is surrounded with attendants of "thousands of *g*she*d*. O! you! having received this ransom, do not "injure the dispenser of these gifts, and expel all the eating-demons, "ghosts and the evil spirits towards the boundary of the south- "west.

"*Hung!* The *g*she*d* of the north-west is the dog-headed woman, "riding on a pig. She is surrounded by thousands of her attendants. "O! you! having received this ransom, do not injure the dispenser of "these gifts, and expel all the eating-demons, ghosts and all the evil "spirits towards the boundary of the north-west.

"*Hung!* The *g*she*d* of the north-east is the bull-headed woman, "riding on a buffalo. She is surrounded by thousands of her atten- "dants. O! you! having received this ransom, do not injure the "dispenser of these gifts, and expel the eating-demons, ghosts and all "the evil spirits towards the boundary of the north-east.

"O! you flesh-eating demons, ghosts of the dead, life-cutting "demons, breath-taking demons, death-causing demons, and all kinds "of evil spirits! I here drive you all away. If you don't go instantly, "I, 'the Great One of Foreknowledge,' will smash your head into a "hundred bits and cut up your body into a thousand pieces. So you "had better go away instantly and not disobey my commands. *Om* "*mama khamkham chhuye swahah!*

"Now they are all driven away to the extreme boundaries of the "four directions. *Om su su ta ta ye swahah!* (Here the people shout "joyously '*God has won!*' '*The demons are defeated!*')

"*Kye! Kye!* O! you! frog of precious gold, made from the thunder- "bolt of 'Byam-*m*gön' (pronounced Cham-gön), or 'The loving "protector,' please remain in the south and there become the king of "all the evil spirits.

"We pray you remain also in the vast ocean, where the rains are "deposited and the clouds originate, and there become the overruling "emperor of 'the land-owning demons' and of 'the kings.'

"Upset also all the *g*she*d* of the bad planets, of the stars, mewa, "time, day, month and year; upset all the *g*she*d* of bad luck; I give "you from the depths of my heart the offerings of the five sublime "namkha-masts, the *r*gyang-bu, etc. Upset the inimical *g*she*d! Bhyo!!*

"Upset the inimical *g*she*d!!! Bhyo!!!!*

"Let glory come! *Tashi-shok!*
"Let virtue increase! *Ge-leg-phel!*"

Death Ceremonies.

As the rites in connection with a death include a considerable amount of devil worship, I notice the subject in this place.

Death ceremonies.

On the occurrence of a death the body is not disturbed in any way, until the "*h*pho-bo" (pronounced "pho-o") lāma has extracted the soul in the orthodox manner. For it is believed that any movement of the corpse might eject the soul, which would then wander about in an irregular manner and get seized by some demon. Immediately on death, therefore, a white cloth is thrown over the face of the corpse, and the "*h*pho-bo," or Soul-extracting Lāma, is sent for. On the arrival of this lāma all *weeping* relatives are excluded from the death chamber, so as to secure solemn silence, and the doors and windows closed, and the lāma sits down on a mat near the head of the corpse, and commences to chant the *h*pho-bo service, which contains directions for the soul to find its way to the Western Paradise (dewa-chén) of the mythical Buddha—Amitabha. After advising the spirit to quit the body and its old associations and attachment to property, the Lāma seizes with the forefinger and thumb a few hairs of the crown of deceased's head, and plucking it forcibly is supposed to give vent to the spirit through the roots of these hairs; and it is generally believed that if the "*h*pho-bo" is, as he should be, a lāma of exceptional virtue, an actual perforation of the skull occurs at this instant through which passes the liberated spirit. The spirit is then directed how to avoid the dangers which beset the road to the Western Paradise, and instructed as to the appearance of the demons and other personages who are to be met with *en route*, and it is then bid God-speed. This ceremony lasts about an hour.

The extraction of the soul.

In cases where, through accident or otherwise, the body of deceased is not forthcoming, this operation for the extraction of the soul is done by the lāma spiritually while engaged in deep meditation.

Death-horoscope.

Meanwhile the *Tsi-pa*, or astrologer-lāma, has been requisitioned for a death-horoscope, in order to ascertain what is the age and birth-year of those persons who may approach and touch the corpse, and the necessary particulars as to the date and mode of burial, and the necessary worship to be done for the welfare of the surviving relatives.

The nature of this horoscope will best be understood by an actual example, which I here give, of the death-horoscope of a little girl of two years of age, who died at Darjeeling in 1890.

"Hail to Lāma Manjusri!

"The year of birth of this female was the Bull-year, with which the Snake and the Sheep are in conflict; therefore those individuals born in the Snake and the Sheep-year cannot approach the corpse. The death-demon was hiding in the house inside certain coloured articles, and he now has gone to a neighbouring house where there is a family of 5 with cattle and dogs (therefore that other family needs to do the necessary worship). The death-demon will return to the house of the deceased within three months; therefore must be done before that time the 'za-de-kha-gyur' service.

Death horoscope of a girl.

Her PARKHA being *Dvā* in relation to her death, it is found that her spirit on quitting her body entered her loin girdle and a sword. [In this case the affected girdle was cast away and the sword was handed over to the lāma.] Her life was taken to the east by Tsán and King (gyalpo) demons, and her body died in the west; therefore small girls, cousins, sisters and brothers in that house will be harmed. The deceased's death was due to Iron. And the death-demon came from the south and has gone to the east.

Her MEWA gives the '3rd Indigo blue.' Thus it was the death-demon of the deceased's paternal grandfather and grandmother who caused her death; therefore take (1) a Sat*s*-tsha (a miniature earthen chaitya), and (2) a sheep's head, and (3) earth from a variety of sites, and place these upon the body of the deceased, and this evil will be corrected.

The DAY *of her Death* was Friday. Take to the north-west a leather bag or earthen pot in which have been placed four or five coloured articles, and throw it away as the death-demon goes there. The death having so happened, it is very bad for old men and women. On this account take a horse's skull[1] or a serpent's skull[2] and place it upon the corpse.

Her DEATH STAR is 'Gre.' Her brother and sister who went near to her are harmed by the death-messenger (shin-je). Therefore an ass's skull and a goat's skull must be placed on the corpse.

Her death HOUR was soon after sunset. And in the 12th month her life was cut. The death-demon therefore arrived in the earthen cooking pot and bowl of a man and woman visitor dressed in red who came from the south. Thus the deceased's father and mother are harmed, and especially so if either is born in the Sheep-year.

---

[1] A fragment of such a skull or its image made of dough is usually all that is used.
[2] Dough also will do.

"*Precautions to secure a* Good Rebirth.—It is necessary to prepare an image of Vajrapani, Vajra-satwa, and before these to have prayer[1] done for the good rebirth of the girl's spirit. If this be done, then she will be reborn in the house of a rich man in the west.

For deceased's Spirit.—It is necessary to get the lāmas to read the service (*s*mon-lam) praying for rebirth in The Paradise of Deva-chhen.

For Survivors *of family*.—It is necessary to have read the prayers for Long Life, *viz*., 'tshe-*m*do' and 'tshe-*gz*ungs.'

Directions for Removal of Corpse.—Those who remove the corpse must have been born in the *Dog* or the *Dragon* year. The body must be taken outside of the house on the morning of the third day following the death, and it must be carried to the south-west, and be *buried* (not burned, or given to birds or dogs)."

Location of corpse.

On obtaining the Death Horoscope the body is then tied up in a sitting posture by the auspicious person indicated by the horoscope, and placed in a corner of the room which is not occupied by the house-demon.

Invitation and entertainment of friends.

Notice is sent to all relatives and friends within reach, and these collect within two or three days and are entertained with food of rice, vegetables, &c., and a copious supply of *murwa* beer and tea. This company of visitors remain loitering in and around the house, doing great execution with hand-prayer-wheels and muttering the "*Om-mani-padme-hung*;" until the expulsion of the "*shen*," or death-demon[2] which follows the removal of the body, in which ceremony they all have to join. The expense of the entertainment of so large a company is very considerable.

Feasting the deceased.

During this feasting the deceased is always, at every meal, offered his share of what is going, including tobacco, &c. His own bowl is kept filled with beer and tea and set down beside the corpse, and a portion of all the other eatables is always offered to him at meal times; and after the meal is over his portion is thrown away, as his spirit is supposed to have extracted all the essence of the food, which then no longer contains nutriment, and is fit only to be thrown away. And long after the corpse has been removed, his cup is regularly filled with tea or beer, even up till the 49th day from death, as his spirit is free to roam about for a maximum period of 49 days subsequent to death.

[1] It has frequently been asserted that no prayer is practised in lāmaism. This is not true: real prayer is frequently done; the word used here is *g*sol-wa-*g*tab.

[2] Fully described hereafter, *vide* page 383.

The lāmas chant by relays all night and day the *De-wa-chan kyi monlam*, or the service for sending the soul of the deceased direct to "The Western Paradise" of the mythic Dhyani Buddha—Amitabha. According to the means of the deceased two or more lāmas are entertained to read this service in chorus, as the more frequently it is repeated the better for the deceased. And a special reading of this service by the assembled monks in the Gompa is also arranged for by those who can afford the expense.

The Litanies.

For "The Western Paradise."

One or more lāmas also read at the house of the deceased the "thos-grol" (pronounced "*thö-dol*"), or guide for the spirit's passage through the valley of horrors intervening between death and a new rebirth. This passage is somewhat suggestive of Bunyan's "Pilgrim's Progress," only the demons and dangers which beset the way are much more numerous and awful. But full directions are read out for the benefit of the deceased as to how to avoid these pitfalls and ogres, and how to find the proper white-coloured path which will lead to a good rebirth. It is, however, rather incongruous to find that while the lāma reading this service is urging the spirit to bestir itself to the necessary exertions for a good rebirth, the other lāma by his side in the *De-wa-chan* service is sending the spirit direct to the Western Paradise—a non-Buddhist invention which is outside the region of rebirth.

For "The Valley of the Shadow of Death."

Though it is scarcely considered orthodox, many of the lāmas find, by consulting their lottery books, that the spirit of the deceased has been sent to hell, and the exact compartment in hell is specified. Then must be done a most expensive service by a very large number of lāmas. First of all is done "*d*ge-ba" or "virtue" on behalf of the deceased; this consists in offerings to The Three Collections, viz.—

Litanies for extraction from hell.

1st.—Offerings to the *Gods* of sacred food, lamps, &c.
2nd.— ,, ,, *Lāmas* of food and presents.
3rd.— ,, ,, *Poor* of food, clothes, beer, &c.

The virtue resulting from these acts is then supposed to tell in favour of the spirit in hell. Then many more expensive services must be performed, and especially the propitiation of *Thuk-je-chhen-po*, or "The Great Pitier," for his intercession with the king of hell (an offshoot of his own self) for the release of this particular spirit. Even the most learned and orthodox lāmas believe that by such a service may be secured the release of a few of the spirits actually in hell. But in practice every spirit in hell for whom its relatives pay sufficiently may be released by the aid of the lāmas. Sometimes a full course of the necessary service is declared insufficient, as the spirit has only got a short way out of hell—very suggestive of the story of the priest and his client in Lever's story, and then additional expense must be incurred to secure its complete extraction.

Removal of corpse.

Before removing the corpse from the house, an especial feast of delicacies, including cooked pork and drink of sorts, are set before the body of the deceased. And a lāma presenting a "scarf of honour" to the corpse thus addresses it:—"You! (and here the deceased's name is stated) now have received "from your relatives all this good food and drink; partake freely of "its essence, as you won't have any more chances! For you must understand that you have died, and your spirit must be gone from here, "and never come back again to trouble or injure your relatives. Remember the name of your spiritual lāma-teacher (*r*tsa-wa *b*lama), "which is . . . . . and by his aid take the right path—the white one. "Come this way!"

The funeral procession.

Then the lāma, with a thigh-bone trumpet in the one hand and a hand-drum in the other, and taking the end of a long white scarf, the other end of which has been tied to the corpse, he precedes the carrier of the corpse, blowing his trumpet and beating the drum and chanting a liturgy. He frequently looks back to invite the spirit to accompany the body, which he assures it is being led in the right direction. And the corpse-bearer is followed by the rest of the procession, some bearing refreshments, and last of all come the weeping relatives. The ceremony of guiding the deceased's spirit is only done for the laity—the spirits of deceased lāmas are credited with a knowledge of the proper path, and need no such instruction. The body is usually carried to the top of a hillock for burial or cremation. The scarf used in the funereal procession may probably represent the Chinese *hurin-fan*, or "soul's banner," which is carried before the coffin in China.

Expelling the Death-Demon.

Exorcising the death-demon.

The exorcising of the death-demon is one of the most common lāmaic ceremonies. It is entitled Za-de-khā-gyur,[1] or "The turning away of the face of the eating devil," *i.e.*, "The expulsion of the Eating or Death-demon." It is always done after a death, within two days after the removal of the corpse, in order to expel from the house and locality the demon who caused the death.

[1] Za-*h*dre-kha *s*gyur.

This ceremony, which requires the presence of four or five lāmas, is as follows:—

The images of himself and attendants.

On a small wooden platform is made the image of a tiger by means of the grass and mud plaster; it is fashioned in a walking attitude, with mouth wide open. The mouth and tusks are made of a dough, and the body is coloured with yellow and brown stripes, in imitation of a tiger's markings, and around its neck is tied a rope of threads of five colours.

Then a small image of a man is made by kneaded dough in which are incorporated filings from the alloy known as the Rin-chhen sna-nga *r*dar, or the five precious things, viz., gold, silver, copper, iron, and tin. Into the belly of this image, which is called "the eating-demon," is inserted a piece of paper, on which is written the following banishing spell[1]:—"Go, thou eating devil, having your face turned to the enemy!"[2] It is then clad in pieces of silk, and is placed sitting astride the tiger's back.

Another figure is made of human form, but with the head of a bird. Its face is painted red; in its belly is inserted paper on which is written "You eating devil, don't remain in this village, but go to the enemy's country." It is then placed in front of the tiger, and is made to hold the free end of the rope attached to the tiger's neck, as a groom.

Another figure of human shape, but with an ape's head, is placed behind as driver.

Then with a piece of "father" tree[3] shape a label like this:—

containing the spell therein inscribed, which is an order to take away the "Eating-demon," and plant this in the shoulder of the bird-faced[4] figure. And making a similar stick out of a "son" tree[5] and inscribed with another spell,[6] plant it in the shoulder of the tiger-riding figure, *i.e.*, the death-demon himself. And with black thread make a geometrical figure *nam-jang nak-po*, as figured in the *nam-gô*-mast already described. And make four arrows of wood with red painted shafts named "*m*dah khra," and place one on each shoulder of the tiger-seated demon-figure and of the bird-faced figure.

[1] *g*zlog-pa-hi *s*nag*s*.
[2] za-hdre-kha *s*gyur *d*gra phyog*s*.
[3] pho shing is interpreted "male" tree, but might possibly be intended for "bamboo."
[4] Za *h*dre *d*gra phyog*s* su-kha *s*gyur ro.
[5] pu shing.
[6] za *h*dre kha *s*gyur ro.

Food and drink offerings.

Then around these figures strew morsels of every kind of eatables, grains, fruits, spices, including raw meat and spirits; also a few small coins of silver and copper.

Enchanted weapons.

The following weapons are then enchanted for the conflict, viz., pieces of iron, copper, small stones, preferably of white and black colours, grains, the root of rampu[1] for the use of the lāmas. And for the lay army of the household and neighbours, a sword, knives, reaping hook, yak's tail, a rope of yak's hair with hook at end as figured with the Fierce *Gonpa*-demons.

The act of exorcism.

When these preparations are completed *and the sun has set*—for demons can only move in the darkness—then the ceremony begins. The head lāma invokes his tutelary deity to assist him in the expulsion of the death-demon. He then chants the following Sanskrit spell:—

"Om! dudtri mārayā srogla bhyo! bhyo!
Raja dudtri mārayā srogla bhyo! bhyo!
Nagpo dudtri mārayā srogla bhyo! bhyo!
Yama dudtri mārayā srogla bhyo! bhyo!"

Immediately on concluding this spell, the lāma with an imprecatory gesture blows his breath spiritualized by his tutelary deity upon the images. And the other lāmas loudly beat a large drum, cymbals, and a pair of *kang-ling* thigh-bone trumpets. And the laymen armed with the afore-mentioned weapons loudly shout and wildly cut the air with their weapons.

On silence being restored the lāma chants the following:—

"*Hung!* Hear you eighty thousand demons![2] In olden time in "the country of India the King Chakra . . . .[3] was taken ill, being "attacked by all the host of gods, devils, 'eating-demons,' and the acci- "dent-causing[4] demons. But, learned and revered Manjusri by doing "the following worship reversed the devils and cured the king. With "the five precious things he made a shapely image of the eating-demon, "and on it planted 'nam-*m*kha *r*gyang-bu, *m*da*h*-khra and phang-khra,' "and writing on slips of wood the *gyur-yik* spells, he stuck them into "the demon's image, and he heaped around it the nine sorts of eatables "as a ransom from the householder, the dispenser of gifts, and he "said, 'Now O! devil! the sun has gone. Your time too for going "has arrived in the black darkness, and the road is good. BEGONE! "Begone to the country of our enemies and work your wicked will

[1] Sweet *Calamus*.
[2] *bgags*.
[3] lkhor-lo-tuk-pa, "the noisy wheel."
[4] *Sri*.

"there! Quickly begone! Jump! Turn about (reverse)!' And thus "the devil was turned away and the king was cured. Again in the "Indra country in the south of India was a king named Dana-aso, "&c., &c. (here are cited several additional examples of the efficacy "of this rite)

"*Hung!* O! Yamantaka. Thou greatest of the gods, the Des- "troyer, the King of the dead! Let the death-demon be sent off "to our enemy!

"O! Ekajati, thou chief of the Ma-mo fiendesses, let the death- "demon be sent off to our enemy!

"O! one-eyed white devil! let the death-demon be sent off to "our enemy!

"O! Hanubhati, flesh-eating demon, chief of all the demons, "let the death-demon be sent off to our enemy!

"O! Nanda and Takshaka, chiefs of the Nāgas, let the death- "demon be sent off to our angry enemy!

"O! Red Father Shü,[1] chief of all the Tsén, let the death-demon "be sent off to our enemy!

"O! 'The well-filled One,'[2] chief of all the Yākshas,[3] let the "death-demon be sent off to our enemy!

"O! Eastern King,[4] the chief of all the Gandharva, let the "death-demon be sent off to our enemy!

"O! Western King, the chief of all the powerful Nāgas, let the "death-demon be sent off to our enemy!

"O! Northern King, the chief of all the givers, let the death-demon "be sent off to our enemy!

"O! Guardians of the ten directions and your retinue, let the death- "demon be sent off to our enemy!

"O! all you Tsén, Ma-mo from the grassy valleys and all Men-mo, "let the death-demon be sent off to our enemy!

"O! all male and female Gong-po, who abstract the essence of "food and your retinue! let the death-demon be sent off to our enemy!

"O! Death-demon, do thou now leave this house and go and "oppress our enemies. We have given you food, fine clothes, and "money. Now be off far from here! Begone to the country of our "enemies!.! Begone!!!"

The ejection of the effigy of death-demon.

Here the lāma smites his palms together, and all the lāmas beat their drums, &c., clamourously, and the laymen wield their weapons, shouting "Begone! Begone!" Amid all this uproar the platform containing the image and its attendants is lifted up by a layman, one of the relatives,

---

[1] Shu*d*="active."

[2] kang-wa bzang-po.

[3] *g*nod-*s*byin.

[4] *r*gyal-po.

selected according to the astrologer's indications, who holding it breast high, at arm's length, carries it outside, attended by the lāmas and laity, shouting 'Begone!' and flourishing their weapons. And it is carried off for about ⅛th of a mile in the direction prescribed by the astrologer of the enemy of the people, and deposited, if possible, at a site where four roads meet.

Subsequent ceremonies.

Meanwhile, to make sure that the demon is not yet lurking in some corner of the room, the sorcerer-lāma[1] remains behind, with a *dorje* in his right hand and a bell in his left, and with the *dorje* he makes frantic passes in all directions, muttering spells, and with the forefinger and thumb of the right hand, without relinquishing the *dorje*, he throws in all directions hot pebbles which have been toasted in the fire, muttering his charms, and concludes:—

"Dispel from this family all the sorceric injury of Pandits "and Bons!!

"Dispel all strife. Dispel all the mischief of inauspicious planets, "and the conjunction of the red and black *Mewa*. Dispel all the evil "of the 8 'parkha.'

"Turn to the enemy all the misfortune.

"Turn to the enemy all plagues, loss, accidents, bad dreams, the "81 bad omens, unlucky years, months, and days, the 424 diseases, the "360 causes of plagues, the 720 causes of sudden death, the 80,000 "most malignant demons.[2]

"Turn all these to our enemy! *Bhyo! Bhyo! Bhyo!* Begone!" And the lāma adds—"Now by these angry spells the demon is "expelled! *O! Happiness!*"

Then all the people triumphantly shout:—

"*Lha-gyal-ō-ō!* *Lha-gyal-ō-ō!!*
God has won!!
Dü pam-bo!! *Dü pam-bo!!!*
THE DEMONS ARE DEFEATED!!!!"

The Lay Figure of the Deceased, and its Rites.

Effigy of deceased.

The interment or cremation of the corpse does not terminate the rites in connection with the disposal of the soul and body of the deceased. That same day, after the removal of the corpse, a lay figure of the deceased is made by dressing a stool or block of wood in the clothes of the deceased, and for a face is inserted the printed paper called *m*tshan *s*pyang or "*s*pyang-pu"—pronounced *chang-ku.*

The face paper.

[1] Ngag-pa.

[2] *b*geg*s*.

Schlagintweit gives a specimen of one form of this print,[1] but he has quite mistaken its meaning. The figure in the centre (see PLATE XXI) is not "the Lord of the Genii of Fire," but it is merely intended to represent the spirit of the deceased person who sits or kneels, and sometimes with the leg bound, in an attitude of adoration. And before this paper figure, occupying the position of the face, are set all sorts of food and drink as is done to the actual corpse.

This is essentially a Bon rite, and is referred to as such in the histories of Guru Padma Sambhava, as being practised by the Bon, and as having incurred the displeasure of the Guru Padma Sambhava, the founder of Lāmaism.

Its inscription usually runs:—

"I, the world-departing One, ... (and here is inserted name of "the deceased), adore and take refuge in my lāma-confessor, and all "the deities, both mild and wrathful,[2] and 'the Great Pitier'[3] forgive "my accumulated sins and impurities of former lives, and show me "the right way to another good world!"

And in the margin or adown the middle of the figure are inscribed in symbolic form the six states of rebirth, viz., S=*sura* or god, A=*asura*, NA=*nara* or man, TRI=beast, PRE=*preta*, HUNG=hell.[4]

Around the figure are depicted "the 5 excellent sensuous things," viz., (1) body (as a mirror), (2) sound (as cymbals, a conch, and sometimes a lyre), (3) smell (a vase of flowers), (4) essence or nutriment (holy cake), (5) dress (silk clothes, &c.)

The lāmas then do the service of the eight highest Buddhas of medicine (Sang*s*-*r*ya*s* man-*b*la), and also continue the service of the Western Paradise.

The duration of this service.

Next day the lāmas depart, to return once a week for the repetition of this service, until the 49 days of *bar-do* have expired; but it is usual to intermit one day of the first week, and the same with the succeeding periods, so as to get the worship over within a shorter time. Thus the lāmas return after 6, 5, 4, 3, 2 and 1 days respectively, and thus conclude this service in about three weeks instead of the full term of 49 days.

Meanwhile the lay figure of the deceased remains in the house in its sitting posture, and is given a share of each meal until the death service is concluded by the burning of the face-paper "*chang-bu*."

[1] *Op. cit.*, page 252.
[2] Of the hundred superior deities, 42 are supposed to be *mild*, and 58 of an angry nature.
[3] An aboriginal or Chinese deity now identified with Avālokita, with whom he has much in common. Other deities are sometimes also addressed.
[4] This also is a mystic interpretation of Avālokita's mantra, the 6th syllable of which is made to mean hell and is coloured black.

THE EFFIGY OF THE DEAD PERSON.

1. *Mirror*
2. *Comch*
3. *Lyre*
4. *Vase with flowers*
5. *Holy Cake*

Reg. No. 398, Fin.—July 94.—500.

Photo., S. I. O., Calcutta.

This paper, on the conclusion of the full series of services, is ceremoniously burned in the flame of a butter-lamp, and the spirit is thus given its final *congé*. And according to the colour and quality of the flame and mode of burning is determined the fate of the spirit of deceased. This process usually discovers the necessity for further courses of worship.

The burning of the paper.

The directions for noting and interpreting the signs of this burning paper are contained in a small pamphlet which I here translate, entitled :—

"*The mode of* DIVINING *the signs of* THE FLAMES *during the Burning of the 'Chang' paper.*

"Salutation to 'Chhe-*m*chhog, Heruka,' or 'The most Supreme Heruka!' The marking of the five colours of the flames is as follows :—

"If the flames be white and shining, then he has become perfect and is born in the highest region of Ok-min (*i.e.*, The Supreme).

Divination by the fire.

"If the flames be white and burn actively with round tops, then he has become pious and is born in the Eastern '*m*ngön-*d*gah,' or 'The Paradise of Real Happiness.'

"If they burn in an expanded form, resembling a lotus (*padma*), then he has finished his highest deeds and has become religious.

"If they be yellow in colour and burn in the shape of '*r*gyal-*m*tshan,' or 'Banner of Victory,' then he has become religious nobly.

"If they be red in colour and in form like a lotus, then he has become religious and is born in *b*de-wa-chan, or 'The Paradise of Happiness.'

"If they be yellow in colour and burn actively with great masses of smoke, then he is born in the region of the lower animals, for counteracting which a *g*tsug-lag-khang, or 'An Academy,' and an image of the powerful and able Dhyāni Buddha (*s*nang-par-*s*nang-*m*dsa*d*) should be made; then he will be born as a chief in the middle country (*i.e.*, The Buddhist Holy Land in India).

"If the fire burns with masses of dense smoke, then he has gone to hell, for counteracting which, images of Vajra . . . . (Dorje-*r*nam-*h*joms) and Vajra-pani should be made; then he will be born as a second daughter of a wealthy parent near his own country, and after his death in that existence he will be born in the fairy land.

"If the fire burns fiercely, with great noise and crackling, then he will be born in hell, for preventing which, images of Mi-*h*khug-pa and Vajra-Satwa and Avālokita should be made, and 'the hell confession of the hundred letters' (yig *r*gya-na-rag *s*kang-*b*shag*s*) should be repeated. Then he will be born as a son of a wealthy parent towards the east.

"If the flames be blue in colour and burn furiously, he is born in hell, for preventing which have read Yige-*br*gya-pa ki-ka-ni dri-med-*b*shag*s*-*r*gyüd, *m*do-thar-chhen-tshe-*h*bar, *s*dig-*b*shag*s*, *l*tung-*b*shag*s*, mani-*b*kah-*h*bum, and *s*pyan-*h*byed must be repeated; then he will either be born as a son of a carpenter towards the east or again born in his late mother's womb. But if this is not done, then he will again be born as a dog, who will become mad and harm everybody, and then he will be born in the ngu-hböd compartment of hell.

"If the flames burn *yellow, without any mixture of other colours*, he will be born in the region of the Yidags (*vide* Wheel of Life, page 266), for preventing which make images of the Dhyani Buddha Ratna Sambhava surrounded by the Nye-sra*s*, also images of Manjusri and of Shakya Muni surrounded by his disciples; then he will be born as a Lāma towards the south and will devote himself to religious purposes.

"If the flames are *yellow in colour and burn furiously*, then make *g*tor-ma-*br*gya-tsa and offer extensive charity to the poor; then he will be born again in his own family. Failing to do this he will be born in the region of the Yidags.

"If the fire flames be *white and burn furiously*, he will be born as a Lha-ma-yin (*vide* Wheel of Life, page 266). Then images of Mahāmāya (Yum-chhen-mo) and Amitayus should be made. Then he will be born in the Happy Paradise of Dewa-chan. If only Tshog*s*-*r*gya be done, then he will be born as a son of wealthy parents.

"If the fire burns furiously in *red*, *emitting sparks*, he will be born as a Lha-ma-yin, for preventing which do *d*kön-*br*tsegs, and thös-grol must be read, and then he will be born as a son of a blacksmith.

"If the fire burns furiously without any colour, then he will be born as a Garuda towards the north, for preventing which make images of Dön-yöd-grub-pa (Dhyāni Buddha *Amogha Siddhi*), *r*Nam-*h*jom*s*, *s*grolma-*h*jig*s*-pa-*br*gyad-*s*kyob*s* (Dolma—The Defender from The Eight Dreads[1]), *s*Man-lha (The God of Medicine), and the worship of Maitreya must be repeated; then he will be born as a son of a famous chief, or he will be born again in his own family.

"If the fire burns of a *bluish-black* colour, then repeat *g*zung-hdüs (*i.e.*, The '*Dô-Mang*'), *m*tshan-*br*jöd, Sang*s*-*r*gya*s*-*m*tshan-*h*bum (The Hundred Thousand Holy Names of Buddha); then he will be born as a chief. By doing these services here prescribed his birth will be good

[1] "The Eight Dreads" are dread of Fire, Prison, Plunder, Water, Enemy, Elephants, Lions, and Snakes:—*Vide* my article "On some Ajanta paintings" in *Indian Antiquary* for the current year (1892).

in every case. 'O! Glorious result! *Sarba mangalam!* All happiness!"

Miniature Chaityas made from the ashes.

The ashes of this burned paper are carefully collected in a plate, and are then mixed with clay to form one or more miniature Chaityas named Sa-tschha. One of these is retained for the household altar, and the rest are carried to any hill near at hand where they are deposited under a projecting ledge of a rock, to shelter them from the disintegrating rain.

On the burning of this paper the lay figure of the deceased is dismantled, and the clothes are presented to the lāmas, who carry them off and sell them to any purchasers available and appropriate the proceeds.

After the lapse of one year from death it is usual to give a feast in honour of the deceased and to have repeated the *s*man-hla service of the Medical Buddhas. On the conclusion of this the widow or widower is then free to re-marry.

To Exorcise Ghosts.

A ghost is always noxious.

A ghost returns and gives trouble either on account of its inherent wickedness, or if the ghost be that of a rich man, it may come to see how his property is being disposed of. In either case its presence is noxious. It makes its presence felt in dreams or by making some individual delirious or temporarily insane.

How exorcised.

Such a ghost is disposed of by being burned. For this purpose a very large gathering of lāmas is necessary, not less than eight, and the service of "byin sreg*s*," or "burnt offering," is done. On a platform of mud and stone outside the house is made, with the usual rites, a magic circle or "kyil-*h*k*h*or," and inside this is drawn a triangle named "hung-hung," as in the diagram here annexed Small sticks are then laid along the outline of the triangle, one piled above the other, so as to make a hollow three-sided pyramid, and around this are piled up fragments of every available kind of food, stone, tree-twigs, leaves, poison, bits of dress, money, &c., to the number of over 100 sorts. Then oil is poured over the mass, and the pile set on fire. During its combustion additional fragments of the miscellaneous

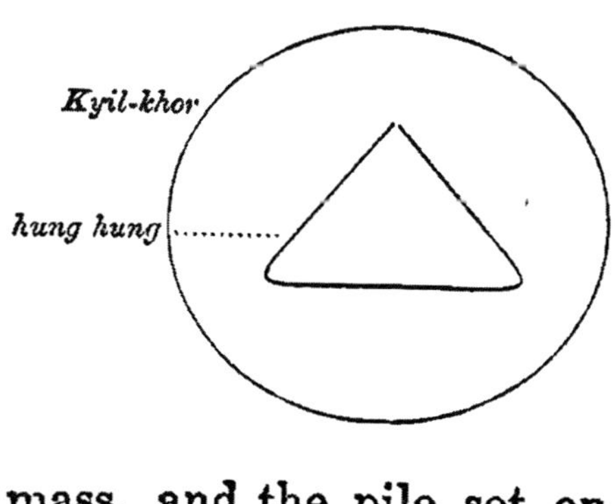

ingredients reserved for the purpose are thrown in, from time to time, by the lāmas, accompanied by a muttering of spells. And ultimately is thrown into the flames a piece of paper on which is written the name of the deceased person—always a relative—whose ghost is to be suppressed. When this paper is consumed the ghost has received its quietus, and never gives trouble again. Any further trouble is due to another ghost or to some demon or other.